Library of
Davidson College

In *The Victorian Achievement of Sir Henry Maine*, some of the world's leading scholars in the fields of anthropology, sociology, linguistics, legal history, jurisprudence, South Asian studies and the history of ideas come together to consider the extraordinary achievement of Sir Henry Maine, Master of Trinity Hall, Cambridge (1877–88) and one of the most powerful and original minds of the Victorian age. The disciplinary range and scholarly stature of the contributors is itself testimony to the fascination of Maine's work, which, after a period of relative neglect, is now recognized as a seminal contribution to the development of social scientific study.

The book is divided into four parts, dealing with the principal strands of Maine's life and writing: his views on social and political progress, his anthropological and social scientific works, his legal and jurisprudential thought, and finally his writings on Indian affairs, the product (in part) of his experiences as the Legal Member of the Council of the Governor-General from 1862 to 1869. The book also contains a comprehensive bibliography covering all of Maine's works, and a substantial array of secondary sources in the various disciplines represented in this volume. The whole amounts to a major reconsideration of a particularly eminent Victorian, and will complement neatly the detailed study of Maine's jurisprudence by Raymond Cocks, published by Cambridge University Press in 1988.

THE VICTORIAN ACHIEVEMENT OF
SIR HENRY MAINE

THE VICTORIAN ACHIEVEMENT OF SIR HENRY MAINE

A centennial reappraisal

EDITED BY ALAN DIAMOND

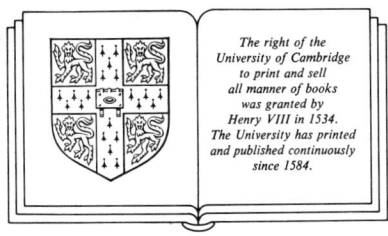

CAMBRIDGE UNIVERSITY PRESS

*Cambridge   New York   Port Chester
Melbourne   Sydney*

Published by the Press Syndicate of the University of Cambridge
The Pitt Building, Trumpington Street, Cambridge CB2 1RP
40 West 20th Street, New York, NY 10011-4211, USA
10 Stamford Road, Oakleigh, Melbourne 3166, Australia

© Cambridge University Press 1991

First published 1991

Printed in Great Britain at the University Press, Cambridge

British Library cataloguing in publication data
The Victorian achievement of Sir Henry Maine: a centennial reappraisal.
1. Jurisprudence. Theories of Maine, Henry Sumner 1822-1888
1. Diamond, Alan II. Maine, Henry Sumner *1822-1888*
340.109

Library of Congress cataloguing in publication data
The Victorian Achievement of Sir Henry Maine A Centennial Reappraisal / edited
by Alan Diamond
p. cm.
Proceedings of the Trinity Hall Henry Maine Centenary Conference.
Includes bibliographical references and index.
ISBN 0 521 40023 6
1. Maine, Henry Sumner, Sir, 1822-1888. Ancient law – Congresses.
2. Law, Ancient – Congresses.
3. Sociological jurisprudence – Congresses.
4. Social sciences – Congresses.
5. Progress – Congresses.
I. Diamond, Alan. II Maine, Henry Sumner, Sir, 1822-1888.
III. Trinity Hall Henry Maine Centenary Conference.
K190.M353A3 1991
340'.115–dc20 90-28233–CIP

ISBN 0 521 40023 6 hardback

CE

*To the memory of Martin Hinds, Fellow of Trinity Hall,
1972–1988*

Contents

Notes on contributors	*page*	xii
Foreword by Sir John Lyons		xiv

	Introduction Alan Diamond	1
1	The Victorian values of Sir Henry Maine George Feaver	28

PART 1	MAINE AND THE IDEA OF PROGRESS	53
2	Henry Maine and mid-Victorian ideas of progress John W. Burrow	55
3	Maine, progress and theory Raymond Cocks	70
4	Maine and the theory of progress Krishan Kumar	76
5	Democracy and excitement: Maine's political pessimism Stefan Collini	88

PART 2	MAINE AND THE SOCIAL SCIENCES	97
6	The rise and fall of Maine's patriarchal society Adam Kuper	99
7	Some contributions of Maine to history and anthropology Alan D. J. Macfarlane	111

8	Henry Sumner Maine in the tradition of the analysis of society *Edward Shils*	143
9	Maine as an ancestor of the social sciences *J. D. Y. Peel*	179
10	*Ancient Law* and modern field work *Ray Abrahams*	185

PART 3 MAINE ON LAW, LEGAL CHANGE AND LEGAL EDUCATION 193

11	Maine and legal education *Peter G. Stein*	195
12	Maine and legal education: a comment *William Twining*	209
13	A wake (or awakening?) for historical jurisprudence *Calvin Woodard*	217
14	Further thoughts on Maine's historical jurisprudence *David E. C. Yale*	238
15	Fictions, equity and legislation: Maine's three agencies of legal change *Alan Diamond*	242
16	Law and language: a metaphor in Maine, a model for his successors? *Bernard S. Jackson*	256
17	Linguistics and law: the legacy of Sir Henry Maine *John Lyons*	294

PART 4 MAINE AND INDIA 351

18	The influence of Sir Henry Maine on agrarian policy in India *Clive Dewey*	353
19	India and Henry Maine *Gordon Johnson*	376

| 20 | Maine and change in nineteenth-century India
C. A. Bayly | 389 |

Appendix: the conference programme   398
Bibliography   401
Index   447

Notes on contributors

GEORGE FEAVER is Professor of Political Science at the University of British Columbia

JOHN BURROW is Professor of History at the University of Sussex

RAYMOND COCKS is Lecturer in Law at the University of Sussex

KRISHAN KUMAR is Professor of Social Thought at the University of Kent

STEFAN COLLINI is University Lecturer in English and Fellow of Clare Hall, Cambridge

ADAM KUPER is Professor of Anthropology at Brunel University

ALAN MACFARLANE is Professor of Anthropological Science and Fellow of King's College, Cambridge

EDWARD SHILS is Professor of Sociology at the University of Chicago

J. D. Y. PEEL is Professor of Anthropology and Sociology, with reference to Africa, in the School of Oriental and African Studies at the University of London

RAY ABRAHAMS is University Lecturer in Social Anthropology and Fellow of Churchill College, Cambridge

PETER STEIN is Regius Professor of Civil Law and Fellow of Queens' College, Cambridge

WILLIAM TWINING is Quain Professor of Jurisprudence at University College London

CALVIN WOODARD is Professor of Law at the University of Virginia

DAVID E. C. YALE is Reader in English Legal History and Fellow of Christ's College, Cambridge

ALAN DIAMOND is a partner in the law firm of O'Neill and Lysaght in Los Angeles, California, and a member of Trinity Hall, Cambridge

BERNARD S. JACKSON is Queen Victoria Professor of Law at the University of Liverpool

Notes on contributors

SIR JOHN LYONS is Master of Trinity Hall, Cambridge

CLIVE DEWEY is Lecturer in Economic and Social History at the University of Leicester

GORDON JOHNSON is Director of the Centre of South Asian Studies and Fellow of Selwyn College, Cambridge

CHRISTOPHER A. BAYLY is Professor of Modern Indian History and Fellow of St Catharine's College, Cambridge

Foreword

Of all the tasks that have fallen to me ex officio, as Master of Trinity Hall, none has been at once so agreeable and so intellectually stimulating as that of presiding at the Conference organized by the College, in September 1988, to mark the centenary of the death of my illustrious predecessor, Sir Henry Maine, Master of the College from 1877 to 1888.

Like all academics, I have been to many conferences in my time. But I cannot recall ever having attended one which was as completely and as genuinely interdisciplinary as the Trinity Hall Henry Maine Centenary Conference, the proceedings of which are published in this volume. It was unique, in my experience, in that not only did all the participants attend all the sessions and contribute knowledgeably to the discussion of one another's papers, but the same general themes constantly recurred throughout the Conference and proved to be equally relevant to the present-day concerns of all the disciplines represented. It was a particularly convincing demonstration of the continued fecundity of Maine's ideas in what are normally thought of as separate scholarly fields: legal history, political science, sociological theory, the history of ideas, anthropology and linguistics.

This aspect of the Conference is emphasized by Alan Diamond in his editorial Introduction and need not be developed further here. My function is to express the College's gratitude to all those who contributed to the success of the Conference and have ensured that the book which issues from it will be equally successful.

Our thanks go first of all to the speakers who accepted the Organizing Committee's invitation to participate in the Conference, all of whom are well-known authors and experts in their individual fields: Christopher Bayly, John Burrow, Owen Chadwick, Rajnarayan Chandavarkar, Raymond Cocks, Stefan Collini, Clive

Dewey, George Feaver, Bernard Jackson, Gordon Johnson, Krishan Kumar, Adam Kuper, Alan Macfarlane, Rosalind O'Hanlon, J. D. Y. Peel, Edward Shils, Peter Stein, William Twining, Calvin Woodard and David Yale. All but two of the papers that were given at the Conference are published here; several of them have been revised and expanded for the purpose. The full programme of the Conference is given in the Appendix.

The College owes a very particular debt of gratitude to Alan Diamond, who did most of the day-to-day organizing of the Conference and has put a vast amount of work into the editing of the proceedings and the compilation of the bibliography, which includes all the works referred to by the authors of the several chapters, as well as a large number of other works relevant to the issues discussed.

Next, I must thank those Fellows of the College who served on the Organizing Committee together with Alan Diamond and myself, and gave us the benefit of their editorial advice after the Conference had been held: John Collier (who was Vice-Master at the time), David Fleming, Graham Howes and Jonathan Steinberg (the current Vice-Master). One other Fellow of Trinity Hall, Martin Hinds, served on the Organizing Committee until he was prevented by illness from continuing in this role, in the summer of 1988; he was not able to attend the Conference itself and died some two months after it was held; in recognition of his very considerable involvement in the organization of the Conference and his academic interest in the themes that were discussed, we have gratefully dedicated this volume to his memory.

I should also like to thank Mrs Thelma Jeffs and Mrs Maureen Elvin, the former for assisting with the organization of the Conference, and the latter for typing the bibliography in its several successive versions, and for retyping two or three of the contributions. Finally, I wish to thank Richard Fisher and Pauline Marsh of Cambridge University Press for their expert assistance in the completion of what has proved to be an unusually complex editorial task.

For a variety of reasons, including the difficulty of collating the several individual bibliographies and adding to them as comprehensive a list of Maine's own publications as it has been practicable to do, this volume has taken longer to produce than we had anticipated. But in apologizing to the contributors for the unexpected delay I cannot resist quoting from one of the prize-winning poems that Maine himself wrote as an undergraduate and expressing the hope that, now that it has appeared, this book will prove to be one of those 'sweetest things' which 'long delayed /Are by their lingering yet more precious made' (Maine B2, 1842a).

Trinity Hall SIR JOHN LYONS
Cambridge MASTER

Introduction
Alan Diamond

It might be said of Maine, as Sir Carleton Allen said of Maine's great antagonist Austin: 'a student must feel that he reads Austin only in order to controvert him' (1964: 7). Allen goes on to observe, however, that

> For a systematic exposition of the methods of English jurisprudence, we still have to turn to Austin. Nobody has replaced him. Austinian jurisprudence ... so far maintains its influence that it may still be described as the characteristic jurisprudence of England ... (1964: 7)

Surveying the scene 100 years after his death, an unbiased observer would be hard pressed to say as much about the current reputation and influence of Sir Henry Sumner Maine. Those who read Maine may indeed feel that they do so 'only in order to controvert him', but how many in fact read him at all? Certainly, he seems all but forgotten today in those fields in which he hoped to exercise the greatest influence: jurisprudence and legal history. The very dominance – until recently, at least – of Austinian jurisprudence suggests that Maine's historical outlook has become peripheral to the concerns of legal philosophy. The battle for the soul of legal philosophy today is a battle between utilitarianism and natural law, both of which Maine criticized as ahistorical. Maine's own historical approach, like historical jurisprudence in general, has been largely discredited, or at least marginalized. As for legal history, it is to Maitland rather than Maine that legal historians look for inspiration, and Maine's self-confident, universalist generalizations have given way to a more precise study of the actual records of individual legal systems. Moreover, to the extent that modern legal history does deal with the issue of legal change, it seems to by-pass Maine. Not once is Maine mentioned in Baker's study (1978) of how the Tudor common law reformed itself from within; and Milsom (1981) seems to develop his theory of reclassification as an agent of change without reference to the famous Mainian triad of fictions, equity and legislation.

In this volume, Professor Woodard relates the melancholy story of the way in which historical jurisprudence in general and Maine's ideas in particular have, by a process of guilt by association, fallen into academic disfavour. Not only are there 'no contemporary advocates of historical jurisprudence' within the study of jurisprudence (see p. 228 below), but that side of historical jurisprudence which remains 'robust in the form of legal history' (p. 228) is a legal history which is closer 'to the ultra-nationalistic version of Savigny and Puchta' than to the cosmopolitan comparative law version of Maine (p. 224). This may be overstating the matter, but it is difficult to quarrel with Woodard's judgement that 'Maine is better remembered and more discussed by anthropologists than he is by lawyers' (p. 228).

The banishment of Maine to the margins of legal history and jurisprudence is confirmed by Professor Twining. He confesses to having 'actually managed to finish' *Ancient Law* as a freshman at Oxford in the 1950s; but it had been 'recommended and perceived as general background to our degree course'; and for historical jurisprudence, which was covered in a week, including Maine, he 'relied on secondary sources' (pp. 209–10). And it appears that Maine has remained as marginal to Twining's teaching as he was to his studies, so that during the past twenty years, he does not 'recall having recommended any student, undergraduate or postgraduate, to read *Ancient Law* or anything else by Maine, except perhaps his discussion of fictions' (p. 210).

The picture in legal history seems equally bleak. In one of the two leading textbooks on the subject (Milsom, 1981), Maine is not even mentioned, although the author was no less concerned than was Maine with the agents of legal change, and his own original contribution to that subject was to some extent anticipated by Maine himself. An important use of Maine's ideas is made by Baker in his legal history textbook (1979: 169ff.), where the chapter on 'Law making' is structured around Maine's identification of the agencies by which law is brought into harmony with changes in the wider society as fictions, equity and legislation. But Baker uses these categories merely as a set of convenient section headings, and the broader definitions given to these mechanisms of change by Maine

Introduction

as well as his assertions about their historical sequence are rejected as 'difficult to square with the English experience' (1979: 170).

And, if Maine has been eclipsed by Maitland in the field of legal history, and driven to the margins in jurisprudence, his reputation has experienced only a slightly better fate in other fields on which his work impinges. In sociology, Maine's name appears infrequently, and his influence seems peculiarly marginal when compared to that of Marx, Weber or Durkheim; while in the field of Indian studies, Maine's influence has been weakened from two related directions: his association with imperialism and an increased tendency to study India through indigenous sources. In Victorian studies, despite the extravagant praise of one commentator, who referred to the 'epoch-making influence' of *Ancient Law* as 'not unfitly [to] be compared to that exercised by Darwin's *Origin of the Species*' (Morgan, Introduction to *AL*, 1917: v), his name has never carried the cachet of men like Mill and Bentham, not to mention such giants as Marx, Darwin and latterly Freud. And, despite the fact that 'comparative philology was, after historical jurisprudence, the chief influence upon [Maine]' (Burrow, 1966: 152), most modern linguists 'will never have heard of Maine in connection with linguistics' (Lyons, p. 294). Nor is he 'mentioned in any of the standard histories of nineteenth-century linguistics' (p. 295). He was, Professor Lyons concludes, merely 'a borrower' (p. 295).

Only in anthropology does Maine seem to have found a secure home. Thus, Professor Kuper recalls in his chapter that, when he first came to Cambridge as a research student twenty-five years ago, *Ancient Law* was one of the first books which he was assigned to read, not as general history or background, but 'as an authority', whose 'theoretical conceptions' were of current value (p. 99). Dr Abrahams testifies to a similar experience at Manchester: 'Maine ... figure[d] prominently in my first apprenticeship in anthropology; and my sense of his significance was also reinforced while writing up my doctoral research' (p. 186). In short, Maine's insights seem to have been more relevant to the relatively youthful fields of anthropology and sociology than to a legal history which was already seeking actual evidence from the archives or to a jurisprudence which already had a surfeit of *a priori* generalizations. Indeed, we might say of Maine that he was abandoned by law and rescued by the social sciences.

Yet even in these fields, Maine's reputation has been problematic.

His patriarchal theory, the central pillar of Maine's anthropological outlook, was attacked only a few years after its original formulation in *Ancient Law*, and today is fully discredited. In the words of Kuper, it 'is a very dead corpse' (p. 99). Worse still, it is not merely the particular answer which Maine gave to the question of the form of primeval society which is rejected, but the very question itself:

> Within anthropology there is fairly general agreement today that we cannot reconstruct very early social forms in any detail ... In short, the issues which were crucial for Maine have passed from academic debate, and there seems little chance that his patriarchal theory will be revived within anthropology. (Kuper, p. 109)

In sociology, as Professor Shils tells us, Maine's name has fallen out of the tradition of the study of society:

> or perhaps it should be said that it never made its entry. Histories of sociology scarcely mention Maine. Sociologists do not read his works very often. When his name is mentioned, it is mentioned very cursorily ... (Shils, p. 143)

And Professor Macfarlane, a self-confessed Maine addict, concedes that: 'An intelligent undergraduate could undoubtedly make a strong case for dismissing Maine.' On the basis of subsequent assessments of his work, the undergraduate would learn that each of 'Maine's supposed achievements ... was deeply flawed'. In the end, the student might be driven to ask his supervisor why he should 'waste time on a thinker whose methodology was based on an outworn paradigm, whose scholarship was shaky, whose findings were unoriginal or wrong' (Macfarlane, p. 111).

And, beyond questions as to his method, his scholarship and his conclusions, there is the related problem of what Collini calls the 'almost blatantly ideological cast of much of his writing' (p. 93). Maine's political outlook undoubtedly infiltrated his scholarship, and in *Popular Government* seems to have secured a dominant foothold. Indeed, for Professor Kuper, even *Ancient Law* 'was in essence an attack on the political and legal theories of Jeremy Bentham and the utilitarians' (p. 100). And Collini, in discussing *Ancient Law*, observes that Maine 'takes for granted the superiority of certain qualities of character, and then finds them at work in those developments he regards as progressive' (p. 90). There are, according to Collini, 'connections between this cluster of values and his individualist politics' (p. 90). Beyond this, his 'Anglican superiority to the values of other societies' (Woodard, p. 219), his 'rhetoric of sobriety and realism, which has the effect of casting opposing views as self-indulgent or weakly deluded' (Collini, p. 91), the extent to which his ideas and expressions reflected 'the biases and prejudices common among the upper classes of his day' (Woodard, p. 218), his deployment of a 'habitual tone of grim realism ... to provide a kind of scientific legitimation for the prejudices of the governing class' (Collini, p. 92), or a tone of voice, which 'seems to have assumed that his readers were, or should be, members of the Athenaeum Club, all of whom shared with him the values and opinions that really counted' (Woodard, p. 218), and 'the pessimistic anti-populism of his later years' (Abrahams, p. 185) – all this contributed to the decline in Maine's reputation and the marginalization of his work in this century.

But it is Maine's close association with three of the most characteristic notions of the Victorian era, 'evolution-cum-progress', 'German historical jurisprudence' and *laissez-faire* individualism' (Woodard, pp. 221, 223, 226), which has served to render his work and ideas unfashionable, embarrassing, and to some even repellent. To a large extent, however, this is unfair, not only because what is worth preserving in Maine has been tossed out with what is expendable, but also because clearly Maine has become a victim of what Woodard calls 'guilt by association'. Yet his connection with these 'high-Victorian notions' (Woodard, p. 221) was considerably qualified. Our century may no longer hold self-confident beliefs in the certainty of progress, but then neither did Maine. Moreover, while evolutionary theory was undoubtedly abused in the form of social Darwinism, or as an apology for imperialism, this is not something with which Maine can be charged, at least not when his work is viewed as a whole. Maine could indeed be embarrassingly patronizing and insensitive: as, for example, when he went 'before the assembled students and faculty of the University of Calcutta, scions to one of the world's oldest and most sophisticated cultures, and solemnly advis[ed] them that "Except the blind forces of nature, nothing moves in this world which is not Greek in origin"' (Woodard, p. 219).

On the whole, however, Macfarlane is right in acquitting Maine of an ethnocentric abuse of evolutionary theory on the basis of a 'wide and relativisitic mind that can suspend moralizing, and a curiosity that bridges different worlds' (p. 137). With rare exceptions, 'When we read Maine today we do not feel a patronizing, or incomprehending, tone creep into his explanations and descriptions (p. 137).

Indeed, some Anglo-Indians saw Maine's evolutionary perspective as a positive contribution towards racial understanding. 'Mutual tolerance', observed Sir Lewis Tupper, 'is easier when educated Indians and Europeans perceive that the India of today teems with analogies to the past of Europe' (Tupper, 1898: 399). Sir Courtenay Ilbert echoed the sentiment. As Darwin had shown that 'the commonest wayside flower' was related 'to the whole animated world', so Maine brought 'the most ordinary phenomena of Indian social life into organic relation with the world-wide evolution of legal and institutional ideas', thereby changing 'the attitude of the English mind to the world of India from an attitude of indifference to one of sympathetic insight' (1898: 403).

In any event, with few exceptions[1], Maine's ideas about progress seem to have involved no assumption of European racial superiority, since those races which had made a successful move beyond status had done so not because of any superior genetic make-up, but simply because of their fortuitousness in getting past the stage at which law and religion are intertwined, and custom, embodied in a code, is given a sacred cast, and rendered unchangeable. Thus, there was no reason why Indians could not progress as far as Englishmen; what had held them back was not their race, but the fact that they had become stuck in the groove of an earlier stage of development, from which British ideas and administration would free them. Those Anglo-Indians who sought to preserve indigenous institutions, or at least to slow the pace of utilitarian-driven change, found support in Maine's theory of stages of development. (See also Tupper, 1898: 399). Thanks to Maine, they were not compelled to rest their case on the proposition that Indians were incapable of enjoying a system of relations based on contract. In time, they believed, that would be possible. For now, however, being at an earlier stage of development, India could not absorb the wholesale importation of British institutions; the diffusionist method of moving her forward required incremental rather than radical change.

The guilt by association which finds its source in Maine's connec-

---

[1] See *AL*: 23; cf. Bayley, p. 396.

tion with German historical jurisprudence is doubly unfair: first, to the extent that the reaction against historical jurisprudence comes simply from its German roots, this is both unreasonable, and particularly unfair to Maine, who 'was not ... as much a Germanophile as many of his contemporaries', including Maitland, who 'was an unabashed admirer of things German' (Woodard, pp. 224, 225). Second, to the extent that modern hostility to historical jurisprudence is to be explained by its 'ultra-nationalistic' character, this is also unfair to Maine, whose outlook was always cosmopolitan and detached, and who was 'much closer, doctrinally, to pan-nationalistic comparative law' than to any particular German school of historical jurisprudence (Woodard, p. 224).

Finally, it would be difficult to defend from the charge of *laissez-faire* individualism the man who gave the world one of the most famous epigrams on the subject: 'the movement of the progressive societies has hitherto been a movement *from Status to Contract*'. His memorable formulation 'provided an entirely original justification' for *laissez-faire*. 'His conclusion was not based on legal theory; nor was it based on morality or religion ... [but] on the long-term historical tendency of "progressive societies" which ... had been "*from Status to Contract*" ' (Woodard, pp. 226, 227). Maine's own views of morality need not have corresponded with the historical tendency which he identified; but, in fact, his generalization has both an historical and a definitional aspect: freedom of contract is 'an aspect – perhaps the most important ... of what makes it proper to call ... [societies] progressive' (Burrow, p. 56). The movement from status to contract 'for Maine expresses not merely an historical truth ... but a moral polarity, which no future social development could cancel' (Burrow, p. 56). If Maine's generalization constituted a law of progress, it was 'not because future progress was certain but because no other comprehensive social development would count as such' (Burrow, p. 56).

None the less, Maine's ideas, at least when placed in the context of his methodology, are far too complex and ambivalent to be dismissed as merely a pseudo-scientific defence of a political and economic order based on *laissez-faire* individualism. Thus, Dr Bayly refers to Maine's disciples as 'conservative imperialist thinkers' (p. 393) and to their ideas as 'the natural ideology for a fragile colonial dominion' (p. 390). Yet, it was these very ideas which 'prepared the ground' for Indian nationalism (pp. 396–7). Similarly, in discussing the active reception of Maine's ideas by the Indian civil service during the final quarter of the nineteenth century, Dewey remarks that the civilians

> took over his combination of historical and comparative method, and applied his insights to Indian institutions with immense vigour and considerable subtlety. As a result, the 'lessons of Maine' were a great deal more ambivalent than the 'lessons of Bentham'. So many implications had to be teased out of an active collaboration with Maine that advocates of diametrically opposed policies could appeal to his authority. (p. 356)

What is most germane for our immediate purpose is the fact that Maine's ideas were enlisted by his disciples to reverse the *laissez-faire* policies of the Government of India and to effect a regression from contract to status; or, more accurately, from *laissez-faire* to government paternalism.

In short, whether deservedly or not, and despite pockets of resistance, from the late nineteenth century onwards, Maine's reputation declined, and his work was disregarded, if not entirely discredited, in virtually every field of intellectual endeavour which he touched. It would not be unreasonable, then, to expect a group of scholars gathered to commemorate the centenary of his death to have come, despite the inevitable pieties, finally to bury Maine's reputation, not to resurrect it. Yet, the chapters in this volume will show that something quite different has occurred: the rediscovery of Henry Sumner Maine as one of the modern age's seminal thinkers.

To Professor Jackson, it is Maine's 'attitude to history – as an ongoing process in which we continue to be implicated – [that] today once again strikes a contemporary chord' (p. 271). Moreover, Jackson finds Maine's evolutionary model a source of current 'social-scientific inspiration' (p. 272). According to this model, all societies, or at any rate all Indo-European societies, pass through certain states of legal development leading the few fortunate ones from status to contract. According to Jackson, Maine may have been correct to analyse historical development in terms of a sequence of stages, but the discipline from which he borrowed his model, comparative philology, was ill chosen, whereas modern cognitive developmental psychology, inspired by the work of Piaget, which 'relies fundamentally upon notions of systemic equilibrium within "stages", as well as suggesting universals of development from one stage to another', might more appropriately provide support, not only for Maine's status-to-contract generalization, but for the stages in the legal development of progressive societies, fictions, equity and legislation, which he identified (Jackson, pp. 272–3).[2]

For Woodard, Maine, 'in the course of a few volumes ... transformed "law" from a technical and professional "box of tools" ... into a museum of past civilizations and remote societies all teeming with unexpected associations with our own legal system ... No member of the Anglo-American Bar, however rigorously disciplined to "think like a lawyer", can ever see his or her subject – law – in quite the same light again, after having been exposed to this man's works' (p. 217). For David Yale, the 'current utility' of Maine's works 'lies in his method' (p. 238). Despite its errors and omissions, '*Ancient Law* is a book which ... remains alive' because of the 'advice Maine offers on how to look for change' (p. 239).

According to Shils, 'no one writer has entered, so penetratingly and so pervasively, into the fundamental outlook of sociologists of the twentieth century as has Maine' (Shils, p. 144). Maine is a genuine, though forgotten, ancestor of sociology, whose ideas live through the 'prominent descendants' he formed (p. 143). For Macfarlane, Maine is one of the fathers of anthropology: 'much of what we are flows from his thought ... both historical and anthropological theory today would be very different without his inspiration' (p. 141). For Professor Peel, Maine is not just a founding father of the social sciences, but an ancestor, one of the 'beings of the past' who though dead 'interact[s] with the living' (p. 179). Despite 'certain vagaries in Maine's posthumous reputation ... the insistent fact', Peel observes, 'is of Maine's relative modernity, compared with many of his contemporaries' (p. 179). And this modernity is testified to by Dr Abrahams, whose 'relation to Maine ... is a working one' (p. 186). In attempting to make sense of the material he had gathered in a recent field study of succession to family farms in Finland, he:

turned to a variety of texts for guidance, and these more or less automatically included *Ancient Law*. I found it a felicitous choice, full of far more than I remembered, and anticipating much that I had learned from later

---

[2] Lyons, in contrast, sounds a cautionary note with respect to both the accuracy of Piagetian stages of language development and the utility of any analogy from the phylogenetic or ontogenetic development of language to the development of legal systems or other human institutions (p. 321).

writers. The result is that the paper in question, which was not written explicitly to extol or assess Maine, is littered with references to his ideas and comments. (Abrahams, p. 187)

If Maine's place in contemporary thought needs reconsideration, so too may the seemingly more settled question of his influence on his own time. It is not that anything contained in this volume casts doubt on Professor Feaver's judgement that 'The life of Sir Henry Maine was an achieved Victorian life' (p. 34) or that his work 'epitomized the spirit of an age' (p. 28). The transforming influence he exerted on the intellectual life of the nineteenth century is beyond question. Stein refers to *Ancient Law* as one of the two works (the other being Austin's *Province of Jurisprudence Determined*) 'which had greater influence on English jurisprudence than any other in the nineteenth century' (1980: 85). The judgement is echoed by the recent biographer of James Fitzjames Stephen, who concludes that the publication of *Ancient Law* 'arguably ... [did] for social science what Darwin had recently done for natural science' (Smith, 1988: 48). And as Burrow and Collini have observed:

the extent and profundity of Maine's influence among the intellectual class would be hard to exaggerate: he set the terms of debate not only for legal historians but for a generation of writers ... who could not easily or exclusively be classified as historians, political theorists or economists. Both Pollock and Vinogradoff virtually lived off his intellectual capital. (Collini et al., 1983: 210)

What has not been generally known or has been too often forgotten is the extent to which Maine's ideas influenced the more mundane realm of practical politics and government, particularly in British India, where he served for seven years as the Legal Member of the Governor-General's Council. During his service in India, Maine seems to have been both pragmatic and visionary; in the latter role, communicating not revolutionary idealism, but a sense of purpose and direction to those charged with the carrying out of day-to-day tasks; or, in Holme's words, 'imparting a ferment' (quoted in Howe, 1942: 1,31). It was this extraordinary combination of the qualities of the clear-sighted lawyer and the far-seeing scholar which made Maine, in Dr Johnson's phrase, 'wonderfully fitted to serve [India] well' (p. 382). While he was, as Johnson informs us, responsible for over 200 separate Acts, none of them were 'striking laws', and most of them were 'recast before the century was out' (pp. 382–3). To his contemporaries this was simply evidence that Maine 'was no adventurous law-giver'; but, as Sir Lewis Tupper noted, he 'limited himself to the actual requirements of his time' (1898, quoted in Johnson, p. 383). It is in the 'valuable services [he performed] in his professional character as a lawyer' that Maine's 'low-key' pragmatism manifested itself (Johnson, pp. 382, 383).

But Maine was also a thinker. He came to India after having written *Ancient Law*, and considering Maine's penchant for 'theorizing ahead of the evidence' (Yale, p. 240), this sequence seems appropriate. Thus, he came with certain large ideas about primitive societies and one might even say a vision of the British role in India, forged not out of the usual imperial rhetoric, or out of missionary zeal, but out of his insight that the movement of progressive societies was from status to contract. It is his possession of a superstructure of ideas, and of course the particular aptness of those ideas to the Indian sub-continent, which made it possible for Maine to make 'the whole country, and the problems of governing it, seem intelligible to his contemporaries' (Johnson, p. 382). Dewey refers to 'the density of the allusions' to Maine: 'his ideas ... crop up in official reports, in secretariat files, in speeches in the legislatures.' (p. 355). And because his writings were 'not only coherent and compelling but also ambivalent and ambiguous' (Johnson, p. 385), 'advocates of diametrically opposed policies could appeal to his authority' (Dewey, p. 356). In short

> For the very best minds who applied themselves to the daunting task of observing, recording and explaining India, it is remarkable how often Maine is the point of departure, even when the new work sets out to modify or to disagree with his own arguments ... (Johnson, p. 385)

Maine's ideas may not have been wholly original, since they harked back to an 'older pre-utilitarian tradition ... [which] had celebrated the virtues of India's institutions ... [and] To a large extent ... had also inherited the "stage theory" of historical development' (Bayly, p. 390). Maine's ideas may not have been wholly accurate: 'In many cases what was perceived as a tradition was in fact the product of the relative economic stagnation' brought about by East India Company rule (Bayly, p. 395). 'The self-contained and ageless Indian village is another myth' (Bayly, p. 395). And the influence of Maine's disciples may have been overstated: to some historians, 'The influence of policy-makers and their ideologies now appeared strictly limited ... Real change emanated from the rhythms of the Indian economy' (Bayly, pp. 391, 392). For these and other reasons, 'At first sight Maine might appear an irrelevance to modern Indian historiography' (Bayly, p. 397). None the less, 'as the ideological shadow of both nationalism and communalism, [Maine] deserves the attention of historians of the non-European world' (Bayly, p. 397).

A TALENT FOR GENERALIZATION

No aspect of Maine's work is more celebrated than his talent for brilliant generalization. The force of his generalizations is such that, according to Yale, they 'must command attention whether they attract or repel the reader' (p. 240). Sir Alfred Lyall refers to Maine's 'luminous generalisations' (1899: 245–6, quoted by Dewey, p. 363) and to his ability to take 'a set of facts, or a certain number of ideas and suggestions ... [and] suddenly set them all in order by one of his weird and wide generalisations' (1898: 402, quoted by Johnson, p. 386).

According to Stein, Maine's generalizations were constructed out of the materials of an elementary course in Roman private law, but were dressed up in such 'vivid imagery and phraseology', were stated with such self-confidence, and presented themselves as so intrinsically plausible, that the reader was persuaded 'that he was being given the results of a scientific investigation' (Stein, p. 208). Peel refers to Maine's most famous generalization, the movement of the progressive societies from status to contract, as having 'so deeply entered the routine stock of social theory that we are hardly aware of it – like genes from a real biological, but forgotten, ancestor' (pp. 179–80). Maine's generalizations remain persuasive today because of their 'brilliance and authoritative air'; at the very least, they offer 'type-situations that we look out for in approaching an unfamiliar legal system' (Stein, 1980: 101,106).

How accurately Maine's generalizations reflect the historical facts is a matter of considerable debate. As we have seen, Stein criticizes Maine for viewing 'all legal systems through the eyes of the categories established in Roman law' (p. 208), and Yale takes him to task for 'theorizing ahead of the evidence' (p. 240). Part of the problem lies in the nature of generalization itself, which, as Maine

Introduction

himself wrote, 'consists in dropping out of sight a certain number of particular facts, and constructing a formula which will embrace the remainder' (*PG*: 107). 'Scholars ... are usually chary, sometimes morbidly chary, of generalization' (Allen, Introduction to *AL*,1931: xviii); and the device is particularly problematic when applied to social and legal change over many centuries in many different societies. Maitland has adverted to this problem:

We are moderns and our words and thoughts cannot but be modern ... Every thought will be too sharp, every word will imply too many contrasts. We must ... use many words and qualify our every statement until we have almost contradicted it. The outcome will not be so graceful, so lucid, as Maine's *Ancient Law*. (Pollock & Maitland, 1968: II, 240–2).

On the other hand, there seems to be a core of truth in most of Maine's great pronouncements; in Macfarlane's words, they are at least three-quarter truths, 'enormously suggestive and almost right' (pp. 133, 134). James Fitzjames Stephen speaks of the 'intrinsic probability' of Maine's generalizations, even though they were reached 'not by any elaborate study of detailed evidence, but by a kind of intuition' (1888: 150). And Professor Fuller insists that 'we cease to worry ourselves about [the] literal accuracy [of Maine's account of the development of law] and treat it as a kind of allegory, full of insight into the processes by which law grows' (1968: 49).

Yet, if there is disagreement over the validity of Maine's generalizations, there is unanimity about their superior literary quality, a fact noted by virtually every writer on Maine, critic and celebrant alike. Dr Cocks speaks of Maine's 'lively generalizations' and of 'the succinct and assertive quality of his sentences' (p. 70). According to Woodard, Maine was 'a genuine "man of letters"' (p. 217). Sir Carleton Allen observes that 'There is scarcely a page [in *Ancient Law*] in which some memorable sentence does not stand out commandingly' (Introduction to *AL*, 1931: xviii). Johnson refers to Maine's 'talent ... for lucidly setting out complex matters' (p. 384); in an era when most books written about India were unreadable, Maine clothed his description of the essential principles of Indian institutions 'in language of consummate literary art' (Johnson, p. 384, quoting Ilbert (1898: 403)).

The question of Maine's style is, however, a tricky one. The more one identifies the literary quality of Maine's writings as the reason for their original success and their continued popularity, the more one implies that Maine's reputation has been a victory of style over substance. Stein's remarks to some extent reflect this double-edged quality. Thus, in *Legal Evolution*, Stein writes that 'The style of *Ancient Law* was an important part of its enormous influence' (1980: 97). And, in referring to Maine's status-to-contract generalization, he notes that 'The force and style of this passage explain in part why *Ancient Law* made such a tremendous impact on publication. The authoritative ease and fluency with which Maine formulated his ideas carried great conviction' (1980: 97).

An earlier description of Maine as 'a lawyer with a style ... [who] belongs, by method and genius, among men of letters' (Wilson, 1898: 363) is also double-edged. The appreciation was by Woodrow Wilson, who added that Maine's reputation would survive 'not ... by reason of the abundance and validity of his thought, but by reason of his form and art' (1898: 364, quoted by Feaver, p. 35). This is not so much a case of damning with faint praise as of dismissing with praise which is inapt. The abundance of Maine's thought is testified to by the many fields which his work has influenced, the wide range of subjects which his books address and, most immediately, by the genuinely interdisciplinary nature of this volume. As has been observed in a recent book on Maine's jurisprudence:

> There is an almost bewildering variety of topics in his work. It seems that he was prepared to discuss any subject. He wrote about ancient customs, modern politics, scientific theories, the development of languages, statute law, poetry, philosophy, literature, whether women are more conservative than men, the extent to which law changes society and society changes law, Roman agriculture, Greek civilization, the caste systems of India, the failings of Bentham, the achievements of Bentham, the consequences of imposing British law on societies governed by custom, the merits of American social values and many, many other matters. (Cocks, 1988: 13)

We have already discussed the controversy over the validity of Maine's thought, which may turn less on the literal accuracy of any given generalization than on the general purpose and utility of Maine's pronouncements. Indeed, even where Maine is in error, his work has proved fruitful. Stein talks of Maine 'provoking a brilliant piece of corrective research by Maitland'; in that case on the matter of the extent of Roman law influence in the thirteenth-century treatise popularly known as Bracton (1980: 109). What provoked this research was precisely, as Stein puts it, the 'lofty and authoritative' way in which Maine discussed the matter and English legal history in general (1980: 109), or what Dr Cocks refers to as his 'tone of dismissive confidence' (p. 70). Clearly Maine never flinched from throwing down the scholarly gauntlet. His style, however, seems itself to have invited attack, 'as if the succinct and assertive quality of his sentences has stimulated attempts to rebut them' (Cocks, p. 70).

GENERALIZATIONS AND PARADIGMS

The power of Maine's language, the vividness of his imagery, the economy of his expression all contributed to transforming mere insights or ideas, however powerful, into axiomatic principles, or paradigms. Thus,

> [Maine's] theory of 'status to contract' is couched in terms at once specific and general but with sufficient vividness to enable it to outlive such rival claimants as Herbert Spencer's more obtuse *First Principles* notion that 'Evolution ... is a change from an indefinite, incoherent homogeneity, to a definite coherent heterogeneity.' (Feaver, p. 51)

Maine's style is undoubtedly a large part of the reason why his generalizations have remained memorable; more importantly, it is an essential ingredient in the mix of qualities which raises them to the status of paradigms. By 'paradigm' – the term is, of course, borrowed from Kuhn (1970) (as will be immediately evident, my usage does not necessarily follow his or that of his many followers) – I mean a particular formulation of a theory or a generalization which is at once authoritative and open-ended, concise and suggestive, capable of providing a principle for selecting and organizing facts or historical experience and fruitful of further research, speculation and debate. Johnson, for example, talks of Anglo-Indians stumbling upon 'a set of facts, or a certain number of ideas and suggestions ... in a confused, unfinished way ... [and Maine] would suddenly set them all in order by one of his weird and wonderful generalizations' (p. 386, quoting Lyall (1898): 402).

Popper and Kuhn have shown, not without controversy, that paradigms play an indispensable part in the workings of the natural sciences. Fact-gathering without the direction of a paradigm is a 'random activity' (Kuhn, 1970: 15) presenting 'a too sizable and inchoate pool of information' (Kuhn, 1970: 17). Observation 'needs a chosen object, a definite task, an interest, a point of view, a problem'; and, above all, something 'in the nature of a theory,' (Popper, 1963: 46). All factual statements are 'interpretations in the light of theories' (Popper, 1980: 107); for 'some theory is presupposed by any observation' (Magee, 1985: 29). The alternative to seeing, say, a swinging stone as a pendulum 'is not some hypothetical "fixed" vision, but vision through another paradigm, one which makes a swinging stone something else' (Kuhn, 1970: 128). And the more ambitious the theory, the more fruitful the observation:

Most of the great revolutions in science have turned on theories of breathtaking audacity not only in respect of creative imagination but in the depth of insight involved, and the independence of mind, the unsecured adventurousness of thought, required. (Magee, 1985: 22)

What is true for the natural sciences is true as well for other disciplines. Linguistics, for example, to the extent that it is concerned with language-systems, rather than languages, depends on 'vision through [a] paradigm', since such systems 'are theoretical constructs which depend on a motivated process of idealization' (Lyons, p. 324). Law and the social sciences also rely on organizing principles to make sense of the factual universe, whether concepts such as contract or fault, theories such as evolution, or the wealth of categories in each into which facts are routinely slotted, thus at once tainting them with theory. The need for a theory, a generalization, or an organizing principle, then, is critical to all intellectual endeavour.

Several of Maine's generalizations qualify to be called paradigms, at least in the specialized sense in which I am using the term. A point of departure for legal historians, for example, is routinely provided by Maine's assertion that in the infancy of a legal system 'substantive law has at first the look of being gradually secreted in the interstices of procedure' (*ELC*: 389); according to Maitland, 'one of Maine's most striking phrases' (Maitland, 1909: 295). Even more famous is Maine's identification of the agencies of legal change as fictions, equity and legislation. The tripartite scheme is discussed in detail elsewhere in this volume (Diamond, pp. 242–55). Maine's best-known generalization, and the one which most closely approximates the features of a paradigm, is the famous sentence which concludes Chapter 5 of *Ancient Law*: 'The movement of the progressive societies has hitherto been a movement *from Status to Contract*' (*AL*: 170).

The grip of this dictum on the academic mind has been nothing short of astonishing. The phrase turns up in the most unlikely places and has been put to the most various uses. The chapters in this volume attest to this fact. Even a subsidiary word like 'hitherto' has commanded attention and provoked debate. The very rhythm of Maine's formulation has proved irresistible, even when the context has nothing whatsoever to do with a contrast between primitive and modern society; as, for example, in Yale's observation that the development of writs of assistance in the Court of Chancery 'is closely related to the movement of Equity from discretion to definition' (Yale, 1965: 28). The generalization has been praised and damned, celebrated and dismissed, invoked and rejected, but it continues to fascinate. It has been pressed into service in anthropology, sociology, jurisprudence and legal and intellectual history. It has even served the end of biography: to Feaver, who entitled his definitive biography of Maine *From Status to Contract*, the generalization captures the essence of Maine's public and intellectual career. What Johnson says about Maine's work in general is certainly true about this, his most famous, generalization: 'It is remarkable how often Maine is the point of departure, even when the new work sets out to modify or to disagree with his own arguments' (Johnson, p. 385). The value of Maine's insight lies in the fact that it is stated with sufficient clarity and conviction to command attention and yet manages to be many things to many people, without somehow losing its core integrity. Or, to quote Johnson again, Maine's 'brilliant prose is not only coherent and compelling but also ambivalent and ambiguous' (Johnson, p. 385).

Shils notes that 'Maine's contribution to sociology may be summarized in the pregnant sentence which ends with the clause: "the movement of the progressive societies has hitherto been a movement *from Status to Contract*" ' (p. 144). The particular aspect of this pregnant sentence which has been most fruitful in the sociological tradition is not the moral aspect of Maine's definition of progress, which Burrow discusses (pp. 55–7), or the historical aspect of Maine's formula, i.e. the movement from status to contract seen as a law of progress, as Maine himself at one point characterizes it (*AL*: 170), but its typological aspect, i.e. Maine's use of two ideal types of society represented by status relationships on the one hand and contractual relationships on the other. Or, as Shils defines them, one society 'in which the collectivity was dominant and the individual recessive, the other in which the collectivity was recessive and the individual dominant' (pp. 144–5). The sharp dichotomy between status and contract, with all that entails in terms of a dichotomy of values and beliefs, is 'the aspect of Maine's work which has lived forward into sociology' (p. 145).

For over a century, this dichotomous scheme has operated as a paradigm, to the extent that it has provided a pair of concepts, status and contract, and an analytical assumption that sharply distinguished one from the other. Maine's generalization is at once part and a source of 'the tradition of the dichotomous classification of societies which had been in the process of formation from, at the latest, the seventeenth century onward' (Shils, p. 175). Tönnies, for example, may not have borrowed directly from Maine in fashioning his own distinction between *Gemeinschaft* and *Gesellschaft*, since he 'must have been pregnant with the contrast ... when he first encountered Maine's ideas' (Shils, p. 153). None the less, 'He clearly saw that what Maine called "status" was very close to what he called the *Gemeinschaft*, and what Maine called "contract" corresponded to what he called *Gesellschaft*' (Shils, p. 153). And it may turn out that there is a so far unacknowledged parallel between Maine's status-to-contract distinction and Malinowski's 'distinction between societies in which language is used primarily for communion and those in which it is used primarily for communication', since Malinowski's distinction 'is evidently very close to the distinction drawn up by Tönnies and his followers between a *Gemeinschaft* and a *Gesellschaft*' (Lyons, pp. 331–2). However that may be, so influential has this dichotomist tradition been that Shils refers to it as tyrannical and attributes to 'the rigours' of its tyranny the failure of 'eminent scholars to see that a national society must have some other elements in it than contracts, bureaucracy, rational bodies of knowledge of thought and rationalized economic organizations. Novel lines of understanding would have been opened to them had the rigour of the tyranny of tradition been eased' (Shils, p. 178). Thus, for better or worse, Maine's most famous generalization has operated, as any great paradigm operates, to preordain the selection and interpretation of the factual universe.

THE REDISCOVERY OF POPULAR GOVERNMENT

Even the most avid votaries of Maine have spoken cautiously of the place to be accorded to *Popular Government* in the canon of Maine's works. Indeed, that is putting the matter rather generously. If Maine went into rhetorical high gear in *Popular Government*, so too have his critics. It is 'his most disappointing book', a 'tawdry crown of his achievement' (Burrow, 1966: 173). Kumar speaks of 'the splenetic outpouring of *Popular Government*' (Kumar, p. 79); Yale contrasts *Popular Government* with *Ancient Law*, the latter 'full of optimism', and the former 'a profoundly pessimistic book, deeply depressing to read' (p. 238). Abrahams speaks of 'the pessimistic anti-populism of [Maine's] later years' as being 'unattractive to many, including myself' (p. 185). Burrow, too, sees *Popular Government* as 'giv[ing] voice to the pessimism of [Maine's] later years' (p. 62). Woodard is particularly pointed in his description of *Popular Government* as revealing a supple mind 'grown dry, brittle and fanatically political', and a 'baleful vision of the future' (pp. 218, 234).

The most serious charge against the book, both at the time of its original release, and from then on, was its partisan nature: Maine had produced not a work of scholarship but a political polemic. Lord Acton called it 'a Manual of unacknowledged Conservatism' (Paul, 1913: 169). Moreover, in taking a strongly anti-democratic stance, Maine swam against the popular current of his own day and was certainly on the wrong side of history as far as much of the next century was concerned. There had always been what Feaver calls a certain 'implied political philosophy' in *Ancient Law*, and one which while it gave 'much solace' to 'Whiggish liberals' also contained 'a definite Tory strain' (p. 46). The explicit political philosophy of *Popular Government*, however, may have caused later commentators to find in Maine's earlier works more of a political message or more of an ideological motive than was actually intended or present; although few have, I think, gone as far as Professor Kuper, who finds the very structure of *Ancient Law* determined by Maine's desire to use 'The history of the development of law ... as a stick with which to beat the modern radicals, beginning with Rousseau and ending with his particular antagonist, Jeremy Bentham' (p. 100).

Maine's modern biographer concludes that 'While *Popular Government* enjoyed a wide circulation in the months following its publication, and continued to be much admired by conservatives like [James Fitzjames] Stephen, it ultimately proved to be harmful to Sir Henry's standing as a scholar' (Feaver, 1969: 238). In his recent work on Maine, Cocks, speaking from what he describes as 'a jurisprudential point of view', rates *Popular Government* 'as a remarkable failure', a book in which Maine 'completely failed to develop any of his thoughts about legal philosophy. It was, and it remains, a great disappointment' (1988: 140). And Cocks concurs with Feaver that *Popular Government* 'did very little for Maine's reputation as a scholar' (1988: 139). Thus, there has been a tendency, among Maine's defenders as well as his critics, to slice off *Popular Government* from the rest of Maine's output, to see it as an aberration, which in no way detracts from the genuine scholarship in Maine's earlier works.

None the less, like it or not, there has been of late a revival of interest in *Popular Government*, and the chapters in this volume attest to this fact. It is difficult to ignore the obvious links between *Popular Government* and Maine's earlier works, even if *Popular Government* is, for good reasons, 'deeply depressing to read' (Yale, p. 238). Kumar, for example, while recognizing the 'difference in the style and mood' of *Ancient Law* and *Popular Government*, and a 'clear difference of intent', warns that we may be 'in danger of ... making too much of the distinction between the two works' (p. 80), between which there may be 'a good deal of compatibility' (p. 81). At a minimum, *Popular Government* casts considerable light on Maine's general ideas and method (see, for instance, Yale, pp. 239–40). Moreover, the more one views Maine's earlier works as essentially political, the less one will find *Popular Government* to be an aberration. Maine's famous theories, and even his methodology, have been pressed into service as proof of his political agenda. Thus, for Kuper, 'The patriarchal theory is best read as a direct inversion of the radical notion of the state of nature' (p. 104). The famous status-to-contract generalization had even more obvious political implications; and 'the dictum was ... received by Maine's contemporaries as vindication of the leading ideological currents of European society during the period of optimistic industrial expansion' (Feaver, 1969: 53). Moreover, Maine's use of the historical method was 'likely to breed caution and even inertia, a resistance to change on the grounds of the historical and "organic" complexity of society' (Kumar, p. 81). To that extent 'Maine himself was partly to blame for undermining

Benthamite individualism' (Kumar, p. 80). This was the view of Dicey, for whom there was:

> no discrepancy between the spirit and intent of *Ancient Law* and that of *Popular Government*. It was the 'historical method' of the former that, breeding nationalism, racialism and imperialism, had been one of the prime agents of the break-up of Benthamite cosmopolitanism and *laissez-faire*. 'It is no mere accident', wrote Dicey, 'that Maine, who in his *Ancient Law* undermined the authority of analytical jurisprudence, aimed in his *Popular Government* a blow at the foundations of Benthamite faith in democracy.' (Kumar, pp. 80–1, quoting Dicey, 1962: 461n)

Moreover, the distrust, if not the outright terror, of legislative activity which is the hallmark of *Popular Government* may also be seen as a natural outcome of the historical method. To quote Dicey again:

> Historical research ... just because it proves that forms of government are the necessary outcome of complicated social conditions ... suggests the ... inference that it is a waste of energy to trouble oneself greatly about the amendment of the law. (Dicey, 1962: 460–1)

There is yet a more substantive basis on which to connect *Ancient Law* and *Popular Government*, for the latter may be seen as providing a kind of closure for the evolutionary scheme introduced by Maine in *Ancient Law*. The centre-piece of the scheme is the movement from status to contract, from a condition where a man's rights and duties arise out of status in the family, or the tribe, or the community, to a condition where his rights and duties are largely decided by his free agreement with otherwise unrelated individuals. There is, as well, another kind of movement associated with the progressive societies: a movement from rigid adherence to a primitive code to amelioration of the code, first by fictions, then by equity, and lastly by legislation. Maine himself restricts this sequence to the progressive societies (*AL*: 23–4). He does not make it clear, however, how the two developments interrelate. The movement from status to contract is essentially a legal development, contract being in essence 'a juridical conception' (*EHI*: 357). And we can assume therefore that the movement to contract depends in some way on the ability of a society to move beyond the confines of an early code, which undoubtedly provided little scope for contractual relations. In *Ancient Law*, the synchronization is left unclear, though both the Roman and the common-law experiences provide examples of an older order of remedies serving a society based largely on property in land being supplanted through the use of fictions, equity and legislation by a new scheme of remedies serving a growing commercial society. While Maine is not much more explicit in any of his later works, in *Popular Government* he does demonstrate, if not the way in which the synchronization works, at least the way in which the parallel movements can get 'out of synch'. Man can be toppled from the progressive pinnacle of contract by the abuse by popular majorities of legislation, the ultimate result of the parallel evolutionary sequence. Now, we might be tempted to connect the arrival of a society at the final stage of the ameliorating instrumentalities, legislation, with its arrival at the final stage of progress, freedom of contract. To begin with, as previously noted, in *Ancient Law*, Maine does not explicitly attack the instrumentality of legislation as intrinsically inferior to fictions or equity, although he does observe that, in theory, 'There is nothing to prevent [the legislature] legislating in the wantonness of caprice' (*AL*: 177). As for public opinion, it seems in *Ancient Law* to be a wholly benign influence restraining the legislature, from imposing 'what obligations it pleases on the members of the community' (*AL*: 177). Moreover, in discussing fictions, Maine notes that 'They have had their day, but it is long since gone by. It is unworthy of us to effect an admittedly beneficial object by so rude a device as a legal fiction' (*AL*: 16).

In short, each instrumentality was merely appropriate to its 'day'; and legislation, because of its rationality and its open and avowed manner of changing the law, was consistent with the rationality which underpinned a modern, capitalist, contractual society. Moreover, legal fictions were harmful to the cause of 'the symmetrical classification' of law: in other words, the codification of law. A code is a kind of legislation; and, Maine is clearly not averse to codification, at least in the limited form of an 'adaptation and simplification of existing law' (Feaver, 1969: 100).

In *Popular Government*, however, Maine takes a different view of legislation, or at least of a particular stage in the use of the legislative instrumentality, the stage at which the power of legislation falls into the hands of a popular majority. This results not in a codification of the legal system limited to pruning away archaic law and fictions and arranging what remains in a systematic order, all carried out by members of the legal profession, but the enactment upon the agitation of the masses of regulatory legislation, which restricts freedom

Introduction

of contract, and which assigns rights and duties on the basis of factors other than the free agreement of man and man. The end result is an end to progress, and a regression to status. Thus, *Popular Government* ties together Maine's two historical schemes: the development of societies from status to contract, and the development of legal systems, once custom has been codified, from the concealed changes associated with fictions to the open and avowed changes associated with legislation. And it turns out that the two movements are in conflict, since popular legislation is inimical to the maintenance of a contractual order. To the extent, then, that Maine's status-to-contract dictum claims to be a law, *Popular Government* makes explicit that it is a law based on the imagery of the life-cycle.

Thus, the 'characteristic element of caution' in Maine's famous dictum ('hitherto') which qualifies its character as a 'law of progress' becomes, in *Popular Government*, a clear prediction of moral decay and death. To quote the sentence which so engaged David Yale: 'We are propelled by an irresistible force on a definite path towards an unavoidable end – towards Democracy – as towards Death' (*PG*: 170, quoted in Yale, p. 238). Thus, as Woodard observes, Maine's pessimism about the future of law causes him to change his imagery in an important way. Whereas 'His notion of "progress" carried with it the idea of motion in one direction ... from a state of moral inferiority ... to a "higher" state of moral development', i.e. from status to contract,

his notion of 'evolution' carried with it, in a human context anyway, the idea of a life-cycle ... ending inevitably in death. When, therefore, he began to doubt that his own society was moving towards a higher moral level of existence, he ... switched to the 'life-cycle' imagery of legal evolution – the last stage of which is death. (Woodard, p. 235)

And death, in the sense of the end of progress, coincided with the arrival of the final stage in the development of the legal system: legislation.

The most important reason for rediscovering *Popular Government*, however, is the astonishing topicality of many of its ideas. This is the view of Professor Feaver, who urges that 'the polemics that have contributed to make *Popular Government* so unattractive to democrats ... be balanced against the many important insights of the book' (1969: 238). Thus:

Sir Henry's concern over the potentials for political manipulation in an age increasingly preoccupied with the authority of public opinion ... continues to have relevance, as does his critical assessment of the Parliamentary form of government as an agency for recruiting and controlling those possessed of scientific and technological knowledge. Moreover, a case can be made that the spirit of the work, in which Maine attempted to get behind the ideological beliefs of his contemporaries to reveal the gulf separating political theory and practice, makes *Popular Government* one of the earliest of the truly modern studies of British political institutions ... [Moreover] few social scientists would nowadays dispute his assertion that great difficulties surround the creation and maintenance of democratic political systems ... (Feaver, 1969: 240)

Indeed, in some ways Maine did not go far enough in identifying the difficulties surrounding 'the creation and maintenance of democratic political systems'. His insistence that democracy 'is simply and solely a form of government' (*PG*: 59–64), which may have been understandable at a time when the wisdom of democratic political systems was being widely debated, is a positive hindrance now, when virtually all nations pay lip-service to the democratic ideal, but when in reality few real democracies exist in the world. It is arguable that, contrary to Maine, the word does a great deal more than simply describe a system of government in which the suffrage is extended to a large portion of the entire nation. Nowadays, the word also reflects a set of attitudes and beliefs, which in fact make democracy possible. We have learned in this century that democracy, in the strict sense of popular government, cannot be imposed where democratic values do not exist, or cannot be created simultaneously with the democratic infrastructure. It is curious that Maine did not say more about this, because he clearly appreciated that the American constitution was a product in large part of an English inheritance, which included a respect for the rule of law, something essential to a constitutional system, like the American, in which the final word on the constitutionality of any action belongs to a judiciary which, as Hamilton put it, has 'neither force nor will, but merely judgement' (Hamilton et al, 1961: 490). Had Maine paid more attention to the need for a value-system to undergird a democratic political structure, he could actually have argued that a successful democracy was even more difficult to envisage; but he would not have been able so lightly to cite examples from antiquity and from the then recent history of the South and Central American republics.

If Maine failed to consider the importance of a nation's historical experience in determining the likelihood that democracy as a form of government would be sustainable there, a prospect which engages twentieth-century political scientists, he did anticipate many of the other modern concerns about democratic government. Maine already saw that Cabinet government resulted in transferring much of the legislative power from the House of Commons to the Ministers of the Crown. Not only has the Cabinet succeeded to whatever legislative powers previously resided in the Crown, but, 'it has taken to itself nearly all the legislative power of Parliament, depriving it in particular of the whole right of initiation' (*PG*: 115). The power to initiate legislation, in effect to define the legislative agenda, remains a matter of contention in the United States, where a President may be of one party and the majority in the legislature may be of another, and where, even when President and legislature are of the same party, there is a tradition of legislative independence foreign to the British model, facilitated perhaps by the fact that the President serves out his term of office, irrespective of the success or failure of his legislative programme. None the less, the leadership role taken by the President in setting priorities and focussing public attention on his agenda demonstrates that Maine's insight is as relevant to constitutional government in the United States as to Cabinet government in Britain. Moreover, one reason Maine identified as to why the initiative would pass to the executive remains relevant today: 'the inevitable difficulties produced by ... [the] numerousness' of the legislative branch (*PG*: 94): 'it now appears that the scanty attendance of Members [of Parliament], and the still scantier participation of most of them in debate, are essential to the conduct of business by the House of Commons ...' (*PG*: 94).

Maine also anticipated the problem of public opinion: how it was formed, how it was to be ascertained, the ease with which it could be manipulated. This has been a continuing theme of modern writers on democracy; and, if Maine did not foresee the effect which the extension of education to the masses would have on their ability to participate in the public debate, he has been proven prescient in recognizing the impact on what he called 'The ruling multitude' of the opinion 'of a great party leader', 'of a small local politician', 'of an organised association', or of 'an impersonal newspaper' (*PG*: 92).

Maine's discussion of the difficulty of determining what constitutes a mandate from the electorate, particularly in the context of the power of the House of Lords to meddle with legislation passed by the Commons, is as pertinent as the recent controversy over the attempt by the Lords to amend or entirely reject the Local Government Finance Bill. In *Popular Government*, Maine noted that 'the most influential members of the House of Lords allowed that it would act improperly in rejecting a constitutional measure, of which the electoral body had signified its approval by the result of a general election' (*PG*: 118–19). One hundred years later, in the midst of a contentious debate over the Community Charge, a form of poll tax introduced by the Local Government Finance Bill, Lord Hailsham asserted in a letter to *The Times* (28 April 1988) that 'It is now generally considered unconstitutional for the House of Lords to reject on second reading a Government Bill introduced after a general election when the proposal embodying it was contained in the manifesto before the election.' Yet, how valid is this assumption of a popular mandate? What are its contours? In an editorial, *The Times*, for example, insisted on distinguishing between the general philosophy behind the Community Charge and the actual detail of the tax, 'which emerged later, much of it after the manifesto' (*The Times*, 20 April 1988, p. 15). A century earlier, Maine had expressed similar sentiments about the vagueness of the concept of a mandate:

What is a mandate ...? I can conjecture that it ... means an express direction from a constituency which its representative is not permitted to disobey, and ... to imply that the direction may be given in some loose and general manner. But in what manner? Is it meant that, if a candidate in an election address declares that he is in favour of household suffrage or woman suffrage, and is afterwards elected, he has a mandate to vote for it, but not otherwise? And, if so, how many election addresses, containing such references, and how many returns, constitute a mandate to the entire House of Commons? (*PG*: 118–19)

Despite all that has been said about the value of *Popular Government*, of its insights, of its connection with the ideas rehearsed by Maine in *Ancient Law*, of the sense of closure which it may be seen as giving, even if in a direction which many of us deplore, to the ideas of *Ancient Law*, still, as Professor Feaver says, 'it remains ... an unsatisfactory book' (Feaver, 1969: 240). Feaver points out a great many of the theoretical shortcomings of Maine's thesis (240–1); but beyond that, and beyond the view of so many that *Ancient Law* is Maine's optimistic work and *Popular Government* his pessimistic one, and a pessimisim of a particularly disagreeable sort, it is simply the case that whereas *Ancient Law* is rich and dense and pregnant with speculative possibilities, *Popular Government* seems, at least in contrast, schematic and superficial; above all, it is virtually bereft of the brilliant generalizations of Maine's earlier works: memorable phrases still abound, but they do not make the kind of 'unexpected associations' (Woodard, p. 217) which provide the reader with grand principles for ordering the world.

CHAPTER I

The Victorian values of Sir Henry Maine

George Feaver

I

It is best that we begin our re-examination of a life notable for the ideas associated with it, as near as we are able, at the beginning. It was in Cambridge, in the middle years of the nineteenth century, that the ground was made ready for a much wider appreciation to come, in Great Britain and abroad, of a distinctive intellectual talent in legal scholarship and social theory. It was a talent that would ultimately win for him in his later lifetime and in the tumultuous century which has passed since his demise the rare intellectual accolade that Maine was the author of a book that epitomized the spirit of an age, a book regarded by posterity as a classic.

It was at Trinity Hall, in the late summer of 1844, that fresh from his brilliant undergraduate studies at nearby Pembroke College, Henry Maine was to take up rooms near what was then the mathematics lecture-room in the principal court and to begin his career as a junior classics tutor. That tutorship was only the first step of a personal and public progress – he would leap-frog from the tutorship in a matter of only three years to become, in June 1847, the very youthful Regius Professor of Civil Law in unreformed Cambridge, and simultaneously, in another display of an unerring penchant for accumulating public appointments, Reader in Jurisprudence and Civil Law at the Middle Temple, London – that would carry Maine in the span of his relatively short lifetime from modest and even obscure beginnings to a position high on the ladder of arrived Victorian social mobility. Indeed, the prestigious university and public-service appointments which, in the 1840s, lay still in the future, appear in retrospect as way points in an aspiring life lived with more than a passing resemblance to that triumphal theoretical movement 'from status to contract' with which, as a juridical scholar and social scientist, Maine has ever since the publication of *Ancient Law* in 1861 been so inextricably linked.

Some years after Henry Maine began his junior classics tutorship at Trinity Hall, though in the same place, he was to be installed as Master in a special ceremony held in the College Chapel, on Christmas Day 1877. In becoming Master, Maine was the real-life beneficiary of complex behind-the-scenes manoeuvres aimed at breaking an electoral deadlock calling to mind C. P. Snow's fictional account of a similar episode in *The Masters* (1951). 'The Fellows of Trinity Hall have been engaged for nearly six months in a struggle to elect one of two candidates out of their own number', Sir Henry wrote sanguinely after the fact to Lord Salisbury. 'They were divided six against six, and the man who should have given the casting vote is a lunatic in confinement. They therefore put strong pressure on me to accept the office before the nomination lapsed' (cited in Feaver, 1969: 174).

Like other Maine letters which have survived, this one suggests a biographical figure not lacking in skills of self-promotion, though Maine was never a physically robust man. As the *Dictionary of National Biography* notes, a lifelong delicacy of constitution contributed to what it calls his 'inability for drudgery' (1963–4: XII, 789). But the skills made up for the delicacy, as is reflected in the fact that, by the date he became Master of Trinity Hall, Maine, in lieu of an apparently disappointed hope for a Privy Councillorship, was styled 'Sir Henry Sumner Maine, KCSI', celebrated author of *Ancient Law* and other pioneering studies in Roman and Aryan legal antiquities deftly drawing upon the 'historical and comparative method'. A fuller account would include the information that Sir Henry was erstwhile Legal Member of the Governor-General's Indian Council at Calcutta, 1862–9, and subsequently, life member of the Secretary of State for India's Indian Council: that he had been lately Corpus Professor of Jurisprudence in the University of Oxford: that he had continued over the years as a frequent and valued contributor to the quality periodicals of the nation's capital: and that he was a member (indeed an apparent *habitué*), of the Athenaeum Club in London's Pall Mall. All of which is to say, reading between the lines of this gloss of a hypothetical *Who's Who* entry for the rising Master of Trinity Hall in 1877, that by that date, Sir Henry Maine was a member in good standing of the newer Victorian Social Establishment.

The guests at a Trinity Hall Christmas banquet to mark Sir Henry's installation in the Mastership included the Master of his own undergraduate college, Pembroke, and his tutor there, the now aged Dr Guillemard. And when a special memorial service was held in the Trinity Hall Chapel, eleven years later, on the occasion of Maine's burial in February 1888, it was attended among others – to bring this brief academic curriculum vitae from its 'end-point' back to its 'beginnings' – by Dr C. E. Searle, the then Master of Pembroke who had been a lifelong friend of Maine dating from their pre-Cambridge schooldays together at the London charitable school, Christ's Hospital.

II

We know in sufficient detail all that we need to know of Sir Henry Maine's literal biographical 'end-point'. He had written to Lord Acton from the Master's Lodge, Trinity Hall, on 7 December 1887 informing him of his plan, for reasons of ill health, to spend a period of a month or so on the Riviera in the New Year, unaccompanied by Lady Maine, and seeking Acton's help in finding 'a quiet hotel not too much on the slope and not at too vast a distance from your quarters', taking pains to impress upon his correspondent that his request was 'not by any means intended as a covert invitation of myself to La Madeleine', Acton's villa at Cannes. He was to write again, this time from the Athenaeum Club, ten days later, acknowledging Acton's help, and informing him that he would leave England on Wednesday 4 January 1888, en route to the Mediterranean and the Montfleury Hotel, Cannes, which had been recommended to him by Acton (Acton Papers a, 7 and 17 December 1888). In a letter sent to Prime Minister Gladstone on 19 January from his Riviera residence, Acton mentions that 'Maine is on my hands, laid up with overwork'; to Gladstone's daughter, Mary, he confided under separate cover that Maine seemed 'at times ... nearly as good as ever, and quite happy about himself, only disinclined to study, and a Tory of the most ordinary and uninteresting type' (cited in Feaver, 1969: 259). Then, on 1 February, Maine suffered a stroke and lay in a coma at the Montfleury for two days before dying, on Friday 3 February 1888. As a consequence of these circumstances of his passing, his remains, like those of his contemporary and fellow English luminary, J. S. Mill, were interred in France.

We know, then, a good deal of detail about the circumstances surrounding Maine's death, even though his own private papers were alas subsequently destroyed. It was an event which attracted more than the usual amount of public attention because by the date of his demise, Maine's achievements were widely perceived to be those of a truly 'eminent Victorian' of the pre-Lytton Strachey sort – and they were hailed as such in a lengthy obituary in *The Times*, in which he was depicted as an English Montesquieu. Public recognition of this elevated stature would find its ultimate expression in the form of an honour reserved for few of his countrymen, when a commemorative medallion was unveiled in Westminster Abbey paying tribute to Maine's signal contributions as one who had 'investigated the learning of the ancients, Framed new legislation for India, Laid open the sources of ancient law for his own people'.

When we turn from a consideration of the detailed circumstances surrounding Maine's 'end-point' to those of his beginnings, we cannot say nearly as much with certainty. Henry Maine was not by birth a member of what Lord Annan once described, in a well-known paper, as 'The Intellectual Aristocracy' of England (1955: 243–87). 'I have never known such a mystery' is the testimony of one who by dint of his own family ties could claim full membership in that elite circle, Sir James Fitzjames Stephen. 'Intimate as we have been, I know absolutely nothing of [Maine's] family connections', Stephen was to write of his longtime friend and fellow jurist in his unpublished autobiography (cited in Feaver, 1969: 4). Another friend of long standing, and his Victorian biographer, the Liberal politician and diarist Sir M. E. Grant Duff, likewise alludes to Maine's habitual reticence about his origins, in informing us that Maine was born 'near Leighton' (Grant Duff, 1892: 2).

But Venn's *Alumni Cantibrigienses* gives Maine's birth as occurring at Hockcliffe, Bedfordshire, on 15 August 1822. And in the earliest surviving documentary evidence known to me, the *Childrens' Register* of Christ's Hospital, recording Maine's entry there as an Almoner in April 1829, it is striking that the year of Maine's birth should differ from that given in both Grant Duff and Venn, and that there is no direct information at all about the place of birth. 'Henry Ja^s Sumner Main, Son of James Main', runs the entry (Christ's Hospital MSS 12818 (15)), 'Born 15 Augt 1821; admitted from Henley-on-Thames, Oxfordshire'. Accounts later in his life were variously to portray Maine as a native of Scotland, Ireland and India.

Certainly Maine had Scottish relations. He was to marry his cousin Jane, a native of Kelso, Roxburghshire; and his father, it seems, was a Scots physician who we may assume migrated to England around 1818 since he is entered as a medical graduate *in absentia* of Aberdeen University in November of that year. But this 'Dr Main' remains a shadowy figure, and we do not know exactly when his eventual marriage to Eliza Fell of Caversham Grove, Oxfordshire, occurred. It is equally unclear what became of him after Henry's arrival on the scene, although the *Lincoln's Inn Admission Records, 1800–93*, in its entry for Henry Maine, refers to his father as 'of the Province of Hindustan, dec'd.'. Grant Duff offers no explanation of just why, as he says, Maine's earliest years were spent in Jersey; nor does he provide elaboration of an oblique reference to 'family difficulties soon supervening', which, according to him, led to Henry's removal to England, where 'he was brought up thenceforward exclusively by his mother' (1892: 2). Nor do we know anything about the circumstances surrounding the upwardly mobile Maine's singular good fortune, for one otherwise bereft of claims to privileged social pedigree, to have had as his godfather John Bird Sumner, who was in the period of young Henry Maine's birth Vicar of Mapledurham, but was to become in due course the Archbishop of Canterbury.

Although we know little of Maine's earliest years, there is a hitherto unpublished letter in the Guildhall Library, London, sent 'with extreme regret' from Christ's Hospital to 'Mrs. Eliza Jean Main, Henley-on-Thames' and dated 10 Feby 1830', informing her that

> your Son, Henry James Sumner Main, now a boy of this House, has contracted such inveterate habits of personal uncleanliness, as to render him unfit for the society of the other Chil^n; and the medical officer of the Establish^t, under whose care he has been placed, having failed in effecting his cure, I am directed to request that you will remove him to your own house, until such time as, by your maternal attention, he is reclaimed from his disagreeable habits. (Christ's Hospital MSS 12828 (12))

We learn nothing more from the Hospital's records of this evocatively Dickensian incident, evidence perhaps of a profound infantile insecurity. But it is pleasing to note an item in the letterbooks some ten years on, recording more auspicious news of young Henry Maine – news calling to mind Dr Johnson's tongue-in-cheek observation about Lord Mansfield, who was educated in England, that 'Much may be made of a Scotchman, if he be *caught* young.' 'It was agreed to recommend to the Court', runs the entry, 'that Henry James Sumner Main be sent to Pembroke Hall in the University of Cambridge ... with an Exhibition of £60 p Annum for 4 years ... with the usual allowances for Apparel, Caution Money, Settling Fees and Books ... to commence from Michaelmas 1840', and a standard caveat to the effect that in case he 'marry, misbehave or absent himself from College, to cease immediately' (Christ's Hospital MSS 12806 (15), ff. 478–9).

Another entry two years later, the first documented instance of the Anglicized spelling of Henry Maine's surname, suggests the evident irrelevance in his case of this proviso, and good reason for the confidence of his Christ's Hospital mentors in the young scholar's promise. In it, a letter from the Upper Grammar Master is read into the record. 'Since [the Rev. Dr Rice] had the honour of communicating ... the gratifying circumstances that Henry James Sumner Maine, one of the Scholars of the House, had gained two of the annual Prizes in the University of Cambridge ... *another* of these Prizes has been adjudged to him, viz. the Latin Alcaic Ode; and he should perhaps observe, in illustration of the meritorious exertions of this young man, that, though this Prize was established nearly 90 years ago, he is the first Scholar of Christ's Hospital that has obtained it.' The entry continues with a resolution

that this gratifying communication be reported to the General Court this day, with a recommendation that the compliment of Thirty Guineaus proposed to be given to Mr. Maine in the Committee's Report of the 7th inst. be increased to Fifty Guineaus as a token of the Governors' approbation of these honourable exertions of his abilities by which he has reflected so much credit on this House as the place of his education. (Christ's Hospital MSS 12806 (15), f. 566)

The Court's action brought forth a fulsome response from the pen of the client of its generous patronage. Sent from Pembroke College, Cambridge, on 23 July 1843 under the signature of 'Henry J. S. Maine', the letter acknowledges 'the munificent encouragement you have lately bestowed on my humble endeavours', while protesting that 'I have received too much at your hands to allow me to think otherwise than that any success of mine at the University is but a tribute already due to you.' It is the earliest extant Maine letter known to me (Christ's Hospital MSS 23806 (15), f. 569). Some five years before it was written, the Victorian age, with the young

Queen's succession to the throne in 1837, had already technically begun. The public *ethos* that would come to be known as 'Victorian' still awaited the achievement of its self-conscious voice. But it seems clear that it was in the ferment of these years, impressionable youthful years for Maine at Pembroke College and Trinity Hall, Cambridge, that there were first nurtured in him his 'Victorian values'.

III

Ideas, like individual lives, have figurative pedigrees and biographies. The life of Sir Henry Maine was an achieved Victorian life; but our interest in it is not an interest exclusively in terms of the significance of its literal biographical 'beginnings' and 'end-points' and of 'what happened' between the two. Historians of ideas, as Sir Isaiah Berlin once observed, however scrupulous and minute they may feel it necessary to be, 'cannot avoid perceiving their materials in terms of some kind of pattern' (1969: 1). And our interest in the life of Henry Maine is drawn by the relation of his characteristic ideas to the fortunes of liberal thought in nineteenth-century Britain, and so to the question of whether or not a renewed assessment of his standing as a 'representative' thinker of the Victorian age is perhaps merited. It is the interest of a successor scholarly generation undertaking to pronounce, at the convenient if arbitrary juncture of the passage of a century since our principal's death, upon the continued relevance or irrelevance of his characteristic ideas, theories and polemizing discontents (cf. Cocks, 1988).

That said, if there is such a thing as a right fit between a man and the age into which he is born, then Henry Maine seems an apposite instance, inasmuch as he was a direct beneficiary of a new atmosphere of opportunity centred upon the emergent Victorian age in the years of his early adulthood. In the ancient universities, outmoded curricula and a ramshackle system of corporate governance, dating from the late medieval world but still largely intact near the close of the eighteenth century, were to be gradually modified if not transformed in the course of a dawning era of liberalism characterized by the erosion of religious belief and the rising prestige of science and individualism and the spirit of reform.

Now, the genius of Sir Henry Maine, as has been remarked, was a highly idiomatic genius, in mood certainly Victorian and yet something more, said perceptively at the time of his death by the American jurist Oliver Wendell Holmes Jr to have consisted in 'the gift of imparting a ferment' (Howe, 1942: 1, 31). At the same time, Maine's works display a trademark stylistic flair reflected in Woodrow Wilson's admiring tribute to the author of *Ancient Law*, near the close of the nineteenth century, as 'a lawyer with a style, [who] belongs, by method and genius, among men of letters' (Wilson, 1898: 363). Maine was, as the future President of the United States astutely noted, in a certain sense a paradoxical pioneer of modern social science, because his claims to greatness would survive 'not ... by reason of the abundance and validity of his thought, but by reason of his form and art' (Wilson, 1898: 364).

It was an age of progress; and at the time of Henry Maine's early years in Cambridge, change was in the air, in the ancient universities as in the nation at large. Sir James Stephen, LL B, Trinity Hall, 1812, recollected sardonically of his own undergraduate years in the unreformed university several decades before Maine's own arrival at Cambridge, that they had been akin to a three- or four-year residence in 'a pleasant, though not a very cheap, hotel ... if they had been passed at the Clarendon, in Bond Street, I do not think that the exchange would have deprived me of any aids for intellectual discipline, or for acquiring literary or scientific knowledge' (cited in Roach, 1959: 133). But by mid-century, when Stephen's son Leslie followed in his footsteps at Trinity Hall (himself close on the Cambridge undergraduate years at Trinity Hall of his brother, and Maine's close friend, James Fitzjames Stephen), the universities were rousing from their long scholarly torpor and beginning to exhibit a renewed sense of responsibility in their role as stewards of intellectual discipline and the acquisition of literary and scientific knowledge.

In religious matters, the Tractarian Movement 'against Popery and Dissent', centred in the 1830s on Oxford's Oriel College and aimed at restoring moribund Anglican High Church liturgical traditions, had aroused heated controversy in what was becoming a more self-consciously tolerant and reformist age, and was by the mid 1840s in retreat; at the same time, Cambridge, with its own spiritual inheritance of eighteenth-century Evangelicism, had witnessed a growing acceptance of more intellectually accommodative attitudes towards questions of religious belief. As Leslie Stephen was to recall of Cambridge in the 1850s, 'Individuals might belong to what were then called the "high", "low" or "broad" parties, but their differences did not form the ground for any division in University politics. We left such matters to Oxford' (cited in Harvie, 1976: 29).

Henry Maine himself, it seems, had been little troubled by religious matters throughout what would have been for him these formative years. Circumstantial evidence, in the form of a number of articles he wrote for the *Saturday Review* in the 1850s, suggests a temperamental distaste for religious enthusiasm; as for the Oxford Movement, on the other hand, Grant Duff suggests that 'although he was too civil to say so, except to those with whom he was very intimate, Maine regarded most of his Oxford contemporaries as just a little off their heads' (1892: 10). He offers no explanation for Maine's antipathy towards the Tractarians; but one reason might have been the Oxford Movement's sensitivity to the social obligations of the Church.

At any rate, prior to taking up the junior classics tutorship at Trinity Hall, Maine had apparently sought a position at his own undergraduate college, Pembroke, but this avenue had been blocked to him by the requirement that a fixed number of Fellows be in Holy Orders. He had settled for the Trinity Hall tutorship rather than the Fellowship that usually accompanied it for similar reasons – and it is interesting to note his somewhat brittle aside, in an article in the *Saturday Review* some five years before the publication of *Ancient Law*, concerning 'the intolerable and irreligious obligation of taking orders as a condition of holding or retaining a College Fellowship' (cited in Burrow, 1966: 139). As Henry Adams comments of the intellectual progenitorship of mid-century figures like Maine and Rudolph Sohm, 'convinced that the clue of religion led to nothing, and that politics led to chaos, one had turned to the law, as one's scholars turned to the Law School, because one could see no other path to a profession' (cited in Feaver, 1969: 265 n. 7).

In a word, then, an intellectually talented and ambitious Henry Maine, with no apparently pronounced religious inclinations, had arrived on the academic scene at the outset of an age in which the growing prestige of the natural sciences was to underlie what Owen Chadwick has aptly called *The Secularization of the European Mind in the Nineteenth Century*. 'The first word we must consider', Chadwick observes, in a passage which applies as readily to the tensions of Henry Maine's individual biography as it does to the dominant intellectual current of the century in which he lived out his life, 'is the word *liberal*. Confused, vague, contradictory, the idea of liberalism dominated the nineteenth century, more a motto than a word, more a programme of what might be than a description of what was; a protean word, which some claimed to rest upon coherent philosophies and economic theory and other saw as the destruction of the stable structure of a reasonable society' (1975:21). In Victorian Britain, the dissolving agency of this emergent liberal *ethos* would result in a reformed system of higher education aimed at serving the professional aspirations of the new Victorian middle classes. And Henry Maine's thought, as well as his life, is appropriately contextualized in terms of these far-reaching developments that would yield in time a more fully institutionalized professoriate wedded to an increasingly secular appreciation of the criteria governing intellectual merit.

IV

Basing his case on an ingenious reading of classical Roman and modern European sources, Maine was to argue in *Ancient Law: Its Connection with the Early History of Society and its Relation to Modern Ideas* (1861) that the characteristic legal arrangements of progressive societies had involved a broad historical movement 'from status to contract', that is, from an early phase of family-based ascriptive statuses in the law of persons to one in which personal relations were deemed to reflect the free agreement of contracting individuals. He also held that consanguinity rather than territoriality had formed the socio-legal basis of primitive Indo-European political society.

Maine's deft conjectures on these topics of a legal and institutional nature, and many others bearing upon what would come to be broadly subsumed under the separate disciplinary interests of sociology and anthropology, including, as Sir Frederick Pollock was to observe (*AL*, 1906a: xvii), the sentiment of reverence evoked by the mere existence of law in early communities, the essential formalism of archaic law, the predominance of rules of procedure over rules of substance in early legal systems, the fundamental differences between ancient and modern ideas as to the legal proof, the relatively modern character of the individual citizen's disposing power, especially by will and freedom of contract, and the still more modern appearance of true criminal law – were further elaborated in a series of books, including *Village-Communities in the*

East and West (1871) (the third edition of which contains the important 1875 Rede Lecture on 'The effects of observation of India on modern European thought'), *Lectures on the Early History of Institutions* (1875), and *Dissertations on Early Law and Custom* (1883).

Now, as Collini, Winch and Burrow have suggested, it requires the cultivation of 'a mood of vicarious euphoria' for us to recapture the sense in which, in the mid-Victorian era, 'the map of learning seemed, to many members of the educated class in England, about to be re-drawn in an exhilaratingly comprehensive and coherent way' (Collini et al., 1983: 209). Maine's writings in advocacy of what was termed the 'historical and comparative method' were centrally important to the fostering of this atmosphere of promise. As Collini and Burrow observe, 'The extent and profundity of Maine's influence among the intellectual class would be hard to exaggerate: he set the terms of debate' (210). Of course, as the authors of the book in which these comments occur also intimate, the aspiration to develop a 'science of politics' in nineteenth-century Britain was an instance of a larger modern project 'in some sense perpetually falling short of its realisation' (3). But at the close of the book, the authors, accepting that 'large ambitions invite tart judgements', none the less submit that the pioneers whose works they have passed in review in this engaging study 'may stand in need of being rescued from the enormous condescension of posterity' (376–7; Gellner, 1974: 195 *passim*).

And so, initial hopes for a new human science 'not less valuable than the sciences of language and of folk-lore', as Maine was himself to assert in his 1875 Rede Lecture – 'I hesitate to call it Comparative Jurisprudence because, if it ever exists, its area will be so much wider than the field of law' (*VC* 1876: 210–11) – were destined to be disappointed in the course of a century of exploration and discovery. In the first place, the findings of prehistoric archaeology would contribute to undercut the generalizing promise of comparative philology, to which Maine here alludes. Evidence that European man had once lived, 'many thousands of years before any period of language which could be reconstructed by even the most speculative uses of comparative philology', much as primitives still did along the upper Amazon and in the Australian bush in the nineteenth century, effectively exploded the claims of philology to have gained real methodological purchase on the remoter reaches of human society (cf. Burrow, 1967: 180–204). At the same time, the rather different approach of the newly arrived social anthropologists, who aimed to study modern savages on the assumption that they had much to teach us of the prehistoric ancestors of civilized man, had the effect of squeezing this historical and comparative method, as it were, from the other end of the historical line of development.

And yet, a century after Maine's death, his famed generalization concerning the movement of progressive societies from status to contract continues to command textbook respect as a leading nineteenth-century attempt at formulating a putative social scientific 'law' comparable in power to Marx's generalizations about class war or Michel's 'iron law of oligarchy' (see, for example, Raphael, 1970: 2; Nisbet, 1986: 79–80). It is this widely acknowledged sense of his standing as an important pioneer of modern social science that draws our attention away from the circumstances surrounding Maine's literal biographical beginning and ending to the somewhat different matter of the life and times of Sir Henry Maine's ideas. But if, following the procedure adopted for examining his biography, we begin as near as we are able at the beginning, we find that satisfactory answers to questions about the origins of Maine's ideas involve their own fair share of mystery.

v

J. W. Burrow has suggested that 'The germination of *Ancient Law* ... lies somewhere in the decade 1843–53 ... the crucial years in the development of Maine as a social theorist' (1966: 140). He contends that, in common with other students of society, Maine owed considerably more to the new philological learning publicized by Max Müller and the London Ethnological society during these formative years than he did to biological evolutionism. In an unsigned review essay on the patriarchal theory that appeared late in his life, Maine does mention a certain Baron von Haxthausen (B3, 1886: 193), who 'appears to have been the authority followed by Maine in his earlier works'. 'Baron von Haxthausen's volumes', Maine observes, 'which appeared in 1849 and 1852, were at once felt throughout Europe to be the revelation of a new social order, having no counterpart in the West, though it had some in the East' (193). Haxthausen was a rather obscure writer on Russian landholding and early Slavonian social organization; an awareness of his work, construed in the context on the new methods of comparative philology, might well have facilitated Maine's intellectual passage towards the self-conscious elaboration of his own, highly idiosyncratic, 'historical and comparative' method in the years prior to the composition of *Ancient Law*.

It was in this early period, too, that Maine first befriended Whitley Stokes, who was his law student during the crucial Middle Temple years. Stokes had by early adulthood become an enthusiastic follower of the German-dominated 'science' of comparative philology, and this interest was reflected in his authorship of a number of scholarly monographs and papers – earning him the accolade, in a Memorial Discourse delivered at Dublin University in 1951, that he was Ireland's greatest philologist (Best, 1951: 3). Maine's *Early History of Institutions*, an attempt to extend the leading generalizations of *Ancient Law* to early Irish legal usages, is dedicated to Stokes, the only book of Maine's with a dedicatory Preface. But comparative philology *per se* cannot be said to be the whole story in these years. Another of Maine's students at the Inns of Court was Frederic Harrison, who was to become England's leading 'positivist', and whose witness, along with that of Grant Duff, corroborates the view that, at the time, Maine was already delivering as law lectures in London the gist of his *Ancient Law* (see Harrison, 1911: 152, cited in Feaver, 1969: 26–7, 268 n. 31). Harrison had actually met the French sociologist and positivist Auguste Comte in Paris during the summer of 1857, the year before Maine became his law tutor. He must have brought his enthusiasm for positivism to his friendship with Maine – an enthusiasm much evidenced, in fact, in a lengthy review of *Ancient Law* in the *Westminster Review* (19 April 1861: 457–77), where Harrison is at pains to depict his law tutor's book approvingly as the product of a capacious intellect more scientifically historical than juristic in the narrow descriptive sense. As Noel Annan rightly suggests (1959), we ought not to underestimate the extent to which even mid-Victorian figures of Maine's subtlety of intellect were touched by a potent intellectual current more robustly embraced by dedicated positivists such as Frederic Harrison.

There was also, of course, the rising prestige of science in general – and this, in the years of Maine's primary intellectual formation, alongside a pronounced tendency in all post-Enlightenment secular learning to couch social scientific discourse in a broadly evolutionary frame of reference. Ernest Gellner has noted how anthropology and sociology thus arose out of 'an evolutionary or Jacob's ladder vision of human societies, the idea of Progress'. The difference between the two, in his view, was that whereas sociology was to take root in a primarily *historical* evolutionism traceable to Condorcet and Hegel, anthropology, a somewhat later, mid-nineteenth-century creation, was destined to be more *biological* and Darwinian in point of evolutionary departure (1988b). Sir Henry Maine does not quite fit the Darwinian part of Gellner's equation, excepting perhaps in his avowedly political writings: but the historical reference, in a figure often remarked on as displaying affinities with von Savigny and the German Historical School (Stein, 1980: Chapter 3), is closer to the mark. The more general point, concerning the allegedly 'scientific' inspiration of much evolutionist imagery, is amply illustrated in a perusal of Maine's writings – even early on, as in his well-known comment that the 'rudimentary ideas' he had undertaken to examine in the surviving legal records of classical antiquity 'are to the jurist what the primary crusts of the earth are to the geologist' (*AL*: 3).

From a rather different angle, one ought also to note the not insignificant fact that, in 1848, Andrew Amos had been appointed Downing Professor of the Laws of England at Cambridge. Amos, who was previously the first incumbent of the Professorship of English Law at University College London, was an authority on Bentham's legal thought; and his arrival in Cambridge cannot but have been noticed by Maine, perhaps indeed contributing to his own initial attraction to juridical speculation. While his own work would of course constitute a claim for substantial modifications of the analytical perspective of Bentham and Austin, Maine makes clear his indebtedness to both these thinkers, whose ideas were in important respects the point of departure for his own complementary methods of historical and comparative inquiry.

In Maine's view, Jeremy Bentham was essentially a law reformer; and John Austin's consuming interest in the precise analysis of contemporary legal terminology was preliminary to a larger theoretical enterprise aimed at a comprehensive delineation of the conditions requisite in a formal account of the legal system of a modern state. But while Maine shared the assumption of each that the proper goal of judicial inquiry was to substitute, for groundless conjecture, facts scientifically adduced, he believed that the Benthamite and Austinian projects failed to appreciate the deep historicity of the law, and so tended to ignore the often instructive connections between the history of legal institutions and the emergence in some instances and not in others of modernizing societies.

What Maine's method required, in short, was historical perspective, a backdrop against which to adumbrate evolving usages in progressive legal systems. As he says in an early publication: 'It is not because our own jurisprudence and that of Rome were once alike that they ought to be studied together, it is because they will be alike' (B2, 1856, in *VC*, 1876: 330–83; compare with *AL*: 3–4). The author of *Ancient Law* thus emerges in his early intellectual *persona* as an evolutionist of a general sort, whose writings hint at a broadly diffusionist perspective, to which was added in due course a consciously inductive method of inquiry (Burrow, 1966: Chapter 5; Stein, 1980: especially Chapters 4–5). But there is not much direct evidence of any contribution of evolutionary biology to an innovative and individualistic approach which, as a faithfully admiring Sir Frederick Pollock was somewhat exaggeratedly to claim in retrospect, did 'nothing less than create the natural history of law' (*AL*, 1906 edn: xiv).

General observations such as these about the chief intellectual influences of Maine's formative years remain necessarily conjectural. Fitzjames Stephen recollected in his unpublished autobiography that although Maine had 'derived, in the most beautiful manner, applications of history and philosophy to Roman Law', the sources of his inspiration remained something of a mystery. 'He found it', according to Stephen, 'As he told me once (half in fun), in the Book of Revelation' (Stephen Papers: Add. 7349, f. 38, quoted in Feaver, 1969: 25). Stephen's half-jesting remark unwittingly reminds us that an emphasis on the authority of 'science' carries us only so far in quest of the inspiration of an idiosyncratic authorial self shaped as much in an early academic preparation in classical scholarship and owing much, too, to a temperamental inclination to general literature. William Cory, a Christ's Hospital contemporary, thought Maine destined to be a poet in mature life; and Frederic Harrison recorded that in the period in which *Ancient Law* was gestating in Maine's mind, he had met in his rooms young intellectuals of literary bent and that together they had 'discussed a good deal of general literature and politics' (1911: 152, quoted in Feaver, 1969: 26). The pattern is a persistent feature of the early years. As a Cambridge undergraduate, Maine's best friend in the Apostles Club was Henry Fitzmaurice Hallam, the brother of Arthur Hallam, whose early death is said to have moved Tennyson to compose *In Memoriam*. Maine later recalled sharing many hours with the younger Hallam 'in reading aloud the older English dramatists' (quoted in Feaver, 1969: 11). Others of Maine's youthful Cambridge circle, including Julian Fane, Franklin Lushington and Tom Taylor, rounded out a small and rather exclusive group united by their love of literature.

The retrospective testimony of Oscar Browning was that when he first met Maine in 1871, he found him 'characteristically, reading a novel' (*Cambridge Fortnightly*, February 1888: 48–50). And when Fitzjames Stephen composed a death notice of Maine, it was also to the literary and creative gift that he paid tribute, in saying of Maine's books that 'they were written as if by inspiration. Their author had a power of seeing the general in the particular which we do not think has been equalled in literary history' (Stephen, 1888: 150). Stephen's judgement was shared by *The Times*, which spoke in its own obituary notice of Maine's 'singular charm of style and skill in composition' (6 February 1888: 8). In his *Survey of English Literature, 1830–1880*, Oliver Elton was to venture the institutionally partisan opinion that 'There is no better Cambridge prose than that of Sir Henry Maine' (1920: 1, 102–3). By that date, *The Oxford English Dictionary* had paid Maine the more ecumenically minded compliment of including, amongst its illustrative citations, passages from each of his books.

If, then, the prestige of mid-Victorian scientific learning must have impressed itself early on upon the mental sensibilities of Henry Maine, the concomitant influences of a formal classical education and a taste for humanistic and creative literature were to play their own part in moulding his characteristic style and mature outlook. With Maine, as with others amongst the greatest innovators of modern social thought, there seems so powerful a personal stamp on his work that search though we may for definitive influences, we find ourselves acknowledging, in a finally irreducible sense, that his intellectual product is an instance of what Robert Nisbet has called *Sociology as an Art Form* (1976: especially Chapters 5–6).

VI

There is the not unrelated matter of the origins of Maine's interest in India. The internal evidence of some of his *Saturday Review* articles in the mid 1850s suggests that he was by then in possession of more than a mere passing acquaintance with Indian affairs (see Feaver, 1969: 65-6). Maine's family on his mother's side seems to have had business dealings in the East Indies prior to 1858. And we have seen that his father had apparently migrated to India at an early, undetermined date. But that is all we can say with any assurance of the intellectual and personal beginnings of an association with the Asian subcontinent – that richly textured panoply of customary practices and 'survivals' which was to exercise so profound an impact on Maine's fertile scholarly imagination and provide the exotic environment in which he would achieve a fame and influence perhaps under-appreciated in our own post-imperial world (cf. Dewey, 1972b; Burrow, 1974).

He was, as John Morley once opined, 'perhaps the most capacious mind ... that England ever sent to India,' (1917: II, 262). Maine had, of course, composed and published *Ancient Law* before his years there from 1862 to 1869. That his first-hand experience of India exercised an indelible influence on his subsequent thought is already apparent in his *Village-Communities in the East and West* (1871), a virtual appendix to *Ancient Law* informed with the generously supportive evidence of almost seven years spent in the East. In a poignant gesture, Maine sent an author's copy of *Ancient Law* to the Viceroy shortly after his arrival in Calcutta, one of a batch he had instructed his publisher to send out from London. British administrators could learn much from absorbing its arguments, the new Legal Member believed. Participating in his first major debate in the Legislative Council, he was to observe that 'the modern progress of society seemed to be intimately connected with the completest freedom of contract, and in some ways, was almost mysteriously dependent on it' (speech of 17 December 1862, in Grant Duff, 1892: 90, quoted in Feaver, 1969: 73).

During his stay in India, and in his years of service as legal adviser to the Secretary of State's Indian Council in London, Maine strove to fashion his celebrated juridical postulates into workable realities. 'From Indian status to British contract' might almost be said to express the *leitmotif* of Maine's Indian connection (cf. Cohn, 1961).

The trick was to get the right mix of modernizing legal initiative and respect for the traditional usages of the Indian village community. The British rulers of India, he was to observe, 'are like men bound to make their watches keep true time in two longitudes at once ... If they are too slow, there will be no improvement. If they are too fast, there will be no security' (*VC*, 1876: 237). Now, there is amply evidenced in Maine's large output of Indian lectures, speeches and minutes, as this passage itself suggests, an internal logical tension more apparent perhaps from the vantage-point of the present than generally perceived at the time. On the one hand, there is an apologia for British imperial hegemony, cast in terms of the responsibilities of a progressive race to oversee the steady administration in a hitherto stationary society of the rule of law. Thus, as Maine was to urge, 'The best relations which can be established between the Europeans and the Natives is surely one of contract, provided only that the contracts are fair ones' (Wood Collection, MSS Eur. F78, quoted in Feaver, 1969: 73). On the other hand, there is the potentially subversive implication of his belief as a student of society in the dissolving power of the movement from status to contract. 'Whatever be the nature and value of that bundle of influences which we call Progress', as he was to reflect, 'nothing can be more certain than that, when a society is once touched by it, it spreads like contagion.' He added that 'though it be virtually impossible to reconcile the great majority of the natives of India to the triumph of western ideas, maxims and practices, which is nevertheless inevitable, we may at all events say to the best and most intelligent of them that we do not innovate or destroy in mere arrogance. We rather change because we cannot help it' (*VC*, 1876: 237).

Passages such as this suggest that, in the conduct of his career in Anglo-Indian administration, Maine was hardly lacking in a sense of delicacy appropriate to the challenges of the undertaking. The surviving evidence is clear indeed that he was an ever-adept legal draftsman in the unflagging service of the political powers that be. 'I remember some years ago', according to the testimony of John Morley, 'that Maine said a serious study of Machiavelli was well worth doing' (Morley, 1917:1, 290). If Jeremy Bentham and James Mill lay boastful claim to be 'the dead legislative of British India (cf. Stokes, 1959), Maine's own role in nineteenth-century Anglo-Indian affairs has about it something closer perhaps to the characteristic machinations of the indispensable Sir Humphrey

Appleby on behalf of Prime Minister James Hacker in the fictional political world of *Yes, Prime Minister*.

Maine's experience of India reinforced what might be called the liberal conservatism of his juridical thought. While it is misleading to regard his status-to-contract theory as nothing other than a vindication of middle-class entrepreneurial attitudes, as Engels first did, in paying Maine the unusual compliment of suggesting that everything useful encompassed by his theoretical insights had already been anticipated by Marx (see Engels, 1884; Krader, 1972; Sugarman, 1983); or, in rather a different manner, as Roscoe Pound contended earlier in this century (see 1925: 55 *passim*; Mensch, 1981: 753–70), it is doubtless the case that Whiggish liberals would find much solace in the most famed generalization of the advancing argument of *Ancient Law*. But one also detects, in what we might loosely call the implied political philosophy of this classic text, a definite Tory strain. There is Maine's famous critique of Bentham's under-appreciation of history; there is the qualification of his admiration of Montesquieu with the observation that he 'looked on the nature of man as entirely plastic ... He greatly underrates the stability of human nature', and the added later assertion that 'The truth is that the stable part of our mental, moral and physical constitution is the largest part of it' (*AL*: 116, 117). And there is his hostility to Rousseau and other moderns who have undertaken to reconstitute the original juridical postulates of a law of nature so as to make them practical (and radical) guides to political action.

Following his return from India, Maine's ostensibly juridical generalizations became more directly political in tone, so that, by the date of his 1875 Rede Lecture, we find him declaring that 'Nobody is at liberty to attack several property and to say at the same time that he values civilisation' (1875c, in *VC*, 1876: 230). And there is, of course, *Popular Government* itself. Posterity has come to view this work as a dyspeptic anti-democratic Tory tract for the times; but Maine himself insisted that the book was merely an extension to the arena of contemporary British political life in the 1880s of the argumentative methods of *Ancient Law*. When the *Popular Government* essay, 'The age of progress', first appeared in the *Quarterly Review*, Maine told Lord Acton that 'I had planned a book applying the principles of my "*Ancient Law*" to Constitutions; and found, just as I did 25 years since, the path obstructed by a priori theories, political rather than juridical' (Acton Papers b, 16 April

1885; *PG*: v–vi, 134). He might have added that his hostility to 'a priori theories' had been steadily reinforced by his experience of Anglo-Indian administration (see Maine, B2, 1887).

VII

A politically unsympathetic Lord Acton was inclined to dismiss Maine's hardened late-in-life political opinions as those of a Tory 'of the most ordinary and uninteresting type'. Yet in an important sense the author of *Ancient Law* had been, all along, an adherent of an essentially liberal outlook, though his own liberalism was of a more old-fashioned, Whiggish variety than that of Acton. What *had* changed was that during the politically eventful later years of Maine's life, the fit between his individualist political beliefs and the increasingly democratic and interventionist direction of public affairs had grown problematic. This was in marked contrast with those more hopeful, early Victorian years, when, in a precocious juristic celebration of the benefits for progressive societies of the movement from status to contract, he had enacted the role of a craftsman setting out a brilliant literary encapsulation of the spirit of the age. Even so, Maine had taken care, in *Ancient Law*, to qualify his views by indicating that the movement from status to contract had '*hitherto*' been the chief engine of progressive advance (*AL*: 170). By the 1880s, when Maine was a fully arrived stalwart of the Victorian Establishment, that qualification had assumed a renewed significance.

Already with the publication of *Village-Communities* in 1871 some commentators had perceived in Maine's findings implications of a radical sort certainly not intended by him. No less a figure than John Stuart Mill had wondered aloud, in the light of Sir Henry's ingenious speculations about the evolution of communal and private property, 'whether the older or the later ideas are best suited to rule the future, and if the change from the one to the other was brought about by circumstances which the world has since outgrown' (1871, in Mill, 1875: IV, 131). Shortly, as the 1880s unfolded, the attention of Britain's radical political intellectuals was drawn to a more self-assured 'socialist revival'; and the foundation of the Fabian Society, in the very year in which Maine's *Popular Government* was published, seemed a poignant harbinger of things to come.

By the century's end, A. V. Dicey (1905) was to confront liberal adherents of Victorian individualism of the minimal state variety with the bold assertion that the period 1865–1900 had been, in fact if not in rhetoric, a period of 'Collectivism', a line of argument that amongst other things set in train a disparate literature of rebuttal and refinement of Maine's original status-to-contract theory stretching down to P. S. Atiyah's recent *The Rise and Fall of Freedom of Contract* (1979). Even as the twentieth century dawned, 'New Liberalism' set the tone for much that was to follow, in insisting that the characteristic socio-political regime of the years ahead would abjure the politics of Tory status and of *laissez-faire* Liberal contract alike in favour of a form of welfare state grounded in a more consensual and semi-communitarian social ethic (see, for instance, Freeden, 1978, Chapters 2–3; 1986: 52–3; Collini, 1979: chapter 1). In a more anthropological perspective, these apparent political trends seemed further to discredit Maine's already deeply embattled patriarchal theory, with its concomitant emphasis on authority, though its reincarnation would be eventually discerned in the form of 'The Patriarchal Welfare State' (Guttman, 1988: 321–60). 'From status to contract', then, cut two ways. And one is reminded of Stanley Baldwin's difficulties when asked which historical thinker had most influenced him. He is reputed to have said firmly that it was Maine. When asked which aspect of Maine's thought he found most striking he said, a little more hesitantly, that it was Maine's view that human progress involved a movement from status to contract. But Baldwin then looked very worried and added, 'or was it the other way round?' (*The Sunday Times*, 9 October 1988: G10).

As the twentieth century itself nears its close, and in the centennial year of Maine's death, it is, then, a fitting time for us to embark on a reassessment of the Victorian political ideas of Sir Henry Maine – the entire range of expressly political-institutional ideas, secreted, as it were, in the interstices of his many contributions to our understanding of progress, of legal education and the social sciences, and of India.

When my biography of Maine was published at the close of the 1960s, the Buskellite consensus was in vogue in British politics. Today it seems to be moribund, and in its place, we have lately heard a good deal of talk about 'Victorian values' (see, for example, Minogue and Biddiss, 1987: 38–54; Jenkins, 1988: 66–7). While the faintly disapproving opening sentence of an anonymous 1969 review of my biography in *The Times Literary Supplement* ran: 'Sir Henry Maine seems almost the "paradigm case" of a Victorian career of Smilesian "self-help"', one notes, as only a very small sign of how things have since changed, that in 1986 there should have appeared a reissue of Samuel Smiles' *Self-Help* – with an admiring introduction by Sir Keith, now Lord, Joseph! More substantial signs of a renewal in recent years of serious interest in libertarian values are to be seen in such scholarly undertakings as Professor W. H. Greenleaf's *The British Political Tradition* (1983), a work of monumental scale aimed at a detailed, multi-volumed charting of Dicey's turn-of-the-century generalizations about the erosion of individualism and the rise of collectivism in Britain. Greenleaf's primary concern is to recount what he regards as a generally melancholy tale; but he detects, from the vantage-point of the late twentieth century, hopeful signs of renewed momentum in the other direction (cf. Letwin, 1978: 52–68; Barry, 1986; Burrow, 1988).

Now, libertarian ideas, in the years in which Maine composed his controversial *Popular Government*, had already come to be closely associated with Conservative parties in practical politics. Sir Henry's preference in the 1880s was thus for the 'libertarian' Conservatism of Lord Salisbury and the Tories, rather than the 'collectivist' radicalism of the Liberal Party under Mr Gladstone (Marsh, 1978: 14–15; P. Smith, 1972: 348n.; Watson, 1973: 86, 156–7). In our own day, of course, libertarian Conservatism has placed great store by the virtues of political economy and an accompanying celebration of the marketplace. But Maine's own point of departure, though he remained insistent on the intimate connection between private property and progressive civilization, lay more directly still in his concern for the continued viability under ostensibly 'popular' government of parliamentary political institutions and for the common inheritance of traditional rights and liberties actually enjoyed by Englishmen (cf. Atiyah, 1987: 22 *et passim*) – a point of departure embedded deeply in a longstanding Whiggish respect for the rule of law. As he was to reflect, almost by way of contrast, of the political economists: 'they are apt to speak of their propositions as true *a priori* and for all time ... they greatly underrate the value, power and interest of that great body of custom and inherited ideas which, according to the metaphor which they have borrowed from the mechanicians, they throw aside as friction' (*VC*, 1876: 233).

One is put in mind of the strictures often levelled by critics at the paradoxical advocacy of libertarian values by champions of the traditional party of authority. As Anthony Quinton has thus suggested, with Lord Salisbury, coincidentally, in mind:

> In the generally Darwinian style of his age, Salisbury was inclined to conceive a successful governing class as the product of natural selection, the result of a competitive struggle in which the ablest rise to the top. But that idea, with the premium it places on change and conflict as conditions required for the selection of ability, is more liberal and individualistic than conservative. (1978: 87)

VIII

It is fitting that these remarks, devoted to a life notable for the ideas associated with it, conclude as near as possible to its ending. But while Sir Henry Maine's literal demise occurred on the French Riviera in February 1888, there was to be no such definitive 'endpoint' for his ideas. That is because Maine's *Ancient Law* is a great book, a classic; and it is primarily as the author of a classic book that we celebrate the achievement of Sir Henry Maine. Thus it was, that while Lord Acton, whose historical learning was legendary, castigated the author of *Popular Government* as a political Tory 'of the most ordinary and uninteresting type', he also took care to include Maine's *Ancient Law* on a list, drawn up in response to a challenge from Mary Gladstone, of 'the hundred best books in the world' (Mary Gladstone Papers, 10 February 1881; Acton Papers b).

Frank Kermode has suggested that a book regarded as a classic has achieved the status of a perpetual contemporary, occupying a place in 'a privileged order of time', where it is immune from qualitative decay. He distinguishes what he calls the Horatian from the imperialist notion of a classic, the first of these signifying a classic by virtue of the fact that it is continually read, the second because it comes to be seen as a timeless reservoir of cultural understanding – as a paradigm of shared experience (cited in Condren, 1985: 214–16). *Ancient Law* corresponds most to Kermode's imperialist type of classic text. A memorable rendering of Victorian values, its theory of 'status to contract' is couched in terms at once specific and general but with sufficient vividness to enable it to outlive such rival claimants as Herbert Spencer's more obtuse *First Principles* notion that 'Evolution ... is a change from an indefinite, incoherent homogeneity, to a definite coherent heterogeneity' (cf. Peel. 1971: 305 n. 24).

In an even more general perspective, Maine's famed description of the legal arrangements of progressive peoples as involving an uncertain progress from status to contract reflects a timeless and expressly English notion of cultural hope and aspiration, tantamount to an antidote to Edward Gibbons' alternative eighteenth-century metaphor of decline and fall. In this respect, Maine's *Ancient Law* is a masterful 'historical and comparative' juridical reworking of the foundation myth of English liberty, an institutional legend finding support in actual historical records pushing back to the thirteenth century a recognizably English sense of individualism based on private property and free contract (cf. Macfarlane, 1978: 186–88).

'When', an aged Maurice Reckitt once asked, 'did Victorianism, end?' (1958: 268–71). It was a question generative of new questions, and of his concluding notion that 'there is a point at which a commentator in a sense says goodbye to "history" and enters upon "the present day"'. Reckitt's words are as relevant to the intellectual legacy of Sir Henry Maine as they are to 'Victorianism'. That is because Maine's very English celebration of the movement 'from status to contract' draws upon the common understanding of an historic people that authority and liberty, so far from being polar opposites, are the mutually complementary safeguards of English liberty. 'One of the paradoxes of history', as Herbert Butterfield once wisely observed,

> has been the way in which the name of England has come to be so closely associated with liberty on the one hand and tradition on the other hand. It seems that freedom amongst Englishmen is not a frisky thing which romps and capers in the spirit of April. Rather it sits into the landscape and broods there like the stain of setting suns. If in some countries liberty is valued as a recent acquisition – treasured as the reward of a battle which was won only yesterday – the British seem to hold it rather as an ancient possession, itself a legacy from the past, almost even the product of tradition. The word liberty is packed with meanings and implications for us ... precisely because it is so ancient a thing and has gathered into itself so much history. (1952: 21; Oakeshott, 1962: 121)

A passage so evocative of the enduring spirit of the civil estate, perenially renewed amidst the changing circumstances of a present situated between obscure historical beginnings and ever-indeterminate end-points, provides an entirely apposite point of entry upon these celebrations of the achievement of Sir Henry Maine.

PART ONE
Maine and the idea of progress

CHAPTER 2

Henry Maine and mid-Victorian ideas of progress
John W. Burrow

The most celebrated and influential of Henry Maine's ideas, adumbrated and repeated elsewhere, received its classic formulation in the two concluding paragraphs of Chapter 5 of *Ancient Law*. 'The movement of the progressive societies has been uniform in one respect. Through all its course it has been distinguished by the gradual dissolution of family dependency and the growth of individual obligation in its place. The Individual is steadily substituted for the Family, as the unit of which civil laws take account ... ' (*AL*: 168). Epitomized in the concept of contract we have 'a phase of social order in which all these relations [of persons] arise from the free agreement of Individuals' (169). The chapter concludes with Maine's best-known phrase to express 'the law of progress thus indicated': using the term 'Status' to exclude powers and privileges which are even remotely the result of agreement, 'we may say that the movement of the progressive societies has hitherto been a movement *from Status to Contract*' (170).

Unquestionably Maine's most famous dictum, it is also arguably one of his more ambiguous ones. The economy of epigram requires a compression of logic. Attention has rightly been drawn by Professor Feaver, in his authoritative study of Maine, to the significance of 'has hitherto', to deny that the tendencies to collectivism later in the century which Maine, like many of his contemporaries, so deplored, contradicted his most famous generalization in the sense that the latter appeared to contain an unfulfilled prediction (Feaver, 1969: 55). It is surely right to protest, as Professor Feaver does, against the interpretation of Maine's dictum strictly as a prediction. But while this caution is perfectly justified, it would be unfortunate if it, and Maine's own cautionary 'has hitherto', led us to treat the statement simply as an historical one, because there is surely a further layer of meaning. There are strong suggestions in Maine's formula not just of an historical generalization but of a definition. Strictly the statement could mean that progress ('the movement of the progressive societies') has been *correlated* with the development of which Maine speaks. But that, in context, is surely not what he means. He means it is an *aspect* – perhaps the most important – of their progressiveness, of what makes it proper to call them progressive. In that sense, with or without the qualification 'has hitherto', the future course of mere events can neither confirm nor disconfirm the dictum. But in that case, what force does 'has hitherto' have? It was, we may note in passing, something of a verbal tic of Maine's. Thus, in *Popular Government* we find 'the progress of mankind has hitherto been affected by the rise and fall of aristocracies', and 'from that form of political and social ascendancy all improvement has hitherto sprung, (*PG*: 42, 189). In *Ancient Law* it consorts badly with the purely definitional aspect of what Maine is surely intending to assert at that point (the societies 'hitherto' progressive may cease to progress, but the criteria of what made them 'progressive' will not change, for Maine, because they are not just a mechanism but part, or more than part, of what it means to progress). But the dictum is historical as well as definitional, and in this sense 'has hitherto' does have a function, introducing a characteristic element of caution – it might be too much at this point to speak of an incipient pessimism – into the formulation of something his contemporaries might well, and perhaps not altogether unjustifiably, interpret predictively and even deterministically: a 'law of progress'. Indeed, they might legitimately have complained that a 'law' is not much of a law if it offers only historical generalizations and no assurances for the future. But what, it seems justifiable to infer, gave it for Maine the certainty (in fact more than the certainty) implied by a law was not its predictive but its moral authority. It formulated the law of progress not because future progress was certain but because no other comprehensive social development would count as such.

I have laboured the ambiguous and dual character of Maine's 'law of progress' in order to begin by insisting on the obvious: the sense in which 'Status to Contract' for Maine expresses not merely an historical truth ('hitherto') but a moral polarity, which no future social development could cancel; a distinction between two moral as well as social worlds: custom set against analysis and intellectual energy, tradition against expediency, dependence against self-reliance, superstitious fear against mutual trust. Maine is strikingly insistent on the moral growth implied by 'the virtues on which Contract depends... good faith and trust in our fellows' (*AL*: 306; cf. 70–1). This, 'which parallels the loyalty of the antique world' (306), represents something he says many are reluctant to admit, but it is for him a demonstration that between the primitive Romans and ourselves 'morality has advanced from a very rude to a highly refined conception – from viewing the rights of property as exclusively sacred to looking upon the rights growing out of the mere unilateral reposal of confidence as entitled to the protection of the penal law' (307; but cf. n. 4 below). Contract is not the primal but the distinctively modern form of obligation.

It is a thought which characteristically gives a sharp-edged and memorable formulation to ideas which reach back far into the Whig tradition and touch those of the Scottish Enlightenment. We may think of Macaulay, his predecessor as Legal Member of the Viceroy's Council, stressing that keeping one's word, standing by one's bond, is the central Whig virtue, which makes the existence of the National Debt a source of strength and not of weakness, compared with the distinctive Tory virtue of loyalty,[1] and insisting too that it is the distinctive European virtue in the East, and the one on which British authority, as 'the one power in India on whose word reliance can be placed', ultimately rests (Macaulay, 1866: VI, 419). It reaches back, of course, beyond Macaulay to the eighteenth-century discussion, above all Scottish, of the ethics of commercial society and of its distinctive (and distinctively modern) forms of interdependence.

In *Ancient Law* the thought had too, perhaps, a topicality which it is easier for us to miss, when Maine uses it to endorse a belief – which he claims is reluctantly accorded – in moral progress. The explicit target is, of course Rousseau, and the cult of primeval goodness or innocence which was always such an irritant to Maine. For contemporary readers there could have been another – Buckle, the first volume of whose *History of Civilization* had appeared in 1857 (the second appeared in the same year as *Ancient Law*), in which, on quite different grounds from Rousseauist ones, he had insisted on the insignificance of moral compared with intellectual progress as a factor in the development of civilization. Maine's account, based on

---

[1] For a discussion of this in Macaulay, see Burrow, 1981: 77.

his speculative reconstruction of the stages of Roman law, and here, particularly, of the law of contract, strikingly and consciously weaves together moral and intellectual considerations in a manner far more subtle than anything in Buckle, and could have been read by contemporaries as a correction, even if it was not Maine's intention to supply one.

Mention of Buckle is, at all events, a reminder both that contemporary accounts of progress or the development of civilization were notably various and also that the early 1860s mark something of a watershed, with Buckle representing an older and Maine a newer way of conceiving it. The year 1861 was, indeed, something of an *annus mirabilis*, seeing the publication not only of *Ancient Law* and of Buckle's second volume but also of Mill's *Representative Government* and Friedrich Max Müller's *Lectures on the Science of Language* (1st series). All of these works made much of their inductive methodological credentials. Buckle, Maine and Max Müller all loudly proclaimed the superiority of 'the historical method' over the 'speculative' and their allegiance to it. Yet there was a cultural fissure none the less, and it is one which, making due allowance for points of continuity, made Maine's and Max Müller's writings portents (with the former's acknowledged borrowing from philology of his conception of the 'comparative method' for studying the primitive 'Aryan' world)[2] in ways that Buckle's and Mill's books, influential in its own way though the latter was to be, were not. It is a contrast worth attending to. Of course, to bracket Mill's conception (the plural would perhaps be preferable) of progress with Buckle's is in many respects to travesty it; the parallels are not close when seen from any other perspective than the one I am adopting here. Yet at least in their omissions it is possible to distinguish them from the representatives of the 'younger generation' for whom Maine was to be the most influential spokesman. Buckle expresses in its purest form the belief in man's tendency to better his condition, above all through intellectual discovery and its application; the complications come in the various impediments to progress, in the form of religious and political establishments, rather than in its innate principle of movement. In him, in a more emphatically positivist vocabulary, we have the complete fusion of eighteenth-century ideas of enlightenment, and denunciations of clerical obscurantism, with economic *laissez-faire*.

---

[2] See, especially, Rede Lecture, reprinted in *VC*, 1876; *AL*: 122.

Mill's conception of progress is more multi-layered and, notoriously, more anxious. Similarly focussed on notions of intellectual freedom and the progressive function of the discovery of truth, it also incorporated a brooding Tocquevillean concern with the implications for European society of the decline of aristocracy and the advent of democracy which left ample room for hesitancies and forebodings. Mill's Francophilia, too, prompted an abiding contempt for the self-satisfaction and narrowness of English provincialism which has more in common with Matthew Arnold than with Buckle's blithe, provincial, *laissez-faire* version of progressive enlightenment. Even so, in turning against Comte and in learning from Guizot and Tocqueville the importance of diversity and the horror of uniformity of opinion, Mill rediscovered something of the hostility to establishments originally learned from his father (Mill, 1873: chapter 1), intensified as an acute sociological anxiety on behalf of the conditions of continued progress. The problem came to seem that of providing the social or political bases for the authority of intellect without sterilizing it by its monopoly as a mandarinate.

But though Mill's thought is so much richer than Buckle's and though the anxieties he expressed about the deadening implications for progress of the pressure of democratic public opinion were to become almost canonical – the central concerns of *Representative Government* are still those of Maine's *Popular Government* a quarter of a century later – *Representative Government* is, for all that, intellectually speaking not contemporary with *Ancient Law*, nor, despite its continuing reputation, does it belong, as Maine's book was so influentially to do, with later works of the seventies dealing with the development of civilization: with Bagehot's *Physics and Politics* (1872), Freeman's *Comparative Politics* (1873) or Stubbs' *Constitutional History* (1874-8).

We can trace in these, of course, as we can in Maine's work, the persisting importance of more or less perennially Whig and Liberal themes, such as the distinctiveness of progressive European civilization and the antithesis it presents to an Orient represented variously by Turkey, Byzantium, China and India (as well as, in the more insular formulations, by France). The positive values of Europe (or England), which in *Ancient Law* are epitomized in contract, are represented by the crucial importance of diversity and of what Stubbs called constitutionalism, Freeman (sometimes) Democracy, and Bagehot 'government by discussion'. (Maine, in upholding the civilizing role of Roman law, which mid-Victorians sometimes viewed with some suspicion as the parent of despotism,[3] took issue with the ultra-Teutonism of many of his contemporaries, but did so, significantly, in terms of the agreed value of 'diversity' (*AL*: 366).)

Yet all these works, if their central themes are in some measure traditional, were also crucially shaped by something which plays no significant part in Buckle's or Mill's conception of the history of civilization, though it had been a concern, earlier, of the Scottish Enlightenment: the central idea of the emergence of European societies out of tribalism into nationality and (with varying degrees of emphasis) individualism, and the notion that the ways that transition was effected had had crucial and abiding consequences, and that they hence constituted vital clues to what Maine, at the beginning of *Ancient Law*, called one of the great secrets which inquiry has yet to penetrate, 'The difference between the stationary and progressive societies' (23).[4] It was this, of course, which gave these apparently remote historical reconstructions their polemical thrust and contemporary relevance, and with it a sense that the advance of Maine's 'communities which were destined to civilization' (*ELC*: 281–2) had been a precarious achievement, as well as providing the historical warrant for such a highly topical, polemical maxim as that 'Nobody is at liberty to attack several property and to say at the same time that he values civilization' (Rede Lec., 1875c, in *VC*, 1876: 230). The effect of stressing, as Maine was so often to do, the normality of the 'unprogressive' condition of mankind, the implacable conservatism and custom-bound rigidity of most human societies, was to make progress seem not so much a self-generating, ultimately invincible process, hindered in different ways and to differing degrees in different societies, which therefore represented different stages of advancement, but rather a rare and fortunate mutation, dependent on a certain set of conditions and vulnerable to their displacement.

---

[3] E.g. Stubbs. See Burrow, 1981: 134.

[4] This famous concession to ignorance seems to have been drawn from Maine by his inability to assimilate what he perceived to be the stagnation of Chinese society to the religious model suggested by India. Conceding the fact that China had passed the point where 'a rule of law is not yet discriminated from a rule of religion', Maine argued that 'progress seems to have been there arrested, because the civil laws are coextensive with all the ideas of which the race is capable'. *AL*: 23. Maine's concession to ignorance undoubtedly reflects his dissatisfaction with this explanation.

Of course we must not overstress the novelty of the newer perspective. Behind the flowering of British interest in the early Aryan (and sometimes more exclusively Teutonic) institutions from the sixties onwards, which some adepts – it was a contentious matter[5] – made coextensive with the early history of civilization, there lay distinguished forebears from the earlier part of the century: Jacob Grimm, Niebuhr, Savigny, Georg von Maurer, in Germany; Grote and Kemble in England. Not all was new, even in the presentation of what Maine called 'the recent inquiries which have extended the history of the human race in new directions' (*PG*: 143). Moreover, though some, like Freeman, concentrated exclusively on the history of institutions (and in his case political institutions), for others, of whom Maine and Bagehot are the most notable, the triumphs of the speculative intellect are given something like their traditional Enlightenment role. We have already seen in Maine the interweaving of moral and intellectual considerations in his account of the development of Roman law. It was, in part, a story of secularization and a distinctly Benthamite triumph of analysis and expediency over ritual and custom. In addressing an Indian audience (the University of Calcutta), Maine allowed himself to speak much more like a full-blooded spokesman of the Enlightenment as the triumph of free intellectual inquiry, and even, it seemed, to withdraw something of what he had said in *Ancient Law* (for example 70–1) about moral advance: 'If the mind of man had been so constituted as to be capable of discovering only moral truths, I should have dispaired of its making any permanent conquest of falsehood' (Add. 2, 1865, in *VC*, 1876: 270). Later, in *Popular Government*, however, he took pains to limit the optimism this seemed to imply. In the West matters were not so simple. In the East 'the most elementary knowledge of geography or physics may overthrow a mass of fixed ideas ... ' (*PG*: 145). Western prejudices, paradoxically, now seem less vulnerable to such a 'revolution of ideas' (146), and in any conflict between Science and Democracy, 'Democracy ... will certainly win' (190).[6] It is not the least of the oddities of Maine's pessimism in

---

[5] I have not been able to deal in this chapter with the important distinction between those who, like Maine, tended to confine discussion to Indo-European or 'Aryan' peoples and those who, like J. F. McLennan, Friedrich Bachofen and Lewis Henry Morgan, took in all evidence promiscuously. For Maine's protest, see, e.g., Maine, A3, 1886: 201, attributed to Maine in Grant Duff, 1892: 67. For a discussion see Collini et al., 1983: 212–14.

[6] The 'opposition between democracy and science' (*PG*: 37) is a recurring theme in *Popular Government*.

Popular Government that at that point the prejudices embodied in modern public opinion are made to seem more impermeable by enlightenment and progress than those of ancient superstition. Yet if Maine here perpetrated an unintended paradox, just as he also implies simultaneously that popular opinion was dangerously innovative and inherently conservative, the two elements he was juggling formed a longstanding polarity: the dynamism of the critical intellect, set by Whigs and Liberals, initially with confidence and later, under Mill's tutelage, with generally diminishing optimism, against public opinion. It was an antithesis which Maine, concurring with a good many of his generation – Bagehot, for example – made crucial to his view of possible future progress.

Anxiety on behalf of progress was hardly new, but it was intensified among liberal individualists in the period of the Second and Third Reform Acts. Gladstone and the Irish Land Act, 'caucuses' and collectivism, public opinion and popular government, were some of its most obvious components, turning (sometimes guardedly) optimistic individualists of the sixties into the Cassandras of the eighties and nineties: Maine, Dicey, Lecky, Spencer. Yet if political events played the most prominent part in this pessimism, the new historical perspectives introduced from the sixties onwards, and often later associated, as in Maine's case, with a loosely worn Social Darwinism,[7] had already provided its theoretical setting. It by no means entailed pessimism, but it can be said, I think, to have fostered anxiety. In widening the chronological and geographical scale within which the concept of progress had to be located, it presented the potentiality of progress, at least in its early stages, as a throw against the odds: what Bagehot, clearly following Maine, referred to in *Physics and Politics* as 'a little seed of adaptiveness' (Bagehot, 1872, in Bagehot, 1965). In Maine's case, if *Popular Government* was to give voice to the pessimism of his later years, the complexity of the account of the progressive development offered in *Ancient Law* was obviously no simple celebration of the inevitability of enlightenment. Civilized, progressive societies were seen as rare, irrigated gardens, flourishing for reasons which were problematic and exceptional, amid the stagnant swamps and featureless deserts which made up the social experience of the bulk of mankind.

Uniformity, in association with despotism, had been a bugbear for

[7] See, e.g., Rede Lec., 1875c, in *VC*, 1876: 203–39; *PG*: 50; see also the tribute to Herbert Spencer, *PG*: 49.

eighteenth-century writers, as it was later for J. S. Mill, but it had represented primarily either a geographical variety[8] or a possible future, as the nemesis of a loss of virtue and energy – a possibility Maine and his contemporaries also, of course, entertained. But to see it as the human norm, and progress as the fortunate exception, was to put an extra edge on anxiety and to attend with a special intensity to the point at which the original break out from the smothering matrix of custom had taken place. This attention, for Maine's contemporaries and followers, was his central contribution to their ideas of progress. Instead of, as in Tocqueville and Mill, and, for that matter, in more populist versions of progress like Cobden's, focussing on the decline of feudalism and its implications and possible hazards, Maine drew attention above all to the initial emergence of the distinction between the progressive societies and the rest, and to a process of individualization of which the development of feudalism was itself a part;[9] although Maine's later work was to develop its comparative aspects, *Ancient Law* remained in many ways the most detailed and sharply focussed consideration of it.

Ancient Law is a complex work partly because, to speak in Victorian terms, it was one in which, as always in Maine, Benthamite rigour and optimism were held in equipoise with a Whiggish sense of the necessary slowness of change and the inescapability of learning by experience, the persistence of the past and the importance of the ripeness of time, and the relative value in their day of institutions and ways of thinking which a more advanced age would find useless or pernicious. Progress is made to depend, as in Bagehot or Stubbs, on a balance, a way of working with the massive solidity of custom and institutions without succumbing to them. Law is seen, as government is seen in the Whig tradition, as for example, by Macaulay, simultaneously as medium, emancipator and the potential strait-jacket of the energies of society.[10] The successive agents of legal adaptiveness are fictions, equity or the law of nature, and legislation; understandably, in *Ancient Law*, attention is concen-

---

[8] A possibility Maine does not discount. See the reference to 'the physical conformation of Asiatic countries' (*AL*: 17).

[9] In *Ancient Law*, with its focus on Rome, feudalism is, understandably, an 'interruption' (*AL*: 16). But see the distinction between feudalism and 'the unadulterated usages of primitive races' (365) and *EHI*: 120.

[10] For a fuller account of this in the Whig tradition, see Burrow, 1988: Chapter 2; and for Macaulay in particular, Collini et al., 1983: 191–8.

trated on the first two. Inherent in them, alongside their capacity to effect the amelioration and, in the latter case, rationalization, of custom, were the dangers peculiar to each. The process of emancipation from custom is a perilous one. In essence it looks like a Spencerian process of specialization, of separating out: 'the severance of law from morality, and of religion from law' (*AL*: 16). But Maine emphasizes the hazards. Codification at the wrong moment may consolidate a theocracy – an historicized version of Mill's fear of a mandarinate, as well as an adaptation of Savigny's notion of the uniquely favourable moment for the formation of a code.[11] In Maine's account progress requires a good fortune stretched to an almost excruciating extent: 'There were one or two races exempted by a marvellous fate from this calamity, and grafts from these stocks have fertilized a few modern societies ... ' (*AL*: 77–8).

The saviour was the concept of the law of nature, but the agencies of progress themselves are liable to self-destructive abuse, the law of nature not least. In escaping from the uncritical rigidities of ritual and superstition there is a danger of over-rationalization and excessive intellectual volatility, exemplified by the Greeks, who at this point play the role also filled for Maine and for many Victorian commentators, including Bagehot, by the French. Law can change too rapidly; too speedy an emancipation from ritual forms produces an *ad hoc* flexibility in which questions of law and fact are confounded. 'The Greek intellect, with all its nobility and elasticity, was quite unable to confine itself within the straight-waistcoat of a legal formula' (*AL*: 75), and hence the Greeks could produce no durable system of jurisprudence. The modern abuse of equity, formulated as the idea of the law of nature, is, of course, that of the French, who, politically inexperienced and misled by Rousseau, in the eighteenth century dragged down the jurisprudential concept of the law of nature 'from the forum to the street' (87). The contrast, in both cases, is with the Romans, for whom 'Its functions were ... remedial, not revolutionary or anarchical ... the exact point at which the modern view of the Law of Nature has often ceased to resemble the ancient' (77). Such restraint, the remedial, not revolutionary use of critical reason, is not common but, on the contrary, very rare: 'One of the rarest qualities of national character is the capacity for applying and working out the law, as such, at the cost of constant

[11] For Savigny, see Stein, 1980: 60–1. Maine seemed to disagree with Savigny on the Twelve Tables.

miscarriages of abstract justice, without at the same time losing the hope or the wish that law may be conformed to a higher idea' (75). The application to the Romans is not made explicit at this point, but it is clear enough. There is, however, another exemplar which must surely have intruded here for Maine's readers, if not consciously for himself at the moment of writing. If the modern counterpart of Greece was France, that of Rome was surely England, and Maine is speaking here, in a jurisprudential context, of precisely that notion of progress as depending on a balance of liberty and order, continuity and innovation, which had become a stock theme of English political science and polemical self-congratulation and which is found in writers as diverse as Coleridge and Macaulay.

But if impatience and volatility, as well as the creation of a pernicious myth of primeval equality, are the abuse of the rationalism exemplified in the concept (benign and indispensable when properly employed) of the law of nature, the earlier agent of legal change, fictions, illustrated the dangers of unreflective extensions of precedent. Fictions, at an early stage of society, provide a necessary mediation between 'the desire for improvement, which is not quite wanting ... and the superstitious disrelish for change which is always present' (26–7). The fact is that the law is changed, the fiction that it remains the same. Maine's endorsement here is retrospective – fictions have performed a function in the history of progress – but his contemporary judgement is more Benthamite than Whig: 'To revile them as merely fraudulent is to betray ignorance of their peculiar office in the historical development of law. But at the same time it would be equally foolish to agree with those theorists who, discerning that fictions have had their uses, argue that they ought to be stereotyped in our system' (27).

This was the modern, Benthamite answer. There were others available, of greater complexity, which raised the question, to which Maine turned in *Popular Government* and often in his journalism, of the persisting irrationality of great populations. The necessary accommodation of the politician and legislator to public opinion was an important strand of political argument in the Whig tradition, and the classic figure at the end of that tradition is, of course, Maine's contemporary Bagehot. Maine himself laid heavy stress on the existence of a non-rational mass conservatism, which he saw as embodied in democracy. In that sense he recognized a persisting irrationality in the majority of the populations of even the progressive societies. The savage lay just beneath the skin (*PG*: 143). But he was not, I think, interested in it as an object of contemplation, as Bagehot so notably was, and as Maine himself was interested in 'earlier' ways of thinking manifested in archaic societies. It is this, I think, as well as Maine's longer life, which exposed him to the increasing liberal embitterment of the 1880s, which helps to account for the irritability displayed in *Popular Government* compared with Bagehot's habitual tone of irony. Yet for all that it seems at least possible that the most famous of all Bagehot's treatments of political irrationality and the contemporary utility of fictions may owe something to Maine's canvassing of the subject in *Ancient Law*.

The suggestion can only be made tentatively, for, as the quotation from Maine above implies, he was by no means the only writer to consider the uses of fictions, and some discussions were more favourable than his. At bottom the notion may be thought of, generically, as a Burkean, as well as, more loosely still, a Whiggish one, and there were more full-blooded Whigs than Maine, whose affiliation to Whig ways of thinking were complicated both by his qualified Benthamism and by an uncharacteristic admiration for Roman law and a disposition to make it central to his account of progress (*AL*: 366). Bagehot had his own impulses to a managerial progressivism, but he never forgot the importance of accommodation to public opinion, to which his attitude is one of resigned fascination as well as impatience. Some common themes in the two writers go far wider than any question of individual borrowing; the central argument of Bagehot's *Physics and Politics* is, even more explicitly than that of *Ancient Law*, concerned with the balance between order and progress, continuity and innovation, and it is, of course, despite the modish Darwinian gloss given it by Bagehot, a highly traditional one. But there is also clearly direct borrowing from Maine in *Physics and Politics*, where Maine is cited more often than any other author except Macaulay, with whom he comes first equal; there are also other clear borrowings from Maine which are not directly attributed by name. If the central theme of Bagehot's essay is a Whig one, some of its distinctive features, the exceptionality of progress and the rare luck required for its origins, seem more directly related to some of the most striking and distinctive features of *Ancient Law*: 'stagnation is the rule of the world and ... progress is the very rare exception' is not a traditional Whig thought, but has Maine's stamp upon it (in Bagehot, 1872 in Bagehot, 1965–86: VII, 107). The argument of

Maine's book too, to use Bagehot's phrases, was the emergence of an 'age of discussion' out of a 'cake of custom', and it seems very possible that at least one of the germs of *Physics and Politics* was the fusion, in Bagehot's mind, of the Darwinian concept of random but favourable mutations with Maine's identification of the sheer good luck exemplified by the origins of progress among the Romans.

There is, of course, no work of Maine's in which Bagehot's hand is evident in this way, though Maine gives him due acknowledgement as an authority on Cabinet government (*PG*: 213). If sometimes, when speaking of politics, Maine seems to have caught something of his tricks of phrase, a common culture – they were both, after all, *Saturday* reviewers in the fifties – may be explanation enough; as when Maine speaks, for example, in *Popular Government*, of the power of habit (138),[12] or when he writes that 'Englishmen would find it almost impossible to conceive what would compensate them for the withdrawal of the enthralling drama which is enacted before them every morning and evening. A ceaseless flow of public discussion ...' (*PG*: 148).[13]

That we should hear Bagehot in some of Maine's reflections on contemporary politics would be as natural as, if less explicit than, Bagehot's dependence on Maine in *Physics and Politics* for accounts of archaic societies. The example to which I want to point in conclusion is less obvious; it certainly offers a kind of parallel, with significant differences to which I shall return, but as a suggested connection it can only be speculative. It is Bagehot's famous account of the dual character of the English constitution, at once archaic and a protective screen for the possibility of progress, an impressive fiction and a rational, working reality.

It is, again, we may agree, in essence a Burkean thought, and certainly one with strong roots in historic Whiggism. Yet the closest contemporary comparison is more precise, even if the lesson Bagehot draws is rather different; it is, surely, with Maine's account in *Ancient Law* of the fictions that make innovation palatable. Just as Maine himself may have borrowed something, in discussing how fictions came to be abused ('usage which is reasonable generates usage

---

[12] The ensuing pages, on fashion, may perhaps owe something to Herbert Spencer's early essay 'Manners and fashion', *Westminster Review* (1854), reprinted in Spencer, 1858–74: vol. 1. Spencer is mentioned sympathetically in *Popular Government* (49), but only with reference to *The Man versus the State*, published in the previous year.

[13] The thought was as old, at least, as Paley, by whom politics is said to supply a 'substitute for drinking, gaming, scandal, and obscenity'. Paley, 1806: 203.

which is unreasonable' (*AL*: 19)), from Max Müller's early adumbration of his famous theory of reified metaphor as a 'disease of language' ('words said more than they ought to say' (Müller, 1856: 40)), so Bagehot, it may be argued, adapted Maine's historical argument for fictions to his own contemporary purposes. Bagehot actually considers this argument of Maine's (without directly attributing it) in *Physics and Politics* at some length. It clearly struck his imagination, because he dramatizes it, as he dramatized the polarities of the English constitution. By discarding Maine's point about the critical moment for codification he makes the history of Roman progress sound more like a story of continuous Whiggish gradualism – more like England, in fact. 'In the thick crust of her [Rome's] legality there was hidden a little seed of adaptiveness. Even in her law itself ... a hidden impulse of extrication *did* manage, in some queer way, to change the substance while conforming to the accidents – to do what was wanted for the new time while seeming to do only what was directed by the old time' (Bagehot, 1872, in Bagehot, 1965–86: VII, 53). The story is one about the success of a benign stealth – the same lesson as the one inculcated in *The English Constitution*: 'it is necessary to keep up the ancient show while we secretly interpolate the new reality' (Bagehot, 1867, in Bagehot, 1965–86: V, 392).

I have dwelt on the similarities between Maine and Bagehot because to do so makes their differences the more revealing and helps to establish at what precise distance the former stands from the traditional Whiggism of which Bagehot, for all his own idiosyncrasies, is the more representative. He too had his rationalizing impulses and moments of impatience, but he was fundamentally more Whiggish and more cynical, and his view of the history of progress made more ample provision for the continuing existence of the past in the present. Maine explicitly acknowledged the latter, and his *hauteur* towards vulgar opinion does not belong only to *Popular Government* but dates back to his early journalism in the fifties. Yet his notion of the intellectual influence of the elite minority, of what Bagehot called 'the central groups of trained and educated men' (Bagehot, 1876, in Bagehot, 1965–86: III, 229), on which, for both of them, continuing progress critically depended, had more in common with Benthamite authoritarianism than with Whiggish (and Bagehotian) notions of benign political manipulation. This is another way of saying that his form of self-confidence was that of the bureaucrat rather than the politician; it was a yearning for influence uncompromised by vulgarity. When placed in a general historical scheme it depended for continuing confidence on a sharper distinction than Bagehot's between the tribal past and the progressive present. This was the distinction which, for Maine in the eighties, seemed anomalously to be breaking down, and it left him despairing and baffled at the apparently retrograde trajectory of modern society. It broke apart, that is, the ambiguity with which we began, the conflation of modernity as a moral and intellectual category and modernity simply as the present, with all its contingencies. What might theoretically have been seen (as by a political analyst like Michels (1915) considering the phenomenon of political parties) as the new 'influential minorities', caucuses and 'wirepullers' (*PG*: 30, 38, 102),[14] were to Maine simply another form of irresponsible vulgarity. He was drawn instead to the reassuring fixity of codification seen through the eyes of nostalgia: to an adulation of the American constitution (which Bagehot had denounced as over-rigid and fostering a narrow legalism) which emphasized its eighteenth-century roots and presented it as a model of how to rescue progress from democracy (*PG*: Chapter 4). With a similar view of the dangers, Bagehot, while deploring a further widening of the franchise, had gambled on deference; Maine, more impatient and, by the eighties, more disillusioned, turned to the legal barriers of a written constitution.

[14] Bagehot too, of course, was opposed to dictation by constituencies: 'it is a government of immoderate persons far from the scene of action' Bagehot, 1867, in Bagehot, 1965–86: v, 298.

CHAPTER 3

Maine, progress and theory

Raymond Cocks

Maine is remembered as a man with firm opinions. He certainly knew his mind in respect of the patterns of legal history. As is well known, in considering the instruments used to bring law into harmony with society he identified legal fictions, equity and legislation and immediately proceeded to the remarkable claim that 'Their historical order is that in which I have placed them' (*AL*: 25). This tone of dismissive confidence is typical of his works. For example, at almost the same time the reader is informed that 'it is indisputable that much the greatest part of mankind has never shown a particle of desire that its civil institutions should be improved' (*AL*: 22); and in considering the entirety of modern Chinese society he insisted that progress had apparently been arrested 'because the civil laws are coextensive with all the ideas of which the race is capable' (*AL*: 23). The same approach may be found in his later works, where he often made observations such as that 'nothing is more certain than that the mental picture which enchains the enthusiast for benevolent democratic government is altogether false' (*PG*: 45).

Since Maine's death most critics had concentrated upon lively generalizations such as these. In particular there have been sustained and hostile debates about his statements concerning patriarchal society and primitive law. There have also, of course, been arguments about his claim that the movement of progressive societies had been 'a movement from Status to Contract' (*AL*: 170). It is almost as if the succinct and assertive quality of his sentences has stimulated attempts to rebut them.

This concentration upon generalizations has concealed serious problems in his analysis of social and legal change. His vivid and frequent descriptions of progress, not least in his references to status and contract, draw attention away from the fact that he does not completely explain progress. It is true that in a few places he candidly refers to his inability to account for progressive change, but the enduring impression given by his generalizations is that he has explained old mysteries and not for the most part merely described certain phases of legal and social development.[1] In other words there is a contrast between the appearance of his analysis and the substance of what he wrote, and this is of importance in considering his account of progress.

It is particularly significant that in *Ancient Law* he failed adequately to explain what it was that he was doing with his numerous references to historical information. Again and again he produced colourful statements to reveal the extent to which Bentham's and Austin's theories of law were defective because they failed to respond to the facts of legal history. For example, such facts showed that law was not always and everywhere the command of a sovereign. He was even more insistent on the historical shortcomings of the natural law theorists. As he put it, 'The Law of Nature confused the Past and the Present. Logically, it implied a state of Nature which had once been regulated by natural law; yet the jurisconsults do not speak clearly or confidently of the existence of such a state, which indeed is little noticed by the ancients except where it finds poetical expression in the fancy of a golden age' (*AL*: 73).

Behind these references to history lies the unexplored problem: what is the correct place of historical observations in legal thought? Maine's continual use of history in *Ancient Law* and his failure to account for what he was doing with history was of immediate concern to Fitzjames Stephen. In his usual blunt way the latter wrote that Maine 'puts forward no philosophical theories at all, but leaves to others the question how far the truth of the theories which come before him is affected by the account which he gives of their origin' (Stephen, 1861: 484).

It is easy to understand Stephen's frustration when one looks at passages in *Ancient Law* such as the one where Maine wrote that

There is such wide-spread dissatisfaction with existing theories of jurisprudence, and so general a conviction that they do not really solve the questions they pretend to dispose of, as to justify the suspicion that some line of inquiry, necessary to a perfect result, has been incompletely followed or altogether omitted by their authors. And indeed there is one remarkable omission with which all these speculations are chargeable, except perhaps

[1] For an example of limited explanations of progress see *AL*: 18–20.

those of Montesquieu. They take no account of what law has actually been at epochs remote from the particular period at which they made their appearance. (*AL*: 118–19)[2]

The reference in this passage to 'a perfect result' is never in fact followed up. It is all a matter of inference for the reader. Maine simply failed to develop a theoretical justification for his references to history and progress.

He was clearly aware of Stephen's criticism, and during the years which followed, when he was in India, he produced an unequivocal answer. In 'An Address to the University of Calcutta', he said that

It is now affirmed, and was felt long before it was affirmed, that the truth of history, if it exists, cannot differ from any other form of truth. If it be truth at all, it must be scientific truth. There can be no essential difference between the truths of the Astronomer, of the Physiologist, and of the historian. The great principle which underlies all our knowledge of the physical world, that Nature is ever consistent with herself, must also be true of human nature and of human society which is made up of human nature. It is not indeed meant that there are no truths except of the external world, but that all truth, of whatever character, must conform to the same conditions, so that if indeed history be true, it must teach that which every other science teaches, continuous sequence, inflexible order, and eternal law. (Add. 2, in *VC*, 1876:265–6)[3]

Obviously in a modern context claims such as these would raise numerous problems for historians and social scientists, but for an understanding of Maine's ideas about progress they are very helpful. Given certain conditions, progress will occur, and its future course may be predicted with such certainty as may be found in any scientific law. By implication, discovering the relevant conditions was only a matter of time.

Unfortunately for those in search of clarity and theoretical completeness, Maine retreated from this position in later years. He expressed caution about the scientific value of the comparative method. He wrote that he would be

making a very idle pretension if [he] held out a prospect of obtaining, by the application of the Comparative Method to jurisprudence, any results which, in point of interest or trustworthiness, are to be placed on a level with those which, for example, have been accomplished in Comparative

[2] For criticism of Montesquieu, see *AL*: 115–17.
[3] The lecture was given in 1865 and reprinted in certain editions of *Village-Communities in the East and West*, beginning with the third edition. See also Stein, 1980: 87–8.

Philology. To give only one reason, the phenomena of human society, laws and legal ideas, opinions and usages, are vastly more affected by external circumstances than language. They are much more at the mercy of individual volition, and consequently much more subject to change effected deliberately from without. (*VC*: 8)

In a later work, he wrote almost sadly that 'The truth is that the facts of human nature, with which Courts of Justice have chiefly to deal, are far obscurer and more intricately involved than the facts of physical nature, and the difficulty of ascertaining them with precision constantly increases in our age, through the progress of invention and enterprise, through the every-growing miscellaneousness of all modern communities, and through the ever-quickening play of modern social movements' (*EHI*: 49).

This later loss of confidence in the capacity for his theories to yield immediate assistance in his discussion of social and political issues had important implications for his ideas about progress. On an elementary level it helps to explain his antagonism towards political extremists who claimed exclusive understanding of the truth about everything. Such men had no awareness of the increasing complexity of social arrangements. In *Popular Government* he criticized the 'Irreconcilables': they were 'associations of men who hold political opinions as men once held religious opinions...' (*PG*: 25). The worst and most simple-minded of these groups were the Nationalists, although those who opposed attempts at scientific advances such as the ones achieved by Darwin were scarcely better.

Unfortunately, when Maine tried to go beyond such observations and attempted to use scientific reasoning, the results in his later years were not impressive and reflected uncertainty in what he was doing. Science provided no mandate for progress. In his last major work he wrote that

Neither experience nor probability affords any ground for thinking that there may be an infinity of legislative innovation, at once safe and beneficent. On the contrary, it would be a safer conjecture that the possibilities of reform are strictly limited. The possibilities of heat, it is said, reach 2,000 degrees of the Centigrade thermometer; the possibilities of cold extend to about 300 degrees below its zero; but all organic life in the world is only possible through the accident that temperature in it ranges between a maximum of 120 degrees and a minimum of a few degrees below zero of the Centigrade. For all we know, a similarly narrow limitation may hold of legislative changes in the structure of human society (*PG*: 149–50)

Also, it could be said that his inability to relate his arguments in a satisfactory way to scientific theory forced him to readjust his ideas about progress. In *Ancient Law* his references to science were never fully articulated, but they were confident, and in the context of his thoughts on progress they gave the reader a sense of participating in an adventure. The outcome of modern social change was uncertain, but there were good grounds for optimism, and, properly understood, science could show the way forward by revealing the phases of historical development.

In later years the mood is much more cautious and there is increasing emphasis on the possible failure to achieve progress. Attention is given not to science but to the political skills of those in positions of power. Bentham is now criticized, because, in Maine's words, he 'greatly overrated human nature. He wrongly supposed that the truths which he saw, clearly cut and distinct, in the dry light of his intellect, could be seen by all other men or by many of them. He did not understand that they were visible only to the Few, – to the intellectual aristocracy' (*PG*: 86). It is in this context that one may agree with Professor Burrow, who, in considering the problems of progress, wrote that 'The lesson, as Maine read it, was to admit the impact, to acknowledge its potential benefits if applied with caution, but also to cushion the shock' (Collini et al., 1983: 216). Maine was now concentrating upon difficulties rather than opportunities, and, in part at least, this was a consequence of his failure to come to terms with the theoretical issues which he had left unresolved in *Ancient Law*. In the absence of clear guidance from theory, or at least the hope of increasing theoretical certainty, he had lost some of his enthusiasm, and this in turn had influenced his ideas about progress. The topic had become a problem, at times almost a tedious problem.

His difficulties with issues relating to the analysis of progress gave him a distinct place in nineteenth-century jurisprudence. He could not be associated with those professional writers who might refer to Burke and defend the common law as an almost mystical product of long experience. For Maine, legal truth could never be reached by a process of prescription. Nor was he attracted to the approach being considered by Dicey during the mid-Victorian decades, when the traditional role of the common law was justified by reference to the valuable everyday experience of practitioners rather than by pointing to a process of historical evolution.⁴ Admittedly, Maine was open in his enthusiasm for the methods of the utilitarian jurists in so far as they at least attempted an analysis of law which explicitly related practical matters to a general theory of law; he admired their clarity. But he could never see himself as one of their number because of their failure to integrate historical information and a correct understanding of human nature into their writings on legal change. His concern for theoretical issues, and his failure to address them in a way which satisfied his own requirements, did much to place him apart from other Victorian writers. His comparative isolation helps to explain why since his death only Vinogradoff has sought systematically to relate Maine's theoretical ideas to his notions of progressive change.⁵

---

⁴ A. V. Dicey's contrasting ideas are considered in Cocks, 1983: Chapter 9.
⁵ Today, there is increasing interest in Victorian legal theory. See, e.g., Feaver, 1969; Burrow, 1966; Stein, 1980; Morison, 1982; Colaiaco, 1983; Collini et al., 1983; Cocks, 1983; Rubin & Sugarman, 1984; and Sugarman, 1986.

CHAPTER 4

Maine and the theory of progress

Krishan Kumar

As is well known, Maine's attitude to progress was complex and not entirely consistent.[1] He was firm in his belief that there *had* been progress, but he was not clear how or why this had happened, nor – unlike some eminent contemporaries – was he confident that there was some general law of evolution which ensured the passage from a non-progressive to a progressive condition of society. Maine's use of the comparative method, and the generally positivistic or scientific bent of his approach, implied and perhaps even required some such general laws of social development (Burrow, 1966: 164). But this positivism – expressed at its clearest and most confident in his 'Address to the University of Calcutta' (1865) – warred with Maine's equally fervent devotion to the historical approach. The English scientist in him, with his desire to establish laws of society similar to those of the physical sciences, sat rather awkwardly alongside a German Romantic historicist who passionately insisted on the unique and the particular in the varied patterns of human social evolution.

The historical approach could show connection and continuity between past and present – could show this even between phenomena so apparently disparate as Indian communal customs, the practices of early Teutonic communities, Roman codes and English common law. It could document the fact of progress, the progress from a 'closed' to an 'open' society, from one based on 'status' to one based on 'contract', that could manifestly be shown to have occurred within Aryan civilization. It could point to the crucial mediation of the Roman legal code, the establishment of which had for the first time made law open to criticism and conscious change. But it could do nothing to guarantee that this progress would be

---

[1] In these early paragraphs I largely follow the accounts in Burrow (1966: 137–78) and Collini et al. (1983: 209–19).

repeatable elsewhere, among other civilizations beyond the Aryan pale. Indeed increasingly, it seems, Maine came to see this as unlikely, or at any rate unpredictable, a matter of luck or happy accident. Progress within Aryan civilization itself had been achieved 'by a succession of near miracles' (Burrow, 1966: 161). What kind of positivist science could incorporate miracles? By the time he came to write *Popular Government* (1885) Maine was unequivocal: 'The natural condition of mankind ... is not the progressive condition. It is a condition not of changeableness but of unchangeableness. The immobility of society is the rule; its mobility is the exception' (*PG*: 170; cf. Collini et al., 1983: 217).

In the end, it seems, Maine was not really interested in providing a *theory* of progress. He wanted to trace the progressive development of the Aryan world, seen as a unique and perhaps unrepeatable achievement. The comparative method allowed him to make some impressive links between the 'primitive' practices of certain non-Western societies and those of the progressive West. Progress was explained, in so far as explanation was seriously attempted, by the existence of a greater degree of rational comprehension within Aryan communities which, combined with a certain historical good luck, gave Roman and post-Roman societies in the West a unique flexibility and capacity for improvement. This 'intellectualist bias' (Burrow, 1966: 169) seriously incapacitated Maine from dealing properly with non-rational and non-utilitarian forms of conduct – the chief province of modern anthropology. But it did not affect his principal interest in primitive societies, which was to find the origin of that progressive condition of society which had been attained with such difficulty, and whose future, in the era of the Third Reform Act, was threatened by demagogic populism. His interest, that is, was almost exclusively in 'the communities which were destined for civilization' – the Aryan communities.[2] Hence, compared with a Spencer or even a Tylor, this severely limited the extent of his evolutionary positivism: 'the whole of his writing has a professedly historical aim; the Comparative Method is placed at the service of history' (Burrow, 1966: 171).[3]

[2] Quoted in Burrow (1966: 171-2). Cf. Maine's other well-known remark in his 1875 Rede Lecture, *The Effects of Observation of India on Modern European Thought*: 'Civilization is nothing more than a name for the old order of the Aryan world, dissolved but perpetually re-constituting itself under a vast variety of solvent influences' (in *VC*, 1876: 230).

[3] Cf. Collini et al: 'the restriction of the scope of the Comparative Method, at least in its early applications, derived essentially from the philological model, with its conception of a single

Dr Cocks in the preceding chapter seems to take issue with the unqualified assertion of Collini and Burrow that 'Maine was unrepentantly a nineteenth-century believer in progress' (1983: 216). But he certainly accepts that at least in *Ancient Law* and the earlier writings Maine held to a view of progress as an accomplished fact, and as in principle amenable to scientific analysis. He would also accept, I think, that Maine believed very much in a 'progressive' state of society – one characterized by the rights of private property and a wide scope for individual freedom – and that he regarded this as a precious though precarious achievement of Western society. Nevertheless, and like Burrow again, he takes the view that for whatever reason Maine's account of progress was incomplete and unsatisfactory. Maine, he argues, simply failed to develop a theoretical justification for his references to history and progress.

Where Cocks parts company with Burrow and Collini, I think, is in his view that Maine's unwillingness or inability to produce a theory of progress led him also gradually to lose confidence in progress as such, and the ideas that sustained it. Maine is quoted as casting doubt on the ability of the comparative method to deliver firm generalizations – even such as were attainable in the field of comparative philology, let alone physics or biology. His own uncertainties and difficulties with the application of the scientific method to jurisprudence undermined his confidence in science as the bedrock of progress. The references to science in *Ancient Law* are, Cocks says, 'confident' and suggest a firm faith in progress. Science could show the way forward by revealing the laws of historical development. Subsequently, however, Maine's mood became more cautious and sceptical. His emphasis was increasingly on the difficulties, rather than the opportunities, of achieving progress. Cocks suggests that, unable to relate his arguments in a satisfactory way to a scientific theory, Maine lost his 'enthusiasm', and that this affected his ideas about progress. Despairing of resolving the theoretical difficulties, Maine became bored with the idea of progress and so lost his belief in it.

There are a number of ambiguities in this position. What, for

Aryan family.' Hence the need to distinguish the comparative method from the 'scientific' (*sc.* evolutionary positivist) approach, despite the attempt by some practitioners, such as Frederick Pollock, to insist on their identity. In general, as practised by Müller, Maine and their followers such as Vinogradoff, 'the adherence to "history" was deep, the language of "science" usually perfunctory' (1983: 212–13).

instance, does it mean to say that, because of his difficulties with the theory of progress, Maine came to believe that 'science provided no mandate for progress'? Does this mean, as it appears to, that though for Maine progress had in fact occurred, was a self-evident reality, scientific analysis provided no means of accounting for it? That there was not in that sense, or could be, a 'science of history'? This might suggest a loss of faith in science, but surely not necessarily a loss of faith in progress. (Burrow and Collini, for instance, seem to accept the first but not the second.) It is true that for some thinkers, such as Herbert Spencer, scientific certainty and the belief in progress went hand in hand, as twin aspects of the same evolutionary process: as witness Spencer's famous statement that 'progress is not an accident ... but a beneficent necessity'. But clearly the two do not have to go together. Max Weber, for instance – whose thinking on contemporary politics often bears striking resemblances to that of Maine – combined a rejection of a positivist 'science of society' with a cautious belief in progress. Progress may be a two-faced thing, alternately sunny and dark, but that it had occurred Weber did not doubt (see, for example, Brubaker, 1984: 101ff.). A similar position was held by many 'nervous liberals,' as Michael Walzer has called them, at the end of the nineteenth century – Durkheim for one. Tocqueville and J. S. Mill, in the earlier part of the century, also seem to fall more or less in this category.

Or does Cocks mean that Maine's theoretical difficulties and declining confidence in science drove him to doubt the very fact of progress? Is this what the splenetic outpouring of *Popular Government* amounts to? Did Maine now, confronted with the pretensions of an ignorant mass electorate, come to think that perhaps Western society had not actually achieved a stable 'progressive state', and that the attainment of such a state lay in the future – or more ominously, the past: that is, that degeneration had set in?[4] If so, this represents a far more serious loss of confidence in the achievement and promise of Western civilization. It would put Maine closer not so much to the nervous liberalism of Weber or Durkheim as to the radical despair of a Burckhardt or a Nietzsche.

These are questions properly to be settled by Cocks, Burrow, Collini and other Maine scholars, of whom I am not one. But there is another issue arising directly out of Dr Cocks' chapter which might

[4] This is hinted at in several passages in *Popular Government* – e.g. pp. 143–4.

well provoke the general reader. He attributes Maine's alleged loss of faith in the idea of progress chiefly to matters of intellectual difficulty and almost of personal psychology: in a word, 'boredom'. Now, no doubt changes of mood can be caused by such a wrestling with intractable intellectual problems. But in Maine's case this seems too intellectualist an explanation, too enclosed within the confines of the study. There were surely events enough in his world, of appropriate magnitude, to shatter the confidence of even the sunniest optimist: the uses of mass suffrage in the empires of Napoleon III and Bismarck, the nationalist wars on the continent, the bloodiness of the American Civil War, and the almost equally bloody civil war in France, in the rise and suppression of the Paris Commune. Most of these are mentioned by Maine in *Popular Government*. Certainly they seem to have been sobering enough to cause many a European intellectual apart from Maine to abandon or severely qualify the belief in progress in the last quarter of the nineteenth century. The decline in the idea of progress at this time was, that is, a general intellectual phenomenon, as has been charted by many people (for example Kumar, 1978: 164ff; Nisbet, 1980: 317ff.). The reasonable thing is to suppose that like general causes had like effects, rather than that Maine's was an individual or idiosyncratic case.

There is another problem with Cocks' explanation. It seems to be offered partly to account for a supposed discrepancy between the more measured and optimistic Maine of *Ancient Law* and the gloomy, bad-tempered, authoritarian of *Popular Government*. That there is a difference in the style and mood of the two books no one can doubt, though this is partly accounted for by a clear difference of intent (*Popular Government* was a self-evidently polemical contribution to political debate rather than, like *Ancient Law*, a scholarly, though very accessible, treatise). And there is the simple matter of time: nearly a quarter of a century separates the two books, and men, like wine, can go sour. I wonder nevertheless whether we are not in danger of creating a false problem, of making too much of the distinction between the two works.

It is interesting in this connection that Maine's younger contemporary, A. V. Dicey, who shared his distaste for the 'collectivist spirit' of the times, still felt that Maine himself was partly to blame for undermining Benthamite individualism. More to the point, so far as this went there was for Dicey no discrepancy between the spirit and intent of *Ancient Law* and that of *Popular Government*. It was the 'historical method' of the former that, breeding nationalism, racialism and imperialism, had been one of the prime agents of the break-up of Benthamite cosmopolitanism and *laissez-faire*. 'It is no mere accident', wrote Dicey, 'that Maine, who in his *Ancient Law* undermined the authority of analytical jurisprudence, aimed in his *Popular Government* a blow at the foundations of Benthamite faith in democracy' (1962: 461n.).

I do not offer Dicey's view as necessarily providing a correct version of Maine's work or influence (and Dicey's own account is somewhat convoluted). It simply serves to illustrate the possibility that there is a good deal of compatibility between *Ancient Law* and *Popular Government*. The link presumably lies through Maine's conservatism, and the place of the historical approach in forming this. This, again, is not uncharted territory (see, for example, Collini et al. 1983: 215–18). Indeed I suppose the novelty to lie in Cocks' claim that there was a distinct shift in Maine's attitude to progress – a move, say, from a liberal to a conservative position – over his lifetime. Once more I leave this to Maine scholars to settle in detail. But I have to say that I find Dicey quite persuasive, in his suggestion that a strong emphasis on the historical method is likely to breed caution and even inertia, a resistance to change on the grounds of the historical and 'organic' complexity of society. Maine may not have been, as many have pointed out, a Burkean conservative, an adherent of tradition as such. But his hostility to doctrines of natural law and natural rights could lead to an emphatic endorsement of inequality, between classes and between nations, as well as to the quenching of that 'confident enthusiasm' which Dicey regarded as indispensable for the carrying out of beneficial reforms (1962: 461). Here too the connection between *Ancient Law* and *Popular Government* seems obvious.

I turn finally to the larger matter of the theory of progress itself. Both Burrow and Cocks charge Maine with a very unsatisfactory account of progress. The former accuses him of an 'intellectualist bias', the latter of not providing a theory at all. But what should a theory of progress contain? There has always been some ambiguity about this – or rather, practically every major theorist of progress seems to have found it difficult to deal adequately with what are analytically two quite separate things. Should an account of progress principally explain how or why societies evolve from one state or another, or should it rather tell us about the substance or content of progress? Ideally both, of course, but it is surprising how rare this has been in the history of the idea of progress.

Eighteenth-century thinkers, such as Turgot and Condorcet, did not get much beyond postulating a 'progressive tendency' in mankind. Evolutionary thinkers of the nineteenth and twentieth centuries, such as Spencer, Durkheim and Talcott Parsons, were very good at describing and analysing particular states or types of society – 'militant society', 'industrial society', 'organic society', etc. But despite hypothesizing a progressive movement between different types of society, these thinkers were casual and rather careless in supplying what Ernest Gellner calls the 'causal mechanics' of the transition (1964: 15ff.). Spencer's 'instability of the homogeneous' as the *primum mobile* of all change is typical of the vagueness of the principles offered. So too is Durkheim's increase in 'material and moral density' as the source of the momentous change from 'mechanical' to 'organic solidarity' in the evolution of society. Only Marx paid serious attention to the question of what drives society onward (and upward) from one stage to the next. But even here the notion of 'contradiction' in the mode of production is fraught with difficulties, quite apart from the fact that it is embedded in a philosophy of history which largely cancels out any independent causal efficacy it may be supposed to have.

Maine is therefore in good – if not the best – company in frequently invoking, without sufficiently distinguishing, progress both as a *form* of change and as a *condition* which, as it were, institutionalizes change. The two meanings are indeed combined in his most famous statement on progress: 'the movement of the progressive societies', he says, 'has hitherto been a movement *from Status to Contract*' (*AL*: 170). Here we first have progress as a condition: progressive societies (or 'advancing communities'), as opposed to 'stationary' ones, are those which contain the seeds of change, and which will eventually reach a point – with the codification of Roman law – where further and in principle unlimited growth and development will continue by a process of self-criticism and conscious change. The progressive society is here a type of society, the modern type, we might say.

But progress here is also more decisively seen as a movement of change: for all its gradualness, a revolutionary, perhaps unique and, Maine suggests, probably irreversible mutation in human social development which lifted some societies on to a new plateau where their evolution was freed from the rigid constraints of the stationary state. The idea of progress as movement, as change from one condition to another (better) one, is quite clear in the passage which leads up to the famous statement, just quoted, at the end of chapter 5 of *Ancient Law*:

Starting, as from one terminus of history, from a condition of society in which all the relations of Persons are summed up in the relations of Family, we seem to have steadily moved towards a phase of social order in which all these relations arise from the free agreement of Individuals. In Western Europe the progress achieved in this direction has been considerable. (169)

It is this process of change which is the same section Maine glosses as 'the law of progress'. Now it is absolutely true, as both Burrow and Cocks show, that this 'law' bears scant relation to anything we might understand as a law in physics or biology, which presumably are the kinds of disciplines to which Maine would have looked for supplying the characteristics of scientific laws (see, again, Maine's positivist credo in the 'Address to the University of Calcutta' (1865)). The initial conditions of progress are nowhere clearly or systematically stated, and the motive force of the change remains somewhat mysterious – or at least, of a contingent, non-lawlike kind. My point is simply that Maine is as much or as little blameworthy as most of his great nineteenth-century contemporaries (since twentieth-century theorists have largely given up the enterprise of reflecting on large-scale social change, their many shortcomings are neither here nor there). What most of them (with the partial exception of Marx) offered were essentially dichotomous typologies of societies: 'militant' and 'industrial', *Gemeinschaft* and *Gesellschaft*, societies of 'mechanical solidarity' and those of 'organic solidarity', 'folk' and 'urban'. Progress was conceived as the movement from one to the other, but precisely how or why that movement took place was often obscure.

Maine's contrast between 'status' and 'contract', or between 'stationary' and 'progressive' societies, fell neatly into this pattern. And as with the other thinkers, the abiding interest in his work lies in his analysis of the contrasting features of 'primitive' and 'modern' societies, rather than in his account of the movement from one to the other. It may be, indeed, that this is the best that social science – as opposed to history – can do. Both sociology and anthropology, certainly, have always been better at explaining social order than social change. The dynamics of large-scale social change, of the kind that interested Maine and his contemporaries, have remained elusive to modern sociologists. One might even say, echoing Dr Cocks, that so intractable have they found the problem that they have become 'bored' with it, and have gratefully relapsed into a concern with the investigation of the structures of particular societies at particular times in particular places. Speculations about large-scale change have been left to 'philosophic' historians such as Spengler and Toynbee.

Maine's failure in providing a 'theory of progress' may in fact be less of an offence than his critics charge, or than he himself may have suspected. In the 'Address to the University of Calcutta' (1865) he wrote: 'if indeed history be true, it must teach that which every other science teaches, continuous sequence, inflexible order, and eternal law' (Add. 2, 1865, in *VC*, 1876: 266). Dr Cocks suggests that Maine reproached himself for not being able to live up to this high ambition, and in his retreat from it lost confidence in the idea of progress which was bound up with it. If this is so, Maine's failure may be a cause for rejoicing rather than regret. The goal that he and other positivistically minded students of society set themselves was an impossible one, and we should be grateful that they did not follow through all the logical implications of it. But that is no reason for abandoning the search for a workable concept of progress, shorn of its positivist trappings. As industrial civilization encircles the globe, it becomes more important than ever to decide what constitutes true progress within the industrial way of life, to draw up a balance sheet and seek to increase the pluses against the minuses (see, for instance, Kumar, 1978: 301ff.). And might one say, without being unduly heretical, that in doing this Maine's pessimistic reflections on modern life in *Popular Government* might prove to be as helpful as his more optimistic analysis in *Ancient Law*?

We might go even further. Though Maine never developed anything like a 'theory of progress' — at least in the sense that he may have understood this — he did drop some tantalizing hints in that direction. In *Popular Government*, for instance, while complaining that progress was 'a word of which I have never seen any definition' (131), Maine nevertheless goes on to offer something like one. Progress, he says, if it is to be understood 'with its only intelligible meaning', must mean 'the continued production of new ideas' (145).

Later in the same work (and quoting himself from the *Early History of Institutions*) he suggests that 'we can only discover the law of this production by examining sequences of ideas where they are frequent and of considerable length' (191). It is this – and this alone – that can justify the focus of an investigation chiefly on Western Europe, since it is only there that 'the multiplication of ideas' has been substantially achieved and institutionalized (193). It is in this sense that Western societies are progressive societies, although Maine perceives in his own time a certain 'weariness of novelty' which, he avers, 'seems at intervals to overtake whole Western societies' (194).

Maine, we know, was not particularly influenced by Darwin's theory of evolution (Burrow, 1966: 142–53). It is interesting nevertheless that Maine's concept of progress is highly susceptible to a Darwinian interpretation – as indeed was vividly shown, using a similar conception, by Walter Bagehot in *Physics and Politics* (1872). This does not mean (as it certainly did not to Bagehot) some 'socio-biological' explanation of progress in terms of genetic transmission or racial inheritance. Nor does it mean any 'Social Darwinist' explanation of progress through the mechanism of the competitive elimination of weaker rivals. The real lesson to be drawn from Darwinism is in fact the exact opposite of that drawn by the Social Darwinists. The elimination of less efficient rivals gives us indeed successful adaptation to the current environment, but at the price of possible extinction in some future changed environment. The condition of continued survival is not simply adaptedness, but also adaptability.

Maine's account of 'progressiveness' – unlike that of many of his evolutionist contemporaries – seems entirely informed by this perception. The progressive societies are those whose institutions, while having sufficient capacity to make for efficient exploitation of the environment at a given time, retain the ability to change, without the violence of war or revolution, in response to changed circumstances. This is the importance of the tradition of criticism and self-conscious reflection embodied in Western institutions (including, we might say, the religious institutions). Maine emphasizes the continuous creation of new ideas, especially scientific and moral ideas (*PG*: 193), but the concept of progress this entails can clearly also be more widely applied to political and economic change.

What Maine points to, in fact, is a comparative historical sociology of the conditions of progress understood in these terms. Why was it only in the West – and *was* it only in the West – that society was able to fulfil the requirements of both adaptedness and adaptability? Maine points to the importance of Roman law in this, but others have seen as equally important the special nature of European feudalism (Wittfogel, 1963) or the particular quality of Western religion (Weber, 1963). Or was it rather – and more in the spirit of Maine – the result of a 'miraculous ... concatenation of circumstances' that combined ideological and institutional features at a particular historical juncture (Hall, 1986: 111)? The recently revived interest in these questions (see, for instance, R. Collins, 1986; Baechler et al., 1988) after more than a half-century of indifference is a sign that far from being a blind alley, the speculations of Maine and his contemporaries still have much to offer us. And if Maine can provide a start, and a very good start, it may be too that we need to reassess Darwin's contribution in this sphere. Not Darwin as literally and positivistically applied by the Social Darwinists, or Darwin as crassly 'rediscovered' by the sociobiologists, but a Darwinism of a truly sociological kind, one that acknowledges that the Darwinian mechanisms of adaptation, selection and variation can be studied without dependence on a belief in biological determinism. Society lives in a natural environment, but it also creates its own cultural environment, which nevertheless exerts precise Darwinian pressures (Kumar, 1975).

Progress as Maine conceived it can then be understood and analysed in Darwinian terms as the achievement of order without the sacrifice of the potential for change. The order of Western society was in truth precarious by virtue of the very looseness of its political organization. The unique pluralism of Western political society, after the fall of the Roman Empire, meant ceaselsss social disruption and many bloody wars; but by the same token the lack of a commanding sovereign power enabled different parts, at different times, to vary their behaviour in such a way as, in changed circumstances, to be the spearhead of new developments within the whole body of Western society (for instance the Renaissance, the Reformation, the Scientific and Industrial Revolutions). Progress was achieved at the cost of relative stability – but the fossil record, geological and historical, is full of the bones of comfortably adapted stable (or 'stationary') societies.

In his study of legal change Maine began the right kind of inquiry into these questions. But his excessively positivistic understanding of 'the law of progress' made it appear to him increasingly impossible to proceed with the construction of a general theory of progress. Here he, like many other social scientists, appears to have had an unduly inflated and unreal notion of what constitutes 'theory' in the social sciences. It has led to mounds of verbiage on the subject of social theory, and precious little of substance. If the kind of comparative historical sociology implicit in Maine's work is not theory, it is difficult to see what is, or could be, in the study of society.

CHAPTER 5

Democracy and excitement: Maine's political pessimism

Stefan Collini

This chapter, which is intended to complement that by Professor Burrow (Chapter 2), deals largely with the obverse of Maine's theory of progress, namely his pessimism about future stagnation or decline. This strategy necessarily entails concentration upon Maine's later work, especially *Popular Government*, in contrast to Professor Burrow's chapter, which naturally focusses upon *Ancient Law* and its various offshoots.

Needless to say, all accounts of progress involve, at least implicitly, some characterization of stagnation, retrogression and decline; and, perhaps a slightly less obvious point, theories of progress are one very effective form of social or cultural criticism in that they are attempts to endow with some kind of scientific or moral authority the discrimination of those current social and cultural developments that are welcome from those that are not. A special piquancy attends the politically conservative varieties of this kind of criticism, where the future figures more as a source of alarm than of hope, and where the last 'healthy' stage of cultural growth tends to coincide with that of the critic's own youth. Looking at Maine in this way, as a pessimistic or conservative social critic and political theorist, I want very briefly to raise three points for examination. The first concerns the way in which his account of both progress and its opposite rests upon certain moral categories, especially qualities of character. The second is simply to draw attention to the kind of 'voice' Maine uses, and the kind of audience he was addressing, which together account for much of the distinctive tone of his writings. And the third addresses, even if it cannot claim to settle, the question of how to characterize Maine's particular form of conservatism and to distinguish it from those varieties which may perhaps be more familiar.

Both Professor Burrow and, by a different route, Dr Cocks conclude that Maine cannot really *explain* progress, or at least that he does not have any general *theory* of progress based on a single motor force, but rather that he offers a selective account of the part legal developments have played in the course of the singular (in every sense of the word) development of those West European and European-influenced societies which merit the label 'progressive'. But what accounts for the difference between the stationary and progressive societies remained, as he put it in a celebrated phrase also cited by John Burrow, 'one of the great secrets which inquiry has yet to penetrate', and again when identifying the forces which have prevented or arrested 'the progress of far the greater part of mankind', he can only suggest that there were one or two races 'exempted by a marvellous fate' from some of these calamities (*AL*: 23, 77).

Now, whether or not we choose to put it in the language of post-modernist literary theory, I think we cannot help but observe how the logical or structural gaps in Maine's argument are in fact filled in by his invocation of certain values whose presence is signalled more by his characteristic choice of adjectives than by explicit acknowledgement. Professor Burrow brings out very well how the advance of the progressive societies as expressed in their legal arrangements has been both an intellectual and a moral achievement, and one could underline this by pointing to the way in which Maine's characterization of the distinctive merits of advanced societies rests upon what Durkheim was later to call 'the non-contractual elements in contract'. Maine's discussion of the assumptions expressed in modern legal arrangements about contract (essentially in England) is littered with references to the advance in 'good faith and trust in our fellows', 'scrupulous honesty', the respect accorded to 'the mere unilateral reposal of confidence', and so on. These terms all appear in the space of little over a page (*AL*: 306–7).

At this point Maine has no elaborate explanation to offer for this fact of moral progress: he does not, for example, try to explain the occurrence of these qualities by presenting them as in some way functionally superior or advantageous, as various social evolutionary theorists did, nor does he present them as the working out of an essentially teleological conception of human nature, slowly overcoming external impediments, as some more philosophical Victorian social theorists did. There is a suggestion of the familiar thought that the pattern of social development can be understood in terms of the life-cycle of the individual, but Maine does not elaborate this. I think, rather, that in a somewhat circular way he takes for granted the superiority of certain qualities of character, and then finds them at work in those developments he regards as progressive. Indeed, even the intellectual achievements which are so crucial to his story are tinged with these moral qualities also – they are very much a matter of restraint, steadiness, prudence, and so on.

I shall return at the end of my comments to the connections between this cluster of values and his individualist politics, but here I want to suggest that this also helps us in thinking about a minor paradox in *Popular Government* alluded to in passing by Professor Burrow, which, spelled out a bit more fully, goes something like this. The natural state of the populace is that of changelessness, sunk in the immobility of habit and custom. In this respect the majority of the population continues to exhibit the behaviour that has characterized most historical societies: as we have seen, innovation and progress, in the rare cases where they have occurred, have been the work of enlightened minorities, minorities which, as Maine became more conservative and more explicitly polemical, he was increasingly willing to allow to be identified with natural aristocracies. But the chief reason why the advent of popular government is such a source of alarm to Maine is not, of course, the prospect of its torpor; he is not, as for example Mill was, haunted by the fear that the imposition of a levelling mediocrity would produce a kind of Chinese stationariness, though there had been hints of such a view in *Ancient Law*. It is, rather, a democracy's excessive *activity*, especially legislative activity, which Maine finds so alarming. Thus, popular government threatens, bizarrely, to be both inert and overactive at the same time.

But once again I think we can make some sense of this, and see what really determines the contours of Maine's anxieties, if we recognize that this portrait of democracy is a transposition of those qualities, seen as defects of character, which Maine and so many of his contemporaries took to characterize the behaviour of the savage, the child and the mass of the working class. In the absence of those qualities of vigour, independence and adaptiveness which distinguish strong characters, the mass of the population remain largely passive and governed by habit and custom; but then, when subject to the temptation of excitement and self-indulgence, they lack the qualities of self-restraint and maturity needed to resist. Only a few have the strength of character not to give in to what he called 'the craving for political excitement which is growing on us every day' (*PG*: 151); the disdain and the dramatization embodied in 'craving' is very expressive.

Unfortunately I do not have space here to substantiate this suggestion in any detail, but let me just point towards the language used in Maine's discussion of the role of political generalizations in stirring a democracy to ill-advised action. To begin with, his description of the activity of framing generalizations nicely displays the way such intellectual activities rest on or express ethical qualities: Maine typically emphasizes the difficulty and complexity of doing so judiciously, and contrasts this with 'the modern facility of generalization' – you can hear the tut-tutting already in 'facility' – which is obtained by 'a curious precipitation and carelessness' in selecting one's facts. Once framed, these generalizations produce 'a loose acquiescence in a vague proposition', and this 'levity of assent' – the headmasterly ticking-off is very pronounced now – is 'one of the most enervating of national habits of mind'. Finally, to drive the point home, there is a suggestion of the classic comparison with the notorious bad character who has been expelled from the school for secret vice: 'It has seriously enfeebled the French intellect' (*PG*: 106–8). I am suggesting, in other words, that the lacunae in his argument reveal that the real dynamic of his position is an untheorized commitment to certain qualities of 'character' (in a sense of the term that was at once descriptive and normative), and for what it is worth I would add that a somewhat similar analysis could be carried out on several other leading Victorian political theorists.

I have already in effect touched upon my second point, the kind of voice Maine uses or the kinds of authority he invokes, and so I shall try to be briefer here. John Burrow mentions Maine's characteristic 'hauteur', and Ray Cocks refers to Maine's 'tone of dismissive confidence'. Maine very clearly cultivated his standing as an expert, something which contributes an uninviting finality to so many of his pronouncements. But beyond this, Maine's prose invokes for itself not just the authority of historical and legal learning, but also a kind of moral authority, the authority of one who unflinchingly faces up to the demands of complexity, however unpalatable (with the strong suggestion that they nearly always will be unpalatable). Just as there was a rhetoric of sincerity among Victorian unbelievers, so there is in Maine a kind of rhetoric of sobriety and realism, which has the effect of casting opposing views as self-indulgent or weakly deluded. It is not as pronounced in Maine as it is in the figure who most naturally asks to be compared in this as in many other respects, namely Fitzjames Stephen, who took more of the exhibitionist's delight in showing off the virility of his mind, and who was arguably an exponent *avant la lettre* of what has since been called 'the "no-bullshit" bullshit'. But you can even hear something of this note of grim satisfaction in that passage which both Burrow and Cocks cite from one of his addresses to the University of Calcutta, where he insists that 'all truth, of whatever character, must conform to the same conditions, so that if indeed history be true, it must teach that which every other science teaches, continuous sequence, inflexible order, and eternal law' (Add. 2, 1865, in *VC*, 1876: 265–6). There is surely a palpable frisson in this famous cadence that comes from associating oneself with this awesome impersonal force, as well as an element of self-congratulation for managing to contemplate it without flinching. Again, the language is an extension of that used to describe a certain ideal of character.

Much of Maine's later writing consisted of deploying both his assiduously cultivated identity as an expert and his habitual tone of grim realism in the face of almost overwhelming complexity to provide a kind of scientific legitimation for the prejudices of the governing class. I think it is important to bear this intended audience in mind. The essays that make up *Popular Government* first appeared, after all, in the pages of the *Quarterly Review*, and during these years Maine was writing a fair amount of political journalism for the *St James's Gazette*, founded in 1880 as a Tory counterpart to the Liberal *Pall Mall Gazette*, and assessed by Lord Cranbrook in 1882 in these terms: 'The paper is addressed to the cultured and critical, who probably do not take it, but read it at their Clubs, and are a class whose tastes and feelings are Conservative' (quoted in Koss, 1981: 1, 231). This was Maine's natural audience by the 1880s. When he died, *The Spectator* observed in an interesting phrase that his great talent was for 'convincing qualified minds'; an alert sensitivity to the workings, and limits, of minds given to electing themselves to this idealized Athenaeum is evident in his later writings, expressing itself in a tone of collusive, head-shaking dismay at the follies of uninstructed mankind. The obverse of this identity was given in the *Saturday Review*, indulging for once in understatement, when it recorded that 'he was not a man of wide popular sympathies', and the point was put more bluntly still by the *St James's Gazette* itself, which called him simply 'a pronounced and uncompromising Anti-Radical' (all quoted in Grant Duff, 1892: 75, 82). My suggestion here, therefore, is that we should not be misled by the tone of weary disinterestedness which Maine affects into forgetting the almost blatantly ideological cast of much of his writing.

This leads on to my third point, which is to try to bring into focus Maine's relation to more familiar forms of conservative political thought. Benjamin Lippincott called Maine 'the first and last "scientific conservative" in English political thought' (1938: 169). Obviously the term echoes the usage of the period when connecting political analysis to larger patterns of historical and legal development could still try to lay claim to the prestige of science, but viewed from further away the label may even call into question the accuracy of calling Maine a 'conservative' at all. On some understandings of conservatism, after all, especially that retrospectively created tradition of English conservatism which likes to invoke the name of Burke, the phrase 'scientific conservative' is almost an oxymoron, and certainly we would search Maine's work in vain for some of the supposed hallmarks of conservative political thought – there is no elevating of tradition over analysis, no preference for the implicit over the explicit, little respect for the irrational or marked sympathy for religion, and so on. He remained too much the legalistic administrator and too responsive to the claims of system and rationality for that. To take just a minor example, when in *Ancient Law* he was insisting that feudalism was quite distinct from and more durable than genuinely archaic communities, primarily on account of the legacy of Roman law, he observed that 'express rules are less destructible than instinctive habits' (365–6), a remark which does not strike the expected Burkean or Oakeshottian note, and there are many more such examples. He was unremittingly hostile to facile *a priori* reasoning, but not to reasoning as such; he retained an admiration for Bentham, for example, arguing, with that measured tendentiousness so characteristic of his late style, that 'there is no political writer whose strongest and most fundamental opinions are so directly at variance with the Radical ideas of the moment' (*PG*: 84). If anything, Maine rather disdained that vulgar irrationality and unreflectiveness in which some kinds of conservative have claimed to detect a hidden wisdom.

Moreover, not only was his account of progress strikingly intellectualist, depending heavily as it did on the role of new ideas, but so was his diagnosis of the current danger of decline: he attributed a quite absurd causal power to the ideas of Rousseau. But in thus shifting the emphasis away from exploring the laudable role of intellectual innovation and towards decrying the pernicious consequences of theoretical fashion, the later Maine was led to express a somewhat more favourable view both of the role of habit and of the value of fixed constitutional forms, two forces which had appeared in *Ancient Law* chiefly as obstacles to progress. There was now a different resonance to his passing, but revealing, reference in *Popular Government* to the way in which human nature, 'when left to itself', is not intrinsically disposed to pursue change (143); there is a suggestion of untoward or 'outside' interference at work here, perhaps the doing of a tightly knit group of politically motivated men. John Morley was surely right, in his review of the latter book, to call attention both to Maine's 'tendency to impute an unreal influence to writers and books altogether' and his tendency to attach 'an altogether excessive and unscientific importance to form', neither of them supposed to be characteristic of what we have come to regard as conservative political thinking. It is always fun, of course, to see the radical berating the conservative for exaggerating the power of abstract political theory, but Morley had a deeper point to press in referring to the absence in Maine's work on democracy of what he called 'anything like a philosophy of society as a whole' or any 'reference to particular social conditions' (in Morley, 1890: 118, 149).

Maine's range of interests, it may be relevant to observe at this point (it was something his contemporaries remarked), was always pretty narrowly legal and political; it is surely rather odd, for example, to see legislation as the principal, and indeed largely autonomous, agent of change in Victorian England, of all places. Like many disillusioned intellectuals, Maine saw the circumstances prevailing in his youth as the last period of sanity, and more concretely this meant that relatively short period after the initial flush of Whig and Peelite reforms in the 1830s and 1840s but before the slide into democracy and demagoguery initiated by the Reform Act of 1867. It is interesting that Grant Duff mentions 'Peelite' as being Maine's earliest political identity (1892: 11); he never really had that period of eager Liberal enthusiasm which so many of his type did, including, for example, Henry Sidgwick, with whom he otherwise has much in common, especially the fact of being a terrible political hypochondriac.

His criticisms belong to a very specific period, too. There is in his work, for example, no criticism of mass culture as such: he is writing before fears about the proliferation of popular media and the 'Americanization' of 'lowbrow' culture gave their distinctive flavour to the cultural pessimism familiar among English literary intellectuals in the early decades of the twentieth century. As Professor Burrow shows, Maine does not really belong in the Whig tradition, to which he had several superficial resemblances, and my suggestion here is that I think he similarly does not really belong among those forms of religious or anti-rationalist or merely nostalgic political thought which have been factitiously erected into 'the conservative tradition'. He belongs, rather, with that group prominent in if not strictly peculiar to this period, such as Sidgwick, Dicey and the elder Stephen, rationalists with strongly individualist social and economic beliefs and deeply anti-democratic sympathies. It was a political identity which surely coloured his account of progress just as it clearly shaped his prognosis of decline.

PART TWO
Maine and the social sciences

CHAPTER 6

The rise and fall of Maine's patriarchal society
Adam Kuper

Ancient Law was one of the first books which Meyer Fortes directed me to read when I came up to Cambridge as a research student, twenty-five years ago. All Fortes' students were supposed to read *Ancient Law*. This was not because Fortes himself was much interested in the history of anthropology: but so far as he was concerned, Maine was no remote ancestor, some fossil figure from the prehistory of the discipline. On the contrary, he appealed to Maine as an authority, and borrowed a number of his theoretical conceptions. Nor was he alone in this. Fortes' great contemporary in British social anthropology, E. E. Evans-Pritchard, also treated Maine's anthropological ideas with respect, and Maine is one of the few ancestral figures to escape condemnation in Evans-Pritchard's *A History of Anthropological Thought*,[1] which was published posthumously in 1981.

So far as Maine and his own contemporaries were concerned, his anthropology began and ended with his 'Patriarchal Theory'. Neither Fortes nor Evans-Pritchard endorsed this theory, or even took it seriously, although they cited Maine's *obiter dicta* on kinship theory and on law. It was rather Maine's very lawyerly view of social structure which most influenced Fortes and his own mentor, Radcliffe-Brown. I shall return briefly to this 'jural model' (as it came to be called among anthropologists), but my central concern is with the patriarchal theory. Not that I have any intention of trying to breathe new life into the theory – this is a very dead corpse; but in good anthropological tradition I will try to make sense of the theory by setting it in context. In this case, that involves placing Maine's

[1] Maine 'gave us ... many of our more important technical terms: contract, status, delict, crime, agnation, etc., with a new sociological significance attached to them. He also gave us several sociological hypotheses of great value and displayed in doing so a clear understanding of sociological method, giving explanations in terms of relations between social phenomena by showing how one set of ideas or institutions affects others' (1981: 89–90).

arguments in an ideological context, for *Ancient Law* was in essence an attack on the political and legal theories of Jeremy Bentham and the utilitarians.

THE PATRIARCHAL THEORY

The original statement of the patriarchal theory – Maine's theory of primitive society – is to be found in the long fifth chapter of *Ancient Law*, but the chapter cannot be understood in isolation. It is the culmination of a phase in Maine's argument. The first three chapters of the book deal with the evolution of legal systems. In the earliest stages, there was virtually no rule of law at all: 'every man, living during the greater part of his life under the patriarchal despotism, was practically controlled in all his actions by a regimen not of law but of caprice' (*AL*: 8). Gradually a system of customary law was established, piecemeal. In a few societies these laws were later codified. Once a code had been established, instruments were required to amend laws from time to time. The first instrument of reform was the legal fiction. Later, appeals to principles of equity were admitted. Finally, legislation became the usual mechanism for legal change.

Of these mechanisms for reform Maine was particularly interested in equity, and in Chapter 3 he concentrated his attention upon equity and the 'Law of Nature', ideas which he traced to the Greeks. The Romans had borrowed the Greek idea of a natural law for a characteristically practical purpose. The foreigners who came within their jurisdiction had a variety of customs and laws, and so it was sometimes necessary to define general principles which overrode particular local laws. The Greek idea of a 'Law of Nature' legitimated such appeals to general principles which reconciled conflicting legal practices. Later, the idea of natural law was to provide a philosophical basis for legal reform, a touchstone of justice and equity.

The reason why Maine should devote a whole chapter to equity, which by his own account is only one of the instruments of legal reform, becomes more evident in Chapter 4. The history of the development of law given in his first three chapters is now used as a stick with which to beat the modern radicals, beginning with Rousseau and ending with his particular antagonist, Jeremy Bentham. Maine condemned all *a priori* approaches to law and to political theory, identifying them with one or other version of natural law theory, which was, he asserted, 'the ancient counterpart of Benthamism' (*AL*: 79). Speculation about natural law might have served its purpose under the Romans, but only because the Romans were sober enough to set limits on their fancy, to refer always to the actual practices of foreigners. However, in modern times the theory had bred wild and dangerous political illusions and 'helped most powerfully to bring about the grosser disappointments of which the first French Revolution was fertile' (*AL*: 91).

This, then, is the build-up to the fifth chapter, in which Maine describes the true original state of society and of law. No theory of jurisprudence should depend upon guesses about a state of nature. The only alternative is to investigate the history of legal systems, to trace them back as far as possible, by drawing upon the accounts left by classical authors of ancient customs or of barbarous peoples, and also by studying directly the documented systems of ancient law, of which the Roman system is by far the richest.

This method yields a clear-cut conclusion. 'The effect of the evidence derived from comparative jurisprudence', Maine tells us, 'is to establish that view of the primeval condition of the human race which is known as the Patriarchal Theory' (*AL*: 122). Of course, many other writers had assumed in a similar way that early societies were patriarchal: among those who influenced Maine, James Mill took this for granted in his *History of British India* (1817), and Grote, for example, represented the origins of the ancient world in similar terms. The patriarchal form of society is also familiar from the Old Testament, and Maine asserts that its traces can be discerned in every Indo-European legal source. There was therefore nothing new about the patriarchal theory in itself.

Maine's crucial contribution was to give the old-established notion of patriarchal society a legal definition. From the legal point of view, the outstanding feature of patriarchal society was the institution of *patria potestas*, whereby the father enjoyed unfettered control over the person and property of his children so long as he lived. Not only his own children were subject to what Maine calls his despotism: his wife, his adopted children, his slaves were equally in his power. Indeed, the notion of kinship was simply a way of categorizing the people subject to a patriarch.

This was the primeval condition – the patriarchal family (and *not* the individual) was the source of society. In the course of time the patriarchal family became a part of more complex institutions – the *Gens*, the Tribe, the Commonwealth – but even these institutions were conceived of as extensions of the patriarchal family. The patriarchal family was 'the type of an archaic society in all the modifications which it was capable of assuming' (*AL*: 133).

Even in ancient times, not all the members of the tribe, or even for that matter of the family, were really blood relatives. The first great legal fiction, adoption, was freely used to incorporate strangers. But if kinship was not the real basis of the polity, it was the only conceivable ideological foundation for political association. Indeed, there have been no 'subversions of feeling, which we term emphatically revolutions, so startling and so complete as the change which is accomplished when some other principle – such as that, for instance, of *local contiguity* – establishes itself for the first time as the basis of common political action' (*AL*: 129).

This revolution was, however, long delayed. Reform of the primeval institution was gradual, but in time the power of the patriarch was watered down and increasing independence given to grown sons and, eventually, to daughters (though not to wives). These gradual institutional changes amounted cumulatively, at the most abstract level, to a transformation in the principle of organization. The forms of the ancient institutions lingered on, and yet a line of progress was clearly to be discerned. Group membership became less crucial, and individual rights more significant. In his famous peroration to the chapter, Maine asserted that 'All the forms of Status taken notice of in the Law of Persons were derived from, and to some extent are still coloured by, the powers and privileges anciently residing in the Family'; but he concluded that 'the movement of the progressive societies has hitherto been a movement *from Status to Contract*' (*AL*: 170).

The remaining chapters of *Ancient Law* treat specific topics in the history of law, testamentary successions, property, contract, delict and crime. The central theme is the gradual development of civil law in place of criminal law, and, within civil law, the emergence of individual rights in property, and the increasing importance of contract.

THE STRUCTURE OF MAINE'S ARGUMENT

Despite Maine's insistent rhetoric, his reconstruction of ancient law was insecurely grounded in empirical data. *Ancient Law* relies on the case-study of Roman legal history, but leaving aside the problem of generalizing from the Roman case – and Maine only referred glancingly to other sources at this stage – Roman legal documents did not provide direct evidence for his patriarchal theory. For instance, on *patria potestas*, Maine wrote: 'No feature of the rudimentary associations of mankind is deposed to by a greater amount of evidence than this, and yet none seems to have disappeared so generally and so rapidly from the usages of advancing communities' (*AL*: 135). The direct evidence proves, however, to be rather meagre. There might be what Maine called 'hints' of the practice in the Homeric literature, but he accepted that Greek law limited parental power to the period of a child's minority. Maine notes that Gaius described *patria potestas* as a distinctively Roman institution, and reported that it was to be found among no other people in the Empire except for the Asiatic Galatae. Even in Roman law, the *patria potestas* did not extend to public contexts, for a son could command his father in the field or judge him in a court. The evidence is indeed so scrappy that Maine was obliged to adduce indirect evidence, notably the fact that the Romans distinguished a special category of relatives, *agnates*, who were related only in the male line. Distinguishing people who were descended through males from a single patriarch only made sense, Maine argued, if this category had formerly been subject to the domination of a patriarch who enjoyed an unlimited *patria potestas*. Later in *Ancient Law* (and in subsequent books) Maine was to draw more upon the evidence of European feudal law and on Indian village organization, but his use of evidence is seldom persuasive.

The structure of Maine's argument is polemical rather than scholarly. As his friend and rival, James Fitzjames Stephen remarked, Maine evoked Roman law as a way of showing up his opponents: 'He was enabled to sniff at Bentham for knowing nothing about it, & writing in consequence about English law, in a merely revolutionary manner' (quoted in Feaver, 1969: 25).

Maine's procedure was, in fact, quite straightforward. He took the propositions of his opponents and stood them on their head.[2] The patriarchal theory is best read as a direct inversion of the radical notion of the state of nature. The traditional radical theory was that men were originally free and equal individuals, who chose to combine, by agreeing to a contract, in order to protect their interests. Later, however, despots had managed to pervert the contractual order, and to subjugate free men. Patriarchal theory asserts precisely the opposite. Maine insists again and again that the original state of society was despotic. It was a society not of individuals but of family corporations, and the patriarch had untrammelled control over his dependants. Only very gradually, and then only in 'progressive' societies, did the individual come to enjoy any rights. The culmination of this development was the freedom to enter into individual contracts. Far from being the point of origin of human society, the emergence of contracts – and even of individual actors capable of entering into contracts – was the highest point of social development.

The political implications of Maine's argument are evident enough in general terms. His immediate political reference was, however, the debate on the future of the Indian Empire, and in particular the controversy about law reform in India. Maine was an active political journalist, and although *Ancient Law* does not directly address the problems of modern India, he discussed Indian affairs in a series of essays written in the late fifties, and the policy message of the book can be decoded quite easily. Bentham, Mill and Macaulay had hoped that India would serve as the laboratory for Benthamite legal codification. Maine was in effect arguing that the model for Indian reform should rather be the reception of Roman law in Germanic Europe.

The inspiration for Maine's argument can be traced to the German school of Roman law studies, which Savigny and his students had linked to the study of cultural history. Indo-European philologists had established historical relationships between India, Greece, Rome and the societies of northern Europe. The German lawyers added a further layer to the Indo-European construct. The legal systems of the Indo-Europeans had a family resemblance, though some were more developed than others. The Romans had

---

[2] Maine identified this technique himself, though he attributed it to his opponents, whose theory of a law of nature, he wrote, 'is still that of the Roman lawyers ... but the theory is, as it were, turned upside down' (*AL*: 88). In *Ancient Law* he returned the compliment.

developed the common legal system to an unprecedented degree, but other Indo-Europeans could borrow from Roman law without perverting their identity. The reception of Roman law by the Germanic peoples was in consequence not an insult to the folk spirit. It was no more than a speeding-up of a general Indo-European evolutionary process, which had proceeded more rapidly in Rome than among the German tribes. Nothing could be more different from the imposition by Napoleon of a rationalist *a priori* legal code; nothing could be further from the programme of the utilitarians.

Savigny and his students had, in short, developed a historical theory to combat radical, Napoleonic attempts to impose a code of laws based on first principles. Maine lifted their arguments and applied them to British India. India should not be subjected to a Benthamite code. Just as the Romans had helped their Germanic brethren along the common path, so the British would now pass on the baton to the Indians. Savigny and Jhering therefore provided Maine with the resources with which to turn Bentham on his head, in order to argue for a pragmatic, reformist, piecemeal application of English legal principles in India.

Within months of the publication of *Ancient Law* Maine was appointed legal member in the Viceroy's Council, and as his biographer remarked, in office 'he strove to make the major theses of his *Ancient Law* a self-fulfilling prophecy' (Feaver, 1969: 73). He had been supported in his bid for office by Lord Acton, but soon Acton was to remark in disillusionment to Mary Gladstone that Maine's nature was 'to exercise power, and to find good reasons for adopted policy' (quoted in Feaver, 1969: 179). Whether or not Maine actually wrote *Ancient Law* with an eye to membership of the Viceroy's Council, there can be little doubt that the inspiration of the work was primarily political and concerned above all with India; and that the structure of the argument has more to do with the refutation of Bentham than with any evidence concerning ancient law.

THE REACTION TO PATRIARCHAL THEORY

In the very year in which *Ancient Law* appeared, a Swiss jurist, Johannes Bachofen – a product of the German school – published a book entitled *Das Mutterrecht*, in which he also drew on classical myth and law but came to the conclusion that the most ancient societies were founded on matriarchy rather than patriarchy. In Britain, however, matriarchal theory was developed independently by a Scots lawyer, J. F. McLennan, in a book entitled *Primitive Marriage*, which appeared in 1865. McLennan's argument was elaborate and subtle, but essentially he turned Maine on his head, doing to him as he had done to Bentham.

McLennan had contributed an essay on law to the *Encyclopaedia Britannica* in 1857, in which he accepted the view that political society was originally patriarchal. His repudiation of this established view a few years later can probably be put down to a reaction against *Ancient Law*, fuelled perhaps by McLennan's distaste for Maine's political ideas. McLennan was at the time secretary for the Scottish Society for Promoting the Amendment of the Law, and his posthumously published collection of essays, entitled *The Patriarchal Theory*, contains virulent attacks on Maine which suggest something more, even, than the heat engendered by scholarly disagreement. Maine himself read McLennan's book, accurately enough, as an elaborate inversion of his own argument.[3]

The argument which McLennan constructed was modelled on evolutionary doctrines. Where Maine had drawn on Savigny, McLennan looked rather to Malthus and Darwin. His starting-point was the assumption that all early human groups were engaged in a life or death struggle. Female membership of the group had to be kept to a minimum, since women were simply an encumbrance to a fighting party. Consequently, men killed female children. For sexual purposes they captured a small number of women, whom they shared. Initially, there were no incest taboos and no marriage arrangements. Men at first lived promiscuously with their own sisters and, later, with captured mates. Consequently the only kinship tie which could be identified was through the mother.

The central thesis of *Primitive Marriage* is that patriarchal society was not the starting point of human history, but a very advanced stage. Maine believed that relationships of agnation provided the framework of early society. McLennan insisted that, on the contrary, in the infancy of mankind only matrilineal kin were recognized. It was only after several phases of social evolution that individual men began to contract marriages which gave them sole

---

[3] Maine wrote that: 'The other theory which is now opposed to that long called Patriarchal is the theory of the origin of society, not in the Family but in the horde ... It derives the smaller from the larger group, not the larger from the smaller' (*ELC*: 199–200).

control over their own wives. This movement was paralleled by the development of private property. As individuals came to own capital, they would naturally wish to pass it on to their own sons. The consequence of these tendencies was the emergence of a patriarchal society.

The evidence for such sensational practices as primeval infanticide and group marriage was necessarily rather patchy. Malthus had cited female infanticide as a method of population control in primitive societies, and in 1857 Cave-Browne had published his influential report *Indian Infanticide: Its Origin, Progress and Suppression*; but in general McLennan was content with indirect and partial indications that some of the institutions he evoked had existed once, somewhere. Nevertheless, McLennan's thesis was welcomed by Tylor, who was rapidly becoming the arbiter of anthropological matters in Britain. It also greatly influenced an American lawyer, Lewis Henry Morgan, who was to initiate a whole tradition of American anthropology.

The title of Morgan's *Ancient Society*, published in 1877, echoed the title of Maine's *Ancient Law*, and reasonably enough, for it belongs to the same universe of discourse; but Maine recognized it as another assault on his patriarchal theory. He had written a conservative history of Indo-European law, which argued that the original society was based upon patriarchal families, and that improvements, such as they were, had depended upon the efforts of lawyers. Morgan wrote a progressive history of mankind, which argued that the original society was based upon group marriage and matrilineal descent, and that moral progress from this shocking start was inevitable, being the realization of God's plan for mankind. In the small but committed circle which concerned itself with theories of primitive society, Morgan and McLennan were cast as Maine's great theoretical rivals.

The theoretical debate was actually quite quickly resolved. Maine lost the argument, although he enjoyed one crucial advantage: both his rivals died in 1881. Two years later he published his *Dissertations on Early Law and Custom*, which contained a long counter-attack on Morgan and McLennan under the title, 'Theories of primitive society'. It is a powerful piece of advocacy, which demonstrated the contradictions between his two antagonists, and criticized their use of sources. However, he now shifted his ground significantly. In his first response to McLennan, in his

Lectures on the Early History of Institutions, published in 1875, he had suggested that while McLennan might be correct so far as primitive peoples elsewhere were concerned, he was wrong with respect to the Indo-European peoples. In consequence, McLennan's arguments 'do not concern us till the Kinship of the higher races can be distinctly shown to have grown out of the Kinship now known only to the lower, and even then they concern us only remotely' (*EHI*: 67). But by the early 1880s the Darwinian view that all mankind had a single origin was in the ascendant, and Maine no longer tried to insist on a separate path of Indo-European social development. Instead he borrowed an argument which Darwin had himself formulated in *The Descent of Man*, when he queried the matriarchal theory on the grounds that it ran counter to a universal instinct of sexual jealousy. Maine now suggested that 'sexual jealousy, indulged through power, might serve as a definition of the Patriarchal Family' (*ELC*: 209); and indeed Darwin's model of primate social groupings did appear to be consistent with Maine's ideas of primeval patriarchal power.

Nevertheless, despite the convenient absence of his rivals, his powers of advocacy and the adoption of Darwinian arguments, Maine was unable to revive his theory. Orthodox anthropological opinion followed either McLennan or Morgan for the next generation, and their work stimulated ethnographic expeditions to collect new, relevant materials. There are various reasons for their influence, but above all they represented a Darwinian form of argument, for they began from the struggle for survival, gave a central place to mating patterns, and identified cultural equivalents of the fossil record. With Tylor and Lubbock, they also insisted on the unity of human history. Only in the twentieth century did the critiques of Boas, Westermarck, Malinowski and Radcliffe-Brown gradually put an end to fantasies of group marriage, matriarchy and marriage by capture. Moreover, Maine's theories of early Indo-European society were also going out of fashion in the late nineteenth century. A revisionist school began to show that the *mark* community allowed private property, serfdom, feudal institutions and even the ownership of property by women and its transmission through women (see Vinogradoff, 1892).

THE JURAL MODEL

The form of the primeval society is no longer debated in the traditional way in anthropology. The contributions of Maine, Morgan, McLennan – and, later, of Freud, Durkheim and Engels, and of so many others – belong not to science but to a genre of science fiction. These writers constructed mirror images of their own society – or rather of some particular interpretation of their times – and projected these back into the distant past, creating anti-Utopias (or, in the case of some romantics, Utopias) which helped to give substance to their dreams for the future.[4] Within anthropology there is fairly general agreement today that we cannot reconstruct very early social forms in any detail, and that the social arrangements of early man were, in any case, probably rather diverse (as are the social institutions of other modern primate groups). In short, the issues which were crucial for Maine have passed from academic debate, and there seems little chance that his patriarchal theory will be revived within anthropology. If he is still to be read, it is for other reasons.

One of Maine's most potent themes was that the family was the basic social institution, providing the model for other associations including, even, the early state. Similar ideas were taken up and developed, in very different ways, by Engels and Freud, and they have been revived by some modern feminist writers. Maine's contrast between the family model of society and a later, revolutionary form, which was based rather on territory, also interested a number of subsequent writers, not all of whom were probably aware of its provenance. Fortes, for one, borrowed Maine's opposition, while playing down its evolutionary formulation.

Within anthropology and the social sciences, however, Maine figures especially as one of the sources of a 'jural' model of social structure. Fortes, for example, drew from Maine (and Radcliffe-Brown) a view of society as being made up not of individuals but of right-bearing entities, persons. These units might be corporations, offices, even roles in a domestic structure. They were linked to each other by reciprocal rights and duties, which were sustained by a body of sanctions. These systems of jural relationships outlived individuals and lent continuity and stability to a community.

---

[4] I have discussed the argument in detail elsewhere (Kuper, 1988).

They also offered the sociologist a realistic map of the social structure.

This jural approach to social structure is associated particularly with the work of Radcliffe-Brown, Fortes, Evans-Pritchard and Gluckman. It was the central orthodoxy for a generation within British social anthropology, although it was always in tension with an economistic view of society, which played down systematic and enduring forms of social order and concentrated instead upon the choices of individuals, who were supposed to maximize their satisfactions, and whose actual choices yielded temporary statistical patterns, which the sociologist tried to explain. The main proponents of this individualist tradition within European anthropology were Malinowski, Firth and Fredrik Barth. More recently, both these approaches have been eclipsed – certainly within anthropology – by a new wave of phenomenological perspectives, which are not concerned with individual manoeuvres or with formal institutions, but deal rather with the ways in which actors conceive of their social experience. But the new solipsism is already looking decidedly threadbare, and I should not be surprised if the jural model becomes of interest once again. This is the one form which a Maine revival in anthropology could conceivably take.

CHAPTER 7

Some contributions of Maine to history and anthropology

Alan D. J. Macfarlane

An intelligent undergraduate could undoubtedly make a strong case for dismissing Maine. Having read through subsequent assessments of his work, he would list Maine's supposed achievements and then show how each was deeply flawed. Such a critic would point to the supposed 'revolutionary' method, comparative and historical, and show how it was deeply imbued with a form of patronizing Victorian evolutionism which is now both morally and intellectually repugnant. The vaunted width and depth of scholarship would crumble before allegations of inaccuracy and over-dependence on an erring memory. The father of kinship studies in anthropology would be shown to have set up a false theory of universal patriarchal origins which was soon refuted. The great insight, of the movement, of progressive societies from status to contract, would be shown not to be true even of all 'progressive' societies, and in any case was already anticipated by many other Enlightenment thinkers, as well as by Marx. The theories concerning the religious basis of law turn out to be a myth, and the theory of the ways in which legal change occurs, to be inappropriate to the common law. The central thesis concerning the original communal nature of property in Indian and Germanic villages was soon shown to be much too sweeping a generalization. The view that simpler societies rest their associations on kinship, and only later move to non-kinship, or territorial, bonds was soon disputed.

After such a survey, the student would end up, if in critical mood, by asking his supervisor why he had been asked to assess a man who might have temporarily been of importance, but could no longer be of interest except from an historical point of view. Why waste time on a thinker whose methodology was based on an outworn paradigm, whose scholarship was shaky, whose findings were unoriginal or wrong? This chapter will explore some of these charges and try to show that Maine survives all his detractors and emerges with that quality which makes him, like Montesquieu or de Tocqueville or Hobbes, immortal: the ability to speak to us directly and still to contribute strikingly to the intellectual puzzles which face historians and anthropologists.

The methodological criticisms are both the most complex and, in some ways, the most interesting, so let us leave them for a moment. On the question of scholarship, the unanswerable criticism is, of course, made by F. W. Maitland. Writing to Pollock in 1901, Maitland wrote: 'You spoke of Maine. Well, I always talk of him with reluctance, for on the few occasions on which I sought to verify his statements of fact I came to the conclusion that he trusted much to a memory that played him tricks and rarely looked back at a book that he had once read ...' (Maitland, 1965: 279). Maitland then gives an example, which he elaborates (Pollock and Maitland, 1968: II, 305 n. 2). Without months of work it would be impossible to assess *how* inaccurate Maine was. But ultimately it is not terribly important. One does not assess him as a scholar in the sense of Maitland or Stubbs or Vinogradoff. The scholarly defect was the price he paid for his enormous breadth and insight. His reputed ability to read and extract the heart of a large book at amazing speed and his power to move over wide areas of literature were what was needed to provide a new synthesis. Maitland's later judgement, quoted above, has to be taken against his earlier one in the year of Maine's death: 'He was much more than learned, but then he was learned, very learned in law of all sorts and kinds. It is only through learning wide and deep, tough and technical, that we can safely approach those world-wide questions that he raised or criticize the answers that he found for them' (Maitland, 1911: I, 486–7). Thus some of the details may be wrong, but at this distance we are more interested in the tree than the separate leaves.

Sir Henry Maine's contribution will be considered under the following headings: kinship theory; political and legal organization; concept of the community; property rights in general; the growth of individual property rights and their relation to feudalism; the movement from status to contract; general methodology; and the evolutionary framework. Each of these sections covers a large area to which Maine and his critics have devoted many hundreds of pages. Necessarily the treatment will have to be brief and preliminary.

Some contributions of Maine to history and anthropology 113

It has been suggested that Maine's contribution to kinship theory has somehow been discredited by the supposed refutation of his theory of patriarchal origins. In fact Maine made several fundamental contributions which helped lay the foundations for much of the modern analysis of kinship. As Evans-Pritchard, Fortes and others have amply recorded, Maine's ideas of lineage identity, of the differences between cognatic and agnatic descent, of the corporate nature of descent groups, of the importance of adoption and many other topics have been an enormous inspiration to one of the major contributions of modern social anthropology. A few quotations from *Ancient Law* will bring home to modern anthropologists their debt: 'society in primitive times was not what it is assumed to be at present, a collection of *individuals*. In fact ... it was *an aggregation of families*. The contrast may be most forcibly expressed by saying that the *unit* of an ancient society was the Family, of a modern society the Individual' (*AL*: 126). And what were these small families? They were corporate groups. 'Corporations *never die*, and accordingly primitive law considers the entities with which it deals, *i.e.* the patriarchal or family groups, as perpetual and inextinguishable' (126). Or again, 'Succession in corporations is necessarily universal, and the family was a corporation. Corporations never die. The decease of individual members makes no difference to the collective existence of the aggregate body' (186). Of course, this idea is straight from Roman law: 'in the pure Roman jurisprudence, the principle that a man lives on in his Heir – the elimination, if we may so speak, of the fact of death – is too obviously for mistake the centre round which the whole Law of Testamentary and Intestate succession is circling' (190). But while the idea was not new, Maine's breadth of interests and reading allowed him to connect it with the kinship systems in the simplest societies. A whole world, the modern study of unilineal descent groups, lineages and so on, was born.

There is little criticism of all this. The dispute is centred on Maine's own application of the theory. This is a deep marsh in which many a scholar has become entrapped, so I will just skirt the edge with a few remarks. The first is to note a well-known irony: in the very year in which Maine propounded his famous theory that in Indo-European societies the original form of the society was based on father right, descent through males, or what he called the 'Patriarchal Theory', was published Bachofen's famous work on *Mother Right*, showing that the original form of the family in the simplest societies was the complete opposite. From then onwards, there was fierce debate, with McLennan and Morgan later joining to propound a third theory, of original 'primitive promiscuity', leading through mother right to father right to modern cognatic systems.

Several things are now obvious. Maine was uncertain at first as to whether his theory should be applied outside the Indo-Aryan culture area of Europe and India from which all his evidence was drawn. He notes that 'the legal testimony comes nearly exclusively from the institutions of societies belonging to the Indo-European stock, the Romans, Hindoos, and Sclavonians supplying the greater part of it', and therefore 'the difficulty, at the present stage of the inquiry, is to know where to stop, to say of what races of men it is *not* allowable to lay down that the society in which they are united was originally organized on the patriarchal model' (*AL*: 123). He leaves the question open, and it therefore seems unfair that he should be branded as having a universal theory of patriarchal origins.

At any rate, the evidence as to which races did not have such an original 'patriarchal model' was soon to hand. Bachofen, McLennan and Morgan soon produced counter-evidence of other early forms, and we now know, of course, that many of the simplest societies have matrilineal or cognatic kinship (for example, Evans-Pritchard, 1981: 89). Maine reacted in a reasonable and flexible way when this new evidence appeared. This can be seen in his comments on Morgan's work. In *Ancient Society* (1877), Morgan had paid a handsome tribute to Maine, 'whose brilliant researches in the sources of ancient law, and in the early history of institutions, have advanced so largely our knowledge of them'. He agreed with Maine's theories about the patriarchal origins of Indo-European civilizations: the patriarchal family, it is true, is the oldest made known to us by ascending along the lines of classical and Semitic authorities'. But he then argued that 'an investigation along these lines is unable to penetrate beyond the Upper Status of barbarism, leaving at least four ethnical periods untouched, and their connection unrecognized' (1877: 514). With his deeper knowledge of tribal societies, he added strong evidence of early matrilineal systems. This and other evidence Maine accepted. In the Preface to the tenth edition of *Ancient Law* (1885), he admitted that

> the Author has not done sufficient justice to investigations which appear to show the existence of states of society still more rudimentary than that vividly described in the Homeric lines quoted at page 124, and ordinarily

Some contributions of Maine to history and anthropology 115

known as the Patriarchal State ... and, in fact, since his work was first published, in 1861, the observation of savage or extremely barbarous races has brought to light forms of social organization extremely unlike that to which he has referred the beginning of law, and possibly in some cases of greater antiquity. (v–vi)

He then referred the reader to his article 'Theories of primitive society', published in *Dissertations on Early Law and Custom* (1883). In that volume Maine very calmly and rationally assesses his own work in the light of McLennan and Morgan's work. In essence, he accepts that they have shown that there are many societies which are not patriarchal in origin. But he effectively criticizes their position, suggesting that by substituting his own supposed universal evolutionary framework by another, they have produced an equally bad distortion. Thus he writes, 'It appears to me that, while the Patriarchal theory and the counter-theory of which I have been speaking each explain reasonably well a certain number of ancient social phenomena, both are open to considerable objection as universal theories of the genesis of society' (*ELC*: 203–4). Thus while he admits that there are 'unquestionably many assemblages of savage men so devoid of some of the characteristic features of patriarchalism that it seems a gratuitous hypothesis to assume that they had passed through it', 'the newer theory is surrounded by difficulties quite as grave or graver' (203–4). He then proceeds effectively to demolish the theory of primitive promiscuity. He also points out, as anthropologists would now accept, that Morgan's theory that matrilineal forms always preceded the later patrilineal forms is wrong. 'One of these two groups did not really succeed the other, but the two co-existed from all time, and were always distinct from one another' (287). He thus accepted that there is no necessary evolution through states, no ascertainable start in one particular form. This is very much the present position in anthropology. Maine put forward an exciting hypothesis, found its limits, and accepted them; much of the subsequent work has been built within the framework which he set up with Morgan, and he is by no means discredited.

There is one further point to add here, however. We cannot now accept uncritically Maine's account of early Indo-European kinship. His theory of its patriarchal or agnatic character has not been sustained by subsequent research in at least one important respect, that is in relation to Anglo-Saxon kinship. Maine recognized that there was something odd about Anglo-Saxon kinship, writing that in the important area of joint property 'the general usage of the old Germanic peoples – it is remarkable that the Anglo-Saxon customs seem to have been an exception – forbade alienations without the consent of the male children' (*AL*: 280). Nevertheless, in general, he tended to assume its basically agnatic quality. As Vinogradoff stressed (1920: 147–8), 'Maitland lays stress on the difficulty arising from the fact that ancient Anglo-Saxon and Germanic law recognized relationship on the female as well as the male side. In his view, there can therefore be no question of grouping the corresponding societies into patriarchal clans, which stand or fall with the conception of agnatic relationship.' Maitland's elegant demonstration that Anglo-Saxon kinship was in fact cognatic and not agnatic (Pollock & Maitland, 1968: II, 240–60), has been supported by anthropological research (see Lancaster, 1958; Fox, 1967).

This revision is extremely important, for it lets Maine out of a corner into which he had boxed himself by his patriarchal theories. Basically, Maine's problem was how to explain the origins of modern civilization in the 'progressive' societies. This consisted in the movement from status, or kinship-based, societies, to the modern contractual society. The essential bridge was the destruction of kinship in the feudal period. But he never solved the problem of where the magic ingredients of feudalism came from. We will return to this when considering his ideas of property. But it is worth noting here that by assuming the uniformity of the agnatic, kinship-dominated stage, he seemed to leave no room for contract. The idea of alienability, or of primogeniture, seemed to spring from a clear sky. Thus, for instance, he says that there is no concept of primogeniture or its associated ideas in Roman law, in Hindu law or in ancient German law. All children were co-owners with their family. Suddenly it emerges (*AL*: 227ff.). He never solved this central puzzle. But Maitland solved it for him. There were elements in the kinship system of the Germanic peoples which already suggested an alternative to joint property and patriarchal organization; the seed was there, and the mystery of feudalism is not quite as deep as it once seemed. We will return to this.

One aspect of Maine's valuable recognition of the dominating importance of kinship in simple societies was his theory that political organization had originally been based on blood or kinship and later moved to territory, which is part of that famous transition from status to contract, or as anthropologists might put it, from tribal to peasant civilization. As a grand theory, this has provided a solid foundation for much work in political anthropology; for instance, as Adam Kuper points out, the work of Evans-Pritchard and Fortes in *African Political Systems* is to a certain extent a matter of taking over this classification and standing it on its side: 'They did not present it as a classification of political systems in time, but rather in space' (Kuper, 1973: 110). The idea is relatively simple. As Maine expressed it, 'The history of political ideas begins, in fact, with the assumption that kinship in blood is the sole possible ground of community in political functions...' (*AL*: 129). Thus 'the idea that a number of persons should exercise political rights in common simply because they happened to live within the same topographical limits was utterly strange and monstrous to primitive antiquity' (*AL*: 131). It is one 'of those subversions of feeling, which we term emphatically revolutions, so startling and so complete' when 'some other principle – such as that, for instance, of *local contiguity* – establishes itself for the first time as the basis of common political action' (*AL*: 129).

This is 'one of Maine's most important generalizations: kinship and *not* contiguity is the basis of common political action in primitive societies' (Evans-Pritchard, 1981: 87). Anthropologists and others have only marginally qualified the insight. Evans-Pritchard leaves it unchallenged, and Sahlins approves it, drawing on Maine to make the distinction between tribal society, where we speak of the 'King of the Franks', and modern states, where we speak of the 'King of France' (Sahlins, 1968: 6). Lowie writes that 'The soundness of Maine's and Morgan's position in drawing a sharp distinction between kinship (tribal) and territorial (political) organization is beyond cavil' (1929: 377). There are only three modifications or criticisms. One is put forward as a question by Lowie himself, namely 'to what extent it is coterminous with the distinction between rude and advanced cultures' (377). Anthropologists would probably answer that there is a broad but not exact correlation. Secondly, Schapera has pointed out that to the two principles of political organization (kinship and territory) should be added a third, namely 'personal attachment to a common leader' (1956: 29). This is to be found in the South African data Schapera considers, and elsewhere. The third is really a criticism of another kind.

In his comments on Maine's book *Lectures on the Early History of*

Institutions (1875), Marx argued that 'the apparent supreme independent existence of the state is itself merely show, and in all its forms it is an excrescence of society'. Hence it 'disappears again as soon as the society has reached a stage not yet reached'. Marx strongly disapproved of 'blockhead Maine', who does not seem to realize that the emergence of the state is a retrograde step, based on class interests, 'and these in the final instance all have economic conditions at bottom. On this basis the state is built and presupposes them' (Krader, 1976: 225–6). This is a moral gulf which is really too deep to bridge with argument. Marx is criticizing Maine's attitude to the State, and his view, widely shared, that it is an irreversible, necessary and probably desirable revolution. The deeper point, that Maine had elaborated and refined the distinction between pre-State and State systems, should not be lost, and is not destroyed by Marx.

The consideration of Maine's contribution to political anthropology provides a bridge to his ideas on the legal systems of early societies. Here again his work provides a foundation which is essentially sound, when modified. One modification concerns his view as to the origins of law. In several places he argued that law grew out of religion: 'We can see that Brahmanical India has not passed beyond a stage which occurs in the history of all the families of mankind, the stage at which a rule of law is not yet discriminated from a rule of religion' (*AL*: 23). Or again, 'the severance of law from morality, and of religion from law, belong[s] very distinctly to the later stages of mental progress' (16). A. S. Diamond devoted much of his 445-page book of 1935, *Primitive Law*, to demonstrating that this is wrong, and without going into the details, his demolition seems fairly convincing.

Related to this is Maine's view that in the absence of the state, in early societies all law was the law of wrongs, or torts. 'All civilized systems agree in drawing a distinction between offences against the State or Community and offences against the Individual ... Crimes and Wrongs, *crimina* and *delicta*. Now the penal Law of ancient communities is not the law of Crimes; it is the law of Wrongs ... of Torts' (*AL*: 369–70). Hence offences such as theft, assault and trespass are treated as torts, and not as crimes. There is clearly some truth in this; crimes are offences against the State, and if there is no State, there are no crimes. But, in fact, this has to be modified in the light of the fact that most anthropologists have found that there are some offences, typically witchcraft, incest and homicide of certain kinds, which are regarded as offences against the whole community rather than the aggrieved individual. Hence, Lowie remarks that 'in the generality of instances primitive man recognizes both torts and crimes', and produces evidence to show this to be the case (1929: 385). Diamond points out that, partly from Maine's work, there 'has been drawn a widespread conception that in primitive law there is no separation between crimes and civil injuries. But it is not so; the distinction is universal ...' (1935: 279).

A further modification can be made to Maine's theory of how legal change is effected. As John Baker has pointed out, the distinctions Maine made between legal fictions, equity and legislation as mechanisms to effect change are theoretically useful. But it 'is difficult to square' this as a universal order with what we observe, for instance, in the history of English common law (1979: 170).

Logically, this would lead us to consider the validity of Maine's most famous generalization concerning the movement from status to contract. But since that is the summation of his theories and deeply related to the whole methodological debate, we will put it on one side for the moment and consider some other features of his work. One of these is his idea of the original village community.

Since Maine's concept of 'community' was so important in his theories, it is worth digressing a little to elaborate some features of his argument. He believed that the difference between community-based and individual-based societies helped him to understand the origins of modern civilization and the difference between modern Europe and India. One of the major lessons, and one which it 'is often said that it takes two or three years' for a new visitor to India to learn, is that 'the vast Indian population is an aggregate of natural groups, and not the mixed multitude he left at home ...' (*EHI*: 30–1). He believed that this had once been the case in England and in Europe, in the Dark Ages. There had been a growth of 'Village-Communities', and the 'historian of former days laboured probably under no greater disadvantage than that caused by his unavoidable ignorance of the importance of these communities ...' (76–7). The 'naturally organised, self-existing, Village-Community' was an institution not 'specially characteristic of the Aryan races' (77). Maine's ideas here were enormously influential since, as Tönnies emphasized, they formed a crucial strand in his own important work on the distinctions between community and association (1887). What, then, did Maine mean by 'community'?

There are a number of characteristics which, according to Maine, constitute a community. Communities are 'naturally organized', that is to say the bond that unites people is a natural, rather than an artificial one. The two major bonds are kinship, in tribal communities, and territory, in village communities. One of the earliest traces of family communities which Maine could find were the 'East European (Slavonic) House Communities'. As he wrote, 'The House Community then is an extension of the Family: an association of several and even of many related families, living together substantially in a common dwelling or group of dwellings, following a common occupation, and governed by a common chief' (*ELC*: 241). This early bond of kinship, however, had given place in both India and Europe to the bond of locality. The 'Indian Village-Community is a body of men held together by the land which they occupy: the idea of common blood and descent has all but died out' (*EHI*: 82). This is still a 'true Village-Community' (78), even though there had been a transition from the earlier form of 'the Village-Community, a brotherhood of self-styled kinsmen, settled on a space of land' (*ELC*: 327). This is a modification of his earlier position. In *Ancient Law* he had put much more stress on kinship: 'The Village Community of India is at once an organized patriarchal society and an assemblage of co-proprietors. The personal relations to each other of the men who compose it was indistinguishably confounded with their proprietary rights ...' (*AL*: 260). Later he accepted that the basic uniting feature of communities was not kinship, but co-ownership of land: 'when a tribal community settles down finally upon a definite space of land, the Land begins to be the basis of society in place of the Kinship' (*EHI*: 72).

The basic feature of such a community was communal land-ownership; 'the Indian forms of property in land are founded on the Village Group as the proprietary unit' (*VC*: 185). There is some ambivalence on Maine's part as to what this communal ownership actually meant. At times he seems to imply, as above, that the village as a whole owned the land, and individuals were merely users: a corporate group ownership which was the spatial transformation of lineage property. This could be read into remarks such as 'the Indian Village-Community is a body of men held together by the land which they occupy' (*EHI*: 82). On the other hand he seems to recognize that in many villages such communal ownership was already a thing of the past. In *Ancient Law* he had written that the 'co-owners of an Indian village, though their property is blended, have their rights distinct ...' (*AL*: 267). This tension between collective and private is expanded when he explains that 'Land belonged to the tribe, joint-family, or village-community before it belonged to the individual household; even when it became private property, the brotherhood retained large rights over it, and without the consent of the collective brotherhood it could not be transferred' (*ELC*: 352). Here a sort of 'private property' with a *restrait lignager* seems to be envisaged. At other times he puts it in another context: the 'common life of the group or community has been so far broken up as to admit of private property in cultivated land, but not so far as to allow departure from a joint system of cultivating that land' (*VC*: 109).

He believed, therefore, that once upon a time the village community had been a collective entity in terms of landholding, both in India and early Europe. This collectivity manifested itself in terms of the absence of individual rights. Maine argued that there was no concept similar to the modern Western one of inalienable human rights in the traditional village community. 'Nor, in the sense of the analytical jurists, is there *right* or *duty* in an Indian village-community; a person aggrieved complains not of an individual wrong but of the disturbance of the order of the entire little society' (*VC*: 68). The growth of individual rights was one of the major transformations which had occurred in western Europe, and would soon break up the natural communities of India.

Another feature singled out by Maine was 'self-existing'. By this he probably meant 'self-sufficient'. He described how Indian villages were 'total' economies, not dependent for goods on the outside world. In fact, he envisaged in the earliest stage 'a territory occupied by village-communities ... at perpetual war with its neighbour' (*VC*: 192). These were little kingdoms. He described how the mixture of occupations in an Indian village seemed to cover all human needs, and wrote that 'the assignment of a definite lot in the cultivated area to particular trades ... allows us to suspect that the early Teutonic groups were similarly self-sufficing' (*VC*: 126). A final feature we may draw attention to is the fact that such communities were governed by customary, unwritten, laws. The elders claim merely to be interpreting the old customs. Maine accepts that this is often a fiction, and that really they are 'legislating' for new situations, 'Yet ... it is always the fact or the fiction that this council merely declares customary law' (*VC*: 116).

Maine thus created a model of a village community, with the natural bonds of blood or locality, rather than artificial bonds of money and contract, with communal ownership of some form, with economic and political self-sufficiency, and with customary law. This he believed was a transitional form between tribal and modern society. He was aware, however, of certain limitations to the model: these village communities, for example, were neither homogenous nor egalitarian: 'The brotherhood, in fact, forms a sort of hierarchy' in an Indian village, in which there are dominant families (*VC*: 177). In fact, Indian village communities 'prove on close inspection to be not simple but composite bodies, including a number of classes with very various rights and claims' (*VC*: 123). This was, in fact, the start of a departure of reality from the model. For Maine was quite aware that his description of the Indian village community was already an idealized model of what had faded away. In Bengal, 'from causes not yet fully determined, the village system had fallen into great decay' (*VC*: 104). He believed that the concepts of private property and individual rights encouraged by British law would lead the village community to disppear (*EHI*: 82); already 'the Indian village-community is breaking to pieces' (*VC*: 112).

What àre we to make of Maine's work on communities? Considering the time it was written and the influence it has had, it is a major contribution to our understanding of the long period between tribal and modern capitalist civilizations. It anticipates and clearly deeply influenced much of the later great sociological work of Tönnies on community and association, Durkheim on mechanical and organic solidarity and even modern peasant studies in the Redfieldian tradition. As long as we remember that Maine was setting up an archetype or hypothetical model, while recognizing that the pure form no longer existed, it can still be a useful starting-point. Yet his work needs to be modified in two major ways to make it even more valuable. In relation to India, it soon became clear that his account was very one-sided. Baden-Powell, in his work on the *Indian Village Community*, pointed out that Maine's description of Indian villages 'cannot be applied at all to one class, and that by far the largest, of Indian villages' (1896: 7). The majority of Indian villages were of the *raiyatwari* form, Baden-Powell argued, where there was no 'ownership in common'. Thus Maine was roughly right about one-quarter of Indian villages, Baden-Powell calculated (8). As with the debate over kinship, it is no longer certain that communal ownership is the earliest form, just as the patriarchal theory had to give way to diversity of early forms.

Maine devotes less attention to the village community in the European sphere, but it is clear that he believed that early Germanic society had passed through this stage of village communities, a view shared by many of his contemporaries such as Seebohm. This view has again been modified by several authorities, and notably by Maitland. As Vinogradoff wrote, Maitland 'in his criticism of Maine's theory of the village community ... held that there is no evidence of original communalism' (1920: 148). He shows, for instance, that the right in the common land 'is not communalism; it is individualism *in excelsis*' (Pollock & Maitland, 1968: 1, 623). On the question of corporate property, 'England affords but few materials for an answer to this important question, for anything that even by a stretch of language could be called a communal ownership of land, if it had ever existed, had become rare and anomalous before the stream of accurate documents begins to flow' (1, 630). Thus as far back as we can go, there is no evidence of village communities in Maine's sense.

Now we may put together Maine and Maitland again, as we did with kinship. Maine provides the hypothesis and the generalization; but is then puzzled because he is left with a problem. In the earlier case, if all Indo-European societies were agnatic, how did kinship become cognatic? Maitland answers by challenging the assumption. Here, if all Indo-European societies went through a stage, after tribalism, of 'village communities', how did the curious privatized property of parts of western Europe emerge? Maitland again answers by challenging the assumption – leaving it open; communal ownership of land 'if it had ever existed'.

The idea of 'community' was not as important to Maine as the nature and basis of an individual's property rights. His ideas on property are very rich and complex, and only a preliminary sketch of a few of them can be given, in order to see how they can and have influenced us.

As a jurist, Maine realized that property did not consist in an object, corporeal or incorporeal, but in the relationship between a human being and another human being and such an object. As he memorably put it, the 'rights of property are, in the eye of the jurist, a bundle of powers, capable of being mentally contemplated apart from one another and capable of being separately enjoyed' (*VC*: 158). Like marriage, the 'bundle of powers' will have some of the same elements, but also vary from society to society. Hence he doubts 'whether proprietorship in India is to be taken to be the same assemblage of powers which constitutes the modern English ownership of land in fee-simple' (157). Property is an amalgam of rights; the task of the analyst, whether historian or anthropologist, is to unravel 'the apportionment of the rights of which property is made up' (*EHI*: 207). This notion, of a multitude of powers or rights which, like strands, could be feathered apart into different people's hands, or all come together to form the tough rope of that very recent and very extraordinary form of ownership, English freehold landholding, has great value in the comparative study of non-Western economic systems. It helps us to understand, for instance, how different rights in a woman, as labourer, childbearer, sexual partner, and so on can be 'owned' by different people in tribal societies. It enables us to understand how the rights in a resource could be allocated not as actual partitioned and permanent chunks of that resource, half an acre of a particular field, for example, but more abstractly and flexibly, as shares in the produce or as areas which changed from year to year.

As befits a jurist, Maine distinguishes these various separate rights: the right to occupy, the right to use, the right to bequeath to an heir, the right to alienate by sale or gift, the right to alienate temporarily for the purposes of drawing rent, and the right to lay conditions upon the future ownership and use of a resource, for instance by entails. Each of these is a strictly separable power, and each may be held by a different individual or larger group. Much of Maine's work is concerned with showing the way in which rights which had originally been mixed and shared by many people were narrowed down and taken over by the individual.

This is all fundamental for an anthropologist, as is Maine's discussion of the way in which resources are differently classified in different societies. For example, the Romans classified resources (or 'commodities', as Maine refers to them) into *res mancipi* (chained things), which were land, slaves, horses and oxen, and *res nec mancipi* (free things), which were the rest (*ELC*: 337). English law, however, used a different distinction, between immovable objects, such as house and lands, and moveable objects, such as goods and chattels. The individual's rights in a particular resource will vary depending on where it falls in the classificatory scheme of a society. Thus moveables or 'personality' may be subject to individual control, while the estate is beyond such control. Another classificatory difference which has proved useful for anthropologists (for instance Lowie, 1929: 232) is between inheritances and acquisitions (*AL*: 281), the latter often being disposable by the individual while the former are not.

The difference between the Roman and the English classification was related to another difference which Maine considered to be of absolutely fundamental importance, namely the degree to which an asset was regarded as potentially divisible or indivisible. Again, this did not lie in any physical fact about the resource, but in the way it was classified. The Romans had a 'view of land as essentially divisible'. They note, 'as a fundamental difference between immovable and movable property, that land is divisible *ad infinitum*, and may be always so conceived though actually undivided, while movables are not properly capable of division' (*ELC*: 343). This is a widespread feature of peasant civilizations, where land is infinitely divisible into smaller and smaller parcels between all the children.

The revolutionary change which heralded the birth of a new order of things occurred with the arrival of the belief that land was indivisible, that it was a unit which could and should be preserved undivided over long periods. This was the basis of the 'feu' or 'fee', in other words one of the basic features of feudalism. The crucial exposition of this change occurs in Maine's *Early Law and Custom* (341–6). Maine dates the change in England between the later twelfth century (Glanvill) and later thirteenth century (Bracton), which he says was 'the time when the most widely diffused of English tenures – socage – was just putting off the characteristics of the alod, and putting on those of the feud ... the feudal view of land, which is that, when held in individual enjoyment, it is primarily impartible or indivisible' (341). The change, he believed, was enormous. 'Nothing can be more singularly unlike than the legal aspect of allodial land, or, as the Romans would have called it, land held *in dominium*, and the legal aspect of feudal land. In passing from one to the other, you find yourself among a new order of legal ideas' (342). The basis of this new world was the concept of the impartible, individually owned, estate – the basis of modern individualism and the Western industrial world, as both Marx and Maine would have argued.

Maine's elaboration of this major difference deserves full quotation, but here we will just excerpt a few fragments. There 'is no symptom that a Roman lawyer could conceive what we call a series of estates – that is, a number of owners entitled to enjoy the same piece of land in succession, and capable of being contemplated together ... if a Roman lawyer had been asked to take into his mental view a number of persons having rights together over the same property, he would have contemplated them not as enjoying it in turn, but as dividing it at once between them ... A long succession of partial ownerships, making up together one complete ownership, the feodum or fee – could not have been dreamed of till a wholly new conception of landed property had arisen' (*ELC*: 343–4). The basic change was, therefore, from a system in which the land was infinitely divisible between a number of individuals, each of which held identical rights in it, to a system where the estate was indivisible, but different kinds of right, stretching over a long period of time, were shared out between different people. This was one of the essential ingredients of modern individualistic property systems.

It seems unlikely that the contrast between Roman and common law was quite as stark as this. Nor would historians now accept that the concept of indivisibility was invented in the period between Glanvil and Bracton, for there is no trace of an allodial landholding system in England from before the Norman Conquest. Yet Maine's insight into the importance of a new way of looking at property should not be abandoned, especially if we add to it the other two ingredients that laid the foundation for modern individualistic property law, namely primogeniture and the last will and testament.

Maine pointed out that if we add to the rule that property is indivisible the rule that it should be assigned to one individual in each generation, the eldest male, we then have the makings of modern estate property. Maine devotes considerable space to the peculiarity and uniqueness of primogeniture, originally found nowhere outside north-western Europe, and lately developed. But he is very puzzled as to its origins: this is 'one of the most difficult problems of historical jurisprudence' (*AL*: 227). Maine found it difficult because he could not find its antecedents. He believed that no trace of primogeniture could be found in Roman law, in Hindu law or in the ancient German law (228). 'No sooner, however, has the feudal system prevailed throughout the West, than it becomes evident that Primogeniture has some great advantage over every other mode of succession' (231). Where, then, had it come from? Here Maine privides an intriguing hint. At first he seems to rule out a connection with the customs of the Germanic invaders: 'Primogeniture did not belong to the Customs which the barbarians practised on their first establishment within the Roman Empire' (229). But soon after this, Maine muses: the 'examples of succession by Primogeniture which were found among the Benefices may, therefore, have been imitated from a system of family-government known to the invading races, though not in general use. Some ruder tribes may have still practised it' (235). It does indeed seem likely that male primogeniture was related to earlier forms of inheritance and succession; for instance the prevalence of gavelkind in certain parts of England shows that the various Anglo-Saxon tribes that invaded England had different customs, some primogeniture, other ultimogeniture.

If we then graft the use of wills on to indivisible estates and succession by one child, we have a formidable new property system. The importance of the will cannot be overlooked. Maine thought that 'next to the Contract' it 'has exercised the greatest influence in transforming human society' (*AL*: 194). He saw how the written will was breaking up tribal and peasant societies in India, as he believed it had done in the European past. 'Testaments were the principal instruments employed in producing inequality' (225). But their power was only unshackled when it became possible to use them to direct inheritances away from the automatic rights of heirs. This faces Maine with a problem similar to the one he faced over indivisible property and primogeniture: where did the idea of using wills to alienate property come from?

On the one hand he was convinced that the Romans invented the device – 'to the Romans belongs pre-eminently the credit of inventing the Will' – while the 'barbarians were confessedly strangers to any such conception as that of a Will' (*AL*: 172, 194). And yet the Roman will lacked the essential power of free disposal. 'It is remarkable that a Will never seems to have been regarded by the Romans as a means of *disinheriting* a Family, or of effecting the unequal distribution of a patrimony' (217). If this is true, then where did the power of alienation come from? Part of the answer, of course, lies in Christianity. If we apply Jack Goody's argument about the Church destroying the family in order to allow itself to expand in this area, then the Anglo-Saxon Church, as Eric John has shown in his work on 'Bookland', supported those who wished to dispose of their wealth away from their kin (Goody, 1983b; John, 1960), To this, however, we need to add the insight which Maine had concerning the peculiar nature of Anglo-Saxon kinship, already quoted, namely that 'it is remarkable that the Anglo-Saxon customs seem to have been an exception' to the general customs of the 'old Germanic peoples' that 'forbade alienations' (*AL*: 280). Here we have an example of the way in which, by adding Maine's Roman framework to refinements from other traditions, Christian and Anglo-Saxon, we can build up some picture of how this legal revolution occurred.

Let us approach these same problems from a slightly different angle and examine Maine's ideas about the growth of private property. Like Marx, Maine believed that one could speak about 'communal' ownership of land, or perhaps the absence of any private ownership, as the original state out of which all societies have evolved. Thus he speaks of 'that collective ownership of land which was a universal phenomenon in primitive societies' (*VC*: 141). He argues concerning India that 'there has been sufficient evidence to warrant the assertion that the oldest discoverable forms of property in land were forms of collective property' (76). In this way, he believed that India followed the pattern of all early Aryan societies (*ELC*: 235). At the most developed, this was a system of allodial holding, with individuals and households holding temporary rights of usufruct, impermanent shares in a common resource: 'the primitive conveyances of allodial land were before all things public. Land belonged to the tribe, joint-family, or village-community before it belonged to the individual household' (352). He believed that this was a system characteristic not only of ancient and oriental societies, but even of Scotland and Ireland into the seventeenth century. The joint ownership of land whereby 'a definite area of land is occupied by a group of families', individual strips in it being allocated to each according to their need on a lottery system, prevailed quite recently in the Scottish Highlands and Ireland in the 'rundale' system (*EHI*: 102–3). The development of private, individual, property out of such communal property, 'the process by which the primitive mode of enjoyment was converted into the agrarian system, out of which grew the land-law prevailing in all Western Continental Europe before the first French Revolution', was, Maine declared, 'the great problem of legal history' (*VC*: 131).

Now we can easily point to exceptions and qualifications in Maine's stark contrast. We have already seen that India provides evidence of non-communal systems which also seem very ancient. We can find private rights of a kind in the very simplest hunter-gatherer societies. Robert Lowie long ago provided a useful survey of 'primitive communism', and while showing it to be wrong as a generalization, he agrees that 'while full-fledged communism, to the exclusion of all personal rights, probably never occurs, collective ownership, not necessarily by the entire community but possibly by some other group, is common' (1929: 196). He concludes that 'A review of the systems of land tenure ... establishes beyond doubt the reality of that primitive joint ownership which so strongly impressed Sir Henry Maine' (220). But this joint ownership is not usually on the part of a territorial group, but 'only within a strictly limited body of actual kindred. Further, joint ownership, while frequent, is not universal' (221). Thus, in a modified form, 'the great problem of legal history' remains. How did Maine attempt to solve it?

An oversimplified, single-word, answer is 'feudalism'. In earlier societies and civilizations there had certainly been the concept of private property, in other words private, individual ownership of certain commodities. In Rome, for example, all things except slaves, land, oxen and horses could be treated by an individual as his private property (*ELC*: 337). But the great transformation, and the one to be explained, was the emergence of private property in land. This was inextricably linked to the development of the 'feu' or indivisible estate which I discussed earlier. Feudalism introduced the new notion of indivisibility, and the collapse of feudalism set the individual free to dispose of all objects on the market as his own. Without the collapse of feudalism, 'we should never have had the conception of land as an exchangeable commodity' (*EHI*: 86–7).

Maine saw a number of threads coming together to endow feudalism with this new arrangement. Partly it was the unrestrained power of manorial lords over their own demesne land. The 'emancipation of the lord within his own domains from the fetters of obligatory agricultural custom' suggested 'a plausible conjecture that our absolute form of property is really descended from the proprietorship of the lord in the domain' (*VC*: 162, 165). Other powerful forces were the development of written wills, encouraged by the Church, and the granting of land by 'book' to religious bodies. Gradually rights to land came to be looked on as a personal commodity, which could be sold or exchanged just like any other commodity. He pointed out that in England titles to manorial estates, and to the copyholds within those estates, were conceived of as having been originally purchased or acquired (*ELC*: 325). Hence, they could be sold on to others. The internal dissolution of feudalism in England started as soon as feudalism itself, many centuries before the 'bastard feudalism' of the fourteenth and fifteenth centuries. Feudalism was the catalyst, and primogeniture was linked to 'the crucible of feudalism' (*AL*: 237): for instance 'the Feudal law of land practically disinherited all the children in favour of one' (225). This made it possible that 'the equal distribution even of those sorts of property which might have been equally divided ceased to be viewed as a duty' (225).

Maine's characterization of the nature of property rights within feudalism is still valuable today. He saw the central feature as the mixing of political and economic power. Feudalism 'mixed up or confounded property and sovereignty' (*ELC*: 148), every lord of a manor having both economic and judicial rights. Political power and economic power were both delegated down the same hierarchical chain. A second feature was the ability to conceive of different layers of ownership or possession within feudal tenures: 'the leading characteristic of the feudal conception is its recognition of a double proprietorship, the superior ownership of the lord of the fief co-existing with the inferior property or estate of the tenant' (*AL*: 295). A third feature is that the whole system was based not on inherited relations of 'status', but on acts of will or 'contract'. In feudalism, the famous bridge from societies based on status to those based on contract was, perhaps for the first and only time, crossed. This point was memorably emphasized by Maitland. 'The master who taught us that "the movement of the progressive societies has hitherto been a movement from Status to Contract", was quick to add that feudal society was governed by the law of contract. There is no paradox here. In the really feudal centuries men could do by a contract of vassalage or commendation, many things that can not be done now-a-days ... Those were the golden days of "free", if "formal", contract' (Pollock and Maitland, 1968: II, 232–3).

If the gateway from ancient to modern civilizations as both Maine and Marx believed, is feudalism, we are pushed back to considering the origins and nature of feudalism. All that can be said here on this large and vexed question is by means of a summary of a few of Maine's insights. Both Marx and Maine saw that modern individualistic, bourgeois society had developed out of one particular form of society, the feudal one. They were alike in then tracing this feudal system back to Germanic roots. But here their paths diverged. Marx saw feudalism as a specifically Germanic system, arising out of the Anglo-Saxon social system, and basically different from the other major early systems which he delineated, the Asian, Ancient and Primitive. Maine, on the other hand, was interested in the similarities over a much wider area. He posited primitive roots which led into Indo-Aryan systems. The mixture of Roman and Germanic civilization was a particular branch of a tree which also had major branches in Celtic and Indian civilization. Yet he tacitly accepted that in the other two branches, the major transition beyond a very early sort of quasi-feudalism had not occurred and might never have done so without the pressure of British civilization.

Marx never really tried to push back his researches into the origins of feudalism in England, but Maine tried to do so, though his account is clouded for lack of data, which are still not available. His view was that while it was the legal orthodoxy of his time that all that was important in feudalism dated from after the Norman invasion, much that was characteristic of the fully developed feudal system was already present in Anglo-Saxon England. The court leet, he argued, arose from the old township assemblies rather than from royal (Norman or Angevin) grants, as lawyers had argued (*VC*: 139). The common-field and three-field systems were present in Germanic societies (85); 'the three-field system was therefore brought by our own Teutonic ancestors from some drier region of the Continent' (200–1). The whole manorial system was pre-Norman, both the concept of the manor and that of copyhold tenure (*ELC*: 300, 302ff.). Thus while 'the ordinary text-books ... practically trace our land-law to the customs of the Manor, and assume the Manor to have been a complete novelty introduced ... during ... feudalization' (*VC*: 11), in fact, he argued, the Germanic landholding systems did not just die out at the Conquest, but very greatly influenced subsequent land-law (83, 11). He argues that 'the primitive Teutonic proprietary system had everywhere a tendency ... to modify itself in the direction of feudalism' (21). This tendency was particularly marked in England because Germanic customs were not destroyed by the reintroduction of Roman law: 'English institutions have never been so much broken as the institutions of other Germanic societies ... by Roman law' (*ELC*: 167). Yet there was some trace of Romanism, an essential ingredient, for the ground in England had been prepared by a previous Romanized population (*VC*: 147).

This tracing of the origins of feudalism in England to before the Conquest needs modification, but the central thesis was magnificently endorsed in Maitland's *Domesday Book and Beyond* (1897), and still stands. And Maine's attempts to solve the riddle of what lay in the Germanic system to give it, when mixed with Roman civilization, a new property law, are still suggestive. He believed that he had found in early Irish law 'a feudal system (if we may so call it) dependent on cattle and kinship instead of land and tenure' (*ELC*: 348). The model of the central principle of feudalism, the 'Benefice or Feud', was, he argued, 'mainly taken from that which the men of primitive Aryan race had considered as appropriate to chiefships or sovereignties' (349). The origins of private property thus arose from 'the ever-increasing authority of the Chief, first over his own domain and "booked" land, and secondarily over the tribe lands', a process which was beginning long before the Norman conquest (*EHI*: 115). The chiefs or kings then granted benefices, or permanent, indivisible blocks of land to others (*ELC*: 345). Thus, in some strange way, feudalism 'had somehow been introduced into the Western world by the barbarous conquerors of Roman Imperial territories' (149). These are sweeping theories, but the general drift would be acceptable to many scholars, though Maine was one of the first to examine these themes in a critical way.

Maine's ideas are deeply interlinked and difficult to separate out. Another way to approach them is to examine his central and most important generalization, that concerning the movement from societies based on status (kinship, tribe) to societies based on contract (the State). One part of this theory is shown in his treatment of individual rights. His wide sweep allowed him to see 'by what insensible gradations the relation of man to man substituted itself for the relation of the individual to his family, and of families to each other'; 'Ancient Law ... knows next to nothing of Individuals. It is concerned not with Individuals but with Families, not with single human beings, but with groups.' 'The point which before all others has to be apprehended in the constitution of primitive societies is that the individual creates for himself few or no rights, and few or no duties' (*AL*: 185, 258, 311). If we take all these points together, and then look at nineteenth-century England, Maine argued, echoing his other famous formulation, the 'movement of the progressive societies has been uniform in one respect ... The Individual is steadily substituted for the Family, as the unit of which civil laws take account' (168).

One could, of course, quibble with this, showing that in some very simple societies there is extreme individualism, and little group feeling, and so on. But as a broad characterization, it has all the power and insight of a three-quarter-truth, and when restricted to the major civilizations, the vast land-based peasantries of classical Europe, China, India and elsewhere, it is even more than three-quarters true. Thus, one of Maine's most thoughtful critics, Vinogradoff, agreed with him that 'the most profound difference between modern and ancient organization consists in the fact that modern society starts from individuals and adjusts itself primarily to the claims of the individual, whereas ancient society starts from groups and subordinates individual interests to the claims of these groups' (Vinogradoff, 1920: 299). It is indeed a profound difference and Maine contributed to our understanding of it.

This contrast between group-based and individual-based society, the 'defamilization of society', as Weber would put it, is part of that movement from status to contract which Maine thought was the greatest of all changes. Let us first restate Maine's view of what this change was, before examining it.

'Starting, as from one terminus of history, from a condition of society in which all the relations of Persons are summed up in the relations of Family, we seem to have steadily moved towards a phase of social order in which all these relations arise from the free agreement of Individuals' (*AL*: 169). Thus, the relations of parent to child, master to slave, male to female, based on birth and ascribed status, melt before the negotiated relations of free individuals. It is in this sense that 'we may say that the movement of the progressive societies has hitherto been a movement *from Status to Contract*' (170). Thus, 'the society of our day is mainly distinguished from that of preceding generations by the largeness of the sphere which is occupied in it by Contract ... old law fixed a man's social position irreversably at his birth, modern law allows him to create it for himself by convention' (304).

The first thing to be said about this vision, like so much of Maine, is that at the broadest level it is both enormously suggestive and almost right, but that it needs to be qualified in certain ways. The qualifications are well known. Firstly, as Evans-Pritchard noted, 'Maine exaggerated the victory of Contract over Status' (1981: 89); as Maitland, Pound and others have shown, civilization depends to a certain extent on limiting the freedom of contract. In the same passage that Maitland noted that feudalism provided 'golden days' for contract, he continued that 'If there is to be any law at all, contract must be taught to know its place' (Pollock & Maitland, 1968: II, 283; see also Smellie, 1933). Consequently, as Hoebel argues on the basis of Pound's work, Maine's dictum, 'while it held for the historical development of Roman law ... does not comfortably fit the phenomenon of the common law' (Hoebel, 1964: 328). Likewise Hoebel, summarizing work on primitive law, suggests that 'In surveying the truly primitive societies ... no specific trend in the separation of the individual from his kinship groups as a legal entity can really be discerned ... the "Mainean shift" does not really become effective until after the beginning of the urban revolution in full neolithic times' (1964: 328; cf. Diamond's criticism, in 1935: 391).

A second and completely different kind of criticism is that Maine's major idea was not, in any case, original. The classic charge is, of course, made by Engels, writing after 1875 in a book published in 1884. Engels argues that capitalism,

By changing all things into commodities ... dissolved all inherited and traditional relations, and replaced time hallowed custom and historical right by purchase and sale, by the 'free' contract. And the English jurist H. S. Maine thought he had made a stupendous discovery by saying that our whole progress over former epochs consisted in arriving from status to contract, from inherited to voluntarily contracted conditions. So far as this is correct, it had already been mentioned in the Communist Manifesto. (1884: 96)

On the surface this seems a rather silly claim. If Marx, who read and commented on a number of Maine's works, had himself realized that he had anticipated Maine on such a well-known theory, it seems likely that he would have said so. While he was often rude about the 'blockhead' Maine, he did not claim that Maine's major ideas were merely elaborations of his own. As the editor of Marx's *Ethnological Notebooks* puts it, 'The theory of the development of society from status to contract, formulated by Maine in *Ancient Law* (1861), was implicitly accepted by Marx, who cited as an example of this theory the conversion of personal service to slavery in Russia' (Krader, 1972: 36–7). Yet the claim is taken seriously by Marvin Harris in *The Rise of Anthropological Theory*, where he has a section boldly titled 'Marx anticipates Maine'. There he quotes from the recently discovered manuscripts of 1857–8, the *Grundrisse*, where Marx wrote 'The tribes of the ancient states were constituted in one of two ways, either by *kinship* or by *locality*. *Kinship* tribes historically precede locality tribes and are almost everywhere displaced by them' (1968: 227). Harris argues that this supports Engels' claim, though to us it looks like such a general formulation that it is not strong evidence.

Reading the *Communist Manifesto* it is difficult to see where, exactly, Engels thought Marx anticipated Maine. The most likely area concerns the famous passages on the triumph of the bourgeoisie over feudalism. Starting at the passage (p. 70) 'The bourgeoisie ... has put an end to all feudal, patriarchal, idyllic relations. It has pitilessly torn asunder the motley feudal ties that bound man to his "natural superiors", and has left remaining no other nexus between man and man than naked self-interest, than callous "cash payment" ... It has resolved personal worth into exchange value ...", there are several paragraphs which comment on the change from inherited, natural, non-monetized relations to those of money and, implicitly, contract. Standing in a poor light at a considerable distance, a phrase such as 'The bourgeoisie has torn away from the family its sentimental veil, and has reduced the family relations to a mere money relation' (Marx & Engels, 1848: 70), might seem identical to some of Maine's theories. Yet while it would be silly to deny an overlap, to which we shall return, it would be equally foolish to deny that there are deep differences. There is no talk here of status or contract explicitly, there is no realization that the shift had occurred before feudalism reached its peak, and there is little realization of the political and legal correlates.

And yet there is something in what Engels says. That something arises from the fact that both Marx and Maine, along with all the great thinkers of the middle and later nineteenth century, were working within a general framework of evolutionary or semi-evolutionary thought which gave them common problems – the reasons for the emergence of modern capitalist and individualist civilization. And they all drew on overlapping traditions of thought, particularly the prophets of the Scottish Enlightenment.

This leads us to our last major concern, Sir Henry Maine's methodology. As usual, there are two contrasted views on this. On the one hand there are those who feel that his greatest claim to our interest lies in his methodological achievement, that he introduced and exemplified a new comparative and historical approach which laid the basis for the discipline of anthropology and comparative jurisprudence. Others try to extricate him from his methodological framework, 'saving' some of his best 'insights' from what they consider a totally unsatisfactory evolutionary paradigm. As usual, both are partly right.

Before considering the central question of Maine's relation to evolutionism, we may briefly note some of his other contributions to modern anthropological method; in these he was not the only proponent of the views, but one of the earliest and clearest. Maine, like other great thinkers, was able to stand back and question his own society's assumptions, and to see the apparently natural as cultural. This is anthropology's main task today, as it has always been; he saw 'the difficulty of believing that ideas which form part of our everyday mental stock can really stand in need of analysis and examination' (*AL*: 171). He saw the need to go back deep into history and to distant lands. Speaking of earlier works, 'there is one remarkable omission with which all these speculations are chargeable, except perhaps those of Montesquieu. They take no account of what law has actually been at epochs remote from the particular period at which they made their appearance' (118–19). Like Durkheim later, he saw that in order to understand the complex, one should understand the simpler. 'It would seem antecedently that we ought to commence with the simplest social forms in a state as near as possible to their rudimentary condition ... we should penetrate as far up as we could in the history of primitive societies' (119). This is another major feature of social anthropology.

Maine clearly distinguished between the contemporary function, and the reasons for the origins of institutions. 'But the warning can never be too often repeated, that the grand source of mistake in questions of jurisprudence is the impression that those reasons which actuate us at the present moment, in the maintenance of an existing institution, have necessarily anything in common with the sentiment in which the institution originated' (189).

All this pushed him into considering the institutions which existed as described in very early documents, or in accounts of primitive societies in Europe and India. He was well aware that this effort of imaginative reconstruction, the leap of intellect involved, was extremely difficult. He warned of several of the dangers, and heeded the warnings, on the whole, in his own work. 'The mistake of judging the men of other periods by the morality of our own day has its parallel in the mistake of supposing that every wheel and bolt in the modern social machine had its counterpart in more rudimentary societies' (310). He stressed again and again the difficulty. 'At the beginning of its history we find ourselves in the very infancy of the social state, surrounded by conceptions which it requires some effort of mind to realize in their ancient form' (171). This was particularly hard for an affluent Victorian lawyer and academic surrounded by what all considered to be the summit of civilization. 'The favourite occupation of active minds at the present moment ... is the analysis of society as it exists and moves before our eyes; but, through omitting to call in the assurance of history, this analysis ... is especially apt to incapacitate the inquirer for comprehending states of society which differ considerably from that to which he is accustomed' (310). When we read Maine today we do not feel a patronizing, or incomprehending, tone creep into his explanations and descriptions. He has the wide and relativistic mind that can suspend moralizing, and a curiosity that bridges different worlds. By placing his own civilization alongside remote ages and the simplest societies, he foreshadowed much that was best in the anthropology of the next century.

The question of Maine's methodology inevitably leads us to consider his ideas of change and evolution. Here there is a muddle. This confusion is partly the result of Maine's own writings, which can be contradictory, and partly the result of a misunderstanding both of the evolutionary paradigm and its effects.

To paraphrase Maitland on feudalism, it would be possible to argue that Maine was one of the most evolutionary of social thinkers, or one of the least evolutionary. Indeed, an assortment of distinguished writers have argued both positions with confidence, and we may cite just a few. A number of anthropologists seem to assume that Maine was one of the central 'evolutionary' thinkers. Thus, David Pocock feels that we can 'excise the genetical argument and still profit from the discussion that remains' (1961: 24); Adam Kuper writes of 'classical evolutionist anthropology (notably Morgan and Maine) ...' (1973: 110); Marvin Harris lumps Maine with Morgan and the other evolutionists and rejects Lowie's attempt to suggest that he was not an evolutionist (1968: 189–90). On the other side, Robert Lowie devoted considerable effort to arguing that 'that profound and in the highest sense historically-minded thinker, Sir Henry Maine', 'that champion of sane historical method' (1929: 383, 423), 'may occasionally drop a word of homage to "continuous sequence, inflexible order, and eternal law in history", but this sop to regnant fashion agrees neither with his practice nor with his philosophy' (1937: 51). Evans-Pritchard has argued that Maine 'broke away from the attempt to formulate general laws of universal validity' (1981: 89), and Gellner, in his Introduction to Evans-Pritchard (1981), believes that 'Maine constituted an interesting exception' to nineteenth-century evolutionary thinking. 'Maine's vision of human history was rather of the characteristically twentieth-century "Gatekeeper" kind: "the stationary condition of the human race is the rule, the progressive the exception" ...' (Evans-Pritchard, 1981: Introduction, xxviii). Interestingly, Gellner's quotation here, presumably from *Ancient Law*, is almost word for word identical to a passage by Maine in his last work, *Popular Government*, where he affirmed that 'The natural condition of mankind ... is not the progressive condition. It is the condition not of changeableness but of unchangeableness. The immobility of society is the rule; its mobility is the exception' (*PG*: 170, quoted in Burrow, 1966: 160).

This whole problem has been elegantly discussed by John Burrow, who shows that Maine was both a dichotomist and an evolutionist. Maine thought 'in terms of a dichotomy of progressive and unprogressive. Maine was not a determinist evolutionst ...' On the other hand, much of his inspiration and several quotations do suggest that he thought in terms of stages, one likely to lead into another. Yet, after considering Maine's views on Roman codes, for instance, Burrow suggests that 'Maine, far from being one of the leaders of evolutionary thought, is rather behind the times – thinking in terms of conscious adaptation to circumstances rather than the mechanical, involuntary adaptation of Spencer and the neo-Darwinists' (1966: 163, 169). Looking at it from another angle, a large part of Marx's later irritation with Maine seems to have derived from the fact that Maine was not evolutionist *enough*; Maine thought that time had stopped with the supreme achievement of the modern individualist nation state and could not see, as Marx saw, that this was just another stage through which societies must pass towards nirvana.

It is tempting to leave the argument here, to agree with Burrow that 'Because Maine was not a systematic thinker, and because he never fully recognized the conflict between the historical and scientific elements in his intellectual equipment, it would be possible, by selective quotation, to make out a convincing case for either view of him', and that all we can do is to show both aspects of his work and agree that they are not compatible (1966: 164).

Or we can avoid the dilemma by arguing that the contradictions can be explained by the fact that Maine's thought and writing straddle a major paradigm shift. Ideas which developed before 'Evolutionism' was developed were pre-Evolutionary. Then came Darwin and 1859. Thereafter, attempts were made to try to fit them with a completely new set of theories. This seems to be the recent interpretation put forward by George Stocking. He argues that 'Maine's thinking was defined in a pre-evolutionary epoch, and in nonevolutionary terms', but 'quickly found a place in the postevolutionary milieu' (1987: 117). Thus 'Maine's later works all reflect a continuing attempt to sustain the argument of *Ancient Law* in a postevolutionary temporal and developmental context' (126). There is something in this, but it gives far too much weight to the publication of the Darwin–Wallace thesis in 1859. Arguments about evolutionary development had been much in the air throughout the decade when *Ancient Law* was being drafted, and it is difficult to believe that Maine was unaware of them. Instead of looking at the contradictions as negative and needing to be explained away or apologized for, it is more fruitful to see that both evolutionary and non-evolutionary strands were necessary for Maine's work.

Without the evolutionary impetus, not specifically of Darwin, but of a mood that was much deeper and which we witness in many of the works before the publication of *The Origin of Species*, for example the work of Robert Chambers and Herbert Spencer, it is difficult to see how Maine could have been pushed into progressing beyond the

Developmentalist theories of the later eighteenth century. In a broad sense, Vinogradoff must be right that to the Darwinian and evolutionary tendency 'we are indebted for the rise of anthropology, and of sociology, of the scientific study of man and of the scientific study of society' (Vinogradoff 1911: 581). It is thus a necessary ingredient, and it is significant that one of its most noted qualifiers, F. W. Maitland, 'challenged not the method itself, but rather the indiscriminate way in which the comparative anthropologists worked out their ideals' (Vinogradoff, 1920: 148). Without some deep interest in long-term changes and the possible relations of cultures over long periods, without asking the large questions concerning the origins and development of man and civilization, Maine's work would have been impossible.

On the other hand, as a man open to empirical refutation, as an historian and lawyer, he was simultaneously aware of the dangers of mechanical evolutionary thought. This was an opposition based on the external evidence, the obvious facts of no simple progression of stages, but also from a theoretical objection: 'no universal theory, attempting to account for all social forms by supposing an evolution from within, can possibly be true' (Burrow, 1966: 165, quoting Maine). Diffusion was too patently the cause of much change, as Maitland was again to stress.

One could have several reactions to discovering that there is a basic contradiction in Maine's thought. One is to sigh, to lament the fact that he was 'not a comprehensive or systematic thinker', that 'his views were, in fact, something of a rag-bag', and, as one treats rag-bags, pull out of them bits of cloth when needed to fill in the holes in one's arguments. I think we proceed further if we see the contradictions, which we still face today, as necessary and productive tensions. It was necessary for Maine *both* to believe in a certain evolutionary framework *and* to show, in practice, the exceptions to the evolution. Evolutionism provided the guiding hypothesis, the assumption of links, which he could then explore, but only partially confirm.

We may illustrate this interpretation with one example. Maine has often been criticized for having an evolutionary view concerning the movement from status to contract, and more specifically the movement from patriarchal, kin-based, societies, to modern cognatic, state-based systems. As we have seen, he was heavily criticized by McLennan, Morgan and others for this evolutionary perspective.

The difficulty is that it is not all clear how widely Maine meant his theory to apply. On the one hand there are chance remarks which suggest that he hoped that the theory would be valid as a description for all human societies. On the other, as many authorities have pointed out (for instance, Schapera, 1956: 2; Burrow, 1966: 232), Maine was usually careful to insist that he was only talking about the Aryan groups, not all societies. As Vinogradoff put it, 'And yet Maine set very definite boundaries to his comparative surveys ... he upheld the ethnographical limitation confining them to laws of the same race. In his case, it was the Aryan race, and in his *Law and Custom*, he opposed in a determined manner the attempts of more daring students to extend to the Aryans generalizations drawn from the life of savage tribes unconnected with the Aryans by blood' (Vinogradoff, 1911: 582). The truth is that in *Ancient Law*, Maine left the question deliberately open as to how far his series of changes was likely to apply beyond the area from which his data were drawn. As further evidence emerged, he saw that he was describing the characteristics of just one civilization. The hope and belief of the possibility of general laws of evolution provided the impetus for the search; the results of his own and other research provided the limits of the generalizations. If we think in terms of models, the contradiction in Maine's thought is not quite so bizarre. Like Weber, he contrasted ideal types, benchmarks, extremes of society. He then looked to see how far societies had moved between these extremes. We can see with hindsight that his belief that such tendencies were irreversible and his belief that societies always moved, if they moved at all, in one direction are both wrong. But the ideal types he set up, the benchmarks he gave us, are indispensable guides.

Lucy Mair wrote that Tylor is 'often described as the father of British anthropology', though 'some of us might prefer to trace paternity to Maine or even Morgan' (Mair, 1972: 23). In true promiscuous mode, anthropology has many fathers, and it is clear that Maine is one of them. Like all fathers, he was reacted against by the next generation, often unfairly. We, the grandchildren and great-grandchildren, can now look back with a mixture of admiration and affection. We recognize that much of what we are flows from his thought; there can be no doubt that both historical and anthropological theory today would be very different without his inspiration. As with all ancestors, we need not approve his every action. But despite all the limitations, he still lives and speaks to us.

It is perhaps not inappropriate for one of his great-grandchildren to end by quoting Pollock's tribute to him in the year of his death: 'Maine can no more become obsolete through the industry and ingenuity of modern scholars than Montesquieu could be made obsolete by the legislation of Napoleon ...'; for 'At one master-stroke he forged a new and lasting bond between history and anthropology' (quoted in Grant Duff, 1892: 48, 76).

The contributors to this volume, an unusual combination of lawyers, historians and anthropologists in this age of specialization, attest to that lasting bond.

CHAPTER 8

Henry Sumner Maine in the tradition of the analysis of society

Edward Shils

In the past quarter of a century, the academic study of sociology has been given several adoptive ancestors. Karl Marx and Alexis de Tocqueville have been retroactively installed into the ancestry of sociology; they are now thought of as having always been there. They are now regarded as the forefathers of sociology although, in fact, until relatively recently, neither of them was regarded by practising sociologists as a sociologist or even as a proto-sociologist.

There is nothing at all wrong with bringing into an intellectual tradition authors and ideas previously disregarded; it is perfectly reasonable to assimilate into a tradition patterns of thought or propositions which have long been neglected or not previously been regarded as parts of a particular tradition. Intellectual disciplines often benefit from drawing into themselves traditions hitherto remote from them. When this happens, it is perfectly reasonable that the scholars who generated or sustained the newly assimilated tradition should take their place in the ancestral pantheon. When they do so, however, a false view of the historical development of the tradition is suggested.

There are other sources of distortion of the image of the historical form of a tradition. An ancestor – a chronologically genuine ancestor – might be forgotten, so that only his descendants are prominent. The remoter ancestor who formed those prominent descendants has been diminished in the memory of later generations.

This is the situation of Henry Sumner Maine in the tradition of the study of society. The name of Maine has fallen out of the tradition, or perhaps it should be said that it never made its entry. Histories of sociology scarcely mention Maine. Sociologists do not read his works very often. When his name is mentioned, it is mentioned very cursorily. It is true that he did not conceive of himself as a sociologist. He had nothing to do with what was called sociology in his own lifetime. He was no admirer of the ideas of Auguste Comte or of those of Herbert Spencer. Other writers who were called or who called themselves sociologists in his time – Schaeffle, Lilienfeld, Worms – were, as far as I know, unknown to him. He seems to have known about the British Social Science Association and found it repugnant. Yet, no one writer has entered, so penetratingly and so pervasively, into the fundamental outlook of sociologists of the twentieth century as has Maine.

I

Maine's contribution to sociology may be summarized in the pregnant sentence which ends with the clause: 'the movement of the progressive societies has hitherto been a movement *from Status to Contract*' (*AL*: 170). For Maine, the term 'status' does not mean 'high' or 'low social status', 'high' or 'low social rank', or a high or low position in a hierarchy of deference. It means only acting and being treated as a member and only as a member occupying a particular status and hence performing and corresponding to a particular role within a collectivity. The action of an individual in accordance with his 'status' means action in accordance with the norms referring to the status and contained in the collective consciousness of the collectivity. The collectivity Maine had in mind was a primordial collectivity, i.e. one constituted by reference to common biological relationships (descent, ties of blood (kinship) and sex) and territorial locality.

Action in a contractual relationship, as understood by Maine, means that the individual parties to the contract act towards each other without regard to any properties other than the capacity of each to fulfil the terms of the contract. Each party to the contract is in principle considered by his partner to the contract entirely apart from any properties or features ascribed to him in his capacity as a member of a collectivity or as a participant in its collective consciousness. He is self-contained, delimited, the objectives he pursues through the contract are objectives conceived by him and anticipated by him as being of advantage to him. The same obtains where the contracts are between corporate bodies.

Maine was referring to two types of societies, one in which the collectivity was dominant and the individual was recessive, the other in which the collectivity was recessive and the individual dominant. Maine was, in the terminology made popular by Karl Popper, a 'methodological individualist'. Although every society was made up of physically separate individuals, in the collectivistic society each individual was regarded, by others and himself, not with respect to his unique properties and actions but with respect to the properties imputed to him or possessed by him by virtue of his status as a member of the collectivity.

According to Maine, although such members are individuals biologically, they are not acknowledged in the legal order – and in society more generally – as individuals empowered to make decisions for which they alone are responsible and which are intended to be for their own individual advantage. Individuality is not imputed to them by their fellow members of the primordial collectivity; they are cognized and assessed primarily as incumbents of a status within the primordial collectivity or simply as members of the primordial collectivity. They have status within their collectivity. They are not considered to possess individually distinctive qualities or a distinctive individuality outside or apart from that status or that membership. The individual might have sentiments and a self-image which include more than his status, but his fellow members do not consider that: his image of himself as an individual is faint and recessive. Likewise his demands or desires on behalf of himself, as distinct from his demands or desires prescribed or permitted by his status, are faint and recessive.

One may generalize Maine's proposition by saying that every living human being, between infancy and advanced senility, acts both as the incumbent of a prescriptive status within a collectivity and as an individual. Although the balance between the two determinants may differ not only from individual to individual and from situation to situation, it was the variation from society to society which interested Maine. There is a shift in the balance from action as a member of and, hence, an incumbent of a status within a collectivity – primarily a primordial collectivity – to action in an individual or personal capacity, without regard to status, when a society moves from a condition in which 'status' is the dominant feature to one in which 'contract' is dominant.

Maine did not set this forth explicitly. Nevertheless, it is worth while for us to do so, because that is the aspect of Maine's work which has lived forward into sociology.

The schema of the two kinds of societies was central to Maine's intellectual interest. His interest in the history of law was intended to elucidate the difference between them. His application of the comparative method in the study of the history of law had the same intention: to distinguish between the two major classes of societies – those in which the individual has no freedom of choice or action, where he is not regarded as an individual and is not permitted to act as an individual in disregard of the obligations of his particular status as a member of the collectivity and as a representative of the collectivity, and those in which the individual is perceived only with respect to the likelihood of his performance of a specific action in return for a specific reward. Maine chose his examples of the status–dominated society from primordial collectivities such as nuclear families, lineages, or villages settled by lineages. He does not deal with collectivities which are not primordial at all such as social classes, religious institutions and communities, professional associations, or occupational categories; nor does he deal with quasi-primordial collectivities – like nations, national states, or ethnic groups. All these collectivities confer kinds of status on the members, but except for the national or sovereign territorial states, he does not consider any of these. But even the national or sovereign territorial states he regards as completely disjunctive *vis-à-vis* the status-pervaded societies.

In the latter, primordial referents – kinship, real, presumed or fictitious, and locality – are the criteria of membership, the society is small in size of population and in territorial extent, magical and religious practices and beliefs are pervasive and consensual, rules of law and morals tend to be concrete and particular, traditionality is preponderant, and economic activity is almost entirely agricultural or pastoral; economic units tend to be self-sufficient (*bedarfsdeckend*), and exchange is occasional. This primordial society is hierarchical, with authority in the hands of the older generation; literacy is usually non-existent or very restricted. Government tends to be congruent with the authority of the kinship groups or lineage; often the primordial society lives in a territory dominated by an imperial or monarchical power, but it maintains some considerable measure of autonomy within that setting.

In the kind of society in which contractual relationships are prominent, membership in the society is determined by reference to residence in a bounded territory subject to a common sovereign authority. Ratiocination and utilitarian calculation are increased at the cost of traditionality, and secular attitudes are widespread; literacy too is relatively widespread, and legal regulations are written, explicitly enacted and systematic or rationalized; economic activity is differentiated, occupations are diverse and specialized and their products are sold in the market, as is the labour-power of their incumbents, etc. In this type of society, the individual acts freely and rationally for the realization of ends which he has decided for himself. The individual is recognized as morally significant, while his status in a kinship or lineage collectivity is relatively insignificant in determining the responses of others to him.

Maine thought that the movement from status – the primordial society – to contract – the individualistic society – was a progressive one. Maine's progressive view is not to be rejected out of hand, but that is not a question which I wish to discuss here. Nor will I discuss his conception of social evolution or the evolutionary sequence of societies, to which he attributed much significance. The merit of the comparative method and its assumptions will likewise be passed over here. There is much more to Maine's ideas than the distinction between 'status' and 'contract'. This distinction was essential to his idea of progress; it was also fundamental to his application of the comparative method, because it provided the categories which permitted diverse societies in diverse epochs to be compared with each other.

I intend to disregard these aspects of Maine's work, just as I will disregard his achievements as an historian of Roman, Hindu, Irish and early German law, although these were the topics to which he devoted much of his scholarly powers. His work on common ownership of land and on succession and testaments will likewise be passed over here. Nor will I consider the validity of Maine's contentions regarding the patriarchal character of the Indo-European societies. I will pass over all of these topics except occasionally to draw on them to illustrate the distinctive patterns of each of the two major types of societies.

The reason for this disregard for so much of the substance of Maine's work is simple. The efforts to improve sociological knowledge over the century which followed the publication of *Ancient Law* were not vitally interested in the stages of the development of society, nor were they concerned with the relative prevalence of patriarchy and matriarchy or with the universality of common as against private possession of landed property in primordial societies.

Evolutionary conceptions receded from sociology earlier than they did from other branches of learning: so did the comparative method as Maine thought to practise it. Sociologists lost the confidence in the philosophy of history which Comte and Spencer had possessed. Comte and Spencer had both been preoccupied with the present state of modern Western societies, but they placed their ideas in the context of a view of the progressive development of mankind or in the setting of a biological evolutionary pattern. The interest of the leading sociologists of the century following the publication of *Ancient Law* lay in the feature which distinguished modern Western societies from the societies which had gone before them, mainly in the West. For this interest, Maine's conceptual scheme seemed to go to the heart of things. It perceived a traditionless society of individuals, rational and rationalizing, cutting through the encrustations of status, attending only to the performances of individuals and rewarding them commensurately.

Maine's schema avoided the intellectual embarrassment of having to analyse the great oriental and occidental empires by concentrating attention on the small primordial societies in which most of the subjects of these empires lived. Thus the schema was made adequate for the purpose of elucidation of the distinctive features of modern Western societies.

II

The distinction had been adumbrated in many forms by many writers, long before Maine's birth, and by his contemporaries. The observations of the Greeks about barbarians were a step towards such a classification. Hesiod's views about the societies of different ages was another such step, and the ideas about the succession of empires in the Book of Daniel, conceivably affected by knowledge of Hesiod diffused in the Near East in the Hellenistic age, was still another. Christian travellers in Central Asia – diplomats, merchants and missionaries – observed the differences between pagan and Christian societies. It was, however, through the observations by Europeans in the Pacific and in the Western hemisphere in the seventeenth and eighteenth centuries that the outlines of the classification which distinguished savage societies from civilized and Christian societies were fixed. In the eighteenth century, this became the distinction between societies of rude and societies of polished manners. The societies of rude manners had not developed the arts, and were mentally paralysed by traditions fixed by superstitious fear; the advantages of reasoning were unknown to them. (There was, of course, a transvaluation of values when these 'savage' societies were declared to be superior to the advanced Western societies; the transvaluation did not, however, reject the classification.)

The development of a theory of the stages of human history from Turgot and Condorcet to Saint-Simon and Comte followed the same pattern, with variations and changes of nuance. In all of these constructions of types of societies, and of the sequences in which they succeeded each other, the constant was the contrast between a society of unreasoning submission to custom, reinforced by the superstitious fear of spirits, and a society free from the domination of tradition and from the intrusion of mischievous spirits, acting rationally in the fulfilment of objectives which individuals chose for themselves.

In Germany, the ideas of Herder and Hegel offered other variants of this dichotomy. Herder's apostrophe of the *Volk*, of the ordinary people, living steeped in traditions of belief and conduct, expressing themselves anonymously, unconsciously and collectively, reverently deferential towards their ancestors and their 'betters', carried with it a contrast with the sophisticated, ratiocinative, self-centred outlook of the educated classes of urban society. Hegel's conception of the 'civil society' – *die bürgerliche Gesellschaft* – oriented towards the rationally calculating exploitation by the individual of the opportunities offered by the market stood in contrast with the family.

In Great Britain, similar patterns of thought existed. On the one side, there was Romanticism, with its appreciation of the ordinary uneducated countryman; on the other side, the world envisaged and recommended by the economists and the Benthamites, the world of the individual who acts rationally on his own behalf.

In the French and British traditions, the rational thought and the scientific knowledge of individuals emancipated from superstition provided the theme of one pole of Maine's schemas. In the German traditions, the major theme was the dominance over the individual by the collectivity to such an extent that the very conception of an individual separate from his status in the collectivity scarcely existed.

These were some of the materials of thought which were available to Maine while he was conducting his study of the common law and Roman law in connection with his work as reader at the Inns of Court. The writings of Georg von Maurer on the constitution of the early Germanic village offered learned support for his image of a primordial society, in which membership was determined by kinship and lineage and in which the individual counted only when he was perceived as the incumbent of a particular status in his kinship group.

His experiences in India as Legal Member of the Governor-General's Council between 1862 and 1869 confirmed and enriched the ideas which he had put forth in *Ancient Law*. In India he took on himself the two tasks of understanding Hindu customs and particularly Hindu customary law, and of creating a modern, codified rationalized legal system for India. The contrast between the traditional society which he wished to understand and reform and the image of the modern society which he thought India ought to become corresponded to the difference between the two types of society which he had delineated in the year before the assumption of his responsibilities in India. I doubt whether, except for the section on the territorial referent in the constitution of modern societies, he advanced any further in the analysis of the fundamental concepts which underlay the three substantial books which he wrote in the more than two decades following the publication of *Ancient Law: Village-Communities in the East and West* (1871), *Lectures on the Early History of Institutions* (1875) and *Dissertations on Early Law and Custom* (1883). It might even be said that though he continued to adhere to the basic ideas in his analysis of Indian and Irish legal ideas, his mind was hindered from pressing more deeply by his preoccupation with arguing for his own ideas of patriarchy, succession and common ownership as features of primordial societies. His ideas about the 'contractual society' were not called upon in his last book, *Popular Government* (1885), although that book offered a very good occasion for the further elaboration of an idea which he only sketched in *Ancient Law*.

III

Maine's ideas about societies in which the individual is submerged by the obligations and benefits of his status and those societies in which the individual is free to enter into contracts in which his status is of no consequence have been the least discussed of his ideas. In his own lifetime, *Ancient Law* became entangled in controversies about the universality of the patriarchate in Indo-European societies. Then and for a long time thereafter, the validity of the comparative method engaged attention. Legal historians found fault with his proposition about the far-reaching similarity of the early German and the early English forms of landed property and of the scale of common land. His arguments about the universal prevalence of property vested in the collectivity rather than in the individual likewise called forth much discussion and disagreement.

The reception of Maine's view on status-orientated and predominantly contractual societies had to await the appearance of a mode of thought which had largely freed itself from the comparative method in the sense in which Maine had practised and espoused it. The new mode of thought had appeared in Great Britain in economic theory which underwent increasing refinement in the course of the nineteenth century. Likewise, a more analytic theory of law had appeared in England. Both of these were criticized by Maine for their claims to universal validity, particularly the latter.

The new mode of sociological thought into which Maine's conceptual schema was assimilated offered no more than categories for the description of widely divergent types of societies, and it did not purport to provide either a closed explanatory system or an accurate short-hand account of the history of institutions. The categories were appropriate to the formulation of ideal types, not for causal explanation. They permitted the appreciation of the distinctiveness of societies while viewing them *sub specie aeternitatis*; they did not require that the societies which they helped to describe must be arranged in a determinate sequence.

IV

This kind of thought about societies did not exist in Great Britain during Maine's lifetime. It did not exist in Germany for most of his lifetime. Indeed, it made its first appearance in 1887, one year before Maine's death. The new mode of analytical study of societies was the achievement of Ferdinand Tönnies; the book in which it appeared was *Gemeinschaft und Gesellschaft*.

Tönnies had spent about ten weeks in England in 1878, where he intended to pursue his studies of Hobbes, to whom his attention had been directed by his friend, Friedrich Paulsen. It is not certain that he knew about Maine while he was in England. In describing his time in Leipzig in the winter of 1879–80, he says – in an account of the books he studied during this period – that 'I think that I had become acquainted with Sir Henry Maine's *Ancient Law* somewhat earlier' (Tönnies, 1922: 214). On 21 November 1879, he wrote to Friedrich Paulsen, 'grosse Lust habe ich, die Werke von Sir Henry Maine *1*) *Ancient Law, 2*) *Village-Communities, 3*) *Lectures on Ancient Institutions* [presumably *Lectures on the Early History of Institutions*] anzuschaffen, wenn sie (was zu vermuten) auf der Bibliothek nicht zu haben sind. Nach Anzeigen in englischen Revuen, die ich las, ... müssen sie ganz überaus vortrefflich sein' (Tönnies–Paulsen, 1961: 67).

Maine was already a prominent figure of the intellectual life of Great Britain when Tönnies came to England. *Ancient Law* had gone through several reprintings, and *Village-Communities* and *The Early History of Institutions* had already been published. But it is very likely that Tönnies did not read any of those books while he was in England, since he was so preoccupied with Hobbes.

Tönnies himself was born into a prosperous peasant family in Schleswig-Holstein and lived there until he went to the University of Strasburg in 1872. He then returned to Schleswig-Holstein. He remained there for many years after he completed his studies. Much of his academic career was spent in or near his original home. Despite his travels, Tönnies lived for a large part of his life close to a society in which *Gemeinschaft* was a prominent constituent. Thus, quite apart from the numerous intellectual sources – of which Maine's *Ancient Law* and Gierke's *Das deutsche Genossenschaftsrecht* (1868–1913) were surely important ones – from which Tönnies might have drawn some of the elements of his idea of *Gemeinschaft*, he also had ample opportunity to observe it in the region in which he was brought up.

As far as *Gesellschaft* was concerned, his study of the British economists of the last part of the eighteenth and the early part of the nineteenth centuries, his study of Hobbes and Hegel – especially the *Philosophie des Rechts* – as well as his reading of Marx and Engels surely gave him enough scholarly knowledge about the properties of the modern contractual society. There were numerous other sources as well in his observations of the contemporary world.

In the Germany of his boyhood, while at the beginning of its career as a powerful industrial capitalistic society, enough of the traditional rural and small town regime which had enraptured many German writers still flourished. From his study of Hobbes and his sojourns in the then leading capitalistic country of the world as well as from his studies of the rationalistic theories of natural law of the seventeenth century on the one hand, and from his own observations of the local society in which he had grown up, on the other, Tönnies must have been pregnant with the contrast between *Gemeinschaft* and *Gesellschaft* when he first encountered Maine's ideas.

Tönnies was a point of focus of many intellectual influences. Nevertheless, he himself acknowledged the prominence of Maine among these influences, and so too will any objective reader of Tönnies' own writings.

V

Tönnies certainly did much more than merely accept Maine's analytical distinction. He clearly saw that what Maine called 'status' was very close to what he called *Gemeinschaft*, and that what Maine called 'contract' corresponded to what he called *Gesellschaft*.

Although Maine was critical of 'political economy', it was primarily because the 'political economists' believed that their theories presented a truthful account of the societies governed by 'ancient law', i.e. societies in which criteria of status or membership in kinship groups prevailed (that is, in what I call 'primordial societies'). He did not doubt that their theories applied truthfully and fruitfully to the existing individualistic contractual society, and he approved morally of those features of that society in which the theory was fulfilled. He said relatively little about the consequences of that fulfilment. In this respect Tönnies saw the ramifications of the principles underlying the contractual society with far more clarity and differentiation than did Maine.

Tönnies connected *Gemeinschaft* and *Gesellschaft* respectively with two different kinds of dispositions, desires and evaluations ('wills'). *Gemeinschaft* was infused with *Wesenswille* ('essential will', sometimes called 'natural will'), which was affective and spontaneous. It demanded nothing from others. The actions which were impelled by *Wesenswille* were goods in themselves. Tönnies said *Wesenswille* was 'organic'; it was an expression of tendencies inherent in the biological organism. Arising out of the biological organism, *Wesenswille* focussed on the biological facts: ties of kinship and sexual relations. Thought engendered by *Wesenswille* envisaged 'wholes'. *Wesenswille* was directed to the collectivity as a 'whole'; it did not dissolve a collectivity conceptually into individuals. Individuals were incomplete except when they were incorporated into 'wholes'.

There is an obvious affinity between Tönnies' views of *Gemeinschaft* and Maine's conception of the society in which individuals are seen and see themselves predominantly as the incumbents of a particular status and the performers of roles prescribed by that status. But it is equally obvious that Tönnies was seeking to reach a deeper level of understanding of the sources of primordiality. He was also more alert than Maine to such factors as love, gratitude, common memories, reverence and awe, which sustain the solidarity of a kinship group or family. There is nothing like this in Maine.

Tönnies' ideas were vague, and they were formulated in an idiom derived from a literary and philosophical romanticism which is now difficult to comprehend, but they were the results of an attempt to see what it was in the constitution of the human organism and the human mind that produced these two fundamental patterns of society. Maine took a more agnostic view on this matter; he said that the motives of persons no longer living cannot be discovered. Yet, in the last of his major books, he did adduce sexual jealousy to account for patriarchy, and he referred to a propensity to imitate in order to explain the diffusion of institutional patterns from one society to another. Thus, he did not adhere to his own self-denying ordinance, but his divergence from it is rather superficial.

Much more was said by Tönnies than by Maine regarding the ramifications of ratiocinative *Kürwille*, or rational will, by the widespread application and calculation in *Gesellschaft*. He also had much more to say about the public character of *Gesellschaft*. Maine did say in passing that when society extended beyond the limits of the family and lineage and when spheres of activity emerged which could not be covered by the traditional norms and legal fictions of the primordial society, a qualitatively different kind of regulation was needed. Written, codified, sanctioned, legislated regulation became necessary, according to Maine; he also hinted that the body of legal regulations becomes more interconnected or more logically consistent. Tönnies moved further along the same lines.

Although three of Maine's four major works were written after his experience in India of the strains between traditional – status-dominated – law and codified, rationalized, market-oriented law, he did not give much attention to the resistance of traditional primordial, ancient law to rationalized law or to the ravages brought by the new legal order on the primordial society. Tönnies had more to say on both of these subjects, and he said it more vividly. He was also much more ample and realistic in his examination of the repercussions in many spheres of life of the increased prevalence of contractual relationships, their consequences for the weaker parties to the contract, the instability of the contractual society arising from the operation of the capitalist economy and the internal opposition to it on the part of those who were at a disadvantage in the making of contracts.

Similarly there is in *Gemeinschaft und Gesellschaft* a deeper analysis of the mode of thought or outlook which sustains *Gesellschaft* than Maine produced in his account of the contractual society. *Gesellschaft* was made possible by its own distinctive mode of thought, i.e. *Kürwille*, purposeful, instrumental, rational, voluntarily initiated choice. It is, Tönnies said, 'mechanical'; it thinks in terms of cause-and-effect, of the rational adaptation of means to ends, in accordance with empirical or scientific knowledge of the causal relations between the factors or resources chosen as means and the end which is deliberately desired. Unlike *Wesenswille*, *Kürwille* did not arise out of the constitution of the human organism and the human mind. It is a specialized outgrowth of a certain potentiality of *Wesenswille*. Again, Tönnies' analysis of the genesis of *Kürwille* is not persuasive, but it is an effort to link one of the most fundamental patterns of social life with the nature of the mind. Maine, who had an affinity with Benthamism despite his criticism of Benthamite and Austinian jurisprudence, did not draw on Benthamite psychology to account for the two types of society.

In this respect, Tönnies' work represents a considerable advance on that of Maine. Tönnies' analysis of *Wesenswille* and *Kürwille* was an effort to construct a 'philosophical anthropology' which would demonstrate the relationship between fundamental properties of the human body and mind and main patterns of human society. I do not think that Tönnies' plan was successfully carried out, but it was an important attempt. Unfortunately, it has disappeared without a trace.

VI

Just as Tönnies went further than Maine in the extension of the analysis of types of societies and more deeply into their roots in human nature, so he also went further than Maine in his analysis of the ramification of the contractual relationship into the society in which it prevailed.

Gesellschaft lacks solidarity. Conflicts are inherent in it, although the conflicts may be held in check by the recognition of the mutual dependence which also is inherent in the complex division of labour in an economy formed around exchange in the market. Earlier perhaps than any other student of European societies, Tönnies saw that the then contemporary capitalistic order – *Gesellschaft*, in the terminology of his sociology – was the manifestation of a fundamental moral and intellectual orientation. This orientation was given by the 'rational will' – *Kürwille*. The rationalistic orientation was the condition of *Gesellschaft*, not its consequence, as a Marxist interpretation would have it. The rational will, with its 'mechanical' outlook and procedure, in contrast to the 'organic' character of the *Wesenswille*, was to be found in many spheres of life. It was not confined to economic activity; moral and political attitudes and activities and the understanding of nature were dominated by the 'rational will'.

While he was elaborately aware of the steady extension of the contractual relationship into parts of society which had previously been alien to it, Tönnies also saw the resistive power of traditional *gemeinschaftliche* institutions which were being eroded but not totally obliterated by that extension. He also thought that the *Gesellschaft* was being resisted by those who suffered from it – mainly the working class – and that they would attempt to establish a type of society which, although industrialized and urbanized, would have the organic features – solidarity, mutual attachment, etc., – of a *Gemeinschaft*. Tönnies, who was generally sympathetic with the Social Democratic Party and with the ideas of Karl Marx, although never a member of the former or an adherent of the latter, thought the instability of the modern *Gesellschaft* would be overcome by the establishment of socialistic arrangements.

Maine, in contrast with Tönnies, never expressed any doubts about the endurance or stability of the contractual society. However, in his last book, *Popular Government*, he did think that it might be disordered by the unthinking interference of a popularly elected government, which had acceded to office on the basis of unfulfillable promises to the electorate. Maine did speak of 'trituration' of modern societies into their constituent individuals, i.e. what later writers have called the 'atomization' or the 'alienation' of individuals. Like Tocqueville, Maine thought that the dissolution of the plurality of corporate institutions like municipalities, estates and guilds was an outcome of the growth of the power of the central government and its ambition to extend its sovereignty into every sphere of life. He did not however, attribute the 'trituration' of society to the pervasiveness of the contractual relationship or to modern capitalism, as many more recent writers have done. Indeed, Maine was singularly reticent about the social consequences of the erosion of status, in his sense of the word, from modern societies, and of the extension of the sphere of contract. Nevertheless, the formative influence of his ideas was very considerable.

Although written in a rebarbative and archaic idiom and from a philosophical and psychological standpoint which was no longer in wide currency in Germany, even in the last part of the nineteenth century, the analysis offered in 1887 in *Gemeinschaft und Gesellschaft* of the constitution and prospective development of capitalistic society – a society of private property, freedom of contract, the rational organization of labour power, the rational application of scientific and empirical knowledge to technological tasks, the rational calculation of returns on the alternative opportunities for the investment of resources – received a very favourable response among educated Germans. Like *Ancient Law*, which was written with force and lucidity, *Gemeinschaft und Gesellschaft* went through seven reprintings between 1912 and 1935. It left its mark on several generations of German opinion, academic and lay. In addition to giving a fillip to the romantic attachment to traditional village and small-town life of a pre- or non-capitalistic society, it also provided an idiom for the condemnation of the individualism, impersonality, specialization and calculating attitudes of the modern *gesellschaftlich* society.

After the end of the National Socialist rule in Germany, a Danish sociologist, Svend Ranulf, charged Tönnies with having contributed, by his sympathetic portrayal of the *Gemeinschaft* and his condemnation of modern liberal society, to the formation of a matrix of opinion which made the oncoming of National Socialism a welcome prospect for many Germans. Tönnies himself said almost as much shortly before he died in 1936. In his Introduction to the eighth edition of 1935, he said that it had not been his intention either in 1887 or since then to offer an 'ethical or political tract' in *Gemeinschaft und Gesellschaft*. This is undoubtedly true with respect to the situation prevailing in Germany when he wrote that new Introduction, but it is permissible to doubt the disavowal regarding the original intention. At the same time, it should be strongly stressed that Tönnies himself was one of the few German academics who supported the Weimar Republic against its internal enemies. He was, of course, an adamant opponent of National Socialism.

VII

The German sociologist closest in age to Tönnies was Georg Simmel, who was born in 1858 (Tönnies was born in 1855). Simmel was a philosopher with an extraordinary range of interests ranging from aesthetics and moral philosophy to sociology. He was a writer of great subtlety on every topic he touched. His interest in sociology was relatively brief – about fifteen years altogether. One of his main themes was the wide ramification of the individualism of modern societies, which produced both the impersonal, emotionally or psychologically passionless individual, unattached to any person or any institution, and the person who has developed genuine individuality. Two of his most famous essays are on the 'stranger', and on 'the metropolis and mental life'. The 'stranger' is a person without attachment to other individuals or to collectivities. He is the prototypical modern urban resident, but he appears in all societies. The other characteristic essay tells the same story, except that it has its point of departure in the pattern of urban life, with its highly specialized division of labour and the large number of impersonal and transient relationships. In his great work on *Die Philosophie des Geldes* (1900), and in the essays which formed his *Soziologie* (1908), calculation of the value of all social relationships in monetary terms is seen as one of the most prominent features of modern life. There is a close similarity here to the contractual society as generally adumbrated by Maine and to *Gesellschaft* as represented in Tönnies' *Gemeinschaft und Gesellschaft*.

The question whether Simmel derived any of his ideas about modern society from Maine or from Tönnies is difficult to answer. He knew Tönnies quite well personally through their association in the Deutsche Gesellschaft für Soziologie. Whether the similarities in their conception of modern society is attributable to Tönnies' influence on Simmel cannot be determined. There is no evidence that Simmel read *Ancient Law* or any of the other works of Maine. Yet, it is not impossible that Maine's ideas about status and contract did enter Simmel's thought about society through Tönnies' ideas, which, thanks to the bringing together of many of the parallel and convergent currents of thought which were prominent in Germany in the last quarter of the nineteenth century, drew attention to itself as a work which went to the heart of the matter.

Yet it should be borne in mind that Simmel was an extremely imaginative, sensitive and widely cultivated person who might well have thought out his ideas completely independently of Tönnies.

VIII

The greatest sociologist of all in the history of the subject is Max Weber. He clearly stands in the tradition of Maine and Tönnies, although other traditions also come together in his work. Weber does not acknowledge any influence from Maine. He might well have read Maine, but he never referred to him.[1]

He does not refer to him by name in his larger chapter on the sociology of law in *Wirtschaft und Gesellschaft*. Professor Max Rheinstein in his annotations to the English translation of the *Rechtssoziologie* does refer a number of times to Maine, but there is no clear indication that Weber did in fact draw on the books mentioned by Professor Rheinstein; the latter does say that Weber used Maine's books, but he presents no proof of his statement. Johannes Winckelmann in his annotations also referred on numerous occasions to Maine's books, but he does not say whether the references are intended to illuminate passages by Weber or whether he thinks that Weber did in fact have those books in mind when he wrote those particular passages (Winckelmann, 1976).

Weber certainly acknowledged the affinities of some of his own fundamental ideas with some of those expounded by Tönnies in *Gemeinschaft und Gesellschaft*. Many of Tönnies' ideas, such as those on *Wesenswille*, Weber did not take up, but the dichotomous schema of

---

[1] In view of the paucity of scholarly books available to Weber when he wrote the second volume of the *Gesammelte Aufsätze zur Religionssoziologie (Hinduismus und Buddhismus)*, it is noteworthy that nothing of Maine on India is cited in that volume.

Gemeinschaft and *Gesellschaft* certainly was assimilated by Weber and greatly elaborated, well beyond any point ever attained by Tönnies. It is quite possible that Maine, through Tönnies, had a great influence on Max Weber. None the less, despite the advance made by Weber over Tönnies in the study of economic and political institutions and religious institutions, the imprint of Tönnies' schema remained. With that imprint the possibility of the persistence of Maine's imprint on Weber also exists.

Of course, Tönnies was not the only influence on Max Weber's substantive sociology. Weber's first scholarly experiences which laid the foundations for his work as a sociologist were his legal and economic-historical studies. He began as a student of Roman law and Roman agricultural history, then he worked on medieval commercial organization and later on agricultural labourers in Prussia. In this period he was still very much under the influence of Theodor Mommsen's ideas; Mommsen's *Römisches Staatsrecht*, which was analytically rather than purely historically expounded, seems to have left its mark on Weber's approach to the formulation of his sociological ideas in *Wirtschaft und Gesellschaft*. Mommsen's influence was then partially displaced by that of Eduard Meyer's *Geschichte des Altertums*. It was this work which launched Max Weber on his comparative studies of ancient Mediterranean societies. It was the beginning of his career as a 'sociologist'. He had never before regarded himself as such. From the end of the first decade of the century, when he began to plan the *Grundriss der Sozialökonomik*, a nine-volume compendium of economic knowledge, including economic theory, and made preparations for the writing of *Wirtschaft und Gesellschaft*, which was to be the third volume of the *Grundriss*, he entered on a new phase of his intellectual life.

At this time, Tönnies and Simmel were the two major sociological writers in Germany. *Gemeinschaft und Gesellschaft* had established a good name for its author in a small circle, and Georg Simmel, through his two brilliant books, which are exceptionally rich in penetrating ideas but unsystematic in construction and lacking a deliberately promulgated central theme, also became well known. Weber certainly read *Die Philosophie des Geldes* with much appreciation for its scintillating ideas, but also with some dismay because of its amorphousness. Tönnies' *Gemeinschaft und Gesellschaft* and his booklet *Die Sitte* must have appeared to Weber to supply the theme lacking in Simmel. Not only the distinction between *Gemeinschaft* and *Gesellschaft*, but also certain elements of the distinction between *Wesenswille* and *Kürwille* which underlay the distinction between *Gemeinschaft* and *Gesellschaft* were employed by Max Weber as a point of departure of his own sociological work. Both pairs of concepts were much modified by Weber, particularly certain features of the distinction between *Wesenswille* and *Kürwille*, but traces of their presence remain noticeable.

Wirtschaft und Gesellschaft began, like any German university textbook of the time, with definitions of categories. Next, Weber differentiated the basic categories into a series of elaborate analyses of types of economic activity, of legitimate political authority, the legal order, types of religious beliefs and institutions and the relationships between religious and political authorities. These parts of the work are relatively concrete comparative analyses of Western societies, ancient, medieval and modern, and ancient oriental societies; modern oriental societies are scarcely noticed. The work as a whole was enriched by the knowledge which Weber was simultaneously acquiring about China, India and Islam for his studies of the world religions.

Of course, it would be wrong to expect an intelligence as forceful and as capacious as Weber's to content himself with filling in the very general schema set forth by Tönnies. Weber had too much ratiocinative power, too strong a demand for clarity and too great a sense of the concrete to allow himself to be confined by any analytical scheme, including his own; he also had too great a demand for precision to be satisfied with Tönnies' passionate but very vague description of *Wesenswille*. As far as *Kürwille* was concerned, Weber knew much more about economics and religion than Tönnies did to do no more than repeat them. The categories of the introductory chapters are far from being a decorative exercise in definition and classification. The contents of the categorical chapters do pervade the more particular parts, but they are very flexibly interpreted. Moreover, Weber never hesitated to improvise in the use of his fundamental categories, but his improvisations too were guided by what is contained and suggested in the categories set forth in the first chapters.

I will give a few instances of the great affinity between Weber's fundamental sociological categories and those of Tönnies. A first example: in his classification of the four fundamental categories of social action, Weber lists: *Zweckrationales Handeln* (instrumentally rational action); *wertrationales Handeln* (intrinsically valuable action); *affektuelles Handeln* (emotionally impelled action) and *traditionelles Handeln*. Instrumentally rational action, which is concerned with the most efficient or the most economical way to achieve a given end, is the kind of action which prevails in *Gesellschaft*; it is, like *Kürwille*, deliberately, rationally chosen action which selects means in accordance with their anticipated instrumental efficacy to the achievement of any given end. Weber broke down the single type of action which Tönnies called *Wesenswille* into three categories: *wertrationales Handeln* (intrinsically valuable action), traditional action and affectual or emotional action. Although Tönnies in his characterization of *Wesenswille* had mentioned tradition and emotion, he had amalgamated those three types of action into one.

In the subsequent parts of *Wirtschaft und Gesellschaft*, echoes of Tönnies' ideas recur repeatedly. The fundamental contrast between, on the one hand, the self-sufficient household and the moneyless economy – the economy of the *Gemeinschaft* – and, on the other, the extensive money economy oriented towards the urban translocal, national and world economies – *Gesellschaft* – is certainly a central feature of Weber's work. It appears as early in his work on the Protestant ethic and the spirit of capitalism in the first half of the first decade of the twentieth century as it does in his analysis of the economies of the ancient Mediterranean and Near Eastern societies in his essay on 'Die Agrarverhältnisse ...'. It appears also in a fundamental way in his study of Chinese society, as well as in his studies of ancient Israel and ancient India. Here too there is not only an echo of Tönnies – and Karl Bücher – but also, and clearly visible, a parallel with Maine's analysis of the difference between the society in which status is salient and in which the ties of kinship absorb and control practically all of the constitution of society and the contractual society, in which they have become very attenuated. Weber's analysis of the household and the *Sippe*, which are so prominent in *Wirtschaft und Gesellschaft* and in the *Gesammelte Aufsätze zur Religionssoziologie*, moves very much along the lines laid down by Tönnies – and Maine.

Let us turn briefly and illustratively to Weber's three-fold classification of types of legitimate authority. This too is nearly parallel with Tönnies' ideas. *Gesellschaft*, according to Tönnies, is the realm of rationality, but he did not come to grips with the functioning of the State in *Gesellschaft*. This is where Weber moved far beyond

Tönnies. Tönnies was so preoccupied with the expansion of rationalistic individualism that he relegated the functioning of the State to two short sections (Tönnies, 1935: 231–3, 250–1). Weber was never so forgetful. Although he was never backward in his awareness of the expansion of, first, a religiously impelled individualism, and then, a more earthly individualism, his attention to the presence and power of governmental authority was never diverted. He was above all alert to the relationship between the State, law and society.

The modern national state, governing *Gesellschaft*, i.e. 'civil society' in the Hegelian sense, governed in accordance with the prevailing rule of rationality. In the pattern of legitimate governmental authority, this took the form of rational–legal authority. Weber's delineation of rational–legal authority bears many resemblances to the social order portrayed by Tönnies as *Gesellschaft*, and it also has some of the properties of the legal order of the contractual society, as conceived by Maine, tending towards an internally consistent, logically rationalized system of rule and laws, created by enactment or legislation. Maine's conception of the legal order of the modern national State, although brief and offered only for the purposes of delineating more sharply the legal order of primordial societies, went further than Tönnies in the explicitness of its focus on the legal order, but not as far as Tönnies in the understanding of the ramifications of the power of the State. Tönnies saw with certainty the application of rationality and of the instrumental rational attitude almost universally diffused in *Gesellschaft*. (Simmel, in his *Die Philosophie des Geldes*, published about thirteen years later, had the same idea, which he illustrated with extraordinary profusion.) Neither Tönnies nor Simmel traced the ways in which the principle of rational analysis and rational organization pervaded the organization of the State. Weber went further than any of his predecessors in his analysis of the rationalization of the organization of government and of the legal order.

Weber contrasted rational legal authority with the traditional and charismatic types of authority. Traditional authority, as Weber conceived of it, prevailed in the system of authority obtaining within *Gemeinschaften*, with their respect for the authority of the aged and their reverence for custom, in the system of authority of the larger ancient near Eastern and Asian imperial and monarchical societies, and in European feudal societies within which such *Gemeinschaften* were situated. Traditional authority at the centres of these large political structures, as well as authority in the *Gemeinschaften* or societies in which status predominated, combined stereotyped actions and arbitrary actions on the part of the ruler, elder, chief or head of the kinship groups.

It may be pointed out that Tönnies did not deal with these large imperial and monarchical institutions, apparently because they appeared to be neither *Gemeinschaften* nor *Gesellschaften*. Maine was more aware of these imperial and monarchical formations, and his fundamental insight into their working was very acute; but his interest was in the smaller village communities, and he never elaborated his understanding of the pattern of traditional authority in the way in which Weber did. Maine does deal at length with feudalism, but mainly he discusses its genesis, not its structure. Nevertheless, Maine's ideas about traditional authority were very realistic. It is a pity that his fundamental insights on these more important matters were obscured by his and his critics' unfruitful preoccupation with the universality of common property, the universality of patriarchy and the celebration and criticism of the comparative method.

Authority legitimated by tradition was the type of authority which corresponded most closely to Maine's conception of the pattern of ancient law. The status of any individual in what I am calling a primordial society was, according to Maine, entirely prescribed by tradition; there might be biological necessity which required patriarchy, but the substance of authoritative patriarchial decisions were traditionally fixed stereotyped judgement and arbitrariness, exactly in the pattern portrayed by Weber.

The line from Maine to Tönnies to Weber is clear in the line of traditional authority. Tönnies did not merely repeat Maine; Weber certainly did not merely repeat Tönnies. Weber clarified Tönnies' ideas and made them far more precise and orderly, and added to them as Tönnies had done with Maine's ideas.

Weber entered much more elaborately into the analysis of legal order of primordial societies than did Tönnies or even, for that matter, than Maine, although law was Maine's special interest. Nevertheless, when they are at the same level of generality, their views are quite similar. For example, Maine, Tönnies and Weber all said that law in primordial societies is concrete and particular, and is not asserted with any claim to generality or universality. All three of them distinguished this kind of law from custom, in which the normative element is more prominent but which again is neither systematic nor universal or general in its claims to validity. Very similar conceptions of the most elementary forms of law are likewise to be found in Weber. For all three writers, the 'laws' of primordial society are not enacted. Weber and Tönnies also provide a place for these proto-legal declarations in their distinctions between *Brauch* (usage), convention and *Sitte* (custom). In fact, Weber closely approximates Tönnies' classification, and he does so quite explicitly. Both Tönnies and Weber are in accord with Maine's assertion that the most elementary form of traditional regulation of conduct is that which rests on a belief of the obligatoriness of the merely given. They are also in accord with Maine in his assertion that the normative force of custom is given weight only by opinion and that law exists only where there is institutionally established machinery for enforcement by the threat of the imposition of sanctions. Although Maine rejected the Austinian conception of law as it applied to ancient village societies, he allowed that its notion of law as the rationalized or systematized command of the sovereign power was a valid account of law in the modern national state. Weber went very much further than this, but in the same direction.

All three of the writers being considered here regarded 'rationalization' – including rational–legal authority – as bound to triumph over traditional patterns of institutions and thought, once the former began to invade the sphere of the latter. Yet in the matter of rationalization, Max Weber, with his point of departure in the conception of modern society as a contractual or *gesellschaftliche* one, went much further than any of his forerunners, including Maine and Tönnies. Weber saw rationalization as a process which went far beyond the contractual pattern envisaged by Maine and the *gesellschaftliche* one envisaged by Tönnies. For Weber, rationalization could occur in the organization of military forces and in the conduct of war, and in the organization of religious institutions, governmental institutions and legal systems; it could occur in the intellectual activities of scientific research and theology, and in technology and in the organization of the pursuit of learning. The conceptions of contract and of *Gesellschaft*, even though they are very akin to rationalization, are also very much narrower in their range of reference.

Weber's extension and clarification of rationalization already present in Maine's, Tönnies' and Simmel's writings is a good instance of the growth of a tradition through rigorous analysis and reinterpretation. Elements within a given tradition which had been regarded as indissolubly associated with each other are separated from their 'traditional' context and interpreted as independent variables which are seen to be at work in new contexts. In this case, Weber improved the traditional conceptions of the contractual society, of *Gesellschaft*, by breaking them down analytically and then observing the working of the various component elements in other contexts. But despite this enrichment of the tradition through decomposition and rearrangement of the elements into new patterns and in novel contexts, the tradition remains an effective symbolic configuration comprehending its diverse phases and patterns. Thus it was that Maine became installed in the sociological tradition.

It is also possible to improve a tradition by amalgamating it with other traditions, with new and important results. This is what Max Weber did with regard to religion.

IX

Well before he began to conceive of himself as a sociologist, Weber had been sensitive to the importance of religion not just as a department of human life but as a factor in the life of society outside what is conventionally called the 'religious sphere'. His early studies of the Protestant ethic are evidence that he did not have to wait until he began to study Hinduism, Buddhism, Taoism and Confucianism and ancient Israelite religion to see the ways in which religious beliefs enter into other spheres of social life.

It was this understanding that led Weber to construct a third class of legitimate authority, namely charismatic authority. Religious beliefs and activities, which focus on charismatic powers deriving from, or imputed to, a sacred centre, when they go beyond magic and become linked to ethical judgements and norms, theological doctrines and differentiated priesthoods and monastic orders, transcend primordial societies and their religions. The religions which interested Max Weber most were 'world religions', or what are sometimes called 'universal religions'. There was no place for such religions in Maine's view of the world, and scarcely any in Tönnies'. A world religion does not belong in a status-oriented village community. It was entirely consistent for him to think that a contractual society has no place for religion except as an archaic survival.

Indeed, Maine paid singularly little attention to religion, which he regarded as superstition; in this respect Maine was very much a rationalist. Tönnies was a little better. He accepted that religion was an integral part of *Gemeinschaft*, but he agreed with Maine that *Gesellschaft* had no place for religion.

Maine and Tönnies seemed to think that translocality, transprimordiality inevitably obliterated the charismatic element from society. Maine's views on this matter are certainly not explicit. He allotted a minor place to religion in his studies of village communities; for Maine religion and law became divorced from each other at an early stage. He regarded the separation of law from religion as a sign of the progress of a legal order from its most elementary to its more advanced state. Once that state was passed, religion, according to Maine, ceased to be a significant part of the societies with which he dealt.

The fact is that Maine was 'unmusical' in his understanding of religion in primordial societies. He thought that brahminical Hindusim was created largely under the influence of the brahmins' interest in strengthening their position in Indian society. He regarded most religious belief and conduct, in so far as it impinged on legal and other institutions, as 'superstitions'. For Tönnies, religion – largely magic and the cult of ancestors – was part of the culture of *Gemeinschaft*. By its nature it was excluded from *Gesellschaft*. Tönnies had no place for universal or world religions in either *Gemeinschaft* or *Gesellschaft*.

For Weber, in contrast with his two predecessors in sociological studies, charismatic authority is a permanently recurrent feature of all societies, including modern liberal-democratic societies, ruled by bureaucrats and legislators. Max Weber did not think that the functions of charismatic authority were exhausted by religious prophecy or, in an institutionalized form, in monarchies, empires or plebiscitary republics. He thought that it had an important part to play in liberal-democratic societies with parliamentary institutions.

Neither Maine nor Tönnies had any place for charismatic authority. The distinction between traditionality – 'status' or *Gemeinschaft* – and rationality – 'contract' or *Gesellschaft* – seemed to them to be adequate to describe the patterns of societies and their changes. Weber saw the inadequacy of this dichotomous pair of concepts for the purpose of a more truthful account of societies. In trying to provide such an account, Weber went beyond them in a quite fundamental way.

Maine and Tönnies both saw the two types of societies which they had discerned as antithetical to each other and as unable to coexist in a single society. Max Weber saw what Tönnies and Maine failed to see, which is that no society could ever operate according to a single principle. It was of the nature of societies to incorporate antithetical elements. So it was that charismatic authority could become 'routinized' (*veralltäglicht*) and both rationalized and traditionalized.

X

Emile Durkheim is generally and justly regarded as the other great figure of modern sociology. He is regarded by many connoisseurs as being of the intellectual stature of Max Weber. He was three years younger than Tönnies, and six years older than Weber. He was of the generation of sociologists who could have been influenced by Maine and by Tönnies; it is uncertain whether he was so influenced. His main sociological works were written before Max Weber appeared on the scene as a sociologist, so that chronology alone might account for his silence about Weber. He died before the appearance of most of Weber's important sociological works; and the rupture of learned communications between France and Germany from 1914 until his death in 1917 would have made it improbable that he would have seen even those which were printed (with the exception of the *Protestantische Ethik*).

But there need be no hesitation about examining the relationship between Durkheim's ideas, on the one side, and the ideas of Maine and Tönnies, on the other. The legitimacy of the question is increased by the high degree of similarity between some of Durkheim's basic sociological ideas and those of the other two authors.

Emile Durkheim's ideas – at least some of the most important of them – bear a marked resemblance to the main themes of Tönnies' *Gemeinschaft und Gesellschaft* and Maine's *Ancient Law*. In *De la division du travail social*, in *Les Formes élémentaires de la vie religieuse* and in *Le Suicide*, there is a recurrent contrast, sometimes explicit but more often implicit between a primordial society, highly solidary, and according sacred value to the collectivity as a whole while denying significance or value to the individual, and a society with a very differentiated division of labour, and a marked development of individualism. The former is an undifferentiated society with very little division of labour, a very powerful and comprehensive collective self-consiousness, and very little appreciation of its members as individuals; Durkheim called it a society of 'mechanical solidarity'. In his discussion of this kind of society, the *Gemeinschaft*, Tönnies frequently used the term 'organic'; Durkheim used the term 'mechanical' to describe the society which, as he conceived it, bore such a close resemblance to what Tönnies called 'organic'. Durkheim's conception of the society of 'mechanical solidarity' also bears a close affinity to the society described by Maine in which an individual's status is all, his individual features naught.

Durkheim's dichotomizing procedure required that the other type of society be one with a very differentiated division of labour, a high prizing of individuality as an ideal, and a pronounced prominence of individually instigated action and of individual claims to the benefits of action. This society, Durkheim said, was characterized by 'organic solidarity'; Tönnies referred to this kind of society as 'mechanical'. Tönnies and Durkheim employed very similar classifications of societies; Durkheim simply reversed Tönnies' terminology.

This individualistic society is territorially extensive, although its most prominent and distinctive features tend to be found in large cities rather than in the countryside. The conduct of the individual is not comprehensively or deeply controlled by the collective self-consciousness, which is necessarily weak. The similarity between Durkheim's views about the two main types of societies and those of Maine and Tönnies is very far-reaching. However, Durkheim was not by any means confined to the reiteration of the ideas which he shared with Maine and Tönnies. His books *Les Formes élémentaires de la vie religieuse* and *Le Suicide* go much more deeply into the religious foundations of society than did either Maine or Tönnies; in *Le Suicide*, by the use of quantitative methods with an exactitude unusual at the time, he portrayed the consequences of the weakness of the collective self-consciousness in modern societies.

Unlike Maine but much more like Tönnies, Durkheim did not think that the 'organically' solidary society was a realm of unqualified harmony. Conflict, criminality and suicide interested him greatly; he was as observant about the costs of 'organic' solidarity as Tönnies was about the 'costs' of *Gesellschaft*. Durkheim emphasized the importance of legislated law – here the affinity with Maine is striking – as the replacement of usage and customary law which obtain in the society of 'mechanical' solidarity. According to Durkheim, the different kinds of solidarity have their distinctive modes of responding to breaches in solidarity. A state of intense moral solidarity is characteristic of the response of the society of mechanical solidarity to criminal infringement on customary law; and the response is to punish and repress the criminal. In the society of organic solidarity, the response is less intense, and action which accompanies that response aims at restitution. There is some resemblance between these propositions and Maine's, and Durkheim acknowledged as much.

In his treatment of modern society, Durkheim, like Tönnies, but more so, was at odds with himself. On the one side, he argued that modern society is entirely individualistic and the collective self-consciousness very faint. On the other, he contended that no society can exist without a collective self-consciousness which controls and guides action. If that collective self-consciousness does not exist or is not effective, then *anomie* is bound to spread over the whole society. It was to supply such a guiding and restraining self-consciousness that in the Introduction to the second edition of *De la division du travail social*, he proposed the creation of moral codes for occupational groups. He apparently did not believe it possible to dispense with a collective self-consciousness, shared however lightly by most of the members of the society. This resembles Tönnies' view about the moral state of *Gesellschaft*.

Durkheim clearly has a place in the lineage which Maine and Tönnies had themselves already established. But whether Durkheim's position in that lineage is genetic or entirely an outcome of independent development from a common matrix of European intellectual traditions is not easy to determine in any definitive way. Unlike Tönnies, who acknowledged his affinity with Maine, Durkheim acknowledged affinity neither with Maine nor with Tönnies. He cited Maine in a few very specific contexts, once with agreement about the prominence of criminal law in primordial societies, once to disagree with Maine about the grounds for that prominence. There was no acknowledgement of any connection between Maine's conception of the society in which the individual was not perceived as such but was seen only as a member of a collectivity and his own conception of a society of mechanical solidarity. Likewise he did not allude to the similarity between Maine's idea of a society pervaded by contractual relationships and his own idea of a society of organic solidarity, with its highly differentiated division of labour and the interdependence of the individual members of the system for the exchange of goods and services. Despite Durkheim's failure to refer to this similarity, the similarities have been evident to many students of the history of sociological thought.

Durkheim's refusal to place himself in the line of Maine and Tönnies is all the more perplexing since in 1889 he wrote a long review of *Gemeinschaft und Gesellschaft* in the *Revue philosophique*. He expressed agreement with Tönnies' views on *Gemeinschaft*, although he had what were really marginal and trivial reservations about the use of the word 'organic' to refer to the type of primordial society which he designated several years later as a society of 'mechanical solidarity'. At one point in his review of *Gemeinschaft und Gesellschaft*, Durkheim (1889: 418), in summarizing Tönnies' argument, reproduces the terms 'status' and *contrat* taken over by Tönnies from Maine in a passage in which Tönnies quoted Maine explicitly (1935: 184-5). In the same review, in reference to locality as a property of *Gemeinschaft*, he equates it with 'what Sumner Maine has called the village community' (Durkheim, 1889: 418). Durkheim never again cited Tönnies in any of his books or articles, nor did he ever refer to the similarity of Maine's categories with his own. Nevertheless, it is perfectly clear that he was aware of these lineal affinities, and he could not have failed to know that they had anticipated his ideas. Whether Maine and Tönnies were among the sources of his ideas is another matter. It certainly cannot be demonstrated in any conclusive manner. It is entirely possible that Durkheim's ideas of mechanical and organic solidarity were entirely his own discovery; however, that does not seem to me to be very probable. After all, his careful study of Tönnies' *Gemeinschaft und Gesellschaft* preceded the publication of *De la division du travail social* by about four years; in the review he says in the course of a discussion of the nature of *Gesellschaft* and its relations to *Gemeinschaft* that in order to prove his contention, which is scarcely different from Tönnies', 'il faudrait un livre' (1889: 421), but he does not announce that he is writing that book. At the same time, it should be pointed out that he presented a course of lectures on 'Social Solidarity' at the University of Bordeaux in 1887-8 (Lukes, 1972: 138-9), when it is not likely that he could have read *Gemeinschaft und Gesellschaft*.

XI

Although the United States has not produced any sociologists of the intellectual power, depth and erudition of Max Weber, or on a slightly lower level, Emile Durkheim, Ferdinand Tönnies and Georg Simmel, by the beginning of the twentieth century it had become the country where sociology was most widely and actively taught and where sociological research was most amply practised. European sociology was the first source of American sociology. The leading American sociologists of their time had studied at German universities, although sociology was not an academically established subject there. Albion Small, W. I. Thomas, Robert Park, Edward A. Ross, Charles H. Cooley and William Graham Sumner were the leading figures of the last part of the nineteenth century and the early part of the twentieth century. In the second and third quarters of the present century the leading American sociologist was Talcott Parsons; he had studied in Germany in the 1920s, perhaps the last important American-born academic to obtain a doctorate from a German university. (American social scientists did not study in France or in the United Kingdom, where sociology was even less well developed as an academic subject than it was in Germany.)

Henry Sumner Maine's ideas became a significant influence in American sociology through the writings of German sociologists. Simmel was the first German sociologist to be taken up in the United States. He became an associate editor of *The American Journal of Sociology* from the very beginning. A considerable number of his most outstanding essays were published in that journal before the First World War. Simmel's influence was particularly mediated to the United States, with a considerable delay, through Robert Park, who attended Simmel's lectures in Berlin in 1899 and then received his doctorate at Strasburg in 1903.

Simmel made a profound impression on Park, who did not become an academic sociologist until 1912; he had previously studied philosophy and then worked as a journalist for a newspaper in a large American city. Simmel's conception of modern urban society remained with Park for the rest of his life, and the Simmelian conception of urban society was then carried forward by Louis Wirth.

Park was not a field worker himself, but he put his pupils to work in the field – in the city of Chicago and in small towns in the Middle

West – and he supervised their research in the field with intense watchfulness. In some respects, many of the pieces of field work done by Park's students were in fact done collaboratively with Park, because he would spend time in the field with his pupils showing them what to observe, how to interview, etc. Thus German sociology was put to work in Chicago.

In one way or another, most of these investigations dealt with the disintegration of primordial ties – kinship relationships and the ties of locality – through international and intranational migration. They dealt with the isolation of individuals in the metropolis, with the crises of families, the difficulties of life for those from rural societies in a large city with an economic life dominated by the market, with the relations of ethnic, national and linguistic communities in a great city, and the diminution of the authority of parents over their children in such a city.

Park was definitely influenced by Simmel. Park certainly read several of Maine's books; he cited them on several occasions in crucial passages. He also read Tönnies. His vision of urban society and its contrast with rural and small-town society show very convincingly that Maine and Tönnies as well as Simmel left a mark on his way of viewing the world; his mind often returned to the dichotomous ideal-typical patterns. In this regard, he was closer to Maine and Tönnies than he was to Simmel, who was not inclined to order his ideas in such a schematic form.

William I. Thomas was another notable American sociologist who looked on society through the kinds of categorial spectacles offered by Maine and Tönnies. Before he began to work on *The Polish Peasant in Europe and America*, he had studied the literature of *Volkskunde* and *Völkerpsychologie*, so he was bound to be sympathetic with the idea of *Gemeinschaft*. His close association with Robert Park, whom he persuaded to accept an appointment at the University of Chicago, would almost certainly have brought him into contact with the tradition of Maine–Tönnies–Simmel. His own major work, *The Polish Peasant in Europe and America*, echoed all the themes of the conceptual scheme of the two types of societies.

Charles Horton Cooley was an Emersonian sociologist, gently reflective but with an almost unerring sense of what was important. Although he was trained as an economist, he deserted that discipline for sociology. His name is now associated with the 'primary group', the small collectivity, the family, the neighbourhood and the village, which had a high degree of solidarity, a strong sense of 'we-ness'. It was, in short, the *Gemeinschaft* about which Cooley was writing. He did not refer to Tönnies, but he did mention Maine.

Cooley regarded the 'great society', the large national society, in very much the terms applied by Tönnies to *Gesellschaft*, and wished to check the ravages of its contractual individualism. Like Tönnies, who saw a new extended form of *Gemeinschaft* as the redeemer of the troubled *Gesellschaft*, and like Durkheim, who saw a new corporate professional ethic as a source of a new solidarity which would offset the anomic damages in the life of modern society, Cooley saw the remedy for the excessive egotism and competitiveness of the contractual society in a diffusion of the collective consciousness of the primary group into society at large.

Talcott Parsons acceded to a position of ascendancy in American sociology for about a third of a century after the Second World War. More perhaps than any other major sociologist since the period when any professor worth his salt had to create a 'system', Talcott Parsons attempted to construct a comprehensive sociological theory. He joined to a powerful intelligence a considerable sense of reality and an architectonic passion. He began in the 1930s with a grandiose synthetic effort to lay the foundations for the further development of this comprehensive theory by attempting to find the common and mutually complementary elements in the work of Alfred Marshall, Vilfredo Pareto, Max Weber and Emile Durkheim. It would not be unjust to say that when the journey really got under way, Pareto was forgotten, Alfred Marshall put to one side, and Durkheim employed and then relegated; only Max Weber remained a continuous presence. But behind Max Weber, *Gemeinschaft und Gesellschaft* threw an illuminating shadow over the entire undertaking. I once said that the monograph which Talcott Parsons and I wrote, *Values, Motives and Systems of Action* (Parsons & Shils, 1951), was an effort to put into explicit and systematic order the first chapter of *Wirtschaft und Gesellschaft*. I would now say that it was really an attempt to perform that task for the first book of *Gemeinschaft und Gesellschaft*. The 'pattern variables' were the result of that effort, as Professor Parsons himself came near to saying in a later essay (Parsons, 1973).

A certain disaffection from Professor Parsons' ideas began among sociologists in the 1970s. His 'system' was never wholly accepted by any sociologists except a handful of his pupils. Nevertheless, fragments of his elaborate theoretical achievements entered into American and, to a lesser extent, into European sociology. The 'pattern variables' are the most pervasively surviving fragments. They are *Gemeinschaft und Gesellschaft* in a more differentiated and exact form. Thus at several stages' remove, the ancestral power of Henry Sumner Maine has still been at work.

Of course, it is impossible to draw a straight line to modern sociological theory from Maine's proposition regarding the progress of society 'from status to contract'. Nevertheless, Maine's schematic ideas and Tönnies' scarcely less schematic pair of concepts have had a long life. One cannot but be impressed with how long Maine's own ideas, and Tönnies' combination of Maine's ideas with those of Hobbes and the ideas of the German ethnographers and of Marx have continued to be effective.

XII

It is possible that some of the indeterminateness of our observations about Maine's entry into and his place in the tradition of the analysis of society is inherent in the way in which intellectual traditions operate. Maine's 'success' and the uncertainty which dominates our observations about that 'success' are both linked to the prior and contemporaneous prevalence in sociological thought of the tradition of the dichotomous classification of societies which had been in the process of formation from, at the latest, the seventeenth century onward.

This is usually how traditions are assimilated. The recipients of a tradition, either accidentally or because of their appreciation of its intellectual quality, choose one or another of the particular variants of the wider tradition to which they are already potentially disposed.[2]

---

[2] A marginal reflection on the accidents of the character of the flow of tradition might be in order at this point: Maine read German well, and he was well informed about the literature of German economic and social history in so far as this bore on his interest in landed property, village constitutions, etc. Otherwise he seems to have had little interest in Germany. Unlike his friend Acton, who was of partly German extraction and who was intimate with leading German intellectual and public figures of his time, Maine seems to have had few of the personal connections through which knowledge of his work could have spread in Germany. *Ancient Law* was translated into German by a Hungarian admirer of Maine, but within the limits of my present knowledge, it was never taken up by German legal, social and economic historians. As far as I know, German sociologists, even those who, like Theodor Geiger, Josef Pieper and Alfred Vierkandt, took the concepts of *Gemeinschaft*

Whether the taking of Henry Sumner Maine into the tradition of sociology was an accident arising from Tönnies' interest in Hobbes and his consequent sojourn in England cannot be resolved in any definitive way. What is important is the fact that Maine's conceptual scheme was assimilated into the tradition.

Nevertheless, not all of Maine's ideas about society were taken into the tradition of sociological analysis. His ideas about common or collective and individual property in land or about the universality of patriarchy or about primogeniture, or about the identities of Indo-European societies, etc., have fallen out of our field of attention after some initial contention. None of these was really necessary to his conceptual scheme, although they were generally compatible with it.

There are other parts of his theories which are closer to the central conceptual scheme which have not been taken up, discussed, revised and assimilated. I cite, for example, his ideas on kinship and territoriality as mutually exclusive criteria for the determination of membership in a particular society. Similarly, his few but pointed observations on the tendency to describe membership in territorially bounded, more or less contractual societies in the metaphors of kinship. Likewise his observations about the resistances likely to be encountered by an absolute sovereign in a society with traditions of primordial autonomy. Maine has interesting if very fragmentary things to say about nationality; he himself did not treat them except in passing. Subsequent writers have not given any attention to his ideas on nationality, although they are very worthy of such attention. For some obscure and rather complicated reasons, sociologists have been resistant to the analysis of nationality, and there was no tradition which could receive Maine's ideas on this subject. Tradition does not flow in a straight line.

XIII

About two decades ago, I wrote a short essay entitled 'The tyranny of tradition' (Shils, 1970). It was really about the tyranny of the traditional distinction between *Gemeinschaft* and *Gesellschaft*. I do not disparage the tradition; I do not wish to leave an impression that it has been intellectually fruitless. Any idea which could leave a

und Gesellschaft very seriously, did not read Maine. But they did read Tönnies with the utmost assiduity, and that brought the ideas of Maine into their possession.

determinative imprint on the works of Max Weber, Emile Durkheim, Georg Simmel, Robert Park, Talcott Parsons and conceivably William I. Thomas was certainly not intellectually fruitless.

Nevertheless, I think that the time has come to modify that tradition further, as it has in fact been modified ever since Maine entered into the tradition of the continental European and then the American analysis of society. One of the reasons for this recommendation is that the idea of modern society which it has offered is manifestly insufficient. The ideal-typical conception of the contractual society, which was so scantily sketched by Maine and much more elaboratedly portrayed by Tönnies and Durkheim, has set going a quite false account. It is an account which reduces modern capitalistic society to a photomontage of the Hobbesian account of the state of nature and of the conception of society in *The Communist Manifesto*.

This picture of *Gesellschaft* has survived in the most hard-headed empirical investigators, in whom the postulates of the choice of categories of their inquiries and the principles of interpretation are highly individualistic and utilitarian, even where such interpretation flies in the face of common sense and serious sociological observation and reflection.

The way in which this tyranny has been modified into a more realistic conceptual regime was illustrated by Max Weber's introduction of the category of the sacred or the charismatic into his specifically sociological studies of religion. Another line to be followed in the qualification of the misleading picture – even as an ideal type – is to recognize that *gesellschaftliche* or contractual societies are also national societies. Neither Tönnies nor Durkheim gave much weight to this fact. Weber himself was very weak in dealing with the phenomenon of nationality. Interestingly enough it was Maine who perceived this more sharply than any of the great ancestors who have been treated here. He did so not in *Ancient Law* but in *The Early History of Institutions*, in the course of another of his assessments of the limits and validity of the Austinian theory of law (385ff.). Attention to the component of nationality in the modern national State would show that modern societies are not simply contractually controlled or governmentally dominated states of nature. However inchoate and motley they are in their composition, however individualistic and pluralistic they are, however marked they are by conflict among and within their constitutent collectivities, they are territorially bounded societies. Maine was aware of this, but he did not connect that insight with his observations about the sovereign territorial State. He failed to see that the collective solidarity which he said was associated with 'status' lives on, in an attenuated condition, in the modern national State. Max Weber defined the State as a *Gebietsanstaltsverband*, but the significance of that fact was neglected by him when he discussed 'nation' and 'nationality'.

I lay stress on this neglect because it was associated with the failure of these eminent scholars to see that a national society must have some other elements in it than contracts, bureaucracy, rational bodies of knowledge of thought and rationalized economic organizations. Novel lines of understanding would have been opened to them had the rigours of the tyranny of tradition been eased.

To modify a tradition is not to obliterate it. Intellectual traditions can sometimes be modified by approaching a given topic from an entirely different field or discipline. Even in such evasions, the 'new' approach often makes a belatedly independent rediscovery of the tradition, or it succumbs to it through reading some of the older, more traditional literature. In any case, the ideas of status and contract, of *Gemeinschaft* and *Gesellschaft*, and of mechanical and organic solidarity, and the various attendant ideas such as the division of labour and rationalization contain too much that is reasonably sound for it to be discarded. It is more important to correct the tradition by adding to it as Weber did in his sociological studies of religious beliefs, practices and institutions, or by differentiating it and drawing on its own potentialities as Parsons sought to do.

In either case, the tradition, in the development of which Maine's ideas were a nodal point, has remained alive and fertile for more than a century. It is greatly in need of improvement, but its merits have demonstrated themselves in the enrichment of our understanding of society.

CHAPTER 9

Maine as an ancestor of the social sciences
J. D. Y. Peel

In a well-known paper, 'Pietas in ancestor worship', which chiefly concerned itself with ethnographic data from West Africa, Meyer Fortes (1970) sought to extend his generalizations about ancestor worship to other situations where men feel awe and respect towards the founders of the groups to which they belong. He instanced the sentiments that might be felt by the Fellows of a Cambridge college towards their predecessors. Of Trinity Hall's *pietas* towards Sir Henry Maine we are in no doubt. The chapters of this volume are evidence of the great respect in which Maine has long been held as an ancestor of the social sciences.

I say 'ancestor' rather than 'founding father' – the sobriquet more commonly applied by sociologists to those whom they claim as the founders of their discipline – to indicate that paradoxical combination of qualities which West Africans attribute to *their* ancestors. Ancestors are dead beings of the past, who are yet a present force, beings who interact with the living. L. T. Hobhouse will serve as an example of a founding father who is *not* an ancestor in the lively West African sense (notwithstanding Collini, 1979:5). As Edward Shils reminds us (p. 143 above), intellectual ancestors are different from biological ancestors – yet not so different from the socially recognized ancestors of West Africa – in that to a large extent they may be adopted posthumously by those who choose to regard themselves as their descendants. Adam Kuper is right to draw our attention to certain vagaries in Maine's posthumous reputation (see pp. 99–110 above). Nevertheless, the insistent fact is of Maine's relative modernity, compared with many of his contemporaries. My question is: why is this so?

Three general aspects of Maine's thought engage our attention. Firstly, there is 'status to contract', which has so deeply entered the routine stock of social theory that we are often hardly aware of it –

like genes from a real biological, but forgotten, ancestor. Parsons' 'pattern variables' bear its imprint, and so does every casual reference to 'tradition versus modernity', though here it usually is hard to disengage Maine's specific influence from Tönnies' or Durkheim's, for reasons which Shils makes plain.

Secondly, there is the 'jural model', highly influential in British social anthropology for a long generation. It is not Maine's influence on anthropologists of law, such as Gluckman and Bohannan, which I have chiefly in mind here, though certainly Maine's analysis of specific topics to do with law and inheritance can still be highly pertinent to the work of contemporary anthropologists, as Ray Abrahams' chapter shows. Maine's greater influence was on the way that social anthropologists conceived of social relations in general, as the enactment of rights and duties. Kuper is right to observe that this view is now deeply in eclipse. Indeed, so far has the opposing view – which stresses the pragmatic strategies of social actors – carried the day, that several fine field studies have appeared which present a decidedly 'non-jural' view even of legal processes, tending to assimilate law to politics (see Comaroff & Roberts, 1981; Moore, 1986). A nice question arises here: how far the appeal of Maine to a generation of British anthropologists who were primarily grounded in African ethnography may be related to the imperative of the colonial order under which they worked to 'process' indigenous social relations into a form in which they were amenable to specifically judicial forms of control. 'Native Law and Custom' was required to exist; the job of the anthropologist was to determine what it was. Maine's Indian experience may be highly relevant here. If so, it would not be the only case in African colonialism where *nihil est in Africa, quod non prius fuerit in India*.

Thirdly, there is his fundamental style of argument, 'comparative historical' in contrast to the evolutionism of so many of his contemporaries, which is so much more to our taste. To assert this is to take sides, as Macfarlane shows, in a dispute about how Maine should be interpreted. But Burrow (1966: 153–4) and most recently Stocking (1987: 128), despite some more minor disagreements, are surely right in contrasting Maine here with Tylor, Lubbock, Spencer and the matriarchalists. Certainly Maitland, when he attacked the evolutionary style of theorizing in the person of Spencer and challenged anthropology with 'the choice between being history and being nothing' (1936: 249), was gunning for something very different from the core of Maine's writing.

Yes, there *is* in Maine's writing quite enough of evolutionary metaphors, expressions redolent of uniformitarianism (for instance 'insensible gradations'), positivistic declarations of the universality of Law in Nature, and so on – most ringingly in the 'Address to the University of Calcutta' (1866) – to pose real interpretative dilemmas. There seem to be two main ways of proceeding. One, which is manifestly more congenial to the social scientist who finds in Maine an ancestor of living relevance, is to present the two sides of Maine, the comparative historical and the evolutionist, as an integrated whole. Here 'Maine' stands for a system of ideas, rather than a sequence of utterances. Contradictions in the body of writings, radical changes of approach, the pull of motivations extraneous to the writer's central purposes, the 'forensic' or audience-orientated aspects of a work, will all tend to be reduced or even effaced. It hardly derogates from the learning and insight of Macfarlane's appreciation of Maine to note that he is drawn in this direction. Ancestors, if they are to be communed with, *have* to be to some degree historically decontextualized. The other approach, that of intellectual history in the fullest sense, is not troubled by these concerns, for it has no reason to be embarrassed by the full otherness of the past. When Burrow opines that 'Maine was not a systematic thinker' (1966: 164), we might perhaps think his judgement hard, but at least we don't suspect him of an interested piety.

Macfarlane, by contrast, looks to resolve the paradoxical contradiction between the two sorts of things Maine wrote by showing how 'both parts were needed' (pp. 137–140 above). Very rightly, Macfarlane as an historical anthropologist finds particular value in Maine's use of historical comparison to bring out key institutions and circumstances in the emergence of modern forms of property, law, community, etc. The apparent contradiction is reworked as a 'necessary and productive tension': evolutionism was a source of hypotheses, which comparative history could test. Such claims for the logical 'necessity' of certain elements in an author's thought have an uneasy double character. On the one hand their alleged necessity makes these elements seem integral and important. On the other, to invoke the logical necessity of an element is a rather weak way of explaining its presence, since it is tantamount to supplying the author with an argument which seems cogent to the critic rather than finding empirical evidence of the author's actual motives or perceptions. Maine's undoubted evolutionary utterances seem sufficiently explained by the mid-Victorian climate of ideas, his inclination to positivism, his sense of the superiority of Western civilization and (perhaps above all) his readiness to use fashionable idioms and arguments. While all this gave Maine reason enough to sound like an evolutionist on occasion, his essential project – and Macfarlane certainly does not mistake this – was very different. It is for what was thus distinctive in Maine that his writings still engage our interest.

Strong endorsement of what they called 'the comparative method' united Victorian historians and social scientists of a very diverse stamp, and even modern discussion of it (for example Ginsberg, 1961; Evans-Pritchard, 1963) has all too often ignored major differences in what was being attempted by it. Its two great sources of inspiration – comparative anatomy and comparative philology – carried quite different implications for the analysis of historical or ethnographic data and were taken up very selectively. The first of these points to a single, general history of human society, normative in relation to all particular histories, whose universality is grounded in *nature*, in 'the psychic unity of mankind'. The second, based on the philological model, pointed to several actual histories, which, being paths of divergence from a common source, are grounded in a specific *cultural* unity. Whereas the first model directs attention to a course of change or sequence of stages, as well as to some regular mechanism of advance along it, the main focus of the second is on the reconstruction of the *ur*-form and the specification of the, necessarily particular, points of departure or divergence from it.

There can be no question but that Maine's use of the comparative method was overwhelmingly philological in inspiration and thus appropriately historical in its application (cf. Stocking, 1987: 121). Whether we see the evolutionist side of Maine as complementary to this (like Macfarlane) or as substantially rhetorical (like Stocking), or as useful to his views in some respects yet essentially contradictory to the historical side (like Burrow) is a more contested, but less central issue. Macfarlane refers to Burrow's identification of the 'two sides' to Maine: one which employed 'a dichotomy of progressive and unprogressive [societies]', and one which hinted at evolutionary laws of development (pp. 138–9 above). That way of describing two theoretical options is fair enough provided we recognize the ambiguity of dichotomous conceptions within the whole field of discourse of nineteenth-century social theory. With this I return to the links between Maine and classical sociology that Shils examines elsewhere in this volume.

The dichotomy progressive/unprogressive is not itself evolutionary, since it does not refer to two distinct phases in a scheme of development applicable to all societies, but to two concrete categories of societies, i.e. 'the West' versus 'the rest'. However, it does relate to that other dichotomy, status/contract, for which Maine has often been considered an evolutionist. This is because, in the famous words at the end of Chapter 5 of *Ancient Law*, 'the movement of the progressive societies has hitherto been a movement *from Status to Contract*'. Its applicability is thus limited to societies of the Aryan stock. Maine himself, as Macfarlane shows, was cautious about extending his argument beyond the Aryan races, but logically status/contract proved itself readily adaptable to evolutionary forms of argument. *Social* evolution, in so far as it is concerned to give a scientific guarantee to some scheme of progress, *requires* a dichotomy to express the overall direction of social change. As Kuper (p. 109 above) rightly says, 'primitive' (or whatever is the chosen label for the first term of the dichotomy) is typically a state of affairs rhetorically opposed to the present or to some idealized conception of the future. At the same time its source is less likely to be pure projective fantasy than an extrapolation from some real feature of recent social change in Europe. This was the experiential bedrock which accounts for the affinities between Maine's status/contract and Spencer's militancy/industrialism, Tönnies' *Gemeinschaft/Gesellschaft* and Durkheim's mechanical/organic solidarity. Spencer's version was the most thoroughly embedded in an evolutionary scheme: the trajectory from militancy to industrialism (in itself pre-evolutionary) was presented as the outcome of a secular process of adaptation of man's character to 'the social state' (Peel, 1971: Chapter 8). Maine's status/contract dichotomy, though later than Spencer's, owes nothing directly to it, but was in fact easily taken up by Spencer in later expressions of his own system (for instance Spencer, 1884: 1).

But when we compare Maine with these other social theorists and concentrate on how he *uses* the status/contract dichotomy, then we are brought back again to the fundamentally historical, not evolutionist, character of his thought. As far as its content goes, Durkheim's distinction between mechanical and organic solidarity, taking as it does the prevailing character of law as the chief index of the changing nature of the bonds between man in society, has a particularly close affinity with Maine's dichotomy. 'Mechanical' and 'organic' refer, of course, to two extreme cases, poles of a continuum which defines the course of evolutionary development from the most primitive to industrial society. Yet Durkheim is quite uninterested in what happens in the middle, between the two poles (which is where the great bulk of knowable history lies). His basic incuriosity about *why* the progression from mechanical to organic occurred – still less about why organic solidarity emerged most fully in Western Europe – is evident in the utterly reach-me-down quality of the explanations he does give: population pressure, struggle to adapt and survive, occupational differentiation ... themes well-worn for over a century of social thought. Durkheim's own drift away from evolutionism – whose first indications are evident even in *The Division of Labour in Society* (1893) – was not in the direction of history, but towards sociological constants. Here too, when he wanted to demonstrate the universal conditions for social solidarity, he turned to what he supposed to be the most primitive religion, the totemism of the indigenous Australians.

Durkheim, then, used the mechanical/organic dichotomy to elide the historical societies between the primitive and the modern. Maine, in stark contrast, uses it to open out the historical societies – 'the long period between tribal and modern capitalist civilizations', as Macfarlane puts it – as a field of inquiry. If 'status' was the starting-point and 'contract' is where we have got to, the interesting questions – for the comparative historian, that is – concern how and why the movement occurred. Hence Maine's concern is to discriminate between the characteristics of different national or cultural traditions and the desire to pinpoint in time and place those institutional factors (such as primogeniture, or testamentary succession) which engendered the emergence of modernity. The obvious affinity here is with Max Weber, the only one of the classical sociologists on whom, by Shils' careful analysis, Maine had no *direct* influence. Weber too was not without evolutionist elements or passages, but the central drive of his work – even at its most abstract and typological – was to specify the distinctiveness and explain the emergence of the uniquely rationalized society which he saw in the modern West. It is their shared devotion to a common project, which we may call historical sociology, which gives Maine and Weber, rather than (say) Spencer and Morgan, their lively contemporary relevance.

CHAPTER 10

'Ancient Law' and modern field work

Ray Abrahams

Like many of the peoples whom they study, anthropologists frequently express their identity in genealogies. Who they are, and sometimes more importantly who they are not, is proclaimed through the intellectual ancestry they cite and pay respect to in their work. Again, like many tribal genealogies, such academic pedigrees are not usually to be taken literally. They are constructed charters, and they are not without some elements of fiction. Names drop out and others are inserted in ways which may reflect the fashions and alignments of the day more accurately than the history of ideas.

The case of Sir Henry Maine marks a partial exception to this common fictive pattern, at least as far as many modern British anthropologists are concerned. Despite an early period of relative neglect, the line of descent through later central figures such as Evans-Pritchard, Fortes, Gluckman, and more recently, Jack Goody, is extremely well attested.[1] Of course, much of the detail of Maine's writing is quite understandably discarded by most modern scholars, and the pessimistic anti-populism of his later years is unattractive to many, including myself. None the less, because of the significance of the contribution which he made to the identification and elucidation of a number of quite fundamental issues, our intellectual relation to him seems to approximate in some degree to the character of 'universal succession', which he himself delineated in sharp contrast to the mere inheritance of a few bits and pieces. For better or for worse, many of Maine's ideas and concepts still infuse

[1] See, for example, Evans-Pritchard (1951: 27ff.), Fortes (1953: 26; 1969: Chapter 14), Gluckman (1965: 48, 118; 1972: xvi, 127), Goody (1976: 77, 138). The likely role of Radcliffe-Brown as a link in the chain between Maine and such writers is harder to document, since Radcliffe-Brown is very sparing with his references. The direct impact of Maine on his thought can be inferred most clearly from his discussion (1935) on patrilineal and matrilineal succession, and there was in any case an indirect connection via Durkheim (cf. Stocking, 1987: 296).

and influence the ways in which we think, talk and write about social systems. At the same time, I have found that it is also worth while on occasion to make conscious efforts to renew acquaintance with him and examine his opinions on specific problems.

As the title of my chapter suggests, the relation to Maine which I want especially to examine here is a working one, and I hope that this focus will complement that of my colleagues, Dr Macfarlane and Professor Kuper. I am, like them, a social anthropologist, and have much in common with them. Dr Macfarlane and I largely share the teaching of the anthropology of law in the Cambridge department, and Professor Kuper and I have shared many interests in the study of African polities and kinship systems over the years. But although I have also worked in Europe, I am not, like Dr Macfarlane, a historian of European culture and society or, as he has humorously described himself, 'a Maine addict'. Nor am I, like Professor Kuper, an historian of anthropology. My aim is therefore not to write chiefly historically, in either of those contexts, about Maine and his work, but to concentrate more on the present. If there is an historical element in what I have to say, it is mostly, though not wholly, a more personal and recent one. In his chapter, Professor Kuper mentions that it is some twenty-five years since Meyer Fortes told him to read *Ancient Law*. A few years earlier the same thing happened to me, and I also came across many references to the book in undergraduate supervision work for Edmund Leach and in lectures. Maine thus figures prominently in my first apprenticeship in anthropology; and my sense of his significance was also reinforced while writing up my doctoral research.

My first field research area was Tanzania, where I carried out a study of Nyamwezi social and political organization and the changes it was undergoing at the end of the colonial period. Maine's concepts of the corporation sole and aggregate were a special help to me, as they have been to many others, in my efforts to understand the forms of kingship and of kinship I encountered. I must confess too that if I had read more widely in his work by then, or even if I had merely absorbed more fully what I had already read, I would certainly have gained a quicker understanding than I did of the village communities of often unrelated neighbours which I also found there. These Tanzanian villagers collaborated in a wide range of contexts on the basis of their common neighbourhood, and I have spent much of my academic life studying their interactions under a variety of regimes.

The attempts of the first President, Julius Nyerere, and his colleagues to interpret such collaboration as a vestigial form of 'African socialism', whose 'true' quality they then tried to resurrect in *ujamaa* collectives, have much in common with the many nineteenth-century discussions of Maine, Marx and others which were aroused by the discovery of the Russian 'mir'. In my own early attempts at a theoretical understanding of my first findings on these neighbourhood communities, I turned to Ferdinand Tönnies' classic study of *Gemeinschaft und Gesellschaft* (1887), in which Tönnies of course quotes at length in generous acknowledgement of his own intellectual debt to *Ancient Law*.[2]

In 1980, after further work in this and other areas of eastern Africa, I began a new phase of research in Finland. I made a study of eastern Finnish family farmers, and it is part of this work which is most directly relevant to my discussion here. Not surprisingly – given the influence in Cambridge of both Fortes and Jack Goody – I paid a great deal of attention to the many problems of maintaining viable connections between farm and family through the generations. In a recently completed paper (Abrahams, 1989), I have analysed some features of succession to these family farms, including the use of wills and, more commonly, of transfers *inter vivos* between holders and their heirs. As I began to put together my material and tried to make sense of some of its characteristics, I turned to a variety of texts for guidance, and these more or less automatically included *Ancient Law*. I found it a felicitous choice, full of far more than I remembered, and anticipating much that I had learned from later writers. The result is that the paper in question, which was not written explicitly to extol or assess Maine, is littered with references to his ideas and comments.

Firstly and most simply, as I revisited the book, I was struck by the immediate close relevance to my material of what he had to say. I was also struck quite sharply by the clarity and, at times, the acerbity of how he said it. All this was immediately obvious in his discussion of the history of wills. The first few pages of Chapter 6 on 'The early history of testamentary succession' contain a remarkable number of bull's-eye shots at various targets. In the course of a powerful assertion of the value of 'the historical method' within jurisprudence, he pauses briefly to explain the crucial role of the

---

[2] As Professor Shils acknowledges, his own work with Talcott Parsons on the 'pattern variables' in role systems was itself partly an attempt to clarify and develop some of the fundamental ideas Tönnies drew from Maine (cf. Parsons & Shils, 1951).

Church and its economic interests in the development of free testation. He then goes on to show that an attempt to understand the form and function of early wills in terms of one's ideas about modern ones is doomed to failure, since the two forms differ in almost every basic respect. Then he notes, in a passing potshot at the natural law school, that far too many law students are taught that testamentary succession is 'the mode of devolution which the property of deceased persons ought primarily to follow' and that intestate succession rules constitute 'the incidental provision ... for the discharge of a function which was only left unperformed through the neglect or misfortune of the deceased proprietor' (176). Then he moves on to announce that 'The conception of a Will or Testament cannot be considered by itself. It is a member ... of a series of conceptions' (177). Lastly, I may also note how a few pages further on he remarks that early wills were not designed to allow a testator to alienate the members of his family from their property. As I will mention in a moment, there is in fact an interesting twist to this with many modern wills.

All this, plus some of his comments on Germanic notions of the inalienability of inherited property, was of interest and help to me as I looked at Finnish farm succession. One of the main points which I had noticed in my study was that wills are very rarely used by farmers as succession instruments. It appears in fact from other data that little more than one in eight Finnish farmers make a will, and the transmission of a farm to a son or daughter by will, as opposed to other forms of transfer, is much rarer than even this low figure might suggest. I was also drawn to look at some of the contexts in which wills were used. It would be foolish to claim that the expression of individual wishes through free testation was absent from the scene. Some people left varying amounts of property to the Church, or to an unrelated individual. But it was clear that there has been a long history in Finland of the use of wills for more complicated reasons than a simple opposition between individual freedom and ascriptive obligation would suggest. For often enough a will has been used to by-pass the *legal* rules of inheritance in favour of a *customary* preference for certain patterns. Many modern Finnish rural wills, for instance, are drafted mainly to protect the lifetime interest of a surviving spouse from the exercise by children of their own full legal rights in an unresolved intestate situation. Comparably, many seventeenth-century wills seem to have been aimed at avoiding the partition of a farm which the law allowed, and some nineteenth- and early twentieth-century wills which I have seen appear to be designed to maintain customary practice by avoiding the egalitarian transmission of land and other property to women in accordance with then modern legislation. The new laws had been vigorously opposed by many eastern Finnish farmers. They favoured the retention of traditional inequalities in both size and content between sons' and daughters' portions in inheritance, and they also preferred to grant a daughter at least partial pre-inheritance in movables through dowry payments when she married.

While Maine's work helped to throw light on such practices, this use of wills to strengthen customary rights and obligations, as against their legal counterparts, also poses questions about his and others' ideas of the form and force of change from a society based on status to one based on individual freedom of contract. Put simply, one might expect much greater use of wills to distribute wealth beyond the confines of the family. Of course, it might be argued that the case of rural society, and especially family-centred agriculture on the edge of Europe, does not really typify 'modern' society. While this is clearly true up to a point, I consider that the issue goes considerably further than such an argument would suggest. Finland is very much a part of modern Europe, and its rural areas are deeply involved in the life of the country as a whole (see Abrahams, 1985). In addition, the doubts which my findings raise are reinforced by recent studies of a wide range of British and American wills respectively. In one, Horsman (1978), an economist examines wills in England and Wales as evidence of the extent to which property remains in families, and he shows that, in general terms, the vast majority of wills leave the bulk of property to the testator's nearest and dearest rather than to more mercurial objects of affection. In another study (Smith et al., 1987), a group of American socio-biologists find that most American wills follow a comparable pattern of leaving wealth within the immediate family, though not everyone will want to accept the authors' conclusion that this is evidence of an innate tendency to protect the future of one's genes. I might add as an aside that the widely different points of departure of these two investigations seem to me to give strong support to Maine's insight into the significance of wills as an index of important qualities of a society. And if, as in the present case, such findings do not altogether fit his theories, one can still say that he did enough to formulate the nature of some vital questions, and ways of approaching them, without having to provide *all* the answers.

Like his comments on the Church, Maine's argument that the various instruments of succession form a set has more recently been valuably reiterated and expanded by Jack Goody (1976, Chapters 6 and 7; 1984). Certainly, it has made sense to me to look at different Finnish forms together. The most common pattern is succession through transactions *inter vivos*. This has a long history in northern countries and elsewhere, and it has some advantages over a will for the transmission of a working family farm. The general pattern in Finland is for a son, or occasionally a daughter and her husband, to purchase the farm and, often, to agree to look after the retiring owners. At the same time arrangements are made for them to buy out their siblings' rights to a share. The terms of these agreements and arrangements are typically laid out in documents, and the formality of many of these, with their carefully spelled-out conditions for monetary payments and the provision of services to the retiring owners, poses an interesting problem. Thus the purchasing children are typically contracted, in addition to making stated payments within set periods of time, to provide their parents with specified facilities such as subsistence, a dwelling including heating and lighting, cleaning if the sellers cannot do this for themselves, and in due course a decent funeral in accordance with local custom. Goody (1986: 146) has recently commented upon this with regard to comparable documents from other countries. 'Reading such documents', he writes, 'one is astonished to see the way that filial piety has to stand up and be counted, spelt out in exact quantities and decked out in lawyer's jargon.' I myself have written that such documents can easily appear at first sight to mark the full invasion of the family by the form and spirit of legal rationality and capitalism, and that Maine's posited movement from status to contract has apparently been completed with the take-over of the family itself.

Not surprisingly, the truth about such documents, at least in Finland, is more complicated than this, though I can only outline some of its main features here. An important aspect of the situation was brought home to me on one farm when I began to discuss the details of a particular transaction between a father and his children. In this case, land was being sold to the father rather than vice versa, but the principles involved turned out to be of more general relevance. The mother of the children had died, and they had inherited a share of the farm from her. The document set out the terms whereby the father reacquired rights of ownership in this. I had carefully and painfully translated the array of details about payments which were drawn up in legalistic Finnish, only to be told that 'of course no money actually changed hands'. Many of the documents of transfer from parents to children, and of buying out of siblings, also appear to contain some fictional elements; and one finds – perhaps predictably – that the families concerned are using the trappings of legalistic bureaucracy and formal contracts for their own timeless ends of mutual support, and not least for tax and credit purposes. They are not genuinely captured by such forms, but rather use them to achieve as profitable an accommodation with the formal sector as they can. As with the use of wills, one sees quite clearly that the family is alive and well in rural Finland, as indeed elsewhere, and that the processes of individualization within modern society are more complex than Maine and others sometimes seem to have assumed. Nor does one need to adopt an especially radical view of a plurality of interests in order to recognize that the law and its instruments may mean different things to different people even in a relatively homogeneous society.

And yet in the final analysis, I am not sure how much of this would have surprised Maine, even though he puts considerable emphasis on the development of institutional forms. For there are many contexts in which he shows himself keenly aware that truth is importantly and sometimes usefully different from surface appearance. His insistence on the need to look beneath the surface for the true character of other people's institutions – even if he sometimes gets them wrong or fails to follow his own injunction – is one of the more general features of his appeal to anthropologists. And I have often been struck by the powerful and shrewd streak of 'legal realism' in him which again makes him attractive to the anthropological field worker. I first noticed this when reading *Ancient Law* as a student. There, in a well-known passage early in the book, he discusses the idea of legal fictions, and he asserts that he uses the term 'fiction' in a broader sense than English lawyers are accustomed to. He then goes on to argue that in this sense English case law rests upon a legal fiction, and he proffers an analysis of the legislative role of courts which anticipates some of the perceptions, if not the politics, of later legal realist writing. As legal fictions of the common people, if one can extend his usage even further, wills which by-pass law for the sake of custom and morality, and sale and pension agreements which express the unity of families while appearing to be the legalistic symbols of their division, would probably have ruffled his anti-populist feathers without causing him undue – though perhaps one also should say '*due*' – intellectual surprise.

PART THREE
Maine on law, legal change and legal education

CHAPTER 11

Maine and legal education
Peter G. Stein

The thesis that I wish to put forward is that many of Maine's basic ideas about law were closely linked to the particular needs of legal education in England in the 1850s, as he perceived them. That was the period when Maine was giving the lectures which became the basis of *Ancient Law*, and his perception of what students of law should be taught coloured what he included in his lectures. So our first concern is with the state of legal education at that time.

The great movement for the reform of English law, which began in the 1830s, had lost none of its momentum in the 1840s. It was a movement largely inspired by the ideas of Jeremy Bentham, and it aimed to make the law simpler and more rational, by eliminating antiquarian relics which had served their purpose and could no longer be justified. In a general way it may be said that the reforms that were proposed aimed to make English law more scientific than it had been. As long as the law is perceived as essentially a matter of custom and practice, it follows that the proper way to learn the law is to attach oneself to a practitioner and watch what he does with the aim of following his example. Once law is seen as in some sense a science, the method of learning by watching and copying appears to be manifestly inadequate, and some kind of systematic instruction is required.

In 1846, the House of Commons set up a Select Committee to review the state of legal education in England and Ireland (the original proposal was limited to Ireland and the terms of reference were later extended to include England). It received evidence of the situation in the two countries and also in the main comparable countries abroad, such as Germany, France and the United States (the Harvard Law School), and in Scotland. Its conclusion did not mince words: 'no Legal Education, worthy of the name, of a public nature is at this moment to be had' in either England or Ireland. This situation was in 'striking contrast and inferiority to such education, provided as it is with ample means, and a judicious system for their application, at present in operation in all the more civilized states of Europe and America'. The Report especially deplored the lack of literature on the scientific aspects of law, and found the cause in the absence 'of a most important class, the Legists or Jurists of the Continent, men who, unembarrassed by the small practical interests of their profession, are enabled to apply themselves exclusively to Law as to a science.' (Report of the Select Committee on Legal Education, 20 August, 1846, House of Commons Proceedings 686, Conclusions 1, 3, 6; hereinafter '1846 Report'; cf. Stein, 1979: 185ff).

Although the Inns of Court had once constituted a legal university, they no longer provided courses of instruction. The Universities of Oxford and Cambridge each had two professors, the Regius Professor of Civil Law, who gave elementary instruction in Roman law to those preparing for the BCL or LLB degrees, and a professor of English law, the Vinerian Professor at Oxford and the Downing Professor at Cambridge, who gave occasional lectures. The situation in London was a little better, but still left much to be desired. As long as no examinations were required to become a barrister, students had little incentive to study law academically, whether in the universities or in the Inns.

The Report showed that the Committee was particularly impressed with the German system of legal education, which prefaced any instruction in the practical application of law by several years of courses in universities devoted to the history and principles of the law. It was to the 1846 Report that we owe the distinction between the academic stage and the professional stage of legal education, which had such influence on the subsequent course of legal education in England. It encouraged the universities to improve their offerings and urged the Inns to provide parallel courses. It also recommended the introduction of examinations for admission to the Bar.

It was in the immediate aftermath of this Report that Maine first became interested in legal education. Since he was not ordained, there was no Fellowship for him in his own college, Pembroke, and in 1844, at the age of twenty-two, he became the junior tutor in classics at Trinity Hall. Three years later the Regius Chair of Civil Law, which had been occupied since 1814 by James Geldart, also a Fellow of Trinity Hall, became vacant. Geldart, like many holders of the Chair before him, was in holy orders. His family had the right of presentation to the rectory of Kirk Deighton in Yorkshire, and on the death of his father, who was rector, Geldart had in 1840 presented himself as rector, while continuing for some years to hold the Chair. The duties were not onerous and could be carried out during occasional visits to Cambridge. Geldart had tried to make the course more serious by introducing terminal examinations in place of the stylized Latin 'act' at the end of the course, which had become purely a formality. However, the evidence given to the Select Committee had revealed that, far from being the subject of a higher degree, the civil law was studied because it was an easier option than the degree in arts but was nevertheless accepted by most bishops, in substitution for a degree in arts, as a qualification for Holy orders (1846 Report, Evidence, paras. 534–5, cited in *Law Magazine* 7 (1847), 4).

The appointment to the Regius Chair was, as it still is, in the hands of the Prime Minister, who was then the reformist Lord John Russell, one year into his first administration. He would have looked for someone who would stimulate the study of the civil law in the light of the previous year's Report. Maine was appointed, but to a post that carried but small emolument, little more than £100 a year (Feaver, 1969: 19). That he was sympathetic to the views of the Select Committee is clear from the evidence that he gave to the Oxford and Cambridge Commissioners three years later in 1850 (Feaver, 1969: 20). His lectures, he said, were concerned with general jurisprudence, illustrated by Roman and English law, and he pleaded for greater recognition of their merits by way of an increased stipend. When he said that, however, Maine's thoughts were already moving away from Cambridge, for he had moved his residence to London, and in the same year he was called to the Bar, and his wife, whom he had married in 1847, produced their first child. Maine kept the Cambridge Chair until 1854, but it was no longer the focus of his interests.

The publication of the 1846 Report created passionate debate in London on what the Inns of Court should do for legal education (Stein, 1980: 79). At first they refused to act collectively, and it was left to each Inn to take whatever steps it thought fit. The Middle Temple set up a committee which recommended that 'the first step for the promotion of Legal Education to be taken by this House, should be the appointment of a Reader on Jurisprudence and the Civil Law'. The appointment went to George Long, professor of Latin at University College London. He was a disciple of Savigny, but it was the Savigny of the system of present-day Roman law, rather than the promotor of historical jurisprudence, who inspired him. In his inaugural address he argued that 'Roman law, by reason of its universality, approaches nearer to a system of general jurisprudence than any other' (Long, 1847: 7). Long's lectures attracted only sparse attendance, and the appointment lapsed.

In 1851 Sir Richard Bethell, the Solicitor-General, persuaded the Inns to join together to establish a Council of Legal Education which proposed a programme based on five Readerships, whose holders would give courses of lectures and hold examinations (Manchester, 1980: 56). The main problem was that it was not made compulsory for an entrant to the Bar to attend the lectures and pass the examinations. It was held that he could do either one or the other, so that a candidate who had failed the examination was allowed to be called to the Bar on proof that he had attended the lectures. In 1852 the Council advertised a Readership in Jurisprudence and Civil Law with funds provided by the Middle Temple, offering a salary of £300 per annum, which, with the addition of fees, was expected to come to about £600, thus making it, as the *Law Times* commented, 'an acceptable post for a Barrister, in the present prospects of that branch of the profession' (19 (1852), 74).

Maine had tried to practise at the Bar, but without much success, and was eking out his professor's stipend by journalism. His appointment to the Readership, which for a couple of years he held with his Cambridge Chair, must have done much for his financial independence. He determined to make himself one of the first scientific jurists in England, whose absence was bemoaned by the 1846 Report.

Meanwhile the movement to improve legal studies in the Inns of Court was being kept up by a pressure group called the Law Amendment Society and by the *Law Magazine*. In 1854 a Royal Commission was set up to look into the arrangements made by the Inns for promoting the study of law and jurisprudence. *The Times* commented that 'out of revenues amounting to more than £80,000 a year, the Benchers have at length been persuaded to spend about £1700 in the formation of legal readerships, and some trifle more in prizes and scholarships. But, though induced to go thus far, they could not prevail upon themselves to make the system really efficient, by having recourse to the only means which could elevate the standard of knowledge in the legal profession' (cited in *Law Mag.*, new series, 21 (1854), 58), namely the introduction of compulsory examinations for call to the Bar. The *Law Magazine* was not optimistic that the Commission, constituted largely of 'establishment' figures, would recommend the necessary changes. 'If the Inns of Court were designed as lounges for the monied members of the profession, and (like quasi fellowships) as luxurious berths for Queen's Counsel ... the commission would have been suitable to its purpose, – that of maintaining the present system, with some slight modifications, on its old basis' (*Law Mag.*, new series, 21 (1854), 52).

In fact the Commission, to general surprise, reported that the community was entitled to some guarantee and security as to 'the intellectual qualifications and the professional knowledge of a barrister' (*Law Mag.*, new series, 24 (1856), 77). It recommended two compulsory examinations, one for the admission of a student at the Inns, largely in English History and Latin, and another at the end of the course, consisting of two branches. The first branch would consist of Constitutional Law and Legal History, Jurisprudence and the Roman Civil Law, and the second of Common Law, Equity and the Law of Real Property. In order to achieve this, it recommended the establishment of a legal university, with power to grant degrees, based on the Inns. The existing universities should concentrate on providing 'a sound and liberal training' for prospective lawyers, limited, so far as legal studies were concerned, to 'general principles' (*Law Mag.*, new series, 24 (1856), 88). These proposals were ahead of their time, and nothing came of the recommendations. Indeed it was not until 1872 that examinations for Bar students became compulsory.

During the 1850s and 1860s much of the debate on legal education centred around the question of what the student should be taught at the outset of his studies. If law was a science, he should first be introduced to its 'general principles'. In the eighteenth century these might have been taken to be the principles of natural law, but in the nineteenth century natural law was considered to be incompatible with true scientific inquiry, which had to be based on actual institutions and not on purely mental constructs. The closely woven mesh of the English common law made it difficult, if not impossible, to isolate any general principles. On the other hand, that was exactly what Roman law was seen to offer.

Today we are impressed by the similarities between Roman law of the classical period and English law. Both systems are characterized by a pragmatic, casuistic approach to problems and by an emphasis on remedies rather than on rights, producing rules of narrow scope. Nineteenth-century lawyers saw Roman law very differently; they viewed it through the eyes of its foremost contemporary exponents, the German pandectists, who had categorized and conceptualized it into a coherent system. This in fact owed much to the systems of natural law, which were so much out of favour, but was presented as Roman law shorn of purely antiquarian details – 'the system of present-day Roman law', as it was expressed in the title of Savigny's treatise.

An important feature of pandectist works was 'the general part', which set out ab initio principles which applied throughout the various branches of law that followed. In 1855 Nathaniel Lindley, later to become Lord Lindley, who, like John Austin before him, had studied Roman law at Bonn, published an English translation of the general part of Thibaut's *System des Pandektenrechts*. The title was *An Introduction to the Study of Jurisprudence*. The reviewer in the *Law Magazine* commended it, both to 'those who ignorantly prate of the utter worthlessness of the study of Roman jurisprudence and those who in a more humble spirit entertain misgivings as to its importance'. Its value was that it would 'teach them a habit of generalization, in which we fear English lawyers and law writers are as a body singularly deficient' (*Law Mag.*, new series, 23 (1855), 200).

It was in this climate that Maine published his opening salvo on 'Roman Law and Legal Education', which first appeared in *Cambridge Essays* in 1856. Its thesis is 'the immensity of the ignorance to which we are condemned by ignorance of Roman law' (Maine, B2, 1856, in *VC*, 1876: 333). For Maine Roman law was the law as set out in the Corpus Iuris; it 'is not a system of cases, like our own. It ... consists of principles, and of express written rules' (*VC*, 1876: 333–4). There are many cases in the Corpus Iuris, to be sure, but 'they are in no respect sources of rules – they are instances of their application ... problems solved by authority in order to throw light on the rule' (334). Maine understands 'written law' in its literal sense, as law evidenced in any kind of writing, rather than in the sense understood by Blackstone (1979: I, 63), as law formulated in a fixed and authoritative text, such as a statute. For he declares that 'the proper business of a Roman jurisconsult was therefore confined to the interpretation and application of express written rules' (*VC*, 1876: 335). The Roman lawyer had none of the embarrassment that the English lawyer feels when confronted by a statute. 'Nothing can be more peculiar, special, and distinct than the bias of thought, the modes of reasoning, and the habits of illustration, which are given by a training in the Roman law' (336).

The value of this for Englishmen is to be seen in a number of different areas. First, 'all discussion concerning Moral Philosophy has for nearly two centuries been conducted on the Continent of Europe in the language and according to the modes of reasoning peculiar to the Roman Civil Law' (337). The older school of casuists, 'in spiritual communion with the Roman Catholic Church', borrowed little from it, but the system of Grotius, by contrast, 'is implicated with Roman law at its very foundation' (337, 338), and it is that system which has prevailed in the field of ethical science. Because of our ignorance of the subject, we in England fail to take account of 'that remarkable tinge of Roman law which is all but universal in the moral and political philosophy of Continental Europe' (341). In view of 'the intimate relation of moral philosophy to jurisprudence' (342), this ignorance has implications for legal studies. Maine admits that Locke and Bentham provided an ethical system which took little from Roman law, but observes that 'The latest and most sagacious expositors of Bentham [i.e. John Austin and his followers] have formally declared their preference for the phraseology and the methods of Roman jurisprudence'. Wherever English law touches moral philosophy most obviously, as in early Equity cases, it is there that 'it is most deeply implicated with Roman law' (343).

The second area in which ignorance of Roman law impoverishes us is the English language. The words and phrases which indicate fundamental legal ideas, such as 'obligation', 'consent' and 'possession', are rarely derived from English law and 'come to us, almost without an exception, from Roman law' (345). Yet we use them imprecisely, as popular expressions. Thus, as with all popular language, when lawyers use such expressions, they have to qualify and limit them at inordinate length in order to achieve precision. 'The evil consequences of our indifference' to this problem manifest themselves 'in the lengthiness of our Law Reports' and 'the miscarriages of our Acts of Parliament' (348–9). With the help of Roman law, English legal terminology could be improved 'almost indefinitely' (349), for 'Perhaps the greatest of all the advantages which would flow from the cultivation of the Roman jurisprudence would be the acquisition of a phraseology not too rigid for employment upon points of the philosophy of law, nor too lax and elastic for their lucid and accurate discussion' (350).

Thirdly, in the area of international law, no English lawyer can consult 'foreign writers of repute without feeling that he is in most imperfect contact with his authorities' (351). In this field especially, we 'are met at every point by a vein of thought and illustration' which seems strange, since we do not recognize its basis in Roman law (353). This has serious consequences in our negotiations with foreign powers: 'It is a downright absurdity that, on the theatre of International affairs, England should appear by delegates unequipped with the species of knowledge which furnishes the medium of intellectual communication to the other performers on the scene' (354).

Again, foreign legal systems increasingly can be understood only by those who have some knowledge of Roman law. 'The steady multiplication of legal systems, borrowing the entire phraseology, adopting the principles, and appropriating the greater part of the rules of Roman jurisprudence, is one of the most singular phenomena of our day, and far more worthy of attention than the most showy manifestations of social progress' (355). This diffusion of Roman ideas is due largely to the popularity of the French codes and to their adoption even in countries whose social condition is quite unlike that of France, such as the Kingdom of Naples.

It might be argued that 'against these conquests of a Romanized jurisprudence in Europe' (359) should be set the extension of the common law in America. However, Maine refutes this idea, citing the work of Edward Livingston, 'the first legal genius of modern times'. It was he who produced the 1825 Louisiana Civil Code, 'of all republications of Roman law the one which appears to us the clearest, the fullest, the most philosophical and the best adapted to the exigencies of modern life. Now it is this code, and not the Common law of England, which the newest American States are taking for the substratum of their laws' (360). Maine seems to be thinking of the civil law institutions of Spanish origin which were being incorporated in the laws of certain Western states, and which he attributes, without much evidence, to the influence of the Louisiana Civil Code. Indeed he even credits to the success and popularity of that code 'the greatest experiment which has ever been tried on English jurisprudence, – the still proceeding codification and consolidation of the entire law of New York' (361).

The conclusion is that Roman law 'is fast becoming the lingua franca of universal jurisprudence' and as such demands a place in the new system of legal studies (361). In the minds of many, however, Roman law is associated with codification, and Maine now confronts that issue. The word 'codification' has two senses: it may mean the conversion of unwritten law into written law, and in that sense English law is already codified; but it may also mean 'the conversion of Written into well Written law' (364), and in that sense English law is certainly not codified. Yet surely codification in the latter sense is 'one of the highest and worthiest objects of human endeavour'. At this point Maine adopts (without acknowledgement) an argument from Savigny. Codification should only be undertaken when there are sufficient jurists with the necessary training to carry it out: 'badly expressed law, thoroughly understood and dexterously manipulated, is better than badly expressed law of which the knowledge is still to seek'. The study of Roman law 'would arm the lawyer with new capacities for the task' (365). A code would not eliminate the need for judicial decisions to interpret it, but would, as the experience of Louisiana shows, greatly reduce it.

The contribution of Roman law in the area of legislation is that it would enable English lawyers to handle statutes with the same dexterity as they handle cases. The Bar currently blames the legislature for the difficulties of interpreting statutes, but the fault lies with 'the special mental habits of the English Bar' (370). The only remedy is a uniform system of legal education, 'in which proper attention was paid to the dialect of legislation and law' (372). English law lacks rules for construing statutes as a whole. As a result legislative draftsmen must 'deal not so much with principles as with applications of principles', and try 'to anticipate all the possible results of a fundamental rule' instead of trying 'to modify and shape anew the fundamental rule itself' (375).

There are those who deprecate Roman law as being of no 'practical' value. The term 'practical' 'serves a large number of persons as a substitute for all patient and steady thought' (376). If the *Institutes* are first mastered, the rest of Roman law is 'little more than child's play' (378) compared with English law. In England we could concentrate on 'pure classical Roman law', without bothering about the scholastic accretions of its later expositors (378). (Maine overlooks the fact that much of the technique of interpreting statute law was the product not of the Roman jurists but of the later commentators.) In a final exordium he points to social pressures which in the classical period turned the best minds towards law, and asks what would have been the state of English law if it had counted Locke, Newton, and the whole strength of Bacon, Milton and Dryden among its chief luminaries. Such is the quality of Roman jurisprudence 'that the language of conventional panegyric may even fall short of the unvarnished truth' (383).

The whole essay is a plea for the acceptance of Roman law as the grammar of all advanced legal systems. It was not so much a knowledge of its particular rules but rather an understanding of its concepts and its ways of thinking that was essential for the new generation of educated lawyers, who, he hoped, would drag English law into the modern world. A theoretical structure was necessary for an advanced system of law, but English law had a dearth of theory. Sooner or later English lawyers would have to accept Roman ideas, which were technically superior to anything they could find in their own system. In fact 'we in England are slowly, and perhaps unconsciously or unwillingly, but still steadily and certainly accustoming ourselves to the same modes of legal thought and to the same conceptions of legal principle to which the Roman jurists had attained after centuries of accumulated experience and unwearied cultivation' (332–3). In a word, Roman law was more advanced than English law, and so a progressive lawyer was necessarily a Romanist. In reaching this conclusion Maine adopts the contemporary German view of Roman law as consisting of Pandect science, and he attributes to the Roman jurists of the second century many of the characteristics of the pandectists of the nineteenth century.

It is possible to discern in the essay of 1856 a number of the features which characterized *Ancient Law*. Despite its title, and the reference in the sub-title to the 'early history of society', that work was not concerned with the primitive societies which had so interested Montesquieu and his followers in the eighteenth century, such as that of the North American Indians. Given his aims, Maine concentrated on societies which progressed, as opposed to those that remained stationary, and such societies, as he pointed out, were the exception rather than the rule: 'nothing is more remarkable than their extreme fewness' (*AL*: 22). This method of selecting only a small number of societies which served his purpose to illustrate his argument was again taken from Savigny. The latter's theory of legal evolution was presented as characteristic only of 'the nobler nations', which conveniently turned out to be the Roman and the German (Stein, 1980: 59).

Maine seems to have derived the distinction between progressive and stationary societies from the work of Charles Comte, who was often coupled with Savigny in English legal writings of the first half of the nineteenth century. Charles Comte (1782–1837) should not be confused with his namesake Auguste Comte, the founder of positivism, who also had an influence on radical thinkers in England.[1] Charles Comte's *Traité de législation* was published in 1827 in four volumes and purported to identify 'the general laws according to which peoples progress, decline or remain stationary'. He put particular emphasis on geographical and racial factors as accounting for the progress of some societies and lack of progress of others, and asserted the superiority of people of the Caucasian race over others; in the latter regard he relied on the lectures of the English physiologist William Lawrence. These findings seemed confirmed by Max Müller, the philologist, who stressed the way in which the development of the languages related to and popularly thought to be derived from Sanskrit proved the essential unity of 'the Indo-European or Arian family'.

Maine does not expressly say that progressive societies are to be found only in this group of peoples, but that is a tacit assumption and his interests are confined to them. In asserting the proposition that the era of heroic kings is uniformly followed by an era of aristocracies, he says that it 'may be considered as true, if not of all mankind, at all events of all branches of the Indo-European family of nations' (*AL*: 7). In the chapter on 'Theories of primitive society' in *Early Law and Custom*, Maine admitted that his generalizations on the prevalence of patriarchal power were confined to Indo-European races (194, 220).

Ancient Law is essentially structured around the development of the institutions of Roman Law, with occasional references to Greek, English, Germanic and Indian institutions, when they seemed to

---

[1] I myself have been guilty of such confusion (Stein, 1980: 73ff.). For my correction, see Stein, 1986: 295.

confirm his conclusions. Roman law provided Maine with a unique model of a legal system which had progressed over a thousand years, from the Twelve Tables to the codification of Justinian, each stage of the development being evidenced by written records. As he acknowledged in the Preface to *Ancient Law*, without Roman law he could not have written the work, for he was bound by 'The necessity of taking Roman Law as a typical system'.

According to his account of the earliest period of society, divinely inspired kings hand down isolated judgements, the *themistes*. Subsequently they lose their sacred power and are replaced by small groups of aristocrats. The latter have a monopoly of knowledge of the customs which have come to be accepted, but they abuse it and so there is popular agitation to have the customs recorded in what Maine calls Ancient Codes. All this is based on what happened in Rome, where the monarchy was replaced by a republic, dominated by patricians, whose interpretation of the *ius civile* provoked the plebeians to demand the enactment of the Twelve Tables. But the scheme is not readily discernible elsewhere. There is little, if any, parallel to this development in England, the other society which Maine intends his scheme to exemplify. What is the English equivalent of an Ancient Code?

Again, when dealing with the substantive law of the family, he assumes that the powers of the Roman *paterfamilias* were found in all early societies. 'In truth in the primitive view, Relationship is exactly limited by Patria Potestas. Where Potestas begins, Kinship begins' (*AL*: 149). In fact the Romans themselves recognized that *patria potestas* was peculiar to Roman citizens and did not apply in other communities (Gaius, *Institutes* I. 55).

As Maine tacitly accepted, Roman law was anything but a typical system. What he meant when he referred to it as such was that Roman law demonstrated what heights of technical legal science could be achieved by an exceptional, progressive society. In its earlier periods, it adopted certain mechanisms of legal change which could also be found in the early stages of English law, such as fictions and equity. There was considerable interest in fictions in England in the 1850s. George Long discussed them in his lectures, and an anonymous article on them appeared in the *Law Magazine* for 1857. Having shown that in their formative periods, Roman law and English law adopted similar techniques, Maine intended his readers to infer that if the developed English law now followed the example of Roman law in its later stages, it would progress more rapidly.

In a revealing passage copied verbatim from the 1856 essay, Maine argues that a society's technical superiority in law derives from the share of the national intellect which that society has invested in it. Generalizing flagrantly from the case of Rome, he states that 'the earliest intellectual exercise to which a young nation devotes itself is the study of its laws'; Roman history shows that this monopoly is broken as 'Art, Literature, Science and Politics claim their share.' It is the same in England, for, as he observes a little wistfully, 'The students are counted by hundreds instead of thousands in the English Inns of Court' (*AL*: 361).

Maine recognized that there was an alternative theory which could compete with his as the basis of the jurisprudential preparation of law students, namely that of Bentham. He acknowledged the influence of Benthamism in the reform legislation of his own time. But, he argued, by viewing all law as legislation, Bentham obscures the nature of legal change. It is 'unfruitful' to say that societies modify their laws according to modifications of their views of general expediency, for that merely recognizes that change takes place. 'There is such widespread dissatisfaction with existing theories of jurisprudence, and so general a conviction that they do not really solve the questions they pretend to dispose of, as to justify the suspicion that some line of inquiry necessary to a perfect result' has been overlooked. No one, except perhaps Montesquieu, has taken account of what the law has actually been in periods earlier than his own (*AL*: 118–19).

A proper jurisprudential inquiry must be scientific, and as such must be based on observations rather than assumptions. The mistake of theorists such as Bentham is 'analogous to the error of one who, in investigating the laws of the material universe, should commence by contemplating the existing physical world as a whole, instead of beginning with the particles which are its simplest ingredients'. Why should 'such a scientific solecism ... be more defensible in jurisprudence than in any other region of thought?' (*AL*: 119). In fact the farther we go back in time, 'the farther we find ourselves from a conception of law which at all resembles a compound of the elements which Bentham determined' (7–8). The natural science which Maine chose as his model was geology. Early in Chapter 1 he says that the rudimentary ideas of law found in the literature of early societies 'are to the jurist what the primary crusts of the earth are to the geologist' (3).

Maine claimed that when he taught Roman law at Cambridge, he made his course, as many teachers do, an introduction to the basic elements of a private law system. When he moved to the wider forum of the Inns of Court, where his subject was officially Jurisprudence and Civil Law, he did not find it necessary to make a significant change of approach. When he came to write *Ancient Law*, he discussed family law, property, contract and delict, as they developed in Roman law, adding references to English and other laws only when they confirmed his generalizations from Roman law. He then wrapped it all in the vivid imagery and phraseology for which the work is famous. Many of his aphorisms doubtless arose from the oral instruction that he gave at the Inns. This consisted not only of formal lectures but also of informal exercises in which teacher and students discussed the topics of the lectures.

Such was its effect, that he persuaded the reader that he was being given the results of a scientific investigation. Just as Blackstone in the eighteenth century presented English law for the first time in a manner fit for a gentleman, so Maine now presented law in a manner fit for a scientific man. So plausible were his generalizations, and such was the confident manner in which they were expressed, that *Ancient Law* was received everywhere as a work of scientific truth. Yet it is no exaggeration to claim that Maine viewed all legal systems though the eyes of the categories established in Roman law. When, after he had completed *Ancient Law*, he came to learn more about Hindu law and old Irish law, what he discovered never altered his ideas, but was assimilated to the schemes that were already stated in *Ancient Law*. As he himself admitted in a revealing aside, 'Let us fix our ideas, as it is always desirable to do, by looking at the ancient Roman law' (*ELC*: 222).

CHAPTER 12

Maine and legal education: a comment

William Twining

As a freshman at Oxford in the 1950s I was told that I was expected to 'read round the subject'. We were presented with a 'general reading list' that read like a list of Great Books about law. Knowing no better, during the next two years I read a reasonable number of items on the list: Maitland's *The Forms of Action*, Holmes' *The Common Law*, Friedmann's *Law and Social Change in Contemporary Britain*, Hewart's *The New Despotism* and several works by C. K. Allen. *Ancient Law* was on the list and I read it one vacation. I remember thinking that it was not quite as racy or as readable as its reputation suggested, but on rereading it this summer I was surprised that as an undergraduate I had actually managed to finish it. Perhaps this was only possible because I had already studied some Roman law and I could see its relevance to my three papers in Roman law and to analytical jurisprudence. Significantly it was recommended and perceived as general background to our degree course, which was highly integrated and very particularistic: in Oxford at the time English legal system was mainly the history of English courts (contrast, for example, René David's *Les Grands Systèmes de droit contemporain*); legal history was largely the history of the sources of law and of contract, tort and land law – all in English law; I had but four tutorials, on Saturdays, on constitutional law; and Roman law consisted mainly of parsing Latin texts and the study of contract, sales and delict, sometimes in detailed comparison with their modern English counterparts. Even analytical jurisprudence was highly particular, a substantial proportion dealing with the concepts of personality, possession, ownership, legal rights and legal duties in English law. The rationale for studying Roman law was said to be to help one to see a legal system (i.e. a body of principles) whole and to enhance one's understanding of the detailed rules of English private law. In this context *Ancient Law* was relevant as background, but was insufficiently detailed to be of much help. We 'did' historical jurisprudence in a week, including Maine's most famous generalization, but for this I relied on secondary sources.

I have now taught jurisprudence for nearly thirty years. During the past twenty I do not recall having recommended any student, undergraduate or postgraduate, to read *Ancient Law* or anything else by Maine, except perhaps his discussion of fictions. Recent surveys on the teaching of jurisprudence in the United Kingdom in 1973 and 1984 suggest that this is fairly typical (Cotterrell and Woodliffe, 1974; Barnett and Yach, 1985). Peter Stein and a few brave souls keep the flag of historical jurisprudence flying alongside the tattered banner of Roman law, but one wonders how many undergraduates in 1988 read *Ancient Law in toto*. One suspects almost none. Some of the reasons for this are indicated in Stein's chapter: Roman law, analytical jurisprudence and even English private law have a significantly diminished place in the total picture of undergraduate legal education. Normative jurisprudence and much else besides have edged out the detailed analysis of 'fundamental legal conceptions' that took up so much of Salmond, Holland, Paton and latterly, Dias. I do not expect students to read *Ancient Law*, first, because hardly any of them have a Roman law background; secondly, its direct relevance to their other studies would be difficult to establish; and thirdly, because teachers of jurisprudence more than ever suffer from an *embarras du choix*.

The title 'Maine and legal education' could be interpreted in several ways. It could refer to Maine's views about legal education; the relationship of those views to his general ideas; the influence of either or both of these on the subsequent development of legal education in England; and Maine's ideas as a subject of study within legal education. Peter Stein in his excellent chapter and in his other writings in this area has shown how these are all intimately related (Stein, 1979, 1980); in so far as I am competent to judge, I agree with his general thesis and with most of his specific interpretations. In particular, I agree with the following points:

(1) Maine's general ideas and the scope and emphasis of *Ancient Law* are closely connected with his views on legal education in the aftermath of the famous Select Committee Report of 1846;

(2) One of his central concerns was to establish the study of law on a 'scientific' basis;

(3) For Maine, Roman private law, as interpreted by the pandec-

tists, provided the best exemplification of the general principles and fundamental concepts of law in maturer systems;
(4) In all of these respects Maine was quite close to Austin; and his version of historical jurisprudence was perceived by his contemporaries to be compatible with and complementary to Austinian analytical jurisprudence;
(5) However, over time a narrow interpretation of Austinian particular jurisprudence came to dominate English legal education at least until after the Second World War, and this prevailed over the broader conception of academic law that underlay *Ancient Law*. Accordingly neither Maine's general ideas nor his conception of legal education ever had more than a marginal place in mainstream legal education.

I wish to consider these general themes in the light of two classic distinctions: Bentham's sharp differentiation between expository and censorial jurisprudence and Austin's distinction between general and particular jurisprudence. These, I will suggest, are useful aids to interpreting and explaining the relationship between Bentham, Austin and Maine and the subsequent story of English academic law.

If we treat Bentham, Austin and Maine as the three great figures in English legal thought in the mid nineteenth century, a good starting-point for comparison is their respective conceptions of jurisprudence as the most general or theoretical part of the science of law. In so far as each had developed views on legal education, these stem in large part from their conceptions of their general intellectual enterprises. Apart from a few asides, Bentham only wrote one paper on legal education, in which, not surprisingly, he argued for a School of Legislation (Bentham MSS, *c.* 1794). Austin's most important statement is contained in his well-known lecture 'On the uses of the study of jurisprudence' (1954: 363ff.). This is reported to be the text of his opening lecture, but was not included in *The Province of Jurisprudence Determined* and was first published in 1863 (1954: ix). Maine, as Stein has shown, was more actively involved in the mid-century debates on legal education. He probably devoted more thought to the specifically educational aspects than the other two. It is no doubt true that the form, scope and emphasis of *Ancient Law* are intimately related to his view of the needs of legal education in general and of his students at the Inns of Court in particular. But this view was based on his conception of law as a discipline.

The relations between the ideas of Bentham, Austin and Maine are open to a variety of interpretations. They are too complex to be extensively canvassed here. One theme that links them is in contrast to the prevailing spirit and routine ways of thought of the common law: they were all committed to the 'scientific' study of law. Interpreting what this meant in each case is one key to locating them in the history of English legal education.

Here the two distinctions mentioned above are crucially important. The first, Bentham's distinction between expository and censorial jurisprudence, is generally interpreted as the foundation of modern positivist jurisprudence. The classic formulation is in *A Fragment on Government*: 'To the province of the *Expositor* it belongs to explain to us what, as he supposes, the Law is; to that of the *Censor* to observe to us what he thinks it *ought to be*' (1977: 397).

The second distinction, to be found in Bentham but more fully articulated by Austin, is between general and particular jurisprudence (Austin, 1954: 365-73). Particular or national jurisprudence is concerned with the positive law of a single system. Austin states:

I mean, then, by General Jurisprudence, the science concerned with the exposition of the principles, notions, and distinctions which are common to systems of law: understanding by systems of law, the ampler and maturer systems which by reason of their amplitude and maturity, are pre-eminently pregnant with instruction.

Of the principles, notions and distinctions which are the subject of general jurisprudence some may be esteemed necessary. (367)

Before considering these distinctions in relation to Maine and English legal education, it is worth examining them briefly in relation to Bentham and Austin. First, as is well known, Bentham concentrated on censorial jurisprudence, and Austin on expository jurisprudence, although he was not unconcerned with the former. Both of them considered that censorial jurisprudence could be 'scientific' – witness the term 'Science of Legislation'. More significant is the point, forgotten by some critics of positivism, that Bentham considered the principle of utility to be the foundation of his system of thought, including, as Gerald Postema has reminded us, his epistemology, based on his theory of fictions. We construct our knowledge of the world through language, which is a technological apparatus determined by 'pragmatic strategies of the mind' in the service of human needs and interests (Postema, 1983: 54). In an important sense for Bentham 'the ought' was anterior to 'the is' and, unlike Austin and most subsequent English academic lawyers, he did not consider that exposition should precede criticism (Twining, 1987: 274).

Secondly, both Bentham and Austin were primarily concerned with general jurisprudence. But here again their paths diverged in a crucial way. For Bentham 'the *Expositor* is always the citizen of this or that particular country: the *Censor* is, or ought to be, the citizen of the world' (1977: 398). Austin, while not denying the possibility of a universal science of legislation (1954: 373), puts the emphasis quite differently: 'Legislation supposes (expository) jurisprudence, but jurisprudence does not suppose legislation' (372). One must study law as it is before law as it ought to be; the study of law in a given system presupposes a scientific understanding of general jurisprudence. But the science and art of legislation involve knowledge of the particularities of what is. Whether or not this represents a disagreement between Austin and Bentham or merely a shift of emphasis, Austin's position was subsequently interpreted and adopted by English academic lawyers – including critical scholars such as Wedderburn and Kahn-Freund – to mean that students should not be encouraged or even allowed to criticize before they have mastered the particularities of English legal doctrine (Twining, 1987: n. 63). In this view particular expository jurisprudence is antecedent to censorial jurisprudence.

Thirdly, Austin and Bentham both insisted on a sharp distinction between 'is' and 'ought', but recognized that the distinction between general and particular is relative. Nevertheless, for Austin, the distinction between science and art was quite emphatic: 'the only practical jurisprudence is particular', he wrote, but the science of law is, in the first instance, general (1954: 372).

Austin anticipated the modern distinction between the academic and vocational stages: science is for the academy; art is for lawyers' offices. Both are forms of useful knowledge. Austin's proposed curriculum concentrated on general expository jurisprudence, with logic as a necessary foundation and a strong emphasis on Roman law. English law was given a restricted place. Significantly, he pointed out that 'In the Prussian Universities, little or no attention is given by the Law Faculty to the actual law of the country' (381). The same could be said of the national law schools in the United States, where from a relatively early stage the primary object of study was, and still is, largely a fictitious entity – American law. The 1846 Committee shared Austin's admiration for the Prussian (and to a lesser extent, the American) model. They drew a sharp distinction between 'the practical and mechanical side' and 'the higher and doctrinal side' and provided that even in the professional law schools, which have been and remain a distinctive feature of the English tradition and its imitators, the latter should concentrate on 'general principles'. To begin with these were not just general principles of English law. Roman law and jurisprudence in Maine's time occupied half of the curriculum of the Inns of Court and were interpreted in a way which approximated more closely to general than particular jurisprudence. Later, in a process that has been well described by F. H. Lawson (1968) and David Sugarman (1986), the 'academic side' became more and more orientated towards the particular and particularistic study of English law in the universities as well as the Inns and on the solicitor's side. Giving some part of the academic side to the profession made the particularization virtually inevitable.

Thus Bentham was primarily concerned with the censorial or normative aspects of general jurisprudence. The science of legislation was general, but its application was to some extent dependent on time and place. What became known as analytical jurisprudence was also general, primarily concerned with the fundamental concepts (and distinctions) in which laws could be expressed anywhere. But for Bentham, the science of legislation was not confined to prescribing rules of positive law. He was not only concerned with codification and commands addressed to the will; he was also concerned with designing institutions and recommending correct ways of thought. This is illustrated by his treatment of judicial organization and adjective law, which are among his most extensive works. His writings on adjective law constitute on the negative side a sweeping attack on all formal regulation; on the positive side he is concerned with both institutional design and 'instructions' addressed to the understanding: so, for example, he has a lot to say on the evaluation of evidence, a matter on which modern expository textbooks are largely silent, just because we have almost no rules of weight to expound (Twining, 1986; 1990: 41, 66–7). It is symptomatic of later positivist thought that Thayer says that Bentham's *Rationale* 'is not a law book' (Thayer, 1898: 279n.).

Austin narrowed down Bentham by concentrating on positive law and expository jurisprudence. But he too was more concerned with general than particular jurisprudence and hence with necessary and general conceptions and principles that 'occur very generally in matured systems of law' (1954: 369).

It is relatively easy to fit Maine into this scheme. Like Bentham and Austin he was concerned with developing a 'scientific' approach to law through general jurisprudence; like Austin he was primarily concerned with the 'is' rather than the 'ought' – perhaps for political as well as 'scientific' reasons; as with both of them the analysis of what Hohfeld called 'fundamental legal conceptions' was central to his concerns; like Austin he regarded Roman law as the exemplar of legal thought in maturer systems. Both at Cambridge and the Inns of Court he treated Roman law as *illustrating* the general conceptions and principles of such systems. In several important respects he was broader than Austin: for example, he was more directly concerned with law in societies that have been variously designated as ancient, early, primitive, pre-literate, simple or traditional, and he did much to stimulate interest in them. But this was a matter of interest and emphasis: for Austin allowed that 'the principles, notions and distinctions which are the subject of general jurisprudence' are to be found 'more or less nearly conceived' in the 'rude conceptions of barbarians' (1954: 366–7). And Maine, as we have been reminded, was also more interested in 'progressive' than 'static' societies (Stein, Chapter 11 above). Secondly, while his conception of legal science naturally gave a central place to general principles, notions and distinctions, his conception of 'legal institutions' was much broader than that. Historical and sociological discourse about the evolution of modes of dispute-settlement or legal change or institutions such as courts or law-making bodies or lawyers cannot be conducted solely in terms of the 'internal' 'folk concepts' of doctrinal discourse, even that of the exponents of general expository jurisprudence. Such discourse also needs the 'analytic concepts' of social scientists and historians which describe, interpret and explain them from an 'external' point of view, which, of course, takes into account the internal ways of thought of participants within a legal system, including jurists, but treats them as objects of study. Maine's 'science' naturally included legal doctrine, but much else besides.

This is also true of Bentham, and to a lesser extent, of Austin. However, subsequent developments can be broadly interpreted in terms of a Maine-like hypothesis: between 1850 and 1950 the movement of academic law in England was a progressive narrowing from general jurisprudence, broadly conceived, to particular expository jurisprudence, concerned almost exclusively with the exposition and analysis and application of English legal doctrine. This was illustrated not only by the content and scope of the professional examinations and the rise of the expository textbook, but also by the history of taught jurisprudence in that period. Bentham was side-lined; the followers of Austin used him selectively and developed a narrower and more particular conception of analytical jurisprudence; and Maine was marginalized. Like Maine's grand hypotheses, this is vulnerable to particularistic attack as being simplistic and over-generalized. But it contains a core of truth sufficient to provide the basis for a plausible and coherent story about English academic law over a hundred years. General jurisprudence and legal science, as these were variously interpreted by Bentham, Austin and Maine, never took root in England – for fairly obvious reasons.

CHAPTER 13

A wake (or awakening?) for historical jurisprudence
Calvin Woodard

I

I start with the proposition that Henry Maine is something of a puzzle. On the one hand, he was one of the two or three most formative thinkers in my own life. He was the first legal scholar I read, as a law student, who was also a genuine 'man of letters'. It seemed to me that, in the course of a few volumes, he transformed 'law' from a technical and professional 'box of tools' (to borrow a phrase the late Joan Robinson applied to economics) into a museum of past civilizations and remote societies all teeming with unexpected associations with our own legal system; he brought the whole range of classical mythology into the realm of legal learning; and he humbled the student of the common law, making him feel ignorant, even naked, before the magisterial eminence of Roman law. Along the way, he offered marvellously perceptive critiques of various 'schools' of legal theory, ranging from natural law to positivism, together with insights into the leading exponents of each, such as Grotius and Austin, including everything from Bentham's 'Political Economy' to chips from Max Müller's philological workshop. His withering dismissal of Rousseau and his 'romanticism' remains, to this day, a devastating argument against easy assumptions about a Golden Past of 'Noble Savages'. I thought then, and I still think that no member of the Anglo-American Bar, however rigorously disciplined to 'think like a lawyer', can ever see his or her subject – law – in quite the same light again, after having been exposed to this man's works.

With all his virtues, however, there are things about Maine that repel even his most ardent champions. On the personal level, for example, there is no doubt that he was a vain, wife-debasing if not abusing, and aggressively ambitious person. Indeed, some of his contemporaries thought it characteristic of him that he ended his illustrious career in a vulgar power struggle to garner yet another trophy to add to his list of triumphs. Thus while Master of Trinity Hall, full of years and fuller still of honours, he insisted on standing for the newly created Whewell Chair of International Law, a field that was not really his own. By throwing his weight around in a most unseemly manner, he won the election – but only at the cost of leaving behind the not very pleasant image of an old man driven relentlessly by an insatiable appetite for ever more public recognition. To many, he must have been reminiscent of the pluralists and tuft-hunters of an earlier era.

Nor were his ideas and expressions always rendered in a form free of the biases and prejudices common among the upper classes of his day – as one, perhaps unfairly, expects of a scholar of his intellectual eminence. Time and again he demonstrated, in his writings and elsewhere, an appalling insensitivity to the concerns and values of 'others'. Indeed, he seems to have assumed that his readers were, or should be, members of the Athenaeum Club, all of whom shared with him the values and opinions that really counted. He addressed them accordingly.

Worse yet, his later writings reveal a supple mind, once remarkable for its fertile expansiveness, grown dry, brittle and fanatically political. Like many of his learned contemporaries – such formidable thinkers as Fitzjames Stephen, A. V. Dicey and the earlier deceased John Austin, to mention only a few lawyers – he experienced, in his later years, what John Roach called 'a crisis in Liberalism'. As a result, he ended his days lamenting the excesses of the French Revolution and other more recent revolutions; reflecting on the fall of empires, not only the Roman, at the hands of barbarians; and despairing of a future in which some form of 'mobocracy', 'collectivism' (to use Dicey's term) or (in Carlyle's Germanesque word) 'swarmerei' – the American Vernon Parrington would speak of those roiling times as 'the Great Barbeque' – overran and ultimately destroyed civilization itself. He was rather like the caricature of a retired civil servant, safely returned from foreign postings and comfortably settled in one of the Home Counties: his horizons seemed to shrink until, at the end, he worried himself endlessly about local rates and election returns.

Consequently, many readers of different political persuasions and circumstances, including some fellow members of the Athenaeum

Club, found his later works both offensive and disappointing. Likewise, his non-English readers, among whom he had enjoyed a large following, felt the sting of his imperious observations. For example, all Americans, like myself, must flinch when they run across his assertion that 'most English democratic philosophy translates itself into (the proposition that) if you vote straight with the Blues (Tories), your great-grandchild will be on a level with the average citizen of the United States'. That surely puts a new twist on the much bruited-about 'special relationship' between the two nations.

Maine's insensitivity to the concerns of those outside his charmed circle not only put many Americans on edge. Indians, especially, must have rolled their eyes when they read his words. Thus though a certain Anglican superiority to the values of other societies was assumed in Maine's day – he was, after all, an elder contemporary of Lord Curzon – most modern readers are embarrassed, as well as amazed, by his colossal temerity in going before the assembled students and faculty of the University of Calcutta, scions to one of the world's oldest and most sophisticated cultures, and solemnly advising them that 'Except the blind forces of Nature, nothing moves in this world which is not Greek in origin.'

On such occasions he surely made 'the White man's Burden' heavier – and not only for the white man. I cannot say that I lament the passing of that aspect of Maine. If he had taken it to the grave with him, he would have done us all a great service.

In addition to his less than winning personality and his occasional imperious manner of expression, however, there are still other, more substantive factors that have worked to debase (and possibly conceal) the continued importance of this remarkable man's ideas to jurisprudence. In the first place, subsequent generations of Roman law scholars have found blunders and mistakes in his works, thereby undercutting his reputation as an authority in that field in which he was, in England anyway, an acknowledged master. Today, most Roman law scholars probably share Alan Watson's doubts about the reliability of many of his conclusions about Roman law.

Again, comparative law, the field that many of his contemporaries, such as Sir Paul Vinogradoff and the young John Henry Wigmore, expected to be the most enduring monument to his creative genius, somehow never quite attained that exalted status. Though a subject of that name still survives in the curricula of many law schools, it scarcely resembles that new 'scientific discipline' inspired by Maine's example: the quest for the 'natural history' of law by applying 'the comparative method' to the various legal systems of the world. Indeed, in 1966, when the late Professor Otto Kahn-Freund delivered his inaugural lecture in comparative law at University College London, he described himself as an academic anomaly: the incumbent of a professorial Chair in a non-existent subject.

Though Professor Kahn-Freund purposely overstated his case, it is clear that, in so far as Maine was regarded as the modern founder of that amorphous subject, his reputation has not been enhanced by its subsequent history. Indeed, one question anyone curious about Maine's influence in the modern world must consider is: why, in an age of burgeoning inter- and multi-national legal relationships, did not comparative law, as he envisioned it, blossom into one of ever-increasing speculation and interest? Why not, indeed?

II

One clue to many of the puzzles concerning Maine's posthumous fate is that he was *too* much of a nineteenth-century man for his ideas to appeal, at least in the form in which he presented them, to denizens of the twentieth century. Hence his diminished reputation reflects, in part, the depreciation that *all* eminent Victorians (and, as Lytton Strachey's own current reputation suggests, Edwardians as well) have suffered in the twentieth century. In fact, if we set our clocks and calendars by Elie Halévy Time, we see that the nineteenth century did not really end until 1914 – and, I would add, the twentieth century did not begin until *c*. 1920; and Maine's reputation flourished, after his death in 1888, down to the First World War. Increasingly thereafter, however, his works, like those of so many of his well-known contemporaries, became more a target to be shot at than a source of scholarly inspiration.

This reaction is not altogether surprising, for Maine's 'eminence' was, in the popular mind, largely based on his close association with three of the most characteristic notions of the Victorian era; and each of those notions was part of that metaphysical lumber that so many members of the younger generations, especially those returning from the First World War, wilfully left behind with a jeering 'farewell to all that'.

The three high-Victorian notions with which Maine was so closely associated were:

(1) *'Evolution-cum-progress'*

Perhaps the most seminal of all nineteenth-century ideas, 'Evolution', took many forms, including Hegel's idealism, Marx's materialism, Lyell's geology, Comte's sociology, L. H. Morgan's primitive societies, and Matthew Arnold's culture. Of course, Darwin's biological version was the most influential, and 'social Darwinism' its most conspicuous off-shoot. When 'Evolution' was crossed with Victorian optimism (or Biedermeier *Fortschritte* or Yankee 'Manifest Destiny'), it became 'Progress', a moral principle as well as a philosophy of history, of immense appeal and influence in the last century.

One significant form of this mixture was 'Legal Evolution', a concept widely identified with Maine. How law, as a subject, came to be seen as evolving is itself a remarkable story well told by Professors Burrow and Stein. The pre-nineteenth-century assumption (with a few Scottish exceptions) had long been that law – real 'law' – was immutable. After all, Moses had received the authoritative Word carved in stone; continental lawyers had long associated it with a finite text (such as the Code of Justinian or Napoleon); and Blackstone had, as recently as the mid eighteenth century, analogized English law to an ancient Norman fortress, a 'noble pile', that had withstood the forces of change through five hundred turbulent years of English history.

By the end of the nineteenth century, however, the opposite notion – that law was (to quote Justice Holmes) 'constantly changing' – had gained wide acceptance. Maine deserves much of the credit for this remarkable jurisprudential innovation, for he was the leading exponent of 'Legal Evolution' in the English-speaking world. Moreover, his celebrated dictum about the movement of Western societies 'from status to contract' firmly linked him (at least in the minds of his nineteenth-century readers) to the idea that legal evolution led, through contract, to 'human progress'.

In the twentieth century a powerful reaction arose against both the notion that law constantly changes and the idea of progress. The reaction against the latter came first and was most thorough. The First World War put a great damper on the easy optimism so prevalent in England during the *Pax Britannica* of the last century. But it was the horrors of the Holocaust that killed all lingering belief in the idea that human history was a chronicle of progressive triumphs of reason over ignorance and unreason. As a result, the second half of the twentieth century has been lived under a Calvinistic cloud of deep, primordial evil pervading all human affairs despite outward commitments to scientific rationalism. Thus despite the extraordinary advances of twentieth-century science, few commentators have dared talk of 'progress': we all know too well that every advance' has a 'down-side'; and where, and to what ends, our innovations are leading us are more matters of despair than of hope. In such a context, Maine's links to 'progress' have served neither him, nor us, well.

The same circumstances that undermined confidence in the heady nineteenth-century versions of 'progress' also led many legal scholars in the second half of the twentieth century to resist the idea that law not only changes but is constantly evolving. On the whole, these critics of 'legal education' took 'Positive Law' – a form of law which is, by definition, purely human in origin, conceptually distinct from morality, and eminently useful as a 'tool' for implementing social policy – to be a prime twentieth century villain. In attacking it, the anti-positivists rejoined, unconsciously or otherwise, the age-old jurisprudential quest for a form of law based on some authority more permanent than capricious human will and morally superior to vulgar political power.

Thus the reactions to legal evolution – the idea that law is ever in a state of flux – have engendered a minor natural law revival in a most unlikely place at a most unexpected time. In the post-industrial world of science and technology during the late twentieth century, thinkers as different as Maritain, Fuller, Finnis and Dworkin have all contributed to a quickened interest in a jurisprudential theory many legal thinkers had assumed to be long dead.

As noted above, modern efforts to limit the scope of legal change have focussed mainly on the shortcomings of 'positivism', meaning *either* the abstractions of Austinian legal theory *or* the realities of social policy implemented through legislation of the Welfare State/ New Deal genre. Maine, I scarcely need add, would have heartily joined in attacks on both these forms of positivism: Austin, as a theorist, and 'legislation', as a form of law, were among his favourite targets. But he was also an implacable foe of natural law, and he would not, I think, ever endorse a return to any legal theory based on *a priori* assumptions about man, nature or any superhuman power.

Modern thinkers who share his distrust of positive law might have been better served, jurisprudentially anyway, if they had considered some of Maine's own ideas about the shortcomings of positivism and natural law. But few did. Interestingly enough, the contemporary legal philosopher who appears to have learned most from Maine may well have been the celebrated positivist H. L. A. Hart, who clearly incorporated some of Maine's ideas into his own elegant restatement of Austin's theory.

Maine identified a kind of 'legal change' that was not the result, but the cause, of the most common form of positive law, legislation. In his scheme, legislation was a stage in the natural evolution of legal systems. Whether those stages were (like 'adolescence') inexorable, and whether legislation was the final stage of a kind of life-cycle leading inevitably to a Roman Empire-like collapse, is not altogether clear. He left no doubt, however, that the stages of legal change were inherent in the institutionalized process of law itself.

The full development of that process, however, culminated in two slightly inconsistent ends: (1) a 'progressive' social order based on contractual, rather than status, relationships; and (2) a legal system in which legislation is the dominant form of law.

Maine, being the Victorian that he was, focussed his attention in his earlier works, most notably *Ancient Law*, on the development of the 'contract' relationships as the indicia of social 'progress'; and in his later essays, most notably *Popular Government*, he lamented the tendency of democracies to enact more and more legislation abridging the freedom of contract. Thus, though he was a champion of legal evolution, he ended up deploring the end to which late nineteenth-century law seemed to have evolved; and many readers who admired his jurisprudential analysis of legal evolution differed sharply with his political views about the uses and consequences of legislation.

(2) *(German) historical jurisprudence*

Much nineteenth-century German scholarship focussed on the *Volksgeist*, a concept reflecting Aryan values that was embodied in German culture, especially language and law. It also found expression in the great German universities which, throughout much of the nineteenth century, were the envy of scholars throughout the entire Western world. They were the acknowledged leaders of the most advanced forms of science, legal and social as well as physical; and Germanic learning and German 'research' methods, including doctoral degrees and seminars, became models to be emulated in institutions of higher education throughout both Britain and America.

In the twentieth century, however, after two world wars in which Germany was the enemy, coupled with the scourge of Nazism, the admiration countless Anglo-American intellectuals, including legal scholars, held for Germany and things German came to a bitter end. (One recalls, for example, Holdsworth's dedication to a wartime reissue of one of the volumes of his *History of English Law*: 'To The Unspeakable Bestiality of the Germanic Peoples'.)

Everything German became suspect, including 'Historical Jurisprudence', with its great emphasis on custom. And not only in the Anglo-American world: I well recall causing a minor Ice Age when, in 1969, I innocently expressed admiration for Rudolf von Jhering in a jurisprudence seminar in Munich. Afterwards, I was solemnly advised that von Jhering, who died in 1892, was *persona non grata* in post-War Germany because his legal theories had contributed (through the likes of Carl Schmitt) to the rise of Nazism.

Maine was the Englishman most closely associated with historical jurisprudence. He was not, however, as much a Germanophile as many of his contemporaries. Though he was surely influenced by Savigny, and possibly by von Jhering, the extent, and indeed the nature, of that influence is not at all clear. In fact, Maine's historical jurisprudence – the 'English variant' – was much closer, doctrinally, to pan-nationalistic comparative law than it was to the ultra-nationalistic version of Savigny and Puchta.

Oddly enough, it is what we now call 'English legal history', the systematic study of the early records of one particular nation's legal institutions, that is closest in both aim and method to (German) historical jurisprudence. For English legal historians are attempting to reconstruct the past, primarily from archival sources, in order to enable us today to understand realistically, rather than romantically or mythically, the history of English law.

That past we are all seeking to understand also embraces the aspirations and values of earlier generations of Englishmen, which, we are often told, gave rise to and are embedded in the English common law. Often called the 'spirit of the English people', those aspirations and values are really an extension of what the Germans meant by the *Volksgeist*.

Of course, modern English legal historians wisely do not now speak in those suspect terms. Not so those of earlier generations. Such notable nineteenth-century historians as E. A. Freeman and J. M. Kemble, Maine's fellow Apostle, and even Bishop Stubbs, came remarkably close to emulating the German concept of institutional history based on ancient (Anglo-Saxon, i.e. Teutonic) custom. Also, of course, the father of English legal history, Maitland, was an unabashed admirer of things German. His regard for the works of Otto von Gierke, Henry Brunner and Felix Liebermann is well documented; he named two of his daughters Ermengard and Fredegond; and he went so far as 'to thank God for German nannies' who taught him the Teutonic language as a child. He died in 1906, however, well before the Great Change of 1914; and most of the best English legal history has been written under the aegis of Maitland's Selden Society, a name deeply rooted in English history and safe from any obvious associations with Germany and 'German Historical Jurisprudence'.

So, paradoxically, Maitland, the Germanist, and *his* (German-style nationalistic) legal history have flourished during the very period that Maine, the British imperialist, and *his* (non-German, comparative law) version of historical jurisprudence went into decline. For after 1914, *all* forms of 'Historical Jurisprudence' became, jurisprudentially speaking, nullities. Most Anglo-American scholars linked with historical jurisprudence prior to 1914, such as the American James Coolidge Carter, were, if not forgotten, left to sleep deeper sleeps. 'Deep underneath deep', as Emerson said.

A few erstwhile champions of historical jurisprudence who were still alive after 1920 – such as Roscoe Pound and H. Kantorowicz – managed to save their scholarly credibility by distancing themselves from ideas with obvious German associations, chiefly by turning their scholarly attention elsewhere. Indeed, it is instructive to note the sharp decrease in the number of references Pound made to von Jhering, Ehrlich, Kohler and Stammler – his earlier heroes – in the period *after*, as compared to the period *before*, the First World War. Increasingly after 1920 he became a vocal champion of English law rather than German legal thought; and he wrote about such topics as 'the Common Law Tradition', 'the Spirit of the Common Law' and the common law influence during 'The Formative Era of American Law'.

The fact that Maine's reputation survived the anti-German onslaughts following the two wars that virtually exorcised historical jurisprudence of *all* kinds, German and otherwise, from Anglo-American legal thought for most of the twentieth century, is a measure of his genuine intellectual power. It is also a measure of his personal influence, not of his 'school' of jurisprudential thought.

(3) *Laissez-faire individualism*

The role of government, especially in economic affairs, during the nineteenth century has long been a hotly disputed historical question. One can debate endlessly whether that period was a 'golden' (or, as may be, 'cruel and selfish') Age of Individualism, in which the State did virtually nothing; or whether it was an era of fertile experimentation during which the 'Victorian origins' of the modern Welfare State were firmly established. Even so, I think that Dicey was right when he said:

From 1832 onwards the supremacy of individualism *among the classes then capable of influencing legislation* was for many years incontestable and patent. (my italics)

Maine became one of the standard-bearers of late Victorian *laissez-faire*. Despite the fact that most of his writings dealt, at least ostensibly, with such remote subjects as ancient law, early custom and non-English (Roman, Indian and Brehon, for example) legal systems, they all seemed to lead to the same political conclusion. However, the most obvious link between Maine and the idea of *laissez-faire* was 'contract', the sanctity of which had been traditionally anchored in some form of natural law theory. The intellectual basis of all such theory was seriously weakened by Benthamite positivism/utilitarianism in the nineteenth century; and of course the ever-widening extension of the franchise created an ever more practical (and therefore a more dangerous and realistic) threat, from legislation, to the sanctity of contract, property and everything else.

Maine's works provided an entirely original justification for opposing all governmental activities interfering with or curtailing the right to contract. His conclusion was not based on legal theory; nor was it based on morality or religion. Rather, it was (as already noted) based on the long-term historical tendency of 'the progressive societies' which, he noted, had been *'from Status to Contract'*.

To his propertied contemporaries terrified by the prospect of Demos controlling government to radical egalitarian ends, his message meant that more than one person's, or one family's, or even one class's, interests were endangered by interferences with 'freedom of contract'. The course of history itself was at stake. Tamper with contract, and not only would all 'progress' cease; society would degenerate, as tyrannical, stultifying 'status' once again supplanted 'contract' and defined, as in ancient law, the limits of human possibilities. The dynamic modern nation would, in short, revert to a dismal, stagnant 'stationary state' of the kind evident everywhere in the darker regions of the globe.

Maine thereby revealed the traditional strictures against radical reform, especially through social legislation, in a new light. He also identified a new order of danger lurking in the best intentions of sentimental do-gooders. Through his works, especially the later essays, judges, legislators, statesmen and the public-at-large all learned about the dire consequences of governmental interference with contract.

The fact that Maine's elegant work on the most esoteric subjects was so easily reduced to such an obvious defence of *laissez-faire*, a conservative political maxim congenial to the upper classes, made him appear, in many circles, to be a genuine political prophet. But not to everyone. In the early years of the century, even before 1914, change was in the air, and many persons, including members of his own class, found his politics less than persuasive, even obnoxious. Thus his jurisprudence often got lost, or became fatally entangled, in the furious political controversies that raged over the role of the modern State during the first half of the twentieth century.

The various political developments that culminated in the modern Welfare State were led by parties and persons who did not subscribe to the three basic notions upon which much of Maine's popular reputation, as a Victorian, depended. After 1914, when everything changed – including (to quote Dicey again) 'the classes then capable of influencing legislation' – many younger persons and most of the newer political parties (1) rejected the idea of legal evolution-cum-progress, (2) renounced or recanted all deference to

Germany and Germanic learning, including 'Historical Jurisprudence', and (3) engaged in open war over the policy of *laissez-faire*.

In that world, Maine ceased to be regarded as either a paragon or a prophet. Also, in that world, his jurisprudential theory often got overlooked or left behind.

III

So Maine and historical jurisprudence both fell from lofty perches. Today, I dare say, Maine is better remembered and more discussed by anthropologists than he is by lawyers. Also, as indicated earlier, historical jurisprudence is, realistically speaking far more robust in the form of legal history than it is as a part of jurisprudence as such. In fact, so far as I know, there are no contemporary advocates of historical jurisprudence, in any form, on the scene today.

I find this circumstance most troublesome. For if Maine teaches us anything at all, it must surely be that 'law', whatever it is, not only exists *in*, but also *through* time. Neither legal philosophers, who tend to focus on abstract theory, nor legal historians, who are primarily concerned with archival research, are likely to deal directly with the jurisprudential problems Maine, and others of the school of historical jurisprudence, identified. As a result, modern jurisprudence is, I think, the poorer – not because we no longer agree with Maine's conclusions, but because lawyers are denied the invitation, and opportunity, to share in speculation about such matters.

Indeed, Maine's major contribution to law, as we know it today, may well have been simply to have induced, by the sheer brilliance of his writings, one and possibly two generations of tough-minded, hard-headed lawyers into thinking about their subject in a totally new and fresh way. For he redefined the scope, in both time and space, of a subject which had been, in England anyway, for some five hundred years moulded and shaped by the legalistic conventions and practices of the monopolistic Inns of Court. The 'legal mind' – that proud hallmark of the common law Bench and Bar – brought much-needed discipline, including reason and patience, to a cadre of practitioners dealing with the numerous knots and fiendish backlashes which bedevil human existence. It did so, however, at the cost of forcing life into a narrow-necked bottle: the public knew nothing about the 'mysterious science of law', and the lawyers did not want to know about anything else

In England, Maine managed to drag the concept of law itself outside the confines of the legal monasteries, the Inns of Court, where it could be thought about and discussed in the context of extra-legal (historical, theological, moral, economic, social and political) influences. To traditional lawyers, he raised marvellous questions, offered improbable comparisons and inconceivable solutions to age-old legal puzzles, threw out elegant, unprovable generalizations, and then – died. As noted above, however, his legacy survives more under the rubrics of Legal Anthropology, Legal Sociology and Legal History than it does among lawyers.

Even so, however, once law (and here I mean the 'common law') was drawn outside its traditional confines, no one has succeeded in getting it altogether back in; and I dare say a major difference between late twentieth-century British and American law is that American law schools have been, comparatively, more responsive to demands to integrate the 'new' (i.e. since c. 1870) social sciences into legal education than have English law faculties. 'Sociological Jurisprudence', 'Legal Realism' and, more recently, 'Law and Economics' – to mention but three twentieth-century 'schools' of legal thought that have all stressed the importance of extra-legal factors in judicial law-making while discounting the value of traditional legal analysis (now disparagingly called 'formalism') – have exerted considerably more influence in America than England. Some of the major divergences in the development of the two common law-based systems in this century can be attributed to this difference.

Maine stimulated much of the interest that inspired the extra-legal approaches to law. Though it may be doubted that he would have taken much pride in many of the results of those particular movements, a conference commemorating the centenary of Maine's death is, nevertheless, an appropriate occasion to call – *à la* Savigny – for a revival of interest in some form of historical jurisprudence. Moreover, there can be no better place to initiate a revival of interest in such matters than in that bundle of provocative ideas Maine himself left behind. Accordingly, I shall, in the remainder of this chapter, consider briefly what I conceive to be the central jurisprudential issue running through Maine's work.

If we strip Maine's work of his personal biases and 'Victorian' mannerisms — all of which deflect our attention from his primary concern — we are left with his deliberations on the issue of 'legal change': where law comes from; why and how it changes; the stages legal systems pass through as they develop in complexity and sophistication; and, perhaps most important of all, the relationship between legal and social change. As would be expected, Maine gives us a plethora of hints, clues and possibilities about all these matters.

In the first place, he reminds us of a fact more familiar to the common-law world than to that of the continent: 'law' consists of more than a body of rules and theories; it embraces legal institutions, including pre-eminently courts, as well; and it is the procedures and practices pursued in those institutions — far more than any codified body of positive law itself — that determine the nature and role of the law of a given society.

Rather like the German historical school, Maine thus reminds us that law takes different forms in different societies, an observation that led him not to the extreme nationalism of the 'Germanists' but to wonder why such differences exist. Consequently, his concern about the different forms of legal institutions leads him to ponder, in a legal context, one of the questions that has haunted our century: why some societies are (in modern terminology) 'developed' and others remain 'undeveloped'. (Not surprisingly, he spoke of 'progressive' and 'stagnant' societies.)

He suggests that the kinds and forms of legal institutions adopted in a given society are of capital importance in answering the question. Unfortunately his idea has not been properly developed, in part because social scientists, particularly anthropologists, economists, sociologists and political scientists, rather than lawyers, have been most concerned with 'Third World' problems. Traditionally, social scientists have evaluated law and legal institutions from a quite different perspective from lawyers, who invariably see their subject from an 'inside', not to say proprietary, point of view. Thus in addressing the question, modern social scientists have emphasized such factors as economic growth and political power structures. Little attention has been given to the conditions conducive to the development of a cadre of legal officials committed to preserving and promoting the integrity of a legal process. Historical jurisprudence could, I think, develop the idea to our advantage.

Secondly, Maine suggests that those institutionalized procedures, as developed and refined by legal practitioners, not only become the essence of a slowly emerging body of 'substantive' law; they also make for (some) change and give (some) direction to change that is not predetermined by those who, at any given time, wield political power. He perceived, in short, that law – institutionalized law administered by a group of legal experts – develops, to some extent, a life of its own, a life than even sovereigns cannot change by fiat. (He leaves open the question whether the independent life of the law, as he describes it, stems from ideas inherent in the concept of 'law' itself, as the late Lon Fuller suggested, or whether it really depends upon the nurturing of a cadre of intellectually superior, politically discrete, and possibly economically motivated legal experts – similar to the jurisconsults of Roman law or the serjeants of the common law – who asserted such formative influences in shaping not only legal rules but the institutional practices themselves.)

Thirdly, we also learn, more from Maine's example than from his teachings, that the course of change in legal institutions does not necessarily stop at the point where the historian concludes his studies. Historians, like the rest of us, live in the latest, not the last, stage of historical change. Even so, if Maine described the process of legal change down to his own day in a plausible way, it is reasonable to assume that that process can be a basis for explaining the legal changes that have taken place since his death. That is, Maine's approach may be a key to understanding legal change in the twentieth century, a period during which the changes in the role, nature and uses made of law have been remarkable even in the long run of history as he defined it.

As is well known, Maine suggested that legal systems developed in ancient societies out of the chaos of anarchy. In fact he seems to have imagined a three-stage development: (1) ancient (pre-law) developments; (2) the legal stage, properly speaking; and (3) the post-law, or legislative, stage of popular governments.

The pre-law developments included vesting authority to resolve specific disputes in one person; generalizing such authority to extend to all disputes and vesting it in a king; and regal abuse of that authority leading to the enactment of a code by the aristocracy to define (and thereby curtail) the power of kings.

The second stage in the development of legal systems begins only after a code comes into being. Then, a legal system, including a cadre of legal experts and judges responsible for interpreting, applying and implementing the code, gradually emerges. Also, law (that is, the code plus the legal institutions making up the legal system) begins to take on a life of its own, one distinct from vulgar power-politics, religion, morality and even custom. That 'life' is shaped by various techniques devised by the legal experts who have, on the one hand, a personal stake in preserving the authority of the code itself and, on the other hand, practical incentives to make the legal system work with sufficient fairness to establish its credibility in the eyes of a suspicious and unforgiving public.

In order to ride these two horses at the same time, Maine recognized that the lawyers resorted, first, to legal 'fictions': they 'interpreted' the law so as to avoid the hard results occasioned by the rote application of the literal letter of the code to all cases. Thus, for example, the word 'man' might, in an appropriate contact, be construed to include (or exclude) 'woman', 'child' or 'slave'. In this piecemeal fashion, the lawyers gradually formulated certain 'canons of interpretation' similar in character to the hermeneutic tradition developed by the rabbis in interpreting the Torah and the exegetical conventions adopted by canon lawyers in expounding the New Testament. They thereby introduced nuance into the black letter of the monolithic code, and with it came the possibilities of adding new meaning and hence an unsuspected modicum of flexibility. No less important, the lawyers infused this dynamic element into law even as they publicly vindicated the authority of the code: rather than yielding to the public clamour to amend the code (and thereby weaken the idea that it was invincible), they accomplished the same result, while upholding the code, through fictitious interpretation.

In time, however, such acrobatic interpretations of the code become so far-fetched that the fictions strained the credulity of even legal minds. Thus the lawyers developed a second means of getting around the rigidity of the code without abrogating it. That is, they looked to a 'higher' authority than 'law'. In certain instances, they resorted to principles of 'equity' or 'conscience' or 'justice', extra-legal standards that 'transcend' rather than contradict the law. In the name of these higher principles, legal officials came to wield a kind of 'equitable discretion' authorizing them, in appropriate circumstances, to ignore the black letter. Thus, once again, the lawyers had introduced a new method of legal change, and a new source of flexibility, into the legal system, in a way that preserved the integrity of the code. For they firmly anchored the new, potentially disruptive authority/power of 'equitable discretion' in the legal system itself. Though the Roman praetors were laymen, they operated in a well-defined legal context; and the English chancellors, who were originally clerics acting in the name of 'good conscience', gradually became, literally, lawyers who wielded their 'equitable powers' in a Court of Chancery that increasingly reduced that discretion into 'Chancery law'.

So, Maine believed, legal systems developed their own internal means of propagating innovation, flexibility and the capacity to respond to changing social circumstances. Moreover, those forms of legal change remained within the control of members of the legal profession who had their own incentives to strengthen the legal system and the role of law in social affairs. Thus there emerged a kind of 'rule of law', to borrow his friend Dicey's famous phrase, that embodied its own internal values, including a powerful commitment to the procedures and processes of the legal system itself and a measure of genuine political independence. It allowed for some (anyway) legal change through its ordinary operation; and that leeway, combined with the autonomy inherent in a legal system's relative freedom from external (political) interference, gave rise to an institution with unique potential to accomplish major social change. That potential was realized by individuals freed from the tyranny of 'status' who sought a forum that would lend the force and authority of law to their private 'contracts'. The legal system became, in short, the vindicator not only of law but, no less important, of individual freedom to contract. Together, the two added up to that extraordinary 'progress' that catapulted the nations of Western Europe to a unique place in world history.

With the emergence of popular government, however, Maine seemed to imply that this remarkable stage in the development of law – I think he regarded it as the Halcyon Stage – was coming to an end. Legal evolution had moved to a totally different (post-law) stage. Whereas earlier power and authority over law had developed, via the code, from the king to the aristocracy–legal profession, it now gravitated from the lawyers to the representatives of 'the people'. As a result, law itself becomes increasingly less 'legal' and more 'political' in character as the major means of accomplishing legal change comes through the politically based legislature rather than the professionally controlled judiciary. Thus Maine feared that the integrity of the code and the rights of individuals (including the sanctity of contract) were at the mercy of a newly enfranchised mob possessing the power to change the law by new legislation whenever or wherever a majority of votes could be garnered.

So Maine seems to have envisioned the life-cycle of law: beginning in the chaos of anarchistic no-law, it ends in the chaos of too much law, a Niagara of ill-advised legislation. (He actually said that the greatest legal system the world had ever seen, that of Rome, 'begins with a code (the Twelve Tables) and ends with a code (the Code of Justinian)' – though, of course, the Empire came to an end not because of the code but because of the lawless Vandals.) Clearly his fear of democracy stemmed from the belief that the lower classes of Englishmen were tantamount to a horde of Vandals bent on destroying civilization. The only difference was that the Vandals used bludgeons while the English electorate would use legislation.

Such, is, I take it, a not unfair rendering of what Sir Frederick Pollock called Maine's 'natural history of law', though I have stressed the jurisprudential rather than the anthropological aspects of the matter. It was a heady account of the role law had played in bringing society out of the stagnant doldrums of pre-law custom and nudging it persistently, over long spans of time, to the modernity of Maine's own day. But from then on, his vision of the future became progressively gloomier.

I think Maine's baleful vision of the future, especially his predictions about the future of law, have proved to be wrong in some instructive ways. For both civilization and law did survive the crises he anticipated. Indeed, it may be that in the United States, anyway, the life of the law (in the sense of legal change brought about by judicial, rather than legislative, action) is more robust today than it ever was during his lifetime. Hence it seems fair to ask what has happened, jurisprudentially, since Maine's day. Or, more bluntly, where did Maine go wrong?

In one sense, Maine's pessimism about the future of law reflected the limitations of the imagery associated with his own ideas about 'legal evolution'. His notion of 'progress' carried with it the idea of motion in one direction, if not in a straight line; and that direction was from a state of moral inferiority (custom-enforced status) to a 'higher' state of moral development (law-sanctioned contract). At the same time, his notion of 'evolution' carried with it, in a human context anyway, the idea of a life-cycle consisting of various stages of development ending inevitably in death. When, therefore, he began to doubt that his own society was moving towards a higher moral level of existence, he stopped thinking in terms of 'progress'. He then switched to the 'life-cycle' imagery of legal evolution – the last stage of which is death. The death of civilization, I might add, was a recurrent theme in *fin de siècle* Europe, especially Vienna. As noted earlier, many of Maine's contemporaries experienced the gravest personal crisis as Great Britain faced and underwent its greatest social and constitutional upheaval since Cromwell's day.

IV

If one wished to build on Maine's jurisprudential speculations about the course of legal change, one should perhaps start by rejecting his imagery. Rather than thinking, as he did, in terms of law evolving either in straight-line lower-to-higher 'progress' or in a birth-to-death 'life-cycle', one might imagine his history of law describing a helix. Starting in the chaos of (no-law) anarchy, law emerges as a spiral circling upwards to higher levels not of morality but of legal/institutional complexity. So conceived, Maine described several turns of the helix before he summarily assumed the process was about to end.

Starting from the chaos of no-law, the *first* turn of the helix included the rise of the kingship as a solution to the problem, but culminated in a new crisis stemming not from no-law anarchy but from the threat of tyranny by a lawless king. Thus the *second* turn began with the search for a means of curbing the power of the crown and ends with a code defining the scope of the king's authority. The *third* turn begins with the king constrained by the code and ends with a new crisis caused by the rigidity of the code itself. The *fourth* turn begins with the threatened legal paralysis of the code and ends with an autonomous legal system that has developed its own internal means of accomplishing legal change within the code. The *fifth* turn begins with a legal system administered autonomously by legal professionals and ends with a political struggle between the professionals, who claim the authority to control the legal system, including the manner and the means of legal change, and the public who claim, as free citizens, the right to make and to change law through legislation in accordance with social needs rather than strict legalistic standards. To Maine, 'politicizing' law, by allowing indiscriminate change through legislation, was tantamount to the death of law itself.

At that point in the history of the helix, Maine concluded his analysis. Also, of course, it is at that precise point that his analysis would be most pertinent to modern jurisprudence. For he clearly saw the impending crisis that would set the stage for a new turn of the helix. He also anticipated many of the problems with which legal thinkers of the twentieth century have had to grapple; and, even without providing answers to those problems, his elongated perspective is, at least to me, most suggestive.

For example, if Maine were right – if, that is, the lay public's claim to the right to control law through legislation reduced all law to politics – we might expect one response to that threat to be similar to that of an earlier stage in the history he himself described. As early societies created kings to bring order to the chaos of anarchy, so modern societies might be expected to look for a king-like 'strongman' to bring order to the chaos created by the lay public's having the power to change law. Controlling the electorate, in short, would be seen as a major problem calling for extreme measures. This is to say that the emergence of right-wing (law-and-order) strong-men, such as Mussolini, Hitler and Franco, in the wake of growing working-class political power, cannot be a great surprise. After all, the threat of chaos brought about by radical legislation is not that different from chaos brought about by anarchy. Nor is it surprising that left-wing strong-men, sympathetic to the causes of the working classes rather than to the established legal order, came to power in the same circumstances.

Interestingly, both disciplinarians of Demos – the Fascists on the right and the Communists on the left – deplored and distanced themselves from the relatively autonomous and non-political legal system. (Hitler's Werner Best demeaned the legal process with a disdain similar to that which Pashukanis expressed in his Marxist jurisprudence.) Oddly enough, it was chiefly in the United States where the philosophy of judging and the theory of legal change underwent the most profound jurisprudential change, largely as a result of the Legal Realists, that the legal (Bench-and-Bar) profession kept the firmest grip on legal change.

Maine would probably be pleasantly surprised to see a judiciary maintaining firm control over legal change in an alleged egalitarian society. Whether he would approve the decisions of American courts, or even the directions in which American law and society appear, at any point in time, to be moving, is another matter. Only someone interested in historical jurisprudence is likely to care.

CHAPTER 14

Further thoughts on Maine's historical jurisprudence
David E. C. Yale

Popular Government, the last of Maine's publications, seems to me a profoundly pessimistic book, deeply depressing to read. Having come to doubt political progress, Maine regards with horror the prospect of the enfranchised mob throwing its weight on the lever of legislation: 'we are', he thinks, 'propelled by an irresistible force on a definite path towards an unavoidable end – towards Democracy, as towards Death' (*PG*: 170). Whether the life-cycle analogy is valid, I don't know, but I do know that it was a relief to turn back to *Ancient Law*, the younger book, full of optimism, and opening doors in so many directions.

Ancient Law has been much discussed in the context of Maine's own day, in the writings of Burrow, Stein and others, as well as in this volume, and rather than attempt to add to that, it seems to me that I should offer some remarks on what I think Maine has still to say to us today. I think the residual value lies in his method. Though Maine does not explain his methodology in any one place, there are remarks and recommendations scattered through his writings. These are well worth looking for, since they are often of current utility. Some examples:

(1) When discussing intestate succession, he comments that 'the grand source of mistake in questions of jurisprudence is the impression that those reasons which actuate us at the present moment, in the maintenance of an existing institution, have necessarily anything in common with the sentiment in which the institution originated' (*AL*: 189). This is a lesson which it has taken legal historians a long time to learn, particularly those brought up in a school of law, and the advice applies to rules and principles as well as to institutions. The reasons which sustain rules change, even if the rules do not. The forces tending towards preservation or perishing are of an ever-changing nature.

(2) Another example might be Maine's remark that ancient concepts and ancient terms are 'subjected to a process of gradual specialization. An ancient legal conception corresponds not to one but to several modern conceptions. An ancient technical expression serves to indicate a variety of things which in modern law have separate names allotted to them.' Later on change occurs, and we find that 'the subordinate conceptions have gradually disengaged themselves and that the old general names are giving way to special appellations. The old general conception is not obliterated, but it has ceased to cover more than one or a few of the notions which it first included. So too the old technical name remains, but it discharges only one of the functions which it once performed' (*AL*: 316).

Now, one might associate this last example with an idea of variation or differentiation of species, or the first example with a principle of survival through adaptation. But what is of current value here, I suggest, is the advice Maine offers on how to look for change, the frameworks for perspective which he provides; and *Ancient Law* is a book which (despite its errors and omissions) remains alive for that reason.

(3) Again, in Maine's discussion of occupancy as a root title and of the origins of property, one reads that 'The sentiment in which this doctrine [*occupatio*] originated is absolutely irreconcilable with that infrequency and uncertainty of proprietary rights which distinguish the beginnings of civilization. Its true basis seems to be, not in an instinctive bias towards the institution of Property, but a presumption arising out the long continuance of that institution, that *everything ought to have an owner*' (*AL*: 256).

Whether Maine is right or wrong about the way in which early societies regard the acquisition of *res nullius*, an object not previously acquired or an object previously abandoned, is beside my point. He alerts one here to the process of *ex post facto* legal rationalization when he suggests that the acquirer becomes the owner because things are presumed to be someone's property, and then the legal notion is grafted on to the fact of sole possession and retention by the first acquirer. The legal concept is not anterior to the practice; it simply tries to explain the fact.

(4) One obvious feature of Maine's method is that he worked with a broad brush. This was evident to his earliest reviewers, as it is to us. Thus Fitzjames Stephen said that Maine 'made in the most

beautiful manner applications of history and philosophy to Roman Law, and transfigured one of the driest of subjects with all sorts of beautiful things without knowing or caring much about details' (quoted in L. Stephen, 1895: 101).

Today we may not take Maine's Roman law on trust. Anyone expounding the subject now needs to depart frequently from Maine's view of certain matters. But the generalizations must command attention whether they attract or repel the reader. Maine himself described this process of abstraction by writing that 'all abstraction consists in dropping out of sight a certain number of particular facts, and constructing a formula which will embrace the remainder; and the comparative value of general propositions turns entirely on the relative importance of the particular facts selected and the particular facts rejected' (*PG*: 107). This selectivity is, I suppose, one reason why Maitland distrusted Maine's approach to historical exposition, that is, the exclusion of the qualifications, and it is of course the case that Maine disdained footnotes and detailed deployment of the evidence. And he could be guilty of distortion, as when he rebuked Blackstone for 'elaborate sophistry' in explaining the exclusion of the half-blood in inheritance and then forced the rule into his own view of the agnatic family. But to be fair to Maine, it seems to me that though he appears all too often to be theorizing ahead of the evidence when his generalizations appear in the form of conclusions, and unqualified conclusions at that, nevertheless these generalizations still can be usefully taken as hypotheses, and have value if we read them as questions rather than as answers. Moreover, Maine was capable of some caution. We have heard some discussion of 'hitherto' in the status-to-contract theory. He does offer some cautionary remarks on the famous fiction–equity–legislation sequence. He does not offer it as an invariable historical sequence.

Finally, it seems to me, as one interested in the history of the common law, that it is strange that Maine did not make more use of that customary law which in a sense lay closest to hand. True, he started as a classicist, he took up Roman law, and then widened his jurisprudential horizons (there is comparative use of Indian legal customs in *Ancient Law*, though later he needed to change some of his views in that direction). But apart from Kemble and Anglo-Saxon texts he was not much beyond Blackstone, a hundred years earlier, in his use of native customary law. Yet in his own time books were beginning to appear quite modern in style compared with Blackstone and Reeves: Forsyth on the history of trial by jury, Wilson on the history of English law since the Middle Ages, and Digby on the history of the land law. Was it that the literary state of the materials for early English law was obscure to him, or that he lacked the willingness to embark on the detailed examination undertaken a generation later by Vinogradoff and Maitland? Certainly, he does not seem as at home in the common law as in the civil law, and the deficiency is apparent in *Ancient Law* as a work of comparative jurisprudence. But perhaps the residual value of Maine today is not in the information he gave us about evolving or static legal systems, but in his thoughts on the processes by which societies come by their own laws and how those processes may be interpreted.

CHAPTER 15

Fictions, equity and legislation: Maine's three agencies of legal change

Alan Diamond

Maine's great contribution to the study of legal change is his identification of fictions, equity and legislation as the mechanisms by which law is brought into harmony with changing social conditions. Maine was clearly not the first person to recognize the utility of these mechanisms, but his crisp formulation remains memorable, and the evolutionary twist which he gave to this scheme has proved to be fruitfully controversial.

The first three chapters of *Ancient Law* are concerned with the evolution of legal systems. According to Maine, all societies (or at any rate, what he referred to as the Indo-European societies) evolve from a stage at which there is virtually no rule of law at all, where men are subject only to the caprice of 'the patriarchal despotism' (*AL*: 8), to an 'epoch of Customary Law, and of its custody by a privileged order' (13). From there, 'We arrive at the era of Codes, those ancient codes of which the Twelve Tables of Rome were the most famous specimen' (14). With the adoption of a code, which according to Maine was simply the embodiment in words of the existing customs, the 'spontaneous development' of law comes to an end (21). It is with the coming of the epoch of codes that 'the distinction between stationary and progressive societies begins to make itself felt' (22). In part, the progressive societies are distinguished by the fact that their codes were obtained at an earlier stage of their social progress, a stage at which 'usage was still wholesome' (16, 20). Moreover, these codes were merely codifications of the existing customs of the people, whereas 'the codes obtained by Eastern societies [which] were obtained, relatively, much later than by Western . . . wore a very different character' (17). For one thing, they were composed 'not so much of the rules actually observed as of the rules which the priestly order considered proper to be observed' (17). For another, they were compiled after the customary rules had been subjected to 'a law of development which ever threatens to operate upon unwritten usage', so 'that usage which is reasonable generates usage which is unreasonable' (19). More importantly, in time the codes, whether embodying wholesome or unwholesome usage, became rigid, and remote from contemporary life. In the progressive societies, there is a gradual amelioration of the rigidity of the codes; in the stationary societies, there is none (22–4). In the progressive societies, law is made to be responsive to 'social necessities and social opinion', but in the stationary societies, 'instead of the civilization expanding the law, the law has limited the civilization' (23). It is at this stage that we encounter Maine's famous generalization about the agencies of legal change:

A general proposition of some value may be advanced with respect to the agencies by which Law is brought into harmony with society. These instrumentalities seem to me to be three in number, Legal Fictions, Equity and Legislation. Their historical order is that in which I have placed them. (24–5)

Maine's scheme, however, has been found 'difficult to square with the English experience' (Baker, 1979: 170). There are two reasons for this, the first of which arises from the generalization itself: the English experience suggests an interplay among these instrumentalities, rather than an evolution from fictions to equity, and then to legislation. Second, Maine defines his terms 'in a broad sense rather than in the technical sense familiar to English lawyers' (Baker, 1979: 170). Thus, Maine defines fictions so as to include both statutory interpretation and judicial decision-making, and equity so as to emphasize not the procedural advantages offered by the Court of Chancery, which allowed that court to supplement, correct and aid the common law, but a view of equity as a superior kind of law, as a kind of natural justice, with an inherent claim to override the municipal law. Despite these shortcomings, if shortcomings they are, Maine's tripartite scheme has proved invaluable; indeed Baker himself presses it into service to describe the various ways in which law is made (1979: Chapter 12). Moreover, the very breadth of Maine's definitions and the ambitiousness of his claim that the instrumentalities of legal change can be placed in historical sequence make his generalization enormously suggestive. Most importantly, Maine's dictum served in its time, and continues to serve, to concentrate the minds of lawyers on law, 'not only [as it] exists *in*, but also *through* time' (Woodard, p. 228 above). And, to borrow Professor Shils' term, it provides a useful set of 'categorial spectacles' with which to view the history of widely disparate legal systems (see p. 173 above). In the end, Maine's definitions may call into question the validity of the tripartite scheme itself.

Maine admits to employing 'the word "fiction" in a sense considerably wider than that in which English lawyers are accustomed to use it, and with a meaning much more extensive than that which belonged to the Roman "fictiones" ' (*AL*: 25). In its strictest sense, in both Roman and English law, the term 'fiction'

signifie[d] a false averment on the part of the plaintiff which the defendant was not allowed to traverse [the purpose of which was invariably to give the court jurisdiction]; such, for example, as an averment that the plaintiff was a Roman citizen, when in truth he was a foreigner ... [or] the allegations in the writs of the English Queen's Bench and Exchequer by which those courts contrived to usurp the jurisdiction of the Common Pleas. (*AL*: 25–6)

In fact, even as so strictly conceived, fictional allegations had a purpose beyond the merely jurisdictional:

Fictions were also used to extend substantive remedies, the most familiar examples being the false allegation of deceit in assumpsit, the false allegation of a loss and finding in trover, the false allegation of a lease and ouster in ejectment, and the collusive common recovery. (Baker, 1979: 175–6)

Maine, however, uses the term 'fiction' in a far broader sense, one which includes the classic fictions just mentioned, but which refers as well to 'any assumption which conceals, or affects to conceal, the fact that a rule of law has undergone alteration, its letter remaining unchanged, its operation being modified' (*AL*: 26). Each such fiction performs the 'two-fold office of transforming a system of laws and of concealing the transformation' (30). This definition throws a revealing light on the very nature of the common-law system. For it is not only the most obvious fictions which transform the law while concealing the transformation; the case-law method, the very heart and soul of the common law, does so as well. Maine calls the process of judicial decision-making 'virtual legislation', a procedure which 'is not so much insensible as unacknowledged' (31). In this regard, he comments:

When a group of facts come before an English court for adjudication, the whole course of the discussion between the judge and the advocates assumes that no question is, or can be, raised which will call for the application of any principles but old ones, or any distinctions but such as have long since been allowed. It is taken absolutely for granted that there is somewhere a rule of known law which will cover the facts of the dispute now litigated ... Yet the moment the judgement has been rendered and reported, we slide unconsciously or unavowedly into a new language and a new train of thought. We now admit that the new decision *has* modified the law. The rules applicable have ... become more elastic. In fact they have been changed ... (31–2)

Since the time that Maine wrote, we have come to recognize that many allegations which become fictional begin in situations of genuine uncertainty. For example, allegations of deceit in actions of assumpsit (essentially actions for breach of oral contracts) first appear in situations where there really is an element of sharp-dealing. Similarly, the assertion that judges simply declare the already existing law but do not change it, or make new law, is, as applied to the Middle Ages, more a statement of actual fact than a fiction calculated to conceal judicial legislation. In the Middle Ages, the common-law courts 'made' law infrequently; and, when they did, it was usually in the course of pleading, and it was often implicit, to be gathered from the fact that one counsel withdrew a point, rather than explicit, i.e. pronounced from the bench. Moreover, this law 'was not law laid down by the court so much as law which was accepted learning within the profession: "common erudition", as it is called in the old books' (Baker 1979: 172).

Thus, it could be said that the early common-law courts essentially did declare existing law, rather than creating new law. But for the post-medieval legal world, Maine's insight is valuable. Even today, when a precedent is overruled, the courts usually find that the original decision was wrongly decided; rarely do they own up to the fact that a change in social conditions has necessitated a change in the law. Maine also perceived a fictional element in the act of interpreting the written word, whether embodied in reports of case decisions, or in legislative enactments. Maine's view was that the act of interpretation was itself a kind of legal fiction which permitted the judges in effect to amend or ameliorate the written law without in fact being seen to do so; while the act of interpretation left the black letter of the code, the statute, and the case decision unchanged, it altered their scope and operation. The judges had made no overt amendment to the authoritative legal source, but had simply engaged in the inescapable act of interpreting its meaning. By creative interpretation, troublesome precedents could be confined; or, to use Professor Allen's phrase, 'sterilise[d] by the semi-fictions of "distinguishing" them on tenuous grounds of fact or law' (1964: 357). Statutory terms could be expanded or contracted as the judges saw fit.

Maine illustrates this by reference to 'A body of law bearing a very close and very instructive resemblance to our case-law' – the Responsa Prudentum of the Roman law (*AL*: 33). The Responsa were the answers of the learned Roman jurists to questions of law, and largely 'consisted of explanatory glosses on authoritative written documents, and at first they were exclusively collections of opinions interpretative of the Twelve Tables' (33). These glosses proceeded on the assumption 'that the text of the old Code remained unchanged'; its express rules 'overrode all glosses and comments, and no one openly admitted that any interpretation of it, however eminent the interpreter, was safe from revision on appeal to the venerable texts' (33–4). Yet, the responses of the leading jurists 'obtained an authority at least equal to that of our reported cases, and constantly modified, extended, limited or practically overruled the provisions of the Decemviral law' (34). The jurists 'professed the most sedulous respect for the letter of the Code. They were merely explaining it, deciphering it, bringing out its full meaning' (34). By the art of interpretation, however, the jurists 'introduced nuance into the black letter of the monolithic code, and with it came the possibilities of adding new meaning and hence an unsuspected modicum of flexibility' (Woodard, p. 232 above). Indeed, by their efforts the jurists 'educed a vast variety of canons which had never been dreamed of by the compilers of the Twelve Tables and which were in truth rarely or never to be found there' (*AL*: 34).

The breadth of Maine's definition of fictions compels us to rethink the basis on which Maine distinguishes equity, 'The next instrumentality by which the adaptation of law to social wants is carried on' (*AL*: 28). Equity as defined by Maine is 'any body of rules existing by the side of the original civil law, founded on distinct principles and claiming incidentally to supersede the civil law in virtue of a superior sanctity inherent in those principles' (28). Equity, 'whether of the Roman Praetors or of the English Chancellors, differs from the Fictions which in each case [i.e. Rome and England] preceded it, in that the interference with law is open and avowed' (28). In the English experience, there is some truth in this distinction, but perhaps less than meets the eye. For it is the central boast of English equity that it acts in personam only; that it never interferes with the law, but only with the conscience of the defendant; that, indeed, it comes not to destroy the law, but to fulfil it. In fact, the interference is considerable and, as a result of the in personam distinction, as covert as in the case of fictions.

In the common law, for example, if a debtor paid his debt, but failed to obtain back his bond, or otherwise to have it cancelled, he could be forced to pay the debt a second time, on account of the rule that the bond was conclusive evidence of the debt. Under these circumstances, the Chancellor took to relieving debtors, by enjoining creditors from proceeding at law, and ordering them to turn over the cancelled bonds to their debtors. Of course, the rule remained the same: in all cases, a bond was conclusive evidence of a debt, and the defendant at law could not raise a defence of payment. In practice, however, looking at the English legal system as a whole, the rule had been modified. Even more problematic was the equitable practice of enjoining a successful plaintiff at law from enforcing his judgement. Again, the party line of Chancery's defenders was that the injunction operated on the party, and did not purport to interfere with the legal rule, or the legal judgement. But, of course, in practice the judgement was useless, and the rule of law on which the judgement had been based had no practical value. In short, the claim by the Court of Chancery that it operated only on the person, not on the rule, seems simply to be a device, to use Maine's definition of a legal fiction, 'which conceals, or affects to conceal, the fact that a rule of law has undergone alteration, its letter remaining unchanged, its operation being modified' (*AL*: 26). Indeed, there is the recent phenomenon of the *Anton Piller* order, by which a plaintiff, or his nominees, may obtain access to a defendant's residence or business premises and search for and remove documents and physical property relevant to the claim. In defending the order against the charge that it constituted a civil search warrant issued to a private party, Lord Denning relied on a variation of the traditional Chancery distinction between declaring rights and ordering the performance of duties, between operating on or declaring the legal rule and acting in personam on the conscience of the party. On the one hand, he affirmed that if a 'constable or bailiff... knock[s] at the door and demand[s] entry so as to inspect papers or documents, the householder can shut the door in his face and say "Get out." ' On the other hand, Lord Denning insisted:

> the order sought in this case is not a search warrant. It does not authorise the plaintiffs' solicitors or anyone else to enter the defendants' premises against their will ... The plaintiffs must get the defendants' permission. But it does do this: it brings pressure on the defendants to give permission. It does more. It actually orders them to give permission – with, I suppose, the result that if they do not give permission, they are guilty of contempt of court. (*Anton Piller KG* v. *Manufacturing Processes*, [1976] 1 All ER 779 at 782–3)

In some sense, then, English equity, like English case law, can be seen as resting on a fiction. Indeed, even legislation, the most open and avowed form of legal change, may be seen as implicated with the notion of fictions. I am not here speaking of the kind of fiction which is suggested by Maine himself when he speaks of the legislature as 'the assumed organ of the entire society' (*AL*: 29). For that is not a fiction which conceals the fact that a rule of law has undergone alteration. I am speaking once again of the art of statutory interpretation. As Professor Allen has observed:

> a very great, and perhaps the most important, part of the operation of statute is indissolubly dependent on the function of the judge. To ignore this intermediate stage between the 'will' of the Sovereign and the 'obedience' of the subject is to falsify completely the actual operation of statutory law and society. It is the unfortunate but inevitable consequence of this fact that interpretation sometimes results in the opposite of what the legislator seems to have intended ... (1964: 502)

May we not say of this result what Maine says of legal fictions: 'the *fact* is ... that the law has been wholly changed; the *fiction* is that it remains what it always was' (*AL*: 26)?

We have seen that Maine's insistence that his three agents of legal change appear in an invariable historical sequence has been criticized as inconsistent with the English experience. And it is certainly true that fictions continue to play a role in legal development after the establishment of the Court of Chancery, and that legislation plays a role in the legal development of the common law from the very outset, and an important role during the reigns of Edward I and Henry VIII. Still, Maine's sequence seems roughly right, particularly when we remember that he limits his proposition 'respecting their order of sequence to the periods at which they exercise a sustained and substantial influence in transforming the original law' (*AL:* 25). Surely, for example, we can recognize the nineteenth century as ushering in the age of legislation, in a way which was not true of the age of Edward I or even of Henry VIII. Beyond this, however, Maine's historical sequence, right or wrong, has proven to be fruitful.

As we have observed, after embodying customary law in a code, some societies, the progressive societies, go on to develop, in Professor Woodard's words, 'their own internal means of propagating innovation, flexibility and the capacity to respond to changing social circumstances' (p. 233 above). These are, in fact, the three instrumentalities of legal change identified by Maine: fictions, equity and legislation. If the movement from status to contract takes society to the apex of progress, can the same be said of the movement from fictions to legislation? Is legislation the final ameliorating instrumentality, or is there some agent of change that takes over after the era of legislation arrives? In answering these questions, we first may observe that Maine does not seem to see the coming of the era of legislation as a negative development in and of itself. It is simply the appropriate agent of change for the appropriate stage at which the legal system has arrived. Maine is not reactionary. Fictions, for example,

> have had their day, but it is long since gone by. It is unworthy of us to effect an admittedly beneficial object by so rude a device as a legal fiction ... If the English law is ever to assume an orderly distribution, it will be necessary to prune away the legal fictions which, in spite of some recent legislative improvements, are still abundant in it. (*AL:* 27–8)

The same could be said of equity in that, as we have seen, it also keeps alive legal rules which have been altered or voided by its operation. It is only when legislation is co-joined with popular government, when the levers of legislation are controlled not by legal experts but by the common man, that the movement from fictions to legislation can be seen as a movement in the direction of decline. In this volume, Woodard speaks of 'law itself becom[ing] increasingly less "legal" and more "political" in character as the major means of accomplishing legal change comes through the politically based legislature rather than the professionally controlled judiciary' (p. 234 above). Viewed this way, Maine's description of the development of legal systems envisions a 'life-cycle of law: beginning in the chaos of anarchistic no-law, it ends in the chaos of too much law, a Niagara of ill-advised legislation' (p. 234 above). Yet, even if the advent of popular government was, for Maine, the beginning of the end of a life-cycle, his tripartite scheme need not be interpreted so pessimistically. Essentially adopting Maine's own evolutionary scheme, one commentator has seen a stage beyond legislation, marked by judicial review of legislative enactments (White, 1973: 655). And perhaps Maine himself perceived this later stage in his description of the American constitutional process in *Popular Government*.

In identifying legal fictions and equity as primary instrumentalities of legal change, Maine focussed attention not only on the way in which law adapts itself to the changing conditions of the larger society but on the way in which legal systems reform themselves, develop 'their own *internal* means of propagating innovation, flexibility and the capacity to respond to changing social circumstances' (see Woodard, p. 233 above). In this, Maine anticipates the work of modern legal historians like Professors Baker and Milsom. While I would not wish to try to pin-point the areas in which Maine may have directly influenced either man, it seems abundantly clear that their work is part of a tradition of legal history and jurisprudence of which Maine is a prominent ancestor.

In his Introduction to the reports of John Spelman, Professor Baker has demonstrated the way in which the common law, faced with a renaissance in legal ideas and fierce competition from newer jurisdictions, particularly the Court of Chancery, reformed itself from within, providing litigants with new remedies and streamlined procedures, while leaving the old forms of action in place and theoretically inviolate. Where once an action for breach of contract would have been brought by a writ of covenant or of debt, now the action of assumpsit was available, and with it the assurance that questions of fact would be tried by jury, rather than by wager of law. Where once title to land had to be tried in one of the slow, archaic real actions, now, through the use of perhaps the most blatant fictions ever practised in English legal history, title could be tried in the new action of ejectment, which provided a speedy remedy and a streamlined procedure. We cannot ignore Maine's scheme if we are to understand this change, for much of it is accomplished through the use of fictions and by an appeal to the Chancellor's equitable powers. On the other hand, we need to go further than Maine if we are to understand fully the dynamics of the process by which the common law reformed itself.

Viewing the English legal system as a whole, there is no question that the remedies given by the Court of Chancery did much to ameliorate the rigidities of the common law, and to bring the legal system into the modern age. The common-law system was rooted in the feudal era, and was concerned primarily with questions of the possession and ownership of land; and its procedures, including trial by jury, were peculiarly appropriate to such questions, but were less satisfactory, indeed often inimical, to the kinds of disputes thrown up by the commercial society which England was rapidly becoming. Moreover, this commercial society required legal remedies beyond those which the common law was prepared to give: remedies like specific performance, accounting and injunctive relief were available exclusively from the Court of Chancery. It was, however, equity's enforcement of the use (what we today call the trust), by which the legal and beneficial ownership of land was separated, which most vividly illustrates the way in which equity relieved litigants from the strictures of outmoded legal rules. According to the rule of primogeniture, all of a man's real property descended upon his death to his eldest son. He might, during his lifetime, make *inter vivos* grants of such land to others, subject to certain constraints to preserve the eldest son's inheritance, but he could not leave real property by will; whatever had not been conveyed to others at his death passed automatically to his eldest son. By conveying property to third parties to hold to his own benefit during his lifetime, and to convey to other persons, younger sons or daughters, for example, upon his death, a landowner could in effect make a will. The common law, however, did not recognize, and to this day does not recognize, beneficial ownership in land. The persons to whom the land had been conveyed, to hold in trust for the benefit of the original landowner, had the sole legal title. In enforcing the use, the Chancellor did not meddle with this legal title. He did not allow men to make wills. He did not purport to repeal the rule of primogeniture. In reality, however, the common-law rules were completely circumvented whenever a man chose to place his property in trust, with instructions to the trustees to deliver the property in accordance with his instructions at death. In short, the distinction between operating only on the conscience of the party and meddling with the rule itself was so refined in practice as to amount to a fiction. None the less, this is an important distinction, because the Chancellor's intervention was indeed open and avowed, despite the unreality of his assertion that the legal rule was never disturbed.

But the English legal system was not only reformed by recourse to the Chancellor's jurisdiction, since the greater part of the reform came from within the common-law system itself. Some of this was accomplished by fictions as strictly conceived; but much change was the result of a fourth agent of change, one which Professor Milsom has identified as reclassification. In order to understand this process, we must say something about classification in the law. At the most elementary level, the common law distinguished between claims to enforce a right and claims to obtain compensation for a wrong. Two families of writs grew up reflecting this elemental difference: the *praecipe* writs involved claims in which, at least in theory, the defendant could still put the matter right by performing his obligation: repaying the loan, building the house, delivering the goods, vacating the land from which the plaintiff had been ejected, and so on. The second family of writs, the *ostensurus quare* writs, involved situations where the defendent had done an irreparable wrong; there was nothing to put right, and the plaintiff's only remedy was in damages.[1] Within each family of writs, there were further classifications of claims, and these came to be known as the forms of action, legal boxes into which claims had to be fitted if they were to be cognizable at common law. A choice of a form of action was a choice as well of a particular procedure and even a particular substantive law (see, for example, Maitland, 1909: 298; Baker, 1979: 52).

The separation of various claims into different legal pigeon-holes created the conditions by which law could be reformed from within. The process of reclassification involves taking a set of facts, a claim for relief, which naturally falls within one class of writs, and reclassifying it so as to bring it within a different form of action in the other class of writs. So, in the classic common law, an action to recover for damages for breach of a promise to perform services would sound in covenant, i.e. the plaintiff would be required to purchase a writ of covenant, and would be bound by all the procedures associated with that particular writ or form of action, one of which was the require-

---

[1] In fact, at an early date, the common law limited itself to giving damages, whether the claim sought performance of an obligation or compensation for an irreparable wrong, except in real property actions, in which the common-law courts continued to award the return of the property.

ment that no action could be brought except on a written promise under seal. A plaintiff who had not obtained a written agreement under seal was thus left with the choice of suing in the local courts, where no such requirement obtained; but, in the event that his claim was in excess of forty shillings, he had to sue in the royal courts, and without a document under seal, he was in effect without a remedy. But if his claim could be seen not as one sounding in covenant but one sounding in trespass, i.e. not as a question of a performance of a right but of compensation for a wrong, he could avoid the requirement of a document under seal, and bring an action for damages in the royal courts. Thus legal change 'is largely brought about by re-classification, by transferring the matter from, say, contract to tort' (Milsom, 1981: 7). And this involves nothing less than 'the abuse of [the] elementary ideas' of the common law, so that:

If the rules of property give what now seems an unjust answer, try obligation ... If the rules of contract give what now seems an unjust answer, try tort ... if the rules of one tort, say deceit, give what now seems an unjust answer, try another, try negligence ...' (Milsom, 1981: 6)

As with the operation of legal fictions and equitable remedies, the legal rule, the requirement of a document under seal, was not directly altered or repealed. But the consequence of the legal rule was avoided by reclassifying the claim as one of trespass. Legal change by reclassification thus 'has the appearance of a conjuring trick: out of the old hat there comes a new rabbit' (Milsom, 1985: 150). The sleight of hand is important, for the court cannot be seen to attack the legal rule directly, nor can anyone be explicitly granted an exemption from the operation of the rule. Rather, the case itself must be removed from the operation of the rule, and this is done by giving it a new name, a new classification. What was essential was the existence of different compartments, because 'the rabbit is really taken from a different hat' (Milsom, 1985: 152). Thus,

The abolition of the forms of action may well have made major change more difficult for the courts, by making it harder to reverse the result without openly reversing the rule. The continued existence of a partially formal barrier between law and equity may be a condition of the continued potency of equity as a means of law reform; its *in personam* operation has always been the most artless means of making a change without actually saying so ... (Milsom, 1985: 153)

Whether expressly intended as such or not, Milsom's work, it seems to me, builds upon and modifies Maine's original scheme. Moreover, Maine in some ways anticipates Milsom's reclassification theory, or at least that part of the theory which recognizes the importance of legal classification as a means of facilitating legal change. To appreciate this, we need to turn to Maine's discussion of the distinction in Roman law between *res mancipi* and *res nec mancipi*, which he called 'the type of a class of distinctions to which civilization is much indebted' (*AL*: 279). The *res mancipi* were those things capable of being transferred only by the mode of transfer known as *mancipatio*, and included land, slaves and such animals as horses and oxen. The *res nec mancipi* were things which could be conveyed by a mode other than *mancipatio*, primarily the informal mode of conveyance known as *traditio* or tradition.

The treatment in Roman law of the *res mancipi* was, according to Maine, typical of 'the universally unmalleable character of the ancient forms of property'. Thus:

Sometimes the patrimony of the family is absolutely inalienable ... and still oftener, though alienations may not be entirely illegitimate, they are virtually impracticable ... from the necessity of having the consent of a large number of persons to the transfer ... [Or] ... the act of conveyance itself is generally burdened with a perfect load of ceremony, in which not one iota can be safely neglected. (*AL*: 271–2)

How then are 'These various obstacles to the free circulation of the objects of use and enjoyment' surmounted? (272). There are various 'expedients by which advancing communities endeavour to overcome' these obstacles, including legal fictions and equity (272). In England, as we have seen, a landowner is able to circumvent the rule of primogeniture by granting his property to trustees, who are obligated at his death to convey the property in accordance with his instructions. And Maine recognizes that fictions and equity played a role in reforming the Roman law of property as well, since these 'Two ... agents of legal amelioration ... were assiduously employed by the Roman lawyers to give the practical effects of a Mancipation to a Tradition' (278–9). But reform in the law of property was also brought about by the manipulation of legal classification, i.e. by an expedient 'which takes precedence of the rest from its antiquity and universality', the expedient of 'classify[ing] property into kinds', a higher order and a lower one (272). This is seen in the division between the higher order of *res mancipi* and the lower one of *res nec mancipi*, one requiring archaic ceremonies to effect its transfer, the other not; and also in English law, in the distinction between moveables and immovables. In time, objects originally classified among the lower order of property, and thus relieved from the obstacles placed on alienation, increased in value, or a new awareness grew that their value or prominence was equal to, if it did not surpass, the objects placed among the more dignified class of property. Yet, they were not reclassified, for *res mancipi* 'never varied once the category had been established' (Thomas, 1976: 129); or, as Maine puts it, 'the list of the *Res Mancipi* was irrevocably closed' (*AL*: 278). Thus, for Maine, 'the grand point of interest' is

the continued degradation of these commodities when their importance had increased and their number had multiplied ... [the] disposition to keep these last at a lower grade in the arrangements of Jurisprudence, and to permit their transfer by simpler processes than those which in archaic conveyances, serve as stumbling-blocks to good faith and stepping-stones to fraud. (275-6)

Thus, the existence of two kinds of classifications allowed societies to reform the law by isolating the items subject to conveyancing restrictions, while extending the items included among the lower order of property. And as 'every fresh conquest of man over material nature' added to the items included among the lower order (278), it became increasingly difficult to maintain the distinction between higher and lower orders of property; in other words, the logic of the separate classifications itself became suspect. This is what occurred in Rome as the simple formality attached to the *res nec mancipi* was, with the help of actions in equity, transferred to the *res mancipi*. And, at the time of Justinian, 'the difference between *res mancipi* and *res nec mancipi* disappears, and tradition or delivery becomes the one great conveyance known to the law' (279). In short, 'The history of Roman Property Law is the history of the assimilation of *Res Mancipi* to *Res Nec Mancipi*' (273). And the linchpin of this reform was the existence of 'The distinction between *res mancipi* and *res nec mancipi* ... the type of a class of distinctions to which civilization is much indebted'. (279).

CHAPTER 16

Law and language: a metaphor in Maine, a model for his successors?

Bernard S. Jackson

ABSTRACT

Part A of this chapter considers Maine's conception of the relationship between law and language. For him, comparative philology was the dominant paradigm of linguistics. He used it for the most part non-technically, as a model to support his view of parallel development within a particular family of legal systems: the Indo-European group. But the model does not fit Maine's views in all respects. Most importantly, Maine failed to grasp the significance of the distinction between merely semantic parallels and historical etymological derivations.

Part B considers whether the parallel between law and language can claim any greater status today. I argue that it can, even though the dominant paradigm of linguistics is now one of synchronic language-systems. We are better placed today to assess the parallels between law and language because we have a range of inter-disciplinary models which identify and speak to that which is common to law and language. I offer some examples of these from cognitive developmental psychology and from Greimasian semiotics (discussing, in both cases, some ancient law by way of illustration), while taking a more critical view of law/language parallels based on Chomskyan linguistics and on New Criticism in literature.

PART A: A METAPHOR IN MAINE?

There has been much discussion of the relations between different disciplinary models — biological, geological, linguistic — in the writings of Maine's period. No simple picture emerges.[1] Biologists

[1] Burrow, 1966: 109f.: 'When G. L. Gomme suggests that folk-lore may be accounted for "by some law analogous to Grimm's law in the study of Language" (*Folk-lore as an Historical*

Law and language

and linguists cite each other,[2] and both they and Maine also cite the geologists. Vinogradoff (1911: 581) saw comparative philology as the principal single influence on Maine. While Feaver appears less sure,[3] Burrow agrees that this seems to be Maine's own perception.[4] He notes that there is a far greater number of references to comparative philology (sometimes bracketed with comparative mythology) in Maine's works than to any physical science (1966: 148).

At the same time, Burrow rightly ponders the reality of the influence on Maine. He asks whether such interdisciplinary references in the works of the nineteenth-century writers are intended to be 'merely persuasive analogies, picturesque metaphors, interesting parallels, or clarifying illustrations of the methods of new subjects by reference to better known ones; or do they represent actual, if vague, influences?' (11). For Maine, specifically, he observes: 'to notice a parallel, though it proves knowledge, does not necessarily indicate that it has influenced one's thinking; one might merely have used it to make a point more effectively' (148).

We may seek to answer this question in a number of ways: (a) by investigating the actual sources available to and used by Maine, and comparing them with Maine's approach; (b) by considering Maine's own statements regarding the use and status of comparative philology; (c) by examining instances of Maine's deployment of linguistic arguments; and (d) by relating the law/language comparison to

---

Science, 1908), when Max Müller speaks of "the Stratification of Language" and says that he doubts whether "we should have arrived at a thorough understanding of the real antecedents of language, unless what happened in the study of the stratification of the earth, happened in the study of language" (Müller, 1868: 12), when Maine says that the evidence for the patriarchal theory "appeared to me very much of the same kind and strength as that which convinces the comparative philologist that a number of words in different Aryan languages had a common form" (*Dissertations on Early Law and Custom*, 194; *Village-Communities*, 6), and, in *Ancient Law*, says that "these rudimentary ideas are to the jurist what the crusts of the earth are to the geologist" (2), the situation is far from clear.'

[2] Burrow notes that Darwin (1874: 19–91 vol 2) uses philology to help illustrate the concept of rudimentary organs, and compares Jacob Grimm as quoted in Pedersen, 1965: 262 (Burrow, 1966: 109). Schleicher, if not Grimm or Müller, viewed language as a natural organism and in 1863 published *The Darwinian Theory of Linguistics*. Both disciplines constructed theories of stages. See also Burrow, 1967: 186, 198, 200ff.

[3] In describing the Oxford scene when Maine joined it in 1871, Feaver, 1969: 111, puts comparative philology (here embodied by Müller) on a par with other social scientific disciplines.

[4] 'The most powerful parallel to his own method seemed to him to be that of comparative philology' (Burrow, 1966: 149). He quotes (149, n. 3) in particular *VC*: 6, 8; Add. 2, in *VC*, 1876: 267ff.; *EHI*: Chap. II; Rede Lec., 1875: 8–10.

Maine's general intellectual (and political) concerns. I shall comment briefly on each of these.

(1) *Maine's sources*

Nineteenth-century linguistics,[5] inspired by the discovery of Sanskrit by Sir William Jones and his announcement of the existence of an Indo-European group of languages 'sprung from some common source' (quoted in Jespersen, 1922: 33), had by Maine's day generated an extensive technical literature in comparative philology, much of it in German, but already claiming classic status. Already in his *Über die Sprache und Weisheit der Indier* of 1808 Friedrich von Schlegel had advocated a 'comparative grammar' and indicated some sound-shift patterns (Jespersen, 1922: 34f.). The modern period of linguistics, however, is attributed by Pedersen to the work of Rask[6] and Bopp.[7] Also notable, though too late to have influenced *Ancient Law*, was the work of August Schleicher,[8] who attempted the first serious reconstruction of the phonological system and individual words and forms of the parent language of the Indo-European group (Pedersen, 1965: 267). From a later perspective, it is true, the really significant developments in nineteenth-century comparative philology only occurred from the 1870s. Beginning about 1870, Pedersen suggests, 'a series of splendid discoveries made by scholars of various nationalities accounted for the most striking cases of apparent irregularity in the Indo-European laws of sounds' (1965: 243f.). Nevertheless, the basic agenda of comparative philology – the inquiry into comparative morphology and comparative phonology – was already well established before Maine's day.

[5] For my information on nineteenth-century comparative philology, I have relied principally on two works: Jespersen (1922); and Pedersen (1965).

[6] Pedersen, 1965: 248–54; cf. Jespersen, 1922: 36–40). Rask was the first to explain vowel changes in terms of the approximation of the vowel of the stem to that of the ending (Jespersen, 1922: 37). He published the first usable grammar of old English in 1817 (Pedersen, 1965: 37). But Rask did not study Sanskrit, and most of his writings were in Danish.

[7] Pedersen, 1965: 254–8; Jespersen, 1922: 47–55. His *Über das Conjugationssystem der Sanskritsprache in Vergleichung mit jenem der griechischen, lateinischen, persischen und germanischen Sprache*, of 1816, treats the verbal inflection of Sanskrit in comparison with Greek, Latin, Persian and Germanic (Pedersen, 1965: 254). His comparative grammar is best expressed in his *Vergleichende grammatik des sanskrit, zend, armenischen, griechischen, lateinischen, litauischen, altslawischen, gotischen und deutschen*, of 1833–52. Jespersen, 1922: 255f., is critical of his approach to phonology, and suggests that here he added nothing new.

[8] Pedersen, 1965: 265–72; Jespersen, 1922: 71–6. Author of *Compendium der vergleichenden Grammatik der indogermanischen Sprachen* (1861–2).

It was Grimm,[9] of the classical nineteenth-century writers, whose work seems to have impinged most on Maine's consciousness. But the reason for this probably lies in Grimm's non-linguistic interests. Grimm's first research was in Germanic poetry and folklore, and he became known (in conjunction with his brother) as much for his comparative mythology as for his philology.[10] Moreover, Grimm himself studied law and assisted Savigny (to whom he dedicated his *Deutsche Grammatik*) with his legal-historical research. Jespersen suggests that Savigny's view of legal institutions 'as the outcome of gradual development in intimate connexion with popular tradition and the whole intellectual and moral life of the people' appealed strongly to Grimm; indeed, the latter speaks of the *Sprachgeist* – the spirit of a language (1922: 40, 45). This view came to be reflected in Grimm's interest in popular dialects, and his refusal to follow the 'old philology' in dealing only with the two classical languages and the upper-class literature embodied in them (41). Here we see a reciprocal influence of historical jurisprudence and comparative philology. From *Village-Communities*, at least, Maine took the same direction.

Grimm applied the ideas of Savigny not only to the choice of data, but also to his approach to it. As Jespersen puts it: 'He charges them [previous German grammars] with unspeakable pedantry; they wanted to dogmatize magisterially, while to Grimm language, like everything natural and moral, is an unconscious and unnoticed secret which is implanted in us in youth' (42). Nevertheless, Grimm went on – inspired by Rask in particular – to develop the study of the 'sound shift', which Müller came to term (somewhat generously, Jespersen suggests) 'Grimm's law'.

Grimm's popularity is explained by Jespersen thus: 'he gave fuller word lists than people had been accustomed to, and this opened the eyes of scholars to the great regularity reigning in this department of linguistic development ... He speaks of law ... in connexion with the consonant shift, and there recognized that it serves to curb wild etymologies and becomes a test for them ... The consonant shift thus

[9] Pedersen, 1965: 37–42, 258–62; Jespersen, 1922: 40–3, 60–2. Author of *Deutsche Grammatik* (1819–37): 'Grimm's strength lies not so much in the phonetic description of sounds as in the determination of their etymological value and in the exact statement how the sounds of the various dialects correspond to one another ... In addition, Grimm explained accurately and clearly the changes in sounds which we now know by the name he used, *umlaut*' (Pedersen, 1965: 38). Grimm restricted his studies to the Germanic languages. He advanced, in particular, the study of consonantal sound-shifts in the Germanic languages.
[10] *Über den altdeutschen Meistergesang* (1811); *Kinder- und Hausmärchen* (1812). See Jespersen, 1922: 41.

became *the* law in linguistics, and because it affected a great many words known to everybody, and in a new and surprising way associated well-known Latin or Greek words with words of one's own mother-tongue, it became popularly the keystone of a new wonderful science' (46). Here again we see elements that were particularly attractive to Maine, for whom comparative jurisprudence was not merely an exercise in ancient legal history, but – as he put it in the Preface to *Early Law and Custom* – an attempt 'to connect a portion of existing institutions with a part of the primitive or very ancient usages of mankind, and of the ideas associated with these usages'.

It was at the most general methodological level that Maine derived inspiration from Grimm, not from his technical linguistic studies. Pedersen, following Grimm's own view, notes that '[Grimm] has often been designated as the founder of historical rather than comparative linguistics, and he has been contrasted with specialists like Rask and Bopp' (1965: 258). One of Grimm's historical claims (in which he was not alone[11]) is of particular interest in this connection. As Pedersen notes: 'Grimm is more or less consciously involved in the belief that the comparative linguistics of which Gothic and Sanskrit are the foundations leads us back to the very beginnings of language' (40). A similar equivocation – between the history of a particular family and comparative studies designed to reveal the evolutionary origins of a particular institution – was to emerge in the status claimed by Maine for the patriarchal theory.

It is also noteworthy that Grimm offers an evaluation of contemporary German language, and that 'in many passages ... he places the old stages of the language very much higher than the language of his own day'.[12] Maine too regards authenticity to the historic roots of a legal system as a test of the value of its later development. Yet Grimm came also to contradict the widely held view that the history of language in general is one of decline. Jespersen quotes him thus: 'Human language is retrogressive only

---

[11] Pedersen quotes Bopp as having regarded 'the investigation of the relationships of languages not merely as an end in itself, but also as a means of penetrating the secrets of the evolution of language' (1965: 258). This claim, Pedersen comments, 'does no serious harm' to Bopp's work. Jespersen takes the view that discovery of 'the ultimate origin of grammatical forms' was Bopp's chief aim (1922: 48).

[12] Jespersen, 1922: 60, on Grimm's *Über das Pedantische in der deutschen Sprache* (1847). Cf. Burrow, 1967: 185f., associating this degenerationist view of language with German Romanticism.

apparently and in particular points, but looked upon as a whole it is progressive, and its intrinsic force is continually increasing' (1922: 62). Taken literally, this might appear to run counter to Maine's ideas on progress within legal systems. However, given the exclusively Germanic context of Grimm's work, such a remark could have provided Maine with grounds for his distinction between Indo-European laws (regarded as 'progressive') and the generality of legal systems (non-progressive).

What methods and claims were being made in this newly invigorated discipline of comparative philology? The foundations were laid by the methods elaborated and applied by the Danish linguist Rasmus Rask. He stressed the importance of the study of the grammatical system[13] rather than individual words, since the latter are often transmitted from one language to another, while this occurred very rarely with the former: 'Grammatical agreement is a much more certain indication of kinship or of original identity, because a language which is mixed with another seldom or never takes over morphological changes or inflections from it' (quoted in Pedersen, 1965: 250–51). In addition, however, some types of word, such as pronouns and numerals, were so 'essential, concrete, indispensable', that if the points of agreement between them in two languages were sufficient to frame rules for the transition of sounds, the languages may be related by way of kinship.[14] For example, as Pedersen notes (1965: 252), in his study of the Thracian group of languages, Rask compiled a list of 352 vocabulary items, arranged according to their meaning, in order to show how the most important and most necessary words in language, words which indicate the first objects of reflection, are the same in both branches of the language. But these parallels in vocabulary were to be considered significant only if the laws of sound-change operative in that family of languages could be established.[15] In other words, the data on the basis of which linguistic kinship could be established were, on the one hand, grammatical in the sense of morphology (inflectional changes), and lexical on the other, where the same word (its identity established through the operation of laws of sound-change) was used to designate the same concept in the different languages. It was not, as

---

[13] On Bopp's comparative studies on the inflectional system of the verb in Indo-European languages, see Jespersen, 1922: 48–52.
[14] Pedersen, 1965: 251; Jespersen, 1922: 38.
[15] For examples, see Jespersen, 1922: 252–3.

sometimes occurs in Maine, a process of semantic comparison, whereby word X in language A has a comparable semantic range to word Y in language B.

In another respect, however, Maine's invocation of comparative philology was exact. Once given the establishment of a family relationship between the languages, the results could be used to fill in gaps in the history of particular members of the family. The following quotation from Bopp certainly adumbrates Maine's general approach:

> I do not believe that the Greek, Latin, and other European languages are to be considered as derived from the Sanskrit in the state in which we find it in Indian books; I feel rather inclined to consider them altogether as subsequent variations of one original tongue, which, however, the Sanskrit has preserved more perfect than its kindred dialects. But whilst therefore the language of the Brahmans more frequently enables us to conjecture the primitive form of the Greek and Latin languages than what we discover in the oldest authors and monuments, the latter on their side also may not infrequently elucidate the Sanskrit grammar.[16]

Burrow has observed that comparative philology was becoming fashionable in England in the early 1860s, and was first popularized in England in two series of lectures by Max Müller[17] at the Royal Institution, in 1861 and 1863.[18] However, Maine must have been familiar with comparative philology before these lectures were delivered. Burrow points out that between 1846 and 1860 Müller had published a number of papers on linguistics (1966: 150). Maine's interest may well have been attracted by Müller's first paper published in England, which was read to the British Association in 1847, and which gave considerable space to a discussion of the principles of comparative philology.[19] Stein has pointed to Müller's review of Bopp's *Comparative Grammar* in the 1851 *Edinburgh Review*, in which he argues (Stein's words with quotations from Müller):

[16] Quoted in Jespersen, 1922: 48. He comments: 'Herein subsequent research has certainly borne out Bopp's view' (*ibid.*).
[17] On whom see Jespersen, 1922: 85f., taking the view that Müller was a popularizer, and of no great academic importance. Pedersen does not mention him at all.
[18] Published as *Lectures on the Science of Language*.
[19] *Report of the British Association*, No. 17 (1847). See also Burrow, 1967: 193ff. on Müller's relationship to Bunsen. Amongst other papers of Müller which Burrow notes (1966: 150f.) is that on comparative mythology in *Oxford Essays* (1856) and his *History of Ancient Sanskrit Literature* (1859), which contains an introductory section on the Aryan 'race' and the methods of comparative philology. However, as Burrow points out, Müller himself had objected (*Lectures*, 314), to this process of tracing racial affiliations by means of comparative philology.

Languages must be classified into groups 'according to the peculiar character of their etymological and grammatical structure' (p. 305). The only group seriously studied so far is that comprising 'the languages of the Indo-European or Arian family' (p. 310). 'As soon as Sanskrit appeared above the horizon, the broad fact of the connexion of the Arian languages became as clear as daylight', but the establishment of connection is only a first step to 'penetrating into the secrets of lingual development' (p. 317). More than that, it enables us 'to reconstruct on a firmer basis the oldest history of the whole Arian family' (p. 328). (Stein, 1980: 92)

Whether Maine was personally acquainted with Müller before being elected to the Corpus Chair at Oxford in 1869 (taking it up in 1871) is unknown (to me). Undoubtedly, the personal connection was to strengthen Maine's interest; and references to comparative philology are in fact more frequent in the later books than in *Ancient Law*. There was, however, an earlier personal contact of Maine which may have been significant in this regard. Feaver points to the possible influence of Whitley Stokes, whom Maine knew at the Middle Temple, and whom he appointed Head of his Legislative Department in Calcutta in 1862, and indeed Stokes' opinion (impliedly from personal contact, not scholarly writing) is explicitly invoked by Maine (*EHI*: 216) in connection with 'Geilfine' (see below).

(2) *Maine's statements regarding comparative philology*

A second approach is to consider Maine's own statements about comparative philology. From them we certainly get the impression that Maine was interested in comparative philology's general conclusions rather than its methods: there was an Indo-European family of nations, and if its linguistic development could be traced back to a common origin, why not also its legal development? As Maine argued in a famous passage regarding the patriarchal theory:

We have not indeed knowledge of any working system of institutions in which the Family exactly corresponds to the primitive family assumed by the theory. The Roman law, as a working system, takes a view of Family and Kinship not very different from that accepted in modern societies, but we happen to have unusual facilities for ascertaining a very ancient condition of this law, and it is not possible to doubt that, when the law was in this state, the Family and the Kinship of which it took cognisance had for their basis the authority of the eldest male ascendant. Other bodies of old usage and legal rule, less perfectly known to us than the Roman from the scantiness of the inferior quality of their materials, seemed to me to suggest that a Family organised on the Patriarchal model had been the near or remote antecedent of the Family which they reflected. The Hindu law appeared to me to suggest this very strongly. So did Slavonian law, as far as it was known. Greek law seemed to point to the same conclusion, less distinctly yet not very obscurely; and, more doubtfully, the ancient law of the Teutonic races. The evidence appeared to me very much of the same kind and strength as that which convinces the comparative philologist that a number of words in different Aryan languages had a common ancestral form in a now unknown ancestral mother tongue.[20]

To us, today, such rhetoric would hardly be persuasive. The reason for the difference perhaps resides in our later appreciation of the basic *arbitrariness* of much of linguistic development, as compared with the far greater social or human constraints which appear to limit the range of possible legal developments. In the nineteenth century, on the other hand, linguistic development appears to have been regarded as *natural*, simply by virtue of the fact that it was *spontaneous*. If there existed a *spontaneous* development of language within defined families, why should there not also be spontaneous development of law within those same families? But Rask, as Jespersen observes (1922: 38), had himself stressed the difference between law and language in this respect: whereas religion, customs, laws and institutions may change completely, language remains recognizable after thousands of years.

It is possible to view Maine's invocation of comparative philology in *Early Law and Custom* as a defence *against* such anthropological evidence (produced by J. F. McLennan and L. H. Morgan) as favoured matriarchy, since comparative philology implied the peculiarity of family groups, and the patriarchal theory – Maine now accepted – might well be peculiar to the legal family he was studying.

Undoubtedly, Maine sought to appropriate for his own theories the image of scientific exactitude and reliability which attached to comparative philology, and there was no better way of doing so than to deny such pretensions explicitly:[21] 'I should, however, be making

[20] *ELC*: 193–4. Interestingly, he goes on: 'but I stated with some caution the opinion that, at that stage of the inquiry, "the difficulty was to know where to stop and to say of what races of mankind it was not allowable to lay down that the society in which they were united was originally organised on the patriarchal model" ('Ancient Law', 123)' (194).

[21] Cf. Burrow, 1966: 148, who accepts that 'Often he seems not merely to be pointing to comparative philology as an interesting analogy, but actually to be using it as a justification of his own method' (citing Rede Lec., 1875c: 20, 25, 30 in *VC*, 1876). He too quotes *Early Law and Custom* (193–4) (on the patriarchal theory, see n. 20 above) in this connection.

a very idle pretension if I held out a prospect of obtaining, by the application of the Comparative Method to jurisprudence, any results which, in point of interest or trustworthiness, are to be placed on a level with those which, for example, have been accomplished in Comparative Philology' (*VC*: 8).

Maine was not unaware of the political potential of the comparative philology he was using. In *Lectures on the Early History of Institutions* he suggests that those particular forms of the theory of nationality represented by Pan-Slavism and Pan-Teutonism 'are in truth a product of modern philology, and have grown out of the assumption that linguistic affinities prove community of blood' (*EHI*: 75). In fact, Müller had come to reject just this proposition.

(3) *Maine's deployment of linguistic arguments*

When we examine Maine's actual use of linguistic data, we in fact encounter relatively few genuine philological arguments. He is aware, and mentions in passing, that 'dooms' are 'the exact Teutonic equivalent' of *themistes* (*AL*: 4). But the fact of a common root is not here given any special weight. But this is a rare example in Maine of the invocation of semantically related terminology in different languages which can be shown, by operation of sound-change regularities, also to be genetically related (a methodological approach which remains in use a century later[22]). More typical in Maine is an interest in parallel semantics rather than etymology, as

[22] See Watkins, 1970: 322, who offers the following strong statement of his methodological assumptions: 'Given linguistic evidence in the Indo-European languages for common etyma in form and function for a given social or legal institution – and an obvious example is the system of kinship terms – it is a necessary fact that social or legal institutions existed in the society of speakers of Common Indo-European. To deny this is to deny to the reconstructed language the status of a vehicle of human communication. This implication may then be recast in its proper historical context: the linguist who makes such a reconstruction, by the techniques of the comparative method, from the data of legal language in the various Indo-European languages, has thereby furnished incontrovertible formal evidence for the common Indo-European origin not merely of a given vocable, but of salient features of the different historical legal systems themselves. The linguist at this point finds himself in a wholly new domain: that of comparative law in the genetic sense. That there should be a close analogy between the comparative method in language and in the law follows from the identity of the problem in each. Any linguistic comparatist will state that there are basically three possible explanations for similarity between languages: borrowing or diffusion, common inheritance, and independent creation due either to universality or to chance.' Watkins in this essay provides detailed studies of *usurpare, aut noxiam sarcire aut noxae dedere* and the Roman law of theft, from a comparative linguistic viewpoint. He warmly endorses (1970: 326) Maine's interpretation of *usurpare* in terms of a break in *usus*, in his discussion of *usucapio* (*EHI*: 315f.).

in the link between 'chattels' and 'capital', and the usage of *pecunia* for money as well as cattle; equally, in discussing the importance of horned cattle, the Brehon usage of *sed* and *cumhal*, as standards of value, is explored (*EHI*: 147–9). At best we have here parallel semantic ranges or semantic oppositions, reflecting parallel social developments.

Perhaps the most detailed linguistic comparison offered by Maine was in support of his theory of the common existence within the Indo-European family of the institution of patriarchal authority:

> Now, Mr. Whitley Stokes has conveyed to me his opinion that 'Geilfine' means 'hand-family'. As I have reason to believe that a different version of the term has been adopted by eminent authority, I will give the reasons for Mr. Stokes's view. 'Gil' means 'hand' – this was also the rendering of O'Curry – and it is, in fact, the Greek word χείρ. In several Aryan languages the term signifying 'hand' is an expressive equivalent for Power, and specially for Family or Patriarchal Power. Thus, in Greek we have ὑποχείριος and χέρης, for the person under the hand. In Latin we have *herus* 'master', from an old word, cognate to χείρ; and we have also one of the cardinal terms of ancient Roman Family Law, *manus*, or hand, in the sense of Patriarchal authority. In Roman legal phraseology, the wife who has become in law her husband's daughter by marriage is *in manu*. The son discharged from Paternal Power is *emancipated*. The free person who has undergone manumission is *in mancipio*. In the Celtic languages we have, with other words, 'Gilla,' a servant, a word familiar to sportsmen and travellers in the Highlands and to readers of Scott in its Anglicised shape, 'Gillie'.
>
> My suggestion, then, is that the key to the Irish distribution of the Family, as to so many other things in ancient law, must be sought in the Patria Potestas. (*EHI*: 216–17)

In the context of his argument, this appears as a very telling point: very commonly within the Indo-European family, 'the term signifying "hand" is an expressive equivalent for Power' (though Maine does not distinguish, for this purpose, between those terms which are etymologically connected – such as χείρ and *herus* – and those not etymologically connected – such as *manus*).[23] Its value is consider-

---

[23] Compare the following argument: 'Feodum, the later Teutonised name of the Beneficium, is now allowed to have been derived from the old Gothic word *'fihu'*, or *'fiu'* – cattle. The term is supposed to have come to mean "property", just as *pecunia*, from *pecus*, contracted this meaning. A few years ago, after pointing out the great part played by cattle in converting Irish tribal holdings into something like feudal tenures, I stated that I suspected 'feodum' to have a closer connection with cattle than the usual etymology implied. M. de Laveleye, commenting on this remark, has stated that he has no doubt of the association; and he observes that we thus see the meaning of the original contrast between allodium and

ably diminished, however, by consideration of the fact that the Hebrew word for hand, *yad*, appears commonly in exactly the same context, a fact which anyone with a knowledge of biblical Hebrew would have confirmed to Maine, had he been concerned to inquire about it. Given this fact, Maine really does need to establish etymological connections, and not merely semantic parallels. But he neither appreciated the need for this nor drew upon the technical resources of the discipline whose support he prayed in aid.

(4) *Relation to Maine's overall theories*

Finally, we may attempt to relate Maine's use of comparative philology to his general scholarly objectives. It is useful, first of all, to note some aspects of the intellectual context within which Maine worked.

Burrow has drawn attention to the differences in approach between two influential scholarly societies in Victorian England, the Ethnological Society and the Anthropological Society. An interest in comparative philology was taken by the members of the Ethnological Society. But Burrow notes that this society was predominantly diffusionist rather than evolutionist. The method of tracing origins which it favoured was philology, but philology used not as a model for and guarantee of evolutionary social theory, but as a means of tracing actual historical affinities. He contrasts the approach of the Anthropological Society, which was more concerned with the possibility of establishing sociological laws. Maine's approach, Burrow suggests, was closer to that of the Anthropological Society (1966: 122–3).

But this view is not universally held. The Ethnological/Anthropological debate continues to be echoed in modern appreciations of Maine. Julius Stone regarded Maine as a unilinear evolutionist, whose denials of that role amount only to a 'formal caveat' (1966: 120). Evans-Pritchard, on the other hand, denied that Maine sought to formulate laws of historical development according to which all human societies pass through a succession of stages, and saw him rather as seeking 'to explain any institution in terms of its origins, or

---

feodum – al-od, the complete property; fe-od, the cattle property. Plausible as this is, I should have hesitated to build on it as a basis but for the remarkable results disclosed by the examination of the Salic Law. It undoubtedly shows that an ancient Law of Movable Property may deeply affect a Law of Land' (*ELC*: 346).

at any rate of its antecedents' (1961: 1). My own view is closer to that of Evans-Pritchard.[24] I prefer to look at the intellectual debate within which Maine himself located his work. This was not the evolutionist/diffusionist debate, but rather the attempt to substitute real for conjectural history, the latter represented by the theories of natural law. In *Early Law and Custom*, he defended his patriarchal theory against those who took it to be a theory of origins: 'It was not part of my object to determine the absolute origin of human society. I have written very few pages which have any bearing on the subject ... The undertaking which I have followed ... has been to trace the real, as opposed to the imaginary, or the arbitrarily assumed, history of the institutions of civilised men' (192). The patriarchal theory, he stressed, had claims 'to be considered a real historical theory; that is, as a theory giving an account upon rational evidence of primitive or very ancient social order' (192). In the Preface to *Ancient Law*, Maine described his principal objective as 'to indicate some of the earliest ideas of mankind, as they are reflected in Ancient Law, and to point out the relation of those ideas to modern thought'. As Pollock stressed, this was not an attempt to account for the 'ultimate origin of human laws' (*AL*, 1906: xiv). In *Village-Communities*, Maine set out 'to point out the importance, in juridical enquiries, of increased attention to the phenomena of usage and legal thought which are observable in the East' (*AL*, 1906: vii) and show their relation to 'the laws and usages, past and present, of other societies' (*VC*: 3). In particular, the book was designed to show a connection between systems of landholding observed in contemporary India and the historical systems of Germany and England. We have here the model of an assumed parallel development, from which data from one

---

[24] At least if one gives Maine the benefit of the kind of reading advocated by Pollock (1890b: 163f., Section A5 below). It is significant in this context that nowhere did Maine make the concept of 'stages' the pivotal point of his theories – unlike, for example, his American contemporary Lewis Morgan (e.g. 1964: 7ff.). Maine was wary of describing his object in terms of the identification of general stages of progress, preferring to talk about 'parallel phenomena ... in the order of historical succession' (*VC*: 6). He does, however, often identify stages in the development of specific legal institutions. Maine rejected Spencerian evolution based on spontaneous rather than conscious adaptation – at least as a universal explanation of all social development. In *Early Law and Custom*, he writes: 'no universal theory, attempting to account for all social forms by supposing an evolution from within, can possibly be true' (*ELC*: 285). The context shows that the emphasis of this statement lies on the words 'from within'. In the same book, he confessed a distaste for such 'inquiries which, when I have attempted to push them far, have always landed me in mudbanks and fog' (192) – apparently a reference to evolutionary claims beyond the Indo-European family.

society can be used to fill in gaps, or add to our knowledge of, data in another – a model to which comparative philology, as we have seen, lent support. His objective, he wrote, was to

> examine a number of parallel phenomena with the view of establishing, if possible, that some of them are related to one another in the order of historical succession. I think I may venture to affirm that the Comparative Method, which has already been fruitful of such wonderful results, is not distinguishable in some of its applications from the Historical Method. We take a number of contemporary facts, ideas, and customs, and we infer the past form of those facts, ideas, and customs not only from historical records of that past form, but from examples of it which have not yet died out of the world, and are still to be found in it. (*VC*: 6–7)

The vital question, of course, was the basis on which such inferences were to be made. But the difference between the comparative agenda (typical developmental patterns) and the historical (diffusionist) is not unimportant here, in connection with the precise use being made by Maine of comparative philology. Typical developmental patterns might well be shown on the basis of parallels in the semantic range of etymologically unrelated lexical items; historical connections, on the other hand, required the full techniques of comparative philology, with their attention to connections between *arbitrary* types of linguistic data – parallels which could be explained only on the basis of historical connection.

In other respects, too, Maine's invocation of comparative philology fails to cohere fully with other aspects of his theories. Whereas the patriarchal theory may have related to the period of the spontaneous development of law, it was Maine's contention that the Indo-European family was exceptional in that it was *progressive*. After the period of spontaneous development, it underwent phases of *conscious* reformulation. Support here could hardly be taken from comparative philology.[25] But in fact it was this 'progressive' phase of the history of Indo-European law that attracted most of Maine's attention.

Progress, for Maine, was far from inevitable. 'When primitive law has once been embodied in a Code, there is an end to what may be

---

[25] Pedersen comments thus on the approach of Schleicher: 'In all seriousness Schleicher conceives of language as an organism, and reckons linguistics as one of the natural sciences. The ancient languages, which were the cardinal points of departure for comparison, were regarded quite differently from the modern. Schleicher even maintained that the evolution of language took place only in prehistoric times, while historical times have known only linguistic decay' (1965: 242).

called its spontaneous development' (*AL*: 21). Beyond that point, progress occurred by conscious adaptation.[26] It was 'endemic' in only one society, the Greek (*VC*: 238). 'The natural condition of mankind ... is not the progressive condition ... The immobility of society is the rule, its mobility is the exception' (*PG*: 170). Outside 'progressive societies', comparative jurisprudence showed the 'fewness of ideas and the slowness of additions to the mental stock' as among the most general characteristics of mankind (*EHI*: 225). Again, this model of exceptionality fits rather badly with comparative philology.

But there is another reason why Maine was so wedded to the historical rather than the comparative agenda. The history of the progressive societies culminated in – the British Empire, and in the responsibilities thereby incumbent upon its administrators. Hence this remarkable passage from the Rede Lecture, delivered in Cambridge in 1875:

> To one small people, covering in its original seat no more than a handsbreath of territory, it was given to create the principle of Progress ... That people was the Greek. Except the blind forces of Nature, nothing moves in this world which is not Greek in its origin. A ferment spreading from that source has vitalised all the great progressive races of mankind, penetrating from one to another, and producing results accordant with its hidden and latent genius, and results of course often far greater than any exhibited in Greece itself. It is this principle of progress which we Englishmen are communicating to India. We did not create it. We deserve no special credit for it. It came to us filtered through many different media. But we have received it; and as we have received it, so we pass it on. (*VC*, 1876: 238f.)

(5) Conclusion

Most writers have seen Maine as multi-faceted, and have attempted, in one way or another, to take account of the different aspects of his academic persona. Burrow suggests that Maine was 'not a systematic thinker ... it would be possible, by selective quotation, to make out a convincing case for either view of him – that he was a legal historian with perhaps too great a fondness for cross-comparison and "brilliant" generalisation, or that he was a rigid evolutionary determinist' (1966: 164). Pollock sought to resolve the dichotomies in Maine's

---

[26] *VC*: 8; for Maine's view of limitations on conscious adaptation, see *EHI*: 227.

writing in his favour, by attributing them primarily to his style: 'Few great writers are so easy as Maine to criticise superficially, for he constantly seems to be laying himself open by wide assertions. Few are so hard to criticise thoroughly, for the more carefully one studies his language, and with the greater knowledge of the subject-matter, the more real caution and the more subtle discrimination does one find, both in what he says and in what he abstains from saying' (1890b: 163f.).

Both these judgements seem applicable to Maine's use of comparative philology. But before we reach too negative an evaluation, we should perhaps adopt a discursive rather than an historical approach: what we should judge – all, perhaps, that we *can* judge – is Maine's construction of comparative philology for the purposes of his own discourse. In looking at the passages in which he makes use of the argument from comparative philology, we may not be able to gauge, for example, whether he would have arrived at his theories without the existence of this model. We may not even be able to determine with certainty the extent of his knowledge of that model. What we can assess is the rhetorical construction of comparative philology in Maine's writings, which tells us (a) what version of comparative philology made sense to him, and (b) what version he felt could be used in order to persuade the audience (not a technical linguistic audience, of course) which he was addressing of the validity of his general theses. And these general theses were by no means antiquarian. However much we may disagree with Maine's sense of historical mission, his attitude to history – as an ongoing process in which we continue to be implicated – today once again strikes a contemporary chord. In this respect, at least, the law/language parallel is more than metaphorical.

PART B: A MODEL FOR HIS SUCCESSORS?

(1) *Historical jurisprudence and cognitive development psychology*

Today, comparative philology is no longer the paradigm form of linguistic study. Comparative philology survives, but the emphasis in theoretical linguistics has shifted from the diachronic to the synchronic dimension: the snapshot image of a language, taken in order to study it as a system, within which the meaning of each part is to be determined by reference to its relations to others.

Such a development in linguistics might suggest – in so far as the analogy between law and language remains valid – that the era of historical jurisprudence is over, and this indeed seems to be suggested by Stein in a recent work (1980: 124ff.). But in fact, historical jurisprudence is not necessarily left stranded amongst the receding waters of social scientific inspiration. Help is at hand, and from a source which – though not primarily linguistic – seeks to take account of modern synchronic linguistics, and indeed regards the problem of language acquisition as central to its concerns. I refer to modern cognitive developmental psychology, particularly the theories of Jean Piaget and Lawrence Kohlberg. Over fifty years ago, Piaget hailed Brunschvig's *Progrès de la conscience dans la philosophie occidentale* as 'the widest and the most subtle demonstration of the fact that there exists in European thought a law in the evolution of moral judgements which is analogous to the law of which psychology watches the effects throughout the development of the individual' (1932: 402). Similarly, Kohlberg concluded that the stages of moral evolution of culture identified by Hobhouse 'parallel our own stages in many ways' (1971: 178).

This is not to be seen as a reversion to nineteenth-century evolutionary models. It relies fundamentally upon notions of systemic equilibrium within 'stages', as well as suggesting universals of development from one stage to another. It is surely significant, in this respect, that Piaget (1965: 65) expressed some sympathy for the jurisprudential theories of Kelsen; in particular, he saw a parallel between the psychological notion of auto-regulation and the dynamic character of Kelsen's legal system, wherein the law itself could regulate its own creation.[27]

What links the modern cognitive developmentalists with nineteenth-century social evolutionary thought is the retention of increasing differentiation as a central feature of development. It is this, for example, that leads Piaget to suggest (1965: 201) that primitive peoples differentiate between law, religion and morality only by nuances (though this should perhaps be taken more as an external claim which appeals to Piaget, rather than a result of his own psychological investigations). For Kohlberg, the introduction of great flexibility, or 'equity', into a hitherto legalistic morality is a distinguishing feature of stage 5 moral development: it is difficult not

---

[27] For a fuller discussion, see Jackson, 1989b.

to detect traces of Roscoe Pound's stages of 'strict law' and 'equity and natural law' (1959: 1, 382–421). Perhaps the most striking parallel is that between Piaget's view that in law bilateral relations tend (with democracy) to gain ascendence over unilateral relations (1965: 117), and Maine's movement from status to contract.

Such substantive resemblances are less important than the conceptual differences in the model which the cognitive developmentalists use. Piaget eventually turned against the idea of gauging the logical level of a society by reference to its already crystallized cultural products: rather, he argued, attention should be directed to the manner in which these products are used in the reasoning processes of members of that society – thus, in the process of further construction (1971: 116–18). Secondly, the conservative ethnocentric biases of historical jurisprudence are replaced by universal developmental tendencies. This is not the place to discuss the validity of such cross-cultural claims. The important thing, for present purposes, is that the claims are made, that Piaget and Kohlberg hold out their sequences to be universal – quite unlike the movements which Maine described within 'progressive' societies. That is not to say that progression to the highest stages of moral development is regarded as inevitable (barring pathological disorders) for each individual. Kohlberg has contrasted the acquisition of morality with that of grammar by saying that whereas, following Chomsky, there may be only 'one grammatical system of intuition, known to all children of five ... the only "competent moral speakers" are the rare individuals at stage 6 (or more tolerantly at stages 6 and 5)' (1971: 225–6).

It is the choice of a cognitive base for the evolutionary progression which represents the distinctive contribution of the cognitive developmentalist. Historical jurisprudence lacked a strong response to the problem of choosing an appropriate measure of evolutionary advance. The cognitive developmental approach comes far closer to satisfactory solutions to these problems. In this respect, Kohlberg has gone further than Piaget (cf. Mays, 1974: 241): while Piaget, at least in his early work, regarded logic and morality as parallel phenomena, the one regulating thought while the other operated on action and the affective life (1932: 404–5), Kohlberg has demonstrated, particularly in respect of the first four stages, the dependence of moral upon cognitive development (1971: 166, 182, 183, 186, 187ff., 197f., 203). Nevertheless, differences in social environment (particularly, for Kohlberg, the opportunities for moral role-taking) continue to play a vital part in the constructivist process. It is this that enables Piaget, for example, to explain the differences between primitive societies and children as regards collective responsibility: the child at the egocentric stage lacks the feeling of unity and solidarity with the group which is an essential condition of the development of collective responsibility (1932: 249–50).

It is this choice of cognition as the base of the evolutionary theory that enables Piaget and Kohlberg (particularly the latter) to provide a more satisfactory account of the nature of 'stages' than was available to Maine and his school. Through their concepts of equilibration and structure, Piaget and Kohlberg are able to show distinctions in kind rather than degree within the constructivist process: the determination of whether x is within a stage or between stages is no longer an arbitrary labelling process, and the structural nature of 'stages' has (as a result of its formal character) considerable explanatory power.[28]

The cognitive developmental model has not lacked its critics. But support for it has recently come from an unexpected quarter. I would hazard that perhaps the most stimulating source today for a revived historical jurisprudence lies in the evolutionary theories of Habermas, which place both speech and language at the centre of social evolution, in the search for a theory of universal pragmatics. But that is a topic which cannot usefully be pursued in this chapter (see further Jackson, 1989b).

(2) *Towards a cognitive developmental theory of legal drafting*

One strong implication of the work of the cognitive developmentalists is that we are more likely to identify evolutionary progressions within the form of institutions rather than their substance. But what is 'form' for present purposes? How are we to identify the cognitive structure of a particular institution? These questions suggest a multiplicity of answers. Piaget himself, as we have noted, stresses the process of justification. But this is for the purposes of his account of *moral* development, which is only one aspect of the cognitive development of the child. Looking at Piaget's work more broadly, we may identify forms of rationality on the one hand (closer here to

---

[28] See, e.g., Piaget, 1932: 77; 1971: 141; Kohlberg, 1971: 169, 184, 186, 225f., 226, 230.

Weber than to Maine) and types of relationship of the self to others on the other hand as amongst the most important reflections of cognitive developmental stages.

The process of language acquisition may also be argued to reflect the child's cognitive growth. A few years ago, I suggested that there might be a direct parallel with legal development in this area. I argued that, within a particular culture, we might identify a process of legal language acquisition, manifested (where we have the appropriate evidence) in the development of the techniques of legal drafting. I suggested that insights from both cognitive development and language-acquisition studies could be used in the comparative analysis of the drafting of ancient codes – particularly where, as in ancient Babylonia and in the Bible, we have a succession of documents from the same culture, whose relative chronology is established (Jackson, 1980). I limit myself here to some illustrative examples.

(a) Increasing combination of variables within a single clause

The child in the stage of concrete intellectual operations deals with each problem in isolation (Piaget, 1980: 61), and cannot focus simultaneously on more than one aspect of a situation.[29] Compare with this the following two stages of Accadian drafting, from second-millennium Babylonia. In the earlier text, the Laws of Eshnunna, the same rule regarding an intruder caught in the act is repeated verbatim in separate clauses, to take account of a simple variation in the context: in clause 12 the intruder is caught in a field, in clause 13 in a house:

LE 12: A man, who will be seized in the field of a *muškenum*, in the crop, in broad daylight, shall weigh out 10 shekels of silver. [He] who will be seized at night in the crop – he shall die, he shall not live.
LE 13: A man, who will be seized in the house of a *muškenum*, in the house, in broad daylight, shall weigh out 10 shekels of silver. [He] who will be seized at night in the house – he shall die, he shall not live.[30]

Compare with this the much more complex combination of variables found in the Laws of Hammurabi, as in the following example:

[29] See Ginsburg and Opper, 1969: 115, for an example from the child's moral judgement: he cannot consider both degree of damage and intention, and bases his judgement solely on the former.
[30] Translations of Eshnunna from Yaron, 1969.

LH 8: If a man has stolen an ox or a sheep or an ass or a swine or a boat, if [it is the property] of a god [or] if [it is the property] of a palace, he shall pay 30-fold; if [it is the property] of a villein, he shall replace [it] 10-fold ...[31]

(b) Reasons for action

The incapacity of young children (the data is drawn mostly from 4–7-year-olds) to give reasons or justifications for their assertions is taken to reflect an incapacity to recognize the possibility that others may take a different view from their own – an aspect of the well-noted characteristic of 'egocentricity' (Ginsburg & Opper, 1969: 89). Michel (1975) has compared this with the development of law at Rome: the pontiffs did not justify their decisions, which were handed down like oracles and accepted only by reason of the authority (*auctoritas*) of their authors; it was only towards the end of the Republic that reasoning appears in legal argument, under the influence of Greek philosophy. We may add data from the ancient Near East. Motive clauses are far more frequent in the later than the earlier legal collections within the Bible. Moreover, no such clauses are found in Eshnunna, while the Laws of Hammurabi do exhibit the phenomenon: where someone finds property he claims to be his in the possession of another, but is unable to produce witnesses corroborating his identification of the property, he is described as 'a felon since he has uttered a slander' (§11).

This example illustrates another facet of cognitive development: the overt use of classification ('he is a felon') in order to produce, or justify, a legal conclusion. Such a form is also found (late) in the Bible. Daube has called it the 'diagnosis' form.[32] An example occurs in the priestly account of the law of homicide:

But if he struck him down with an instrument of iron, so that he died, he is a murderer; the murderer shall be put to death. (Num. 35: 16)

The text displays more than the usual two-part structure, the protasis containing the facts and the apodosis the legal consequences. In the diagnosis pattern there is a third element, the designation of the facts as falling into a recognized category: 'He is a murderer.' Thus the legal consequences are impliedly derived not directly from the facts, but from the categorization of the facts as falling within an

---

[31] Translations of Hammurabi from Driver & Miles, 1952–5.
[32] 1944–5: 39–42, and 1981: 100–6. See further Jackson, 1987b: 3–5.

accepted legal class. We have here an expression of the consciousness of the draftsman of the importance of classification – a vital step, one might think, towards the propositional logic that Piaget has identified as a principal characteristic of the stage of abstract intellectual operations. The incidence of this form suggests the existence of a developmental pattern. In the Bible the diagnosis pattern occurs only in priestly sources;[33] in the Accadian tradition we find it in LH (7, 9, 10, 11, 13) but not in LE. At the same time we may note Daube's observation that the form is *not* met in Greek or Roman legislation. That in no way detracts from its cognitive significance in the Semitic sources. Conceptual advance is not coterminous with its particular expressions in classical culture. While cognitive analysis suggests the universality of underlying developmental sequences, it does not claim that the particular forms expressive of those universal sequences will equally be universal.

I shall not repeat here the other examples provided in my earlier study, other than to note the principal phenomena which I take them to illustrate:

(a) What Beseler termed the 'completomania' of some forms of Roman drafting seems to parallel Piaget's observation of legalistic elaboration at the beginning of the stage of abstract intellectual operations, where children 'seem to take a peculiar pleasure in anticipating all possible cases and in codifying them' (1932: 40).

(b) Studies of language acquisition show that the very young child (ages 2–4 years) is inconsistent in the use of words, and only gradually acquires a usage that is internally consistent and convergent with that of his environment (Ginsburg & Opper, 1969: 81). I have not observed any notable *semantic* inconsistency in early codes (which, after all, are not far distant from the semantics of the ordinary literary language of their age). But we do find a progression from the use of a variety of drafting *forms* towards convergence upon formal consistency. This is particularly notable in the relationship between the Laws of Eshnunna and those of Hammurabi.

(c) The development of the capacity to integrate previously isolated units into a system is a theme of both cognitive and linguistic development; in the latter, it may be measured by the degree of

---

[33] E.g. Lev. 11: 4, 41; 13: 3, 40; Num. 35: 16, 17, 18, 21. Cf. Ezek. 3: 18, 18: 5, 9, 10, 13.

grammatical complexity represented by sentences with more than a single verb, often linked by conjunctions (Limber, 1973; see also Crystal and Davy, 1969: 203f.). We find comparable developments both in the Bible and the ancient Near East. The maximum number of clauses which the Laws of Eshnunna is able to combine into a single paragraph is five; in Hammurabi, we find up to fourteen.

(d) The movement from the concrete to the abstract is a theme of both legal history and developmental psychology. Many examples could be noted at the level of drafting. We may take an example from Roman law, provided by Fritz Schulz (1946: 64, 66). A man who borrowed a horse to ride from Rome to Aricia, but rode through Aricia up the hill beyond, was held liable for *furtum*; in the second century B.C. the jurist Brutus advanced one step beyond the reported case, laying down the rule that one who borrowed the animal was guilty of theft if he took it elsewhere or further than he had stated when borrowing it; Q. Mucius then increased the level of abstraction of the rule, making it apply to any *res* handed over under *depositum* or *commodatum*; ultimately the matter was further generalized, the principle now being expressed as *furtum fit si quis usum alienae rei in suum lucrum convertat*. At the grammatical level, the process is often associated with the movement from the use of the verbal form (for example 'if a man steals') to a nominal form (or 'action noun', as Daube, 1969: 11–63, has called it) derived from it (for example 'theft').

(3) *Modern structural linguistics*[34]

Modern linguistics has not abandoned the problems addressed by Jones, Grimm, Müller et al., nor (so far as I can judge) has the methodology substantially altered. No doubt techniques have become more refined as our knowledge, for example of regularities of phonetic change, increases, but the hypothesis of an original proto-Indo-European language, being that spoken by the Indo-European peoples before their dispersion, is still seriously addressed (see n. 22 above). Indeed, it would be absurd to deny that languages can be grouped in families, and descent from a common parentage (which is

---

[34] I am indebted to Sir John Lyons for his observations on this section, which account for such improvements as I have been able to make to the argument advanced in Jackson, 1988a. This is not to imply his endorsement of what here follows.

not to exclude historical influences) remains the most likely explanatory hypothesis.

However, historical linguistics no longer plays the intellectual role of nineteenth-century comparative philology, as a model – widely diffused amongst the intelligentsia – to which workers in other fields look for inspiration. That role in our day has been assumed by structural linguistics. Here, the emphasis is not upon the development of languages, but rather on the synchronic, or systemic dimension: it is the relation between different elements of the language (to put the matter non-technically) that allows meaning to be constructed and transmitted. Perhaps the two dominant representatives of the synchronic approach are Saussure and Chomsky (notwithstanding the major differences between them), although it would be wrong to attribute to either one of them a total neglect of or disinterest in the diachronic aspects of language.

Links between twentieth-century linguistic and jurisprudential formalism have recently been claimed by Goodrich (1987), who sees a particular similarity between Kelsen and Saussure, though he finds the source of the parallel to reside more in neo-Kantian philosophy than in any direct influence of the modern linguistic paradigm. While the suggested parallel between Saussure and Kelsen requires some care (Jackson, 1988d: 125–31), it is certainly true that jurisprudential formalism in the twentieth century has achieved a dominance over latter-day historical jurisprudence (such as the schemes of Roscoe Pound or A. S. Diamond), in much the same way that synchronic linguistics (in its different forms) has pushed comparative philology from the centre of the linguistic stage.

An attempt has, indeed, recently been made to argue in favour of a particular theory of law by claiming that it exhibits the same features as are found in a leading synchronic theory of linguistics. I refer to the suggestion by Perrott that legal systems themselves have a 'deep structure' comparable to the linguistic deep structures identified by Chomsky. Perrott claims to find the 'deep structure' of a legal system partly in Hart's conception of the union of primary and secondary rules. Using Chomsky's theory of 1957, Perrott seeks to equate Hart's primary rules with Chomsky's 'phrase-structure rules' and Hart's 'secondary rules' with Chomskyan 'transformational rules'. As he puts it, 'Chomsky's conception of linguistic analysis ... also necessarily consists ... of rules of two logically distinct types, phrase structure rules and transformational rules. The phrase structure rules impose direct prescriptions on linguistic behaviour, the transformational rules only do so rather indirectly' (1980: 9). His argument may be reconstructed thus. Phrase-structure rules are an obligatory element of natural languages. They generate the deep structures on which transformational rules operate in order to produce the surface structures. But transformational rules are 'optional' in the sense that natural languages could operate without them (and in the earliest version of Chomskyan theory do operate largely without them), albeit with apparent loss of efficiency. Similarly, on the Hartian account, primary rules (which prescribe patterns of behaviour, typically by imposing duties) are a universal phenomenon of human societies, whereas secondary rules are 'optional', in that they are characteristic of advanced legal systems. Perrott seeks to place a naturalist interpretation upon the apparent structural similarity by emphasizing the substantive universals within the 'deep structure', and by viewing the 'mediating' role of transformational rules in terms of the transformed *status* (as positive law) of such rules, and perhaps also of their more concrete or specific form. Thus he argues that 'the deep structure of law consists only of primary rules ... [which] would impose on all humans certain rather abstractly stated duties, and these duties would be "Fundamental Duties" in an ultimate sense. But they would also be legal, or rather proto-legal, duties and not merely moral (or proto-moral) duties, in that it would be genetically required (to *be* human) that appropriate secondary rules (analogous to syntactic transformational rules) be adopted by particular societies in order to mediate the Fundamental Duties into specific legal duties of the positive legal system' (10). This leads him to suggest that 'the phrase Natural Law perhaps should be used of the *combination* of Fundamental Proto-Legal Duties specified in the deep structure, together with the appropriate mediating secondary rules that make possible the specification of corresponding legal duties in the given positive law system, and together with the deductive inference that some such legal duties are logically necessary to any society' (10).

But there are serious difficulties in this argument. First, Chomsky does not conceive of transformational rules as mediating between a level of universals and one of particular concretizations. Rather, transformational rules mediate between the 'deep structures' and 'surface structures' of particular sentences (the former being no more abstract than the latter), these sentences having already been generated by the phrase-structure rules. Perrott himself seems to recognize this when he writes that the transformational rules 'specify what operations can be performed on or with the products of those other [i.e. phrase-structure] rules' (9). There is, in fact, a clear difference between the function of Chomsky's transformational rules and Hart's secondary rules. The former are, as Perrott puts it, '*about* the phrase structure rules' (7; cf. 9) only in the sense that they alter the form of the deep structures by transposing their elements; Hart's secondary rules, on the other hand, are 'about' primary rules in the sense that they affect their status in law, and their efficiency of operation. One might almost say that Chomskyan transformational rules concern the syntactic dimension of sentence structure, whereas Hartian secondary rules concern the pragmatic dimension of primary rules. In assigning to secondary rules the role of mediation of natural law fundamental duties into specific legal duties of the positive legal system, Perrott retains such a 'pragmatic' role for secondary rules; the syntactic function of transformational rules is not here replicated.

There is, moreover, a more serious difficulty inherent in Perrott's argument. To my mind, he fails to establish in what respect legal theory presents problems analogous to those which synchronic linguistics seeks to explain. One aspect of this failure to identify a genuine parallel in the problem is the confusion in Perrott's argument over the very function of the notion of 'deep structure' in Chomsky. For the latter, the 'deep structure' of sentences is part of their grammatical form (more technically, as Lyons suggests to me, it is 'a sub-level of their lexical and syntactic structure, which is directly related to, but distinct from their syntactic structure, or meaning'): every sentence has a deep structure (or, in the case of ambiguous sentences, two or more deep structures). Deep structure is not, therefore, a characteristic of (far less an invariant, genetically required feature of) entire languages (conceived as linguistic systems).

We must be clear as to what Chomsky claims to be innate. He has shown some irritation at misunderstandings of his work on this point:

I have read many criticisms saying how ill-conceived it is to postulate innate deep structures. I never said that, and nothing I have written suggests anything of the sort, though such a view has been maintained by others. Similarly I have often read that what I am proposing is that deep structures do not vary from one language to another, that all languages have the same deep structure: people have apparently been misled by the word *deep* and confuse it with *invariant*. Once again, the only thing I claim to be 'invariant' is universal grammar. (1979a: 171f.)

For Chomsky – leaving aside, for present purposes, the modifications which he has made to his theory over a period of a quarter-century – 'deep structures' are properties of sentences, not of grammars. Every sentence has its 'surface structure', an analysis into grammatical categories not far removed from the traditional 'parsing' of sentences into the explicit formal components of the surface grammar of the language. However, the immense variety of sentences, and the difficulty in accounting for the process of learning them on the basis of the explicit grammar of the language alone, leads Chomsky to require the analysis of such sentences in terms of a system of relations between a much smaller group of elements. It is this set of relations – phrase-structure grammar or, more recently, the 'base component' – which generates the 'deep structure' of sentences, in the sense that it is that set of relations which provides a precise, structural description of the elements of the 'deep structure' of the sentence itself, and of their interrelationship. Hence, the 'deep structure' of a sentence is nothing other than an integral part of the formalization of the grammatical structure of that sentence, accorded a special status as 'deep' in virtue of its scientific importance in enabling us to construct an intelligible grammar of that language, and for its contribution to the process of learning the language.

Every natural language is taken to have its own 'base component'. But only some aspects of the base component are taken to be universal, and it is these alone which make up what Chomsky calls 'universal grammar' – the only part of his account for which he claims that we must assume the existence of a physical representation within the genetic endowment.

The deep structure of particular sentences, therefore, is a reflection of the particular grammatical structure of a specific language. Chomsky clearly does not suggest that any part of the grammar specific to a particular language is innate. What he claims to be innate is no more than a part of the capacity to learn some (any) particular language.

For Chomsky, such a limited claim to innateness presents the best hypothesis available to account for three particular features of linguistic communication, which otherwise would appear difficult to explain in psychological terms. These features are: first, the fact that there appears to exist a capacity to construct an infinite set of complex linguistic sentences on the basis of the child's much more limited experience of such sentences; secondly, there appears to exist a capacity to recognize sentences presented to us as either well-formed or not, according to the rules of well-formedness of our particular natural language, without conscious knowledge of or instruction in those rules of well-formedness and without prior experience of judging the well-formedness of the particular sentence presented to us; thirdly, these capacities are universal to the members of any particular linguistic community, barring pathological incapacities such as deafness or language disorders. For convenience, we may refer to these problems as those of construction, recognition and universality.

It is far from clear that law presents comparable problems. Although legal systems undoubtedly contain rules for the construction of further rules (implicit within Hart's rules of recognition), there is no suggestion that the child has a capacity, comparable to his linguistic capacity, to generate *legal* rules. Secondly, while the psychological recognition of rules as legal (well-formed according to the legal system) is indeed a problem which legal theory is required to address, there is no suggestion (within positivism, to be sure) that such recognition proceeds upon the basis of some unconscious knowledge; quite the contrary, Hart's theory requires the deployment of an 'internal point of view' by the officials, who consciously use the secondary rules as reasons justifying their action (creation or application of the primary rules). Nor is it at all clear that legal systems are universal in human society, such that we could say that a society without one was pathologically flawed (whatever that might mean).

Lyons has attempted to detach the psychological/genetic problematic from Chomsky's theory. Even if we ignore the problem of language learning, he argues, Chomsky's theory still provides us with the best formal account of what is common to all languages. In other words, he claims that we can have 'generative grammar' without presupposing any form of innate capacity (1970b: 83ff.; 1981a: 125, 228, 235). Whether Chomsky would agree is somewhat debatable. There are indications that he views his theory as the best formal account *given* the need to account also for psychological competence; thus, that without that latter need, alternative formal accounts would do just as well. We need not enter into this debate.

Let us assume, for present purposes, that Lyons is right. Comparison between law and language would appear to be rather more promising, if we confine ourselves to a formal, rather than a psychological/genetic problematic.

If we accept this standpoint, we may quite validly ask whether it is useful to model the structure of an individual law upon the structure claimed within linguistics to underlie an individual sentence. For example, we might profitably review Kelsen's theory of norm structure in the light of transformational grammar. But then, we must be clear about the kind of claim being made. If the individual norm is itself regarded as a particular form of linguistic proposition, then the findings of contemporary linguistics will, indeed, be pertinent. For the norm, in that event, will fall directly into the class of phenomena which linguistics claims to study. But Kelsen himself insists on a distinction between the norm and its linguistic expression, and this distinction is common within the tradition of the logical analysis of law. In that event, we have to ask how far the analogy between law and language (being treated as different phenomena) extends.

Whether we take law to be a species (or sub-set, or register) of language, or to be a dual semiotic system – a system of signification which is communicated in language, even though it is not itself language (arguably, like the novel), the Chomskyan model loses any claims to special privilege. At least two alternatives open up. One is represented by the work of Kalinowski, who sees law as consisting in a multiplicity of language-systems (legislative, adjudicatory, doctrinal, etc.), each one of which can be analysed for its specific syntactic, semantic and pragmatic features.[35] This tradition draws upon the logic of Carnap, Frege, and latterly Montague. But there is also another tradition, represented by structural semiotics, which draws inspiration from an extension of Saussurian linguistics to the discursive level. Here, it is claimed that models developed for the understanding of lexical meaning and sentence meaning may also provide clues for the understanding of larger units of discourse. Indirectly, I suggest, the modern movement which sees law as analogous to literature stands in this tradition, and it is to this that I next turn, albeit briefly.

[35] Kalinowski, 1965, and numerous other works. See further Carrión-Wam, 1985: 32–43.

(4) Law as literature

One of the most discussed topics in modern jurisprudence is the use of literature as a model for the understanding of legal systems (Jackson, 1988c: chapters 1 and 5). Ronald Dworkin, in particular, has urged that we view legal systems not as mere collections, or lists, of independent rules or norms, related to each other only by the law of non-contradiction (as is suggested by many versions of positivism), but rather holistically, paying attention to the 'integrity' of the system, taken to reflect as coherently as possible a set of underlying principles (1978; 1986). The law – or at least its judicial elaboration – should be viewed as a chain novel, wherein each judge adds a new chapter, paying maximum regard to coherence with what has gone before.

It may be thought that this takes us some distance from Chomskyan – or any other formal system of – linguistics. And indeed it does. Dworkin's immediate source of inspiration appears to be New Criticism in literature, which stresses the constructive role of the community of interpreters. In terms of our earlier argument against the direct applicability of the Chomskyan model as a 'deep structure' of the legal system, Dworkin's account remains closer to law as we traditionally understand it than to language. For the processes he seeks to describe are entirely explicit and rational; they do not depend upon either arbitrary associations of signifiers and signifieds, or upon any notion of unconsciously deployed knowledge (on the importance of which for law, see Jackson, 1987a). Nevertheless, I have argued that Dworkin's literary model does contain significant features which link it with the traditional structure of linguistics. In particular, Dworkin sees law as a system within which meaning is constructed intensionally: meanings are constructed *within* and for the purposes of law, and through the relationship to each other of legal signifiers. Dworkin remains wedded to the importance of distinguishing the legal function from the non-legal (including the political); hence, his insistence that the judge ought to base his reasoning upon 'principles' as opposed to 'policies'. It is, of course, true that Dworkin sees his jurisprudence as, in a different sense, 'political': his ideal judge must base his reasoning upon the best version he can produce of the political morality of the community he serves. But such a judicial political theory is produced within, and for the purposes of, the law: we may compare (though

Dworkin does not) the adoption and use of loan-words taken from a foreign language, or the construction of images in the press which purport to reproduce a particular form of specialized discourse, but which clearly reconstruct it for their own purposes.

In a second respect, Dworkin's position shares a problematic common to linguistics and literature: the role attributed (or not attributed) to authorial intention. Legislative intention is not seen by Dworkin as a paramount criterion of legal interpretation, just as much of modern literary criticism refuses to accord exclusive validity to those interpretations which can be shown to have been within the intention of the original author. But there is, I would suggest, a deeper issue inherent in this problem, one drawn from linguistics. There, we encounter much debate as to whether it is possible or desirable to separate meaning (or signification) from communication. Chomsky provides one classical version of the theory that language is an abstract system of meanings, while its use for communication is something entirely different. In a different way, Saussure distinguished *langue* from *parole*. Modern pragmatics has stressed the importance of distinguishing a sentence from its utterance, the latter normally implying an intentional act on the part of the utterer.

Such issues have been reflected in modern jurisprudence. They are not, however, to be restricted to the applicability of the literary analogy. I have argued (1985: chapter 7) that Hart strongly endorses a 'communicational model' of law, wherein law works if and to the extent that the messages sent by the legislator are successfully received, decoded and applied by the judge. Hart is fully aware that the legislator may use a form of encoding which is explicitly designed to delegate to the judge a creative function – as where phrases like 'reasonable care' or 'fair wage' are used. But equally, he sees the open texture of language as inevitably creating some situations in which the judge is not able, immediately and unambiguously, to decode a legislative expression for the purposes of application to a particular case before him. Where this occurs, we have, in Hart's terms, a 'crisis in communication'.

It is clear from this that our understanding of law, like that of literature, requires us to face some very fundamental issues. Is law to be regarded as a dual semiotic system, one where language (or a particular register of a language) is used in order to express a set of meanings which possess their own rules and system of signification, in the same way that we may offer a linguistic description of a painting? And if so, do such interlocking semiotic systems have anything in common? Are any common semiotic features to be regarded as universals, valid for all signifying systems in society? Clearly, if we offer an affirmative answer to the last question, we have a new means to answer some of the questions posed by Maine. For we may adopt semiotic criteria in the search for legal universals, and equally we may look to non-universal semiotic characteristics in any search for family relationships between legal systems. It is, for example, a matter of active debate at present whether the procedural and evidentiary differences between systems of common law and civil law are significant, at the semiotic level (Jackson, 1988c: chapter 1).

The argument in this section has thus far suggested that contemporary debates in legal philosophy do reflect some important linguistic issues, even though the protagonists do not identify their problems as primarily falling within this field. I turn now to a different model of 'law as literature', which stems from a source which is quite explicit about the relationships between law, literature and linguistics. I refer to the structural semiotics of the school of Greimas.[36] Greimas, unlike Chomsky, claims that we may identify common structures within semiotic systems. These common features may be explained in terms of linguistic categories. Indeed, much of the French structuralist tradition, to which Greimas belongs, is premised upon the belief that the categories which explain the relations between different signifying elements within a sentence may also be used in order to explain the semiotic structures of larger units of discourse. However, this does not lead Greimas to accord a primacy to linguistic structures. They, like the structures of other systems of signification, reflect in a particular manner what Greimas takes to be universal semiotic structures.

Within what he calls the 'structures élémentaires de la signification', Greimas identifies two interacting axes: a paradigmatic axis and a syntagmatic axis. The paradigmatic axis concerns the constraints upon choice in any semantic context (for example oppositions such as 'good' versus 'bad', or choice of colours, where substitution is possible while still making sense). The syntagmatic axis concerns sequential (rather than substitutory) constraints on

---

[36] For a full account, see Jackson, 1985: Part 2, and for a less technical summary, 1988c: chapter 1. For a comparison of legal and semiotic notions of 'structure', see Jackson, 1988b.

intelligibility: sense depends upon the reducibility of that which is signified to a basic 'narrative' structure. (In effect, this amounts to a claim that our systems of signification commonly presuppose an identification of intelligibility with purposive action.) Specifically, intelligibility consists of three parts: the setting of goals, the performance (or attempted performance) of those goals, and retrospective recognition of the performance (or non-performance) of those goals. In literature, such goals, performances and recognition processes may be 'fictional'.

In law, this syntagmatic level may be expressed (I do not suggest exclusively) in the communicational process itself. Parliament is set a goal of communicating a particular message to a judge. It promulgates a set of words to do so. When we read the court's judgement, we may recognize whether, and to what extent, the 'performance' of Parliament has achieved such objectives. I put the matter in such simplistic terms purely by way of illustration. Of course, the judge himself is also an agent, or a 'subject' in Greimasian terminology, in the sense that he too has been set a goal. The many different processes of law (for instance fact-finding, doctrine-writing, judicial decision-making, advocacy, client-counselling) are each capable of bearing meaning because they reflect those same basic underlying patterns of goal–performance–recognition as underlie all construction of meaning. To say this is not to explain what it is that makes such processes appear legal. But that question – the construction of the appearance of a particular form of sense, legal sense – is itself answerable in terms of the particular ways in which the 'structures élémentaires de la signification' are expressed in those texts and activities we designate as 'legal'. To ask that latter question is to proceed to a level closer to the surface, which involves the use of cultural artifacts which no one would suggest are universal.

(5) *Law and religion revisited*

All this might seem to have taken us far away from the concerns of Maine's historical jurisprudence. Let me suggest, however, that these apparently abstract concerns may nevertheless contribute to our understanding of some of the issues which Maine discussed. I confine myself here to one example, Maine's treatment of the relationship between law and religion.

Of the 'primitive' codes, Maine observed:

Quite enough too remains of these collections, both in the East and in the West, to show that they mingled up religious, civil, and merely moral ordinances, without any regard to differences in their essential character; and this is consistent with all we know of early thought from other sources, the severance of law from morality, and of religion from law, belonging very distinctly to the later stages of mental progress. (*AL*: 16)

This passage is not uncharacteristic of Maine's methodology. He accepted from others (for instance Spencer, 1858: 1, 34) that at an early stage of mental progress, man did not differentiate the ideas of law, religion and morality. But his principal concern was to show a particular effect, within law, of what he took to be a generally accepted view of that stage of mental development. His theory of the intermingling of law and religion in primitive codes was not, I suggest, designed as *proof* of the absence of, or incapacity to form, a distinction between law and religion; it was simply a particular legal reflection of what he took to have been established on other grounds.

We may note, at the same time, that Maine was not attributing this lack of differentiation to the very earliest stage of social development, nor indeed was he claiming it to be universal. Such propositions were not required for Maine's purposes. His most famous statement on the matter contained within it its own limitation: 'There is no system of recorded law, literally from China to Peru, which, when it first emerges into notice, is not seen to be entangled with religious and ritual observance' (*ELC*: 5). Maine here refers to systems of *recorded* law, which to him did *not* represent the earliest stage. Nor did he purport to *prove* that no distinction was perceived between law, religion and ritual. He asserted only the coexistence and lack of differentiation of these elements within the ancient codes.

The evidence on which Maine based his claims was largely that of the Roman and Hindu law-books. However, he also referred to Leviticus (*ELC*: 5–6). Since Maine's day, considerable evidence has come to light of 'law-codes' from the ancient Near East, and some later writers (for example Diamond, 1971: 47–8; Sawer, 1965: 62) have seen them as supporting the very reverse of Maine's theory: the earliest stage of recorded law is in fact 'secular', and 'religious' (or priestly) elements only come to be added later.

However, both Maine's theory, and its negation, simply presuppose the applicability of our modern concepts of 'law' and 'religion' to the ancient sources. Maine's version also imputes a certain view of primitive mental incapacity to differentiate these concepts. I would like now to offer an alternative view, one informed by the structural semiotics of Greimas, to which reference was made in the last section.

The document of ancient lore which seems, on the surface, most clearly to exemplify Maine's claims is the Bible. The Pentateuch, in particular, seems to the modern eye to present multiple conflations of categories, amounting to a veritable literary hotch-pot. Not only does there appear to be no distinction between law, morality and ritual; there is also a fluid relationship between the presentation of norms, and the narrative context in which they appear. Even within such modest collections of 'civil law' which may be identified, scholars have found great difficulty in detecting principles of arrangement. Biblical critics, armed with modern conceptions of literary coherence, have accordingly resorted to scissors and paste. The 'literary-historical' approach, descended (conventionally) from Wellhausen, might only with moderate unkindness be described as neither literary nor historical. But that would be going too far. Suffice it to stress the importance of recognizing that any such method presupposes the universality, or at least the applicability, of a particular form of underlying rationality to the texts in hand. My contention is that modern biblical scholarship in this area has too uncritically presupposed the applicability of modern Western rationality. In saying that, I do not suppose that we can discard our modern spectacles, and attain direct access to the rationality of the past. But modern thought presents us with a range of models of rationality, amongst which we may choose. My choice – if a crude characterization may be in order – is closer to Lévi-Strauss than to Kant.

I suggest that we can find a particular manifestation, within biblical literature, of the underlying Greimasian 'deep structure' of signification. The key to it resides in the use of repetition as a mode of recognition. 'Repetition' itself is found in a number of different modes. One is 'thematic repetition'. That is the function, for example, of the valedictory addresses of Moses, which comprise the bulk of the Book of Deuteronomy, and which seek to validate, in this way, both the giving of the Law at Sinai, and the (polemic) course of the history of the Israelites, in being released from the slavery of Egypt and approaching the conquest of the promised land. The validation, by such repetition, of that combination of themes is given particular theological expression in the concept of 'covenant', which is itself given narrative form in ritual ceremonies said to have occurred at various points in the history. Biblical scholars reading such accounts through the eyes of New Testament theology have seen in these repeated covenants a notion of change or supersession: the 'covenant renewal ceremony'. That, in its own way, is just as anachronistic (for the Old Testament) as are some of the modern readings of biblical law which I have mentioned.

Again, there is thematic repetition in the biographies of significant leaders: that of Joshua is closely modelled upon that of Moses, and indeed Deuteronomy 18 promises quite explicitly the re-emergence in any generation of a 'prophet like Moses'. There was nothing strange, therefore, when in a later epoch Jesus self-consciously sought to fulfil the same role.

There are multiple links between these narratives and the collections of law found in the Pentateuch. The 'Exodus' theme – liberation from slavery – occurs, hardly surprisingly, at the head of the first collection of laws which follows the release from Egypt (Exod. 21: 2–11), and this theme is repeated in the laws, not only directly in the later collections, but also by way of (apparent) 'motive clauses' justifying norms of other kinds – especially social norms concerning charity or debt-relief (Jackson, 1989c). Moreover, it is the theme of slavery which provides the organizing principle of the first section of the so-called 'Book of the Covenant' in Exodus (Jackson, 1988e). For slavery is the theme of a chiasmus which provides the only satisfactory explanation of the arrangement of this group:

Chiasmus in Exodus 21:2–27

A   Exod. 21: 2–11   Liberation of male and female slaves

B   Exod. 21: 12–17 Capital provisions

C   Exod. 21: 18–19 Injuries from a brawl

D   Exod. 21: 20–1   Fatal assault on one's own slave

C   Exod. 21: 22–3   Brawl affecting pregnant woman

B   Exod. 21: 24–5   Talionic provisions

A   Exod. 21: 26–7   Liberation of male and female slaves

'Chiasmus', of course, is a sophisticated literary form, but based nevertheless upon repetition. Much of the arrangement of the rest of this collection is also based upon repetition of themes, though not in such a highly structured literary fashion. Carmichael (1972) has called attention to the existence of a number of 'double-series' in the 'Book of the Covenant', the elements of the second series repeating the themes in the same order as they appear in the first. Of course, this begs the question: 'What is a theme?' A negative criterion may be stated readily enough: thematic repetition is not negated merely because the elements concerned fail to fall within the same *modern* category. At this literary level, we do find connections between 'law' and 'narrative' on the one hand, and 'law', 'morality' and 'ritual' on the other.

To state the positive principle of connection is more difficult. It is sometimes claimed (by Schacht, 1974: 397, for example) that Western rationality is 'analytical', Eastern 'analogical'. But it is not easy to find in the literature any account of the 'analogical' which goes beyond claiming that it is a wider conception that that of Western analyticity. Often, we find it presented as a somewhat arbitrary association of ideas. As regards the biblical material, I have suggested (1989a) that analogical connections are identifiable as ones where the mode of expression is to be found as much in the *form* of the legal texts as in their content; and where the systematicness of the values underlying the law is identifiable more as a matter of narrative fit than by reasoning through different levels of abstraction. Analogy thus does not have to be explicit in the advancement of its own argument: it can proceed by the collocation of different sets of binary oppositions; and its resemblances and differences may be based upon social–experiential narrative frameworks, rather than abstract legal concepts. In this sense, the legal text both creates and is expressed in its own language. It is relatively easy to demonstrate this through the study of material from cultures far removed from our own. But on principle, the same types of signification may be found to operate within our own legal system. The study of ancient law, so viewed, remains pertinent to the analysis of contemporary legal problems, and language is an even more important model for law today than it was for Maine.

(6) Conclusion

The account of the relations between law and language which I have offered in this chapter should be sufficient to warn us against any simple, positivistic retrospective judgement upon Maine – one which says that science has progressed, that we now know better, and that we can specify in which respects Maine was right or wrong. To say this is not merely to deny that later scholarship is necessarily better than earlier scholarship. Even more important, we should be wary of our competence to construct an historical Maine with any degree of objectivity (cf. Jackson, 1988c: chapter 6). In reading Maine, we are necessarily – to some extent – rewriting him in the light of modern preoccupations and interests. What we can do, however, is to read him in a dialogic spirit – to see what he would say about *our* preoccupations and concerns, and to ponder what we should now say about problems and hypotheses as he formulates them.

CHAPTER 17

Linguistics and law: the legacy of Sir Henry Maine

John Lyons

INTRODUCTION

The title of my contribution, it will be noted, is slightly, though significantly, different from that of Professor Jackson's. I have reversed the order of the two keyterms, putting the word 'linguistics' before 'law', in order to reflect the fact that I, in contrast with him (and with Maine himself), am looking at the issues, not with the eyes of a lawyer, but with those of a linguist: i.e. with those of a professional student of language. And I have used 'linguistics' rather than 'language', partly to reinforce this fact, but also to eliminate certain troublesome ambiguities associated with the word 'language' in English.

The linguist, nowadays, finds it essential to draw a clear distinction, conceptually, if not always terminologically, not only between language and the study of language, but also between different senses of the word 'language' (construed generically), between language (in these several senses) and languages, and between language and the use of language (or the products of the use of language). My substitution of 'linguistics' for 'language' is associated with the adoption of a particular, late twentieth-century, theoretical framework within which the distinctions to which I have referred find their place (see Lyons, 1981a). Maine himself, of course, employed the characteristically nineteenth-century term 'philology', rather than 'linguistics'. Nowadays, 'linguistics' is generally taken to be the broader term; and 'linguistics', quite rightly, is the term that Jackson uses in the second part of his chapter.

As to my sub-title, which also relates to, but differs from, Jackson's: this will no doubt greatly surprise my colleagues in linguistics. Most of them, I am sure, will never have heard of Maine in connection with linguistics.¹ Maine is not mentioned in any of the standard histories of nineteenth-century linguistics. Nor, to the best of my knowledge, do studies of Maine which mention his appeal to the findings and methods of comparative philology, as many do with different degrees of emphasis, suggest that he was anything other than a borrower.

In this respect, of course, Maine stands in striking contrast with Sir William Jones, who, in one of his addresses to the Royal Asiatic Society of Bengal a hundred years earlier, had delivered himself of those now famous words (quoted by Jackson, p. 258), which, many would say, initiated, or at least prophesied, the beginnings of the new discipline of comparative philology. Jones' work was, of course, well known to Maine. And their careers have much in common. There is no doubt about the dramatic effect that Jones' long period of service in India had, both upon Jones himself and also upon what came to be seen later as the scientific study of language, and, indirectly, upon the history of ideas (cf. Cannon, 1964: 1979). But, as is clear from some of the preceding chapters, scholars differ considerably as to the influence that Maine's much shorter stay in India had either on Maine himself or on India. Others may challenge the view that he 'returned to England remarkably undisturbed by the experience of Calcutta' (Cocks, 1988: 88). But it seems clear that, unlike Jones, not only did he not learn Sanskrit or study with the brahmins while he was in India, but he did not show evidence, either then or subsequently, of any particular interest in language and languages different in degree or kind from that of any well-trained classicist.

However that may be, none of the ideas for which Maine is known to students of legal history or of anthropology and sociology is associated with him and discussed in terms of this association by historians of nineteenth-century linguistics. But these ideas – in particular, the idea of evolutionary progress from more primitive to more advanced stages of social and cultural development and of the possibility of reconstructing aspects of past stages of civilized human societies from their fossilized relics or vestiges in contemporary societies judged to be less advanced – were of course components of

[1] I myself had not heard of him in this connection (though I was aware of his work, in a general sort of way and at second hand, in other fields) until I had been elected to the Mastership of Trinity Hall and my Sussex colleague, Dr Raymond Cocks, who was at that time writing his now recently published book (1988), drew my attention to Maine's interest in comparative philology.

the Victorian *Zeitgeist* (as several of the other contributors have reminded us). They played their part in the development of linguistics, and in the mid nineteenth century they drew support from the findings of that branch of linguistics which came to be called comparative philology. But they did not originate in comparative philology; nor did the mid- and late nineteenth-century comparative philologists or the theorists of the emergent discipline of linguistics look to the writings of Maine for what Jackson aptly refers to as their models and their metaphors. I shall have more to say about this presently.

What I want to emphasize here is that I have deliberately chosen both my title, and more particularly, perhaps, my sub-title, in the spirit of Jackson's proposal that we should 'read Maine in a dialogic spirit – to see what he would say about *our* preoccupations and concerns, and to ponder what we should now say about problems and hypotheses as he formulates them' (p. 293). And I have been pleased to note that several of the other contributors have adopted the same viewpoint, emphasizing Maine's role, especially in the development of the social sciences, as being that of an ancestor, rather than a founding father: one of those 'beings of the past', as Professor Peel puts it above, 'who yet are a present force, beings who interact with the living' (p. 179); one of those beings, with whom we, their descendants, can commune (though regrettably we can no longer communicate with them) in the present. This sense of communion is for me the more exciting in that I was not aware, until now, that Maine was, or could reasonably be adopted as, an intellectual ancestor in my own field.

Like Professor Jackson, I will divide my contribution into two parts: Part A, 'Maine and [nineteenth-century] comparative philology'; and Part B, 'Linguistics and the study of law'. In each case, I will comment briefly, and selectively, on points made by Jackson in his chapter, and will add one or two of my own.

PART A: MAINE AND COMPARATIVE PHILOLOGY

As far as Maine's appeal to comparative philology is concerned, I see no reason to challenge Professor Jackson's conclusions or to question any part of his presentation, but it might be worth making a few supplementary comments from the viewpoint of modern linguistics.

(1) The comparative method

Let me begin by commenting upon the rather special sense in which the word 'comparative' was employed by philologists in Maine's day, and still is employed in present-day linguistics, in such phrases as 'the comparative method'. 'comparative philology' or 'from a comparative point of view'.

Languages may be compared with one another, in principle, from many points of view and for any of several different purposes. But when nineteenth-century comparative philologists set about comparing languages, they did so, primarily if not exclusively, from a diachronic, or historical, point of view and for the very specific purpose of demonstrating that the languages in question either did or did not belong to the same so-called family of languages – that they were or were not genetically related. And the method that they applied – the so-called comparative method – was associated with this point of view and this specific purpose. It was supported, moreover, by a particular set of assumptions about the nature of language and about the way in which languages develop through time, which, though they may not have been made explicit initially, came to be recognized for what they were in the course of the nineteenth century, and were challenged or reasserted, as the case may be, as the comparative method itself was refined and submitted to critical examination, in what we may now think of as the classical period of comparative philology. Several of these assumptions can no longer be accepted without qualification.

Maine's interest in comparative philology may well have been stimulated a decade or so before the publication of *Ancient Law* (during the period when he was first of all assistant tutor at Trinity Hall, 1844–7, and subsequently Regius Professor of Civil Law in Cambridge, 1847–62). But it is generally accepted that one of Maine's principal sources for his knowledge of the findings and theories of comparative philology was the work of Max Müller, who, as Jackson notes, did more than anyone else to popularize the subject and make its findings known to the educated British public in the mid-century. Maine may have become personally acquainted with Müller, when he returned from India, during the time that he spent in Oxford (1871–8). Whether or not this is so, although Maine continued to refer to the findings of comparative philology as support for his views in his later works and in later editions of *Ancient*

Law, there is no evidence that he kept up to date with developments in the subject. It was mid-century comparative philology, therefore, that Maine drew upon – the comparative philology (or comparative grammar) of what one may now characterize as the pre-classical period. This was the period which followed that of the founding fathers, Rask, Bopp and Grimm, and preceded that of Brugmann and the other great Neogrammarians, who emerged as self-conscious revolutionaries in the 1870s and within a relatively short space of time had established a new orthodoxy and constructed what we may now think of as the classical synthesis (see below). What were the characteristics of this middle, pre-classical, period of comparative philology in contrast with those of later periods? At the risk of grossly oversimplifying what is a complex set of similarities and differences, of continuities and disjunctures, I would mention the following points as being of particular relevance in the present context.

(i) 'Race', 'language' and 'culture'
Although many mid-century philologists (including Müller) may have explicitly rejected the equation of language with race and culture, it is arguable that much of their thinking and theorizing was still influenced by earlier attitudes. It must not be forgotten that the founding fathers, including Rask, Grimm and Bopp had been strongly motivated in their researches (and Grimm more strongly, perhaps, than the others) by German Romanticism and by its assertion of an intimate association between language, culture and nationhood. The philologists of the mid nineteenth century were certainly more ready than were most of their late nineteenth-century successors to assume that some languages are more primitive than others and to correlate the development from a more primitive to a more advanced stage in language with a development from a more primitive cultural level to a more advanced level.

(ii) The terms 'Indo-European' and 'Aryan'
The assumption that changes in the structure of languages correlate with, and are in phase with, stages in the development of culture (regardless of whether this development is seen as having directionality and as being describable in terms of progress or decline) cannot but have been encouraged by the potentially equivocal use of such terms as 'Indo-European' and 'Aryan', or 'Germanic', 'Celtic', 'Slavonic', etc., by comparative philologists.

There are in fact two possibilities of equivocation, and they may be conflated. The terms in question have frequently been employed until quite recently, even by specialists, on the one hand to label not only languages but also peoples and cultures, and on the other, to label not only a particular family of languages and its members, but also the so-called parent-language (*Ursprache*), attested or hypothetical, from which the so-called daughter-languages were said to be descended. Maine's own speculations about the prehistory of the various peoples and cultures to which he refers may not have been seriously affected by the equivocal use of terms which properly apply only to languages, but there are certainly passages in his writings where 'Aryan', in particular, appears to be used equivocally.

Nowadays, most linguists distinguish systematically between terms for language-families ('Indo-European', 'Germanic', etc.) and terms for parent-languages ('Proto-Indo-European', 'Proto-Germanic', etc.), while 'Aryan', if it is used at all by linguists, covers a narrower range of languages than 'Indo-European'.[2]

(iii) Sanskrit and Proto-Indo-European

Not surprisingly given the relative antiquity of the earliest extant written records, when the Indo-European hypothesis was first clearly formulated and for some considerable time thereafter, much greater weight was given to Sanskrit (and more especially to the Sanskrit of the Vedic hymns) in the reconstruction of the parent-language than to Greek or Latin or to any of the Germanic, Celtic or Slavonic languages. Correspondingly more weight was similarly given to the Indian evidence in the reconstruction of Proto-Indo-European (so-called Aryan) mythology and institutions. And the original homeland (*Urheimat*) of the speakers of Proto-Indo-European was generally thought to be in Asia, rather than Europe.

---

[2] Jespersen (1922: 19–99) and Pedersen (1931) are still invaluable for much of the detail that they include, and for their accessibility and readability. But it must now be recognized that the account that they give of nineteenth-century linguistics is very much that of Neogrammarian 'Whiggism'. A more recent, and more up-to-date, brief history of linguistics is Robins (1967). There has been a very considerable amount of work done in the historiography of linguistics in the last few years, the results of which have not yet found their way into general textbooks on the subject. The following will give entry to the field: Bynon (1986), Hoenigswald (1977; 1978; 1986), Hymes (1974), Koerner (1981; 1983a, b), Maher (1966), Morpurgo-Davies (1975; 1986), Robins (1978), Sebeok (1975), *TPS* (1978) and Wilbur (1977). For historical and comparative linguistics, as it is practised at the present time, reference may be made to: Aitchison (1981), Anderson & Jones (1974), Antilla (1972), Bynon (1977), Coates (1987) and Lass (1980).

Later research, and the more systematic application of the comparative method, as this was refined and further developed by the Neogrammarians in the classical period, showed that Sanskrit (or rather, the sub-family to which it belongs) was in certain respects less conservative than some of the other Indo-European languages. More generally, by the late 1870s it had become clear that no one of the earliest-attested languages, or sub-families of languages, could be thought of as being, globally, more conservative, and thus closer to Proto-Indo-European, than any other. It is of course understandable that even Maine's later writings should continue to reflect the older, pre-classical, view of the status of Sanskrit and Indian culture in the Indo-European context. This view has, after all, endured among non-specialists down to the present day. It is important, however, that we, reading Maine today, should know that it is erroneous.

Even more strongly to be condemned, of course, is the view that either Sanskrit or Proto-Indo-European is in any interesting sense more primitive – more representative of an earlier, less highly evolved, stage of human language – than any of the Indo-European languages spoken today; and it is important not to read this implication into the prefix 'proto-', as it is used in this context by linguists and philologists. We shall come back to this point. There is no trace of any such view, I think, in Maine. I mention it here because it is found in others and because it is relevant to the general question of progress and evolutionism. And, as I will explain immediately, it has perhaps been encouraged by the potentially equivocal use of the German term *Ursprache* ('original language') by mid-nineteenth-century philologists.

(iv) The Ursprache, *the origin of language and the thesis of uniformitarianism*

When the founding fathers set about the task of reconstructing what we now call Proto-Indo-European (initially, by the standards of the later period, unsystematically and without the aid of what we would now recognize as the comparative method), they could be excused for believing that the prehistory of human languages, whether they all went back to a single source or not, could be measured in terms of no more than six or seven thousand years (cf. Lyons, 1987b). It was reasonable for them to believe, therefore, that they were reconstructing, if not the primeval human language or one of the primeval human languages, at least a language that was significantly closer to it in time, and therefore more similar to it structurally, than it was reasonable for their successors of the classical, and even the pre-classical, period to believe. And, once again, confusion or equivocation was no doubt fostered by the use of the ambiguous German word *Ursprache* both for the reconstructed, or hypothesized, parent-language and for the postulated original, primitive, language from which the attested human languages were assumed by many to have evolved.

By the late nineteenth century, however, philologists had been supplied by palaeontologists, not to mention geologists, with a much longer timespan with which to operate. They also had, by then, a better understanding of the nature of language-change (if not of its determinants) and a better sense of the rate at which the phonological and grammatical structure of languages could be expected to change over time. And they had come to realize, not only that the comparative method could not, in principle, take them back to anything approaching an original, primeval, language, from which all extant or attested human languages might plausibly be derived, but also that there was no linguistically meaningful sense of 'primitive' in which any reconstructed parent-language could be said to be more primitive than the daughter-languages derived from it. The search for extant primitive languages, spoken by so-called savages in remote parts of the world, continued, unsuccessfully, throughout the nineteenth century. But by the 1870s specialists in comparative philology had for the most part come to the conclusion that their discipline had nothing to contribute to discussions of the origins of language. There have been exceptions to this generalization, notably Jespersen (1922); but he was deliberately challenging what, by then, had long been the orthodox view of the matter.[3]

(v) The normality and (partial) regularity of language-change
Earlier generations of scholars may be excused for believing (as many did) that language-change was abnormal and, in some sense, pathological. And they were, no doubt, encouraged in this belief by what I have elsewhere referred to as 'the classical fallacy'. This

---

[3] Such linguists as have contributed to recent discussions of the origin of language have tended to do so within an interdisciplinary context and have made little or no use of the findings of historical and comparative linguistics: for a personal, and somewhat unorthodox, view of the question, with references to other work, see Lyons (1987b).

combines a number of attitudes which linguists frequently associated, more generally, with what is commonly called traditional grammar: a more or less exclusive concern with the language of literature; the belief that the literary language is, in some sense, inherently purer or more correct than colloquial or vernacular languages and that its purity is maintained by the usage of the educated and corrupted by the illiterate; and the conviction that it is the duty of grammarians to prescribe the norms of correct usage and to be vigilant against their infringement (Lyons, 1968: 9; 1981a: 179–80). This combination of erroneous beliefs and assumptions was fostered by the peculiar status of the classical languages of Europe, Greek and Latin.

The status of Latin is especially important in this connection. It had been used for centuries in Western Europe as the language of scholarship, administration, religion and international diplomacy. By the nineteenth century it was close to being a dead language, but it still enjoyed a prestige that set it apart from most other languages. And it does so to this day for traditionally minded grammarians. The importance of the special position of Latin in the present context is that, until well after the Renaissance, scholars could reasonably think of it as having existed as a living language, more or less unchanged, for some two thousand years and as having been preserved from corruption, throughout this period, by the usage of the educated and by the rules and precepts of the grammarians. Much the same attitude was adopted towards the modern literary languages of Europe when they came into being – or, more precisely, when they came to be recognized as languages that could be used for literary purposes – in the post-Renaissance period. Any differences that were noted by grammarians between the literary and the colloquial, or between the standard language and non-standard dialects, tended to be condemned and attributed to slovenliness or lack of education. Few, if any, realized the significance of the fact that the transmission of the literary languages of Europe from generation to generation is highly untypical of the way in which people acquire, as children, their native, spoken, languages.

Nor was sufficient attention paid to the fact that in the case of many modern languages, notably English and French, the spelling system, which is still based on the pronunciation of centuries ago, conceals most of the sound-changes that have taken place in their development as now more or less standardized, non-colloquial (even literary), spoken languages.

It was only after a great deal of detailed work had been done during the nineteenth century, in what I am referring to as the pre-classical and the classical periods of comparative philology, that scholars came to a better understanding of the relation between written and spoken languages, on the one hand, and between standard and non-standard languages, on the other. And with this understanding there developed gradually the belief that language-change is universal, continuous and, to a very considerable degree, regular. The regularity of language-change – and more particularly of change in the sound-systems of languages – is something that we shall look at more carefully below. For the moment, however, let me simply note that the famous principle of the absolute regularity of the so-called sound-laws ('die Ausnahmslosigkeit der Lautgesetze') proclaimed by the Neogrammarians in the 1870s is better understood as a methodological postulate than as a fully substantiated empirical discovery. It is only with the twentieth-century structuralist reinterpretation of the sound-laws that it became clear what the classical comparative philologists were really doing and that the validity of their findings, limited but real, could be justified within a general, and theoretically satisfactory, framework.

The point that I have just made in relation to the principle of the regularity of sound-change is of much more general applicability. The classical, late nineteenth-century, view of language-change is the one that guides a good deal of current research; and it is the one that is still propagated in many textbooks and popular accounts of linguistics. It is important for me to emphasize, therefore, that the classical view of language-change and language-families espoused by the Neogrammarians and their followers is now itself out of date and, in certain respects, untenable. This is something that needs to be taken into account by anyone who (unlike Jackson) is thinking of updating Maine's appeal to the methods and findings of historical linguistics and comparative philology in support of, or as a model for, present-day comparative law and historical jurisprudence. In particular, theoretically sophisticated practitioners of historical and comparative linguistics now have a very different understanding of the nature of reconstruction.

But before turning to the question of reconstruction, I must also emphasize that much of what I have said in this section about the normality (and inevitability) of language-change and about the relation between written and spoken language, and between standard and non-standard languages (or dialects), is more immediately relevant to the everyday study and practice of law than might appear to be the case from the context in which I have introduced the topic. Apart from its actual or potential applicability in the philosophy of law, comparative law and historical jurisprudence, it has a direct bearing upon the eminently practical, day-to-day, task of legal interpretation. It is widely believed by judges and others whose job it is to interpret the law, as it is by the ordinary citizen, that words and phrases have a determinate and diachronically constant, so-called literal, meaning, which is discoverable, should this prove necessary, by referring to authoritative dictionaries of the language. Some little knowledge of the findings of historical linguistics, on the one hand, and of the principles of lexiocography, on the other, would quickly disabuse them of this belief. This is not to say that the notion of literal meaning, or dictionary meaning, to which lawyers commonly appeal is unjustifiable, but rather that it cannot be taken for granted and needs to justified, on its own terms, in the light of the more sophisticated understanding of the nature of language and its cultural context that modern historical linguistics (and socio-linguistics) makes available to them. This is a point that I will take up in Part B.

(2) *Reconstruction and reality*

The comparative method, as we have seen, has as its goal what is commonly described as the reconstruction of parent-languages or proto-languages: Proto-Indo-European, Proto-Semitic, Proto-Bantu, etc. But what exactly is meant by 'reconstruction'? What precisely is it that is reconstructed? And how much faith can we put in the results of reconstruction? Questions like these were not seriously addressed until well into the post-classical period of comparative philology.

August Schleicher (1821–68) is usually credited with the first detailed and explicit application of the notion of reconstruction in his *Compendium* (1861). By then, he had already written a number of other important works, and had established himself as one of the leading practitioners and theorists in the field of historical grammar and comparative philology. (Schleicher, it will be noted, is roughly contemporary with Max Müller; and the pre-classical period that he represents is the one in which Maine himself first came into contact, directly or indirectly, with the speculations and findings of comparative philology. The year 1861 also saw the publication of Max Müller's first series of Lectures, and has been described by Professor Burrow as an *annus mirabilis*: see p. 58.) Schleicher's most important contribution, as far as reconstruction is concerned, was to make fully explicit the hypothetical status of reconstructed proto-languages and to systematize the genetic relations between their descendants, whether attested or (like Proto-Germanic) reconstructed, by means of the family-tree model. It was in fact Schleicher who introduced the family-tree model of language-change and language-relationship into linguistics.

It was also Schleicher who first made use of the now standard convention of putting an asterisk in front of reconstructed forms in order to make explicit their hypothetical status and to distinguish them from the attested forms which serve as the evidence for the reconstruction. For example, on the basis of a set of attested forms, including Sanskrit *daśa*, Greek *deka*, Latin *decem* and Gothic *taihun*, we can reconstruct the Proto-Indo-European word-form **dekm*, meaning 'ten'. (I have simplified both the process of reconstruction and the notation: I will come back to this.) The asterisk prefixed to the so-called starred form **dekm* tells us that it is hypothetical – hypothetical in the sense of being non-attested.

Schleicher himself would have reconstructed as the Proto-Indo-European (PIE) word for 'ten', not **dekm*, but, for reasons that I have already mentioned, something much closer to the Sanskrit *daśa*. What is of more immediate concern, however, is the fact that he would have been more prepared to say that it was a faithful representation of an actual word of the proto-language than would his immediate successors of the classical period. The technique of reconstruction is still used, and so is the notational convention of the starred form. But no comparative philologist these days would think of publishing a text, as Schleicher did, in what they believed to be what we now call Proto-Indo-European (cf. Jespersen, 1922: 81–2). They would have far less confidence in their ability to reconstruct more than a very small part of the grammar and vocabulary of the proto-language.

Indeed, if they are theoretically sophisticated and have fully appreciated the lessons of twentieth-century Saussurean structuralism, they will realize that what they are reconstructing is not a language as such, but a language-system – or rather, parts of the phonological, grammatical and lexical sub-systems of a set of diachronically distinct language-systems. The theoretically important distinction between a language and a language-system (and its component sub-systems) and Saussure's associated distinction between the synchronic and the diachronic may be left for the second part of my chapter. The points that I want to make here can be made well enough for the moment without using the technical term 'language-system'. It will be evident later, however, that it is not ill-placed pedantry that has led me to introduce it here. The term 'legal system' is, after all, in common usage among the historians of the law; and legal systems or parts of legal systems, I take it, are what Maine and his successors would claim to have been reconstructing when they adapted the methods and assumptions of the mid-nineteenth-century comparative philologists to their own purposes. The question therefore arises whether legal systems and language-systems are sufficiently alike, in relevant respects, for a legal historian's appeal to comparative philology to be either valid or useful. And this is, of course, the central question to which Jackson addresses himself in the first part of his chapter. The conclusions to which I would come, approaching the question as a linguist, rather than a lawyer, are none the less consonant with his.

The main point that I want to make, which might strike non-specialists, initially at least, as paradoxical, is as follows; and it is not given sufficient emphasis in the standard histories of linguistics. On the one hand, with the refinement of the comparative method at the hands of the Neogrammarians and their successors, the method itself is unquestionably more reliable than it was in earlier periods, so that we can say, confidently, that *dekm (in my simplified notation) is, if not right, less wrong than, say, *dakm, *dasa, *teka or *tesm. Our confidence is increased by our better understanding of general phonetics, of the workings both of what the Neo-grammarians called analogy and of the several factors involved in language-change and by the possibility of complementing the comparative method with other methods such as (in principle, though not in the present instance) what is called internal reconstruction. At the same time, however, and – this is where the apparent paradox lies – as a consequence of the refinement and greater reliability of the comparative method, linguists are now less confident than they used to be, not only about the comprehensiveness, but also about the so-called reality of what they reconstruct as proto-languages. For example, they are now less likely to believe that there was ever a language spoken at a particular time, in a particular place, by a particular people, tribe or community, in which the word meaning 'ten' was pronounced as one might pronounced the starred form *dekm*.

The reasons for the increased scepticism of specialists about the reality, or ontological status, of the products of reconstruction are several. First of all, it is now widely accepted that Proto-Indo-European, in so far as it can be reconstructed by the comparative method, systematically applied, was not, and may never have been, a homogeneous language: i.e. it may always have been, and in all probability always was, composed of several more or less different dialects.

I have just used the word 'always', and this brings us to the second reason for scepticism about the reality of the products of reconstruction. Let us grant that the sounds, or phonemes, represented by Sanskrit *d*, Greek *d*, Latin *d*, Gothic *t* (and English *t*, German *z*, etc.) can all be traced back to a single PIE source-phoneme of a particular phonetic quality representable as *d*; that Sanskrit *a*, Greek *e*, Latin *e*, Gothic *ai* = *e* can be similarly traced back to PIE *e*; and so on. It does not follow that there was ever a time in the period accessible to the comparative method when the reconstructed phonemes *d*, *e*, *k* and *m* coexisted in the word meaning 'ten'. There may have been; but we do not, and cannot, know. All that the comparative method tells us, on the assumption that it is based on sound evidence and properly applied, is that there was a time when there was (in the relevant positions of the word meaning 'ten' and in comparable contexts) in the parent-language, or in one of its dialects, a phoneme *d*, a time when there was a phoneme *e*, a time when there was a phoneme *k*, and a time when there was a phoneme *m*. It cannot tell us that these four times (t_1, t_2, t_3 and t_4) are the same. What this means is that, just as the word 'English' covers a whole set of diachronically distinct states of the language separated by several centuries (from, say, the time of Chaucer to the present day), so 'Proto-Indo-European' refers to a language with what might be a comparable time-depth; and the elements of the reconstructed language may come from different periods.

A third reason for scepticism about the reality of what is reconstructed has to do with the variable quality of the evidence upon which the reconstruction is based in particular instances. We can be more confident about the actual phonetic quality of certain reconstructed phonemes than about that of others or about the form and function of certain grammatical endings, either because there is closer agreement among the attested forms of the extant languages or because (on good uniformitarian principles) what is reconstructed fits in with what we commonly find in attested languages. And in the case of some phonemes, word-forms or grammatical constructions we can be almost as confident as Schleicher was. But we cannot be equally sure about everything.

For these and other reasons, then, we have to be more careful than comparative philologists of the pre-classical or classical period were in the claims we make for the reality of Proto-Indo-European and other reconstructed proto-languages. The comparative method does not, and cannot, reconstruct whole language-systems, but only parts of systems; it tends to merge diachronically distinct (i.e. temporally separate) states of reconstructed languages; and, because there is no way, generally, of reconstructing irregularities, it inevitably over-simplifies (over-regularizes) the partial systems that it does reconstruct. It does not follow, however, that we have to reject entirely the findings of historical and comparative linguistics, but simply that we have to interpret them within the framework of a more sophisticated theory of the structure of languages and a better understanding of synchronic variation, on the one hand, and of the distinction between the synchronic and the diachronic, on the other.

All that I have said about the reconstruction of proto-languages would seem to apply – and with equal force – to the reconstruction of the culture and social institutions of the speakers of the proto-languages in question. And Jackson does well to remind us that the reconstruction of language-systems, resting as it does upon the arbitrariness of form and meaning (and the prima facie greater systematicity, or rule-governedness, of language), enjoys an advantage that the reconstruction of past states of society and past cultural beliefs and practices lacks.

To conclude this section, mention should now be made of the family-tree metaphor or model of language-relatedness, introduced into comparative philology by Schleicher and adopted by the Neogrammarians, in association with the comparative method, as part of their late nineteenth-century (classical) synthesis of theory and practice. But this is a separate, and for us irrelevant, issue. The point I want to make here is that the orthodox family-tree model of language-relatedness and language development operates, implicitly if not explicitly, with a notion of languages as homogeneous, dialectally undifferentiated, whole systems (e.g. Proto-Indo-European), which at some point in time suddenly split into new whole systems (e.g. Proto-Indo-Iranian, Proto-Hittite, Proto-Italo-Celtic, etc.), and with the assumption that each so-called daughter-language gives independent evidence for the purpose of reconstruction. We now know that this model, if it is interpreted as a model (i.e. schematic representation) of what actually happens in language-change, is, in several respects, unrealistic. Nor is it simply (as some of the textbooks suggest) that we must merely make modifications for particular cases of demonstrated convergence, as exceptions to what is rightly assumed to be the norm of sudden split and continuous and increasing divergence thereafter. We have to adopt a theoretically more sophisticated concept of language-systems and of the associated (structuralist) distinction of the sychronic and the diachronic. I will say something about these questions, therefore, in Part B. Meanwhile, I will leave it to the legal historians to decide how much of what I have said here about the comparative philologist's notion of reconstruction is also relevant to their concerns.

(3) *Progress and evolutionism*

One of the major themes of the Conference has been the characteristically Victorian notion of progress and Maine's attitude to it. Not much has been said, however, about progress and evolutionism in relation to language.

Is there directionality in the diachronic development of languages? And, if so, does this constitute progress or decline? This was an issue that had long been debated by scholars. Up to and into the pre-classical period of comparative philology, it had been generally taken for granted that a distinction could be drawn between more primitive and more advanced, or civilized, languages and that the classical languages of Europe, Greek and Latin, were the prime examples of highly advanced languages that had developed, prehistorically, out of less civilized, barbarous, languages. Since the earliest practitioners of comparative philology were, for the most part, classically trained, they shared the general tendency to think of the structure of Greek, Latin or Sanskrit as representing the high point of language-evolution. So too, it would appear, did Maine himself.

This general tendency was to some extent counterbalanced, however, particularly in Germany, by the new spirit of Romantic nationalism which developed at the end of the eighteenth century. The leaders of the Romantic Movement rejected the view that the standards of literary excellence had been fixed for all time by the canonical Greek and Roman authors and that classical Greek and Latin were inherently superior to either the older or the modern Germanic languages. Their interest in German antiquities led to the publication and study of texts and glossaries of the older Germanic languages (Gothic, Old High German and Old Norse); and, as we have seen, the researches of such scholars as Rask, Bopp and Grimm into the history and prehistory of German and related languages played a critical part in the foundation of the new discipline of comparative philology. Herder (1772) had maintained that there was an intimate connection between language and national character; and, following him, Wilhelm von Humboldt (1836) had given more definite form to this thesis, saying that each language had its own distinctive structure, which reflected and conditioned the ways of thought and expression of those whose native language it was. This belief in the connection between national language and national character promoted not only the greater interest in the earlier stages of the Germanic languages to which I have just referred, but also a more general enthusiasm for linguistic variety itself and a greater readiness to consider all languages, whether 'civilized' or 'barbarous', on their own terms.

Meanwhile, with the advance of comparative philology in the course of the nineteenth century, it became increasingly clear that Greek and Latin and other languages commonly regarded as civilized, or advanced, did not differ significantly in complexity or grammatical structure from genetically related non-civilized languages. It was gradually recognized that, to quote Sapir, 'When it comes to linguistic form, Plato walks with the Macedonian swineherd, Confucius with the head-hunting savage of Assam' (1921: 219). By what I am calling the classical period of comparative philology, it had become more or less generally accepted that the question whether languages evolved in the course of time, necessarily, from a lower to a higher state (or vice versa), like the broader questions about the origin of language, was unanswerable in the terms in which it had been put. The question continued to exercise the imagination and dialectical skill of a minority of scholars, including Jespersen (1922), until well into the twentieth century. There were some, like Jespersen, who argued for progress; there were others who defended the contrary opinion; and there were yet others who advocated a cyclical theory of language-change.

One version of the cyclical theory popular in the mid nineteenth century was supported, more or less explicitly as the case may be, by the organic model (or metaphor), which conceived of languages, like organisms (and perhaps also species), as being born, passing through periods of growth, maturity and decline, and then dying. This was Schleicher's view of what we might think of as an evolutionary law of language-change (and it fitted very well, of course, with the family-tree conception of language-relatedness). It was also Max Müller's; and, although the organic view of language and a cyclical theory of language-change may not have been articulated explicitly in these terms by Maine, it seems to me that what he has to say about social progress is compatible with such a view. It was, of course, a commonplace of nineteenth-century thought that societies evolved naturally (as it were) from barbarism into civilization and then, subsequently, into decadence (and death). As we have seen, the linguistic correlate of this view had its proponents among mid-nineteenth-century comparative philologists. But it has long been abandoned by most specialists, because it has proved impossible to find empirical support, not only for a cyclical theory of language-change (cf. Aitchison, 1981), but for any general theory of progress or decline in the diachronic development of languages. Indeed, most linguists would say that the very terms 'progress' and 'decline' are uninterpretable in strictly linguistic terms.

The orthodox twentieth-century view is expressed in what is commonly referred to as the thesis of linguistic egalitarianism: the thesis that all languages are equal. Linguistic egalitarianism has had a bad press recently, but what the principle actually says is that all languages – more precisely, all natural, living, human languages (and dialects) – are of equal concern to linguists in their construction of a general theory of the structure and function of language. However, it is usually combined by linguists with the following propositions: (1) that all languages are of roughly equal complexity;

and (2) that all languages are equally well adapted to the communicative and expressive purposes they serve in the societies in which they operate (cf. Lyons, 1981a: 27–8, 329).

These two propositions are more controversial – the more so, if they are misconstrued (by either their proponents or their opponents). First of all, they are best understood as being hypothetical, rather than factual, and perhaps also as being implicitly negative, rather than positive: in other words, linguists who propose them for acceptance should be understood, not as reporting some by now well-established empirical findings, but rather as challenging the commonly held and ill-informed view that (1) some languages are structurally simpler, or more primitive, than others and (2) some languages are functionally better, richer or more expressive (in some unanalysed or absolute sense of these terms) than others. And the reason for challenging this commonly held view is partly that, in the terms in which it is customarily presented, it is descriptively uninterpretable and partly that, when the terms in which it is presented are clarified, it can usually be shown to be based upon a culturally prejudiced and imperfect understanding of the structure and functions of what is alleged to be the more primitive and inferior language (or dialect).

The second point that we have to be clear about is that the principle of linguistic egalitarianism does not, of itself, commit the linguist to the view that all languages are equally suitable for all communicative and expressive purposes. Granted, there are linguists (and philosophers) who do take this view. But I am not one of them. On the contrary, I am on record as saying that 'some languages by virtue of their role as world-languages have a flexibility and a versatility that most languages do not possess'; that it would be 'paradoxical, if not absurd, to interpret the principle of the equality of languages as implying that the language that a person speaks has no effect upon the quality of his intellectual and artistic life, not to mention his career and economic prospects'; and that there are 'eminently defensible reasons why some languages, rather than others, are widely taught in our schools and universities' (1981a: 329).

In short, although it may be impossible to justify the assertion that one language, as a whole, is more advanced than, or superior to, another, it is by no means impossible to demonstrate that some languages are more advanced than, or superior to, others in certain

Linguistics and law: the legacy of Maine

respects or for certain purposes. To the extent that this is true, it is possible to construct a modified version of Maine's thesis relating to the parallel evolution of language and culture – a version of it, moreover, which in my view is both theoretically and empirically justifiable. This is a point that I will pick up and develop in the second part of the chapter.

(4) *The typological classification of languages*

As we have seen, languages may be grouped into what are metaphorically referred to as families by means of the comparative method. They may also be grouped, for different purposes and using different criteria, into structural or functional types.

The most famous of all such systems is one that originated in the eighteenth century, was popularized by W. von Humboldt and was widely used by nineteenth-century comparative philologists, having been put into more or less definitive form by Schleicher. This was a tripartite classification of languages, based on what we now call morphological criteria: on the complexity and grammatical structure of words. Languages in which words are characteristically or predominantly invariable in form (such as classical Chinese or Vietnamese) were said to be isolating (or analytic). Non-isolating (or synthetic) languages were then sub-divided into two sub-classes, agglutinating and inflecting (or fusional), in terms of word-structure. Roughly speaking, an agglutinating language may be defined as one in which the words can be analysed into segments (a root and its affixes), each of which is invariant in form and meaning (or function); and an inflecting (or fusional) language is one in which the words are less readily analysed into segments, and such word-segments as can be identified tend not to be invariant in form and meaning. For example, the Turkish words *evden* and *evlerden* and the Latin words *domo* and *domibus* are more or less equivalent semantically and syntactically, being the singular and plural ablative forms respectively of the word meaning 'house' (cf. Lyons, 1968: 187–92). The two Turkish words are readily analysed into their constituent parts, *ev-den, ev-ler-den*; and each part (or morpheme) has the same form and meaning wherever it occurs (*ev* means 'house', and *den* and *ler* make the words in which they occur ablative and plural respectively). The two Latin words, in contrast, are not so readily analysed into segments (school-grammars frequently give the misleading impression that the boundary between the stem, or root, and the ending is clear-cut, but this is not so in the present case or in most cases); and the affixes, or endings, in so far as they are identifiable as such, tend to combine two or more meanings or functions (and also to vary in form across different classes, or declensions). Thus, there is no part of *domo* or *domibus* that can be said to make the words ablative, rather than both singular and ablative or both plural and ablative; and it is not clear how much of *-o* and *-ibus* belongs to the stem and how much to the ending. There is, as it were, a double fusion – fusion of two grammatical categories in a single ending, and fusion of form between stem and ending. This, then, simplified and, to some degree, updated is the basis of the nineteenth-century tripartite classification into isolating, agglutinating and inflecting languages.

What is of particular interest to us in the present connection is that Max Müller, like many others, correlated this tripartite typological classification of languages both with a developmental sequence in the evolution of languages, from isolating through agglutinating to inflecting, and also with a hypothetical developmental sequence in stages of social organization, from what he called the 'family stage', through the 'nomadic stage', to the 'political stage'. Although Maine may not have taken Max Müller's sociological theorizing very seriously (and probably no one else did) or operated explicitly with this particular language-typology, it is perhaps not too fanciful to see a parallel between Müller's political stage of human society and Maine's postulated advanced stage of human organization, characteristic of what he called the Aryan peoples. At any rate, Maine, like many others of the period, specialists and non-specialists, seems to have associated the term 'Aryan' with both an advanced state of society and also, if only tacitly, an advanced state of language (characterized by inflection).

Although the terms 'isolating', 'agglutinating' and 'inflecting' are still used by linguists in the typological classification of languages, it is now generally accepted that no language is wholly of one type rather than another. (English, for example, has instances of all three kinds of structure, and is not easily classified as being predominantly of one type.) And very few linguists these days would put much faith in a developmental sequence, of putative universal validity, from isolation through agglutination to inflection (or vice versa), or seek to correlate typological differences of language, of the kind we have been discussing, either with cultural differences or with differences in communicative and expressive power, saying that languages of one of these three types are, by virtue of being of that type, better adapted to the expression of more abstract or subtler concepts than languages of a different type. In particular, they would reject the view that Latin, Greek or Sanskrit are, by virtue of their character as inflecting languages, more suitable for the codification of law or the composition of lyric poetry than, let us say, a predominantly agglutinating language like Turkish or a predominantly isolating language like Vietnamese.

Now I do not wish to challenge this consensus. I accept that, just as we cannot say that any one language is superior to another in all respects and for all purposes, so we cannot say that one kind of grammatical structure is, of itself, superior to, or more powerful than, another. It does not follow, however, that typological differences between languages – differences other than those to which nineteenth-century philologists attached so much importance – are never relevant to their expressive power. And it seems to me, if I may register a minority view, that there are indeed typological differences between languages that make them more or less suitable for particular purposes, such as the objectification (and codification) of law and morality. This point supports the point that I made at the end of the last section. These two points will be brought together in the second part of the chapter, where they will be related both to Jackson's discussion of codification and also to Maine's comments on non-written law, written law and well-written law.

PART B: MODERN LINGUISTICS AND THE STUDY OF LAW

I will now turn to a discussion of the links, actual and potential, that Professor Jackson has established, in the second part of his chapter, between law and modern linguistics. I must begin, however, by saying what I mean, in the present context, by the term 'modern linguistics'.

(1) *The periodization of linguistics*

The historiography of linguistics, as of science and scholarship in general, has its own so-called Whiggish tendencies. One of the principal indicators of this is the too ready use of the term 'mainstream', in which certain works by, for example, Saussure or Chomsky are seen as part of an inexorable progression towards present-day (albeit transitory) orthodoxy. Within this framework the publication in 1916 of Saussure's *Cours de linguistique générale* is commonly taken to initiate the period of modern linguistics, and accordingly I shall follow Jackson's example and use the phrase 'modern linguistics' to mean essentially post-Saussurean structural linguistics, contrasting this with nineteenth-century 'comparative philology'. For what it is worth, then, the more or less conventional periodization of linguistics with which I am operating in this chapter recognizes a two-way division by centuries and, superimposed upon this, a five-way division by the publication dates of significant works, each of which we may think of retrospectively, following Kuhn (1970), as having brought about a change of paradigm. As we have seen, nineteenth-century linguistics is characterized, Whiggishly of course, by the predominance of comparative philology and of the historical, or diachronic, point of view; twentieth-century linguistics, by the emergence, triumph and currently unchallenged supremacy of the opposing, synchronic, viewpoint.

As to the five-stage division by dates, the periods in question may be labelled for our purposes as follows (the labels are my own):
1. The age of the prophets: initiated by Sir William Jones (1786)
2. The age of the founding fathers: initiated by Rask (1818) or Grimm (1822)
3. The classical period (of comparative philology): initiated by the Neogrammarians in the mid 1870s (cf. *TPS*, 1978)
4. The post-Saussurean period (of modern linguistics): initiated by Saussure (1916)
5. The Chomskyan – and post-Chomskyan – period (of modern linguistics): initiated by Chomsky (1957).

As I have explained in Part A, it was a fairly popular version of pre-classical, mid-century, comparative philology to which Maine himself appealed for support.

It should be obvious from the above schematic periodization of the subject that what we now think of as twentieth-century linguistics, or modern linguistics, did not start officially until well after the turn of the century. Conversely, nineteenth-century linguistics has not only continued into the twentieth century, but is still practised by many specialists in more or less its classical mode. It must also be emphasized that much of what we think of as modern linguistics can be found in earlier ages. Indeed, there is a sense in which later versions of modern linguistics, in particular Chomskyan generativism, have reasserted many of the aims of traditional, pre-nineteenth-century linguistics (cf. Lyons, 1968; 1981a: 216–36). And to this topic I now turn.

(2) *Deep structure versus surface structure*

Professor Jackson reminds us that the term 'deep structure' has a specialized sense in Chomsky's theory of generative grammar, and more particularly in the so-called standard theory, in which it is first given formal definition (1965). He also tells us, correctly, that Chomsky himself has explicitly argued against the view that all languages have the same deep structure and has pointed out that the thesis which this view embodies is, strictly speaking, nonsensical in terms of the technical definition of 'deep structure'.

At the same time, linguists and others can be forgiven for having drawn from Chomsky's earlier statements about universal grammar a conclusion that can be formulated, loosely, in terms of the distinction between the deep structure and the surface structure of languages. Moreover, it is a conclusion which is in accord with a very traditional view of the grammatical structure of languages: 'Grammar is substantially the same in all languages, even though it may vary accidentally.' This is a famous quotation from the thirteenth-century philosopher Roger Bacon (1214–94). It is cast in the Aristotelian terminology of medieval scholasticism (cf. Lyons, 1968: 15–16). But a very similar view underpins the rationalist, Cartesian, theory of language of the seventeenth-century grammarians of Port-Royal, who have been seen by Chomsky (1966) as precursors of generative grammar and generativism.

It is a view which can be traced back, with the necessary terminological and conceptual adjustments, to the very origins of Western traditional grammar. And it is easy enough to reformulate it, on the basis of Chomsky's distinction between the deep structure and surface structure of sentences, indirectly and derivatively, as a distinction between the deep structure and the surface structure of languages. Every language, let us say with Chomsky, is a set of sentences; to each sentence of any language that is generated by a standard-theory transformational grammar there is assigned, by the rules of the grammar, at least one deep structure and at least one surface structure; and sentences of the same language differ from one another in meaning if, and only if, they are derivable from two or more different, and semantically non-equivalent, deep structures. Let us now go on to say – as Chomsky does not – that the deep structure of a language is either (1) the totality of the deep structures from which it (i.e. the totality of its sentences) is generated (by a standard-theory transformational grammar), considered in abstraction from the actual words supplied by the vocabulary, or (2) the categorial rules of the grammar which (together with a rule of lexical insertion which makes reference to the vocabulary) generate the deep structures of the sentences; and let us, finally, declare or hypothesize that all natural human languages, being intertranslatable and generable from the same universal inventory of syntactic and semantic elements, share the same deep structure. What I have just done is to reformulate, fairly precisely and in theoretically acceptable terms, a Chomskyan version of what I take to be the hypothesis that is at issue: the hypothesis that all languages have the same deep structure. And in the second of the two alternative formulations that I have adumbrated it was explicitly put forward, as the universal-base hypothesis, and defended, in conscious opposition to Chomsky's own theory, or hypothesis, of universal grammar in the late 1960s and early 1970s, by a breakaway group of generativists known, misleadingly, as generative semanticists.

The fact that the linguistic hypothesis to which Perrot (1980) appeals – the hypothesis that the deep structure of language is universal and innate – can be satisfactorily reformulated within the framework of transformational grammar means that it cannot be dismissed as theoretically incoherent within this framework. Chomsky himself would challenge it as empirically unmotivated. But that is another matter. To my mind, neither Chomsky's own theory of universal grammar nor the more traditional theory with which many scholars originally, and reasonably, thought Chomsky was associating himself is to be preferred to its rivals on purely empirical grounds (cf. Lyons, 1977b).

In any case, I am on record, as Jackson observes, as someone who believes that the theory of transformational-generative grammar as such has nothing whatsoever to tell us, in principle, about the innateness of the hypothesized language-faculty or the structure of the mind. This does not imply that I believe Chomsky's ideas on these issues to be wrong or unimportant. On the contrary, they are certainly important; and what he says about universal grammar and innateness may be right. But I think that we have to be very careful – more careful, perhaps, than Chomsky himself has been – to maintain a distinction between generative grammar as such (including transformational grammar) and what I have called generativism (Lyons, 1981a). It is all too easy for non-specialists to get the impression from the arguments of Chomsky and his fellow generativists that the case for his version of universal grammar (and the role that innateness plays in the acquisition of language) is very strongly confirmed by, rather than being more or less strongly supported by or merely compatible with, some of the findings of descriptive linguistics and of data which come from the empirical investigation of the acquisition of language by children. It seems to me that in this area all options, apart from fairly radical behaviourism, are still open; and, as a linguist, one makes one's personal selection from the available options on metatheoretical and methodological, and more or less consciously philosophical, grounds.

For present purposes, then, the question to be answered is whether the appeal that has been made to transformational grammar as a model for the formalization of the distinction between primary and secondary rules in a legal system gains any positive support from linguistics. And I have to agree with Jackson when he suggests that it does not. In the form in which it has been presented, it appears to be based on nothing firmer or more solid than a loosely phrased analogy. As we have seen, it could be reformulated and made at least technically acceptable within the framework of Chomsky's standard theory of transformational grammar. But the possibility of reformulation speaks neither for nor against the empirical validity of the distinction between primary and secondary rules or the hypothesis of the innateness of the former.

I should perhaps add, at this point, that the distinction between deep structure and surface structure no longer occupies the same position of prominence in generative grammar that it once did. The standard theory of transformational grammar, within which the distinction was formalized, was radically modified by Chomsky, in several relevant and important respects, more than a decade and a half ago; and the role of transformational rules has been successively reduced in the various Chomskyan and non-Chomskyan versions of generative grammar that have been developed since then. Any so-called transformational derivation of the secondary rules from the primary rules of legal systems will therefore need to provide its own formal definition of the distinction between the two kinds of rules and its own definition of 'transformation'. It will also need to justify itself on its own terms, either empirically, on the one hand, or, on the other, with reference to such methodological or metatheoretical notions as expressive and descriptive power, generality, simplicity, coherence and elegance. Whether such a venture is worth pursuing is not for me to say.

There is one final point to be made, which, though it does not relate directly to the Chomskyan standard-theory distinction of deep structure and surface structure, has a bearing on the issue of the innateness of universal grammar and its relevance to the comparative and historical study of law. Rightly or wrongly, Chomsky currently takes the view that what he calls the language-faculty – the genetically transmitted knowledge of the principles of universal grammar – is a specialized mental organ, or mental module, which plays no part in our other mental activities and accomplishments and is not connected, developmentally or neuro-physiologically, with intelligence or any other mental organ. And he has recently been defending the more general hypothesis of what has come to be called the modularity of mind: the hypothesis that the human mind is a system of relatively autonomous special-purpose faculties, which have developed independently of one another phylogenetically (i.e. in the evolution of the species) and which also grow, or mature, independently of one another ontogenetically (i.e. in the mind of the individual). Chomsky is far from being alone in subscribing to this hypothesis. It has also been defended by a number of cognitive psychologists, who do not necessarily agree with Chomsky on the issue of innateness. The fact that it is seriously defended, regardless of whether it is true or false, implies that we should not be too hasty in drawing inferences from the linguistic to the legal: from the hypothesized innateness of universal grammar to a hypothesized innateness and parallel evolutionary development of conscience, the moral sense, intelligence, or whatever mental faculty it is whose growth or maturation is held to be responsible for the development of legal systems.[4]

---

[4] The most influential proponent of the hypothesis of modularity (apart from Chomsky himself) is Fodor (1975; 1981; 1983). Professor Jackson has touched on this issue in 1988a: 250, 259.

(3) *Piagetian developmental psycholinguistics as a model for historical jurisprudence*

In Sections 1 and 2 of Part B of his chapter, Jackson suggests that Piagetian theories of language acquisition might replace comparative philology as a more relevant, up-to-date, model for historical jurisprudence. There is very little that I can say, as a linguist, about this suggestion. It does, of course, raise the whole question of the relation between phylogeny and ontogeny. And if it implies a commitment to a psycholinguistic version of Haeckel's (1867) dictum, 'ontogeny recapitulates phylogeny', it must be treated with caution. There is no doubt that a good deal of research on the acquisition of language by children has been guided by what looks like a commitment to Haeckel's principle (although it was abandoned long ago in biology). It is also true that the views of Piaget have been very influential and have led to a good deal of interesting research in child language acquisition. Indeed, I have myself been influenced by Piaget in my own writing on the acquisition of language (Lyons, 1977a: 88–93). But Piaget's views are by no means universally accepted, and I have the impression that they are less widely accepted now than they were ten or fifteen years ago.[5]

Independently of the validity of Piaget's theory of language acquisition, there are two other cautionary points that must be made. The first is that, if the linguist's principle of uniformitarianism is correct (and there is no reason to believe that it is not), it implies that human languages have never passed through a sequence of developmental stages comparable with the sequence of stages through which law or morality is assumed, by Kohlberg (1971), to have evolved.[6] It may be, of course, that the precursors of human language did pass through such a sequence of stages in some remote prehistoric period, but there is no positive evidence to support this view (cf. Lyons, 1987b).

The second point has to do with the assumed parallelism between the development or acquisition of two different cognitive faculties. It has already been made in the preceding section, but it may be

---

[5] For an introduction to the by now voluminous literature on language acquisiton and a summary of the principal findings, see Fletcher & Garman (1986); Ingram (1989).
[6] On uniformitarianism in nineteenth-century comparative philology, see Christy (1983). For recent attitudes and methods in historical and comparative linguistics (which subsume what is traditionally referred to as the comparative method), see references in n. 2 above.

repeated here because it bears directly upon the present topic. Many cognitive psychologists nowadays subscribe to the thesis of the modularity of mind. And Chomsky, rightly or wrongly, has argued strongly for the view that the language faculty, which, as we have seen, he regards as innate, is independent of, and unrelated to, other mental faculties, including intelligence and, presumably, conscience or a sense of right and wrong. Cognitive psychologists who espouse the modular theory of mind may, of course, be wrong; and, even if they are right, it may also be the case that independent modules of the mind develop through a similar sequence of stages marked by increasing complexity. There is nothing implausible about this hypothesis (if we treat it as a hypothesis); and it is not, of course, incompatible with the modular theory of mind as such. But equally there is no convincing reason to believe that it must be true; and, to the best of my knowledge, there is no empirical evidence to support it. What I am saying, then, is simply that we have to be very careful about drawing analogies of the kind that Kohlberg appears to have drawn between the acquisition of language and the acquisition, or development, of moral or legal consciousness.

(4) *The synchronic and the diachronic*

The Saussurean distinction between the synchronic and the diachronic points of view (which both Jackson and I have used to characterize one of the principal differences between nineteenth-century and modern, twentieth-century, linguistics) is, at first sight, straightforward enough: a synchronic description of a language describes that language at a particular point in time (without regard to preceding or following states of the same language); a diachronic description of the language describes the historical development of the language in question through time. The theoretical and practical implications of applying this distinction are, however, far from trivial. And the distinction itself has not always been explicated properly by linguists. It may therefore be worth while making a few brief explanatory comments.

(1) It is frequently said that languages change inevitably as a function of time. There is a sense, of course, in which this statement is true. But it is only true if it is interpreted, loosely, as an empirical generalization. If we press the terms 'inevitably' and 'function' and understand the statement as a whole to have a causal, or nomic,

sense, it is false. The convenient terminological distinction between synchronic and diachronic description must not be understood to imply that time is itself a causal factor in language-change. The passage of time merely allows for the complex interaction of various factors (physiological, social and functional) to bring about what is subsequently describable, from a diachronic or historical point of view, as language-change. This point would not be worth mentioning, if it were not for the fact that linguists sometimes do talk as if it is of the essence of languages that they should change simply by virtue of the passage of time.

(2) The notion of diachronic change – i.e. of transition between successive synchronic states of the same language – makes sense only if it is applied with respect to language-states that are relatively far removed from one another in time. If it is assumed that language-change involves the diachronic transformation of what is at any one time a uniform system, the whole distinction between the diachronic and the synchronic creates insoluble theoretical pseudo-problems. No language is ever stable or uniform; and if we take two diachronically determined states of a language that are not widely separated in time, we are likely to find that most of the differences between them are also present as sychronic variation at both the earlier and the later time. From the microscopic point of view – as distinct from the macroscopic point of view that one normally adopts in historical linguistics – it is impossible to draw a sharp distinction between (diachronic) change and (synchronic) variation.

(3) One pseudo-problem that has troubled some linguists in the past can be formulated as follows: if the English of today is different from the English of, let us say, three hundred years ago, they are not the same language; and, if they are not the same language, what justification do we have for calling them by the same name? Instead of saying that the language, or more precisely the language-system, has changed, should we not say that one language – one language-system – has been replaced by another? And if we do say this, how do we conceive of the process of replacement? Is it gradual or cataclysmic? The notion of the gradual replacement of one system with another hardly makes sense; and the notion of a cataclysmic, or sudden, replacement of one language-system by another at a particular point in time flies in the face of appearances. What we have here, of course, is but a particular version of the more general metaphysical paradox of identity through change. I cannot go into

this question in detail here, and there is no need for me to do so. Suffice it to say that the paradox is resolved, in my view, by recognizing that languages in the sense of language-systems are theoretical constructs which depend upon a motivated process of idealization and that different branches of linguistics operate legitimately with different concepts, or models, of the language-system. And I will return to this aspect of the question in the section devoted to metaphors, models and paradigms.

(4) Saussure's distinction of synchronic and diachronic description is usually taken by structuralists to imply that historical considerations are irrelevant to an understanding of how a language operates at any particular time. It is also commonly held to imply that, whereas synchronic description is independent of diachronic, diachronic description presupposes the prior synchronic analyses of the successive states through which languages have passed in the course of their historical development. We need not be concerned with the principle of the priority of synchronic description in its full generality. But it may be worth mentioning that it implies that the original, or older, meaning of a word has no privileged status and cannot be properly described, on those grounds alone, as the correct or primary meaning. This point is relevant to the notion of literal meaning and its role in the interpretation of statutes, etc. We shall return to it later.

(5) *Models, theories and paradigms*

The contrast that Jackson draws in the title of his chapter between a metaphor and a model recalls the distinction that Max Black drew, with particular reference to the history and philosophy of science, in a now classic article (1962). I too have tacitly invoked Black's distinction above, in my own reference to the metaphorical character of the comparative philologist's family-tree model of the development of languages (Section A1). But in his title, though not everywhere in his text, Jackson appears to be using 'model', if not 'metaphor', at least partly, in a rather different, non-technical, sense: the sense in which a model is held to be a pattern or example to be followed.

Interestingly enough, the word 'paradigm' is also employed in this non-technical sense at times. In my comments on the periodization of linguistics, however, I have used 'paradigm' in its philosophy-of-science, and more particularly its Kuhnian, sense (Section B1): the sense in which we talk of a radical or revolutionary change of method, theory or metatheory as a change of paradigm, which can be seen, either immediately or with hindsight, as introducing a new kind of 'normal science' (Kuhn, 1970). I will continue to use 'paradigm' in this sense.

In fact, each of the three terms that I have used in the heading for this section has several technical, or semi-technical and non-technical, meanings; and in some of its senses 'model' is interchangeable not only with 'paradigm', but also with 'theory'. It is no part of my purpose to compare or contrast these three terms. What I do want to do, however, is to suggest that, if present-day linguistics is to serve usefully as a model (in the sense of pattern or example) for historical jurisprudence or other branches of the study of law, it is important that lawyers should know what linguists are up to when they are theorizing about language or describing particular languages (from either a synchronic or a diachronic point of view). The question is far from being uncontroversial. All I can do, in the space available, is to give, somewhat dogmatically, my own view of the matter. And this will involve me in saying a little more about the use of the term 'model'. For what linguists are doing (whether they express themselves in these terms or not) is constructing models of what is pre-theoretically identifiable as language (Saussure's *langage*). The models may be generative or non-generative. But I will assume that we are working in the Chomskyan paradigm, and that the models we construct are formalized in terms of some theory of generative grammar (not necessarily Chomsky's). The purpose of constructing models is to provide theoretically satisfying answers to the question 'What is language?' – under particular technical interpretations of the word 'language'.

But let me begin by commenting further on two of the technical senses of 'model' (senses in which it is not synonymous with 'paradigm', 'exemplar', etc.). For the mathematician and mathematical logician, a model is a formal system considered from the point of view of its interpretation, or application to some practical problem, rather than abstractly for its own sake. When social scientists or physical scientists employ the term 'model', however, they usually mean some deliberately restricted and abstract representation of the phenomena whose structure or behaviour is being studied, from which hypotheses can be derived for testing. Typical models, in this latter sense of the term, are a physicist's representation of atomic structure or an economist's representation of free-market competition. Since any model of this kind is necessarily based upon an idealization of the data that it is designed to describe or explain, how one decides which variations in the data are of significance and which variations can be discounted becomes a question of crucial importance; and the answer to it will depend upon the nature of the correspondence that is assumed to hold between the data and the model, and upon a fairly precise prior specification of what it is that the model is intended to explain or describe.

The nature and purpose of idealization is crucial. But there are also conflicting senses in the everyday use of the term 'model', and these can affect our intuitive interpretation of its more technical senses. Sometimes we think of a model as a norm to which actually existent objects or actually occurrent patterns of behaviour merely approximate; at other times, we talk as if the model were but an imperfect and purely derivative representation of independently existing objects. Reflected in these alternative ways of thinking of a model are conflicting attitudes with respect to the age-old philosophical controversy between realism and nominalism or idealism and phenomenalism. As we shall see, there are realist and non-realist interpretations of the models that linguists construct when they are describing languages.

The two technical senses of 'model' that I have distinguished are not, of course, incompatible. Moreover, since the term itself tends to be used by those who favour formalization of a mathematical kind in the interests of rigour and explicitness, in linguistics, as in other sciences, the two senses are frequently merged or conflated. There are occasions, however, when it is important to emphasize one aspect of model construction rather than the other and, in doing so, to use the term in one sense rather than the other. In linguistics, the distinction between the two senses is most clearly seen, perhaps, in relation to the distinction between the description of language in general and the description of particular languages. The phrase 'a model of language' is more naturally construed in the mathematician's senses of the term than is the phrase 'a model of English' or 'a model of Chinese'.

Both of the senses of the term 'model' that I have distinguished might be described as relatively strict, or technical, senses. The term has often been employed rather more loosely, by linguists and by others. For example, linguists commonly talk about the generative, or Chomskyan, model (or at a lower level of specificity the 1957 or 1965 models of generative grammar) and contrast this with various non-generative models. It is in this sense that 'model' is more or less equivalent to what I would rather refer to as a paradigm or a theory. So, let me henceforth use the term 'model' in one of the two more technical senses.

What concerns us now is the nature of the linguist's data and the relation between the data and the model. When we say that someone is speaking a particular language, English for example, we imply that he or she is engaged in a certain kind of behaviour, or activity, in the course of which he or she produces language-utterances. Native speakers of English will recognize these utterances as belonging to the language and as being, for the most part at least, grammatically acceptable and meaningful, appropriate to their situation of utterance and interpretable.

So much is a matter of pre-theoretical observation or empirical discovery, and it provides us with our data: a sample of relevant language-utterances, which may be characterized, pre-theoretically, as being utterances in, or of, a particular language; as being similar or different in meaning; as being typical, or diagnostic, of certain social groups; and so on.[7] What linguists do when they describe a language, however, is to construct a model, not of actual language-utterances (and still less of language-behaviour), but of the system of regularities which underly, or are manifest in, utterances which are a product of language-behaviour: a model of what is referred to technically as the language-system. The distinction between language-utterances and an underlying language-system was drawn by Saussure (1916) in terms of the opposition between *parole* and *langue* (both *parole* and *langue* being complementary parts of the more comprehensive *langage*). And Saussure's distinction, which was widely accepted in Europe, if not immediately in America, became the foundation stone of twentieth-century structural linguistics. The same, or a very similar, distinction has been drawn by Chomsky in terms of performance and competence (1965: 4); but Chomsky deliberately adopts a psychological, or cognitive,

---

[7] I use the term 'pre-theoretical' here and elsewhere, advisedly and despite Popper's (1933; 1963) well-known criticisms of the use made of the notion of theory-neutral observation by empiricist philosophers of science. It is only in a loose, or weak, sense of 'theory' that the linguist's data are necessarily theory-laden. For further comments on this issue, see Lyons (1990).

view of language, and, as I will explain shortly, there are other equally valid viewpoints, each with its own concept of the language-system. For the moment, I too will take Chomsky's view: it is probably easier to understand, as well as being more familiar.

When we say that someone speaks English (in the sense of being able to speak English), we imply that he or she has acquired, normally in infancy, the mastery of a system of rules underlying the behaviour (or performance) which we refer to as speaking English. And it is by virtue of competence that one is able to perform: performance presupposes competence, but competence does not logically presuppose performance. This is a crucial point.

Now, it is more or less obvious that no two people speak precisely the same language, or even the same dialect. There will always be differences of vocabulary and there will probably be systematic differences of grammar and pronunciation, which may or may not inhibit communication and of which the persons in question may or may not be conscious. The reasons why communication is not necessarily inhibited by such differences are several. First, conversation and discourse normally proceed on the basis of shared assumptions and expectations, which supplement what is said and forestall many potential ambiguities and misunderstandings. Second, most utterances, in the context in which they occur, contain a good deal of redundancy (i.e. they contain a large amount of information that is predictable from context); and many differences of vocabulary, grammar and pronunciation, as well as slips of the tongue and other so-called performance-errors, are (like misprints when one is proof-correcting) simply not noticed. Third, it is not generally necessary for the listener to extract from an utterance all the information that the speaker, if interrogated, would say it contains. It follows that people may go through life without discovering that they have a different understanding of even quite common words and expressions. It also follows – though I will not develop this point here – that successful communication, or apparently successful communication, by means of language does not presuppose determinacy of meaning.

Not only do no two people speak exactly the same language or dialect (i.e. have exactly the same language-system stored in their brains), but no single person speaks the same language or dialect on all occasions. Everyone switches from one so-called style or register to another – from the colloquial to the formal, from the hortatory to the expository, from the technical to the non-technical, etc. – according to circumstances. Establishing and explaining the correlations between these circumstances, or situations, and the style or registers that are associated with them is the business of such overlapping interdisciplinary sub-disciplines as stylistics, socio-linguistics and pragmatics.

The language-system underlying the utterances of any one person (that person's competence) turns out, then, upon analysis, to be made up of several partially disjoint (not wholly determinate) systems of vocabulary, grammar and pronunciation; and each of these could, in principle, be regarded as separate languages. Furthermore, each of these more or less different language-systems that are combined and integrated in a so-called monolingual's competence first of all changes over time – dramatically during the period of so-called language acquisition, gradually and less noticeably throughout life – and, secondly, is always at any one time more or less indeterminate.

And yet not only the ordinary person, but also the linguist (the latter at least in full cognizance of the facts of the matter) continues to talk as if there are such things as (so-called) natural languages (English, French, German or whatever) and as if they are homogeneous, determinate and well-defined systems, common to all members of a particular community and constant over space, time and situations of utterance: we continue to say, for example, that something is or is not an English word or phrase and has such-and-such a meaning. How can one make sense of this evident mismatch between the facts and the way we describe them?

Quite simply, by recognizing that the word 'language' – and more precisely a phrase like 'the language' or 'a language' – involves different kinds of hypostatization and refers to many different kinds of thing. The psycholinguist's notion of the language-system stored in the individual's brain as what Chomsky calls competence is quite different, ontologically, from the socio-linguist's notion of the language-system as something shared by all members of a given community, and both of them differ in turn from the historical linguist's notion of the language-system as something which endures through time but passes through a succession of synchronically distinct states. Whether these different views of language can ever be satisfactorily reconciled within a single theoretical framework is a matter of controversy. But that is a question that need not concern us here. What I want to emphasize is, first, that each of the different views is theoretically defensible and, second, that each of them involves, whether explicitly or not, the construction of a model which inevitably idealizes what is being described, by discounting, more or less deliberately, a certain amount of indeterminacy and variation in the data.

What I have said will explain why non-linguists should be very careful about adopting any particular model of the structure and function of language without giving very careful consideration to the purpose for which the model was constructed, the particular sense of 'language' that it is intended to explicate and the kind and degree of idealization that has been practised in relating the model to the empirical data. There may or may not be a sufficiently close parallelism between a language and a legal system for it to be profitable for lawyers to look to linguistics for their models and their paradigms. That is for the lawyers, or the philosophers of law, to decide. My primary concern, in this section of my chapter, has been to assist them in coming to that decision and, inspired by both the title and the content of Professor Jackson's chapter, to play my part in ensuring that their appeal to linguistics is not simply metaphorical.

(6) *Communion and communication, and modern semantics*

The most famous dichotomy to be found in Maine is the one that he established between status and contract, and which he himself correlated with his other, possibly less original, distinction between stationary and progressive societies. Several contributors have compared Maine's distinction between these two kinds of societies with the equally famous distinction that Tönnies (1887) drew between *Gemeinschaft* ('community') and *Gesellschaft* ('association', 'society'): between, to quote Shils on Maine's distinction, rather than that of Tönnies, 'Two types of societies, one in which the collectivity was dominant and the individual was recessive, the other in which the collectivity was recessive and the individual dominant' (pp. 144-5 above).

Shils has set both dichotomies within their historical context and has traced for us, in fascinating detail, their subsequent influence upon the development of sociological theory, in the work of Weber, Durkheim and others.[8]

These two dichotomies also have their parallels in twentieth-century linguistic semantics, in a whole cluster of distinctions drawn by a variety of scholars coming from what appear to be, on the face of it, very different intellectual traditions. An especially close parallel is to be found in Malinowski's distinction between communion and communication, as two antithetical functions of language, which he associated, characteristically, with two different kinds of society, primitive and civilized. Indeed the parallel is so strikingly close that I now cannot but believe, though I was ignorant of this before, that it derives from Malinowski's familiarity with some of the late nineteenth-century work to which Shils has referred us. In this connection, I am struck by the latter's account of the part played by 'the observations by Europeans in the Pacific and in the Western hemisphere in the seventeenth and eighteenth centuries' in the delineation of 'the classification which distinguished savage societies from civilized' and of the subsequent, sociological and anthropological, elaboration and theorization of this classification (p. 148 above).

The technical term that Malinowski coined for the function, or kind of meaning, which he saw as dominant in so-called primitive languages (i.e. the languages of primitive societies) was 'phatic communion'. This has now become part of the linguist's stock-in-trade. Regrettably, however, it has been separated from the context in which it originated; and, for this reason, it has been trivialized by many linguists employing it, who put the emphasis on the word 'phatic', rather than 'communion'. 'Phatic' for Malinowski meant nothing more than "by means of speech". The principal terminological and conceptual opposition, therefore, was between 'communion' and 'communication': between participation in the communal life and activities of a tribal collectivity, on the one hand, and, on the other, the transmission of factual information between more or less rational individuals in a civilized, or advanced, society. The distinction between societies in which language is used primarily for communion and those in which it is used primarily for communication, as I have just explicated it, is evidently very close to the

---

[8] Grillo (1989: 23) explicitly relates the *Gemeinschaft/Gesellschaft* distinction to Maine's status/contract distinction and makes considerable use of it in his interesting discussion of language and nationhood.

distinction drawn by Tönnies and his followers between a *Gemeinschaft* and a *Gesellschaft*.

The distinction between 'communion' and 'communication' is but one of many comparable distinctions that have been drawn by semanticists, in recent times, in their analysis of meaning. Others include 'emotive' versus 'referential', 'affective' versus 'cognitive', 'socio-expressive' versus 'propositional', 'interpersonal' versus 'ideational', 'experiential' versus 'historic', 'restricted' versus 'elaborated' and 'participant' versus 'observer'. Some of these dichotomies are, no doubt, closer to Malinowski's than are others. And few of the proponents of any of them, these days, would associate themselves with Malinowski's characterization of languages or societies, as such, as primitive or civilized without further qualification. What many (and I myself) would do is to begin by drawing a distinction between the language itself and the use, or uses, of that language and, perhaps also, another distinction between the language and its component dialects, styles and registers. They would go on to say that no language, and perhaps also no dialect, style or register of a language, is characterizable wholly in terms of the one or the other member of whatever dichotomy or anthithesis they are applying: and they would maintain, rather, that one or other kind of meaning – the emotive or the referential, the experiential or the historic, or whatever – predominates in particular uses of the language and perhaps also that, because particular styles and registers are more appropriate to particular uses (in particular contexts), the various component styles and registers of a language may encode more of one kind of meaning than of the other. This point of view, as far as the structure and function of languages is concerned, is clearly comparable with the sociological viewpoint expressed by Shils in terms of the dominance or recessivity, rather than the presence or absence, of the antithetical traits of collectivism and individualism.

One of the dichotomies that I have mentioned, 'emotive' versus 'referential', has been of particular importance in twentieth-century philosophical semantics and, derivatively, in fields of study as diverse as theology, literary criticism, ethics and the history and philosophy of law. I have no need to elaborate upon this point in the present context. It suffices to mention radical logical positivism with its insistence on verifiability as the touchstone of meaning proper, and the various reactions to it. There were those, on the one hand, who accepted in principle the distinction between scientific and non-scientific discourse and used the distinction between the referential and the emotive to develop so-called emotive theories of religion, literature and law within the framework of a less radical version of logical positivism. There were others who, either initially or subsequently, rejected logical positivism entirely. Notable among the root-and-branch opponents of logical positivism were the later Wittgenstein (1953) and J. L. Austin (1962). It may also be worth noting in passing that the best-known source for Malinowski's notion of 'phatic communion' is his article 'The problem of meaning in primitive languages' (1923), which was published as a Supplement to the later editions of that highly influential work, *The Meaning of Meaning* by Ogden and Richards (1927), which is based on the distinction between the emotive and the referential.

It is obviously not possible, in the space available, to investigate, from a properly historical and analytic point of view, the complex web of interconnections and influences among the several theories of meaning (philosophical, linguistic, social-psychological, anthropological and literary) to which I have referred. In any case there is as yet no comprehensive study of twentieth-century semantics that does full, genuinely interdisciplinary, justice to the topic. I have been concerned merely to establish a link between one of the major themes of this volume – Maine's distinction between status and contract and the characteristically distinct types of societies, stationary and progressive, or *Gemeinschaft* and *Gesellschaft*, with which he associated them – and recent semantic theory. Shils has commented in this connection: 'Max Weber saw what Tönnies and Maine failed to see, which is that no society could ever operate according to a single principle. It was of the nature of societies to incorporate antithetical elements' (p. 168). I have made exactly the same point about the integration of the analytically distinguishable components of meaning which are commonly recognized as antithetical and which I have here summarized, for particular historical purposes, in Malinowki's opposition between communion and communication. The literature of present-day ethnolinguistics, sociolinguistics and pragmatics is full of descriptions of particular languages, or of particular uses of language in general, or of particular styles and registers of particular languages, which can be more or less directly related to the status-versus-contract or the *Gemeinschaft*-versus-*Gesellschaft* distinction, though I, for one, have not previously seen them in this light.

I have written elsewhere of the need to give full weight, in semantic theory, to the socio-expressive and experiential, non-propositional, dimensions of meaning; and I have been more prepared than most linguists are these days to accept that not only different styles and registers of a language, but also different language-systems may differ significantly in grammar and vocabulary, in respect of the degree to which they encode socio-expressive or propositional meaning (Lyons, 1977a; 1981b). I will return, in the final section, to one particular aspect of the more general thesis which seems to me to be highly relevant to another of Maine's themes: the role of codification in the historical development of law as we now understand it. This is a topic that Jackson has addressed, from a different, but complementary, point of view in his chapter.

(7) *Literacy and progress*

Let me turn now, in these final sections, to a set of related topics, which are perhaps latent in Jackson's discussion of legal drafting, on the one hand, and of law and literature, on the other, but which, in my view, could profitably be made explicit and associated with Maine's view of progress.

The first of these is the linguistic, social and cognitive effects of the invention of writing – and subsequently of printing. For some years now, Jack Goody and his collaborators have been arguing the thesis that 'cognitively as well as sociologically, writing underpins "civilization", the culture of cities' (Goody, 1987: 300; cf. Goody, 1968, 1977, 1986). And in the elaboration of this thesis, they have ascribed to societal literacy several historically attested, if not inevitable, consequences, including the following:

(1) the development of logic, grammar and mathematics, and with this the development of a capacity, or facility, for generalization and abstraction;
(2) the codification of laws, both secular and sacral (by listing [them] in an "organized" way [which] pulls them out of their particular contexts of pronouncement (probably in judgements) and collects the rules together in a sequential order like that of the Ten Commandments, ... so that they can be rearranged, reordered, in more "logical" and consistent ways', Goody, 1987: 107–8);
(3) the transformation of oral poetry and narrative into literature (properly so called) and of folklore into scripture;

(4) the promotion of the dialect of one region, class or caste at the expense of others and its standardization as the language of administration, literature and scholarship;
(5) the evolution of a particular style or register of language – for example what may be referred to loosely as Written English – which is characterized by, inter alia, its greater impersonality, its greater independence of the time, place and circumstances of its context of utterance (its 'decontextualization'), its greater syntactic complexity and richness, precision and abstractness of vocabulary and its greater diachronic stability and constancy.

This is by no means a complete list of what Goody sees as the historical consequences of literacy in the world as we know it: I have selected the features that are directly, and obviously, relevant to the themes that are discussed in this volume. Features (2), (3) and, in part, (5) are patently relevant to what Jackson has to say in Sections B2 and B4 of his chapter. As to Goody's general thesis I would suggest that this can be seen as an updated, a more carefully modulated, and a theoretically and empirically better-substantiated version of Maine's thesis about the distinction between static and progressive societies. Maine himself, it will be recalled, drew attention to the importance of written, and then of well-written, laws in the progress from status to contract. And Goody (1987: 286), for his part, refers explicitly to Bernstein's (1964) distinction between so-called elaborated and restricted codes of communication and associates the development of the former with literacy (1987: 286). Bernstein's distinction was of course one of several that I related to Malionowski's distinction between communication and communion.

Now, I am not unaware that Goody's hypothesis (not to mention Bernstein's) is controversial. It has been challenged, both in general and in some of the detail, by anthropologists, linguists and sociologists. At the very least, however, it deserves mention in the present context. And I, for one, would certainly agree with Goody when he accuses 'most linguists in this century' of having 'given their virtually exclusive attention to oral language' and of having failed to recognize the diachronic and synchronic importance of societal literacy (1987: 261). It is certainly not the case that written language can be treated, diachronically or synchronically, as purely derivative and epiphenomenal (cf. Lyons, 1981c).

Moreover, some of the components of Goody's general thesis, controversial though it may be in its full generality, seem to me to be all but incontrovertible. One can hardly deny the importance of societal literacy in the standardization of English and other languages – and also, especially as far as English is concerned, in the uncoupling of accent and dialect (so that contemporary Standard English can be, and is, spoken with many different regional and social accents). Again, it would be perverse to dispute the fact that the relative constancy and stability of written languages over considerable periods of time (and their consequential enhanced authority and prestige) derive from the relative permanence and reliability of written texts, which are available for continuous reference and commentary and are proof against the vagaries and improvisations of oral tradition: even today, with the invention of conveniently portable instruments for sound-recording, the old adage, *Scripta manent, verba volant*, has as yet lost little of its force. Needless to say, the relative permanence and immutability of authoritative written texts can, in principle, work for good and ill. And several contributors have noted that Maine himself emphasized the negative, as well as the positive, effects of written codes of law: their inflexibility and inhibiting force in the face of changed circumstances.

As to the alleged historical role of literacy in the development of more abstract and more impersonal, less context-dependent, modes of expression and reasoning and of appropriate styles or registers of language ('elaborated' rather than 'restricted', to use Bernstein's terminology), this is perhaps more debatable. But, independently of the historical reasons for the difference, I am of the opinion that languages do indeed differ from one another significantly in grammar and vocabulary in some of the ways mentioned by Goody. That they do so differ is evidence against the hypothesis of linguistic egalitarianism, as it is commonly formulated (see Section A3 above). I return to this question, independently of its alleged causal connection with literacy, but with particular reference to legal language and jurisprudence, in the final section. But first I must say something about another topic, which, it has been argued, is also the product of societal literacy, and which is certainly relevant to our present concerns: the concept of literal meaning and the practice of legal interpretation.

(8) *The myth of literal meaning and the rule of law*

There is no need to labour the fact there there is a historical connection between literal meaning and literacy. The word 'literal', like the words 'literature' and 'scripture', wears its etymology on its sleeve; and etymology is usually indicative of some kind of historical connection. The question is whether the connection is essential or contingent.

It is readily demonstrated that literal meaning is not essentially, or logically, dependent upon literacy. It can be defined and explicated without reference to writing or written languages; and it has been so defined and explicated recently, in various ways, by linguists, literary critics and philosophers of language. In this respect the concept of literary meaning is like the concepts of literature and scripture. They too were applied initially to written texts, but they can also be defined to cover the products of either speech or writing. There is nothing self-contradictory about the concepts of oral literature or even oral scripture, as there is nothing self-contradictory about the concept of the literal meaning of spoken utterances.

However, to say that there is no intrinsic or essential connection between the concept of literal meaning and societal literacy does not imply that the connection between them is historically contingent in any trivial sense (as are so many of the connections to which etymology bears witness). The existence of culturally important written texts which, in contrast with the purely oral, untranscribed, products of speech, could endure through time and can be carefully preserved, consulted and venerated, may well have been a precondition of the development of the traditional concept of literal meaning. It is, at any rate, indisputable that this concept did originate, as a matter of historical fact, in literate societies in which there were such written texts, sacred and secular; that these texts were held to be of singular cultural importance; and that the concept of literal meaning derived its significance from their cultural importance and from the need to interpret them correctly. This historical connection between literal meaning and literacy is well documented, as is the role played by priests, judges, rhetoricians, teachers and latterly philosophers in its elaboration and propagation (cf. Coulmas & Ehlich, 1983). It can be seen as part of what Goody has identified as one of the effects of societal literacy: a capacity for objectification and abstraction (see Section B7). And it is supported and reinforced by the phenomenon of intertextuality, itself a product historically of literacy, to which Jackson has appealed in his discussion of law as literature.

There can be no question of providing here a comprehensive

treatment of the concept of literal meaning, whether historical or analytical. With respect to the historical dimension, suffice it to say that the traditional concept of literal meaning is the product of several academic and cultural (Judaeo-Christian and Graeco-Roman) traditions. The most important of these, no doubt, are the scriptural, the legal and the rhetorical (or literary-critical). None of them, of course, is sharply distinguishable, in its origins at least, from either of the others. Jackson has made this very clear, in his chapter, as far as the scriptural and the legal traditions are concerned; and so have other contributors (as did Maine himself). With respect to the analytical dimension, let me simply assert: first, that, in my view, there is room in both law and linguistics (not to mention theology and literary criticism) for a defensible concept of literal meaning; and second, that the linguist's concept of literal meaning – or at least the concept of literal meaning that is current in present-day formal semantics – is likely to be of little direct use to the lawyer. I will briefly develop these two points presently; and I will relate them to Maine's idea of progress and to the role that written law – literally interpreted – plays in the establishment and maintenance of the rule of law in what he would call progressive societies. But I must first say what I mean by the traditional concept of literal meaning; and I must justify the deliberately provocative title that I have chosen for this section.[9]

The non-technical traditional notion of literal meaning used by educated members of Western societies – the pre-theoretical concept with which they operate in everyday situations before they start reflecting upon it or theorizing about it – is essentially negative or oppositional. That is to say, it is non-literalness of meaning (or interpretation) that is positively definable, and literalness is definable only by contrasting it with non-literalness. Moreover, non-literalness is quite heterogeneous. For example, we contrast a literal translation of a text with one that is free, loose or idiomatic; and we may say of one kind of non-literal translation that it is more faithful than a literal translation would be to the spirit of the text (or to the intentions of its author) than it is to the letter of the text. We distinguish literal equivalence (or identity) of meaning from para-

[9] I have borrowed the phrase 'the myth of literal meaning' from Rommetveit (1986), but have given it a somewhat different interpretation. Harris (1988b) has recently employed the phrase 'the myth of Standard English', for which I would provide the same kind of explication and justification as I have done for 'the myth of literal meaning'. The two myths are, of course, intimately associated.

phrase, and a literal interpretation of an expression from one that is metaphorical, allegorical, euphemistic, hyperbolic or otherwise figurative. It requires but little reflection to see that these various kinds of literality and non-literality are different from one another; and it is not clear that it is possible to construct a single unitary theoretical definition of either literality or non-literality of meaning that would usefully cover all of them.

Given the historical circumstances in which the traditional notion of literal meaning originated, it is not surprising that the more technical concepts of literal meaning with which lawyers, linguists, literary critics and others operate should have much in common with one another and also with the everyday pre-theoretical notion of literal meaning current in Western society. But the relevant academic traditions have more recently diverged and become more sharply distinguishable from one another; and the aims of theorists in the various disciplines are different. So, it is also not surprising that, despite the similarities, there should be differences of detail between the lawyer's and the linguist's theoretically defined concept of literal meaning, between the literary critic's and the linguist's, and so on. Indeed, there are often significant differences of detail between one scholar's theoretically defined concept of literal meaning and that of another scholar in the same discipline. But let us leave these differences on one side for the moment.

What the several more technical concepts of literal meaning have in common is the assumption that words and phrases have an inherent meaning (or set of related meanings), which is proper to them, constant and determinate, and more or less independent of the non-verbal context, or situation, in which they are used. It is this assumption that I am characterizing as mythical – its mythical status having been reinforced, if not created, by the physical durability and the imputed authority and impersonality of culturally significant written texts. It is an assumption for which neither traditional grammar and lexicography nor modern descriptive linguistics can supply any empirical justification whatsoever.[10]

But to say that something is a myth is not simply to say that it is empirically unjustifiable; and it certainly does not mean that it

---

[10] Searle (1979) mounts a vigorous attack on the notion of context-independent literal meaning. Much of what he has to say is, on his own terms, reasonable enough. But he does not allow for the possibility of mythical (or metatheoretical) justification. My own thoughts on the notion of literal meaning were strongly influenced some years ago by those of my Ph.D. student Mava Jo Powell (1983; see also 1985).

cannot be justified on non-empirical grounds. To say that something is a myth, in the anthropological sense in which I am using the term, is to emphasize its social role. Myths, whatever their origin, are sustained by, and in their turn support and can be seen as validating or even sanctifying, the beliefs, institutions and practices of the society in which they operate. Their primary function is typically that of maintaining the cohesion and stability of the society and of reinforcing its identity. The question whether they are true or false, in terms of some external (transcendental or positivist) notion of objective truth, is from this point of view of secondary importance. If raised, it might be answered by those who both subscribe to the validity of the myth and are yet intellectually sophisticated enough to understand the question, that the myth is objectively false, but has its own kind or level of truth (allegorical, symbolic, etc.). They might even take Plato's line, admitting that such myths (literally interpreted) are not true, but then going on to say that, as propagated by the wise and the good for the benefit of the State, they are 'noble lies'. In any event, I am not employing the term 'myth' pejoratively.[11]

It is not for me to defend this or that scholar's theory of legal interpretation. I may be permitted, however, to add something from a linguist's point of view to what Jackson has said about Dworkin's (1978) playing down of 'legislative intention ... as a paramount criterion of legal interpretation' and about the related question of 'whether it is possible or desirable to separate [literal] meaning (or signification) from communication' (p. 286). The standard legal concept of literal meaning, as I understand it, differs from the concept of literal meaning with which many linguists currently operate (in the distinction that they draw between semantics and pragmatics) in that those lawyers who use it, either in theory or in

---

[11] Critics of the Platonic ideal of benevolent and beneficent oligarchy, whether they are advocates of the open society or revolutionary proponents of an alternative authoritarianism, will, of course, reject the epithet 'noble' and describe this attitude as cynical or self-interested. These are large issues that I am not concerned with here. I mention them because they do indeed set the larger context for the interpretation of my assertion that the traditional concept of literal meaning current in Western society is a myth. Limitations of space prevent me from addressing such larger questions as the possibility of ideologically neutral socio-linguistic description. I have a good deal of sympathy for those who argue that most of what purports to be value-free sociological or historical analysis is the product of socio-cultural or political bias. There are, however, degrees of ideological commitment, and in the discussion of specific issues it is possible, I believe, to achieve a fairly high degree of objectivity: for a recent discussion of many of the issues (with references to related work), see Grillo (1989).

practice, unlike the linguists to whom I am referring, do not assume that the literal meaning of a text is wholly independent of the intentions of its author or the context in which it was drafted.[12] These differences are readily and satisfactorily explained, to my mind, by the lawyer's need to temper that mythical constancy and determinacy of meaning which is assumed to inhere in the text itself (and whose putative constancy and determinacy it is important not to undermine) with the ability to vary or adjust the interpretation of particular words or phrases in the light of unforeseen or changed circumstances; and he or she must do this, if possible, without having recourse to the device of the acknowledged legal fiction. Looked at in this light, a lawyer's inclusion of authorial, legislative, intention and context-dependence within the definition of literal meaning can be seen as a means of maintaining the rule of law and inhibiting what Maine would have regarded as the excessive use of one of his three agencies for change (see Chapter 15 above).[13]

Linguists, on the other hand, are under no such constraint. If they are theoreticians, their principal concern is not the interpretation of actual texts, but the construction of a model of the language-system within which the grammatical and semantic properties of natural languages can be satisfactorily formalized. For them, the concept of context-independent, literal meaning (like the notion of the synchronic language-system and its regularization and standardization) serves the purpose of theoretical simplification. It rests upon the acceptance of a whole set of interconnected distinctions (each of which can be justified descriptively in particular cases) and their association (in various combinations) with the global distinction between semantics and pragmatics, to which Jackson has referred.

Two of these several interconnected distinctions have been mentioned by Jackson: (1) the distinction between the meaning of a

[12] In personal correspondence Professor Jackson has drawn my attention to the fact that although 'what lawyers might erroneously regard as unproblematic plain meaning is itself taken to represent the legislative intent (as indeed the notion of the rule of law must imply), on the grounds that "Parliament is taken to intend the plain meaning of its words"', there are frequently occasions when lawyers 'do contrast the "plain meaning of the text" with the search for legislative intention (one "rule of construction" being that one seeks the intention of parliament ... only when there is no "plain meaning" available)'. He refers me to Cross (1976) for illustrations.

[13] Alan Diamond has raised the question whether I should also describe the lawyer's concept of 'ascertainable authorial intent', particularly where there is a collective author, as mythical. My own view would be that authorial intent (when it is in fact conscious and determinate) is in principle ascertainable, but is in practice, of course, frequently impossible to determine because the evidence is simply not available.

sentence and the meaning of an utterance; and (2) the distinction between meaning (or signification) and communication (or interpretation). If we combine these and then, as many theoreticians do, identify literal meaning, on the one hand, with sentence-meaning, and on the other, with what is encoded in the grammatical structure and vocabulary of a language-system, we can say that utterance-meaning (i.e. the meaning of either spoken discourse or written texts) is the product of sentence-meaning and of the context of utterance (including the author's intention).

When it comes to the application of the distinction between semantics and pragmatics to the task of describing languages for practical, rather than for purely theoretical, purposes, we find, not only that the language-system is not sychronically homogeneous or diachronically constant, but also that the facts of the matter in particular instances are indeterminate. This is something that should always be borne in mind when we consult a putatively authoritative reference-grammar or dictionary of any language. Much of what is there represented as objective fact (for example that this or that grammatical construction is correct in Standard English, that a particular word has two meanings or three, that two words are synonymous, and so on) is the product of an individual editor's, more or less responsible, but in the last resort arbitrary, decision.

What conclusions can we now draw from this rather abstract and theoretical discussion of the concept of literal meaning? In the present context, the following would seem to be especially important:

(1) Maine's view of the progressive role of written law – and more especially of well-written law – would seem to depend upon its imputed constancy and objectivity and upon its interpretability in terms of some accepted notion of literal meaning.

(2) The traditional notion of literal meaning originated in literate societies and is plausibly associated with the increased capacity for abstraction and objectification which has commonly been seen as one of the effects of societal literacy that makes for progress.

(3) The traditional concept of literal meaning (which presumably Maine accepted) cannot be justified, from the viewpoint of descriptive linguistics, on purely empirical grounds. Like the related concept of synchronically uniform and diachronically continuous national languages (such as Standard English), it is part of a myth to

which Western societies subscribe. As such, it can be seen as supporting the rule of law. Provided that its mythical status is recognized, it is, at least in principle, justifiable. But its justifiability does not fall within the province of linguistics. Nor does its definition for the specific purpose of legal interpretation.

(4) The standard legal definition of literal meaning, which allows for the inclusion of context and legislative intention, might be defended by a latter-day Platonist (as the conservative-minded Maine seems, in this respect, to have been, especially in *Popular Government*) on the grounds that it enables judges to interpret the law with such flexibility as is required without undermining its authority or its reputation for objectivity and constancy. A more liberal-minded lawyer might well reject this argument. But Maine's view of the matter (if I have represented it correctly) cannot be challenged on linguistic grounds. Modern linguistics, in its various branches, is neutral on such questions. It can at most play its interdisciplinary part in the clarification of the issues.

(5) Although current linguistic theories of semantics and pragmatics, properly understood, speak neither for nor against Maine's view of the role of written law in what he identified as progressive societies, they are certainly not incompatible with it.

(6) Independently of its theoretical implications for historical jurisprudence and comparative law, the fact that there is no such thing as literal meaning empirically determinable within the framework of descriptive linguistics (including traditional lexicography) is inescapable. It means that legislators and judges who are concerned with the practical business of establishing or interpreting the law must be careful not to operate on the assumption that there is. They must be especially careful not to identify the literal meaning of words and phrases with what is sometimes referred to as their dictionary meaning – if 'dictionary meaning' refers to the meaning (or meanings) authoritatively established and codified in conventional published dictionaries of the language. And when they have recourse to such invaluable and, properly used, incomparably authoritative works of reference as the *Oxford English Dictionary* (or its recently published successor, the *New Oxford English Dictionary*), which are organized, deliberately and explicitly, on historical principles, they must also be careful not to fall into the etymological fallacy of supposing that an earlier (or earlier-attested) meaning of a word is its correct, literal, meaning, in contrast with a later (or

later-attested) meaning. They must be sensitive, in short, to the distinction between the synchronic and the diachronic – and to its theoretical and descriptive limitations (see Section B4). More generally, they should be aware that any description of the lexical and grammatical structure of a natural language, whether it is presented as such or not, is of necessity an idealized and empirically imperfect model of what it purports to describe (see Section B5).[14]

(9) *The propositionalization of deontic modality and the objectification of ethics, morality and law*

It is a widely held view, among philosophers of language and even linguists, that all natural languages are semantically equivalent and of equal expressive power: that anything that can be said in one language can be said in all. Let us call this the thesis of intertranslatability. Logically distinct from this, but frequently coupled with it, is the thesis of expressibility: whatever can be meant can be said (Searle, 1979: 134). In both cases, it should be noted, the verb 'to say' is being employed, semi-technically, in the sense in which what is meant or implied can differ from what is actually said (compare 'it's not what he [actually] said, it's what he implied' or ' ..., but I know what he [really] meant'). Saying, in this sense, is commonly held to be explicable in terms of literal meaning, or of sentence-meaning (in contrast with utterance-meaning: see Section B8).

Despite their current popularity, both these theses are in my view demonstrably untenable. Indefinitely many everyday examples can be produced from any two natural languages (or any two dialects of the same language) to refute them. In the present context, however, I am concerned with differences of expressive power and semantic structure in one particular domain, deontic modality, and with respect to just two classes of utterances, commands and statements. What I now wish to offer for the consideration of historians and philosophers of law and jurisprudence are the following theses:

(1) that languages differ as to whether they permit or facilitate the propositionalization of the subjectivity of utterance (and more

---

[14] In this section I have not explicitly addressed issues raised by the so-called deconstructionists such as Fish (1982). Professor Jackson himself has dealt with them from a somewhat different point of view in several publications, including (1988c). But I believe that my view of the mythical status of literal meaning allows for the adoption of a via media between the Scylla of extreme critical subjectivity and the Charybdis of semantic objectivity and constancy.

especially, in the present context, of deontic subjective modality);
(2) that propositionalization alters, and may increase, expressive power;
(3) that the kind of expressive power which comes from propositionalization:
   (a) is plausibly subsumed under the general notion of abstraction which has been seen as one of the products, historically, of literacy (see Section B7) and of the development of the (mythical) concept of literal meaning (see Section B8); and
   (b) can reasonably be invoked as a pre-condition of progress in any theory of jurisprudence which sees the process of the objectification and codification of laws as progressive.

I shall first need to explain what is meant by deontic modality and subjectivity, and I shall also need to introduce the concept of propositionalization. I have dealt with these questions at considerable length elsewhere, though without making particular reference to the history and philosophy of law (Lyons, 1977; 1981b). I will make this account as brief and (at the risk of a certain lack of precision) as non-technical as possible.

Deontic modality has to do with the interrelated, and indeed interdefinable, notions of obligation, permission, prohibition and exemption. It has been much discussed by philosophers in recent years and brought within the scope of modern formal logic, which has greatly extended the application of the classical (alethic) modalities of necessity and possibility (Hilpinen, 1981 a, b). Whatever is obligatory is deontically necessary; whatever is permitted is deontically possible; and so on. This much, I trust, will be intuitively clear. So too will be the connection between deontic logic and the logic of commands (sometimes referred to as imperative logic): if X, with the authority to do so and in the appropriate circumstances, commands Y to perform some action a, X thereby imposes upon Y the obligation to do a (he makes it deontically necessary for Y to do a). He may then be said to have created, or brought into existence, the obligation to do a. But the person describing what has happened cannot, of course, make this additional statement unless the language of description provides the means for moving to the higher level of abstraction in which obligations, prohibitions, rights, etc. can be hypostatized or objectified (i.e. referred to as entities). And it is the difference between languages that do and languages that do not provide their users with the means for making such statements that is of primary concern to us in this section.

The expression of deontic modality in English, as no doubt in all natural languages, is not simply a matter of grammar and vocabulary. It is distributed over the whole language-system, including, as far as spoken language is concerned, the intonational sub-system. For example, the declarative sentence 'I am telling you to be quiet' can be used, without change of grammatical or lexical structure, to perform a variety of so-called speech acts – more technically and more precisely, illocutionary acts (see Austin, 1962; Searle, 1969), including those of making a statement and issuing a command. The illocutionary force of the resultant utterance, its status as a command or a statement, may well be evident from the context, but it may also be signalled, in speech, by its intonation-pattern.

At this point, it should be noted, I have been careful to distinguish between the sentence, the meaning of which is determined by the structure of the language-system, and the utterance, the meaning of which (including its illocutionary force) is determined partly by the meaning of the sentence (held to be invariant and context-independent) and partly by the context. As we have seen, this distinction between sentence-meaning and utterance-meaning (which was invoked by Jackson, in a somewhat different connection) is a commonplace of modern linguistic semantics and pragmatics and can be associated with the concept of literal meaning (see Section B7). Nothing but confusion results from the failure to draw this distinction (cf. Lyons, 1981b).

Now for subjective deontic modality. By subjectivity – more precisely, locutionary and illocutionary subjectivity – I mean speakers' (or writers') expression of themselves (i.e. their will, desires, expectations, attitudes, beliefs, etc.) in the utterance that they produce. It so happens that English, and more especially Written English, allows its users to make categorical, unqualified, statements in which there is no indication of the utterer's attitude towards what is said or the grounds, or evidence, or authority for saying it. For example, there is nothing subjective (in the relevant sense) in the grammatical or lexical structure of the sentence 'Smoking is forbidden (here).' In uttering it the speaker (or writer) expresses – and typically, if making a statement, will be asserting – nothing more and nothing less than the proposition that smoking is forbidden (at the time and in the place in which the statement is made): its (literal) meaning can therefore be identified with its propositional content. (In speech, if not in writing, there will usually be some indication of the subjectivity of utterance in the intonation-contour and stress-pattern that is superimposed upon the sentence that is uttered, but it is a matter of dispute whether stress and intonation count as part of sentence-structure.) The proposition that is asserted does not create the prohibition against smoking, but represents it as existing, objectively, prior to and independently of the utterance of the sentence in question, and it can be evaluated for its factual truth or falsity.

Let us now compare the sentence 'Smoking is forbidden' with (a) 'Do not smoke (here)' and (b) 'You must not/may not (cannot) smoke (here).' Of these (a), 'Do not smoke', differs from 'Smoking is forbidden', in that, being in the imperative mood (to use traditional terminology), it would be used, characteristically, not to assert the prior existence of the prohibition, but (provided that the person uttering the sentence has the requisite deontic authority – legal, moral, or whatever) to create the prohibition. In such cases, as generally in languages that have the grammatical category of mood, the imperative mood grammaticalizes (i.e. encodes grammatically, rather than lexically) that part of the subjectivity of utterance which consists in the speakers' expression of his or her deontic authority: his or her authority (acknowledged or assumed) to prohibit, or prevent, his or her addressee, or addressees, from doing what might otherwise be held to be permitted (i.e. deontically possible).

As for (b), 'You must not/may not (cannot) smoke (here)', this is more problematical, in that it is by no means clear whether, literally interpreted, it is more like 'Smoking is prohibited' or 'Do not smoke': the question is empirically undecidable. What is clear, however, is that it can be used, in particular contexts, either subjectively (to create a prohibition) or objectively (to assert that the prohibition exists).

Now, the fact that we can form sentences like 'Smoking is forbidden' in English depends, first of all, on the fact that English, by virtue of its grammatical structure and vocabulary, enables its users to refer to acts and activities as second-order (abstract) entities by nominalizing the verb that denotes them. In this case, nominalization (the formation of a noun or noun-phrase) involves the use of what is traditionally called the gerund (identical in form with the present participle ending in -*ing*). There are many other kinds of nominalization, grammatical and lexical, in English; and associated with them are several important semantic differences, which tend to be obscured in traditional discussions of their meaning by the use of the catch-all term 'abstract': it is important not to confuse the different kinds of abstraction (Lyons, 1989a).

The fact that we can propositionalize and objectify the modality of prohibition depends also on the fact that English provides its users with a set of adjectives, such as 'forbidden', 'wrong', 'immoral', 'illegal', etc., which can be employed to ascribe second-order (abstract) properties to such second-order (abstract) entities as acts and activities. In other words, English allows us to form sentences like 'Smoking is forbidden' which are not only grammatically comparable with 'Snow is white', but can also be interpreted as being semantically and logically comparable, due allowance being made for the ontological differences between concrete (first-order) and abstract (second-order) entities and properties. (The increase in expressive power that is provided by this kind of abstraction is exactly the same as the increase in expressive power that is achieved by the move from the first-order to the second-order predicate calculus in modern formal logic.)

But not all natural languages provide their users with the lexical and grammatical resources to propositionalize and thus to objectify deontic (and other kinds of) modality in this way. And languages also differ with respect to the distinctions that they draw in their deontic vocabulary between what is a matter of religion, law, custom, ethics, morality, and so on. At one extreme we might envisage a language with, let us say, imperative constructions like 'Do not smoke' (or 'Honour thy father and thy mother') and first-order declarative sentences like 'Snow is white' (or 'The table is round'), but no abstract vocabulary (of the relevant kind) and no means of nominalization. In such a language, there would be, ex hypothesi, no way of forming sentences like 'Smoking is forbidden', 'It is wrong to smoke' or even, let us assume, 'You must not/may not (cannot) smoke.' At the other extreme, we find a language like English, furnished with the kind of grammatical and lexical devices for propositionalizing deontic modality that I have mentioned and for differentiating linguistically between what have developed historically, in certain cultures, as different kinds of deontic morality.

As we have seen, most present-day linguists reject the characteristically mid-nineteenth-century view (which Maine may well have accepted) that there are evolutionary stages in the historical development of natural languages, such that some languages can be said to be more advanced (richer, more expressive, more powerful, etc.) than others (see Section A3). And, in doing so, they also reject, *a fortiori*, the view that languages of a particular grammatical type (for example highly inflecting languages like Greek, Latin or Sanskrit) are better adapted for the expression of abstract or complex ideas than are languages of a different grammatical type (see Section A4).

As I have said, I do not wish to challenge the thesis of linguistic egalitarianism (properly formulated). At the same time, I do not believe that it is in principle impossible to evaluate natural languages in terms of their expressive power. Indeed, there is an immediately applicable measure of expressive power which comes from the study of formal languages (i.e. non-natural, or artificial, languages deliberately constructed by logicians, mathematicians and computer scientists for specific purposes). This tells us that if one language, X, properly includes within itself another language, Y, then X is (in this respect) richer, or more powerful, than Y. (For example, the extended propositional calculus which contains modal operators of necessity or possibility is more powerful that the simple propositional calculus; and a higher-order logical language, such as the second-order predicate calculus, is more powerful than a lower-order logical language, such as the first-order predicate calculus.) It follows that, if two natural languages, X and Y, differ from one another only in that, whereas X has the grammatical and lexical resources for the propositionalization of deontic modality, Y does not, X is (in this respect), more powerful, or richer than, Y. And if being able to objectify deontic modality is rightly regarded as a mark of cultural progress, a language which facilitates this ability may also be regarded, in this respect at least, as being more advanced, more progressive, than a language which does not.

However that may be, regardless of whether it is rightly regarded as a mark of cultural progress or not, the objectification and codification of law (and morality) was certainly facilitated, first of all, by the development in particular cultures of a concept of literal meaning and, second, by the development in particular languages of the necessary devices for the propositionalization of deontic modality: i.e. for the construction of declarative sentences, such as 'Smoking is forbidden' or 'It is right to honour one's parents', which can be used, in contrast with imperative sentences, such as 'Do not smoke' or 'Honour your parents', to assert the objective existence of obligations and prohibitions. And both of these developments would seem to have been associated, historically, with societal literacy (see Section B7).

We must, of course, be careful not to assume, as swiftly as Maine and other nineteenth-century thinkers may have done, that such differences of expressive power in different languages as I have mentioned necessarily reflect different stages of mental development in their users. To the best of my knowledge, there is no evidence that this is so, just as there is no evidence of any intrinsic connection between race and language, or between race and intellectual or artistic ability.

PART 4
Maine and India

CHAPTER 18

The influence of Sir Henry Maine on agrarian policy in India

Clive Dewey

I have had in the Punjab and in the Secretariat of the Government of India some special opportunities which have enabled me to trace the living and inspiring influence of Maine's ideas in certain fields of policy and administration ... I heard Maine deliver in the hall of my college at Oxford the lectures which were published in his book entitled *Village-Communities in the East and West*; and his pregnant suggestions have constantly guided my work in India, and throughout my life have chiefly inspired my studies ... [When the appalling number of murders among the Pathan tribes forced us to revive their *jirgas*, or customary courts,] we looked back to another ancient society, to a time in this country when jurymen were in effect witnesses, and when, by the system of frankpledge, the men of a tithing were responsible each for any offence of the rest. We did not, of course, pedantically try to imitate Anglo-Saxon ... institutions. We based our project on the facts we found. But that Maine had taught us to compare one archaic society with another, and to accept as part of the course of nature some of the differences between tribal and civilised society, helped us both in understanding our case and in reporting it. (Tupper, 1898: 390, 396)

A single problem pre-empts the attention of historians working on agrarian policy in British India in the late nineteenth century. Between the two great insurgencies against British rule – between the last of the old rebellions in 1857 and the first of the new nationalist agitations in 1906 – the Government of India altered its entire agrarian strategy. Gradually, inexorably, the promotion of the free market (regardless of the social consequences) gave way to the protection of Indian institutions (regardless of their economic drawbacks). It is impossible to explain this metamorphosis without reference to Sir Henry Maine. As an official, a teacher and an author, he brought historical and comparative method to the attention of the Indian civil service. A number of civilians, fascinated by the potential of the new methodology, revolutionized anthropological research in India. Then 'official anthropology' changed the policy-makers' priorities, by changing their perception of Indian society.

In the 1840s the most representative civilians – the civilians who most accurately reflected the spirit of the age – had no doubts about the sources of India's economic stagnation. They saw the village community, the sub-caste, the feudal estate, as so many shackles on the maximizing entrepreneur; and they were determined to sweep them away. They hated the customs which held traditional collectives together, because they stopped the market fulfilling its appointed functions: allocating resources to their most efficient uses, and rewards to their most efficient users. They detested communal tenures, because communal tenures awarded equal holdings to competent and incompetent cultivators alike – preventing successful farmers taking over their feckless neighbours' land. They despised joint cultivation, because joint cultivation made it harder to adopt new methods and blurred the relationship between effort and reward. Joint responsibility for taxation was worst of all: it destroyed all incentives to exertion, by forcing villagers with savings to pay the arrears of pauper defaulters. The caste system reduced the mobility of labour, locking manpower into hereditary occupations with customary pay-scales. Entail made it impossible for new men to buy up the estates of territorial magnates, even if the magnates' misman-agement laid them waste. Tenant rights stopped landlords replacing unproductive tenants with productive ones. And so on, and so forth.

By the 1890s this indictment seemed hopelessly old-fashioned, and the utilitarians' chosen instruments – the *ryotwari* revenue system and the Benthamite legal system – were largely discredited. The Young Turks of the Revenue and Agriculture Department were much more likely to acclaim the village community, the sub-caste and the feudal estate as the only guarantees of India's social stability. Their organizing obsession was the fear of *anomie*. They had no faith in the 'spontaneous reconciliation' of interests by the market, much less the 'artificial reconciliation' of disputes by the courts. They suspected that if all the traditional collectives dissolved into a pullulating congeries of isolated, hostile individuals, South Asia would become ungovernable. There would be no intermediaries with sufficient authority to transmit the directives of the tiny elite of

British administrators to the mass of the population. In fact, the great mass of the population would have no means of cooperating with one another for any public purpose whatever. Every man's hand would be turned against his neighbour, in a Hobbesian jungle rapidly reverting to barbarism.

Hence the rash of reforms propping collectives up. Legislation protected the integrity of the village community by protecting the *biraderi* – the brotherhood of cultivators – against outsiders with ambitions on their holdings: moneylenders threatening to foreclose their mortgages and rack-renting landlords anxious to break down their tenant rights. The cultivators' property was exempted from seizure by the courts; relief acts gave special judges the power to scale down their debts; a new usury law set limits to the accumulation of compound interest; cooperative societies provided alternative sources of credit; tenancy acts set out the rights of tenants with greater precision, and public registers of rights in land made it much easier to defend their interests in court. The caste system and the great estates were protected in much the same way. The membership of each sub-caste was defined, and the sub-castes were arranged in neat hierarchies; peasant castes were forbidden to sell land to commercial castes; martial castes were drawn into the army; disloyal castes were eased out of government jobs. Courts of wards took over the management of 'encumbered' estates, saving them from liquidation; the introduction of primogeniture put an end to sub-division through multiple inheritance; the revival of entail stopped little kingdoms being sold off piece by piece.

The origins of this revolution in policy lay in a parallel intellectual transformation – in the progressive supersession of utilitarian modes of thought by a sceptical historicism. The early Victorian officials who welcomed the destruction of the collectives were disciples of Bentham, Ricardo and Mill; the *fin de siècle* civilians who were desperate to maintain the cohesion of Indian society were followers – frequently self-professed followers – of Sir Henry Maine. During the debates over the 'great reversal', Maine's authority was constantly invoked. His ideas – about village communities, about tribes, about tenures, about customs – crop up in official reports, in secretariat files, in speeches in the legislatures. The density of the allusions raises two obvious questions. What, exactly, was the nature of Maine's influence? And how did he gain such an ascendancy over the Indian civil service?

THE 'LESSONS OF MAINE'

The larger part of Bentham's output as a philosopher consisted of a series of detailed proposals for administrative reform, interspersed with convenient summaries of the principles from which further reforms could be deduced. Maine never drew up check-lists of things to be done, except in one restricted sphere – codification. It was Maine's methodology, not his prescriptions, that influenced agrarian policy. The civilians took over his combination of historical and comparative method, and applied his insights to Indian institutions with immense vigour and considerable subtlety. As a result, the 'lessons of Maine' were a great deal more ambivalent than the 'lessons of Bentham'. So many implications had to be teased out of an active collaboration with Maine that advocates of diametrically opposed policies could appeal to his authority. This was true especially in the early stages of the great debate, for the biases inherent in Maine's approach to primitive societies were not always immediately apparent. In fact, they became obvious only as his techniques of analysis were applied. In the mean time, as the products of an incompletely reconstructed utilitarian, Maine's ideas were open to conflicting interpretations. Sir Denzil Ibbetson, the moving force behind the Punjab Alienation of Land Act, claimed that Maine's ideas about the evolution of property showed that the 'fatal gift' of individual property in land had been premature – and should be withdrawn, before the peasant proprietors of the Punjab lost their holdings to trader-moneylenders. Sir Dennis Fitzpatrick, the Act's principal opponent, appealed to the same evolutionary framework when he argued that there was no going back, once 'the highest form of property' had been conceded.

But the fact remains that once Maine's techniques of analysis set off an explosion of interest in Indian anthropology, research on Indian institutions was bound to throw the dangers of indiscriminate modernization into high relief. His most ardent admirers – the 'official anthropologists' who wrote the classic studies of Indian villages, castes and estates, with the aid of theories culled from his works – were far more sympathetic to the collectives they studied than their predecessors, the classical political economists and analytic jurists. Three implications of this Maine-derived research were responsible for the sympathy. They were not particularly sophisticated implications: their simplicity was their strength. More abstruse chains of argument would have resisted reduction to the rough rules of thumb that lodged in civil servants' minds and determined the outcome of official controversies. Agreement – between large numbers of civilians, dispersed over different departments and provinces, at every level of the hierarchy – grew out of simple, endlessly repeated axioms, the lowest common denominators of official discourse, not the most original and refined insights.

In the first place, the universal adoption of the evolutionary schema inculcated an elementary relativism. Maine's insistence that the ideas and institutions of late Victorian England – the most advanced industrial society – were, in a sense, superior to all other ideas and institutions worked both ways. It implied that they would be hopelessly inappropriate in a backward agrarian society like India. This was hardly a revolutionary discovery; paternalists had been saying similar things since Plassey. But Maine's disciples applied the general principle to the key issues with such cogency as to force the assimilationists on to the defensive. In effect, they shifted the onus of proof. Before Maine, a strong case had to be made out *against* the introduction of an English law; after Maine, an English law was automatically suspect.

Maine's 'functionalism-before-the-term-was-invented' had a similar effect. His followers rehabilitated the village community, the sub-caste and the feudal estate by showing that each and every mechanism had definite functions to fulfil. Once they were invested with 'manifest social purpose', they stopped being anachronisms. Relics of ignorance and barbarism became rational adaptations to different environments.

The concept of consensus, the third proposition implicit in the mélange of methods and theories the official anthropologists took from Maine, emphasized the interdependence of institutions and ideas. In any given society, every institution interacted with every other institution; and they all interacted with contemporary *mentalités*. From this it followed that modernization could only take place slowly on a broad front. If a particular institution got ahead of itself – if it got out of synchronization with other institutions and the ideas which informed their operation – it was bound to malfunction.

The most notorious example of premature modernization was the Benthamite legal system. The new courts and the new codes 'stank in the nostrils of the people' because they violated popular notions of justice. Village *panchayats* and tribal *jirgas* repaired relationships by shaming defendants who failed to fulfil the obligations attached to their status. They drew everyone with an interest in the defendants' conduct – kinsmen, neighbours, caste-fellows – into the process of conciliation. The new judicial system did nothing to heal the ruptures which threatened groups vital to the individual peasant's survival. On the contrary: British judges awarded victories to one side or another after adversarial combats governed by incomprehensible rules.

Moreover, the new system was vulnerable to manipulation. Witnesses were loath to try and deceive traditional tribunals: they were surrounded by people they knew, and they had to live with their judges. But the British courts – little islands of an alien culture – stood outside the moral community, so none of the normal constraints on perjury applied. Peasant suitors could only hold their own against professional litigants with enough experience to exploit legal technicalities and enough money to fight endless appeals if they and all their friends and relations lied themselves blind. Again and again, one finds civilians complaining that peasant debtors could never defend themselves against rich moneylenders: that the civil courts were 'vast agencies of extortion', churning out decrees for whatever sums the *banias* cared to claim. The criminal courts were no better. Rival factions, struggling for the control of a village or a sub-caste or an estate, constantly got up false cases against their enemies. There was never any difficulty producing bodies to support allegations of murder, or low-caste girls to support allegations of rape. The police solved the cases by selling their support to the highest bidders.

MAINE AND THE INDIAN CIVIL SERVICE

Bentham preached to a self-selected clique and only published a fraction of his voluminous and unbelievably boring manuscripts, so his influence took decades to penetrate the Indian administration. Maine's thought permeated the official mind far faster, because it was more accessible. As a senior official in India and London, he injected his ideas into the heart of the decision-taking machine. He educated his colleagues in the course of business – they recognized his intellectual pre-eminence, and savoured his minutes and speeches. As an academic, he taught the rising generation at Oxbridge and the Inns of Court. A disproportionate number of the civilians who pioneered the anthropological revolution in India were pupils who had sat at his feet. And from the 1860s on, his best-selling books were required reading for the ICS examination. Successful candidates paraded their mastery of Maine's *obiter dicta* in their answer-papers – and went on parading their mastery in the letters, reports and memorandums they wrote in India. Familiarity with the master's theories was a precondition of promotion, as well as appointment.

Ancient Law propelled Maine into high office. Mountstuart Grant Duff – a Whig backbencher, briefly Under-Secretary of State for India – drew Maine's talents to the attention of two crucial patrons: Sir Charles Wood and the Duke of Argyll. Wood sent him out to India as Legal Member of the Viceroy's Council; Argyll put him on the Council of India after he came home. In both capacities, his influence was unique. His advice carried more weight with successive Viceroys and Secretaries of State than any other official. He was Salisbury's favourite counsellor, and he came close to playing the same role for Salisbury's political opponents, Hartington and Kimberley. He inspired confidence because he was the perfect civil servant. He kept his Ministers out of trouble and supplied them with knock-down arguments. What more could they require?

The choleric polemics of Maine's old age disguise the fact that he had an unerring eye for the main chance in a transitional political system. Presented with a potentially explosive problem – the kind of problem that was liable to blow up in a Minister's face – he knew, instinctively, which was the safest course. He had a knack amounting to genius for discovering the resounding general principle which would justify whatever course of action the politicians wished to pursue. There was nothing impractical, nothing 'academic', about his minutes. They leap out of the files – out of the muddled mess of hasty drafts by old India hands – by virtue of the elegance of their exposition. But the real reason they were devoured and reprinted by his colleagues was their realism, as men of affairs measure reality. They were powerful statements of *the case for the winning side*.

Maine's teaching was another conduit taking his ideas straight to the centre of the ruling caste. If Malthus lectured embryo 'writers' at the East India Company's College at Haileybury, Maine lectured at Haileybury's successors. He taught popular courses at Cambridge (1847–53, 1887–8), Oxford (1871–8) and the Inns of Court (1852–61) – at a time when the great majority of Indian civilians went to Oxbridge colleges and Indian judges ate their dinners at an Inn. Some of the pupils who sat at his feet became prominent exponents of his methods in India. Whitley Stokes, Maine's successor as Legal Member of the Viceroy's Council, heard Maine deliver the early drafts of *Ancient Law* at the Middle Temple – and carried out his programme of codification, twenty years on. Sir Lewis Tupper, Maine's most self-conscious acolyte, listened to the 'six lectures delivered at Oxford' which Maine subsequently published as *Village-Communities in the East and West* – and became the *éminence grise*, the ultra-industrious secretary, behind a whole batch of Mainite agrarian reforms in the Punjab. Sir Harcourt Butler stayed on an extra year at Oxford to attend Maine's lectures, after he passed the ICS examination – and became the great architect of the British *rapprochement* with the landlords of Oudh. Butler's policy, 'the policy of sympathy', was Maine at one remove.

Maine's influence as a civil servant and don was highly concentrated; his influence as an author was more diffuse. His books had such an impact on the Victorian intelligentsia that it must have been difficult for an educated man not to know what Maine was on about. As members of the clerisy, Indian civilians responded to the ideas in the air. Sir Denzil Ibbetson, the most brilliant Indian civil servant of his generation, dated his enlightenment from the day *Ancient Law* fell into his hands, some time in the 1860s. Sir Raymond West, the great luminary of the Bombay legal system, published his comments on Maine's theories of tenure a year after the appearance of *Village-Communities*. Sir James Wilson, the head of the Punjab Revenue Department, developed elaborate modifications of Maine's insights into the evolution of property in settlement reports written around 1880.

The introduction of competitive examination for the ICS (after the abolition of the East India Company's patronage in 1855) turned Indian civilians into a class of mandarins educated in response to the dictates of the examination system. One of the demands of the system, from a few years after the publication of *Ancient Law*, was a detailed knowledge of Maine's works. At first sight, there was no obvious reason why this should be so. Most of the successful candidates were high-flying classicists or mathematicians. They had no occasion to study Maine at school or university. But they had every occasion to study him at one of the famous London crammers. If they were to stand any chance of success, the classicists and mathematicians had to sit the seven papers in social science and history which were penetrated by the intellectual controversies Maine provoked. No candidate could get into the ICS on the strength of his classics or his mathematics alone, because they only counted for a fifth of the total possible marks. Candidates could, in theory, attempt all the twenty-odd papers the civil service commissioners set; and it was in their interests to sit as many as they possibly could, because all the marks they received – on as many papers as they chose to try – were added up to make their final aggregate mark.

So normal candidates automatically sat the papers in their specialities, classics or mathematics, and cast about for soft options which they could work up in a limited amount of time. The social science and history papers were the obvious possibilities. Standards were low, because they were neglected by the schools and universities; and they were kinder to newcomers than 'cumulative' subjects such as sciences and languages. Only the most brilliant linguists could hope to work up Sanskrit or Arabic to the required standard in the few months available. But a clever pupil who soaked himself in Maine's books with the aid of an experienced tutor could score a respectable number of marks if the right questions came up in jurisprudence, political science, and some of the history papers.

The infiltration of the ICS examination by historical and comparative method was reflected in the list of texts which the civil service commissioners prescribed. There was no complete *bouleversement*; no total rejection of the utilitarian heritage. Rather, a reaction against utilitarianism coexisted in the book-lists with utilitarianism itself, as if the continued presence of utilitarian works was necessary to throw the reaction into high relief. For the jurisprudence paper an amalgam of Blackstone, Bentham and Austin – in which Bentham and Austin conspired to smother Blackstone – was supplemented by *Ancient Law*. For political economy Ricardo was displaced by J. S. Mill, until Mill, in turn, gave way to Marshall. In history and geography, *Village-Communities* joined Elphinstone in his standing battle against the elder Mill's contempt for India's civilization.

The book-lists were accretive: the civil service commissioners were reluctant to discard books, except on the unanimous advice of several different examiners over several years. The questions set give a far more vivid impression of the turbulence of the academic disciplines Maine did so much to stimulate. Candidates attacked and defended the patriarchal theory of the State; considered kinship and land as rival determinants of ancient societies; explored the origin of individual property rights in land; queried the movement from status to contract; compared and contrasted evolutionary thinkers; reinterpreted ethics in the light of evolution. If only their answers survived, it would be possible to work out the exact impression Maine's ideas made on them. But the general drift seems fairly clear. The sacred texts inculcated a kind of evolutionary relativism: a suspicion that diverse systems of economic thought and policy, differing forms of government and law, apparently exclusive religions, were equally apposite in the particular societies and ages in which they arose.

The fate of classical political economy was representative. In the 1860s Mill's *Principles* enjoyed the status of holy writ; candidates were called upon to regurgitate his doctrines, not criticize them. Then the historicist reaction triggered off a crisis of confidence in classical political economy. The synthesis Mill had so carefully nurtured collapsed. Every question that had seemed closed was reopened. Henceforward it was the errors of the classical political economists, as detected by their successors, that fascinated examiners. W. S. Jevons, the *enfant terrible* of the seventies, set four questions in the 1879 political economy paper which called into question four of the fundamental classical prescriptions: (1) 'Was political economy an inductive or a deductive study?' The historicists' revulsion against inductive logic currently threatened its utilitarian exponents, Bentham and Ricardo in particular; (2) 'What were the true determinants of wages?' Jevons himself had exploded – at least to his own satisfaction – the wages-fund theory, which he regarded as the keystone of the classical economists; (3) 'What constituted 'legitimate' and 'illegitimate' restraint of trade?' The tide was turning in favour of more extensive government intervention; and (4) 'In what ways was Smith's doctrine of rent inadequate?' This was really a question about Ricardo's critics, rather than Smith's. Jevons wanted to know why Ricardo's rent-law was irrelevant to Indian conditions.

The rise of economic history as an academic discipline – with three of Maine's Oxford pupils in the van – went some way towards filling the vacuum created by the collapse of the classical economists' laws. The founding fathers of the subject, Cunningham, Ashley,

Gross, Maitland, Vinogradoff, and Round helped turn the tide against *laissez-faire*, by rehabilitating the whole apparatus of economic regulation. Village communities, guilds, usury laws, protective duties were no longer self-evidently ridiculous or evil. The great evil, at least in Arnold Toynbee's eyes, was the Industrial Revolution: an economic triumph, but a social disaster. The 'anti-industrial spirit' discredited the utilitarians' hostility to Indian institutions by associating their triumph with brutal exploitation, social division and cultural deprivation.

THE REVOLUTION IN INDIAN ANTHROPOLOGY

Sir Henry Maine's remarkable power of insight into the real meaning and connections of archaic customs so alien to modern ideas as to be ordinarily incomprehensible, and his luminous generalisations upon the materials found scattered over these obscure fields of research, have greatly influenced local inquiries in India. He surveys and maps out the whole line of penetration into difficult and entangled subjects, and workers in the field are constantly verifying the extraordinary precision of their chief engineer's rapid alignments. (Lyall, 1899: 245–6)

Indian revenue officers seized on Maine's combination of historical and comparative method as the crucial analytic device unlocking all the secrets of the agrarian institutions they were struggling to understand. Of course, the potential of Maine's methods proved largely illusory. By 1900 no one really believed that the Indian village community – the most contentious agrarian institution – had passed through the same evolutionary states as the Teutonic mark. In fact, it would have been difficult to find a senior revenue officer who still believed that there was such a thing as an Indian village community. There were so many different kinds of village, developing in such diverse directions. But the journey, not the arrival, mattered. Two developments – two consequences of Maine's methods – gave an enormous fillip to anthropological research in India; and the research led to a general rehabilitation of Indian society.

Historical and comparative method taught European scholars to take an interest in the revenue officers' work. If the assumptions underlying Maine's methodology were true – if the present could only be explained by reference to the past, by unravelling the evolution of early institutions; and if India was, as Maine proclaimed, a 'museum of survivals' from a common Aryan past – then South Asia might hold the key to understanding Europe. For the first and last time in the history of the raj, it seemed as if Indian officials might make significant contributions to the progress of knowledge in the West. After a century of isolation and indifference, they were flattered by the attention they received. Maine cited their settlement reports, the great repositories of their accumulated wisdom, in his books; learned societies invited them to give lectures; learned journals invited them to contribute articles; universities showered them with academic honours; Oxford built the Indian Institute to house their publications.

The possibility of developing a new 'science of government' gave the official anthropologists another incentive to publish and be praised. As Sir Denzil Ibbetson put it:

It is only lately that scientific methods have been applied to social, political and judicial phenomena, and the educated European world is watching with interest and expectation the rise of what may be called, under protest, archi-sociology. The new study has already made wonderful strides, and has led to results of absorbing interest – an interest which their applicability to the occurrences of every-day life has extended to the educated world in general, far more than is the case with the majority of scientific results. It requires no very great boldness to prophesy that the time is not far distant when our views on points of administrative policy will be profoundly modified, nay, more probably shaped by, the results of investigation into the history of early institutions, and that this influence will be strongest of all in India, where we have begun to doubt the universal applicability of occidental methods, and are earnestly seeking a new guide for the future.

Settlement officers had all the opportunities they needed to respond to these stimuli. Their sources of information were superb. They were supposed to appraise the tax-paying capacity of anything up to a million fields, and define the rights of anything up to a million proprietors and tenants. They spent years touring the villages, talking to cultivators and landowners about their customs; they had a whole army of subordinate officials at their beck and call, ready to collect data on any subject under the sun; and they could call for any government records they chose. Moreover, it paid them to get things right. An assessment was the settlement officer's chance to prove himself as an administrator: to show that he had the instinctive grasp of agrarian institutions which qualified him for promotion to the select ranks of the policy-makers. As a result, the reports they wrote expanded into major anthropological treatises. In the 1850s and the 1860s, a representative settlement report was a slight affair: an administrative memorandum, listing things done, decked out with a few ethnographic details to add a little light relief. In the 1870s and the 1880s the representative report ran to three or four hundred pages of detailed analysis of every aspect of rural society: village communities, castes, estates; whatever topics excited the settlement officer's interest.

The most famous Punjab reports were landmarks in the development of Indian anthropology. D. C. J. Ibbetson settled the historic shatter-zone to the west of Delhi, the seat of Metcalfe's original 'village republics'. Sir James Lyall, settling the remote foothills of the Himalayas, was fascinated by the caste system, frozen in time by the isolation on Kangra's secret valleys, so old that it antedated the brahmins' assertion of their ritual superiority. In Bannu, S. S. Thorburn studied the communal repartitional tenures of the Pathan tribes which spilled over the mountainous north-west frontier into the settled plains. They preserved their equality and solidarity by regularly redistributing the whole of their arable land among the tribesmen. In Hazara, E. G. Wace found another set of frontier tribes, where over-mighty chieftains were rapidly turning into landlords. In Sirsa, Sir James Wilson grappled with a new society: a society created by hundreds of thousands of peasant immigrants, flocking into an arid tract in response to the extension of irrigation. What united these disparate tracts was the common mental questionnaire: the determination to force every phenomenon on to the same evolutionary bed.

In permanently settled provinces, where the land revenue was fixed at the same level for ever, the place of the settlement report was taken by the district gazetteer. The first of the modern gazetteers, the gazetteers of the Central Provinces and Berar by Sir Charles Grant and Sir Alfred Lyall, were published in 1868–70. They showed that the lessons of *Ancient Law* had been absorbed by the rising generation, and Lyall's gazetteer contained the germs of his *Asiatic Studies* (1882), the most impressive work by any of Maine's Anglo-Indian disciples. Lyall took Maine's ideas on a whole range of issues – from divine kingship to feudalism via 'primitive religion' – and applied them to the parts of India he knew best: Berar, Rajputana, the North-West Provinces. The industrious systematizers soon took over from the men of genius. The Government of Bengal entrusted Sir William Hunter with the compilation of a massive 'statistical account' – one volume per district, around fifty volumes in all. District officers sent up the data Hunter required; then he churned out the gazetteers, using the same format and applying the same theories. His history of property in Orissa was exactly what one would expect: Maine-and-water.

The decennial census reports covered temporarily and permanently settled tracts alike. The first simultaneous census was taken between Lyall's *Berar* and Hunter's *Orissa*. But it was only in 1881 that the census commissioners' forays into Indian anthropology really took off. Ibbetson's Punjab census report was an intellectual *tour de force*. He attempted a classification and an explanation of caste, making such brilliant use of his materials that the relevant chapter served as a model for a whole series of multi-volume surveys covering the tribes and castes of every province, which only came to a close with the tribes and castes of Mysore in the 1930s. The appearance of these overviews stimulated a demand for more detailed monographs. Studies of individual tribes began to appear soon after 1900, but they were restricted to the peripheries of the empire: to the aboriginal tribes of the North-East Frontier, or Chota Nagpur, or the Santal Pargnas. Once again, the biases implicit in Maine's methodology were at work. Compared with the 200 million sedentary cultivators, the aboriginals were socially and economically insignificant. But the more primitive a tribe, the more it had to tell researchers about the earlier phases of human evolution.

Official activity dwarfed private scholarship. There were learned societies and learned journals in India, but they were heavily dependent on government support and government initiatives. The Asiatic Society of Bengal – the great meeting-place of the early nineteenth-century orientalists – was the oldest and most prestigious voluntary association in the sub-continent. It published articles and monographs on anthropological topics and it invited district officers to take part in a national ethnographic survey in the 1860s. But from that point on, it faded out of the picture. More specialized organizations and periodicals were needed: organizations like the Anthropological Society of Bombay (1886), and periodicals like *Punjab Notes and Queries* (1883).

The village community and caste – the most important institutions in Indian society – illustrate the transformation of official attitudes which this explosion of research produced. In the 1850s the village community was the great obstacle to progress in India. Sir John Strachey spoke for his generation when he welcomed the destructions of 'village institutions':

> No great changes can be brought about without some cause for regret. That the full recognition of individual property rights will bring with it the dissolution of the ancient village institutions seems indisputable, but they were necessarily doomed to decay with the establishment of good government and the progress of civilisation. The objects which they were so admirably adapted to fulfil are gradually passing away. The power which their constitution gave them of passive resistance to oppression is now no longer needed. As long as these institutions form the basis of society, any large amount of progress is impossible.

In 1904 the Government of India launched the Indian cooperative movement for the express purpose of enhancing the cohesion of the village community. 'Village institutions' were back where they had been in the 1800s: bulwarks against *anomie*, badly in need of protection.

Attitudes to the caste system went through an even more remarkable metamorphosis. If there was one point that evangelicals and utilitarians agreed on, it was the utter obscenity of caste. Grant and Mill traced the abominable hierarchy to the same fount: a conspiracy against the laity by brahmin priests: an attribution strongly reminiscent of the standard Protestant explanation of the persistence of popery. By the 1890s, the caste surveys had done their work. It was axiomatic that caste was the

> indispensable source of social cohesion, a congenital instinct, an all-pervading principle of attraction and repulsion entering into and shaping every relation of life ... It forms the cement that holds together the wayward units of Indian society. Were its cohesive power withdrawn or its essential ties relaxed, it is difficult to form any idea of the probable consequences. Such a change would be more than a revolution; it would resemble the withdrawal of some elemental force like gravitation or molecular attraction. Order would vanish and chaos would supervene.

AGRARIAN POLICY AND THE ANTHROPOLOGISTS

> The substitition of individual for communal rights in land constitutes the most grievous blunder that we have committed in India. I do not think it is sufficient to answer that [the sale and mortgage of the peasants' ancestral

land is] the inevitable result of a healthy economical process by which the thriftless are ousted in favour of the thrifty. [The alienations are due] to the gradual extension of a sort of law and a system of government unsuited to the people and their circumstances. [Our] insular ignorance of all conceptions of rights in land other than those current in England is only now disappearing under the light of an inquiry first suggested by the facts of Indian landed tenures. [With] obstinate conviction, [we believe that our legal principles] are a sort of necessary truths, wholly independent of the circumstances under which they are to be enforced. What I ask for is that the people should be allowed to manage their affairs in the way in which they, and not we, understand them; and that we should undo the revolution which we have introduced. It is often said that it is too late to go back. But if our first steps were retrograde, then to retrace them will be to advance. We have 'gone back' in this sense in Ireland; we have gone back in the Deccan. (Sir Denzil Ibbetson, Officiating Director of Public Instruction, to the Junior Secretary to the Financial Commissioner, Punjab, 12 August 1885)

There is an obvious way – it may be the only way – to prove that the official anthropologists were the driving force behind the new agrarian strategy. If the crucial policy-decisions were taken by leading anthropologists, at the head of groups of supporters, a prima facie case is made out; and if the anthropologists' ideas dominated the internal debates within the bureaucracy, the argument is stronger still. Identifying the officials involved and unearthing their motives is a great deal easier than strangers to Indian history might suppose. There were no smoke-filled rooms: the ICS conducted its debates on paper and kept detailed records of the few face-to-face meetings that took place. Then it printed the results. The files on complex pieces of late nineteenth-century agrarian legislation would reach the roof. They must constitute the most comprehensive and – once one gets into the relevant archive – the most accessible sources for the study of policy-making anywhere in the world.

There are several policy-decisions which are prime candidates for dissection. Half a dozen acts stand out of the general run of agrarian legislation as clear-cut violations of free-market principles. The Deccan Agriculturists' Relief Act (1879) drove a coach and horses through the sanctity of contract by authorizing judges to revise the cultivators' debts; the Bengal Tenancy Act (1885) deprived millions of tenants of freedom of contract by fixing their rents; the Punjab Alienation of Land Act (1900) infringed the peasants' right to do what they liked with their own, by prohibiting the sale of peasant holdings to urban moneylenders; the Bengal Settled Estates Act (1904) made great estates inalienable by subjecting them to entail; the Indian Cooperative Societies Act (1904) set up government-subsidized sources of credit to compete with private moneylenders; and the Punjab Panchayats Act (1912) substituted customary tribunals (which concentrated on conciliation) for regular courts (which upheld contracts).

Of all these possibilities, the Punjab Alienation of Land Act is probably the most promising. Contemporaries regarded the prohibition of sales between members of different tribes as marking a particularly brutal breach with *laissez-faire*. The campaign for the regulation of the land market was led by some of Maine's most self-conscious followers; it came towards the end of the new strategy, so the full impact of the anthropological explosion is apparent; and it showed the bureaucracy coming to terms with the most-hated institution, caste. The files suggest that around 120 officials took part in the decision-taking process, from the first formal proposals for restriction to the last debate in the legislative council. Sixty-eight backed the bill, 25 opposed it, and the rest hedged their bets. It should occasion no surprise to learn that the most enthusiastic advocates of prohibition were official anthropologists: men who read Maine's books at their university or their crammer, and went on to do research on Indian institutions.

A breakdown of the 93 members of the Punjab commission whose attitudes to restriction are on record shows that ten 'graduate anthropologists' supported the principle of restriction for every one who opposed it. In fact, the number of graduate anthropologists who opposed restriction was so small as to be statistically insignificant. The officials who were neither graduates nor anthropologists clearly thought on different lines. If one splits the waverers down the middle, a majority favoured the maintenance of a free market in land. Breakdowns by seniority imply that the battle over restriction was won by civilians entering the Punjab commission in the 1870s, when Maine's authority was at its height. Two-thirds of the civilians who went out to the Punjab between 1870 and 1879 favoured restriction; half the officials who backed the Act belonged to that cohort. After 1880, there was no support for the free market at all. Of the 27 officials who joined the Punjab commission between 1880 and 1900, only one opposed the Alienation of Land Bill. Clearly, a new orthodoxy had emerged.

Identifying the leaders of the faction which pushed the Punjab Act through is a little harder, though by no means impossible. What one wants to know is how much influence any given official exerted. Influence was a combination of two things: office and advocacy. Certain offices drew their holders into the core of the decision-taking process. After that, it was a matter of effective advocacy – of mobilizing official opinion in favour of restriction. On these criteria, there were four clear-cut leaders surrounded by a penumbra of loyal lieutenants. All four were anthropologists, in the sense that they made substantial contributions to the anthropological literature; and three were graduates who explicitly acknowledge their debt to Maine.

Septimus Smet Thorburn (1844–1924) has claims to be the real architect of the Punjab Alienation of Land Act. He was the first in the field; he conducted the most important surveys of rural indebtedness; and he appealed to the India Office, over his superiors' elevated heads, when the Governor of the day brushed his protests aside. He sent copies of his book, *Mussalmans and Moneylenders in the Punjab* (1886), to every member of the Council of India; the Secretary of State insisted on a full-scale inquiry; and once the possibility of restriction was mooted at the highest level, the pressure of opinion at district officer level stopped the utilitarians in Lahore from suppressing it. In 1897, just as the proposed bill was being drafted, Thorburn became the second-most senior official in the Punjab. As the head of the Revenue Department, he played a prominent part in the crucial conference which insisted on a general prohibition of inter-caste alienations throughout the province, instead of an enabling Act applying to selected areas. He retired before 'the Magna Carta of the Punjab peasantry' passed through the legislative council, but the Alienation of Land Act was acclaimed as a triumph for his persistence.

Thorburn was an anthropologist, but not a graduate. He joined the ICS in 1864, at the age of twenty, straight from Cheltenham. He never went to university; and the ICS examination he sat treated J. S. Mill as if his *Principles of Political Economy* were handed down on tablets from the mountain. It was only after he read Sir Raymond West's *réchauffé* of Maine's thought, *The Land and the Law in India* (1872), that he realized how the Benthamite legal system was bringing about an unwelcome social revolution among the Pathan tribes, elevating the despised Hindu moneylender above the warlike tribesman, and robbing the chiefs of their legitimate influence. The threat of *anomie* stared him in the face, and he decided to dedicate his official career to averting it.

Thorburn's most important contributions to the anthropological literature – his settlement report on Bannu (1879) and his inquiry into peasant indebtedness in the Rawalpindi Division (1896) – were classic pieces of *engagé* research. His account of the communal tenures of the Pathan tribes, regretting their passing, because they maintained the equality and fraternity of the tribe, is still the most sympathetic and informative treatment of *vesh*. His examination of all the debts of all the cultivators in selected villages of the northwest Punjab – some thousands of detailed case-studies – was so exhaustive that none of the subsequent inquiries into rural indebtedness in British India approached its rigour. In many ways, the All-India rural credit inquiry of the 1950s – conducted with a thousand times the resources available to Thorburn, on a national scale – was less informative than his investigations in a dozen villages, conducted in his spare time.

What Thorburn initiated, Sir Denzil Ibbetson (1848–1908) completed. Ibbetson was Revenue Secretary to the Government of India between 1894 and 1898 – the crucial office at the crucial time, while the imperial secretariat was pressing the Alienation of Land Bill on hesitant Governors and an obstructive India Office. He persuaded three successive Viceroys to support restriction, and he won over a significant proportion of the Punjab Commission. His personal authority was unique. He was regarded as the *beau idéal* of an Indian civilian: the paragon who could do everything an Indian civil servant was supposed to do, only twice as well. He drew up the definitive statement of the case for the prohibition of alienation: a sixty-page printed *Memorandum* which stands alone in the history of Indian administration as a *tour de force* of sustained argument. It pillaged Maine's ideas; it was even, up to a point, written in Maine's style.

Ibbetson acknowledged Maine's influence on his research. He was the most distinguished official anthropologist in the Punjab. His report on the settlement of Karnal (1872–80) made his name as a revenue officer and gave his high-flying career a welcome boost; thirty years after it was written, his successors were still turning to his 'scholarly investigation of tribal organisation and the social life of the villages … for information and suggestion'. The analysis of the castes, religions and occupations of the province in his four-volume *Punjab Census Report* (1883) was so detailed, lucid and original that it set the pattern followed by future anthropologists for half a century or more. The most interesting chapters were published separately; a slightly truncated version is still in print.

The 'third man' – Sir Lewis Tupper (1848–1910) – was an exact contemporary of Ibbetson's. Tupper was the guru, the theoretician, of the revisionist lobby. He succeeded Thorburn as Financial Commissioner in 1899 and oversaw the implementation of the Alienation Act. But his work as an officer on special duty, drawing up exhaustive treatises on complex agrarian problems, made a far greater contribution to the cause. As a lowly under-secretary on secondment to the Government of India, he drafted the despatch which vindicated the 'restoration' of occupancy rights to the *ryots* of Bengal. The legislation which followed, the Bengal Tenancy Act of 1885, was the most radical and the most imitated agrarian reform between the mutiny and independence. As a secretary in the Punjab, he championed the revival of customary law and customary courts. He supervised the systematic codification of the customs which protected the village community against the loss of land to outsiders; he wrote the report which led to the recognition of Pathan *jirgas* (assemblies of chiefs) as the best courts to try serious crimes; and he laid the foundations of the Punjab Panchayats Act, which set up councils of elders in thousands of villages. His *magnum opus* – his massive compilation of all the precedents and principles determining the Government of India's relations with the native states – strengthened the princes' autonomy by applying Maine's ideas about the indivisibility of sovereignty to subordinate states. Tupper's *Indian Political Practice* became the Bible of the political officers who served as residents and agents at the Indian rulers' courts.

The last of the leaders – Sir James Wilson (1853–1926) – was an immensely industrious all-rounder. He cut his teeth as a revenue officer settling two of the most drought-stricken districts in the Punjab during the aftermath of the 1878 famine, just as thousands of bankrupt peasant proprietors were losing their holdings and the Deccan Agriculturists Relief Act was bringing the problem of indebtedness to the top of the official agenda. His reports on Sirsa and Gurgaon contained a detailed analysis of the peasant land market and radical proposals for the problem of expropriation. He asked the Government of the Punjab to do two things: to put up the money to liquidate the debts of the most heavily indebted tribe – the Meos of Gurgaon; and to make their land inalienable. The brusque rejection of his plans, on doctrinaire *laissez-faire* grounds, turned him into a lifelong crusader for intervention. As Chief Secretary and Settlement Commissioner, he helped formulate the Alienation of Land Bill; and as Revenue Secretary to the Government of India – in fact, as Ibbetson's successor – he was jointly responsible for the Cooperative Societies Act of 1904. His intellectual credentials were clear from the first. His sketch of the evolution of tenures in Gurgaon, and his pioneer code of tribal custom were property and primitive law seen through Maine's monocle. He may have attended Maine's lectures at Corpus – he was at Balliol in the mid seventies. But it seems probable that he absorbed most of his historical method (and all his social conscience) from Arnold Toynbee. According to Milner, he was a leading member of Toynbee's set.

Analysis of all the other 'historicist' bills, in all the other provinces, reveals a similar pattern. The graduate anthropologists were in the van; the officials who clove to the free market model were neither graduates nor anthropologists. Young revenue officers were more sympathetic to Indian institutions than elderly judges; temporarily settled provinces, with a large number of settlement officers, were easier to move than permanently settled ones; the secretariats fought rearguard actions against pressure from district officers, until they were overrun by exponents of the new ideas.

Historians attempting to explain the far-reaching revival of the paternalist impulse which overwhelmed the Social Darwinists in late nineteenth-century India have generally resorted to 'objective' factors. A particular problem – say peasant indebtednes – became more widespread as a result of the commercialization of agriculture; therefore the Government of India did something about it. The difficulty is making the crucial linkages hold. There was no reason why the curtailment of the free land-market should have followed on, inevitably, from the improvement in the supply of credit. It was perfectly possible to acclaim the increased number of alienations – of sales and mortgages – as signs of economic development. In fact, that is exactly how they were regarded, by most commentators, until the 1870s. Of course, expropriation occasionally led to unrest. But the disorder was on a such a small scale, that it hardly warranted a complete change of agrarian strategy. A determined government would have faced the agitations down. The Deccan riots – which preceded the Deccan Agriculturists Relief Act – were pathetic affairs. They only affected a handful of villages; no one was killed; small detachments of police restored order within a few days. The tenant movements which preceded the Bengal Tenancy Act were more serious; but the most persistent campaigns were localized, and the malcontents could have been bought off by much more limited measures.

The official anthropologists gave the game away in the Punjab, when they argued that the Alienation of Land Act was necessary to stop unrest arising *at some future date*. They expected trouble. They were afraid that the rise of the market would make India ungovernable, because they were operating on a body of social thought which *predicted* social disintegration once South Asia was exposed to the world economy. It was changes in the way of looking at Indian society that produced the reconciliation with Indian institutions, rather than changes in society itself. The official anthropologists lost their collective nerve in the course of their researches. They lost the belief in the beneficence of the free market, which gave the utilitarians the confidence to impose *laissez-faire* regardless of the social costs.

The debates in the legislative council on the Punjab Alienation of Land Bill showed how completely Maine's approach to the analysis of 'early institutions' had come to dominate the official mind. Both sides appealed to his authority. Even the Indian councillors mouthed platitudes ultimately derived from his books. A single exchange sums up the change in the ideological landscape since the utilitarians carried all before them. A Sikh landowner, opposing restriction, invoked the inherent superiority of absolute freeholds, as the highest form of property on the evolutionary ladder. Then a Muslim landowner, primed by Tupper, produced the knee-jerk relativist riposte. Sir Harnam Singh:

> Individual property is being developed by a natural process from collective property, and such development is caused by various social and political circumstances. To throw back the gradual evolution of property now to its old channel would be arresting the march of progress ... Traditional ties of blood relationship, tribal organisations, village-unions, house-communities

and joint families are all disappearing in obedience to a well-established law of nature, and when those ties, which at one time were being considered insoluble and which firmly knitted ancient society are being gradually loosened, no artificial bond ought to be created to prevent disintegration.

Mohammed Hyat Khan:

[There is a reply to those] who judge the measure by the test of abstract principles based on the peculiar conditions of the West and not fully suited to the requirements of this province, or non-officials with modern education bringing their knowledge of the words of Fawcett and of Mill to bear on the hard facts of agricultural indebtedness and expropriation as existing in the Punjab. To the theoretical economist, an answer may best be given in the words of the Hon. Mr. Tupper, 'that laws should everywhere be suited to the existing condition of society'.

If Maine had lived long enough to read the proceedings of the legislative council when they were sent to the India Office, he would probably have cringed to see the use his admirers were making of his methods. But it was too late. The genie was out of the lamp.

CHAPTER 19

India and Henry Maine

Gordon Johnson

Henry Maine was the Legal Member of the Council of the Governor-General of India from 1862 to 1869. The appointment involved serving in India and throwing into appropriate legislative form the policy-decisions of the Viceroy and his Council. Although Maine had doubted whether his health would stand up to extended residence in India (in fact illness had prevented him from accepting the job when it was first offered to him in 1861), the climate and the work suited him extremely well, and his friends were delighted to see how fit he was when he returned to Europe on leave in 1865. The office of Legal Member was a very attractive one for Maine. He had found that the openings for an academic lawyer in Britain were limited for one who could not withstand the rigours of practising at the Bar and at a time when legal studies in the universities were unrewarding both intellectually and financially. The appointment was well paid (Macaulay received £10,000 a year when he held the office in the 1830s) and, following the success of his first major publication (*Ancient Law*) in early 1861, Maine lobbied his political friends to secure him some such well-remunerated public position. His wife was unable to accompany him to Calcutta and so accordingly, as Mountstuart Grant Duff tells us, 'He lived ... the life of a bachelor; but a very hospitable member of that brotherhood. His breakfasts, over which a lady whose many gifts have made her well known in London, as of old in Calcutta society, usually presided, were especially famous' (1892: 31). The service he rendered in India, for which he was rewarded by being created a Knight Commander of the Star of India in 1871, continued after his return to England upon his appointment to a place on the India Council, a body which advised the Secretary of State for India on Indian matters. Maine's election to the Mastership of Trinity Hall, it was noticed, 'gave him a dignified position and a pleasant occasional home at Cambridge, without burdening him with duties sufficiently serious to interfere with his work as a Member of the Council of India' (Grant Duff, 1892: 48).

The overwhelming impression one has from the contemporary record is that Maine's work in its Indian context constituted an important public service and that in the exercise of his duties he was restrained and conservative in his approach. 'Like all sensible men in India', Grant Duff wrote, 'Maine was anxious, whenever he could, to support the man who had to bear the greatest weight of responsibility for all the decisions, and he carried the same habit to the India Office, having as little of the *frondeur* in him as any man I have ever known' (1892: 33). Maine's uncertain social background, together with his dazzling academic success at Cambridge and his subsequent achievement in making a place for himself in English society, had provided him with a set of political attitudes characterized by Professor Burrow as 'hard-headed Peelite elitism varied by a taste for Burkean rhetoric' (1974: 255). Why was it that such a temperament, combined with Maine's considerable academic prowess and his undoubted legal skills, found such a congenial niche in mid-nineteenth-century India?

The question is not an easy one to answer, for India in the 1860s has been rather neglected by the historian. It is difficult to think of any important event which took place during the decade, and impossible to recall the Viceroys. Lord Canning, who presided over the mutiny in 1857 and dealt with its immediate aftermath, gave way to Lord Elgin, who died in the hills. At the end of the decade, Lord Mayo arrived, soon to be assassinated by a prisoner during his tour of the penal settlements on the Andaman Islands. In between Elgin and Mayo, and thus during most of Maine's tenure of office, the Viceroy was Sir John Lawrence, an appointment notable perhaps for the lack of enthusiasm with which it was made, since Lawrence, having served long and successfully in the Punjab, possessed a qualification which was universally held to bar a man from being Viceroy: actual knowledge of India itself. Lawrence was associated – indeed was an essential part of – an approach to Indian administration which stressed direct personal and discretionary rule, and, in the light of his experience in the Punjab, he believed very much in patriarchal government on the spot without too many regulations and without much interference from superiors. Although his government had to stir itself to secure peace on the

North-West Frontier, on the face of it he was determined to do as little as possible: if it was not necessary to do something, then it was absolutely necessary not to do it. In part, the apparently conservative pragmatism which so marked the policies of the 1860s was made easily explicable by reference to the mutiny. As Maine himself put it 'a nervous fear of altering native custom has, ever since the terrible events of 1857, taken possession of Indian administrators' (*VC*: 38–9). It was necessary, therefore, to be cautious and to avoid taking risks if at all possible. But, although the prevailing ethos might appear hostile to change, it is arguable that in the 1860s India underwent a sea-change. In formal terms, the Crown had succeeded the East India Company as government, and there was a lot of detailed tidying up to be done to see the change through. Then the structure of the government of India itself began to move off in ways which made its administration decidedly more modern and uniform in appearance. Both politically and economically, India began to stand in a different relationship to Britain. The extraction of revenue through the operation of revenue systems and the exercise of fiscal and commercial monopolies, together with the indirect trading patterns of the early nineteenth century whereby Indian goods financed Britain's trade with the Far East, gave way in importance to growing bilateral trade, increasing British investment in India, the development of new Indian exports, not only to Asia but to Europe and North America as well, and massive use of India for the purposes of imperial defence. The 1860s ushered in the heyday of empire: the next half-century was to be the truly untroubled decades of British rule in the sub-continent. Such a profound transformation during a period of overt conservatism and caution requires fuller explanation.

Early British government in India depended for its success on a hectic blend of force and political influence. Armed might and subtler politics combined to extract goods and money from a large and, on the whole, poor agrarian economy. This was in the great tradition of Indian government, and the Company simply built upon and improved the native institutions which it found in place. The British in India (in marked contrast to economic policies at home) continued and strengthened State monopolies, and they worked with those social elites who were best able to squeeze money from the rural economy. The Company used its army, on a regular basis, to collect a revenue demand pitched high and in cash (thus also ensuring that commodities needed for trade came on to the market), and it reinforced and developed ways of tying labour to the land and of preventing the free movement of cultivators (particularly important at a time when land was plentiful and labour was not). Success in these hazardous enterprises depended upon securing a reliable army and operating a revenue-collecting system which provided privilege and protection for important elements in society. Although the precise nature of this organization varied enormously across the different parts of India, as Dr Washbrook argues,

> it could be characterised as consisting of corporate, kin-related patterns of land settlement shaped over a long period by the attempts of the state to reduce their autonomy and by a penetration of the caste-system, both of which created internal social and political differentiation. The Company state, following its predecessors, tried to latch on to this differentiation, where it could find it, and turn it into the dominance which could be used to extract surplus. The early raj reinforced the authority of local leaderships (headmen, vatandars, small samindars, single-family mirasidars, malghuzars etc.) and subvented caste-based privileges (through inams and differential rates of assessments). In some cases, it failed to find significant differentiation within the kin-body but was obliged to elevate it in its entirety to privilege over outsiders (bhaiachara, co-sharing mirasi tenure etc.). The key feature of the process, however, was that although the state partially drew out these elements of potential dominance, it neither controlled nor created the context from which they came and in which they remained half-situated. In consequence, actual rights to possess and use the land remained part-conditioned by this context and dependent on the customs and norms of the local agrarian community. These customs and norms (institutionalised in the authority of panchayats, lineage leaders, caste and religous deference, etc.) played at least as large a role in determining the relationship of society to the land as did the granting of state privilege in the first place. (1981: 663-4)

Although the Company had some leverage in rural society, it was never strong enough to control fully local leaderships, far less to redesign the social context from which they came. Thus government was in reality a perpetual struggle with strong elements in rural society to control the economy and share in its profits. The fact that both army and police, as well as all levels of lower or local administration, were part and parcel of the same social network further hampered the freedom of action of policy-makers. The same argument applies in other areas of society as well: the Company was heavily dependent upon the indigenous commercial and banking elites to achieve its fiscal and trading objectives, and it had perforce to draw upon the traditionally literate to staff its administrative offices at the higher levels. The Company's needs were met by the application of force, but in a lively political arena where its wishes were mediated through semi-autonomous social groups and institutions over which the British had no final control. India exhibited, not, then, a series of small, simple archaic societies, but extremely complex sets of social networks which were very difficult to manage. From the earliest governmental experiments in Bengal, fundamental contradictions underlay the Company's rule: while on the one hand it, and some of its Indian supporters, could set out clear, cogent policies for reform, progress and development, on the other, care had to be taken to see that such change was compatible with the maintenance of a perceived status quo and would accommodate local customs and tradition. Hence also the longstanding paradox in Indian law that while, from the eighteenth century, there was a trend to legislate in order to encourage and safeguard the freedom of the individual and his or her rights in property, there was a simultaneous development of personal law which entrenched ascriptive (caste, religous and familial) status as the basis of individual right. At one and the same time policies were conceived which treated of individuals in a world of amoral market relations and of individuals inextricably trapped in joint-families or other communal organizations.

Far from being a static or isolated society, India had come under tremendous pressures, both domestically and internationally, in the late eighteenth and early nineteenth centuries. Natural disaster and the fragile environment for agriculture had led to shortages, famine and large-scale depopulation in the closing decades of the eighteenth century. Internal political turmoil and rapidly changing governments marked the politics of the period. At the same time, various parts of the Indian economy were linked in new ways to international markets, providing both opportunity and enhanced vulnerability to changes over which Indian producers had control. In ways in which historians are only just beginning to fathom, the East India Company and dynamic Indian groups in alliance with it began to provide a more stable political and economic context from the early nineteenth century. The emergence of the new state of things was slow in coming and very uneven, geographically and socially, in its impact. Hence it would be fair to characterize much of the early part of the nineteenth century as a period in which the Company's rule was never totally secure (despite its virtual monopoly of force from about 1820 onwards) and during which it faced chronic unrest in the Indian countryside. There was hardly a year in which the Company was not at war, either on its shifting and seemingly ever-expanding frontiers, or against its own recalcitrant subjects, constantly tussling with the new overlord for shares in resources. In this context, the mutiny of part of the Indian army in 1857, and the serious and widespread disturbances with significant loss of governmental control which followed hard on the initial rebellion at Meerut, were the last, albeit perhaps the grandest, attempt at resistance to the new social and economic order which had been a century in the making. The events of 1857–9 hit British confidence so hard not so much because in objective terms the revolts were impossible to deal with but because loss of control had been so sudden and the close connection between rural society and the army had been underlined in such a striking way. If there was a moral to the tale, it was to err on the side of caution. But in fact there was another side to the coin. Most of India, after all, did not revolt. The Punjab, the most recently acquired of the provinces, and the one which had attracted the most by way of scarce government resources to develop its economy, remained firm, already benefiting from a decade of economic growth. Elsewhere, improved communications in the form of road, canal and, most lately, railway, together with renewed attempts to encourage irrigation, were also beginning to have an effect. There was an increase in the number of schools and in the establishment of the first Indian colleges and universities. Most importantly, groups in the countryside which had become established through the operation of the revenue systems were now launched on a period of unprecedented prosperity: the population increased (thus making labour easier to control), acres of farmland expanded, marginal areas were brought under cultivation, new foreign markets were opening up and, in real terms, the burden of the land revenue demand everywhere began to fall. In some areas, the economic gains were very striking indeed, and, although benefits were far from being evenly distributed, it could not be denied that they were there. Even the government found itself better off than before as inflation and the increased areas under production brought more rupees into the exchequer.

Such developments were not, however, without strain, and the government needed to exercise constant vigilance in its management of the changing situation. As before, it was forced to follow policies riddled with paradox and contradiction: in this sense there is no marked change of policy or of process at mid-century. But whereas the earlier nineteenth century may perhaps have trumpeted reform and change to mask its fundamentally conservative activities, in the second half of the century the prevailing ethos was to hide change under concern for tradition. Thus virtue was made of protecting under-tenants and 'poor' peasants while quietly strengthening the legal and economic position of dominant cultivators; 'moneylenders' became a much-abused class, discriminated against in peculiar ways (for example by preventing certain specified social groups from buying more land outside of towns), but the position of creditors was also improved; a fetish was made of leaving religious and social customs well alone, unless it happened that established usages were so flagrantly opposed to British ideas of right and wrong (such as particular marriage customs or the consequences for ownership of property arising from them), in which case the government stepped briskly forward, irrespective of the critical outcry. And, underneath the policy statements and the laws, there was the continual quest to find those groups in Indian society which could best serve the purposes of the raj. This was a delicate political task at best, society being so open to change; but the invention of social anthropology and the rise of the sociologist in government made men bold. Society was analysed and classified and labels placed unerringly upon the social categories which were deemed reliable or dangerous. Hence the late nineteenth-century view of Indian society as coherent groups, which could be used as building-blocks in the political game: 'peasants', 'proprietors', 'princes', 'Muslims', 'criminal tribes', 'moneylenders' and a myriad of other social descriptions which, whatever their actual justification, became live political categories.

This, then, was the India, to which Maine came, and he was wonderfully fitted to serve it well. Not only did he perform valuable services in his professional character as a lawyer, not only did he make the whole country, and the problems of governing it, seem intelligible to his contemporaries, but he did so in such a way as to give intellectual respectability to the courses of action upon which the government was set.

As Law Member, Maine passed no striking laws, and much of the legislation which was approved in his time was recast before the century was out. Although he was responsible for over two hundred separate Acts, his colleagues are remarkably unanimous in their welcome for his low-key approach. Sir Lewis Tupper found that Maine's virtue lay in the fact that 'he limited himself to the actual requirements of his time' (1898: 391), while Courtenay Ilbert, who was later to prove an extremely controversial Law Member, praised Maine for abstaining 'from passing a great many measures of doubtful utility' (1898: 402). Here was no adventurous law-giver, as Macaulay had been thirty years before, or, it might be argued, as confident a legislator as James Fitzjames Stephen was to prove immediately after him. But his technical skills were without equal, and he established the highest professional standards possible for his department. This high level of technical competence also allowed him to play an influential role as a mediator between conflicting demands made upon the law. The Acts passed through the Council between 1862 and 1869 are very various: some applied to India in a very straightforward way the law as it already existed in England, and these particularly benefited commercial activity and the easy recourse to the courts in support of property and contracts; others gave legislative form to the civil usages and religious practices of particular groups of Indians, and here, while there were some notable exceptions, particularly as regarded marriage, the overall tendency was to put into statute form customary laws and to do so in ways which were prevalent at the time. This gave a specious authenticity to particular versions of Hindu law and, in a sense, worked against the trend of more secular contract-type relations in the society. Maine also saw that the new government of India must rule through laws passed by the legislature rather than by rulings handed down by the courts or by regulations issued by executive authority. His opinion, therefore, was on the side of developing centralized government and of dividing the functions of government into clearly separated departments. But with a Viceroy who in the districts had combined revenue, police and judicial powers all in his own person, such a development was not likely to be welcomed. Maine conceded, therefore, that while the former was to a large degree inevitable, ways might be found of discovering expedients whereby the tendency of legislation to hamper discretion could be minimized. Maine also saw, that, given the size and variety of India, an important feature of law-making in India in the future would be provision for all the regions to be empowered to frame their own provincial legislation (at that time only Bengal, Bombay and Madras could make their own local laws). Much of the work of the law department was on the further codification of Indian laws. Here Maine had to negotiate the results with a law commission sitting in London, and the evidence suggests that for much of the time the two bodies worked at cross purposes. But for Maine codification did not provide an opportunity for a fundamental reconstruction of Indian law (which is what lawyers in London would have liked), but was simply an attempt to 'set forth fundamental principles with as much simplicity as was compatible with accuracy' (Tupper, 1898: 393). Again, the practicalities of the Indian situation were to temper the force of reform. Finally, Maine employed a great piece of legal casuistry to show, from established precedents in international law, that sovereignty could be divided and that, varying as they did in their actual relationship with the British Crown, the princely states in India were, in legality, quite distinct and separate from British India and must be treated as such. Politically, this laid the foundation for the use of princely India as a block on constitutional reform, and it signalled an end to the continued absorption of Indian states into the British raj. Perhaps Sir Alfred Lyall best summed up Maine's legal contribution by pointing out that 'he stood between ancient and modern ideas – between the opinions of Europe and India, and had to find a *modus vivendi* that reconciled both' (1898: 402)

Of course, all Maine's contemporaries recognized that his influence spread far beyond the making of laws. His serious writing – particularly *Ancient Law* and *Village-Communities in the East and West* – had a profound effect on how Indian society was observed and understood. Here his talent for imposing order on chaos and for lucidly setting out complex matters made him compelling reading. 'Many books had been written about India, but most of them were unreadable' (Ilbert, 1898: 403). Maine 'divided the essential principles of Indian institutions and he clothed his description of them in language of consummate literary art' (403). In some respects, Maine cannot lay claim to be a particularly original thinker. Before he had ever set foot in India, Grant Duff tells us, 'he had written admirable papers about the Indian village system' (1898: 399). Baden-Powell pointed out that Maine had had 'no opportunity for "camping out" and personal enquiry on the spot' and hence it was the case that all his knowledge was 'gathered from reading and conversation; he saw with the eyes of others' (1898: 404–5). In fact, Maine drew upon an enormous range of early nineteenth-century writing about India – prominent, no doubt, being works like those of James Mill, Elphinstone, Metcalf, Malcolm and Tod, together with the voluminous published records of the East India Company, particularly revealing for revenue arrangements in Bengal and Madras; and he combined these with fashionable ideas from the German historical school: he took a whole mass of incoherent fact and by applying social theory to it gave it form and shape. 'His mind seemed like a sun shooting forth rays of light which bridged over great intervals of space and time, which brought Indian village communities into relation with village communities in Russia, and associated Rajpootana society today with the society of the Homeric age. His writings were luminous, stimulating and suggestive' (Ilbert, 1898: 403). The last quarter of the nineteenth century saw a tremendous flowering of social studies in India. Census and settlement reports contained miniature ethnographic surveys, and minute inquiry was encouraged into the structure and working of Indian society – its castes, its cultures, its religions and its economies. For the very best minds who applied themselves to the daunting task of observing, recording and explaining India, it is remarkable how often Maine is the point of departure, even when the new work sets out to modify or to disagree with his own arguments; while for lesser minds, the ordinary revenue officers who had read Maine's books as their preparation for government in India, it was easy to pluck from Maine's prose a comforting phrase or paragraph about the true nature of Indian society. Such information would usually be of a conservative nature and would seem to point towards the fineness of simple archaic society and to justify conserving it against change.

Although it would be easy to portray Maine as representing a rather bland conservatism and lending his academic authority to a counter-revolution, it would be a mistake to do so. Besides being an extremely lucid thinker, Maine was also a sophisticated one. The brilliant prose is not only coherent and compelling but also ambivalent and ambiguous. He falls into none of the traps that beset the unwary. He knew that Indian society was not, and never had been, static; he saw clearly that 'the natives of India are not so wedded to their usages that they are not ready to surrender them for any tangible advantage' (*VC*: 39). He argued strongly against there being any uniform or clearly stated set of Indian law: rather the whole was a mass of shifting customs which varied from place to place and over time. He had no truck with the popular impression that 'Indian society is divided ... into a number of horizontal strata, each representing a caste' (*VC*: 56). He told students at Oxford:

> This is an entire mistake. It is extremely doubtful whether the Brahminical theory of caste upon caste was ever true except of the two highest castes; and it is even likely that more importance has been attached to it in modern than ever was in ancient times. The real India contains one priestly caste, which in a certain, though a very limited, sense is the highest of all, and there are, besides, some princely houses and a certain number of tribes, village communities, and guilds, which still in our day advance a claim, considered by many good authorities extremely doubtful, to belong to the second or third of the castes recognised by the Brahminical writers. But otherwise, caste is merely a name for trade or occupation, and the sole tangible effect of the Brahminical theory is that it creates a religious sanction for what is really a primitive and natural distribution of classes. The true view of India is that, as a whole, it is divided into a vast number of independent, self-acting, organised social groups – trading, manufacturing, cultivating. (*VC*: 56–7)

And earlier, in *Ancient Law*, he had encapsulated the Indian village community in a formulation both persuasive and fraught with difficulty: the village community, in reality, was 'at once an organised patriarchal society and an assempiy of coproprietors' (260). As Lyall, no mean scholar himself, told a meeting of the Society of Arts, Maine had not made so many original discoveries as had been supposed. 'Other people had the facts, and knew what they wanted to do, but they did not know how to do it, nor how to justify it; but when they produced their case, Maine found exactly the formula which explained everything. If you put before him a set of facts, or a certain number of ideas and suggestions which most Anglo-Indians had stumbled upon in a confused, unfinished way, he would suddenly set them all in order by one of his weird and wide generalisations, and they discovered that they had been right all along' (1898: 402).

In the surviving literature, not least that which he wrote himself, Maine appears as a decidedly ambiguous figure. Sir Frederick Pollock praised 'the great practical wisdom displayed in everything Maine did, and perhaps also in several things he refrained from doing' (1898: 401). His books were so influential because their clarity does not stand in the way of many interpretations of their content. Conservative in attitude he may have been, but he was historically sensitive, and this lent an ambivalence to his thought. Perhaps this is why Maine provides a good way of looking at the wider questions of India and its government in the later nineteenth century. That society and its administration were shot throughout with contradictions too. But what seems to have been happening was that, from the early 1860s a new balance was struck between British and Indian interests: British rule was re-established after the difficulties of the 1840s and 1850s, on a new basis, and India settled into a new and profitable relationship with Britain. Economic development, reform of the political and administrative structures and a definite move into the international economy all took place within an ideologically conservationist ethos. Those British interests primarily connected with India did well, while significant social groups within India benefited from the economic consequences of rising population, expanded agriculture, growing exports, lessening taxation and increased opportunities for new employment outside their traditional sectors. It was, therefore, an ideal time to be seen to be doing nothing very much and letting nature take its course. The contradictions in society, in the economy and in the political structure did not obtrude. It was perfectly possible, and agreeable, to back both the dynamic and the static; to allow change while protecting an old order; to maintain a fundamentally inefficient order of agricultural production while building canals and railways; to build up native rulers as real princes and to look with pride on colleges and universities.

In the longer term, difficulties would make themselves felt. The social and economic orders were neither efficient enough nor flexible enough to respond to further pressures from within – such as continued growth of population – or to change from without – like new competitors entering the world's marketplaces. The balance achieved in the second part of the century would be destroyed by increased social conflict and economic stratification. There would be no easy evolution of Indian society from the archaic to the modern, and it would be as difficult for a nationalist movement as for an imperial government to make articulate and put in order Indian societies as they buckled under the pressures of the twentieth century.

In retrospect, the later nineteenth century may seem to have been a time of lost opportunity: just when the raj could, perhaps, have pushed ahead and reordered itself on the backs of the more dynamic and entrepreneurial of India's social elites, and given a boost to individual freedoms by attacking more vigorously the mediating social institutions which ensnared men and women in communal and kin associations, it hedged its bets. It felt the need to support and protect a status quo, ever driven by the realization that no government, even the most despotic, can outlast its beneficiaries. And so it balanced the old and the new; it reined back development when it was believed to threaten the stability of order as a whole. It was wisest to play safe. Let Maine throw the argument into clearer form (A2, 1887: 527–8):

I have said that there are many different countries in the remarkable dominion which we call India. But on all of them a double current of influences may be seen to be playing. One of these currents is of foreign origin, and it has done much to shape the mental condition of a relatively small minority, characterised by aspirations with which it is impossible for Englishmen not to sympathise, but too apt to take its opinions from what are called schools of advanced thought, an expression to which I hope I do no injustice by suggesting that it means thought which has shaken itself free from the restraints of human nature and historical fact. The other current arises in India itself, engendered amid a dense and dark vegetation of primitive opinion, stubbornly rooted in the *débris* of the past. It feeds the minds of a majority so large that its very vastness makes it irresistible. I have quoted elsewhere the saying of an eminent Anglo-Indian, that the British rulers of India are like men bound to make their watches keep time in two longitudes at once. Nevertheless, I added, this paradoxical position must be accepted. If they are too slow, there will be no improvement; if they are too fast, there will be no security. The British dominion in India is much too wonderful a creation for despair to be justifiable, but a man must have a very superficial conception of what Indian government is if he thinks that it has been made easier by the necessity for reconciling these two conditions.

CHAPTER 20

Maine and change in nineteenth-century India

C. A. Bayly

Dr Dewey's chapter sees Sir Henry Maine as the prophet and inspiration of the sea-change in policies and attitudes which overtook the British in late nineteenth-century India. The government of the East India Company, in theory at least, had been a rule of modernity, moulded by utilitarianism, Ricardian rent theory and evangelicalism. The eighteenth-century landholding interest had come to be regarded as 'drones on the soil', impeding the improving labour of the yeomanry. The Indian states were faded exemplars of oriental despotisms, to be swept away where possible by escheat when their rulers died without heirs. An English legal philosophy of individualism was to be grafted on to the Hindu law books, and oriental texts were to be superseded by English education. Capitalist enterprise was to transform the Indian economy, and as far as possible the moral reformation was to be completed by the onslaught of Christian missionizing against a dying Hinduism. This modernizing deluge, at its height in the so-called Age of Reform of the 1830s and 1840s, was classically analysed in the first work of Eric Stokes, *The English Utilitarians and India* (1959). Later the supposed utilitarian impact on land revenue and judicial policy was investigated in detail by scholars such as Ravinder Kumar (1968) and Thomas Metcalf (1965). It was this inheritance of ideas and policies that Maine and his pupils are seen finally to have laid to rest.

In a sense, though, one needs to go back even earlier than the utilitarian deluge to put Maine into context. Historians of political thought are wary these days of positing abrupt changes in mentality or ideology. In most circumstances many discourses coexist and struggle for supremacy with each other. Most sets of ideals have deep antecedents in the past. So it was with the conservative historicism of Indian officials. One reason that Maine's thought was well received in the India of the 1870s and 1880s was that it spoke to the older pre-utilitarian tradition represented most notably by Elphinstone, Munro and Tod between 1780 and 1830. Maine himself frequently quotes Elphinstone and Munro as authorities. Though they were by no means as articulate or well grounded in comparative legal theory as Maine, all these individuals and many of their contemporaries had celebrated the virtues of India's institutions such as the Indian village and Indian kingship. To a large extent they had also inherited the 'stage theory' of historical development propagated by Robertson and the historians of the Scottish Enlightenment. Tod in particular drew parallels between European feudalism and the 'stage' of society in Rajasthan in the 1820s in regard to property rights, the feud and feudal obligations. At one point Tod even discerns the emergence of representative institutions among the Rajputs. He notes how what he sees as the feudal government of the Rajput princes was in some places restrained by the corporate religious and commercial privileges of the Jain community (1920: II, 606). Using the same sort of scheme, Tod was prepared to concede that Indian society was capable of reaching a higher stage of development than Maine was to envisage.

It is interesting to find as unlettered an administrator as Sir Thomas Maitland, governor of Ceylon in 1808, disparaging an attempt to substitute cash rent for corvée in the following words:

It was as if one of the ancient barons had pulled out of his pocket Adam Smith: and said I will apply to you vassals principles which will not properly apply to your circumstances for another 500 years. (Lord, 1935: 81–2)

In some ways, then, Maine and his acolytes were merely returning to Anglo-Indian political thought a form of discourse which had been current at a much earlier period and which was the natural ideology for a fragile colonial dominion. Nevertheless, there is a strong case for situating a significant ideological and administrative shift in the 1860s.

Dr Dewey's own dissertation, which concentrated on the recently annexed Punjab, moved Stokes' style of analysis one generation on and discussed the emergence and influence of what he sees as conservative, idealist and historicist thought among the Indian civil servants of the later nineteenth century. Taking as their starting-point Maine's *Ancient Law* and *Village-Communities in the East and West*, these officials were struck by what they saw as the deleterious effects of English individualism and modernizing regulation on Indian societies, which were at a very much more primitive stage of development than Western Europe. The official mind consequently became conservative. A rush of legislation and administrative initiatives, particularly in the Punjab and western India, represented attempts to shore up what were taken to be traditional Indian institutions. A new sympathy for the village community in its many forms was manifested in works such as B. H. Baden-Powell's *The Land System of British India* (1892). Government measures constrained the sale of agricultural lands to moneylenders, protected the Indian aristocracy and princes, and sought to determine and codify the custom of local clan and caste rather than to purvey the general principles of either English or brahminical Hindu law.

This shift in the intellectual culture of colonial administration in India has usually been seen as part of a more general change. The systems of indirect rule pioneered by Sir Frank Swettenham in the Federated Malay States or by Lord Lugard in West Africa seem to embody the same spirit: a desire to preserve native customs and institutions from modernity and to avert the *anomie* which sprang from the erosion of traditional forms of kingship and religious organization. The colonial administrator, it appears, was making a slow transition from the status of social engineer to that of social conservator and anthropologist-as-legislator. Maine therefore stands as the progenitor not only of the conservative administrators of the pre-war Sudan political service, but also of their collaborator and critic Sir Edward Evans-Pritchard.

In the later 1950s, when Stokes wrote *The English Utilitarians*, he felt that the 'locus of historical change' lay in intellectual impulses in Britain and that they worked fairly uniformly and deeply on the structure of Indian society. A generation of historical research, notably by Stokes himself who celebrated the 'return of the peasant' to Indian history, dented these certainties. The influence of policy makers and their ideologies now appeared strictly limited. The minutes and theoretical statements of Mill or Thomason, and for that matter of Maine and Fitzjames Stephen, were no more than examples of 'one clerk talking to another'. Colonial ideology was broken to fragments on the hard edges of Indian society. Where landlords were eliminated, it was not because of the power of pure reason but because their social grip on the land was limited. Where English education and legal institutions were taken up, it was where emerging Indian elites had an interest in doing so. The great ideological changes were no more than surface discourses among officials. Real change emanated from the rhythms of the Indian economy.

In his chapter Dr Dewey has eschewed this reductionist tendency to the extent that Maine appears again almost as Mill once did as the 'true legislator of British India'. Maine's thought, he seems to be arguing, was diffused in India and Great Britain at a critical point when the education of young civil servants was being brought into line with university education more generally. Maine's interests in law and history provided a bonding element in these new studies and therefore had a quite disproportionate influence on a whole generation of officials from Sir Alfred Lyall through Sir Lewis Tupper to Sir Malcolm Hailey. Institutional and educational change provided an enlarged sphere for the action of the new historicist thought.

Dewey does not go on to suggest, however, why teachings in Haileybury, Oxford, Cambridge and London proved particularly relevant to the moral and material conditions in which officials found themselves after 1870. One line of argument might go like this. If there was a single period when the ideological discourse of colonial government was least trammelled by the circumstances of Indian society and most directly influential on agrarian and social policy, it was the years from about 1860, during the post-Mutiny reconstruction, to about 1890, when Indian nationalism began to take root. Colonial government was presented with new room for manoeuvre. The effect of the 1857 Rebellion was to demilitarize India; the expansion of the railway network and the electric telegraph had given the ICS much greater knowledge of the society it was governing and greater leverage within it. A generation of Indian native informants and influential subordinate officials was now in place. In key territories of the raj, the old aristocracy had been severely weakened, but the new clerisy and service class remained weak and dependent. In western India and the Punjab the earlier ruling class had been an amalgam of office-holders and land-revenue farmers. It was easily displaced, and its disappearance made possible deeper intervention by paternalist British officials. The modernizers and utilitarians of the 1830s had been the finer propagandists, but the colonial state at that time was too weak to give them real support, and knowledge of Indian society was too shallow.

The real revolutionaries, one could go on to argue, were the conservative imperialist thinkers of the later nineteenth century. It was they who 'created' Indian caste and religion; they invented the village community and even Indian nationalism itself. For it is important to remember that Maine was read by and indirectly influenced Indians. The school of thought represented by Maine had its counterpart among Indian intellectuals. An important strand within Indian nationalist ideology was also historicist and conservative. It was represented among others by Vivekananda, Dayananda Saraswati, Raja Shiva Prasad and indeed by Gandhi. The difference was that Maine's historical progression was here reversed. For the nationalists, India's traditional institutions were perfectly developed over centuries to guarantee a redistribution throughout society of love and respect. The village community was not simply an economic entity, but a moral economy. The caste system was an ordered and rational system for assigning social groups to occupations where they could best serve the common good. Indian kingship was a paradigm for balancing rights and duties within society. Maine, for his part, thought the problem of Indian polities was that over time politics had been corrupted by the rise of brahminical tyranny. In the West the power of kings had been constrained by corporate bodies and feudal chieftains drawing legitimacy from the inheritance of Roman and tribal law. The ultimate result was representative government. In India, he argued, the power of kings had been usurped by brahmins, but their legitimacy was derived from religious rites which had not been differentiated from civil society and law. The result here, therefore, was tyranny and superstition. But because the West was so much more advanced than India, it was imperative, Maine thought, to build on the existing institutions of Indian society and purge them rather than to overthrow them and impose a wholly inappropriate apparatus of courts and councils.

But for the new generation of Indian thinkers the problem of Indian kingship and the caste system was its perversion by the Muslim conquerors and then by the Western materialism which came with British rule. The progression they saw was not from barbarism to aristocracy and feudalism and then ultimately to representative government, but from the Golden Age through foreign conquest to the Kali Yug, or Era of Destruction of the present age. Sir Henry and the Mahatma would have agreed, nevertheless, if one could imagine them meeting in the corridors of the Middle Temple, that the Indian village, the caste system and tribal custom should be protected.

By 1870, then, both Indian intellectuals and colonial administrators were beginning to fashion ideologies and programmes which stressed 'for somewhat different reasons' the virtue of India's supposed 'traditional institutions', which they perceived as being under threat. Why was this? Modern economic and social historians would agree that change was speeding up in the decades after the Rebellion of 1857. But they would stress the importance of a particular economic conjuncture and would in large degree deny that the institutions of India in the early nineteenth century could be usefully regarded as 'traditional'. The economic conjuncture in question was the recovery of the economy from the relative stagnation which had gripped it from about 1818 to about 1859. The depression which was already ending before 1857 was finally dispelled by the injection of liquidity into the economy, which came about as the result of military expenditure following the Rebellion. The railways, electric steamship, telegraph and the Suez Canal improved the possibilities for internal and external trade, so that land prices began to rise and sticky rent rates began to move. Problems with the bimetallic currency and slowly increasing demand brought about a slow inflation of commodity prices. Cash rents became more general and the land market picked up.

Economic growth and inflation, of course, put pressure on coparcenary and clan institutions, old landholding communities and the profits of village office. But when Maine and his contemporaries saw the decline of pristine institutions, what they were probably seeing was Indian society beginning to employ once again a whole 'library of techniques' of sale, farm, fragmentation, mortgage and lease of property and office which had been quite common before the depression of the 1830s, and which reflected a much more complex understanding of the relationship between property and commerce than these observers were prepared to concede. Speaking of the joint matrilineal and matrilocal property-holding bodies (the *tharavads*), in Kerala, Maine's namesake and echo J. D. Mayne, a judge in Malabar, said in outraged tones:

I have witnessed continued efforts on the part of the natives to cast off their own customs and deal with their property by partition, alienation, and devise, as if it were governed by ordinary Hindu laws. (Mayne, 1914: xi)

But as Menon (1988) points out, there is much evidence that individuals could buy themselves in and out of shares in the *tharavad* in the early nineteenth century and before, and that these institutions had flourished and adapted in the context of a thriving external trade in pepper and other commodities. In many cases what was perceived as tradition was in fact the product of the relative economic stagnation and the administrative freezing of institutions which Company rule had itself brought about.

The self-contained and ageless Indian village is another myth which appealed in a relatively sophisticated form both to Maine and to the conservative nationalists. But the nails have been driven into its coffin with increasing ferocity in the past few years. Perlin (1985) found eighteenth-century aristocrats buying in to village rights. Ludden (1985) and Subrahmanyam (1990) found complex systems of exchange and marketing between villages and a high degree of articulation to external trade as early as the sixteenth century. Property was patrimonial and alienable in the Mughal and other pre-colonial kingdoms, and the State was not 'owner' of all land as Maine thought. Techniques of revenue farming, the splitting and sale of office and status, the development of a Hindu–Muslim culture of accountancy and contract – all these were features of early modern India. At the level of the State, brahmins were not a universal tyrannical force. Here Maine was overinfluenced by what he read of the Marathas of western India, and perhaps by what he was told by Grant Duff, who elaborated the myth of the 'wily' Maratha brahmin. At any rate Indians made a clear distinction between *lokika*, or secular, and ritual brahmins. Again, in much recent research caste appears as flexible, malleable and constructive rather than destructive of the Indian State.

Maine and his followers proceeded on the classical orientalist premise that the brahminical texts or static custom represented a traditional reality. They were therefore not aware of (or ignored) the huge volume of evidence which contradicted their view of the Hindu family, testation in Indian practice, the structure of the joint family, and so on. Above all, the stage theory which equates ancient Germany or early Rome with transitional India is revealed to be totally flawed since the latter had been closely integrated into Asian and intercontinental trade for at least five hundred years. India was also heavily influenced by Islamic forms of government and law which Maine touches on only peripherally. Even if some anthropologists take as their starting-point temples, divine kingship and the rules of purity and pollution in their studies of India, most now accept that these institutions must be understood as operating within the context of a complex and variable culture of commerce and contract.

Perhaps there may not be much utility in exposing the ahistorical and contextless quality of the Victorians' understanding of Indian society. But there are two points which make this deconstruction worth while, rather than a mean exercise of historians' hindsight. The first is that this type of discussion reveals the complete absence in Maine's supposedly historical theory of a real historical dynamic. For instance, there seems no reason, ultimately, why the West developed towards representative institutions and secular law and the Indians towards brahminical tyranny, other than that the Indians were more superstitious while the Romans were somehow imbued with higher rationality and separated off the sacral from the domain of personal and family law. To this extent Maine's ideas and those of his followers were only historicist, not historical, a feature which they shared with Weber, Sombart and the next generation of German sociologists.

Secondly, and more importantly from an Indian perspective, the Maine tradition was highly influential in British attempts to grasp and construct India's late colonial reality. This went beyond the questions of land-revenue policy, interestingly dealt with by Dewey, to politics and the response to nationalism. Maine's emphasis on the inner structure and essential features of clan, village, and the sacral quality of property helped to justify a separatist tradition of administration. The imperative to protect the Indian village from the erosions of commerce soon broadened out to a desire to protect caste, tribe and religious group. The very same officials who were made sensitive to the decline of joint property forms and the integrity of the village community were the ones who argued in the 1880s and 1890s for special representation for Muslims. Soon other species in need of conservation came into view: Sikhs, traditional landholders, non-brahmins and hill-people. Everyone now accepts that conflicts within Indian society helped justify and inform the official policy of separatism. But it is difficult to believe that Indians would have come forward so energetically if the British had not prepared the ground for them. At first sight Maine might appear an irrelevance to modern Indian historiography, but as the ideological shadow of both nationalism and communalism, he deserves the attention of historians of the non-European world.

Appendix: the conference programme

30 September 1988

12.00–1.15   Lunch
1.30–2.30   Luncheon speaker – Professor G. A. Feaver – University of British Columbia
2.30–4.15   **Session 1 Maine and the idea of progress**
  Session Chairman: Dr J. Steinberg – Trinity Hall, Cambridge
  Professor J. W. Burrow, FBA – University of Sussex
  Dr S. A. Collini – St John's College, Cambridge
  Dr R. C. Cocks – University of Sussex
  Dr K. Kumar – University of Kent
4.15–5.00   Tea
5.00–6.45   **Session 2 Maine and the social sciences**
  Session Chairman – G. A. K. Howes – Trinity Hall, Cambridge
  Professor A. Kuper – Brunel University
  Dr A. D. J. Macfarlane, FBA – King's College, Cambridge
  Professor J. D. Y. Peel – University of Liverpool
  Professor E. A. Shils – University of Chicago
  Dr R. G. Abrahams – Churchill College, Cambridge
8.00   Dinner
  Dinner speaker – Revd Professor W. O. Chadwick, OM, KBE, FBA – Selwyn College and Trinity Hall, Cambridge

1 October 1988

9.00–12.15 with 10.30 coffee break   **Session 3 Maine on law, legal change and legal education**
  Session Chairman – The Vice-Master (J. G. Collier)
  Professor B. S. Jackson – University of Kent

Appendix

              Sir John Lyons, FBA – Trinity Hall, Cambridge
              Professor P. G. Stein, FBA – Queens' College, Cambridge
              Professor W. L. Twining – University of London
              Professor C. Woodard – University of Virginia
              Mr D. E. C. Yale, FBA – Christ's College, Cambridge

12.30–1.45   Lunch
2.00–3.45   **Session 4 Maine and India**
              Session Chairman – The Master (Sir John Lyons)
              Dr C. A. Bayly – St Catharine's College, Cambridge
              Dr R. O'Hanlon – Clare College, Cambridge
              Dr C. Dewey – University of Leicester
              Dr G. Johnson – Selwyn College, Cambridge
              Dr R. S. Chandavarkar – Trinity College, Cambridge

The following bibliography includes as complete a list as possible of Maine's own works and a comprehensive list of secondary sources, including all works referred to in the text. Maine's works are divided among four sections: B1, books and pamphlets; B2, articles, reviews and lectures; B3, articles, reviews and lectures in the *Saturday Review*, the *Fortnightly Review*, the *St James's Gazette* and the *Quarterly Review*; and B4, speeches, minutes and memorandums. All references in the text to Section B1 are cited by abbreviations which are furnished below. All citations are to the first edition, unless otherwise noted. References in the text to works by Maine listed in Sections B2 or B3 are in the following form: Maine, B2, 1886: 6. References to separately published works by Maine, listed in Section B1, are abbreviated as follows: *AL* = *Ancient Law* (1861); Add. 1 = 'Address ... University of Calcutta' (1864); Add. 2 = Address ... University of Calcutta (1865); Add. 3 = Address ... University of Calcutta (1866); *VC* = *Village-Communities in the East and West* (1871); *EHI* = *Lectures on the Early History of Institutions* (1875); Rede Lec. = *The Effects of Observation of India on Modern European Thought* (1875); *ELC* = *Dissertations on Early Law and Custom* (1883); *PG* = *Popular Government* (1885).

Bibliography

SECTION A: MANUSCRIPT COLLECTIONS

Acton Papers a, property of Douglas Woodruff, CBE
Acton Papers b, Cambridge University Library
Atkinson Papers, Cambridge University Library
Avebury Papers, British Museum
Bryce Manuscripts, Bodleian Library, Oxford
Christ's Hospital Manuscripts, The Guildhall Library, London
Cross Papers, British Museum
Randolph Churchill Papers, Chartwell
Elgin Collection, India Office Library
Gladstone Papers, British Museum
Mary Gladstone Papers, British Museum
Grant Duff Papers, property of Mrs Sheila Sokolov-Grant
Harrison Collection, London School of Economics and Political Science
Holmes Papers, Harvard University Library and Harvard Law Library
Holt Archives, Princeton University Library
Lawrence Collection, India Office Library
Maine Collection, London School of Economics and Political Science
Maine/Ilbert Letters, India Office Library
Maine/Lyall Letters, India Office Library
Maine/Lytton Letters, India Office Library
Maine/Merivale Letters, India Office Library
Maine Papers (misc.), India Office Library
Maine Papers (misc.), property of H. C. S. Maine, CMG, MVO
Mayo Papers, Cambridge University Library
Mill Papers, London School of Economics and Political Science
Morgan Papers, University of Rochester Library
Murray Archives, John Murray Publishing Company
Ripon Papers, British Museum
Salisbury Papers, Christ Church, Oxford
Sidgwick Papers, Trinity College, Cambridge
Stephen Papers, Cambridge University Library
Wood Collection, India Office Library
Woolsey Papers, Yale University Library

SECTION B: WORKS BY MAINE

I BOOKS, PAMPHLETS, ETC.

(1843) *Plato* [Written for the Chancellor's Medal for English Verse.] Cambridge. (Privately printed.) (Reprinted for J. W. Clark, *Plato: A Poem*, Cambridge, 1894.)

(1851) *Memoir of Henry Fitzmaurice Hallam*. (By H. S. M. and F. L[ushington], for private circulation.) London: Spottiswoode. (Reprinted in H. Hallam (ed.), *Arthur Henry Hallam, Remains in Verse and Prose*, London & Boston: Ticknor & Fields, 1963: xlvii–lx.)

(1861) *Ancient Law: its Connection with the Early History of Society and its Relation to Modern Ideas*, 1st edn. London: Murray. (Reprinted as 2nd edn: 1863.) 3rd edn: 1866 (reprinted as 4th edn: 1870.) 5th edn: 1873, with ms Notes (reprinted as 6th edn: 1876, 7th edn: 1878, 8th edn: 1880, 9th edn: 1883). 10th edn: 1885 (reprinted as 11th edn: 1887, 12th edn: 1888, 13th ('New') edn: 1890, 14th edn: 1891, 15th edn: 1894, 16th edn: 1897, 17th impr.: 1901, 'Cheap edn' (from 10th edn): 1905 (reprinted 1911). (For later Murray edns. see *AL* 1906.)

(186?) *Ancient Law: its Connection with the Early History of Society and its Relation to Modern Ideas*. Unabridged edn. (The Lawyer's Library, 1.) New York: Cockcroft.

(1864) *Ancient Law: its Connection with the Early History of Society and its Relation to Modern Ideas*, 1st American edn (From 2nd British edn), with Introduction by Theodore W. Dwight. New York: Scribner. (Reprinted 1867; 1870; 1871; as 2nd American edn, 1874.)

(1864) *Address Delivered by the Hon. H. S. Maine, Vice-Chancellor of the University of Calcutta, to the Senate and Graduates ... March 1864*, Calcutta. (Reprinted as Address 1, in *VC* 1876: 240–54.)

(1865) *Address Delivered by the Hon. H. S. Maine, Vice-Chancellor of the University of Calcutta, to the Senate and Graduates ... March 1865*, Calcutta. (Reprinted as Address 2, in *VC* 1876: 255–74.)

(1866) *Ancient Law: its Connection with the Early History of Society and its Relation to Modern Ideas*, 3rd edn. London: Murray.

(1866) *Address Delivered by the Hon. H. S. Maine, Vice-Chancellor of the University of Calcutta, to the Senate and Graduates ... 17 March 1866*, Calcutta: Baptist Mission Press. (Reprinted as Address 3, in *VC* 1876: 275–94.)

(1870) *Ancient Law: its Connection with the Early History of Society and its Relation to Modern Ideas*, 4th edn. (Reprint of 3rd edn.) London: Murray.

(1871) *Village-Communities in the East and West: Six Lectures Delivered at Oxford*, 1st edn. London: Murray. (Reprinted as 2nd edn. 1872.) 3rd edn, 1876. (For later editions, see below *VC* (1876).)

(1873) *The Early History of the Property of Married Women: As Collected from Roman and Hindoo Law*. (A Lecture delivered at Birmingham on March 25, 1873. ['This lecture, the substance of which forms part of an unpublished work, is reprinted for the Married Women's Property Committee, with the permission of the author'].) Manchester: Ireland & Co. (Reprinted as Chapter 11, 'The early history of the settled property of married women' of Maine, *EHI*, 1875: 306–41.)

(1874) *Ancient Law: its Connection with the Early History of Society and its Relation to Modern Ideas*, 2nd American edn. (From 2nd British edn), with Introduction by Theodore W. Dwight. New York: Holt.

(1874) *Ancient Law: its Connection with the Early History of Society and its Relation to Modern Ideas*, 5th edn. London: Murray.

(1875a) *Lectures on the Early History of Institutions*. London: Murray, and New York: Holt. (Reprinted as 2nd edn. Murray & Holt, 1878; as 3rd [British] ed., Murray: 1880.) 4th British edn, Murray: 1885 (reprinted as 5th ('New') edn: 1890, 6th edn: 1893, 7th edn: 1897, 1905 (2nd imp.), 1914 (3rd imp.)).

(1875b) *Ancient Law: its Connection with the Early History of Society and its Relation to Modern Ideas*, 3rd American edn. (From 5th British edn), with Introduction by Theodore W. Dwight. New York: Holt. (Reprinted 1877, 1878, 1879, 1883, 1885, 1888.)

(1875c) *The Effects of Observation of India On Modern European Thought*. (The Rede Lecture, delivered before the University of Cambridge, 22 May, 1875.) London: Murray. (Reprinted in *VC* 1876: 203–39.)

(1875d) *European Views of India: The Effects of Observation of India On Modern European Thought*. (The Rede Lecture, delivered in the Senate House, Cambridge, 22 May 1875.) Calcutta: Thacker, Spink, and Bombay: Thacker, Vining.

(1876) *Village-Communities in the East and West: Six Lectures (to which are added other lectures, addresses and essays)*, 3rd (enlarged) edn. London: Murray, and New York: Holt. (Reprinted as 'Author's Edition', Holt: 1880; as '4th edn', Murray: 1881; as '5th edn', Murray 1887; as 'New Edition', Murray: 1890; as '7th edn', Murray: 1895 (with bibliography, 1907; new impression with additional addresses, 1913); as 'Author's Edition', Holt: 1889.)

(1881) *Village-Communities in the East and West: Six Lectures (to which are added other lectures, addresses and essays)*, 4th edn. London: Murray.

(1883) *Dissertations on Early Law and Custom: Chiefly Selected from Lectures Delivered at Oxford*. [With added material comprising Chapters 5, 6, 8, 9, 11, based on articles in the *Fortnightly Review* and the *Nineteenth Century* (see Section B3) and Chapter 7, 'Theories of primitive society'.] London: Murray, and New York: Holt. (British edn reprinted, 1888, 1891, 1901.) (American edn reprinted, 1886.)

(1884) *Lectures on the Early History of Institutions*, 3rd American edn. New York: Holt.

(1885a) *Lectures on the Early History of Institutions*, 4th edn. London: Murray.

(1885b) *Ancient Law: its Connection with the Early History of Society and its Relation to Modern Ideas*, 10th edn. London: Murray.

(1885c) *Popular Government: Four Essays* [from the *Quarterly Review*: see Section

B3), 1st edn. London: Murray. (Reprinted, as 2nd edn. 1886; 3rd edn. 1886; 4th 'New' edn. 1890; 5th edn, 1897, 'Popular edn': 1909; 6th edn: 1918.) (1st American edn, New York: Holt, 1886.)

(1886) *Popular Government: Four Essays*, 1st American edn (from 1st British edn). New York: Holt.

(1888a) *Lectures on the Early History of Institutions*, 4th American edn. New York: Holt.

(1888b) *International Law: A Series of Lectures Delivered Before the University of Cambridge*, (Whewell Lectures, 1887. Edited for publication by Frederick Pollock and Frederick Harrison.) London: Murray and New York: Holt. (2nd British edn, 1894.)

(1889) *Minutes by the Right Honourable Sir Henry Maine, 1862–1869, with a Note on Indian Codification Dated 17 July 1879*. (Government of India, Legislative Department.) Calcutta: Superintendent of Government Printing. (Reprinted, 1892.)

(1905) *Ancient Law: its Connection with the Early History of Society and its Relation to Modern Ideas*. (New Universal Library.) London: Routledge, and New York: Dutton. (Reprinted 1907, 1910, 1913.)

(1906a) *Ancient Law: its Connection with the Early History of Society and its Relation to Modern Ideas*, New edn, with Introduction and Notes by Sir Frederick Pollock. London: Murray. (Reprinted, 1907, 1909, 1912, 1916, 1924, 1927; New edn, 1930.)

(1906b) *Ancient Law: its Connection with the Early History of Society and its Relation to Modern Ideas*, 4th American edn. (from 10th British edn), with Introduction and Notes by Sir Frederick Pollock. New York: Holt.

(1917) *Ancient Law: its Connection with the Early History of Society and its Relation to Modern Ideas*, with Introduction by J. H. Morgan. (Everyman Library.) London: Dent, and New York: Dutton. (Reprinted or reissued, 1920?, 1931, 1936, 1954, 1977.)

(1918) *Ancient Law: its Connection with the Early History of Society and its Relation to Modern Ideas*, ?th edn. London: Murray.

(1931) *Ancient Law: its Connection with the Early History of Society and its Relation to Modern Ideas*, with Introduction by Sir Carleton Allen. (The World Classics.) London & New York: Oxford University Press. (Reprinted 1939, 1946, 1950, 1954, 1959.)

(1963) *Ancient Law: its Connection with the Early History of Society and its Relation to Modern Ideas*, reprint of 1906 British edn (with Introduction and Notes by Sir Frederick Pollock), with new Preface by Raymond Firth: Beacon. (Paperback edn, 1970.)

(1966a) *Lectures on the Early History of Institutions*. (Reprint of 7th British edn) Port Washington, N. Y.: Kennikat Press.

(1966b) *Lectures on the Early History of Institutions*. (Facsimile reprint of 1st British edn, 1875). London: Dawsons of Pall Mall.

(1970a) *Ancient Law: its Connection with the Early History of Society and its Relation to Modern Ideas*, with Introduction and Notes by Sir Frederick Pollock and Preface by Raymond Firth. Boston: Beacon Paperbacks.

(1970b) *Ancient Law: its Connection with the Early History of Society and its Relation to Modern Ideas*, with Introduction and Notes by Sir Frederick Pollock and Preface by Raymond Firth ('by permission of Beacon Press'). Gloucester, Mass.: P. Smith.

(1973) *Village-Communities in the East and West* (reprint of 2nd edn, 1872), with Introduction by Roy M. Mersky and Adrienne C. de Vergie. (Classics in Legal History, 15.) Buffalo, N.Y.: Hein.

(1975) *Dissertations on Early Law and Custom: Chiefly Selected from Lectures Delivered at Oxford*. (Reprint of American 1886 edn ["from a copy in the Princeton University Library].) (European Sociology: An Arno Press Collection.) New York: Arno Press.

(1976) *Popular Government* with Introduction by George Carey (reprinted from 1st British edn, 1885). Indianapolis: Liberty Press.

(1986) *Early Law and Custom*. (Reprint of *Dissertations on Early Law and Custom*, 1883.) New Delhi: B. R. Publishing.

(1986a) *Ancient Law: its Connection with the Early History of Society and its Relation to Modern Ideas* (reprint of 1864 edn), with Foreword by Lawrence Rosen. Tucson: University of Arizona Press.

(1986b) *Ancient Law: its Connection with the Early History of Society and its Relation to Modern Ideas* (reprint of 1st edn). New York: Dorset Press.

2 ARTICLES, REVIEWS AND LECTURES (OTHER THAN ARTICLES FOR THE *SATURDAY REVIEW* (1855–8, THE *FORTNIGHTLY REVIEW* (1873–82), THE *ST JAMES'S GAZETTE* (1880–1) AND THE *QUARTERLY REVIEW* (1884–6) – FOR WHICH SEE SECTION B3)

(1842a) 'The birth of the Prince of Wales' (A poem for the Chancellor's Medal read at the Cambridge Commencement.) In *Prolusiones Academicae [praemiis annuis dignatae et in Curia Cantabrigiensi recitatae Comitiis Maximis ... 1827–1899]* (Cambridge), pp. 5–13. Published in *A Complete Collection of the English Poems which have obtained the Chancellor's Gold Medal in the University of Cambridge. New and enlarged edn.* 2 vols. (Vol. I, Cambridge: Macmillan, 1859). (Vol. II, London: Gibbings, 1894), Vol. I, pp. 233–9. (Other edns of Volume I: 1860 edn, Cambridge: Macmillan & 1894 edn, London: Gibbings.)

(1842b) 'Caesar ad Rubisonem constitit.' (Poema Latinum numismate annuo dignatum et in Curia Cantabrigiensi recitatum Comitiis Maximis.) In *Prolusiones Academicae* (1842), pp. 15–21.

(1842c) 'Navis ornata atque armata in aquam deducitur.' (Carmen Latinum numismate annuo dignatum et in Curia Cantabrigiensi recitatum Comitiis Maximis.) In *Prolusiones Academicae* (1842), pp. 31–9.

(1843a) 'Indus fluvius'. (Carmen Latinum numismate annuo dignatum et in Curia Cantabrigiensi recitatum Comitiis Maximis.) In *Prolusiones Academicae* (1843), pp. 27–34.

(1843b) '*Mia khelidon ear ou poiei*'/'Una hirundo non facit ver,' (Epigrammata numismate annuo dignata et in Curia Cantabrigiensi recitata Comitiis Maximis.) In *Prolusiones Academicae* (1843), pp. 35–7.

(1848) 'Midsummer night's dream', *Edinburgh Review* 87, 418–29 (unsigned).

(1855) 'The conception of sovereignty and its importance in international law' (paper read on 16 April 1855). In *Papers Read Before the Juridical Society, 1855–1858* (London), Vol. I, pp. 26–45.

(1856) Papers on 'Roman law and legal education'. In *Cambridge Essays (Contributed by Members of the University)* (London: John W. Parker & Sons), pp. 1–29. (Reprinted in Maine, *VC*, 3rd edn (1876), pp. 330–83.

(1871) 'A Mahometan revival', *Cornhill Magazine* 24 (October), 421–37, [unsigned].

(1877) 'South Slavonians and Rajpoots', *Nineteenth Century* 2 (December), 796–819. (Expanded version reprinted as Chapter 8, 'East European communities', of Maine, *ELC*, 1883: 232–90.) (1886) 'Mr Godkin on popular government', *Nineteenth Century* 11 (March), 266–79.

(1881) 'The King and his relation to early civil justice'. (Lecture given at the Royal Institution of Great Britain, London: see *Notices of Proceedings* 9.) Published in *Fortnightly Review 31, 603–7 (see Section A3). (Reprinted as Chapter 6 of Maine, ELC, 1883.)

(1887) 'India'. In Thomas Humphrey Ward (ed.), *The Reign of Queen Victoria: A Survey of Fifty Years of Progress*. Vol. I. London: Smith, Elder, pp. 460–528.

3 ARTICLES, REVIEWS AND LECTURES IN NEWSPAPERS AND PERIODICALS

(a) Contributions (unsigned) to the 'Saturday Review', 1855–8 (cf. Bevington, 1941, and Feaver, 1969)

'Our relations with the United States', 1.2 (3 Nov. 1855)
'Our newspaper institutions', 1.2 (3 Nov. 1855)
'Memoirs of James Gordon Bennett and his times', 1.15 (3 Nov. 1855)
'Southwark and public opinion', 1.27 (10 Nov. 1855)
'Laid up in lavender', 1.41 (17 Nov. 1855)
'The war policy of the American government', 1.58 (24 Nov. 1855)
'A burst bladder', 1.75 (1 Dec. 1855)
'The inns of court', 1.76 (1 Dec. 1855)
'Bible burning', 1.90 (8 Dec. 1855)
'Mr. Thackeray and the four Georges', 1.106 (15 Dec. 1855)
'The importunity of truth', 1.111 (15 Dec. 1855)
'American parties', 1.133 (22 Dec. 1855)
'The sound dues', 1.147 (29 Dec. 1855)
'Jeanne de Vaudreuil', 1.157 (29 Dec. 1855)
'Army examinations', 1.167 (5 Jan. 1856)

'A political deadlock', 1.183 (12 Jan. 1856)
'President Pearce and his message', 1.202 (19 Jan. 1856)
'Lectures for senators', 1.222 (26 Jan. 1856)
'A parallel', 1.227 (26 Jan. 1856)
'Mistakes of daily occurrence in speaking and writing', 1.261 (2 Feb. 1856)
'Publicity and the peace', 1.265 (9 Feb. 1856)
'The moral of McNeill', 1.285 (16 Feb. 1856)
'The Crimea commission', 1.310 (23 Feb. 1856)
'The division list on sabbath observance', 1.334 (1 Mar. 1856)
'Your petitioners will ever pray, etc.', 1.358 (8 Mar. 1856)
'Our cousin Veronica', 1.372 (8 Mar. 1856)
'Lord Stratford and General Williams', 1.382 (15 Mar. 1856)
'Leaves of grass', 1.393 (15 Mar. 1856)
'French sketches of English character', 1.549 (5 April 1856)
'Beranger', 1.465 (12 April 1856)
'Medical education', 1.470 (12 April 1856)
'Silly Billy', 1.487 (19 April 1856)
'The language of party', 1.511 (26 April 1856)
'May meetings', 2.2 (5 May 1856)
'The princess's theatre and the winter's tale', 2.3 (5 May 1856)
'Dead men tell no tales', 2.75 (24 May 1856)
'Parma', 2.94 (31 May 1856)
'Academical freedom', 2.118 (7 June 1956)
'Head and tail', 2.142 (14 June 1956)
'Political ultramontanism', 2.166 (21 June 1956)
'Dr Arnold and Jew exclusion', 2.190 (28 June 1956)
'The sorrows of Smith', 2.238 (12 July 1856)
'The Biglow paper', 2.249 (12 July 1856)
'The subalpine kingdom', 2.272,299 (19, 26 July 1856)
'Corrected translation of the Bible', 2.293 (26 July 1856)
'British rank and file', 2.311 (2 Aug. 1856)
'Io triumphe', 2.329 (9 Aug. 1856)
'The Manchester school of Theology', 2.349 (16 Aug. 1856)
'Bathing towns', 2.391 (30 Aug. 1856)
'Panama and Kansas', 2.517 (11 Oct. 1856)
'Scottish University reform', 2.539 (18 Oct. 1856)
'Uncle Tom in politics', 2.562 (25 Oct. 1856)
'Official journals and free newspapers', 2.583 (1 Nov. 1856)
'Anonymous human nature', 2.608 (8 Nov. 1856)
'Lord Ravensworth on "revealed religion"', 2.630 (15 Nov. 1856)
'Circumlocution vs. Circumvention', 2.649 (22 Nov. 1856)
'Political dalliance', 2.672 (29 Nov. 1856)
'Herat and the Shah of Persia', 2.693 (6 Dec. 1856)
'French affinities for England', 2.742 (20 Dec. 1856)
'Naufchatel', 2.745 (20 Dec. 1856)
'Income tax agitation', 2.767 (27 Dec. 1856)

BIBLIOGRAPHY

'Glimpses of justice', 3.1 (3 Jan. 1857)
'Canton and China', 3.21 (10 Jan. 1857)
'Eothen in the South-West', 3.45 (17 Jan. 1857)
'Republican corruption', 3.93 (31 Jan. 1857)
'Dear at the money', 3.142 (14 Feb. 1857) 142,
'Progress of the slavery question', 3.168 (21 Feb. 1857)
'The American Senate', 3.192 (28 Feb. 1857)
'Aspects of things at Canton', 3.213 (7 Mar. 1857)
'Mr Disraeli on India', 4.97 (1 Aug. 1857)
'Wild justice', 4.121 (8 Aug. 1857)
'The solvency of the East India Company', 4.147 (15 Aug. 1857)
'Reactions of public opinion about public men', 4.170 (22 Aug. 1857)
'Lost illusions', 4.214 (5 Sept. 1857)
'Religious influences in Hindostan', 4.233 (12 Sept. 1857)
'Theorizing about India', 4.254 (19 Sept. 1857)
'Indian government', 4.294 (3 Oct. 1857)
'The opposition on the Indian crisis', 4.317 (10 Oct. 1857)
'New schemes of Indian government', 4.340 (17 Oct. 1857)
'Indian statemen and English scribblers', 4.361 (24 Oct. 1857)
'The Indian press', 4.435 (14 Nov. 1857)
'European opinion on Bengal', 4.457 (21 Nov. 1857)
'More assertions and less facts', 4.463 (21 Nov. 1857)
'The abolition of the double government', 4.501 (5 Dec. 1857)
'Control and responsibility', 4.553 (19 Dec. 1857)
'Religion and India', 4.575 (26 Dec. 1857)
'The new Indian department', 5.1 (2 Jan. 1858)
'The middle classes and the abolition of the East India Company', 5.31 (9 Jan. 1858)
'Why is there to be an India Bill next session?', 5.55 (16 Jan. 1858)
'The petition of the East India Company', 5.78 (23 Jan. 1858)
'The incorporation of India and England', 5.101 (30 Jan. 1858)
'Thirty years of improvement in India', 5.129 (6 Feb. 1858)
'The new circumlocution office',, 5.177 (20 Feb. 1858)
'Progress of opinion on the Indian question', 5.207 (27 Feb. 1858)
'Squeezable materials', 5.232 (6 Mar. 1858)
'Administrative Brahminism', 5.259 (13 Mar. 1858)
'What is to be done with the new India Bill?', 5.336 (3 April 1858)
'The friend in need', 5.383 (17 April 1858)
'The India resolutions', 5.409 (24 April 1858)
'Indian legislation', 5.434 (1 May 1858)
'Mumbo-jumbo in parliament', 5.462 (8 May 1858)
'A responsible Indian minister', 5.489 (15 May 1858)
'The moral of the Ellenborough debate', 5.548 (29 May 1858)

Bibliography 409

(b) Contributions (unsigned) to the 'St James's Gazette', 1880–1 (cf. Feaver, 1969: 335–9 and Maine Collection (Manuscripts), Vol. XXII, item 8)

'The future of political ignorance', 1.3 (31 May 1880)
'Hares and rabbits', 1.76 (4 June 1880)
'Goal of democratic progress', 1.115–16 (8 June 1880)
'Franchises and opinions in Ireland', 1.195–6 (14 June 1880)
'Landlordism', 1.243–4 (17 June 1880)
'Radical patriarchalism', 1.259–60 (17 June 1880)
'Rewarding and punishing by legislation', 1.291 (21 June 1880)
'Small pox and small beer', 1.316 (22 June 1880)
'Law, conscience, and Mr Bradlaugh', 1.395–6 (28 June 1880)
'Irish land and English justice', 1.403 (29 June 1880)
'Sabbatarianism and spirit drinking', 1.491–2 (5 July 1880)
'Malthusianism and modern politics', 1.524–5 (7 July 1880)
'Clergymen and laymen at the Universities', 1.579 (12 July 1880)
'The lesson to liberals', 1.611–12 (14 July 1880)
'Dubitations about private property', 1.643 (16 July 1880)
'Possible surprises from the far east', 1.723–4 (22 July 1880)
'Lost political lessons', 1.739 (23 July 1880)
'Imaginary Indian grievances', 1.796 (27 July 1880)
'Property, contract, and the prosperity of England', 1.867 (2 Aug. 1880)
'Probable effects of past blunders', 1.963 (9 Aug. 1880)
'The House of Lords', 1.995 (11 Aug. 1880)
'The House of Commons and its business', 1.1059 (16 Aug. 1880)
'The Whigs', 1.1123 (20 Aug. 1880)
'The misfortune of Ireland', 1.1259–60 (30 Aug. 1880)
'The age of plebiscites', 1.1356 (6 Sept. 1880)
'The farmer's friends', 1.1395 (9 Sept. 1880)
'Hereditary legislators', 1.1443 (13 Sept. 1880)
'Irish distress', 1.1459 (14 Sept. 1880)
'National debts', 1.1523 (18 Sept. 1880)
'Irish agitators and the Church of Rome', 1.1635 (27 Sept. 1880)
'Law and law amendment in Ireland', 1.1755–6 (5 Oct. 1880)
'Now and then', 1.1827 (11 Oct. 1880)
'Some results of nonconformist success', 1.1883–4 (14 Oct. 1880)
'Electoral corruption', 1.1923 (18 Oct. 1880)
'Irish disease and quack remedies for it', 1.1979–80 (21 Oct. 1880)
'Bertrand and Raton', 1.2019 (25 Oct. 1880)
'England under a new dispensation', 1.21265 (4 Nov. 1880)
'Ecclesiastical politics and ecclesiastical teaching', 1.2187–8 (5 Nov. 1880)
'Some advantages of the recognition of barbarism', 1/2251–2 (10 Nov. 1880)
'The judgement of the United States on free trade', 1.2275 (12 Nov. 1880)
'The eccentricities of the University Commissions', 1.2299–300 (13 Nov. 1880)

'Catilinarian victories and their fruits', 1.2332 (16 Nov. 1880)
'Mr. Bright's political and historical philosophy', 1.2379-80 (9 Nov. 1880)
'The agitation against private property', 1.2443-4 (24 Nov. 1880)
'Irish facts and English emotions', 1.2531 (1 Dec. 1880)
'Medicine for the Irish malady', 1.2611 (7 Dec. 1880)
'Why the revolution makes way', 1.2659 (10 Dec. 1880)
'Extraordinary law', 1.2771 (18 Dec. 1880)
'Unnoticed dangers of the Irish example', 1.2795-6 (20 Dec. 1880)
'The survival of the unfittest', 1.2819 (22 Dec. 1880)
'The superstition of ordinary law', 1.2931 (31 Dec. 1880)
'French opinion on Irish affairs', 2.35-6 (4 Jan. 1881)
'The dependence of Ireland on Great Britain', 2.115 (10 Jan. 1881)
'The two voices', 2.139-40 (11 Jan. 1881)
'Mr. Froude and his critics', 2.211 (17 Jan. 1881)
'Remedies for electoral corruption', 2.275 (21 Jan. 1881)
'Radicalism, old and new', 2.331-2 (25 Jan. 1881)
'The populousness of the United States', 2.379-80 (28 Jan. 1881)
'The work of the University commissioners', 2.475-6 (4 Feb. 1881)
'The ordinary law of Ireland and what should be done with it', 2.517 (10 Feb. 1881)
'Disillusion', 2.643 (17 Feb. 1881)
'The land league and the Catholic bishops', 2.692 (21 Feb. 1881)
'Mr. Parnell and foreign opinion', 2.716 (22 Feb. 1881)
'The future of constitutionalism', 2.747-8 (24 Feb. 1881)
'Budgets and land bills', 2.819 (2 March 1881)
'Wiping out conservatism', 2.899 (8 March 1881)
'The measure of English responsibility for Ireland', 2.915 (9 March 1881)
'The Irish nightmare', 2.1004 (15 March 1881)
'Signs of the times', 2.1075 (21 March 1881)
'The latest national humiliation', 2.1123 (24 March 1881)
'Pax britannica', 2.1267 (4 April 1881)
'The Russian conquests in central Asia', 2.1291 (5 April 1881)
'Death duties', 2.1323-4 (7 April 1881)
'The projected economic revolution in Ireland', 2.1379-80 (12 April 1881)
'Some certain results of the land bill', 2.1411 (14 April 1881)
'Patriarchal radicalism', 2.1467-8 (19 April 1881)
'The medicines and the quackeries of the land bill', 2.1531-2 (23 April 1881)
'The Disraeli of foreign opinion', 2.1611-12 (29 April 1881)
'Opium', 2.1635-5 (2 May 1881)
'Missions and their results', 2.1724 (7 May 1881)
'The theory of liberationism', 2.1739-40 (9 May 1881)
'The Irish land court as a school of liberty', 2.1795 (13 May 1881)
'How the Jacobins conquer a nation', 2.1851-2 (17 May 1881)
'The new opinion of the constituencies', 2.1923-4 (23 May 1881)
'The revision of the New Testament', 2.1987-8 (27 May 1881)

'The price of a commercial treaty', 2.2019 (30 May 1881)
'The moral of Monte Carlo', 2.2075–6 (2 June 1881)
'The precedent of fifty years since', 2.2147 (8 June 1881)
'The House of Lords', 2.2211 (13 June 1881)
'Constitutional government in Eastern Europe', 2.2227 (14 June 1881)
'Providence and political economy', 2.2291 (18 June 1881)
'Modern mysteries', 2.2355 (23 June 1881)
'The war against disease', 2.411–12 (27 June 1881)
'The Hanoverian stage of Italian politics', 3.3–4 (1 July 1881)
'Veracity in politics', 3.35–6 (4 July 1881)
'The crime of guiteau', 3.83 (7 July 1881)
'The belief of the original free traders', 3.131 (11 July 1881)
'The Irish land bill as a source of revolution', 3.227–8 (18 July 1881)
'Free trade and foreign tariffs', 3.275 (21 July 1881)
'The true history of free trade', 3.339–40 (26 July 1881)
'A message to a wrong address', 3.467–8 (4 Aug. 1881)
'British trade and British markets', 3.483 (5 Aug. 1881)
'Free contract and free trade', 3.547 (9 Aug. 1881)
'The House of Commons and the French treaty', 3.627 (16 Aug. 1881)
'New theories of the constitution', 3.691 (20 Aug. 1881)
'Orating and legislating', 3.707 (22 Aug. 1881)
'Our commercial difficulties with France', 3.739 (24 Aug. 1881)
'British prosperity and fiscal legislation', 3.835 (31 Aug. 1881)
'Social safeguards in France and England', 3.867 (2 Sept. 1881)
'The past and future of democratic government', 3.899 (5 Sept. 1881)
'The position of the radicals', 3.931 (7 Sept. 1881)
'New economical facts for consideration', 3.1011 (13 Sept. 1881)
'The farmer and his friends', 3.1027 (14 Sept. 1881)
'The radicals and the farmers', 3.1123 (21 Sept. 1881)
'Landed properties, large and small', 3.1187–8 (26 Sept. 1881)
'Orthodoxy and heresy in economics', 3.1251 (30 Sept. 1881)
'Alternatives in legislation', 3.1299 (4 Oct. 1881)
'The demoralization of a people', 3.1317 (7 Oct. 1881)
'Logic at Leeds', 3.1403–4 (11 Oct. 1881)
'What the Boers really want', 3.1442–4 (14 Oct. 1881)
'Remedies for agricultural distress', 3.1555 (22 Oct. 1881)
'The opium trade between India and China', 3.1571 (24 Oct. 1881)
'The Russian return to orientalism', 3.1691–2 (1 Nov. 1881)
'Perils of old and new wealth', 3.1731–2 (4 Nov. 1881)
'Free trade and how it is threatened', 3.1827 (11 Nov. 1881)
'Mr. Bright and his triumphs', 3.1907–8 (17 Nov. 1881)
'Confusion of thought about the land', 3.1979–80 (22 Nov. 1881)
'Surreptitious revolution', 3.2099 (1 Dec. 1881)
'The Irish paradox', 3.2155–6 (5 Dec. 1881)
'The North Borneo Company', 3.2163 (6 Dec. 1881)
'Paying the educational piper', 3.2195 (8 Dec. 1881)

'The new nation', 3.2371 (21 Dec. 1881)
'Realities of Indian taxation', 3.2387-8 (22 Dec. 1881)
'The principles of parliamentary procedure', 3.2483 (29 Dec. 1881)
'The periodical trick', 3.2523 (31 Dec. 1881)

(c) Contributions to the 'Fortnightly Review' (1873-82)

(1873) 'Mr Fitzjames Stephen's Introduction to the Indian Evidence Act', 13 (January), 51-67. (Reprinted as 'The theory of evidence', in Maine, *VC*, 1876: 295-329).

(1877) 'The decay of feudal property in France and England', 21 (April), 460-77 (lecture delivered at the Royal Institution of Great Britain, London). (Reprinted as Chapter 9 of Maine, *ELC*, 1883: 291-328.)

(1979) 'Ancient ideas respecting the arrangement of codes', 25 (May), 763-77, (Reprinted as Chapter 11, 'Classification of legal rules, of Maine, *ELC* 1883: 362-92.)

(1881) 'The King, in his relation to early civil justice', 30 (November), 603-7. (*See also* Section B2.) (Reprinted as Chapter 5 of Maine, *ELC*, 1883: 160-91.)

(1882) 'The King and his successor', 31 (February), 180-94, (Reprinted as Chapter 5, 'Royal succession and the Salic law', of Maine, *ELC*, 1883: 125-59.)

(D) CONTRIBUTIONS TO THE *QUARTERLY REVIEW* (1883-6)

(1883) 'The prospects of popular government', 155 (April), 551-76 (unsigned). (Reprinted as Essay 1 of *PG*, 1885: 1-55.)

(1884) 'The constitution of the United States', 157 (January), 1-31 (unsigned). (Reprinted as Essay 4 of *PG*, 1885: 196-254.)

(1884) 'The nature of democracy', 158 (October), 297-333 (unsigned). (Reprinted as Essay 2 of *PG*, 1885: 56-126.)

(1885) 'The age of progress', 159 (April), 267-98 (unsigned), (Reprinted as Essay 3 of *PG*, 1885: 127-95.)

(1886) 'On Mr Donald MacLennan's "Patriarchal theory"', 162 (January), 181-209 (unsigned).

4 SPEECHES, MINUTES AND MEMORANDUMS, 1862-80 (TAKEN PRINCIPALLY FROM *PROCEEDINGS OF THE COUNCIL OF THE GOVERNOR GENERAL OF INDIA*, CALCUTTA, 1863-9: SEE MAINE, 1889, IN SECTION B1 AND GRANT DUFF, 1892; CF. FEAVER, 1969: 335)

(1862a) 'Suspension and remissions of sentences' (minute dated 29 November 1862). In Grant Duff, 1892: 301-3.

(1862b) 'Breaches of contract committed in bad faith' (speech made on 17 December 1862). In Grant Duff, 1892: 85-91.

(1862c) 'Divorce' (speech made on 24 December 1862). In Grant Duff, 1892: 91–5.
(1863a) 'Divorce' (speech made on 21 January 1863). In Grant Duff, 1892: 95–6.
(1863b) 'Suspension and remissions of sentences' (minute dated 10 March 1863). In Grant Duff, 1892: 304–5.
(1863c) 'Servitude in Oudh' (minute dated 25 May 1863). In Grant Duff, 1892: 305–8.
(1863d) 'Legal education of civil servants' (minute dated 2 December 1863). In Grant Duff, 1892: 308–10.
(1864a) 'Emigration'. In Grant Duff, 1892: 114–20.
(1864b) 'Whipping' (speech made on 17 Feburary 1864). In Grant Duff, 1892: 120–6.
(1864c) 'Official trustees' (speech made on 24 February 1864). In Grant Duff, 1892: 126–8.
(1864d) 'Registration of documents' (speech made on 23 March 1864). In Grant Duff, 1892: 128–30.
(1864e) 'Re-marriage of native converts' (speech made on 4 November 1864). In Grant Duff, 1892: 130–64.
(1864f) 'Specific performance' (speech made on 11 November 1864). In Grant Duff, 1892: 164–78.
(1864g) 'Abolition of grand juries' (speech made on 18 November 1864). In Grant Duff, 1892: 179–92.
(1864h) 'The law of succession' (speech made on 25 November 1864). In Grant Duff, 1892: 192–8.
(1864i) 'Small cause courts' (speech made on 16 December 1864). In Grant Duff, 1892: 209–17.
(1864j) 'Small cause courts' (minute dated 22 February 1864). In Grant Duff, 1892: 311–20.
(1864k) 'The Kathawar states and sovereignty' (minute dated 22 March 1864). In Grant Duff, 1892: 320–5.
(1864l) 'The educational service' (minute dated 12 May 1864). In Grant Duff, 1892: 325–7.
(1864m) 'Study of Persian' (minute dated 19 January). In Grant Duff, 1892: 431–3.
(1865a) 'Partnership' "en commandite"' (speech made on 1 December 1865). In Grant Duff, 1892: 218–26.
(1865b) 'The law of succession' (speech made on 3 March 1865). In Grant Duff, 1892: 199–209.
(1866a) 'Over-legislation' (speech made on 14 December 1866). In Grant Duff, 1892: 227–47.
(1866b) 'Civil liability of military officers' (minute dated 14 December 1866). In Grant Duff, 1892: 227–47.
(1866c) 'Mr. Prinsep's Panjab theories' (minute dated 26 October 1866). In Grant Duff, 1892: 335–40.
(1866d) 'Irrigation-works and railways' (minute dated 8 November 1866). In Grant Duff, 1892: 341–9.

(1867a) 'Judicial taxation' (speech made on 1 March 1867). In Grant Duff, 1892: 247–59.
(1867b) 'Murderous outrages in the Panjab' (speech made on 15 March 1867). In Grant Duff, 1892: 259–62.
(1867c) 'The Judge Advocate General' (minute dated 10 September 1867). In Grant Duff, 1892: 349–54.
(1867d) 'Decentralisation of finance' (extract from minute dated 13 September 1867). In Grant Duff, 1892: 354–8.
(1867e) 'Salt duties' (extract from minute dated 13 September 1867). In Grant Duff, 1892: 358–60.
(1868a) 'Indian municipalities' (speech made on 13 March 1868). In Grant Duff, 1892: 263–8.
(1868b) 'Panjab tenancy' (speech made on 19 October 1868). In Grant Duff, 1892: 268–85.
(1868c) 'Civil marriage of natives' (speech made on 27 November 1868). In Grant Duff, 1892: 285–94.
(1868d) 'Evidence' (speech made on 4 December 1868). In Grant Duff, 1892: 294–300.
(1868e) 'Draft of despatch resulting in Stat. 33. Vic. C. 3' (dated 10 January 1868). In Grant Duff, 1892: 360–2.
(1868f) 'The Bengal legislature' (minute dated 27 February 1868). In Grant Duff, 1892: 362–71.
(1868g) 'Government of Bengal: Simla: Calcutta' (minute dated 15 March 1868). In Grant Duff, 1892: 372–84.
(1868h) 'Indian Universities' (minute dated 29 July 1868). In Grant Duff, 1892: 384–91.
(1868i) 'Kashmir: succession of collaterals' (minute dated 4 August 1868). In Grant Duff, 1892: 391–4.
(1868j) 'Right to cede by Sanad portions of British India' (minute dated 11 August 1868). In Grant Duff, 1892: 395–400.
(1969a) 'Divorce' (speech made on 26 February 1869). In Grant Duff, 1892: 99–114.
(1869b) 'Right of native states to try Europeans' (minute dated 19 August 1869). In Grant Duff, 1892: 400–1.
(1875b) 'Selection and training of candidates for the Indian Civil Service' (minute dated 12 November 1875). In Grant Duff, 1892: 402–11.
(1880) 'Memorandum on Mr. Caird's report on the condition of India' (dated 20 February 1880). In Grant Duff, 1892: 412–31.

SECTION C: WORKS BY OTHER AUTHORS

Aarsleff, Hans (1967). *The Study of Language in England, 1780–1860*. London: Oxford University Press & Princeton: Princeton University Press. (2nd edn, London: Athlone Press, and Minneapolis: University of Minnesota Press, 1983.)
　(1974). 'The tradition of Condillac.' In Dell Hymes (ed.), *Studies in the*

History of Linguistics. Bloomington, Ind. & London: Indiana University Press, pp. 93–156.
  (1982a). *From Locke to Saussure.* London: Athlone Press, and Minneapolis: University of Minnesota Press.
  (1982b). 'Bréal vs. Schleicher: reorientation in linguistics during the latter half of the nineteenth-century'. In Aarsleff, 1982a: 293–334.
Abrahams, Raphael (Garvin) (1985). 'Family farm and wider society: the Finnish case', *Ethnos* 50, 40–59.
  (1989). 'Heating, lighting and a decent funeral'. *Ethnos* 54.
Acton, Lord John Edward Dalberg (1877a). *The History of Freedom in Antiquity.* Bridgnorth: Edkins.
  (1877b). *The History of Freedom in Christianity.* Bridgnorth: Edkins.
  (1895). *A Lecture on the Study of History.* London & New York: Macmillan. (2nd edn. 1905.)
  (1901). *Lectures on the French Revolution* (ed. John N. Figgis & Reginald V. Laurence). London: Macmillan.
  (1949). *Lord Acton on Nationality and Socialism* (with an Appendix on Burke, ed. George Eugene Fasnacht). London: Oxford University Press.
Agnelli, Arduino (1959). *John Austin alle origini del positivismo giuridico,* Pubblicazioni del Istituto delle scienze politiche, Università di Torino. Turin: Edizioni Giappichelli.
Aitchison, Jean (1981). *Language Change: Progress or Decay?* London: Fontana/Collins.
Allen, Sir Carleton Kemp (1964). *Law in the Making.* Oxford: Clarendon Press.
Anderson, John M., and C. Jones (eds.) (1974). *Historical Linguistics.* 2 vols. Amsterdam: North Holland.
Annan, Noel G. (1955). 'The intellectual aristocracy'. In John Harold Plumb (ed.), *Studies in Social History: A Tribute to G. M. Trevelyan.* London & New York: Longman, Green, pp. 243–87.
  (1959). *The Curious Strength of Positivism in English Political Thought,* L. T. Hobhouse Memorial Trust Lecture, 28. London: Oxford University Press.
Antilla, Raimo (1972). *An Introduction to Historical and Comparative Linguistics.* New York: Macmillan. (2nd rev. edn, Amsterdam & Philadelphia: Benjamin.)
Atiyah, P. S. (1979). *The Rise and Fall of Freedom of Contract.* Oxford: Clarendon Press.
  (1987). *Pragmatism and Theory in English Law,* The Hamlyn Lectures, thirty-ninth series. London: Stevens.
Austin, John (1859). *A Plea for the Constitution.* London: Murray.
  (1861–3). *The Province of Jurisprudence Determined.* 2nd edn, with additions, by Sarah Austin. 3 vols. London: Murray. (1st edn, 1832.) (Republished, London: Weidenfeld & Nicolson, and New York: Noonday Press, 1954.)

(1885). *Lectures on Jurisprudence.* 5th edn (revised and edited by R. Campbell). London: Murray.

(1954). *The Province of Jurisprudence Determined and the Uses of the Study of Jurisprudence* (ed. with an introduction by H. L. A. Hart). London: Weidenfeld & Nicolson, and New York: Noonday Press. (1st edn, 1832.)

Austin John L. (1961). *Philosophical Papers.* Oxford: Clarendon Press. (2nd enlarged edn, London: Oxford University Press, 1970.)

(1962). *How to Do Things with Words.* Oxford: Clarendon Press.

Bachofen, Johann Jakob (1861). *Das Mutterrecht: Eine Untersuchung über die Gynaikokratie der alten Welt nach ihrer religiösen und rechtlichen Natur.* Stuttgart: Krais & Hoffmann, and Basle: Schwabe. (English trans. by Ralph Manheim (with a preface by George Boas and an introduction by Joseph Campbell), *Myth, Religion and Mother Right.* London: Routledge & Kegan Paul, 1967.)

Baden-Powell, Baden Henry (1892). *The Land System of British India*, 3 vols. Oxford.

(1896). *The Indian Village Community.* London & New York: Longman, Green.

(1898). In Tupper, 1898.

(1899). *The Origin and Growth of Village Communities in India.* London: Sonnenschein, and New York: Scribner. (Reprinted, New York: Johnson, 1970.)

Baechler, Jean, John A. Hall and Michael Mann (eds.) (1988). *Europe and the Rise of Capitalism.* Oxford & New York: Basil Blackwell.

Bagehot, Walter (1867). *The English Constitution.* London: Chapman & Hall. (2nd edn, 1872.) (Reprinted in Bagehot, 1965–86, Vol. 5.)

(1872). *Physics and Politics.* London: King. (Reprinted in Bagehot, 1965–86, Vol. 7, pp. 17–144.)

(1876). 'Lord Althorp and the Reform Act of 1832' *Fortnightly Review* 20, 574–600. (Reprinted in Bagehot, 1965–86, Vol. 3, 201–31.)

(1965–86). *Collected Works* (ed. Norman St John-Stevas), 15 vols. London: The Economist, and Cambridge, Mass.: Harvard University Press.

(1971). *Historical Essays* (ed. Norman St John-Stevas). London: Dennis Dobson, and New York: New York University Press.

Baker, John H. (1978) (ed.). *Introduction to The Reports of Sir John Spelman*, Vol. 2. Selden Society 94, 23–346. London: Selden Society.

(1979). *An Introduction to English Legal History.* 2nd edn. London: Butterworth. (3rd edn, 1990.)

Banerjee, Anil Chandra (1984). *English Law in India.* New Delhi: Abhinau.

Barker, Sir Ernest (1959). *Political Thought in England, 1848–1914.* London & New York: Oxford University Press.

Barnett H. A. and D. M. Yach (1985). 'The teaching of jurisprudence and legal theory in British universities and polytechnics', *Legal Studies* 5, 151–71.

Barry, Norman P. (1986). *On Classical Liberalism and Libertarianism*. London: Macmillan.
Bateman, Sir Frederick (1877). *Darwinism Tested by Language*. London: Rivingtons.
Baudet, Henri (1965). *Paradise on Earth: Some Thoughts on European Images of Non-European Man*. New Haven: Yale University Press. (Reprinted, Middleton, Conn.: Wesleyan University Press, 1988.)
Baumgardt, David (1952). *Bentham and the Ethics of Today*. Princeton, N.J.: Princeton University Press.
Bearce, George (1961). *British Attitudes Towards India, 1784–1858*. London & New York: Oxford University Press.
Beattie, John (1964). *Other Cultures: Aims, Methods and Achievements in Social Anthropology*. London: Cohen & West, and Glencoe, Ill.: Free Press.
Benn, Alfred William (1906). *The History of English Rationalism in the Nineteenth Century*, 2 vols. London & New York: Longman, Green. (Reprinted, New York & London: Russell & Russell, 1962).
Bentham, Jeremy (1776). *A Fragment on Government*. London: T. Payne. (In Bentham, 1977.)
 (1827). *Rationale of Judicial Evidence* (ed. J. S. Mill), 5 vols. London: Hunt & Clarke. (Reprinted, London & New York: Garland, 1978.)
 (1843). *The Works* (ed. J. Bowring), 11 vols. Edinburgh: Tait.
 (1977). *Collected Works*, ed. J. H. Burns and H. L. A. Hart. London: Athlone Press, and Atlantic Highlands, N.J.: Humanities Press.
Berlin, Sir Isaiah (1969). *Four Essays on Liberty*. London: Oxford University Press.
Berman, Harold J. (1983). *Law and Revolution*. Cambridge, Mass.: Harvard University Press.
Berman, Harold J., and William Greiser (1980). *The Nature and Functions of Law*. Mineola, N.Y.: Foundation Press.
Bernstein, Basil (1964). 'Elaborated and restricted codes', in John J. Gumperz and D. Hymes (eds.), *The Ethnography of Communication*. Washington, D.C.: American Anthropological Association.
 (1971). *Class Codes and Control*, 2 vols. London: Routledge & Kegan Paul. (2nd revised edn, 1974.)
Best, R. I. (1951). *Whitley Stokes, 1830–1909: A Memorial Discourse*. Dublin: Dublin University Press.
Bevington, Merle Mowbray (1941). *The Saturday Review, 1855–1868*. New York: Columbia University Press.
Binchy, Daniel Anthony (1920). *Celtic and Anglo-Saxon Kingship*. Oxford: Clarendon Press.
 (1963). *The Irish Penitentials* (ed. L. Bieler, with an appendix by D. A. Binchy). Scriptores Latini Hiberniae, 5. Dublin: Dublin Institute for Advanced Studies.
Black, Max (1962). *Models and Metaphors: Studies in Language and Philosophy*. Ithaca, N.Y.: Cornell University Press.

Blackstone, William (1979). *Commentaries on the Laws of England*, 3 vols. London & Chicago: University of Chicago Press. (1st edn, 1765–9.)
Blake, Lord, and Hugh Cecil (eds.) (1987). *Salisbury: The Man and his Policies*. London: Macmillan.
Bloomfield, Leonard (1933). *Language*. New York: Holt. (British edn, Allen & Unwin, 1935.)
Boas, Franz (1894). 'Human faculty as determined by race'. *Proceedings of the American Association for the Advancement of Science*, 301–27.
    (1911a). *Handbook of American Indian Languages*, Smithsonian Institution, Bureau of American Ethnology, Bulletin No. 40. Washington, D.C.: Smithsonian Institution.
    (1911b). *The Mind of Primitive Man*. New York: Macmillan.
Bodenheimer, Edgar (1940). *Jurisprudence*. New York & London: McGraw-Hill.
Bopp, Franz (1816). *Über das conjugationssystem der sanskritsprache in vergleichung mit jenem der griechischen, lateinischen, persischen und germanischen sprache*. Frankfurt-on-Main: Andrea.
    (1833–52). *Vergleichende grammatik des sanskrit, zend, armenischem, griechischen, lateinischen, litauischen, altslawischen, gotischen und deutschen*. Berlin: F. Dümmler.
Bowle, John (1954). *Politics and Opinion in the Nineteenth Century*. London: Cape, and New York: Oxford University Press.
Brinsi, Giuseppe (1887). *Il governo popolare e la soveranita popolare secondo due ultime pubblicazioni di E. [sic] Sumner Maine e P. Ellero*. Milan.
Brinton, Clarence Crane (1933). *English Political Thought in the Nineteenth Century*. London: Benn.
Brinton, David Garrison (1890). 'The earliest form of human speech, as revealed by American tongues', in *Essays of an Americanist*. Philadelphia: Porter & Coates.
Browning, Oscar (1910). *Memories*. London: Lane.
Brubaker, Rogers (1984). *The Limits of Rationality: An Essay on the Social and Moral Thought of Max Weber*. London: George Allen & Unwin.
Brugmann, Karl, and Delbrück, B. (1886–90). *Grundriss der vergleichenden Grammatik der indogermanischen Sprachen*, 5 vols. Strasburg: Trübner. (English trans. by Joseph Wright et al., *Elements of the Comparative Grammar of the Indo-Germanic Languages*, Strasburg: Trübner, and New York: Westerman, 1888–95.) (2nd German edn, 1897–1916.)
Brunschvig, Léon (1927). *Le Progrès de la conscience dans la philosophie occidentale*, Paris: F. Alcan.
Bryce, James (1888). *The American Commonwealth*, 3 vols. London & New York: Macmillan.
    (1901). *Studies in History and Jurisprudence*, 2 vols. Oxford: Clarendon Press.
    (1921). *Modern Democracies*, 2 vols. London & New York: Macmillan.
Burke, Edmund (1906/7). *Works*, 6 vols. (with Introductions by W. Willis, F. W. Rafferty and F. H. Willis). London: Oxford University Press.

Burke, Peter, and R. Porter (eds.) (1987). *The Social History of Language*. Cambridge: Cambridge University Press.
Burns, James Henderson (1957). 'J. S. Mill and Democracy, 1829-61', *Political Studies* 5, 158-75, 281-95.
Burrow, John W. (1966). *Evolution and Society: A Study in Victorian Social Theory*. Cambridge & New York: Cambridge University Press.
　(1967). 'The uses of philology in Victorian England', in Robert Robson (ed.). *Ideas and Institutions of Victorian Britain: Essays in Honour of George Kitson Clark*. London: Bell, and New York: Barnes & Noble, pp. 180-204.
　(1974). 'The village community and the uses of history in late 19th century England', in Neil McKendrick (ed.), *Historical Perspectives: Studies in English Thought and Society: In Honour of J. H. Plumb*. London: Europa, pp. 255-84.
　(1981). *A Liberal Descent*. Cambridge & New York: Cambridge University Press.
　(1988). *Whigs and Liberals: Continuity and Change in English Political Thought*. Oxford: Clarendon Press.
Butterfield, Herbert (1952). *Liberty in the Modern World*, The Chancellor Dunning Trust Lectures, Queen's University, 1952. Toronto: Ryerson Press.
Bynon, Theodora (1977). *Historical Linguistics*. Cambridge & New York: Cambridge University Press. (Enlarged edition, 1983.)
　(1978). 'The Neogrammarians and their successors', *Transactions of the Philological Society*, 1978: 111-24.
　(1986). 'August Schleicher: Indo-Europeanist and general linguist', in Bynon and Palmer, 1986: 129-49.
Bynon, Theodora, and F. R. Palmer (1986). *Studies in the History of Western Linguistics: In Honour of R. H. Robins*. Cambridge & New York: Cambridge University Press.
Cahnman, Werner Jacob (ed.) (1973). *Ferdinand Tönnies: A New Evaluation*. With an introduction by the editor. Leiden: Brill.
Cairns, Huntington (1935). *Law and the Social Sciences*. London: Kegan Paul, and New York: Harcourt.
Cannon, Garland (1964). *Oriental Jones: A Biography*. London: Indian Council for Cultural Relations.
　(1979). *Sir William Jones: A Bibliography of Primary and Secondary Sources*, Library and Information Sources in Linguistics, Vol. 7. Amsterdam: John Benjamin.
Cardona, George, H. M. Hoenigswald and A. Senn (eds.) (1970). *Indo-European and Indo-Europeans*. Philadelphia: University of Pennsylvania Press.
Carmichael, Calum M. (1972). 'A singular method of codification of law in the Mishpatim', *Zeitschrift für die alttestamentliche Wissenschaft* 84, 19-25.
Carrión-Wam, Roque (1985). 'Semiotica juridica', in Domenico Carzo

and Bernard S. Jackson (eds.), *Semiotics, Law and Social Science*. Rome: Gangemi, 11–67.

Carter, James Coolidge (1907). *Law: Its Origin, Growth and Function*. New York & London: Putnam.

Cattaneo, M. A. (1962). *Il positivismo giuridico inglese: Hobbes, Bentham, Austin*, Pubblicazioni della Facolta di Giurisprudenza, Universita di Milano. Milan: A. Giuffre.

Cave-Browne, John (1857). *Indian Infanticide: Its Origin, Progress and Suppression*. London: W. H. Allen.

Chadwick, Owen (1975). *The Secularization of the European Mind in the Nineteenth-Century*, The Gifford Lectures in the University of Edinburgh for 1973–4. Cambridge: Cambridge University Press.

Chaudhuri, Nirad C. (1974). *Scholar Extraordinary* London: Chatto & Windus.

CHBE (1929). *Cambridge History of the British Empire*, Vol. 4: *British India, 1497–1858* (ed. H. H. Dodwell). Cambridge: Cambridge University Press.

(1932). *Cambridge History of the British Empire*, Vol. 5: *The Indian Empire, 1858–1918* (ed. H. H. Dodwell). Cambridge: Cambridge University Press.

Childe, Vere Gordon (1926). *The Aryans: A Study of Indo-European Origins*. London: Kegan Paul, and New York: Knopf.

Chomsky, Noam (1957). *Syntactic Structures*. The Hague: Mouton.

(1965). *Aspects of the Theory of Syntax*. Cambridge: Mass.: MIT Press.

(1966). *Cartesian Linguistics*. New York: Harper & Row.

(1972a). *Language and Mind*. 2nd enlarged edn, New York: Harcourt Brace. (1st edn, 1968.)

(1972b). *Problems of Knowledge and Freedom*. London: Barrie & Jenkins.

(1976). *Reflections on Language*. London: Temple Smith. (American edn, New York: Pantheon Books, 1975.)

(1979a). *Rules and Representations*. New York: Columbia University Press. (British edn, Oxford: Basil Blackwell, 1980.)

(1979b). *Language and Responsibility*. Hassocks/Brighton, Sussex: Harvester Press, and New York: Pantheon Books.

(1980). 'Human language and other semiotic systems', in Sebeok and Umiker-Sebeok, 1980: 287–330.

Christie, George C. (1973). *Jurisprudence*. Saint Paul, Minn.: West.

Christmann, Hans H. (1977). *Sprachwissenschaft des 19. Jahrhunderts*. Darmstadt: Wissenschaftliche Buchgesellschaft.

Christy, T. Craig (1983). *Uniformitarianism in Linguistics*. Amsterdam: Benjamin.

Coates, Richard (1987). 'Historical linguistics', in Lyons et al., 1987: 179–99.

Cobban, Alfred B. C. (1964). *Rousseau and the Modern State*, 2nd edn. London: Allen & Unwin, and Hamden, Conn.: Archon Books.

Cocks, Raymond J. C. (1983). *Foundations of the Modern Bar*. London: Sweet & Maxwell.

(1988). *Sir Henry Maine: A Study in Victorian Jurisprudence*, Cambridge

Studies in English Legal History. Cambridge & New York: Cambridge University Press.
Cohn, Bernard (1961). 'From Indian status to British contract', *Journal of Economic History* 21, 613–28.
Colaiaco, James A. (1983). *James Fitzjames Stephen and the Crisis of Victorian Thought*. London: Macmillan, and New York: St Martin's Press.
Collinge, Neville (1986). 'Exceptions, their nature and place – and the Neogrammarians', *Transactions of the Philological Society*, 1978: 61–86.
Collini, Stefan (1979). *Liberalism and Sociology*. Cambridge & New York: Cambridge University Press.
Collini, Stefan, Donald Winch and John Burrow (1983). *That Noble Science of Politics: A Study in Nineteenth-Century Intellectual History*. Cambridge & New York: Cambridge University Press.
Collins, John Churton (1908). *Voltaire, Montesquieu and Rousseau in England*. London: Nash. (Reprinted, Folcroft, Pa.: Folcroft Library, 1980.)
Collins, Randall (1986). *Weberian Sociological Theory*. Cambridge & New York: Cambridge University Press.
Comaroff, John L., and Simon Roberts (1981). *Rules and Processes: The Cultural Logic of Dispute in an African Context*. Chicago: University of Chicago Press.
Comte, François Charles Louis (1835). *Traité de législation*, 2nd edn, 4 vols. Paris: Chamerot, Ducollet.
Condren, Conal (1985). *The Status and Appraisal of Classic Texts: An Essay on Political Theory, its Inheritance and the History of Ideas*. Princeton: Princeton University Press.
Cosgrove, Richard A. (1980). *The Rule of Law: Albert Venn Dicey, Victorian Jurist*. London: Macmillan, and Chapel Hill, N.C.: University of North Carolina Press.
 (1987). *Our Lady the Common Law: An Anglo-American Legal Community, 1870–1930*. New York & London: New York University Press.
Cotterrell, Roger B. M. (1984). *The Sociology of Law: An Introduction*. London: Butterworth.
Cotterrell, Roger B. M., and J. C. Woodliffe (1974). 'The teaching of jurisprudence in British universities', *Journal of the Society of Public Teachers of Law*, n.s., 13 (2) (July), 73–89.
Coulmas, Florian, and K. Ehlich (eds.) (1983). *Writing in Focus*. Amsterdam, New York and Berlin: Mouton.
Cowling, Maurice (1963). *Mill and Liberalism*. Cambridge: Cambridge University Press. (2nd edn, 1990.)
 (1967). *1867: Disraeli, Gladstone and Revolution*. London: Cambridge University Press.
Cranston, Maurice William (1968). 'A dialogue on democracy: Arnold, Maine, Morley', in *Political Dialogues*. London: BBC Publications.
Cross, Sir Alfred Rupert Neale (1976). *Statutory Interpretation*. London: Butterworth.
Crystal, David, and Derek Davy (1969). *Investigating English Style*. London: Longman.

Darwin, Charles (1859). *The Origin of Species*. London: Murray.
  (1871). *The Descent of Man*, 2 vols. London: Murray.
  (1874). *The Descent of Man*, 2nd edn. 2 vols. London: Murray.
  (1956). *A Darwin Reader* (ed. Marston Bates and Philip S. Humphrey). New York: Scribner. (British edn. London: Macmillan, 1957.)
Daube, David (1944/5). 'Some forms of Old Testament legislation', *Proceedings of the Oxford Society of Historical Theology*, 39–42.
  (1969). *Roman Law: Linguistic, Social and Philosophical Aspects*. Edinburgh: Edinburgh University Press, and Chicago: Aldine.
  (1981). *Ancient Jewish Law*. Leiden: Brill.
David, René (1966). *Les Grands Systèmes de droit contemporains*, 2nd edn. Paris: Dalloz.
David, René and John E. C. Brierley (1978). *Major Legal Systems in the World Today*. New York: Free Press, and London: Stevens. (From 6th French edn, 1974.)
Derrett, John Duncan Martin (1959). 'Sir Henry Maine and law in India', *Juridical Review* 4, 44–55.
  (ed.) (1968). *An Introduction to Legal Systems*. London: Sweet & Maxwell.
Deuchar, Margaret (1987). 'Sociolinguistics', in Lyons et al., 1987: 296–310.
Dewey, Clive (1972a). 'The official mind and the problem of agrarian indebtedness in India, 1870–1910'. Unpublished Ph.D. dissertation, University of Cambridge.
  (1972b). 'Images of the village community: a study in Anglo-Indian ideology', *Modern Asian Studies* 6, 291–328.
  (1973). 'The education of a ruling caste', *English Historical Review* 88, 262–85.
  (1991). *The Settlement Literature of the Greater Punjab*. Delhi: Riverdale.
Diamond, Arthur Sigismund (1935). *Primitive Law*. London & New York: Longman.
  (1971). *Primitive Law: Past and Present*. London: Methuen.
Dias, Reginald Walter Michael (1985). *Jurisprudence*. London: Butterworth.
Dicey, Albert Venn (1905). *Lectures on the Relation between Law and Public Opinion in England During the Nineteenth-Century*. London and New York: Macmillan (2nd edn, 1914).
  (1962). *Lectures on the Relation between Law and Public Opinion in England During the Nineteenth-Century*. London: Macmillan. (Reissue of 2nd edn of Dicey, 1914). (New edn, New Brunswick, N.J.: Transaction Books, 1981, with an introduction by Richard A. Cosgrove.)
Driver, Godfrey, and John C. Miles (eds.) (1952–5). *The Babylonian Laws*. 2 vols. Oxford: Clarendon Press.
Durkheim, Emile (1889). Review of Tönnies, 1887. In *Revue philosophique* 27, 416–22.
  (1893). *De la division du travail social*. (Eng. trans., *The Division of Labour in Society*, by George Simpson, New York: Free Press, 1964 and by W. D. Halls, New York: Free Press, 1984.)

(1953). *Montesquieu et Rousseau: précurseurs de la sociologie* (with an introductory note by Georges Davy). Paris: Rivière. (English translation by Ralph Manheim, *Montesquieu and Rousseau: Forerunners of Sociology*. Ann Arbor Paperbacks, 1965.)

Dworkin, Ronald (1978). *Taking Rights Seriously*. London: Duckworth, and Cambridge, Mass.: Harvard University Press.

(1982). 'Law as interpretation'. (Reprinted as 'How law is like literature', in Dworkin, 1985: 146–66.)

(1985). *A Matter of Principle*. Cambridge, Mass.: Harvard University Press.

(1986). *Law's Empire*. London: Fontana.

Eastwood, Reginald Allen, and George W. Keeton (1929). *The Austinian Theories of Law and Sovereignty*. London: Methuen.

Elton, Oliver (1920). *A Survey of English Literature, 1830–1880*, 2 vols. London: Arnold.

Emeneau, Murray B. (1955). 'India and linguistics', *Journal of the American Oriental Society* 75, 145–53.

Engels, Friedrich (1884). *Der Ursprung der Familie des Privateigentum und des Staats. Im Anschluss an Lewis H. Morgans Forschungen*. Zurich. (English translation by Ernest Untermann: *The Origin of the Family, Private Property and the State*, Chicago: C. H. Kerr, 1902; English translation from the text of the 4th edition, Moscow, 1934, by Alick West and revised by Dona Torr, London: Laurence and Wishart, 1940.) (Reprinted in Karl Marx and Friedrich Engels, *Selected Works*. Moscow: Foreign Languages Press, 1958, pp. 117–327.)

Evans, Morgan Owen (1896). *Theories and Criticism of Sir Henry Maine*. London: Stevens & Haynes. (Recent edn, Littleton, Colo.: Rothman, 1981.)

Evans-Pritchard, Edward Evan (1951). *Social Anthropology*. London: Cohen and West.

(1961). *Anthropology and History*. Manchester: Manchester University Press.

(1963). *The Comparative Method in Social Anthropology*. London: Athlone Press.

(1981). *A History of Anthropological Thought*. London & Boston: Faber & Faber, and New York: Basic Books.

Fabian, A. C. (ed.) (1988). *Origins*, The Darwin College Lectures. Cambridge & New York: Cambridge University Press.

Feaver, George A. (1965). 'The political attitudes of Sir Henry Maine', *Journal of Politics* 27, 290–317.

(1969). *From Status to Contract: A Biography of Sir Henry Maine, 1822–88*, London: Longman.

Ferguson, Adam (1767). *An Essay on the History of Civil Society*. Edinburgh: Bell. (Edited, with an introduction, by Duncan Forbes, Edinburgh: Edinburgh University Press, 1966.)

Fifoot, Cecil Herbert (1971). *Frederick William Maitland*. Cambridge, Mass.: Harvard University Press.

Fish, Stanley (1982). 'Working on the chain gang: interpretation in the law and in literary criticism', *Critical Inquiry* 9, 201–16. (Reprinted in Fish, 1989: 87–102.)
  (1989). *Doing What Comes Naturally: Change, Rhetoric and the Practice of Theory and Literary and Legal Studies.* Oxford: Clarendon Press.
Fletcher, Paul, and Michael Garman (eds.) (1986). *Language Acquisition*, 2nd edn. Cambridge & New York: Cambridge University Press.
Fodor, Jerry A. (1975). *The Language of Thought.* New York: Crowell, and Hassocks, Sussex: Harvester.
  (1981). *Representations.* Hassocks, Sussex: Harvester, and Cambridge, Mass.: MIT Press.
  (1983). *The Modularity of Mind.* London & Cambridge, Mass.: MIT Press.
Ford, Trowbridge H. (1985). *Albert Venn Dicey.* Chichester: Barry Rose.
Fortes, Meyer (1953). 'The structure of unilineal descent groups', *American Anthropologist* 55, 17–41.
  (1969). *Kinship and the Social Order.* Chicago: Aldine.
  (1970). 'Pietas in ancestor worship', in *Time and Social Structure*. London: Athlone Press, and New York: Humanities Press.
Fox, Robin (1967). *Kinship and Marriage.* Harmondsworth: Penguin. (Recent edn, Cambridge & New York: Cambridge University Press, 1983.)
Freeden, Michael (1978). *The New Liberalism: An Ideology of Social Reform.* Oxford: Clarendon Press.
  (1986). *Liberalism Divided: A Study in British Political Thought 1914–1939*, Oxford: Clarendon Press.
Freeman, Edward A. (1873). *Comparative Politics.* London: Macmillan. (2nd edn, 1896).
Fried, Charles (1981). *Contract as Promise.* Cambridge, Mass.: Harvard University Press.
Friedmann, Wolfgang Gaston (1951). *Law and Social Change in Contemporary Britain.* London: Stevens.
  (1960). *Legal Theory*, 4th edn. London: Stevens, and New York: Columbia University Press. (5th edn, 1967).
Fuller, Lon (1967). *Legal Fictions.* Stanford, Calif.: Stanford University Press.
  (1968). *Anatomy of the Law.* New York & London: Praeger.
Fustel De Coulanges (1861). *La Cité antique.* Paris: Hachette.
Gardner, Beatrice T., and R. A. Gardner (1980). 'Comparative psychology and language acquisition', in Sebeok and Umiker-Sebeok (1980: 287–330).
Geldart, William (1984). *Introduction to English Law*, 9th edn (prepared by D. C. M. Yardley). Oxford & New York: Oxford University Press.
Gellner, Ernest (1964). *Thought and Change.* London: Weidenfeld & Nicholson. (American edn, Chicago: University of Chicago Press, 1965).
  (1974). *Legitimation of Belief.* Cambridge: Cambridge University Press.

(1988a). 'Origins of society'. In Fabian, 1988: 128–40.
(1988b). 'The politics of anthropology', *Government and Opposition* 23, 290–303.
(1988c). *Plough, Sword and Book: The Structure of Human History.* London: Collins Harvil.
Gierke, Otto Friedrich von (1868–1913). *Das deutsche Genossenschaftsrecht*, 4 vols. Berlin: Weidmann. (Translated with an introduction by F. W. Maitland, Cambridge: Cambridge University Press, 1990).
Ginsberg, Maurice (1961). 'The comparative method', in Maurice Ginsberg, *Evolution and Progress.* London: Heinemann.
Ginsburg, Herbert, and Sylvia Opper (1969). *Piaget's Theory of Intellectual Development.* Englewood Cliffs, N.J.: Prentice-Hall.
Gluckman, Max (1965). *Politics, Law and Ritual in Tribal Society*, Oxford: Basil Blackwell.
(1972). *The Ideas of Barotse Jurisprudence.* Manchester: Manchester University Press.
Godkin, Edwin Laurence (1886). 'An American view of *Popular Government*', *Nineteenth Century* 19, 177–190. (Reprinted in Morton Keller (ed.), *Problems of Modern Democracy: Political and Economic Essays by E. L. Godkin.* Cambridge, Mass.: Harvard University Press, 1966, pp. 68–97.)
Goldman, Lawrence (ed.) (1989). *The Blind Victorian: Henry Fawcett and British Liberalism*, Cambridge: Cambridge University Press.
Gomme, George Laurence (1908). *Folk-lore as an Historical Science.* London: Methuen.
Goodrich, Peter (1987). *Legal Discourse: Studies in Linguistics, Rhetoric, and Legal Analysis*, London: Macmillan & New York: St Martin's Press.
Goody, Jack (ed.) (1968). *Literacy in Traditional Societies.* Cambridge: Cambridge University Press.
(1976). *Production and Reproduction.* Cambridge & New York: Cambridge University Press.
(1977). *The Domestication of the Savage Mind.* Cambridge: Cambridge University Press.
(1983a). 'Literacy and achievement in the ancient world', in Coulmas & Ehlich, 1983: 83–97.
(1983b). *The Development of the Family and Marriage in Europe.* Cambridge & New York: Cambridge University Press.
(1984). 'Under the lineage's shadow', *Proceedings of the British Academy* 70, 189–208.
(1986). *The Logic of Writing and the Organization of Society.* Cambridge & New York: Cambridge University Press.
(1987). *The Interface between the Written and the Oral.* Cambridge: Cambridge University Press.
Gopal, Sarvepalli (1953). *The Viceroyalty of Lord Ripon, 1880–1884.* London: Oxford University Press.
(1965). *British Policy in India, 1858–1905.* London & New York: Cambridge University Press.

Graham, William (1926). *English Political Philosophy from Hobbes to Maine* London: Arnold. (1st edn, 1899.)
Grant Duff, Sir Mountstuart Elphinstone (1892). *Sir Henry Maine: A Brief Memoir of his life ... With Some of his Indian Speeches and Minutes* (selected and edited by Whitley Stokes.) London: Murray and New York: Holt. (Recent edns or reprints: New York: Harper & Row, 1969; Littleton, Colo.: Rothman, 1979.)
  (1897). *Notes from a Diary*, 12 vols. London: Murray.
  (1898). In Tupper, 1898.
Graveson, Ronald Harry (1941). 'The movement from status to contract', *Modern Law Review* 4, 261–72. (Reprinted in *Status in the Common Law*. London: Athlone Press, 1953.)
Green, L. C. (1975). *Law and Society*. Leyden: Sijthoff and Dobbs Ferry, N.Y.: Occana.
Greenleaf, William Howard (1983). *The British Political Tradition*. London: Methuen.
Grillo, Ralph D. (1989). *Dominant Languages: Language and Hierarchy in Britain and France*. Cambridge: Cambridge University Press.
Grimm, Jacob L. K. (1811). *Über den altdeutschen Meistergesang*. Göttingen: Dieterich.
  (1812). *Kinder- und hausmärchen*. Berlin: Realschulbuchhandlung.
  (1819–37). *Deutsche Grammatik*. Göttingen: Dieterische Buchhandlung.
  (1847). *Über das Pedantische in der deutschen Sprache*, Phil. u. hist. Abh., Vol. 32. Berlin: Akademie der Wissenschaften.
Groliter, Eric de (ed.) (1983). *Glossogenetics: The Origin and Evolution of Language*. New York: Harwood.
Guehenno, Jean (1962). *Jean-Jaques Rousseau*, 2nd edn, Paris: Grassett. (English translation by John and Doreen Weightman, 2 vols., London: Routledge & Kegan Paul, 1966.)
Guttman, Amy (1988). 'The patriarchal welfare state', in Amy Guttman (ed.), *Democracy and the Welfare State*. Princeton: Princeton University Press, pp. 321–60.
Haeckel, Ernst Heinrich Philipp August (1867). *Natürliche Schöpfungsgeschichte: Gemeinverständliche Wissenschaftliche Vorträge*. Berlin: Reimer. (Eng. trans., *The History of Creation*. London: King, and New York: Appleton, 1876.)
Hall, John A. (1986). *Powers and Liberties: The Causes and Consequences of the Rise of the West*. Harmondsworth: Penguin, and Berkeley: University of California Press.
Hallam, Henry (ed.) (1863). *Arthur Henry Hallam: Remains in Verse and Prose*. London.
Hamilton, Alexander, James Madison and John Jay (1961). *The Federalist*. Cambridge, Mass.: Belknap Press. (1st edn, 1788.)
Harding, Alan (1966). *A Social History of English Law*. Harmondsworth, & Baltimore: Penguin.
Harnad, Stevan R., Horst D. Steklis and Jane Lancaster (eds.) (1976).

Origins and Evolution of Language and Speech, Annals of the New York Academy of Sciences, 280. New York: Academy of Sciences.
Harris, James William (1980). *Legal Philosophies*. London: Butterworth.
Harris, Marvin (1968). *The Rise of Anthropological Theory*. New York: Crowell.
Harris, Roy (1980). *The Language-Makers*. London: Duckworth, and Ithaca, N.Y.: Cornell University Press.
Harris, Roy (ed.) (1988a). *Linguistic Thought in England 1914–1918*. New York: Routledge.
  (1988b). 'Murray, Moore and the myth', in Harris, 1988a: 1–26.
Harrison, Frederick (1879). 'The English School of Jurisprudence', *Fortnightly Review* 25, 114–30.
  (1911). *Autobiographic Memoirs*, Vol. 1. London: Macmillan.
Hart, Herbert Lionel Dolphus (1961). *The Concept of Law*. Oxford: Clarendon Press. (New rev. edn, New York: Oxford University Press, 1972.)
Harvie, Christopher (1976). *The Lights of Liberalism: University Liberals and the Challenge of Democracy, 1860–86*. London: Allen Lane.
Havard, William C. (1959). *Henry Sidgwick and Later Utilitarian Political Philosophy*. Gainesville, Fla.: University of Florida Press.
Hays, Hoffman Reynolds (1959). *From Ape to Angel: An Informal History of Social Anthropology*. London: Methuen. (American edn, New York: Knopf, 1958.)
Hearn, William Edward (1891). *The Aryan Household*. London & New York: Longman, Green.
Herder, Johann Gottfried (1772). *Abhandlung über den Ursprung der Sprache*. (Reprinted in *Sprachphilosophische Schriften*, ed. E. Heintel. Hamburg: Felix Meiner, 1960.)
Herrick, Jane (1954). *The Historical Thought of Fustel de Coulanges*. Washington: Catholic University of America Press.
Heuston, Robert Francis Vere (1961). 'Sovereignty'. In Anthony Gordon Guest (ed.), *Oxford Essays in Jurisprudence*. London: Oxford University Press. (2nd impression, Oxford: Clarendon Press, 1968.)
Hewes, Gordon W. (1973). 'Primate communication and the gestural origin of language', *Current Anthropology* 14, 5–32.
  (1976). 'The current status of the gestural theory of language origin', in Harnad et al., 1976: 482–584.
  (1983). 'The invention of phonemically-based language', in Grolier, 1983: 143–62.
Hill, Jane H., and R. B. Most (1978). Review of Harnad et al., 1976, *Language* 54, 647–60.
Hilpinen, Risto (ed.) (1981a). *New Studies in Deontic Logic*. Dordrecht & Boston: Reidel.
  (1981b). *Deontic Logic: Introduction and Systematic Readings*, 2nd edn. Dordrecht & Boston: Reidel. (1st edn, 1971.)
Hobbes, Thomas (1650). *De corpore politico: or, The Elements of Law, Natural and Politick*. London: Martin & Ridley. (Ed., with preface and critical

notes, by Ferdinand Tönnies, Cambridge: Cambridge University Press, 1928; first published in 1889.)
  (1651). *Leviathan.* London. (Ed., with introduction, by Michael J. Oakeshott, Oxford: Basil Blackwell, 1946.)
Hobsbawm, Eric J. (1959). *Primitive Rebels: Studies in Archaic Forms of Social Movement in the 19th and 20th Centuries.* Manchester: Manchester University Press.
Hoebel, Edward Adamson (1942). 'Fundamental legal concepts as applied in the study of primitive law', *Yale Law Journal* 51, 951–66.
  (1964). *The Law of Primitive Man.* Cambridge, Mass.: Harvard University Press.
Hoenigswald, Henry M. (1974). 'Fallacies in the history of linguistics', in Hymes, 1974: 346–58.
  (1977). 'Intentions, assumptions, and contradictions in historical linguistics', in R. W. Cole (ed.), *Current Issues in Linguistic Theory*, Bloomington & London: Indiana University Press, pp. 168–94.
  (1978). 'The *annus mirabilis* 1876 and posterity', *Transactions of the Philological Society*, 1978: 17–35.
  (1986). 'Nineteenth-century linguistics on itself', in Bynon & Palmer, 1986: 172–88.
Holdsworth, Sir William Searle (1928). *The Historians of Anglo-American Law.* New York: Columbia University Press.
  (1938). *Some Makers of English Law.* Cambridge: Cambridge University Press. (Paperback edn, 1966.)
Horsman, E. G. (1978). 'Inheritance in England and Wales: the evidence provided by wills', *Oxford Economic Papers*, 30 (3), 409–22.
Howe, M. D. (ed.) (1942). *The Pollock–Holmes Letters*, Vol. 1. Cambridge, Mass.: Harvard University Press.
Humboldt, Wilhelm von, and August Wilhelm Schlegel (1908). *Briefwechsel.* Halle: Niemeyer.
Hunt, Alan (1978). *The Sociological Movement in Law.* London: Macmillan.
Hunter, Sir William Wilson (1870). *Seven Years of Indian Legislation.* Calcutta: Trubner.
Hymes, Dell (ed.) (1964). *Language in Culture and Society.* New York: Harper & Row.
  (1974). *Studies in the History of Linguistics.* Bloomington & London: Indiana University Press.
Ilbert, Courtney (1898). In Tupper, 1898.
Ingram, David (1989). *First Language Acquisition: Method, Description and Explanation.* Cambridge: Cambridge University Press.
Jackson, Bernard S. (1980). 'Historical aspects of legal drafting in the light of modern theories of cognitive development', *International Journal of Law and Psychiatry* 3, 349–69.
  (1985). *Semiotics and Legal Theory.* London: Routledge & Kegan Paul.
  (1987a). 'Rationalité consciente et inconsciente dans la théorie du droit et la science juridique', *Revue interdisciplinaire d'études juridiques* 19, 1–18.

(1987b). 'Some semiotic questions for Biblical Law', in A. M. Fuss (ed.), *The Oxford Conference Volume*, Jewish Law Association Studies, III. Atlanta, Ga.: Scholars Press, 1–25.

(1988a). 'Can one speak of the "deep structure of law"?', in S. Panou et al. (eds.), *Theory and Systems of Legal Philosophy*, Stuttgart: Franz Steiner Verlag, 250–61.

(1988b). 'Structure', in A.-J. Arnaud et al. (eds.), *Dictionnaire encyclopédique de théorie et de sociologie du droit*. Paris: LGDJ, and Brussels: E. Story-Scientia, pp. 399–401.

(1988c). *Law, Fact and Narrative Coherence*. Merseyside: Deborah Charles Publications.

(1988d). Review of Goodrich, *Reading the Law and Legal Discourse*, *Legal Studies* 8 (1), 125–31.

(1988e). 'Some literary features of the Mishpatim', in Matthias Augustin and Klaus-Dietrich Schunck (eds.), *Wunschet Jerusalem Frieden: Collected Communications to the XIIth Congress of the International Organization for the Study of the Old Testament, Jerusalem 1986*, Beihefte zur Erforschung des Alten Testaments und des Antiken Judentums, 13. Frankfurt: Peter Lang, pp. 235–42.

(1989a). 'Analogy in legal science: some comparative observations', in P. Nerhot (ed.), forthcoming.

(1989b). 'Piaget, Kohlberg and Habermas: psychological and communicational approaches to legal theory', in *Investigaciones Semioticas* (Venezuela), forthcoming.

(1989c). *Wisdom-Laws*, forthcoming.

Jenkins, Peter (1988). *Mrs Thatcher's Revolution: The Ending of the Socialist Era*. Cambridge, Mass.: Harvard University Press.

Jespersen, Otto (1922). *Language: Its Nature, Development and Origin*. London: Allen & Unwin.

John, Eric (1960). *Land Tenure in Early England*. Leicester: Leicester University Press. (2nd impression, corrected, 1964.)

Jones, Sir William (1807). *The Works of Sir William Jones*, 13 vols. London: Stockdale.

(1970). *The Letters of Sir William Jones* (ed. Garland Cannon), 2 vols. Oxford: Clarendon Press.

Kalinowski, Georges (1965). *Introduction à la logique juridique*. Paris: LGDJ.

Kantorowicz, Hermann (1937). 'Savigny and the historical school of law', *Law Quarterly Review* 53, 326–43.

Karmiloff-Smith, Annette (1987). 'Some recent issues in the study of language acquisition', in Lyons et al., 1987: 366–86.

Keane, Augustus Henry (1895). *Ethnology*. Cambridge: Cambridge University Press. (2nd rev. edn, 1896.)

Keeton, George William (1949). *The Elementary Principles of Jurisprudence*, 2nd edn. London: Pitman.

Kingsley, Mary Henrietta (1897). *Travels in West Africa: Congo Français*,

Corisco and Cameroons. London & New York: Macmillan. (5th edn, London: Virago, 1982.)

Kirk, Russell (1954). *The Conservative Mind*, 2nd rev. edn. Chicago: H. Regnery, and London: Faber & Faber.

Klima, S. Edward, and Ursula Bellugi (1979). *The Signs of Language.* Cambridge, Mass.: Harvard University Press.

Knickerbocker, Francis Wentworth (1943). *Free Minds: John Morley and his Friends.* Cambridge, Mass.: Harvard University Press.

Knowlson, James R. (1965). 'The idea of gesture as a universal language in the 17th and 18th centuries', *Journal of the History of Ideas* 26, 495–508.

Koerner, E. F. Konrad (1973). *Ferdinand de Saussure: Origin and Development of his Linguistic Thought in Western Studies of Language.* Braunschweig: Vieweg.

(1975). 'European structuralism: early beginnings', in Sebeck, 1975: 717–827.

(1981). 'Schleichers Einfluss auf Haechel: Schlaglichter auf die wechselseitige Abhhangigkeit zwischen linguistischen und biologischen Theorien im 19, Jahrhundert', *Nova Acta Leopoldina*, n.s., Vol. 54, (245), 731–45.

(1983a). 'The Schleicherian paradigm in linguistics', in new edition of Schleicher (1848).

(ed.) (1983b). *Linguistics and Evolutionary Theory: Three Essays by August Schleicher, Ernst Haechel, and Wilhelm Bleek.* Amsterdam & Philadelphia: Benjamin.

Kohlberg, Lawrence (1971). 'From is to ought: how to commit the naturalistic fallacy and get away with it in the study of moral development', in T. Mischel (ed.), *Cognitive Development and Epistemology.* New York: Academic Press, pp. 151–235.

Koss, Stephen E. (1981–4). *The Rise and Fall of the Political Press in Britain*, 2 vols. London: Hamish Hamilton, and Chapel Hill N.C.: University of North Carolina Press.

Krader, Lawrence (ed.) (1966). *Anthropology and Early Law.* New York: Basic Books.

(1972). *The Ethnological Notebooks of Karl Marx: Studies of Morgan, Phear, Maine, Lubbock.* Assen: Van Gorcum.

(1976). *Dialectic of Civil Society.* Assen: Van Gorcum.

Kuhn, Thomas S. (1970). *The Structure of Scientific Revolutions*, 2nd enlarged edn. Chicago: University of Chicago Press. (1st edn, 1962).

Kumar, Krishan (1975). 'Sociological Darwinism', *Biology and Human Affairs* 40, 71–6, 146–53.

(1978). *Prophecy and Progress: The Sociology of Industrial and Post-Industrial Society.* Harmondsworth & New York: Penguin, and London: Allen Lane.

Kumar, Ravinder (1968). *Western India in the Nineteenth Century.* London.

Kuper, Adam (1973). *Anthropologists and Anthropology.* London: Allen Lane.

(1988). *The Invention of Primitive Society: Transformations of an Illusion.* London & New York: Routledge.
Lancaster, Lorraine (1958). 'Kinship in Anglo-Saxon society: II', *British Journal of Sociology*, 359–77.
Landman, Jacob Henry (1930). 'Primitive law, evolution, and Sir Henry Sumner Maine', *Michigan Law Review*, 28, 404–25, (Reprinted, New York, 1930).
Laslett, Peter (1965). *The World We Have Lost.* London: Methuen.
Lass, Roger (1980). *Explaining Language Change*, Cambridge & New York: Cambridge University Press.
Lawson, Frederick Henry (1968). *The Oxford Law School, 17850–1965*, Oxford & London: Clarendon Press.
Lecky, William Edward Hartpole (1892). *The Political Value of History.* Birmingham and Midland Institute Presidential Address.
  (1893). *The Empire: Its Value and its Growth*, London & New York: Longman.
  (1896). *Democracy and Liberty*, London & New York: Longman.
  (1910). *History of the Rise and Influence of the Spirit of Rationalism in Europe*, 2 vols. London: Watts and Longman, Green. (First published 1865).
  (1911). *History of European Morals from Augustus to Charlemagne* 2 vols. London: Longman. (First published 1896).
Lefevre, André (1894). *Race and Language.* London: Kegan Paul and New York: Appleton.
Lehmann, Winfred Philipp (ed.) (1967). *A Reader in Nineteenth-Century Historical Linguistics.* Bloomington & London: Indiana University Press.
Leitzmann, Albert (ed.) (1908). *Briefwechsel.* See Humbold & Schlegal, 1908.
Lepschy, Giulio (1986). 'European linguistics in the twentieth century', in Bynon and Palmer, 1986: 189–201.
Leslie, T. E. C. (1875). 'Maine's *Early History of Institutions*', *Fortnightly Review* 17, 303–20.
Letwin, Shirley Robin (1965). *The Pursuit of Certainty.* Cambridge: Cambridge University Press.
  (1978). 'On conservative individualism'. In Maurice Cowling (ed.), *Conservative Essays.* London: Cassell, 52–68.
Levin, Lawrence Meyer (1936). *The Political Doctrine of Montesquieu's Esprit des Lois: Its Classical Background.* New York: Columbia University Press.
Limber, John (1973). 'The genesis of complex sentences'. In T. Moore (ed.), *Cognitive Development and the Acquisition of Language*, New York: Academic Press.
Linden, Eugene (1976). *Apes, Men and Language.* Harmondsworth & Baltimore: Penguin. (First published, New York: Saturday Review Press, 1974.) (Updated edn, Harmondsworth & New York: Penguin, 1981.)
Lippincott, Benjamin Evans (1938). *Victorian Critics of Democracy: Carlyle, Ruskin, Arnold, Stephen, Lecky.* Minneapolis: University of Minnesota Press, and London: Mitford & Oxford University Press.

Lloyd, Trevor Owen (1968). *The General Election of 1880.* London: Oxford University Press.
Lock, Andrew J. (1980). *The Guided Reinvention of Language.* London & New York: Academic Press.
 (ed.) (1978). *Action, Gesture and Symbol: The Emergence of Language,* London & New York: Academic Press.
Long, George (1847). *Two Discourses Delivered in Middle Temple Hall.* London. (Reprinted in Law Library, Philadelphia: Little, 1848, 60.)
Lord, W. F. (1935). *Sir Thomas Maitland.* London.
Lowie, Robert H. (1921). *Primitive Society.* London: Routledge. (1st American edn, New York: Boni & Liveright, 1920.)
 (1929). *Primitive Society.* 2nd impression. London: Routledge.
 (1937). *The History of Ethnological Theory.* New York: Farrar, and London: Harrap.
Lubbock, Sir John (1965). *Pre-historic Times.* London: Williams and Norgate.
 (1870). *The Origin of Civilization and the Primitive Condition of Man.* London: Longman (2nd edn). (Recent edn, Chicago: University of Chicago Press, 1978.)
Ludden, David (1985). *Peasant History in South Asia.* Princeton, N.J.: Princeton University Press.
Lukes, Stephen (1972). *Emile Durkheim: His Life and Work.* New York: Harper & Row.
Lukes, Stephen, and Andrew Scull (eds.) (1983). *Durkheim and the Law.* Oxford: Martin Robertson.
Lyall, Sir Alfred C. (1888). 'Sir Henry Maine', *Law Quarterly Review,* 4, 129–35.
 (1893). 'Life and speeches of Sir Henry Maine', *Quarterly Review* 176, 287–316 [unsigned].
 (1898). In Tupper, 1898.
 (1899). *Asiatic Studies.* London: Murray. (1st edn, 1882.)
Lyons, John (1968). *Introduction to Theoretical Linguistics.* London & New York: Cambridge University Press.
 (ed.) (1970a). *New Horizons in Linguistics.* Harmondsworth: Penguin, and New York: Viking.
 (1970b). *Chomsky.* London: Collins/Fontana, and New York: Viking/Penguin (2nd edn, 1977.)
 (1977a). *Semantics.* 2 vols. London & New York: Cambridge University Press.
 (1977b). *Chomsky.* 2nd edn. London: Collins/Fontana, and New York: Viking. (First edn, 1970.)
 (1981a). *Language and Linguistics.* London & New York: Cambridge University Press.
 (1981b). *Language, Meaning and Context.* London: Fontana/Collins.
 (1981c). 'Language and speech', *Transactions of the Royal Society,* B295, 215–22. In H. C. Longuet-Higgins, D. A. Broadbent and J. Lyons

(eds.), *The Psychological Mechanisms of Language*. London: Royal Society and British Academy. (Revised and expanded version in Lyons, 1991.)

(1987a). 'Semantics', in Lyons et al., 1987: 152–78.

(1987b). 'Origins of language', in Andrew Faber (ed.), *Origins*, Cambridge: Cambridge University Press, pp. 141–66.

(1989a). 'Semantic ascent: a neglected aspect of syntactic typology', in Douglas G. Arnold. et al. (eds.), *Essays in Syntactic Theory and Universal Grammar*, London: Oxford University Press, pp.153–86.

(1989b). 'The last forty years: real progress or not?', in *Georgetown University Round Table on Languages and Linguistics*. Washigton, D.C.: Georgetown University Press, pp. 13–38.

(1990). 'Linguistics: theory, practice and research', in *Georgetown University Round Table on Language and Linguistics*. Washington, D.C.: Georgetown University Press.

(1991). *Natural Language and Universal Grammar: Essays in Linguistic Theory*, Vol. 1. Cambridge: Cambridge University Press.

(forthcoming a). 'Linguistic theory and theoretical linguistics', in Lyons, 1991.

(forthcoming b). 'Natural, non-natural and unnatural languages', in Lyons, 1991.

Lyons, John, R. Coates, M. Deuchar and G. Gazdar (eds.) (1987). *New Horizons in Linguistics*, Vol 2. London: Penguin.

Macaulay, Lord Thomas Babington (1866). 'Lord Clive', in Lady Trevelyan (ed.), *The Works of Lord Macaulay*. 8 vols. London & New York: Longman, Vol. VI, pp. 381–453.

Macfarlane, Alan (1978). *The Origins of English Individualism: The Family, Property and Social Transition*. Cambridge: Cambridge University Press.

Mack, Mary Peter (1962). *Jeremy Bentham: An Odyssey of Ideas, 1748–1792*. London: Heinemann.

McKinney, John C., and Charles P. Loomis (1963). 'The Application of Gemeinschaft and Gesellschaft as Related to Other Typologies', in Introduction to *Community and Society*, trans. and ed. Charles P. Loomis, New York & London: Harper, pp. 12–29. See Tönnies, 1887.

McLennan, John Ferguson (1857). 'Law', in *Encyclopaedia Britannica*, 8th edn, Vol. 13. Edinburgh: Black, pp. 253–79.

(1865). *Primitive Marriage: An Inquiry into the Origin of the Form of Capture in Marriage Ceremonies*. Edinburgh: Adam & Charles Black (Recent edn, ed. and introduction by Peter Riviere, London & Chicago: University of Chicago Press, 1970.)

(1876). *Studies in Ancient History*. London: B. Quaritch. (New edn with notes and preface by Donald McLennan, London: Macmillan, 1886.)

(1885). *The Patriarchal Theory* (ed. Donald McLennan). London: Macmillan.

(1896). *Studies in Ancient History* (2nd series, ed. by his widow, E. A. McLennan, and Arthur Platt). London & New York: Macmillan.

Macpherson, Crawford Brough (1964). *The Political Theory of Possessive Individualism.* Oxford: Clarendon Press.

Magee, Bryan (1985). *Philosophy and the Real World.* La Salle, Ill.: Open Court.

Maher, John Peter (1966). 'More on the history of the comparative method: the tradition of Darwinism in August Schleicher's work', *Anthropological Linguistics* 8 (3), 1–12.

Mair, Lucy Philip (1972). *An Introduction to Social Anthropology,* 2nd edn. Oxford: Clarendon Press.

Maitland, Frederick William (1897). *Domesday Book and Beyond.* Cambridge: Cambridge University Press, and Boston: Little, Brown.

  (1909). *Equity and the Forms of Action at Common Law.* Cambridge: Cambridge University Press.

  (1911). *Collected Papers* (ed. H. A. L. Fisher), 3 vols. Cambridge: Cambridge University Press.

  (1936). *Selected Essays* (ed. H. D. Hazeltine, G. Lapsley and P. H. Wisfield). London: Cambridge University Press.

  (1965). *The Letters of Frederick William Maitland* (ed. C. H. S. Fifoot). London: Selden Society.

Malinowski, Bronislaw (1923). 'The problem of meaning in primitive languages', Supplementary Essay to Ogden and Richards, 1927: 451–510.

  (1935). *Coral Gardens and their Magic.* London: Allen & Unwin.

  (1937). 'The dilemma of contemporary linguistics', *Nature* 140, 172–3. (Reprinted in Hymes, 1964: 63–5.)

Mallock, William Hurrell (1884). *Property and Progress.* London: Murray, and New York: Putnam.

  (1889). *The New Republic,* new edn. London: Chatto & Windus. (First edn, 1877.)

  (1898). *Aristocracy and Evolution: A Study of the Rights, the Origin and the Social Functions of the Wealthier Classes.* London: Black, and New York: Macmillan.

  (1918). *The Limits of Pure Democracy.* London: Chapman & Hall. (American edn, New York: Dutton, 1917.)

Manchester, A. H. (1980). *A Modern Legal History of England and Wales, 1750–1950.* London: Butterworth.

Mansfield, Harvey Claflin (1965). *Statesmanship and Party Government: A Study of Burke and Bolingbroke.* Chicago: University of Chicago Press.

Marcuse, Herbert (1941). *Reason and Revolution: Hegel and the Rise of Social Theory.* London & New York: Oxford University Press.

Marsh, Peter (1978). *The Discipline of Popular Government: Lord Salisbury's Domestic Statecraft, 1881–1902.* Hassocks, Sussex: Harvester Press.

Martinet, André (1955). *Economie des changements phonétiques.* Bern: Francke.

Marx, Karl (1972). *The Ethnological Notebooks of Karl Marx: Studies of Morgan, Phear, Maine, Lubbock* (transcribed and ed. with an Introduction by Lawrence Krader). Assen: Van Gorcum.

Marx, Karl, and F. Engels (1848). *Manifesto of the Communist Party*. In David Fernbach (ed.), *Karl Marx: The Revolutions of 1848*. London: Allen Lane, 1973.
Mayer, Jacob Peter (1960). *Alexis de Tocqueville: A Biographical Study in Political Science*. New York: Harper & Row.
Mayne, John D. (1885). Review of *The Patriarchal Theory*, Law Quarterly Review 1, 485–95. See McLennan, 1885.
—— (1914). *A Treatise on Hindu Law and Usage*, 8th edn. Madras.
Mayo, Henry Bertram (1960). *An Introduction to Democratic Theory*. New York: Oxford University Press.
Mays, Wolfe (1974). 'Popper, Durkheim and Piaget on moral norms', *Journal of the British Society for Phenomenology* 5, 233–42.
Meillet, Antoine (1903). *Introduction à l'étude comparative des langues indo-européennes*. Paris: Hachette.
—— (1936). *Linguistique historique et linguistique générale*, Vol. 2. Paris: Klincksieck.
Mensch, B. (1981). 'Freedom of contract as ideology', *Stanford Law Review* 33, 753–70.
Metcalf, Thomas R. (1965). *The Aftermath of Revolt*. Princeton, N.J.: Princeton University Press.
Michel, J. (1975). 'How to build a critical jurisprudence' (unpublished Edinburgh lecture).
Michels, Robert Willy Eduard (1915). *Political Parties*. London: Jarrold.
Mill, James (1817). *The History of British India*, 3 vols. London: Baldwin.
Mill, John Stuart (1858). *Memorandum of the Improvements in the Administration of India during the Last Thirty Years, and the Petition of the East India Company to Parliament*. London. (Reprinted, Farnborough: Gregg, 1968.)
—— (1859). 'Recent writers on reform'. *Fraser's Magazine* 65, 489–508. (Reprinted in Mill, 1965– , Vol. 19, pp. 341–70.)
—— (1861). *Considerations on Representative Government*. London: Parker. (Reprinted in Mill, 1965– , Vol. 19, pp. 371ff.)
—— (1863). 'Austin on jurisprudence', *Edinburgh Review* 118, 439–52 (unsigned). (Reprinted in Mill, 1965– , Vol. 21, pp. 165–205.)
—— (1865). 'Auguste Comte and positivism', *Westminster Review and Foreign Quarterly* 83, 339–405 and 84, 1–42. (Reprinted in Mill, 1965– , Vol. 10, pp. 261–368.)
—— (1871). 'Mr Maine on village communities', *Fortnightly Review* 9, 543–56. (Reprinted in Mill, 1875: Vol. 4, pp. 130–3.)
—— (1873). *Autobiography*. (Edited and with Introduction by Jack Stillinger, London: Oxford University Press, 1971.)
—— (1875). *Dissertations and Discussions*. 4 vols. (Vols. 1 and 2, 3rd edn; Vol. 3, 2nd edn; Vol. 4, 1st edn). London: Longman, Green. (1st edn, 2 vols., 1859.)
—— (1950). *Mill on Bentham and Coleridge* (Introduction by F. R. Leavis). London: Chatto & Windus.

(1962). *Utilitarianism, On Liberty, Essay on Bentham, together With Selected Writings of Jeremy Bentham and John Austin* (ed. Mary Warnock). London: Collins.

(1965–). *Collected Works* (ed. John M. Robson et al.). Toronto: University of Toronto Press, and London: Routledge & Kegan Paul.

Milsom, S. F. C. (1981). *Historical Foundations of the Common Law*. London: Butterworth.

(1985). *Studies in the History of the Common Law*. London & Roncervente, W.Va.: Hambledon Press.

Minogue, Kenneth R., and Michael Biddiss (eds.) (1987). *Thatcherism: Personality and Politics*. Basingstoke: Macmillan.

Monboddo, Lord (James Burnett) (1744–92). *Of the Origin and Progress of Language*, 6 vols. London: Thomas Cadell.

Montesquieu, Charles de Secondat, Baron de (1950–5). *Œuvres complètes* (publiés sous la direction de André Masson), 3 vols. Paris: Nagel.

Moore, Robin James (1966a). *Sir Charles Wood's Indian Policy, 1853–1866*. Manchester: Manchester University Press.

(1966b). *Liberalism and Indian Politics, 1872–1922*. London: Edward Arnold.

Moore, Sally Falk (1978). *Law as Process*. London & Boston: Routledge & Kegan Paul.

(1986). *Social Facts and Fabrications: Customary Law on Kilimanjaro, 1880–1980*. Cambridge & New York: Cambridge University Press.

Moore, Terence, and Christine Carling (1988). *The Limitations of Language*. Basingstoke: Macmillan.

Morgan, Lewis H. (1870, 1871). *Systems of Consanguity and Affinity of the Human Family*. Washington D.C.: Smithsonian Institute.

(1877). *Ancient Society: Researches in the Lines of Human Progress from Savagery through Barbarism to Civilization*. New York: Holt. (Ed. with introduction by Leslie A. White, Cambridge, Mass.: Belknap Press, 1964.)

Morison, William Loutit (1982). *John Austin*. London: E. Arnold, and Stanford, Calif.: Stanford University Press.

Morley, John (1886). 'Sir Henry Maine on popular government', *Fortnightly Review* 39, 153–73. (Reprinted in Morley, 1890.)

(1890). *Studies in Literature*. London: Macmillan.

(1917). *Recollections*, 2 vols. New York: Macmillan.

Morpurgo-Davies, Anna (1975). 'Language classification in the nineteenth-century', in Sebeok, 1975: 607–716.

(1978). 'Analogy segmentation and the early Neogrammarians', *Transactions of the Philological Society* 1978: 36–60.

(1986). 'Karl Brugmann and late nineteenth-century linguistics', in Bynon and Palmer, 1986: 150–71.

Mounin, Georges (1967). *Histoire de la linguistique*. Paris: Presses Universitaires de France.

Müller, F. Max (1847). *Report of the British Association*, 17.

(1856). 'Comparative mythology', in *Oxford Essays*. London: Parker.

(Edited with additional notes and an Introductory Preface on Solar Mythology by A. Smythe Palmer, London: Dutton, and New York: Palmer.)
  (1859). *A History of Ancient Sanskrit Literature*. London: Williams & Norgate.
  (1861). *Lectures on the Science of Language*, first series. London: Longman, Green.
  (1864). *Lectures on the Science of Language*, second series. London: Longman, Green.
  (1868). *On the Stratification of Language*. London: Longman.
  (1875). *Chips from a German Workshop*, Vol. 4. London: Longman.
  (1888). *Three Introductory Lectures on the Science of Thought*. London: Longman.
Murray, Robert Henry (1929). *Studies in the English Social and Political Thinkers of the Nineteenth Century*. Cambridge: Heffer.
Nisbet, Robert (1966). *The Sociological Tradition*. New York: Basic Books (British edn, London: Heinemann, 1967.)
  (1976). *Sociology as an Art Form*. New York: Oxford University Press.
  (1980). *History of the Idea of Progress*. London: Heinemann & New York: Basic Books.
  (1986). *Conservatism: Dream and Reality*. Milton Keynes: Open University Press.
Oakeshott, Michael (1962). *Rationalism in Politics*. London: Methuen.
Ogden, Charles K., and I. A. Richards (1927). *The Meaning of Meaning*, 2nd edn. London: Routledge & Kegan Paul, and New York: Harcourt (1st edn, 1923.)
Oldham, James Basil (1913). *Analysis of Maine's Ancient Law*, with notes. Oxford: Blackwell.
Packe, Michael St John (1954). *The Life of John Stuart Mill*. London: Secker & Warburg and New York: Macmillan.
Pal, Dharm (1952). *Administration of Sir John Lawrence of India, 1864–1869*. Simla: Minerva Book Shop.
Paley, William (1806). *The Principles of Moral and Political Philosophy*, 16th edn, 2 vols. London: Faulder. (1st edn, 1785).
Parsons, Talcott (1937). *The Structure of Social Action*. New York & London: McGraw-Hill. (Recent edn, 2 vols., New York: Free Press, and London: Collier-Macmillan.)
  (1973a). 'A note on Gemeinschaft and Gesellschaft', in Cahnman, 1973: pp. 140–50.
  (1973b). 'Some afterthoughts on Gemeinschaft and Gesellschaft', in Cahnman, 1973: pp. 151–9.
Parsons, Talcott, Edward A. Shils, E. D. Naegel and J. R. Pitts (eds.) (1961). *Theories of Society: Foundations of Modern Sociological Theory*, 2 vols. New York: Free Press of Glencoe. (One-vol. edn, New York: Free Press of Glencoe, and London: Collier-Macmillan, 1965.)
Pateman, Trevor (1987). 'Philosophy of linguistics', in Lyons et al., 1987: 249–67.

Patterson, Edwin Wilhite (1953). *Jurisprudence: Men and Ideas of Law*. Brooklyn: Foundation Press.
Paul, Herbert Woodfield (ed.) (1913). *Letters of Lord Acton*, with an Introductory Memoir by the editor. London: Macmillan. (1st edn, 1904.)
Pedersen, Holger (1965). *Linguistic Science in the Nineteenth Century* (trans. John Webster Spargo). Cambridge, Mass.: Harvard University Press. (Reprinted as *The Discovery of Language*, Bloomington, Ind.: Indiana University Press, 1959.) (1st edn, 1931.)
Peel, John David Yeadon (1971). *Herbert Spencer: The Evolution of a Sociologist*. London: Heinemann, and New York: Basic Books.
Perlin, Frank (1985). 'State formation reconsidered, II', *Modern Asian Studies*, 19(3).
Perrot, David L. (1980). 'Has law a deep structure? The origin of fundamental duties', in Dominick Lasok et al. (eds.), *Fundamental Duties*, Oxford & New York: Pergamon, 1–15.
Piaget, Jean (1932). *The Moral Judgement of the Child* (trans. Marjorie Gabain). Paris: F. Alcan; London: Routledge & Kegan Paul; New York: Harcourt Brace.
  (1965). *Etudes sociologiques*. Geneva & Paris: Droz.
  (1971). *Structuralism* (trans. and ed. Chaninah Maschler). London: Routledge and Kegan Paul. (1st edn, Paris: Presses Universitaries de France, 1968; 1st American edn, New York: Basic Books, 1970.)
  (1980). *Six Psychological Studies* (trans. Anita Tenzer; ed. with an introduction and notes by David Elkind). Brighton: Harvester. (1st edn, Paris: Gonthier, 1964.)
Pilbeam, David R. (1988). 'Human origins and evolution', in Fabian, 1988: 89–114.
Pillai, Purnalingam M. S. (1915). *An Epitome of Maine's Ancient Law and Austin's Jurisprudence*. Madras.
Pinto-Duschinsky, Michael (1967). *The Political Thought of Lord Salisbury, 1854–1868*, London: Constable.
Plamenatz, John Petrov (1949). *The English Utilitarians*. Oxford: Blackwell. (2nd rev. edn, 1958.)
  (1963). *Man and Society*, 2 vols. London: Longman.
Pocock, David F. (1961). *Social Anthropology*. London & New York: Sheed & Ward. (2nd rev. edn, 1971.)
Pohlman, H. L. (1984). *Justice Oliver Wendell Holmes and Utilitarian Jurisprudence*. London & Cambridge, Mass.: Harvard University Press.
Pollock, Sir Frederick (1890a). *Oxford Lectures and other Discourses*. London & New York: Macmillan.
  (1890b). 'Sir Henry Maine and his work', in Pollock, 1890a: 147–68.
  (1893). 'Sir Henry Maine as a jurist', *Edinburgh Review* 178 (July), 100–21 (unsigned).
  (1895). *An Introduction to the History of the Science of Politics*. London & New York: Macmillan.
  (1898). In Tupper, 1898.

(1906). *Introduction and Notes to Sir Henry Maine's 'Ancient Law'*. London: Murray. (Also included in Maine, *AL* 1906 and subsequent editions and reprints.

Pollock, Sir Frederick, and F. W. Maitland (1968). *The History of English Law*, 2nd edn. (with a new Introduction by S. F. C. Milsom). 2 vols. London & New York: Cambridge University Press.

Popper, Sir Karl Raimund (1963). *Conjectures and Refutations*. London: Routledge & Kegan Paul.

(1980). *The Logic of Scientific Discovery*. London: Hutchinson. (1st edn, 1933.)

Postema, G. (1983). 'Fact, fictions and law: Bentham on the Foundations of Evidence', in William Twining (ed.), *Facts in Law*, Wiesbaden: Franz Steiner, pp. 37–64.

Pound, Roscoe (1925). *Interpretations of Legal History*. Cambridge: Cambridge University Press.

(1959), *Jurisprudence*, 5 vols. Saint Paul, Minn.: West.

Powell, John Lesley (1891). *Indian Linguistic Families*. Bureau of American Ethnology, Annual Report, 7. Washington. D.C.: Smithsonian Institute.

Powell, Mava Jo (1983). 'The notion of literal meaning in contemporary linguistic semantics'. Unpublished Ph.D. dissertation, University of Sussex.

(1985). 'Conceptions of literal meaning in speech act theory', *Philosophy and Rhetoric* 18, 133–57.

Prasannakumara, Sena (1896). *A Study of Ancient Law; or, an analysis of Maine's Ancient Law*. Konnagar: P.C. Kundu.

Puhvel, Jaan (1987). *Comparative Mythology*. Baltimore & London: Johns Hopkins University Press.

Quinton, Anthony (1978). *The Politics of Imperfection: The Religious and Secular Traditions of Conservative Thought in England from Hooker to Oakeshott*, The T. S. Eliot Lectures delivered at the University of Kent at Canterbury in October 1976. London: Faber & Faber.

Radcliffe-Brown, Alfred Reginald (1935). 'Patrilineal and matrilineal succession', reprinted in Radcliffe-Brown, 1952.

(1952). *Structure and Function in Primitive Society*. London: Cohen & West.

Raphael, David Daiches (1970). *Problems of Political Philosophy*. London: Macmillan.

Rask, Rasmus (1818). *Undersogelse om det gamle Nordiske eller Islandske Sprogsoprindelse*. Copenhagen.

Reckitt, Maurice (1958). 'When did "Victorianism" end?', *Victorian Studies*, 268–71.

Redfield, Robert (1950). 'Maine's *Ancient Law* in the light of primitive societies', *Western Political Quarterly* 3, 574–89.

Renfrew, Colin (1987). *Archaeology and Language: The Puzzle of Indo-European Origins*. London: Jonathan Cape.

Richter, Melvin (1964). *The Politics of Conscience: T. H. Green and his Age*.

Cambridge, Mass.: Harvard University Press and London: Weidenfeld & Nicolson.
Roach, John P. C. (1956). 'James Fitzjames Stephen', *Journal of the Royal Asiatic Society*, 1–16.
  (1957). 'Liberalism and the Victorian intelligentsia', *Cambridge Historical Journal*, 13, 58–81.
  (1959). 'Victorian universities and the national intelligentsia', *Victorian Studies* 2, 131–50.
Robertson Scott, John William (1950). *The Story of the Pall Mall Gazette*. London & New York: Oxford University Press.
Robins, Robert Henry (1967). *A Short History of Linguistics*. London: Longman. (2nd edn, 1979.)
  (1978). 'The Neogrammarians and their nineteenth-century predecessors', *Transactions of the Philological Society* 1978, 1–16.
  (1982). 'Condillac et l'origine du langage', in Sgard, Jean (ed.), *Condillac et les problème du langage*, Geneva & Paris: Slatkine (1985), pp. 95–101.
Robson, Robert (ed.) (1967). *Ideas and Institutions of Victorian Britain*. London: Bell, and New York: Barnes & Noble.
Robson, William Alexander (1933). 'Sir Henry Maine today', in Arthur Lehman Goodhart et al. (eds.), *Modern Theories of Law*. London: Oxford University Press.
Romaine, Suzanne (ed.) (1982a). *Sociolinguistic Variation in Speech Communities*. London: Edward Arnold.
  (1982b). *Socio-Historical Linguistics*. Cambridge: Cambridge University Press.
Rommetveit, Ragnar (1986). 'On literacy and the myth of literal meaning', in Saljo, 1986.
Rothblatt, Sheldon (1968). *The Revolution of the Dons*. London: Faber & Faber, and New York: Basic Books.
Rothermund, Dietmar (1978). *Government, Landlord, and Peasant in India*. Wiesbaden.
Rousseau, Jean-Jacques (1782). 'Essay on the origin of languages', in John H. Moran (ed. and trans.), *On the Origin of Language*. New York: Ungar, and Chicago: University of Chicago Press, 1966.
  (1962). *Political Writings* (ed. Charles Edwyn Vaughan), 2 vols. Oxford: Basil Blackwell, and New York: Wiley. (1st edn, Cambridge: Cambridge University Press, 1915.)
Rubin, G. R., and David Sugarman (eds.) (1984). *Law, Economy and Society, 1750–1914*. Abingdon, Oxon.: Professional Books.
Rumney, Jay (1934). *Herbert Spencer's Sociology: A Study in the History of Social Theory*. London: Williams & Norgate.
Sahlins, Marshall David (1968). *Tribesmen*. Englewood Cliffs, N.J.: Prentice-Hall.
Saljo, Roger (ed.) (1986). *The Written Code and Conceptions of Reality*. (Proceedings of a symposium held at Sydkoster, Sweden, August 1985.) Linkoping.

Sapir, Edward (1921). *Language*. New York: Harcourt, Brace and World.
  (1933). 'Language', in *Encyclopaedia of the Social Sciences*. New York: Macmillan.
Saussure, Ferdinand de (1916). *Cours de linguistique générale* (ed. Charles Bally and Albert Sechehaye). Paris: Payot. (English trans.: (1) by Wade Baskin, *A Course in General Linguistics*, New York: Philosophical Library, 1960 (revised edn, with Introduction by Jonathan Culler, London: Fontana/Collins, 1974); (2) by Roy Harris, *Course in General Linguistics*, with Introduction and annotations. London: Duckworth.)
  (1922). *Recueil des publications scientifiques*. Geneva: Sonor.
Savigny, Frederick Carl von (1814). *Vom Beruf unseren Zeit für Gesetzgebung und Rechtwissenschaft*. Heidelberg: Mohr. (Eng. trans. by Abraham Hayward, *Of the Vocation of our Age for Legislation and Jurisprudence*, London: Littlewood, 1831.)
Sawer, Geoffrey. (1965). *Law in Society*. Oxford: Clarendon Press.
Schacht, Joseph (1974). 'Law and state: (a) Islamic religious law', in Joseph Schacht and C. E. Bosworth (eds.), *The Legacy of Islam*, 2nd edn. Oxford: Oxford University Press.
Schapera, Isaac (1956). *Government and Politics in Tribal Societies*. London: Watts.
Schlegel, Frederick von (1808). *Über die Sprache und Weisheit der Indier*. Heidelberg: Mohr & Zimmer.
Schleicher, August (1861/2). *Compendium der vergleichenden Grammatik der indogermanischen Sprachen*. Weimar: Bohlau.
  (1863). *Die Darwinische Theorie und die Sprachwissenschaft*. Weimar: Bohlau.
  (1865). *Über die Bedeutung der Sprache für die Naturgeschichte des Menschen*. Weimar: Bohlau.
  (1869). *Darwinism Tested by the Science of Language* (English trans., with preface and additional notes, by A. V. W. Bikkers., of Schleicher, 1863). London: Hotten.
Schrader, Otto (1890). *Prehistoric Antiquities of the Aryan Peoples* (trans. by F. B. Jevons). New York: Scribner & Welford, and London: Griffin.
Schulz, Fritz (1946). *History of Roman Legal Science*. Oxford: Clarendon.
Schwarz, A. B. (1934). 'John Austin and the German jurisprudence of his time', *Politica* 1, 178.
Searle, John R. (1969). *Speech Acts*. London & New York: Cambridge University Press.
  (1979). 'Literal meaning', *Erkenntnis* 13, 207–24. (Reprinted in *Expression and Meaning*, Cambridge: Cambridge University Press, pp. 117–36.)
Sebeok, Thomas Albert (ed.) (1975). *Current Trends in Linguistics*. Vol. 13: *Historiography of Linguistics*. The Hague & Paris: Mouton.
Sebeok, Thomas Albert, and Jean Umiker-Sebeok (eds.) (1980). *Speaking of Apes: A Critical Anthology of Two-Way Communication with Man*. New York: Plenum.
Secondat, Charles Louis de Baron de Montesquieu (1950–5). *Œuvres*

complètes (publiés sous la direction d'André Masson), 3 vols. Paris: Nagel. (See also under Montesquieu.)
Shils, Edward A. (1970). 'The tyranny of tradition', *Encounter* 34 (3) (March), 57–61.
   (1975). *Center and Periphery*. Chicago & London: University of Chicago Press.
Shopen, Timothy (1985). *Language Typology and Linguistic Description*, 3 vols. Cambridge: Cambridge University Press.
Sidgwick, Arthur, and E. M. Sidgwick (1906). *Henry Sidgwick: A Memoir*. London & New York: Macmillan.
Simmel, Georg (1900). *Die Philosophie des Geldes*. Leipzig: Duncker.
   (1908). *Soziologie*. Munich & Leipzig: Duncker.
Simpson, A. W. B. (ed.) (1984). *Biographical Dictionary of the Common Law*. London: Butterworth.
Skine, Francis Henry (1901). *Life of Sir William Wilson Hunter*. London: Longman, Green.
Smellie, Kingsley Bryce (1928). 'Sir Henry Maine', *Economica* 8, 64–94.
   (1933). 'Maine, Sir Henry James Sumner', in *Encyclopaedia of the Social Sciences*, Vol. 10 (ed. Edwin R. A. Seligman). London: Macmillan, 49–50.
Smith, Brian C. (1963). 'Maine's concept of progress', *Journal of the History of Ideas* 24: 407–12.
Smith, Francis Barrymore (1966). *The Making of the Second Reform Bill*. Cambridge & London: Cambridge University Press.
Smith, Keith John Michael (1988). *James Fitzjames Stephen*. Cambridge & New York: Cambridge University Press.
Smith, Martin S., Bradley J. Kish and Charles B. Crawford (1987). 'Inheritance of wealth as human kin investment', *Ethology and Sociobiology* 8, 171–82.
Smith, Paul (1967). *Disraelian Conservatism and Social Reform*. London: Routledge & Kegan Paul.
   (ed.) (1972). *Lord Salisbury on Politics*. Cambridge: Cambridge University Press.
Smith, Reginald Bosworth (1883). *Life of Lord Lawrence* 2 vols. London: Smith, Elder.
Southgate, Donald George (1962). *The Passing of the Whigs, 1832–1886*. London: Macmillan & New York: St Martin's Press.
Soyeda, Juichi (1886). *A Comparison between Japanese Village Communities and those Described by Sir Henry Maine*. Cambridge: Cambridge University Press.
Spahr, M. (1962). 'Mill on paternalism in its place', in Carl Joachim Friedrich (ed.), *Nomos IV: Liberty*. New York: Atherton Press, pp. 162–75.
Spencer, Herbert (1851). *Social Statics*. London: Chapman.
   (1858–74). *Essays: Scientific, Political and Speculative*, 3 vols. London: Longman, Brown, Green.
   (1862). *First Principles*. London: Williams & Norgate.
   (1876). *The Principles of Sociology*, 3 vols. London: Williams & Norgate.

(1884). *The Man Versus the State*. London: Williams & Norgate.
Stam, James H. (1976). *Inquiries into the Origin of Language: The Fate of a Question*. New York: Harper & Row.
Stanlis, Peter J. (1958). *Edmund Burke and the Natural Law*. Ann Arbor, Mich.: University of Michigan Press.
Stein, Peter (1979). 'Legal theory and the reform of legal education in mid-19th century England', in A. Giuliani and N. Picarda (eds.), *L'educazione giuridica*, Vol. 2: *Profili storici*. Perugia. (Also in Stein, 1988.)
— (1980). *Legal Evolution: The Story of an Idea*. Cambridge & New York: Cambridge University Press.
— (1984). 'Maine', in Simpson, 1984.
— (1986). 'The tasks of historical jurisprudence', in Neil MacCormack and Peter Birks (eds.), *The Legal Mind: Essays for Tony Honoré*. Oxford: Clarendon Press, and New York: Oxford University Press.
— (1988). *The Character and Influence of the Roman Civil Law: Historical Essays*. London & Ronceverte, W.Va.: Hambledon Press.
Stein, Peter, and John Shand (1974). *Legal Values in Western Society*. Edinburgh: Edinburgh University Press.
Steinberg, Jonathan (1987). 'The historian and the Questione della lingua', in Burke & Porter, 1987: 198–209.
Stephen, Sir James Fitzjames (1861). 'English jurisprudence', *Edinburgh Review* 114, 456–86 (unsigned).
— (1873). *Liberty, Equality, Fraternity*. London: Smith, Elder. (New edn, edited with an introduction and notes by Reginald James White, London: Cambridge University Press, 1967.)
— (1885). *The Story of Nuncomar, and the Impeachment of Sir Elijah Impey*. 2 vols. London: Macmillan.
— (1888). 'Sir Henry Maine', *Saturday Review*, 65, 150–1 (unsigned).
— (1891, 1892). *Horae Sabbaticae*. London: Macmillan.
Stephen, Leslie (1895). *The Life of Sir James Fitzjames Stephen*. London: Smith, Elder.
— (1900). *The English Utilitarians*. 3 vols. London: Duckworth, and New York: Putnam.
Stevens, Robert (1979). *Law and Politics*. London: Weidenfeld & Nicolson. (American edn, Chapel Hill, N.C.: University of North Carolina Press, 1978.)
Stocking, George W. (1968). *From Physics to Ethnology*. In *Race, Culture and Evolution: Essays in the History of Anthropology*. New York: Free Press.
— (1987). *Victorian Anthropology*. New York: Free Press and London: Collier-Macmillan.
Stokes, Eric (1959). *The English Utilitarians and India*. Oxford: Clarendon Press. (Corrected edn, 1963.)
Stone, Julius (1965). *Human Law and Human Justice*. London: Stevens, and Stanford, Calif.: Stanford University Press.
— (1966). *Social Dimensions of Law and Justice*. London: Stevens and Stanford, Calif.: Stanford University Press.
Strachey, Sir Richard (1898). In Tupper, 1898.

Stubbs, William (1874-8). *The Constitutional History of England*, Oxford: Clarendon Press.
Subrahmanyam, Sanjay (ed.) (1990). *Merchants, Markets and the State in Early Modern India*. New Delhi.
Sugarman, David (1983). 'Law, economy and the State in England, 1750-1914, some major issues', in David Sugarman (ed.), *Legality, Ideology and the State in England*. London: Academic Press, 213-66.
 (1986). 'Legal theory, the common law mind and the making of the textbook tradition'. In Twinning, 1986: 266-1.
Szymura, Jerzy (1988). 'Bronislaw Malinowski's "Ethnographic theory of language"', in Harris, 1988a: 106-31.
Thayer, James Bradley (1898). *A Preliminary Treatise on Evidence at the Common Law*. Boston: Little, Brown.
Thomas, J. A. C. (1976). *Textbook of Roman Law*. Amsterdam & Oxford: North Holland.
Thorner, Daniel (1951). 'Sir Henry Maine', in H. Ausubel et al. (eds.), *Some Modern Historians of Britain*. New York: Dryden Press, pp. 66-84.
Tod, James (1920). *The Annals and Antiquities of Rajasthan*. 3 vols. Oxford.
Tönnies, Ferdinand (1887). *Gemeinschaft und Gesellschaft*. Leipzig: Fues's Verlag. English trans. from the 8th edn and introduction by Charles P. Loomis, as (1) *Fundamental Concepts of Sociology*. New York: American Book Co., 1940, and (2) *Community and Society*. London: Routledge, 1955. Paperback edn, New York: Harper, 1963.
 (1922). [Untitled], in Raymond Schmidt (ed.), *Philosophie der Gegenwart in Selbstdarstellungen*, Vol. 3. Leipzig: Meiner, pp. 199-234.
 (1935). *Gemeinschaft und Gesellschaft*, 8th edn. Leipzig: Hans Buse. For English edns, see Tönnies, 1887.
Tönnies-Paulsen (1961). *Ferdinand Tönnies-Friedrich Paulsen: Briefwechsel, 1876-1908* (ed. Olaf Kose, E. R. Jacoby and I. Fischer, with an Introduction by E. G. Jacoby). Kiel: Hirt.
TPS (1978). *The Neogrammarians*, Transactions of the Philological Society, Commemorative Volume. Oxford: Basil Blackwell.
Trudgill, Peter (1978). *Sociolinguistic Patterns in British English*. London: Edward Arnold.
Tupper, Sir Charles Lewis (1874). *Indian Political Practice*. Delhi: BR Pub. Corp.
 (1898). 'India and Sir Henry Maine' (paper read to the Society of Arts, 10 March 1898, together with a report of the discussion following). *Journal of the Society of Arts* 46, 390-405.
Twining, William L. (ed.) (1986). *Legal Theory and Common Law*. Oxford & New York: Basil Blackwell.
 (1987). '1836 and all that: laws and the University of London 1836-1986', *Current Legal Problems* 40, 261-99.
 (1990). *Rethinking Evidence*. Oxford: Blackwell.
Tylor, Sir Edward Burnett (1861). *Anahuac*. London: Longman.
 (1865). *Researches into the Early History of Mankind and the Development of*

Civilization. London: Murray. (Abridged edn by Paul Bohannan, Chicago: University of Chicago Press, 1964.)
(1871a). *Primitive Culture*, 2 vols. London: Murray.
(1871b). 'Maine's *Village Communities*', *Quarterly Review* 131, 176–89 (unsigned).
Vann, Icilio (1892). *Gli studi di Henry Sumner Maine le dottrine della Filosfia del diritto*. Verona: D. Tedeschi.
Vinogradoff, Sir Paul G. (1892). *Villainage in England*. Oxford: Clarendon Press.
(1904). 'The teaching of Sir Henry Maine' (an Inaugural Lecture delivered at Corpus Christi College Hall, London, on 1 March 1904). London: Froude.
(1911). 'Comparative jurisprudence', in *Encyclopaedia Britannica*, 11th edn. London: Cambridge University Press, Vol. 15, pp. 580–7.
(1920–2). *Outlines of Historical Jurisprudence*, 2 vols. London & New York: Oxford University Press.
Voget, Fred W. (1975). *A History of Ethnology*. New York: Holt, Rinehart.
Wallace, Alfred Russell (1895). 'The expressiveness of speech, or mouth-gesture as a factor in the origin of language', *Fortnightly Review* 58, 528–43.
Wanner, Eric, and Lila R. Gleitman (eds.) (1982). *Language Acquisition: The State of the Art*. Cambridge & New York: Cambridge University Press.
Ward, Thomas Humphry (ed.) (1887). *The Reign of Queen Victoria: Fifty Years of Progress*. London: Smith & Elder.
Washbrook, D. A. (1981). 'Law, state and agrarian society in Colonial India', *Modern Asian Studies* 15.
Washburn, Sherwood L., and Elizabeth R. McCown (eds.) (1978). *Human Evolution: Biosocial Perspectives*. Menlo Park, Calif.: Benjamin/Cummings.
Watkins, Calvert (1970). 'Studies in Indo-European legal language, institutions and mythology', in George Cardona et al. (eds.), 1970: pp. 321–54.
Watson, George (1973). *The English Ideology: Studies in the Language of Victorian Politics*. London: Allen Lane.
Weber, Max (1922). *Wirtschaft und Gesellschaft: Grundriss der Verstehender Sociologie* 2 vols. Tübingen: Mohr.
(1963). *The Sociology of Religion* (trans. by Ephraim Fischoff of Chapter 4 of Vol. 2 of Weber, 1922, with an Introduction by Talcott Parsons). Boston: Beacon Press, and London: Methuen.
West, Sir Raymond (1872). *The Land and the Law in India*. London.
White, James Boyd (1973). *The Legal Imagination*. Boston & Toronto: Little, Brown.
Whitney, William Dwight (1870). 'On the present state of the question as to the origin of language', *Transactions of the American Philosophical Association*. (Reprinted in Whitney, 1873).

(1872). *The Life and Growth of Language*. New York.

(1873–4). *Oriental and Linguistic Studies*. New York: Scribner.

Wilbur, Terence H. (1977). *The Lautgestz Controversy*. Amsterdam: Benjamins.

Wilson, Woodrow (1898). 'A lawyer with a style', *Atlantic Monthly* 82, 363–74.

Winckelmann, Jonannes (1976). *Erläuterungen zu Wirtschaft und Gesellschaft*. Tübingen: Mohr.

Wittfogel, Karl August (1963). *Oriental Despotism*. New Haven: Yale University Press.

Wittgenstein, Ludwig von (1953). *Philosophical Investigations*, Oxford: Basil Blackwell, and New York: Macmillan.

Woodruff, Phillip (pseudonym) (1954). *The Men Who Ruled India: The Guardians*, Vol. 2. London: Cape. (Abridged edn, Philip Mason, London: Cape, 1985.)

Wundt, Wilhelm Max (1886). *Ueber den Begriff des Gesetzes mit Rucksicht auf die Frage der Ausnahmslosigkeit der Laugesetze Philosophische Studien* 3, 195–215.

(1900). *Volkerpsychologie. Eine Untersuchung der Entwicklungsgesetze von Sprache, Mythus und Sitte*, B.1: *Die Sprache*. Leipzig: Engelmann.

(1901). *Sprachgeschichte und Sprachpsychologie*. Leipzig. Engelmann.

Yale, David E. C. (ed.) (1965). *Manual of Chancery Practice*. Cambridge: Cambridge University Press.

Yaron, Reuven (1969). *The Laws of Eshnunna*. Jerusalem: Magnes (2nd rev. edn, 1988.)

Young, George Malcolm (1949). *Victorian England: Portrait of an Age*, London: Oxford University Press.

Index

Abrahams, Raphael, 3, 5, 9–10, 19
Acton, Lord, 19, 30, 46, 47, 50, 105
Adams, Henry, 36
agnates, 103
Aitchison, Jean, 311
Allen, Sir Carleton, 1, 13, 248
America, *see* United States
Amos, Andrew, 41
analytical jurisprudence, 214
Ancient Law (Maine), 2, 3, 4, 9–10, 11, 13, 14, 223, 359, 360, 361
   and comparative philology, 263, 268, 297–8
   and evolutionary theory, 139, 141
   and feudalism, 93
   and historical jurisprudence, 238–41
   history and progress in, 71–2
   and ideas of progress, 55, 56, 57, 59, 60, 61, 63–4, 66, 74, 78, 83, 90, 94
   and India, 44, 104, 105, 150, 386
   and kinship, 120, 121
   and legal education, 195, 204–8, 209–11
   and legal fictions, 191
   and legal systems, 243
   and patriarchal theory, 80, 99, 100–2, 106, 107, 113, 114–15, 151
   and *Popular Government*, 19, 21–2, 26–7, 81, 84, 150
   and sociology, 147, 148, 152, 157
   and Victorian values, 37, 39–40, 46, 50–1
Ancient Society (Morgan), 107, 114
Anglo-Indians, 6
anomie in society, 170
Anthropological Society, 267
anthropology, 9, 40–1, 111–42
   Indian, 356, 363–7
   and patriarchal theory, 99–110
   and theories of progress, 83–4
Argyll, Duke of, 359
Arnold, Matthew, 59, 221
Athenaeum Club, 29, 92, 218–19
Atiyah, P. S., 48, 49

Austin, J. L., 333, 346
Austin, John, 1, 10, 41–2, 71, 218
   and legal education, 200, 201, 211, 212, 213–16
authority
   Weber's classification of, 162–6

Bachofen, J. J., 105–6, 113–14
Bacon, Roger, 317
Baden-Powell, Baden Henry, 122–3, 384–5, 391
Baechler, Jean, 86
Bagehot, Walter, 59, 61, 62, 63, 64, 65, 66–9, 85
Baker, John H., 1, 2–3, 119, 243, 245, 250, 252
Baldwin, Stanley, 48
Barnett, H. A., 210
Barry, Norman P., 49
Barth, Fredrik, 110
Bayly, Christopher, 7, 11–12
Bentham, Jeremy, 3, 4, 8, 19, 41–2, 45, 46, 71, 74, 93, 217
   and India, 355, 356, 357–8, 361, 362, 370
   and legal education, 195, 201, 207, 211, 212–13, 214–16
   and Maine's patriarchal theory, 100, 103, 104, 105
Berlin, Sir Isaiah, 34
Bernstein, B., 335, 336
Best, R. I., 40
Bethell, Sir Richard, 198
Bible, the
   law and language in, 276, 277, 290–2
Biddiss, Michael, 48
Black, Max, 324
Blackstone, William, 200, 208, 221, 240–1, 361
Bopp, Franz, 258, 260, 262, 298, 310
British Social Science Association, 144
Browning, Oscar, 43
Brubaker, Rogers, 79

447

Brunschvig, Léon, 272
Bücher, Karl, 162
Buckle, Henry Thomas, 57–8, 59, 60
Burckhardt, Jacob, 79
Burke, Edmund, 74, 93
Burrow, John W., 3, 7, 10, 17, 19, 36, 38, 39, 42, 44, 49, 221, 267, 305
  evaluation of Maine, 180, 181, 182, 270
  and Maine's evolutionary theory, 138–9, 140, 141
  and Maine's ideas on progress, 74, 76, 77, 78, 79, 81, 83, 85, 88, 89, 90, 91, 92, 95
  on Maine's political attitudes, 377
  and Maine's work on comparative philology, 257
Butler, Sir Harcourt, 360
Butterfield, Herbert, 51

Cambridge University
  and legal education, 196–7
  Maine at, 28, 29, 30, 33, 34, 42–3, 359–60, 376–7
  politics at, 35–6
Cannon, G., 295
Carmichael, Calum M., 292
Carter, James Coolidge, 225
Cave-Browne, John, 107
censorial jurisprudence, 212, 213
Chadwick, Owen, 36–7
Chambers, Robert, 139
Chancery law, 233
change, Maine's ideas on, 137–42; *see also* legal change
charismatic authority, 163, 166, 167
Chomsky, Noam, 273, 279, 280–3, 316, 321–2, 327–8
  theory of generative grammar, 317–20, 327
civil service in India, 353, 358–63, 368, 392
civil society, 149
Cobden, William, 63
Cocks, Raymond, 13, 14, 15, 20, 34, 295
  and Maine's ideas on progress, 78, 79–80, 81, 83, 84, 88–9, 91, 92
codification of law, *see* law, codification of
cognitive development psychology
  law and language, 271–8
Cohn, Bernard, 44
Collini, Stefan, 4, 5, 10, 38, 48, 74, 179
  and Maine's ideas on progress, 77, 78, 79, 81
Collins, R., 86
Comaroff, John L., 180
Communist Manifesto, The, 134, 135, 177
community, Maine's concept of, 119–23

Community Charge debate, 26
comparative historical argument, 180, 181
comparative law, 219–20
comparative method
  Maine's use of, 76, 77, 146, 147, 151, 182, 297–304
comparative philology, 3, 8, 38, 39, 40, 72–3, 182, 256, 257, 258, 269, 270, 271, 296–315
Comte, Auguste, 40, 59, 144, 148, 149, 205, 221
Comte, Charles, 205
Condorcet, M., 41, 82, 149
Condren, Conal, 50
conservatism
  and Maine's political thought, 88, 93, 95
Cooley, Charles Horton, 172, 173–4
Cory, William, 42
Cotterrell, Roger, 210
Coulmas, F., 337
Court of Chancery, 250–1
Cranbrook, Lord, 92
Crystal, D., 278

Darwin, Charles, 3, 6, 73, 85, 86, 106, 108, 139, 221, 257
Daube, David, 276, 277, 278
David, René, 209
Davy, D., 278
democracy
  in *Popular Government*, 24–6, 61, 90
Denning, Lord, 247–8
deontic modality, 345–8, 349–50
Descent of Man, The (Darwin), 108
Dewey, Clive, 6, 8, 11, 12, 44
Diamond, A. S., 118, 119, 134, 279, 289
Dicey, A. V., 21, 47–87, 49, 74, 80–1, 95, 218, 226, 227, 233
Dissertations on Early Law and Custom, *see* *Early Law and Custom* (Maine)
Division of Labour in Society, The (Durkheim), 184
Domesday Book and Beyond (Maitland), 132
Durkheim, Emile, 3, 79, 82, 89, 109, 122, 136, 172, 174, 180, 331
  classification of societies, 168–71, 177, 183–4
Dworkin, Ronald, 285–6, 340

Early History of Institutions (Maine), 40, 85, 108, 117–18, 150, 152, 177, 265
Early Law and Custom (Maine), 107, 115, 125, 141, 150, 205, 260, 264, 268
education, legal, 195–216
Ehlich, K., 337
Elphinstone, Mountstuart, 385, 390

Index 449

Elton, Oliver, 43
Engels, F., 46, 109, 134, 135, 152
English law
 common law, 225, 240
 and legal education, 195–208
 property, 124–6
 reform, 250–3
equity, 246–8, 254
Ethnological Society, 267
Evans-Pritchard, E. E., 99, 110, 113, 114, 117, 134, 138, 182, 185, 267–8, 391
evolutionary theory, 5–6, 137–42, 181–3, 221–3
 and cognitive development, 274
 and language, 309–13
examinations, legal, 199
expository jurisprudence, 212, 213, 215, 216

Fabian Society, 47
Fane, Julian, 43
Feaver, George, 10, 14, 15, 17, 19, 20, 22, 23, 26, 29, 36, 40, 42, 43, 44, 45, 55, 103, 105
 and Maine's work on comparative philology, 257
Fell, Eliza (Maine's mother), 32
feudalism, 93, 125, 127, 129–32, 134, 135, 137, 164
 and theories of progress, 86
Finland
 study of farm succession, by Abrahams, 187, 188–91
Fitzpatrick, Sir Dennis, 356
Fortes, Meyer, 99, 109, 110, 113, 117, 179, 185, 186, 187
Fox, Robin, 116
Freeden, Michael, 48
freedom of contract, 227
Freeman, E. A., 59, 61, 225
Freud, Sigmund, 3, 109
Fuller, Lon, 231

Gaius, 206
Geldart, James, 197
Gellner, Ernest, 38, 40–1, 82, 138
Gemeinschaft und Gesellschaft (Tönnies), 151–71, 174, 175, 330, 332
geology, 207–8
Germany
 ancient law, and primogeniture, 116, 126
 classification of societies in, 149, 151–68
 historical jurisprudence, 5, 7, 223–6
 and legal education, 196
 sociologists, 172, 173
Gibbon, Edward, 51
Ginsberg, M., 182

Gladstone, Mary, 30, 50, 105
Gladstone, William E., 30, 49, 62
Goodrich, Peter, 279
Goody, Jack, 127–8, 185, 187, 190, 334, 335, 336, 337
Grant, Sir Charles, 365, 367
Grant Duff, Sir M. E., 31, 32, 36, 40, 44, 93, 94, 142, 359, 376–7, 384, 395
Greek language, 309, 310, 315
Greek law, 103
Greenleaf, W. H., 49
Greimas, 287–8
Grimm, Jacob, 259, 260, 278, 298, 310, 316
Grote, George, 101
Grotius, Hugo, 201
Guillemard, Dr, 30
Guizot, F., 59
Guttman, Amy, 48

Habermas, Jürgen, 274
Haeckel, E., 321
Hailey, Sir Malcolm, 392
Hailsham, Lord, 26
Hall, John A., 86
Hallam, Arthur, 43
Hallam, Henry Fitzmaurice, 43
Hamilton, A., 24
Harris, Marvin, 135, 138
Harrison, Frederic, 40, 42
Hart, H. L., 223, 279, 281, 283, 286
Harvie, Christopher, 36
Haxthausen, Baron von, 39–40
Hegel, G., 41, 149, 152, 221
Herder, J. G., 149, 310
Hesiod, 148
Hilpinen, R., 345
Hindu law, 150, 264, 383, 389
 and primogeniture, 116, 126
 see also India
historical development, 8–9
historical jurisprudence, 1–2, 3, 74–5, 217–41, 279
 and cognitive development psychology, 271–4
 and developmental psycholinguistics, 321–2
 German, 5, 7, 223–6
 teaching of, 210
historical sociology, 184
history, legal, *see* legal history
Hobbes, Thomas, 112, 151–2, 153, 176
Hobhouse, L. T., 179
Hoebel, E. A., 134
Holmes, Oliver Wendell, Jr, 35
Horsman, E. G., 189
House of Lords, 26

Howe, M. D., 10, 35
Humboldt, Wilhelm von, 310, 313
Hunter, Sir William, 366

Ibbetson, Sir Denzil, 356, 360, 364, 365, 368, 371–2, 373
Ilbert, Sir Courtenay, 6, 13, 383, 384, 385
India, 353–95
  agrarian policy, 367–75
  caste system, 354, 355, 366–7, 369, 393, 394
  civil service, 353, 358–63, 368, 392
  government, 377–82, 387–8
  land ownership, 128, 129
  law, 118, 150, 154–5, 382–4; *see also* Hindu law
  and Maine's patriarchal theory, 104, 105
  Maine's studies, 3, 7–8, 11–12, 13, 44–6, 384–8
  property rights, 124
  Punjab Alienation of Land Act, 369–70, 374
  religion in, 167
  village communities, 119, 120–3, 354–5, 357, 363, 366–7, 385, 386, 391, 393, 395
individualism, 48–50
  laissez-faire, 5, 7–8, 48, 226–8
Indo-European languages, 258, 263, 266, 269, 278, 298–9
Indo-European laws, 261
infanticide, 106, 107
Inner Morality of Law, The, 231

Jackson, B. S., 274, 275, 279, 285, 287, 291, 293, 294, 295, 296, 297, 303, 306, 308, 317, 318, 319, 322, 340, 341–2
Jenkins, Peter, 48
Jesperson, Otto, 258, 259, 260–1, 264, 299, 301, 305, 311
Jevons, W. S., 362
Jhering, Rudolf von, 105, 224, 225
John, Eric, 128
Johnson, Samuel, 32–3
Jones, Sir William, 258, 278, 295, 316
jural model, 99, 109–10, 180
jurisprudence
  and legal education, 210–16
  see also historical jurisprudence

Kahn-Freund, Otto, 213, 220
Kalinowski, Georges, 284
Kantorowicz, H., 225
Kemble, J. M., 225, 240
Kermode, Frank, 50
Khan, Mohammed Hyat, 375

kinship
  Anglo-Saxon, 128
  and community, 120
  linguistic, 261–2
  and political organization, 117
  in primitive societies, 135, 146
  see also patriarchal theory
Kohlberg, Lawrence, 272, 273–4, 321, 322
Koss, Stephen E., 92
Krader, Lawrence, 46, 118, 135
Kuhn, Thomas S., 15–16, 316, 325
Kumar, R., 19, 20–1, 80, 84, 86, 389
Kuper, Adam, 3, 4, 19, 20, 117, 138, 179, 180, 183, 186
Kürwille ('rational will'), 155, 156, 161

laissez-faire, *see* individualism
Lancaster, Lorraine, 116
landownership, 124–5, 128–32
language
  classification of, 263, 313–15
  expressive power in, 349, 350
  and law, 256–93
  parent- and daughter-languages, 299, 301
  primitive, 298, 301
  reconstruction, 304–9
  spelling, 302–3
  see also linguistics
language-change, 301–4, 306, 311
  synchronic and diachronic, 322–4
language-systems, 308, 309, 327–30
language utterances, 327–30
Latin language, 302, 309, 310, 315
law
  codification of, 22, 64, 203, 334, 384
  Greek, 103
  in India, 118, 150, 154–5, 382–4, 386
  and language, 256–93
  legal codes, 242–3
  and linguistics, 294–350
  and literal meaning, 340–1, 343–4, 349–50
  as literature, 285–8
  Maine's contribution to, 16, 228–31
  of nature, 64–5
  in primordial societies, 164–5
  and religion, 272, 288–92
  in societies, 37–8
Law Amendment Society, 198
Law Magazine, 198–9, 200, 206
Lawrence, Sir John, 377–8
Lawrence, William, 205
Laws of Eshnunna, 275, 276, 277, 278
Laws of Hammurabi, 275–6, 277, 278
Lawson, F. H., 214
Leach, Edmund, 186

Index 451

legal change, 86, 119, 222–3, 230–7, 242–55
legal drafting
  cognitive development theory of, 274–8
legal education, 195–216
legal fictions, 191–2, 244–6, 247, 248, 249, 250–5
legal history, 2–3, 209, 228
legal systems
  development of, 231–7, 249–50
legislation, 248–9
  in *Popular Government*, 22–3
Letwin, Shirley Robin, 49
Liberal Party, 49
liberalism, 37, 47–50
Lindley, Nathaniel (later Lord), 200
linguistic arguments
  Maine's deployment of, 265–7
linguistic egalitarianism, 311–13, 336, 349
linguistics, 16
  communion and communication, 331–2, 333
  deep structure versus surface structure, 317–20
  and law, 294–350
  models, 325–30
  modern structural, 278–84
  periodization of, 315–17
  see also language
Lippincott, Benjamin, 93
literacy
  and literal meaning, 337
  and progress, 334–6
literal meaning, 336–44
literature, law as, 285–8
Livingstone, Edward, 202
locality tribes, 135, 146
Locke, John, 201, 204
logic and morality, 273
Long, George, 198, 206
Louisiana Civil Code, 202–3
Lowie, Robert H., 117, 119, 125, 129, 138
Ludden, David, 395
Lukes, Stephen, 171
Lushington, Franklin, 43
Lyall, Sir Alfred, 12, 15, 221, 363, 365, 366, 384, 386
Lyall, Sir James, 365
Lyons, John, 3, 16, 18, 283–4, 300, 302, 312, 313, 317, 321, 334, 335

Macaulay, Lord Thomas Babington, 57, 63, 65, 66, 104, 376, 383
Macfarlane, Alan, 4, 5, 9, 13, 51, 180, 181, 182, 183, 184, 186
Machiavelli, N., 45

McLennan, J. F., 106–8, 109, 114, 115, 141, 264
Magee, Bryan, 16
Maine, Sir Henry Sumner
  birth, 31
  character, 217–19
  death, 30–1
  early years, 32–4
  evaluation of writings, 217, 218–19
  family connections, 31–2
  ill health, 29, 376
  language, 15
  marriage, 32
  methodology, 136–7
  public appointments, 28, 29, 196–7, 376
  style, 13–14, 15
Mair, Lucy, 141
Maitland, Frederick William, 1, 3, 7, 13, 14, 16, 112, 116, 123, 130, 132, 134, 140, 180, 240, 241, 252
  and Germany, 225
Maitland, Sir Thomas, 390
Malinowski, B., 18, 108, 110, 331, 332
Malthus, T., 106, 359
Manchester, A. H., 198
mandate, concept of, 26
Mansfield, Lord, 32–3
marriage
  and patriarchal society, 106–7
Marsh, Peter, 49
Marsh, Alfred, 174
Marx, Karl, 3, 39, 46, 82, 83, 118, 131, 152, 156, 187, 221
  and property rights, 126, 128
  and sociology, 143
  and status-to-contract theory, 134–5
matriarchal theory, 106–8, 113–14, 115, 116
Maurer, Georg von, 150
Mayne, J. D., 394
Mayo, Lord, 377
Mays, Wolfe, 273
Mensch, B., 46
Metcalf, Thomas, 385, 389
Michel, J., 39, 276
Michels, R., 69
Mill, James, 45, 101, 385
Mill, John Stuart, 3, 11, 30, 47, 62, 63, 64, 79, 90, 104, 355, 361, 367, 391, 392
  conception of progress, 58, 59, 60
  Principles of Political Economy, 362, 370
Milsom, S. F. C., 1–2, 250, 252, 253–4
Minogue, Kenneth R., 48
Mommsen, Theodor, 160
Montesquieu, C., 46, 112, 136, 142, 204, 207
Moore, Sally Falk, 180

moral development, 272–4
morality
and literal meaning, 349–50
Morgan, Lewis Henry, 107, 108, 109, 114, 115, 117, 138, 141, 184, 221, 264
Morley, John, 44, 45, 94
Moses, 290, 291
Mother Right (Bachhofen), 113–14
Müller, Max, 39, 58, 68, 205, 217, 257, 262, 263, 265, 278, 297, 298, 305, 311, 314

National Socialism (Nazism), 157–8, 224
nationality, 177–8
natural law, 100–1, 268
Newton, Sir Isaac, 204
Nietzsche, F., 79
Nisbet, Robert, 39, 43, 80
Nyerere, Julius, 187

Oakeshott, Michael, 51
Ogden, C. K., 333
Oxford English Dictionary, The, 43
Oxford Movement, 35, 36
Oxford University, 196, 359

paradigmatic axis, 287
paradigms, 15–17
Pareto, Vilfredo, 174
Park, Robert, 172–3
Parliament
House of Lords, 26
Parrington, Vernon, 218
Parsons, Talcott, 82, 172, 174–5, 180
patriarchal theory, 4, 39, 48, 99–110, 113–16, 260, 268
and the Indo-European languages, 266
and linguistic development, 263–4
Paul, H. W., 19
Paulsen, Friedrich, 152
Pedersen, Holger, 258, 260, 261, 299
Peel, John, 9, 12, 183, 296
Perlin, Frank, 395
Perrot, David L., 279, 280, 281, 318
pessimism, 61–2, 88–95
phatic communion, 311, 333
phrase structure
in linguistics, 279–84
Physics and Politics (Bagehot), 59, 62, 66–7, 68, 85
Piaget, Jean, 272, 273, 274, 275, 277, 321
Pocock, David, 138
political anthropology, 116–19
politics
and legal systems, 235–7
Pollock, Sir Frederick, 37, 42, 112, 116, 123, 130, 134, 142, 234, 270–1, 386

Popper, Sir Karl, 15, 16, 145
Popular Government (Maine), 4, 19–27, 46, 47, 56, 59, 66, 68, 77, 79, 80, 88, 92, 94, 238, 250, 343
and *Ancient Law*, 19, 21–2, 26–7, 81, 84, 150
and contractual society, 156–7
criticism of 'Irreconcilables', 73
and democracy, 24–6, 90
pessimism in, 61–2
and theories of progress, 84–5
positivism, 76, 79, 83, 182, 222
Postema, Gerald, 212
Pound, Roscoe, 46, 225, 273, 279
Primitive Law (Diamond), 118
Primitive Marriage (McLennan), 106–8
primitive societies
and Maine's patriarchal theory, 99–110
Maine's study of, 77
primogeniture, 116, 126–7, 130, 251, 254
primordial collectivities/societies, 144, 145, 146–7
Durkheim on, 168–9
religion in, 167
progress
evolution-cum-progress, 221–3
in language, 309–13
in law and language, 269–70
and legal evolution, 234–5
and literacy, 334–6
Maine's ideas on, 6, 70–95
mid-Victorian ideas of, 55–69
modern attitudes to, 221–2
property
corporate, 123
in India, 124, 395
Maine's ideas on, 123–32, 151
and patriarchal theory, 108
private, 107, 108, 121, 122, 128–32
rights, 123–32, 239, 254
Proto-Indo-European languages, 299–300, 305, 307, 308, 309
psychology, *see* cognitive development psychology
public opinion, 25–6

Quarterly Review, 46, 92
Quinton, Anthony, 50

Radcliffe-Brown, A. R., 99, 108, 109, 110, 185
Ranulf, Svend, 157
Raphael, D. D., 39
Rask, Rasmus, 258, 259, 260–1, 264, 298, 310, 316
rational-legal authority, 163, 165

rationalization, 165–6
Reckitt, Maurice, 51
religion, 35–6
    and law, 118, 272, 288–92
    and theories of progress, 85, 86
    Weber on, 166–8
Rheinstein, Max, 159
Ricardo, David, 355, 361
Richards, I. A., 333
rights
    individual, 121, 122, 132–3, 234
    property, 123–32
Roach, John, 35, 218
Roberts, Simon, 180
Roman law, 12, 14, 60, 61, 66, 82, 219, 234, 240
    and feudalism in England, 132
    fiction in, 244
    and language, 277, 278
    and legal education, 198, 200–8, 209, 210–11, 213, 215
    and Maine's patriarchal theory, 103, 104, 105
    and property, 116, 124, 126, 128, 254
    and reasoning, 276
    Responsa Prudentum, 246
    and theories of progress, 86
Romanticism, 149, 310
Ross, Edward A., 172
Rousseau, Jean-Jacques, 19, 46, 57, 64, 94, 217
Russell, Lord John, 197

Sahlins, M. D., 117
St James's Gazette, 92–3
Saint-Simon, C., 149
Salisbury, Robert Gascoyne, 3rd Marquis of, 49, 50, 359
Sanskrit, 258, 262, 263, 300, 315
Saturday Review, 92
    Maine's articles in, 44
Saussure, Ferdinand de, 279, 286, 306, 316, 324, 325, 327
Savigny, Friedrich Karl von, 41, 64, 104, 105, 106, 198, 200, 203, 205, 224, 229, 259
Sawer, Geoffrey, 289
Schacht, Joseph, 292
Schapera, Isaac, 117, 141
Schlegel, Friedrich von, 258
Schleicher, August, 258, 304–5, 308, 311, 313
Schmitt, Carl, 224
Schultz, Fritz, 278
science
    and progress, 73–4, 78–9

scientific conservative, Maine as, 93
Scottish Enlightenment, 60, 390
Searle, C. E., 30
Searle, John R., 344, 346
Selden Society, 225
Shils, Edward A., 4, 9, 17, 18, 179, 180, 183, 184, 244, 330, 331, 332, 333
Sidgwick, Henry, 94, 95
Simmel, Georg, 158–9, 160, 162, 165, 172
Singh, Sir Harnam, 374–5
Small, Albion, 172
Smellie, K. D., 134
Smiles, Samuel, 49
Smith, K., 10
Smith, Martin S., 189
Smith, P., 49
Snow, C. P., 29
social action
    Weber's classification of, 161–2
social sciences, 3–4, 9, 16
    Maine as an ancestor of, 179–84
socialist revival, 47
societies
    contractual relationships, 144, 145–6, 150, 151, 156–7
    group versus individually based, 133, 144–7, 149–51
    primordial, 144, 145, 146–7, 167, 168–9
    progressive/stationary, 21, 182–3, 243, 270, 330–1, 333
    see also status-to-contract theory
sociology, 3, 9, 17–18, 143–78
    and theories of progress, 83–4
Sohm, Rudolph, 36
Spectator, The, 92
Spelman, John, 250
Spencer, Herbert, 15, 79, 82, 139, 144, 148, 180, 183, 184, 289
Spengler, Oswald, 84
status-to-contract theory, 18, 20, 21–2, 23, 39, 45, 46, 47, 48, 51, 116–17, 132–7, 140–1, 144–51, 179–80, 183
    and patriarchal theory, 102
    and progress, 55, 56–7, 76, 82, 83
    and property rights, 130
Stein, Peter, 10, 12, 14–15, 41, 42, 196, 197, 205, 210, 211, 215, 221, 262, 272
Stephen, James Fitzjames, 10, 13, 20, 31, 35, 42, 43, 92, 103, 218, 239–40, 383, 391
    criticisms of Maine, 71, 72
Stephen, Sir James, 35, 95
Stephen, Leslie, 35
Stocking, George, 139, 182, 185
Stokes, Eric, 389, 390, 391
Stokes, Whitley, 40, 45, 263, 266, 360

Stone, Julius, 267
Strachey, Sir John, 367
Strachey, Lytton, 220
Strachey, Sir Richard, 11
Stubbs, William, 59, 63, 112
Subrahmanyam, Sanjay, 395
Sugarman, David, 46, 214
Sumner, John Bird, 32
Sumner, William Graham, 172
Swettenham, Sir Frank, 391
syntagmatic axis, 287–8

Tanzania
  field work by Abrahams in, 186–7
Taylor, Tom, 43
Tennyson, Arthur, Lord, 43
territory
  and community, 120
Thayer, James Bradley, 214
thematic repetition, 290–1
Thomas, J. A. C., 255
Thomas, William I., 172, 173
Thorburn, S. S., 365, 370–1, 372
Times, The, 26
Tocqueville, A. de, 59, 63, 79, 112, 143, 157
Tönnies, F., 18, 119–20, 122, 172, 176, 177, 180, 183, 330, 332, 333
  and Durkheim, 168–71
  Gemeinschaft und Gesellschaft, 151–71, 174, 175, 187
Toynbee, Arnold, 84, 363, 373
Tractarian (Oxford) Movement, 35, 36
traditional authority, 163–4
Tupper, Sir Lewis, 6, 13, 353, 360, 372, 383, 384, 392
Turgot, A., 82, 149
Turkish language, 313, 315
Tylor, Sir Edward Burnett, 107, 108, 141, 180

United States
  constitution, 24, 25, 69
  law schools, 229
  and legal change, 234, 236–7
  legal education, 213–14
  sociologists, 172–5
universities
  German, 224
  Indians at British, 359–60
  and legal education, 196–7, 199
  and Victorian values, 35–6

Victorian values, 34–52
Village-Communities in the East and West (Maine), 37–8, 44, 47, 150, 152, 259, 268–9, 353, 360, 361, 384, 390
Vinogradoff, Sir Paul G., 75, 108, 112, 116, 123, 133, 140, 141, 219, 241, 257
virtual legislation, 244

Wace, E. G., 365
Walzer, Michael, 79
Ward, Thomas Humphrey, 47
Washbrook, D. A., 379
Watkins, C., 265
Watson, Alan, 219
Watson, George, 49
Weber, Max, 3, 79, 86, 133, 141, 174, 178, 184, 275, 331, 333, 396
  and Tönnies, 159–68
Wesenwille ('essential will'), 153–4, 161, 162
West, Sir Raymond, 360, 370
White, James Boyd, 250
Wigmore, John Henry, 219
wills, 127–8, 130, 187–91
Wilson, Sir James, 360, 365, 372–3
Wilson, Woodrow, 14, 35
Winckelmann, Johannes, 159
Wirth, Louis, 172
Wittfogel, Karl, 86
Wood, Sir Charles, 359
Woodard, Calvin, 2, 5, 7, 9, 13, 19, 23, 27, 243, 246, 249, 250
Woodliffe, J. C., 210

Yach, D. M., 210
Yale, David, 9, 12, 17, 19, 20, 23

LIBRARY OF DAVIDSON COLLEGE

Books on regular loan may be checked out for four weeks. Books must be presented at the Circulation Desk in order to be renewed.

A fine is charged after date due.

Special books are subject to special regulations at the discretion of the library staff.